Meade and Lee at Bristoe Station

The Problems of Command and Strategy
from Brandy Station to the Buckland Races
August 1 to October 31, 1863

Jeffrey Wm Hunt

Savas Beatie
California

Library of Congress Cataloging-in-Publication Data

Names: Hunt, Jeffrey Wm. (Jeffrey William), 1962-author.
Title: Meade and Lee at Bristoe Station: The problems of Command and Strategy After Gettysburg, from Brandy Station to the Buckland Races, August 1 to October 31, 1863 / by Jeffrey Wm Hunt.
Description: El Dorado Hills California: Savas Beatie, [2018] | Includes bibliographical references and index.
Identifiers: LCCN 2018030113| ISBN 9781611213966 (hardcover : alk. paper) | ISBN 9781611213973 (ebk)
Subjects: LCSH: Virginia—History—Civil War, 1861-1865—Campaigns. | Bristoe Station, Battle of, Va., 1863. | Brandy Station, Battle of, Brandy Station, Va., 1863. | United States. Army of the Potomac. | Confederate States of America. Army of Northern Virginia. | United States—History—Civil War, 1861-1865—Campaigns. | United States—History—Civil War, 1861-1865—Campaigns.
Classification: LCC E470.2 .H926 2018 | DDC 975.5/03—dc23
LC record available at https://lccn.loc.gov/2018030113

First Edition, First Printing

Savas Beatie LLC
989 Governor Drive, Suite 102
El Dorado Hills, CA 95762
916-941-6896 / sales@savasbeatie.com / www.savasbeatie.com

All of our titles are available at special discount rates for bulk purchases in the United States. Contact us for information.

Proudly published, printed, and warehoused in the United States of America.

Table of Contents

Table of Contents (continued)

Table of Contents (continued)

Maps, photos, and illustrations have been distributed
throughout the book for the benefit of the reader.

Preface

THIS book is the second volume in a three part series that examines the Virginia Theater of the Civil War between the conclusion of the Gettysburg Campaign and the end of the active operations in December 1863. It is the result of 25 years of research. The first volume, Meade and Lee After Gettysburg: The Forgotten Final Stage of the Gettysburg Campaign, covered the 14 days between the Army of Northern Virginia's retreat across the Potomac River and its arrival behind the upper Rappahannock River on July 28, 1863. This volume picks up the story at that point and examines the operations conducted by Lee and Meade between August and October of 1863, the culmination of which is the Bristoe Station Campaign.

Most histories of the War Between the States pass lightly over this period because it did not produce a major battle and its attendant blood bath. That is in stark contrast to the time lavished on these operations in regimental histories, personal memoirs, period documents and the Official Records of the Union and Confederate armies. They reveal months of dramatic combat and maneuvering as fascinating as any of the war's other campaigns. Decisions made by rival leaders during this period had an enormous impact on the war in Virginia and on the course of the conflict in general. The consequences of many of those choices proved monumental in 1864.

The campaigns after Gettysburg and before the arrival of Ulysses S. Grant at the helm of the Union war effort speak to the effect of Gettysburg on the course of the war. They provide the bridge between July 1863 when the North seemingly sewed up victory and the 1864 campaigns that almost led to the Union's defeat. They tell a great deal about Jefferson Davis and Abraham Lincoln as commanders-in-chief. Furthermore, they reveal that Robert E. Lee was unbowed by Gettysburg and determined to continue his aggressive tactical and strategic paradigm. These campaigns show us even more about George Meade. The six months between Gettysburg and the end of 1863 represent the only period in which he had sole responsibility for the war in Virginia. Because Meade would live in Grant's shadow from March 1864 until the end of the war, an examination of his operations in the fall of 1863 represent history's only chance to study Meade on his own terms.

Space prevents me from including all of the dramatic tactical detail that I uncovered in preparing this manuscript. I hope to publish that story at a later date. At the suggestion of my editor, I have kept the story of the cavalry battles in August and September to a minimum. Likewise, this volume's bibliography is restricted to material cited in the footnotes.

*   *   *

It is my great privilege to thank the following wonderful people for their contributions to this work. Among these are Dr. George Forgie of the University of Texas at Austin, who posed the initial question that put me on a quest to understand what happened in the late summer and fall of 1863. My fellow Civil War reenactors who over more than 30 years in the hobby have helped me understand the tactical minutiae of Civil War armies. Gill Eastland, my best friend for over 30 years, who spent an entire week exploring Culpeper Country, Virginia with me. Rob Orrison, Bill Backus, Mike Block and Bryce Suderow for walking the fields with me, giving advice and encouragement, correcting errors, providing critical knowledge and insight. Dr. Gary Gallagher, Kent Masterson Brown and Fred Ray for the encouragement and assistance they have given me during this project. Mark Ragan and Jonathan Wiley, who mined the resources of the National Archives and Library of Congress as well as the North Carolina State Archives and University of North Carolina on my behalf. Sara Buehler, Amanda Shields and Chuck Ulmann deserve special thanks for helping me use the remarkable artwork of N. C. Wyeth that graces the cover of this book. And most importantly my publisher, Theodore P. Savas, managing director of Savas Beatie—an outstanding historian whose passion for bringing fresh perspectives to the reading public has placed Savas Beatie on the cutting edge of Civil War historiography.

In researching this volume I have been honored by the kind assistance of Ronald A. Lee (Tennessee State Library and Archives), Virginia Dunn (Library of Virginia), Ben Tayloe (Thomas Balch Library, Leesburg, Virginia), Corinne Nordin (Indiana Historical Society), Christine Beauregard, (New York State Library), Linda Thornton (Auburn University), Janet Bloom (William Clements Library – University of Michigan), Leah Weinryb Grohsgal, Teresa Burk and Kathleen Shoemaker (Robert Woodruff Library – Emory University), Joan Wood (Stewart Bell, Jr. Archives, Handley Regional Library, Winchester-Frederick County Historical Society), Blaine Knupp and Theresa McDevitt (Indiana University of Pennsylvania), Helen Conger

(Case Western Reserve University Archives), Katherine Wilkins (Virginia Historical Society), Peiling Li and Alyson Barrett (Gilder Lehrman Institute of American History), Matthew Turi and Emma Parker (Southern Historical Collection, University of North Carolina), Vicki Catozza (Western Reserve Historical Society Library and Archives), Jennifer Coleman (Navarro College), Shannon Schwaller (United States Military History Institute), Emilie Hardman (Houghton Library, Harvard University), the Research & Instructional Services Staff of the Wilson Library (University of North Carolina), and the staff of the Museum of the Civil War (formerly the Museum of the Confederacy).

The unsung heroine of this book is my wife, Chris, one of the smartest and most talented people I know. The fantastic maps in this volume are her creations. Her patience and love throughout the researching and writing of this book is the bedrock upon which everything rests.

Jeffrey Wm Hunt
Austin, Texas

*   *   *

For John and Edna

CHAPTER 1

"General Meade . . .
Let the Crop Go to Waste"

Glorious Victories—Lincoln's Distress—Meade's Request—The Gettysburg Campaign
Continues—Blue Ridge Chess Match—Return to the Rappahannock

CHARLES Dickens published *A Tale of Two Cities* in 1859. No one knows if Abraham Lincoln ever read the Englishman's masterpiece. But if he did, the novel's opening lines, "It was the best of times. It was the worst of times," might have resonated with the American president at the end of July 1863. The month had begun with stupendous Union military victories and the possibility of a rapid, successful end to the great rebellion. It had ended in disappointment and frustration.

The scale of July's triumphs was unmistakable. In the Western Theater Major General Ulysses S. Grant had forced the surrender of Vicksburg, Mississippi, and its 30,000-man Rebel garrison on July 4 after a six-week siege. Five days later the capitulation of 9,000 Confederates defending Port Hudson, Louisiana to Maj. Gen. Nathaniel P. Banks ceded the Union control of the Mississippi River and split the Southern Confederacy in two. In Tennessee Maj Gen. William S. Rosecrans had maneuvered General Braxton Bragg's Rebel army out of the middle of the state and back to the outskirts of Chattanooga. The Union Army of the Cumberland stood poised to capture the vital railroad hub in the near future.

In the Eastern Theater the news had been equally glorious. Throughout 1862 and the first half of 1863 the Army of the Potomac had endured a string of embarrassing defeats at the hands of Gen. Robert E. Lee. In June his victorious Army of Northern Virginia had crossed the Potomac River to invade Maryland and Pennsylvania. In the midst of the Confederate offensive Lincoln had dismissed Maj. Gen. Joseph Hooker from command of the Army of the Potomac and replaced him with the leader of its V Corps—Maj. Gen. George G. Meade. Just three days after Meade's appointment, the

President Abraham Lincoln in August 1863.
Library of Congress

forward elements of his and Lee's armies collided at the crossroads village of Gettysburg, Pennsylvania. The bloody and closely fought three-day battle that followed ended in the defeat of the Rebels and their retreat toward Virginia.

In this quartet of Union victories many Northerners, civilian and soldier alike, glimpsed the destruction of the Southern Confederacy and the end of the war. Perhaps no one saw that vision with greater hope and clarity than Abraham Lincoln.

The 54-year-old president of the United States was not a handsome man. He stood well over six feet tall, lean and lanky with long arms, huge hands, big feet, large ears and an enormous mouth. A thick mane of unruly black hair and a somewhat scraggly close cropped beard framed a face dominated by a prominent nose. His deep set dark eyes were in the words of one reporter, "penetrating.' Lincoln had visibly aged since taking the oath of office in March 1861. His already famous visage, made popular by photographer Matthew Brady, reflected the burdens he bore. Always dressed in black, Lincoln invariably inspired strong emotions. Depending on their politics people either hated or revered the Kentucky-born, Indiana-raised, former lawyer-turned-politician from Illinois. Some men looked up to him and others looked down their noses at him. Editors mocked or praised him and sometimes alternated between supporting and attacking him with equal fervor. By and large Northern soldiers felt a deep, almost mystical connection to the man in the White House. Most Southerners utterly detested him. Freed slaves who had escaped bondage courtesy of his armed forces or the stroke of his pen saw him as Father Abraham, the great emancipator.[1]

Lincoln was anti-slavery but no abolitionist. He had tried to avoid the war, but once it began his one goal was to save the Union in as near its antebellum form as possible. His every act, every decision, whether political or military, aimed at that end. The reality of a long and bloody war had forced him to take increasingly stringent

---

1   William Howard Russell, *My Diary North and South* (Boston, MA, 1863) 37-38.

actions, the most radical of which was his emancipation proclamation in January 1863. In the face of enormous challenges Lincoln had held the Northern pro-war coalition together, largely thanks to his talents as a politician and his astute ability to judge public sentiment. But by no means had threats to the North's unity disappeared, and the longer the war went on the larger those dangers loomed.

Lincoln's learning curve in military matters had been steep. He tried to leave military questions to military men, although that had often proven almost impossible. The president had made mistakes while feeling his way forward, but by 1863 he was a proven, although imperfect, commander-in-chief. When Lee's army invaded Pennsylvania in June 1863, Lincoln had perceived enormous opportunity rather than great peril. He was convinced that once the Rebels came north of the Potomac they could, as he put it, "never return if well attended." Meade's Gettysburg victory seemed to vindicate this belief. Nine days after the battle, when the defeated Confederate army found itself trapped around Williamsport, Maryland, with its back against a flooded and unbridged Potomac River, the president—like many Northerners in and out of the Union army—was certain the "substantial destruction" of Lee's command was at hand and with it the virtual end of the war.[2]

It did not happen. When Meade reached Williamsport at the end of a difficult pursuit from Gettysburg, he found Lee strongly entrenched and ready to meet any attack. Despite unrelenting pressure from Lincoln and Maj. Gen. Henry W. Halleck, general-in-chief of all the Union armies, Meade declined to launch an immediate assault. His army had lost more than 22,000 men in the recent battle and was in no better condition than the enemy it confronted. Meade worried that throwing his battered army into a hasty offensive against such a formidable position might result in a bloody repulse and cripple him further. Such a defeat could potentially undo all the North had accomplished at Gettysburg.

Meade hesitated to attack until he could strike a powerful blow with a good chance of succeeding. That would require time to gather a thorough understanding of the enemy position. To that end, the general intended to launch a large-scale reconnaissance against the Rebel works on July 13 in hopes of uncovering a vulnerable spot the army could breach with an all-out assault. But when Meade convened a council of war on the night of July 12, many of his corps commanders disapproved of the proposal. They wanted more time to get ready and bring up reinforcements.

Influenced by his subordinates' reservations as well as his own, Meade decided to take an extra day to prepare. The Rebels could not escape across the flooded Potomac, he thought, which meant the Union army had time to properly organize a powerful

---

2   George Meade, *Life and Letters of George Gordon Meade* 2 Vols. (New York, 1913), Lincoln to Howard, July 21, 1863, Vol. 2, 138.

reconnaissance-in-force to find and exploit any weakness in the enemy front. When word of this decision reached Washington it produced a howl of protest from Halleck, who demanded that Meade push forward at once and fight Lee before he could escape. But it was already too late. On the morning of July 14 advancing Union troops found only empty fortifications. Lee had slipped away the night before and withdrew back into Virginia on a makeshift bridge.[3]

The failure to destroy the virtually surrounded Southern army stunned everyone. Though many of Meade's soldiers were mortified, most of his officers thought the general had acted wisely and avoided a potential disaster. Not so the Northern editors and politicians. Halleck was furious. But no one was more distraught than Lincoln, who felt Meade had missed *the* great opportunity to end the war.

Halleck knew, of course, what Lincoln thought, and on afternoon of July 14 wired Meade a scathing telegram ordering him to pursue the Rebel army and cut it up wherever it had gone. In a biting passage Halleck told Meade "I need hardly say . . . that the escape of Lee's army without another battle has created great dissatisfaction in the mind of the President and it will require an active and energetic pursuit on your part to remove the impression that it has not been sufficiently active heretofore."[4]

Meade was as chagrined at Lee's escape as anyone, but the word "dissatisfaction" stuck in his craw. He had taken command of the army against his better judgment on the president's explicit order a mere three days before the great battle at Gettysburg. The 17 days from then till now had imposed enormous strain. He thought he had done everything possible to prevent Lee's successful withdrawal. Consequently, the general, whose temper was infamously short, immediately telegraphed Halleck a reply. He had performed his duty "conscientiously" and to the best of his ability, he wrote, and in his opinion the "censure of the President" was "so undeserved" he felt "compelled" to ask to be "immediately relieved" from command of the army.[5]

Once Lincoln had seen this response, he sat down to write Meade a letter of reassurance. He began by telling the general that he was "very, very grateful" for the "magnificent success you gave the cause of the country at Gettysburg" and went on to say that he was "sorry now to be the author of the slightest pain to you.'" But as he continued writing, Lincoln's emotional distress at Lee's escape gradually took over. The letter morphed into a reproachful missive castigating the general for letting a

---

3   *The War of the Rebellion: A Compilation of the Official Records of the Union and Confederate Armies* 128 vols. (Washington, D.C., 1880-1901) Series 1, Vol. 27, pt. 1, 91-92. Hereafter cited as OR. All references are to Series 1 unless otherwise noted.

4   Ibid., 92.

5   Ibid., 93.

golden opportunity slip through his fingers. However, Lincoln wisely decided not to send the letter, which would change nothing and only make things worse. He filed it away unsigned.[6]

Unlike the president, Halleck responded to Meade only an hour and twenty minutes after receiving his demand to be relieved. The general-in-chief took a conciliatory tone. The president's "disappointment . . . at the escape of Lee's army," he wrote, "was not intended as a censure, but as a stimulus to an active pursuit." It was hardly a reason for Meade's replacement.[7]

Meade noted that "dissatisfaction" had become "disappointment" and let the matter drop. Others did not, and the press and Washington politicians continued carping at Meade's failure to strike Lee at Williamsport. At a July 17 cabinet meeting several of Lincoln's department heads voiced displeasure at Meade's letting Lee escape and implied that he should be removed from command. The president refused and stood by the general. "He has committed a terrible mistake," Secretary of the Navy Gideon Welles recalled Lincoln saying, "but we shall try him farther." Secretary of State William Seward agreed and declared that other than permitting the Rebel army to get away, Meade had shown real "ability."[8]

The press of course knew nothing of this and continued to fulminate against Meade. These stories so disturbed Maj. Gen. Oliver Otis Howard (commander of the Army of the Potomac's XI Corps) that he wrote the president defending Meade's handling of the Gettysburg battle and his decision to delay attacking at Williamsport. The president responded a few days later. He admitted mortification at Lee's escape, saying "General Meade and his noble army had expended all the skill, and toil, and blood, up to the ripe harvest and then let the crop go to waste." Nonetheless, Lincoln confessed that, having thought things over, he was "profoundly grateful" for what Meade had done "without criticism for what was not done." The general had his confidence, he continued, as a "brave and skillful officer and a true man." Howard shared the president's letter with Meade, who was so pleased with its sentiments he sent a copy to his wife.[9]

*   *   *

---

6   Carl Sandburg, *Abraham Lincoln: The War Years* 4 vols. (New York, 1939) Vol. 4, 352.

7   *OR* 27, pt. 1, 93-94.

8   Sandburg, *Lincoln*, Vol. 3, 354-55.

9   *OR* 27, pt. 1, 700; Sandburg, *Lincoln*, Vol. 3, 354-55.

The Gettysburg campaign did not end when Lee slipped across the swollen Potomac. Meade was under orders to pursue his adversary and bring him to battle. Nonetheless, he was reluctant to follow the Rebels into Virginia. He believed Lincoln ought to be satisfied with having driven Lee out of Maryland and allow the tattered Union army to pause for rest, reorganization, and reinforcement. He knew, of course, that this was politically unacceptable and that the government expected him to push after the Confederates and finish what he had started at Gettysburg. Although he was worried that his army was in no condition to fight another major engagement, Meade threw his troops over the Potomac on July 18 and 19.[10]

The Federals crossed the river at Harper's Ferry, Virginia and Berlin, Maryland, after which Meade concentrated his forces in the northern end of the Loudoun Valley. This strategically sound decision put the Army of the Potomac on the flank of the Confederates who remained encamped in the lower Shenandoah Valley. The rugged Blue Ridge Mountains and a flooded Shenandoah River separated the opposing armies, and for the next week Meade and Lee played a game of cat and mouse across these barriers.

Both generals lacked firm intelligence on the position and movements of their adversary. Meade's cavalry seized control of several important mountain passes as Union infantry gradually moved south. At the same time, a Federal force of 6,000 men under Brigadier General Benjamin F. Kelley crossed the Potomac near Williamsport and advanced to the town of Hedgesville on the western side of the Shenandoah Valley. Halleck ordered Kelley to find some way to damage the Rebel army.

Meanwhile Lee's troops lingered not far from the Potomac around the towns of Martinsburg, Bunker Hill, and Winchester. The failure of the Confederates to rapidly retreat southward perplexed Meade. Virginia newspapers soon reported a possible explanation: massive reinforcements were on the way to Lee. Meade thought these stories were probably true, which would explain why Lee remained in the lower Valley. He was merely awaiting an infusion of strength before undertaking a sudden offensive thrust designed to cut off the Army of the Potomac from Washington.

When Confederate Lieutenant General Richard S. Ewell's Second Corps lunged at Kelley's force on July 21, Meade took it as proof of Lee's aggressive intentions. Determined not to fall into whatever trap his adversary had concocted, he halted the advance of his infantry until he could gather solid information on the enemy's exact position and numbers. The pause lasted for 35 critical hours.

Meade's apprehension was groundless. The Rebels weren't planning an offensive, and had gained only a single brigade in reinforcements. Lee had halted in the lower

---

10 Meade, *Life and Letters*, Vol. 2, 135.

Valley merely to see if Meade would cross the Potomac. But even before Confederate cavalry could confirm that the Yankees had entered the Loudoun Valley, Lee, with his usual decisiveness had put his army in motion for the Rappahannock River. The Confederates aimed to cross the Blue Ridge Mountains at Chester Gap near Front Royal, Virginia. Lieutenant General James Longstreet's First Corps would lead the way, followed by Lt. Gen. Ambrose Powell Hill's Third Corps. Ewell's Second Corps would stay near Bunker Hill for a bit longer, but Lee anticipated it too would shortly shift to the Rappahannock.

Front Royal was a critical spot. Two passes through the Blue Ridge opened onto the town, Manassas Gap to the north and Chester Gap to the south. As the Rebels moved toward the village, Federal horsemen from Brig. Gen. John Buford's 1st Cavalry Division rode for those mountain passes. If they could take and hold them, Meade could lock Lee in the Shenandoah Valley. Then he could shove the Army of the Potomac through one or both passes and destroy the whole or a part of the Rebel army on disadvantageous ground.

The Confederates, not unaware of this possibility, rapidly moved infantry into each pass. On July 21 Rebel foot soldiers collided with a brigade of Buford's cavalry in both gaps. In sharp fighting over the next two days, the Southerners held the Yankees in check at Manassas Gap and evicted them from Chester Gap. Once the latter was open, Longstreet and Hill hurried their infantry and supply trains through the gap toward the Rappahannock and Culpeper Court House.

Not until mid-day on July 22 did Meade have enough incontrovertible evidence from his signal stations and cavalry to convince him that Lee was leaving the Shenandoah Valley. Only then did he put his infantry back into motion, directing a third of his force toward Manassas Gap. Unfortunately, Federal intelligence on Lee's troop locations had become badly confused. Meade thought that only one Rebel corps had slipped through Chester Gap. He incorrectly believed the other two were still in the Valley, one approaching the pass and the other around Winchester. Obviously once the Army of the Potomac cut them off, it could concentrate overwhelming destructive force against them. Thus misconstruing the strategic situation, he ordered an attack through Manassas Gap to trap two Confederate corps no longer there.

Meade gave the job of taking Manassas Gap to Maj. Gen. William H. French, the newly appointed commander of the Federal III Corps. Regrettably for Meade's plan, French advanced cautiously. In charge of a corps for the first time, he was reluctant to risk a major attack until the V Corps under Maj. Gen. George Sykes arrived to reinforce the effort. Thus a brigade of Georgians from A. P. Hill's corps held the Yankees in check until two divisions from Ewell's command reached the scene and plugged the exit to Manassas Gap at the end of the day. The intense fighting inside the pass on July 23 was dramatic and consumed so much time the Federals failed to bull their way through to Front Royal before nightfall.

While Meade tried to shove his way westward into the Shenandoah Valley via Manassas Gap, Longstreet and Hill successfully slipped eastward through Chester Gap just a few miles to the south. At dawn on July 24, the Federals awoke to discover that during the night Ewell had disengaged and escaped to the south. Although French pushed on to Front Royal, the Confederates had already eluded him.

By that point Meade's troops were desperately low on rations. With Lee out of reach, Meade had no choice but to pivot eastward and move rapidly on Warrenton, Virginia where he could connect to the vast supply dumps around Washington, DC via the Orange & Alexandria (O&A) Railroad. As the Yankees trod northeast, Lee's troops concentrated around Culpeper Court House, which lay on the O&A midway between the Rappahannock and Rapidan rivers. From this position Lee could parry any Union thrust toward Richmond.[11]

For the moment the rival armies had lost touch with one another. Each would need a few days to rest and establish a new line of communication. Their pause on the Rappahannock, however, might prove as brief as the pause on the Potomac had been. Although the retreat from Gettysburg had brought the foes back to where they had started their march toward Pennsylvania, it was unclear whether the campaign had come to an end. Meade had failed to finish off Lee at Williamsport or in the Shenandoah Valley. That hardly meant he might not attempt to complete the job somewhere south of the Rappahannock, or that the Lincoln administration didn't expect him to. Sooner, rather than later, Meade would resume his advance. How Lee chose to respond would determine whether the armies fought their next big battle near Culpeper Court House or somewhere much closer to the Confederate capital.

---

11 For a detailed account and analysis of these final two weeks of the Gettysburg campaign, see Jeffrey Wm Hunt, *Meade and Lee After Gettysburg: The Forgotten Final Stage of the Gettysburg Campaign, From Falling Waters to Culpeper Court House, July 14-31, 1863* (El Dorado Hills, CA, 2017).

CHAPTER 2

"Natural and Artificial Obstacles"

Union Challenges—George Meade—Halleck's Rapprochement—Pressure to
Advance— Lincoln Refutes—Draft Riots—Offensive Plans

W HEN Maj. Gen. George Meade rode into Warrenton, Virginia, around noon on July 25, 1863 he had been in command of the Army of the Potomac for exactly 28 days. During the last tumultuous four weeks the press and Lincoln administration had praised the general for winning the fight at Gettysburg and condemned him for allowing the Rebels to escape back into Virginia. And despite Halleck's effort to soften the critique, Lincoln's criticism of the Union army's failure to trap the Confederates north of the Potomac still rankled. Meade's unsatisfying battle of wits with Lee across the Blue Ridge Mountains and the subsequent disappointment at Manassas Gap only exacerbated his frustrations.

As the last week of July dawned, the general and his troops sagged under the strain of an extraordinarily difficult campaign and the war's bloodiest battle to date. The march eastward from the mountains had proven brutal. Temperatures in the upper eighties, hunger, and unrelenting sun had taken a toll. Sunstroke had felled hundreds of men, and some had died. The heat was so intense, complained one Northerner, it seemed "as though lead would melt in the sun;" another attested that even in the shade "the wind will almost scorch you." Despite such conditions, a serious shortage of rations had compelled Meade to keep the army moving swiftly toward the railhead at Warrenton. "[M]arches of 20 & 28 miles per day in about the hottest season of the year are necessary," a tired infantryman conceded, but that men were "marched until they drop dead by the roadside," he thought outrageous.[1]

---

1 Raymond G. Barber & Gary E. Swinson, eds., *The Civil War Letters of Charles Barber, Private, 104th New York Volunteer Infantry* (Torrence, CA, 1991), 137; Edward K. Cassedy, *Dear Friends at*

Hard movement for the foot soldiers was torturous for the artillery. The extreme weather limited battery horses to only eight or ten miles a day. Even that pace was too much for many animals. The experience of Battery D, 5th United States Artillery was typical. Since crossing the Potomac on July 18, the unit had daily abandoned four to ten broken down horses, turning them out to die, an alarming loss even for an army that habitually worked its animals to death. The corpse of a horse or mule and often three or four marked every bad spot in the road.[2]

Regardless of such suffering the Union army completed its strategic redeployment from the Loudoun Valley to Warrenton by July 25. While the Federals had moved east, the Confederates had gone south and were now encamped around Culpeper Court House, some 23 miles distant. For the moment the rival forces had broken contact; danger of further combat was remote. That afforded at least a temporary respite to the worn out Federal army and its commander.

As his troops assumed positions around Warrenton, Meade faced a multitude of serious problems. His army was desperately low on supplies. Cavalry and artillery officers reported a shortage of horses and warned that the animals on hand were in poor shape. Three of the army's seven infantry corps—the I, II, and XI—severely mauled at Gettysburg, were understrength. The III Corps had suffered just as badly and only the recent addition of an extra division kept it up to strength.[3]

The XI Corps presented a special problem, having suffered great misfortune at Gettysburg and Chancellorsville. In both battles Rebel attacks had crushed its flanks. Its reputation in the rest of the army was woefully negative. The fact that a large percentage of XI Corps soldiers were German immigrants and widely looked down upon by native born troops, reinforced such feelings. Many officers had lost faith in the XI Corps and were recommending it be broken up.[4]

Field returns on August 10 showed only 76,000 men present for duty with the army—a far cry from the 88,000 it had taken into Gettysburg and the 120,000 it had carried into the fight at Chancellorsville just three months ago. Battlefield losses and the departure of thousands of men whose two-year enlistments had expired accounted for most of the decrease in fighting power. The Army of the Potomac badly needed

---

Home: The Civil War Letters of Sergeant Charles T. Bowen, Twelfth United States Infantry, First Battalion, 1861-1865 (Baltimore, MD, 2001), 309; Robert Krick, *Civil War Weather in Virginia* (Tuscaloosa, AL, 2007), 104.

2 Oliver Norton, *Army Letters 1861-1865* (Chicago, IL, 1903), 166-171.

3 *OR* 27, pt. 1, 99-102.

4 Ibid, 105-106.

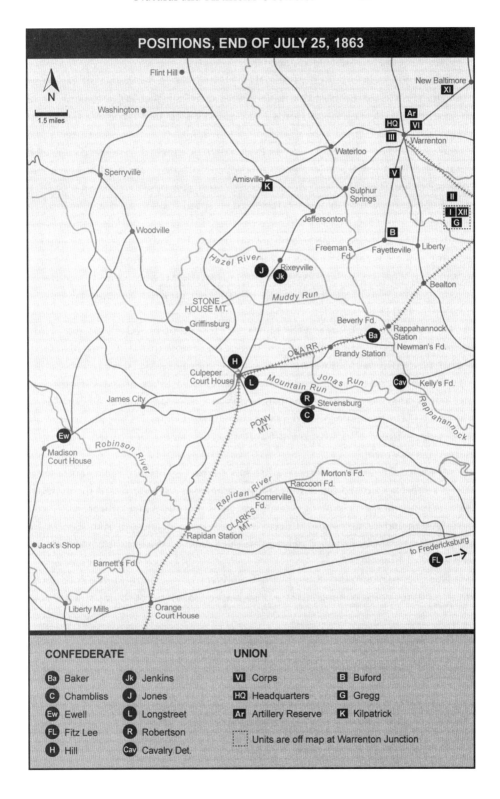

POSITIONS, END OF JULY 25, 1863

N
1.5 miles

Flint Hill
New Baltimore
XI
Washington
Ar
HQ   VI
III   Warrenton
Waterloo
Sperryville
V
Amisville
K
Sulphur
Springs
II
Jeffersonton
I XII
G
B
Woodville
Freeman's
Fd.   Fayetteville   Liberty
Hazel River
Rixeyville
J
Jk
Bealton
Muddy Run
STONE
HOUSE MT.
Griffinsburg
Beverly Fd.   Rappahannock
Ba   Station
O&A RR   Newman's Fd.
H   Brandy Station
Culpeper
Court House   Jonas Run
L   Mountain Run   Cav   Kelly's Fd.
James City   R   Stevensburg
C
PONY
MT.
Ew
Madison
Court House   Robinson River   Morton's Fd.
Raccoon Fd.
Rapidan River   Somerville
Fd.
CLARK'S
MT.
Jack's Shop   Rapidan Station
to Fredericksburg
FL
Barnett's Fd
Liberty Mills   Orange
Court House

CONFEDERATE   UNION

Ba Baker   Jk Jenkins   VI Corps   B Buford
C Chambliss   J Jones   HQ Headquarters G Gregg
Ew Ewell   L Longstreet   Ar Artillery Reserve K Kilpatrick
FL Fitz Lee   R Robertson
H Hill   Cav Cavalry Det.   Units are off map at Warrenton Junction

replacements and reinforcements. Where the government would find those vital commodities, however, remained uncertain.[5]

In addition to manpower, Meade also worried about the caliber of his corps commanders. Two of the most able leaders in the army had fallen at Gettysburg. Major General John F. Reynolds of I Corps had been killed on July 1 and Winfield Scott Hancock of the II Corps badly wounded on July 3. Meade deemed their loss "most serious" and told his wife that "their places are not to be supplied." He also complained about a lack of "active and energetic subordinate officers," upon whom he could "depend and rely" to take "care of themselves and commands."[6]

The general was too circumspect to record his specific feelings about individuals in his letters home. One of his staff officers, Captain James C. Biddle, felt no such constraint. The 27-year old Philadelphian and friend of the Meade family had entered the army as a company commander in the 27th Pennsylvania. Biddle joined Meade's staff in May 1863 and would serve there throughout the rest of the war. Doubtless he echoed opinions at headquarters when he confided unflattering appraisals of the army's principal leaders in a letter to his wife.

Biddle adjudged major generals Oliver O. Howard of the XI Corps and Henry Slocum of the XII Corps as "slow." He had heard rumors that III Corps' Maj. Gen. William H. French was a drunk, and the I Corps commander, Maj. Gen. John Newton, "nervous and fidgety." Furthermore Maj. Gen. George Sykes of the V Corps was suited to command of no more than a division, and Brig. Gen. William Hays, temporary II Corps commander, did "not amount to anything." Only major generals John Sedgwick of the VI Corps and Cavalry Corps commander Alfred Pleasonton escaped his judgment.[7]

Meade could not simply replace his subordinates, whatever their deficiencies. Congressional law limited the number of major generals in the army. At the moment there were no vacancies in that grade and precious few alternative officers to choose from. As an old regular army officer, Meade was disinclined to ruin careers by requesting the transfer of fellow old regulars. He would do the best he could with the men already by his side.[8]

This determination did not apply to Brig. Gen. Hays, whom Meade considered utterly unfit for corps command. As a brigadier he did not merit so important a post

5 Ibid., *OR* 29, pt. 2, 28.

6 George G. Meade to wife, July 18, 1863, *Life and Letters*, 2:136.

7 James C. Biddle to wife, August 13 in James C. Biddle papers, Historical Society of Pennsylvania.

8 *OR* 27, pt. 1, 101.

and Meade was especially anxious to replace him with a competent major general. After consulting with Winfield Hancock, Meade recommended Brig. Gen. Gouverneur K. Warren for promotion and command of the II Corps until Hancock healed and could return to that post. Currently the army's chief engineer, Warren was a man of considerable energy and talent who had played a key role in saving the Union left flank at Gettysburg. Halleck supported this request but could do nothing until successfully shepherding it through the government's bureaucracy.[9]

Lurking in the shadows behind these problems was Meade's distress at what he considered the unfair appraisal of his generalship by Lincoln, the war department, and the press. Halleck's July 14 telegram expressing the president's "dissatisfaction" over Lee's successful retreat into Virginia still bore down on him. It mattered little that the general-in-chief had quickly amended the phrase to "disappointment." Meade continued fretting that Halleck and Lincoln believed he had "failed" to do what he "might and should have done" or what "another would and could have done." It rankled and planted doubts about his standing with the administration.[10]

These difficulties paled in comparison to Meade's greatest worry: the Army of Northern Virginia just over the horizon, a force of hardened veterans under talented commanders, led by General Robert E. Lee, a dangerous and wily foe. He had beaten badly each of Meade's predecessor commanders of the Army of the Potomac. But despite his formidable record, the public and press still expected the Union army to exploit its recent Gettysburg victory by destroying Lee and his army. Given his own command's weaknesses and problems, Meade was certain that task was presently impossible and would remain so until he successfully overcame his own army's difficulties. Confronting all those challenges simultaneously was an undertaking of Herculean proportions. Yet that is precisely what circumstances demanded. Meade would have to do it while still adjusting to his new post and seeking to put his own administrative and operational stamp on the army.

* * *

The fact that George Meade found himself wrestling with these issues was somewhat ironic. The 47-year old Pennsylvanian had never wanted to be a soldier. He had gone to West Point with the goal of a free education rather than a military career. After graduating in 1835 and pulling a year-long tour of duty in Florida during the

---

9   Ibid., 96-97, 101; Stephen W. Sears, *Lincoln's Lieutenants: The High Command of the Army of the Potomac* (Boston, MA, 2017), 595.

10 Meade to Halleck, July 31, 1863, *Life and Letters*, 2:139-40.

Second Seminole War, he had become discouraged with the tedium of army life, low pay, and poor promotion prospects and resigned his commission in October 1836.

But this didn't sever his association with the US Army. His talent for mathematics led to a new career as a contract employee for the war department's topographical branch. He subsequently worked on a host of projects including river and boundary surveys as well as railroad construction. In 1841 he married Margaret Sergeant, the eldest daughter of Pennsylvania congressman John Sergeant—a long-time confidant of the Meade family.

Shortly thereafter the army decided to cease employing civilian contractors. This led to Meade's rejoining the military in 1842 as a second lieutenant of topographical engineers. In 1846, at the outset of the Mexican War, Meade was serving on Maj. Gen. Zachery Taylor's staff. The lieutenant performed commendably at the battles of Palo Alto and Resaca de la Palma and later displayed considerable courage and competence while guiding a flanking column during the three day fight for the city of Monterrey. After the war Meade oversaw lighthouse construction until 1856 when he took control of a geographic survey of the Great Lakes. Promoted to captain in 1858, Meade was in Detroit when the Civil War began, and in September 1861 he received an appointment as a brigadier general of Pennsylvania volunteers.[11]

Meade proved a solid combat leader. He was wounded in the hip and arm at the June 1862 battle of White Oak Swamp. After recovering, he advanced steadily in rank and responsibility. By the fall of 1862 Meade had a division, and he temporarily commanded the I Corps at Antietam. Three months later at Fredericksburg his brigades were the only Federal units to achieve even a temporary penetration of the Confederate defenses. His solid record led to a major general's stars and command of the V Corps in time for the battle of Chancellorsville, where his troops saw only modest action. In the wake of that defeat, many of his fellow corps commanders enthusiastically supported replacing the beaten Joe Hooker with Meade. Those recommendations, Meade's abstention from playing politics, plus his solid record, convinced Lincoln to place him in charge of the Army of the Potomac on June 28, 1863. Less than a week later, the Pennsylvanian was famous for becoming the first Union general to win a clear cut victory over Robert E. Lee.[12]

George Meade was a thorough professional whom his peers respected. Physically brave, modest to a fault, and totally bereft of vanity or pretension, he was, however, touchy about his professional reputation. Tall, erect, with a slight patrician air and

---

11 Ezra J. Warner, *Generals in Blue* (Baton Rouge, LA, 1964), 315-16.

12 Larry Tagg, *The Generals of Gettysburg: The Leaders of America's Greatest Battle* (Campbell, CA, 1998), 1-4.

Major General George G. Meade
Library of Congress

fluent in several languages, he easily charmed visiting foreign military observers. When the occasion required he could look splendid, but he usually dressed carelessly with the look of a busy field commander. He had a high forehead, prominent nose, a lantern jaw adorned by a thick beard and mustache and appeared older than he was. A pair of deep-set eyes perched above bags of drooping skin gave him the aura of a wise judge or family doctor.

Although a devoted and loving husband and father, he was also a stern military disciplinarian. His awful, often uncontrollable and demeaning temper earned him an unpleasant reputation for heartlessness. Meade had the conditional respect of his troops after Gettysburg, but not their affection. The men had endured too many broken promises of victory and had seen too many army commanders come and go for emotional investment in someone like Meade. The general would have to prove that his Pennsylvania victory bespoke war-winning talent rather than a momentary streak of competence or luck. The troops' final judgement on Meade would depend on how he performed in the weeks ahead.[13]

*   *   *

Before the general could do anything to meet the host of hopes and expectations heaped upon him, he first had to cope with a serious supply problem. The army reached Warrenton "short [of] and out of everything," one officer said. The troops desperately needed a quick connection with Washington, DC's vast supply depots. The

13 Robert G. Scott, *Fallen Leaves: The Civil War Letters of Major Henry Livermore Abbot* (Kent, OH,1992), 189; Horace Porter, *Campaigning with Grant* (New York, 1897), 247; Patricia L. Faust, ed., *Historical Times Illustrated Encyclopedia of the Civil War* (New York, 1986), 482-483; "George Gordon Meade, 1815-1872," accessed 30 Apr 2018, www.thelatinlibrary.com/chron/civilwar notes/meade.html.

army's requirements were breathtaking: daily rations for 100,000 men and 8,000 animals, not to mention enormous quantities of ammunition, clothing, medicine, harnesses, horseshoes, and a host of other sundries. Moreover, Meade wanted to have enough additional supplies to fill his wagons with ten days' rations as rapidly as possible.[14]

Fortunately the army's rapid departure from the Loudoun Valley did not take the US Military Railroad (USMRR) system by surprise. Brigadier General Herman Haupt—chief of construction and transportation for the USMRR—had anticipated the necessity of switching Meade's communications to the Orange & Alexandria Railroad (O&A), which ran northeast from Warrenton Junction toward the Potomac. The Union army had all but ignored the line during the Gettysburg campaign. Its tracks, culverts and bridges required serious maintenance before the route could be fully operational. Anticipating this, the highly competent Haupt had concentrated his work crews at Alexandria, Virginia just before Meade crossed the Potomac on July 18. His foresight now allowed his men to descend on the O&A and speedily put it back in working order as far south as Warrenton Junction, where a spur of the O&A stretched westward to Warrenton.[15]

Once the rails were functional, Yankee stevedores and locomotive engineers strained every nerve to meet Meade's immense requisitions. On July 26 Federal quartermasters moved 530 loaded boxcars the 40 miles from Manassas to Warrenton. The following day, another 127 cars traveled the same path. Northern railroad crews emptied Manassas Junction of nearly every operational vehicle in order to transfer 1,272 tons of supplies to the front in a single day. These monumental efforts replenished the army's coffers overnight and solved the first of Meade's post-Loudoun Valley problems.[16]

More imposing difficulties lay in Haupt's near future, however. While his workers struggled to improve the rail line to Warrenton Junction and then southward, an imminent challenge loomed along the banks of the Rappahannock River. Union troops had burned the O&A bridge over that stream in November 1862, and the crossing, located at Rappahannock Station, had lain in ruins ever since. Until this 500-foot span was rebuilt, the Union army could not supply itself south of the river and hence couldn't continue its pursuit of Lee.[17] The continuation of that pursuit was uppermost on Meade's mind. As far as the general was concerned, Halleck's July 14 order that

14 Herman Haupt, *Reminiscences of General Herman Haupt* (Milwaukee, WI, 1901), 246-52.

15 Ibid; *OR* 27, pt. 3, 696.

16 Haupt, *Reminiscences*, 252.

17 *OR* 27, pt. 3, 841-45. The previously noted severe shortage of horses also hindered the plan.

Lee's army should be "pursued and cut up wherever it may have gone" remained in effect. Meade therefore informed the general-in-chief on July 28 that his army was making every effort to prepare for a continued advance. The general confessed that, as usual, the exact whereabouts of the Rebel infantry was uncertain. Intelligence reports were contradictory. Meade thought that Lee's main body was behind the Rapidan. However, a Union scout just returned from across the Rappahannock asserted (incorrectly) that 10,000 troops under Lt. Gen. Daniel Harvey Hill had reinforced Lee, who was preparing to make a stand at Culpeper Court House. News that enemy locomotives were running all the way north to that town supported this troubling prediction.

Regardless of Lee's position or intentions, Meade planned to throw his cavalry across the Rappahannock to "feel the enemy" and secure the south bank of the river. Once Union troopers accomplished this, Haupt's men would rebuild the railroad bridge at Rappahannock Station, and Meade's army would immediately cross the river and advance along the railroad to Culpeper Court House and "as far beyond" as Lee's position would "permit."[18]

As a caveat to his plan, Meade wanted to ensure Halleck understood that this pending offensive would require the O&A to handle all the army's logistical needs. Meade remained uncertain whether the railroad was up to the task. It wasn't merely a question of the single track line's capacity, but also of its vulnerability to Rebel guerrilla attacks. Nonetheless, Meade expressed willingness to "test the question" and resume the pursuit that had begun at Gettysburg. Less than 24 hours later the premise upon which the general was making his plans evaporated completely. The pretext for that change was a memorandum Lincoln sent to Halleck after reading Meade's July 28 telegram promising an advance.[19]

The president wrote that he was disturbed to realize Meade felt the government was demanding a "general engagement with Lee as soon as possible." He was "claiming no such thing" and was against forcing a battle. Obviously still chagrined at Lee's escape after Gettysburg, Lincoln took a not-so-subtle swipe at Meade, observing that it was "absurd" to think the Union army could "safely engage" Lee near Culpeper if it had been impossible to attack him safely in Maryland. Now that the Rebels had been driven back into central Virginia, Lincoln felt that the army had done all that was

---

18 Ibid., 27, pt. 1, 103-104.

19 Ibid; Survivors' Association, *History of the 121st Regiment Pennsylvania Volunteers* (Philadelphia, PA, 1906), 65-66, describes these blockhouses and the requirements to man them.

presently possible. He didn't want Meade to instigate a battle "on the impression" that the administration was "pressing him."[20]

He was not ordering the Army of the Potomac to avoid combat per se: the president told Halleck and Meade they were free to launch an offensive if their judgment was contrary to his own. But he wanted it perfectly understood that Meade should not fight because he felt compelled to do so by the administration.

Although strategically oriented, Lincoln's message was as much a political document as military directive. Although he saw little hope of decisive action in Virginia, there was no reason to prevent his generals from trying to create some. But if Meade incited and lost a battle within the context of government expectations, Lincoln's political foes could claim that defeat resulted from presidential pressure to fight before the army was ready. That would be powerful ammunition to hand to the Democratic Party just two months before congressional elections. By explicitly putting his thoughts in writing Lincoln somewhat shielded his administration from such accusations and threw the question of what to do in Virginia squarely into the laps of Halleck and Meade.

*   *   *

Perhaps no man other than Abraham Lincoln had a more central role in the Union war effort than Henry Wager Halleck. The 48-year old general was a New Yorker by birth whose father had served as an officer in the War of 1812. To escape life as a farmer, Henry ran away from home at the age of 16 to live with his grandfather, Henry Wager, who facilitated his education and appointment to West Point. Halleck excelled there and ranked third in his class when he graduated in 1839. That distinction earned him an appointment in the prestigious corps of engineers. Before embarking on active duty he spent a year teaching French at his alma mater.[21]

Following this brief academic tenure, Halleck steadily amassed a noteworthy set of accomplishments. He penned a lengthy and impressive report on sea coast fortifications for the Senate, spent six months in Europe studying the continent's many armies, and authored *Elements of Military Art and Science*, a treatise that became a standard textbook at West Point. Transferred to California during the Mexican War, Halleck saw little action but gained prominence by assuming an influential role in drafting the state's constitution. Despite a promotion to captain in 1853, Halleck left the United States Army in 1854 for a successful career as both a businessman and an attorney. That same

---

20 *OR* 27, pt. 1, 105. Halleck forwarded a copy of Lincoln's message to Meade on July 29.

21 Stephen E. Ambrose, *Halleck: Lincoln's Chief of Staff* (Baton Rouge, LA, 1996), 5-7.

year he married Elizabeth Hamilton, Alexander Hamilton's great-granddaughter. Halleck excelled in his new profession, and by 1860 he was worth half-a-million dollars.[22]

When the Civil War broke out Halleck returned to uniform as the fourth highest ranking major general in the Federal army. After he took command of the department of Missouri his energy and organizational talents ended the chaos and corruption that marked the initial Union war effort in the West. The orderly system he created ensured that Federal forces were well-supplied, -organized, and -administered. It was within this framework that officers under Halleck's overall direction—John Pope, Ulysses S. Grant, and Samuel R. Curtis—won the North's first significant victories. As a reward, the government gave Halleck overall command of Union forces in the West. With Halleck in charge, the Federal armies, in conjunction with the United States Navy, captured Memphis and Nashville and the vital rail junction of Corinth, Mississippi. These triumphs overshadowed Maj. Gen. George B. McClellan's failure to take Richmond and led Lincoln to name Halleck general-in-chief of all the Union armies in July 1862.

The former California business mogul did not look at all the part of a successful military chieftain. Brigadier General William E. Doster, the provost marshal of Washington, DC, described Halleck as a man of "medium height, inclined to fatness." The general, Doster continued, sported a "double chin, bald forehead and small busy eyes, twinkling under uplifted eyebrows." The general's "carriage and dress were somewhat ungainly and bespoke a solid citizen rather than the active soldier." *A New York Herald* reporter agreed with Doster: Halleck, he explained, didn't look a "whit military in appearance" and even in a new uniform seemed as if "he were in borrowed clothes."[23]

Halleck's demeanor was as unmilitary as his appearance. Major General Lew Wallace, who served under Halleck in the Western Theater, commented on his "sideways carriage of the head and a habit of looking at people with eyes wide open." Doster remembered that Halleck "walked generally with his hands behind his back or in his trouser pockets, slightly stooping, in an apparently meditative attitude." Although Halleck's scholarly attainments resulted in his nickname "Old Brains," Wallace seemed to scoff at the moniker and found nothing professorial in his superior's stare, which he described as having the "dull" lifeless quality of a fish rather than the supposedly wise aspect of an owl. Secretary of the Navy Gideon Welles found

---

22 Ibid, 7. A half-million dollars in 1860 is the equivalent of $14 million in 2017.

23 William E. Doster, *Lincoln and Episodes of the Civil War* (New York, 1915), 178; *New York Herald*, July 21, 1862.

General-in-Chief Henry W. Halleck
Library of Congress

quite annoying the general's habit of rubbing his elbows "as if they were the seat of thought."[24]

A failure to meet pre-conceived expectations did not impinge upon Halleck's professionalism. He firmly believed trained specialists acting in accordance with the immutable axioms of war should handle military affairs. All business all the time, he disdained amateurs and conducted his affairs with the impatience of an expert forced to work with inferior minds. Halleck simply abhorred wasting time, and habitually anticipated what someone had to say and decided how he would respond before the speaker managed to get half way through his discourse. He exhibited neither "humility nor greatness," and "was just General-in-Chief, no more—no less; that he knew and felt and made you know and feel," Doster confessed in a rather damning description. Halleck's subordinates resented his pressure on them to move, and the condescending manner in which he scolded and lectured them. That included George Meade.[25]

Having snapped testily at one another in mid-July after Lee's retreat over the Potomac, the two generals' relationship had remained somewhat tense ever since. Nonetheless, Meade impressed Halleck. On July 11, just days before the disappointment at Williamsport, the general-in-chief confided to Ulysses Grant that Meade had "thus far proved an excellent general" and remarked that he "seems the right man in the right place." Although Lee's escape across the Potomac had dismayed

---

24 Lew Wallace, *Lew Wallace, An Autobiography* (New York, 1906), 570; Doster, *Lincoln and Episodes*, 178; William E. & Erica L. Gienapp, eds., *The Civil War Diary of Gideon Welles: Lincoln's Secretary of the Navy* (Urbana, IL, 2014), 38.

25 Doster, *Lincoln and Episodes*, 178. An excellent administrator who deftly manipulated and maintained the Union military machine, Halleck's contribution to the Northern war effort was important and essential. Victory would not have come without what he gave the cause. But he functioned as a chief-of-staff not a true general-in-chief.

everyone in Washington, Halleck did not lose sight of Meade's vital accomplishment at Gettysburg.[26]

The war would continue, and Halleck needed good rapport with the commander of the Union's principal eastern army. It was time to mend fences with his subordinate for his harsh words about failing to destroy the Rebels at Williamsport. On July 28 Halleck wrote a warm letter to Meade commending his "superior generalship" at Gettysburg and lauding him for bringing all his "forces into action at the right time and place, which no commander of the Army of the Potomac has done before." He urged Meade not to be "vexed" by Lincoln's disappointment at Lee's escape. Those feelings were entirely understandable and certainly shared by Meade. "Such things sometimes occur to us without any fault of our own," he observed and assured his subordinate of his own, the president's, and the country's confidence and gratitude.[27]

Halleck's correspondence arrived at army headquarters the evening of July 30. Meade replied the next morning and "heartily" thanked the general-in-chief for his "kind and generous" letter. Despite his gracious tone, the bulk of Meade's response defended his actions at Williamsport and his reaction to Lincoln's expression of "dissatisfaction." Although he appreciated his superiors' confidence, he reminded them that he had "no pretensions to any superior capacity" entitling him to command the Army of the Potomac. He would "exert" his "utmost efforts" and do his best, but Meade made clear that "the moment" his chiefs decided he was "wanting, or that another would do better," the general "earnestly" wished to be replaced for the good of "country and . . . cause."[28]

Until such a moment, Meade had to deal with Lee. He wasn't overly pleased with his army's current line of operation on the O&A, feeling that it offered many difficulties and few advantages. Although he occupied his current position by happenstance rather than plan, Meade was prepared to see what his command might accomplish by crossing the Rappahannock. Lee would probably be inclined to yield ground in the face of a renewed Federal advance. Just how much territory the Rebel might relinquish easily was hard to predict. Since Gettysburg Lee had evaded every Union effort to force another battle. This evinced either Southern weakness or shrewd strategy.

Meade suspected the latter. It was "evident" Lee was "determined not to fight," he wrote his wife on July 26, until he had drawn the Union army "as far from Washington

---

26 *OR* 24, pt. 3, 498.

27 *OR* 27, pt. 1, 104; Meade, *Life and Letters*, 2:139. Meade's response in *OR* 27, pt. 1, 108-109, says Halleck's letter was received on the evening of July 30.

28 *OR* 27, pt. 1, 106; Meade, *Life and Letters*, 2:138-141.

as possible" and obtained a "position where all the advantages will be on his side." Under that assumption, a Federal thrust beyond the Rappahannock toward the Rapidan would not meet serious opposition. In the best case, it would reveal just how far Lee was willing to retreat before refusing to back up any farther. What would happen then Meade could not yet say. Nonetheless, he was determined to continue his southward march as soon as his army was ready to move. Perhaps that would help dispel doubts in the capital about his aggressiveness.[29]

* * *

Events on the Northern home front soon complicated Meade's plans and scrambled the strategic situation in Virginia. On July 13, a severe riot protesting the Union's newly instituted draft, among other things, had broken out in New York City. Throughout July 13-14 violence ruled parts of the city. The rampage wasn't quelled until militiamen broke up the mobs with gunfire.[30]

In the wake of the riot, the draft was suspended, but the city remained restless. Newspapers claimed 500 people had died in the mayhem and officials feared a reoccurrence if conscription resumed. It was important, however, that the draft resume quickly because, as impossible as it might seem, the North, with its vast preponderance of population over the South, was beginning to face a manpower shortage.

By late summer of 1863, the United States had been at war for 28 months. During that time Union armies had lost tens of thousands of troops killed, crippled or maimed on the battlefield. A far larger number had died or been rendered incapable of further service by disease. These losses alone were enough to present Northern armies with the need to swell their ranks.

But an even greater danger hovered on the Union's military horizon. After the July 1861 debacle at First Bull Run, the Federal government called on loyal states for more men. They produced the required number of regiments and batteries, but most of the soldiers in these units had enlisted for only two or three years. By the end of July 1863, the army had discharged two-year enlistees in droves. Before the next spring, the enlistments of the three-year men, who made up a significant portion of the army, would expire as well. If these trained and battle-tested soldiers did not reenlist, a large portion of the Union's military strength might simply melt away.

---

29 Meade to Wife, July 29, 1863, *Life and Letters*, 2:137.

30 For detailed analysis of the New York City draft riots see, Iver Bernstein, *The New York City Draft Riots Their Significance for American Society and Politics in the Age of the Civil War* (New York, 1990) and Barnet Schecter, *The Devil's Own Work: The Civil War Draft Riots and the Fight to Reconstruct America* (New York, 2005).

The North needed men, a great many of them—and *now*, so they could learn the business of soldiering while veterans remained to teach them. So conscription was imperative. But the draft could not resume at the cost of another riot. The only way to go forward while maintaining law and order was to put enough troops in New York City and other hot spots to deter a recurrence of the violence.

This filtered down to the Army of the Potomac on the afternoon of July 29. Meade was still absorbing Lincoln's message disclaiming any demand for renewed combat with Lee, when a second telegram arrived from Halleck. Cutting right to the chase, he warned that it might become necessary to transfer troops from Virginia to enforce the draft. Meade, therefore, should defer any advance, at least for the moment.[31]

Meade quickly wired a response: his army was on the verge of crossing the Rappahannock which might provoke a battle. Although he believed Lee would retire across the Rapidan rather than fight around Culpeper Court House, the possibility of an engagement was real. If the war department wanted to forestall an advance, it needed to make up its mind quickly. Meade hastened to add that he favored a forward movement and was confident he could defeat Lee, provided the Rebels were not well entrenched in a strong position. In that case, the general feared such "natural and artificial obstacles" would allow even an outnumbered Southern army to prevail.

Should Lee fall back behind the Rapidan the strength of the entire Army of the Potomac would be required to breach the Rebel river defenses. Meade told Halleck that in that case he would very much like reinforcements. If, however, the army was to hold its present position, the shallow waters of the upper Rappahannock wouldn't hinder Lee if he decided to turn the Union army's western flank and force it into retreat. Moreover, Meade didn't think Washington could reinforce the Northern army faster than Richmond could reinforce Lee. For the moment, though, Meade promised not to undertake any movement until Halleck and Lincoln advised him of their wishes.

These were not long in coming. Before day's end, the government instructed Meade to send four regiments of infantry to New York City. The war department contemplated no further reduction in Meade's strength, but Halleck minced no words about how desperate the situation was: "Under no circumstances can we now give you any reinforcements. Every place has been stripped bare." That same afternoon, Meade got a definitive order to halt on the Rappahannock but maintain a "threatening attitude."

Early on the morning of July 31, in compliance with his new orders, General Meade put the 5th Wisconsin, 1st and 37th Massachusetts, and 20th Indiana regiments, a total of 1,643 men, on railway cars for the North. His army thus lost the equivalent of

31 *OR* 27, pt. 1, 105.

one brigade, a diminishment which hardly seemed sufficient reason to switch from an offensive to a defensive stance. But Meade had Halleck's order to halt, and Meade obeyed orders.[32]

However, those same orders also said to maintain a threatening attitude, and Meade thought the best way to do that was to go ahead with the already planned movement across the river. This would allow Haupt to rebuild the railway bridge and permit Meade to test his suspicion that Lee was inclined to continue retreating toward Richmond. If he were right, the Union army might jump two important river barriers without much of a fight. Of course, realization of such hopes relied on the enemy's cooperation. Unfortunately for Meade, Rebel cavalry under Maj. Gen. James Ewell Brown (Jeb) Stuart stood watch along the upper Rappahannock. When the Federals moved south, the Confederates would be ready to fight.

32 Ibid., 106-108.

CHAPTER 3

"No Field . . . For Battle"

Culpeper County—Lee's Decision—Seizing the Rappahannock Fords—
Buford's Drive on Culpeper—The Federals Repulsed—Lee Pulls Back

B ELOW the Rappahannock, Robert E. Lee awaited the Federals' next move. He was grateful that his army had gained some badly needed breathing space in Culpeper and Madison counties after the fight at Manassas Gap on July 23.

For the moment, Longstreet's First and A. P. Hill's Third Corps were encamped around Culpeper Court House. Two divisions of Ewell's Second Corps bivouacked along Robertson's River on the border between Madison and Culpeper counties. Ewell's third division, commanded by Maj. Gen. Jubal A. Early, was concentrated around Madison Court House. Jeb Stuart's cavalry picketed the Rappahannock River and screened the Rebel infantry.[1]

How long these forces would linger in their current locations was an open question. Although the Rebel army had found temporary safety, it was doubtful its retreat from Gettysburg had finally ended. The Confederates were certain that Meade would renew his advance as soon as he had resupplied. The proximity of Union depots around Washington meant that wouldn't take long. Whenever the Federals decided to resume active operations would be too soon for Lee's taste.

The great Confederate general faced a plethora of serious problems. The Pennsylvania invasion had cost his command 27,125 casualties, with losses among officers especially heavy. The enemy had killed, wounded, or captured over a third of the army's leaders above the rank of colonel. Six general officers were dead or would

---

1 Jeffrey Hunt, *Meade and Lee After Gettysburg*, 250, 262-266; Clifford Dowdey & Louis H. Manarin, eds., *The Wartime Papers of R. E. Lee* (New York, 1961), 563-564.

soon die of wounds, eight more were injured, and three had become prisoners of war. Among these fallen commanders were some of the most capable soldiers in the South.[2]

The rank and file reflections on the recent campaign produced a wide variety of emotions and opinions. When the army had moved north at the end of May 1863, it had done so after a string of victories and with full confidence in itself and its leaders. The unexpected outcome at Gettysburg had dismayed and embarrassed many Confederate soldiers. Some were furious at the failure, others were embittered over high casualties resulting from what they saw as questionable strategy and tactics. An unknown percentage of officers and enlisted men felt their once unshakeable faith in the Confederate army's leadership jarred, at least temporarily.[3]

Their commander, too, was troubled and disappointed by his defeat at Gettysburg. General Lee realized that the campaign into Pennsylvania had not been a total failure. His commissary had procured enormous quantities of supplies in the North. His troops had exhibited sublime courage in the battle and the performance of the army had been exemplary during the retreat from Pennsylvania. His men had remained resolute and disciplined throughout the ordeal despite its many hardships and dangers. Their skill had kept the enemy at bay on the Potomac and stymied their attempts to prevent Lee from shifting his command across the Blue Ridge Mountains into central Virginia.

Nevertheless, the army was in rough shape. Uniforms were in tatters, thousands of men lacked shoes, efficiency was impaired, morale badly bruised. Overworked animals needed grain, and everyone required rest. It would take weeks to address these concerns and repair the damage endured in Pennsylvania.

Lee knew the enemy would not willingly grant him time to rehabilitate his command. The Confederates would have to wrest that interval from their opponents by occupying a strong defensive position that Meade would hesitate to challenge. After careful consideration, Lee concluded that his army's current post in Culpeper County was poorly suited to that purpose.

---

2 Stephen Sears, *Gettysburg* (New York, 2003), 498; Douglas Southall Freeman, *Lee's Lieutenants*, 3 vols. (New York, 1944), 3:190.

3 For examples of Confederate opinions and feelings after Gettysburg, see Micajah Wood papers, University of Virginia(UVA); Bell Wiley, *The Road to Appomattox* (New York, 1983), 64-65; Jeremiah Tate letters, (Gilder Lehrman Institute of American History, New York, NY.) (GLIAH); Click letters, United States Military History Institute, Carlilse Barracks, PA (USMHI); Lewis Nunnelee Diary, Museum Of the Civil War, Richmond, VA (MCW), 91; Edward G. Longacre, *Lee's Cavalrymen: A History of the Mounted Forces of the Army of Northern Virginia* (Mechanicsburg, PA, 2002), 237; James Longstreet, "Lee in Pennsylvania," *Annals of the War* (Edison, NJ, 1996), 414-15.

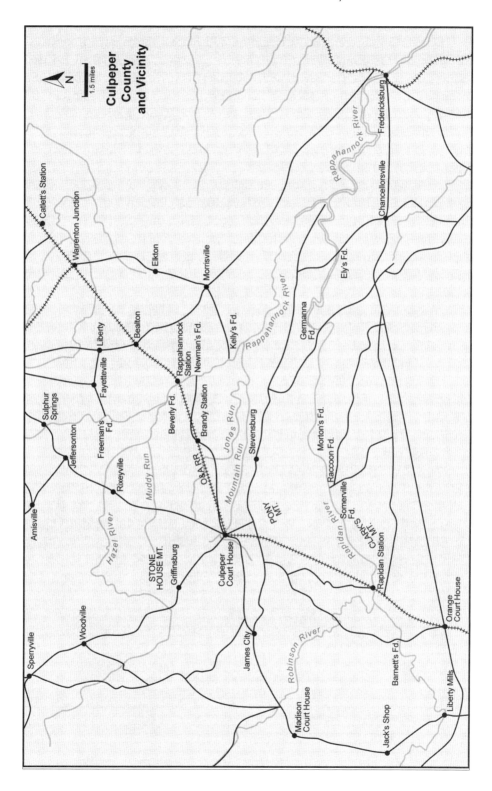

Located mid-way between Washington and Richmond, the county encompassed 383 square miles of gently rolling terrain consisting mostly of open fields interspersed with occasional forest. The county seat, Culpeper Court House, a town of about a thousand people, lay almost exactly in the district's center. George Washington had originally surveyed the village site in 1795, and A. P. Hill had grown up near there. Several smaller communities lay scattered across Culpeper's bucolic countryside, all of them on dirt roads that radiated out of the court house toward various fords on the waterways that marked the region's frontier.[4]

The Rappahannock River formed Culpeper County's northern and eastern boundary, the Rapidan River, its southern boundary, with the diminutive Robertson's River marking much of the county's western extent. North and east of Culpeper Court House the Rappahannock flows northwest to southeast until its confluence with the Rapidan some twenty miles due west of Fredericksburg. From there the Rapidan traces a generally westward line to its intersection with Robertson's River just west of Rapidan Station.[5]

Culpeper County sat inside a large sideways "V" formed by the Rappahannock and Rapidan rivers, with Culpeper Court House located almost exactly in the middle of this space. The western end of this "V" formed by the rivers opened toward the Blue Ridge Mountains and the vital gaps into Shenandoah Valley. Consequently, the farther west one traveled, the more hilly and difficult became the terrain. South of the court house and on both sides of the Rapidan River, high hills abruptly rose one thousand feet or higher above the surrounding countryside. These features dominated the surrounding terrain and provided excellent military observation points that could take in a considerable area.

The O&A bisected the county. The line originated on the banks of the Potomac at Alexandria, Virginia just downstream from Washington, DC and ran southwest to Culpeper Court House, crossing into Culpeper County at Rappahannock Station along the way. At the courthouse, the O&A turned due south toward the Rapidan. Once it crossed that waterway at Rapidan Station the line continued to Gordonsville in Orange County, where it connected to the Virginia Central Railroad which ran west to Staunton in the southern (upper) Shenandoah Valley and east to Richmond. The

---

4 Daniel E. Sutherland, "Culpepper County During the Civil War," Encyclopedia Virginia, Accessed April 17, 2018, https://www.encyclopediavirginia.org/Culpeper_County_During_the_Civil_War#start_entry.

5 Today, the Robertson's River is the Robinson River. The Rappahannock and Rapidan originate in the foothills of the Blue Ridge Mountains. The Robertson flows into the Rapidan, which flows into the Rappahannock, which flows toward Chesapeake Bay and the Atlantic Ocean. Mays in *Tyler's Quarterly* #5, July 1923, 102, said the Robertson was really just a "very small stream" which didn't deserve "the appellation of river."

Virginia Central was a vital Rebel supply line linking the agricultural bounty of the Valley to the Confederate capital. Lee had to defend it at all hazards.[6]

The quirks of geography and the railroad had made Culpeper County a pivotal location in the struggle for Northern Virginia. Both sides had camped on, marched over, and fought for the region incessantly since the war began. Culpeper provided the Confederates a perfect jumping off point for offensive operations in the Valley and the North. As a defensive position, however, the county was less than ideal.

Inside the Culpeper V the distance between the Rappahannock and the Rapidan rivers stood at just 23 miles if one traced the O&A from Rappahannock Station through Culpeper Court House to Rapidan Station, and that distance narrowed geometrically near the intersection of the two rivers. This geography limited maneuver room for any army positioned around Culpeper Court House.

If Lee lost a battle between the V of the rivers he would have to fall back across the Rapidan. Although multiple fords crossed the waterway, all were all susceptible to flooding and therefore potential traps. Moreover, these crossing points were natural funnels that would slow a retreating army and render it vulnerable to attack. And any withdrawal toward the western end of the Culpeper V would virtually sever a Confederate army's line of communications with Richmond and the city itself.

The land inside Culpeper County along the Rappahannock was lower than in neighboring Fauquier County to the north. Thus Yankee troops holding the north bank of the river had the tactical advantage of higher ground as well as the ability to mass unseen opposite any fords for a sudden offensive into Culpeper. The terrain also offered the Federals the opportunity to march unobserved down the Rappahannock's eastern bank toward Fredericksburg. By stealing such a march the enemy might get between Lee and Richmond with potentially disastrous results for the Southern cause.[7]

After careful inspection of the terrain and his maps, Lee found "no field in Culpeper offering advantages for battle." The Federals could easily outflank any position the Army of Northern Virginia might take between the V of the rivers. The high ground north of the Rappahannock rendered it all but impossible to monitor enemy activity, making it difficult to deduce Meade's next move. Lee therefore decided to retire his army behind the Rapidan. A line south of that river offered far greater

---

6   In 1867 the O&A RR merged with the Manassas Gap Railway system. Changes in the line's ownership and affiliation were common throughout the last half of the 19th and early 20th centuries. In 1982 the line became part of the Norfolk Southern Railway System. At the time of this book's publication it remained part of that network and was also used by the Amtrak and Virginia Express commuter train systems.

7   Major General Ambrose E. Burnside had caught Lee by surprise with just such a march in November 1862 before the battle of Fredericksburg.

defensive advantages and better positioned his army to oppose any southward advance Meade might make.[8]

Once Lee determined on his course of action he moved quickly. He told his engineers to begin laying out a defensive line along the Rapidan. On July 30 he ordered Stuart to shift Brig. Gen. Fitzhugh Lee's cavalry brigade and five guns from the horse artillery to Fredericksburg to guard against a sudden Union lunge to the southeast. Major Generals Robert Rodes and Edward "Allegheny" Johnson's divisions of Ewell's corps withdrew south of the Rapidan on July 31. That same day Early's division sidled from Madison Court House to Locust Dale, on Robertson's River just a few miles northwest of Rapidan Station. Early received orders to pull south of the Rapidan on August 1 and take position around Orange Court House.[9]

Lee told Longstreet to move Maj. Gen. John Bell Hood's division—under Brig. Gen. Evander Law since Hood's wounding on July 2—and Maj. Gen. George E. Pickett's division south of the Rapidan as well. Both units would be deployed to guard the lower Rappahannock between its junction with the Rapidan and Fredericksburg.[10]

As soon as these movements were complete, Lee would withdraw Maj. Gen. Lafayette McLaws division of Longstreet's corps and A. P. Hill's three divisions, commanded by Maj. Gens. Robert H. Anderson, Henry Heth and Cadmus M. Wilcox, behind the Rapidan. Stuart's cavalry would remain in Culpeper County as a buffer and early warning system. All Lee needed was a few unmolested days to execute these adjustments and his army would be safely behind the Rapidan where it could truly recuperate from the Gettysburg campaign.

*   *   *

George Meade had no idea of Lee's plans, although he did anticipate that he would retreat closer to Richmond if the Union army advanced. Halleck's order to forego a forward movement meant Meade could not test that suspicion fully. However, the general-in-chief's directive to maintain a threatening attitude opened the door for the army to execute its planned seizure of the key Rappahannock crossings, after which it would rebuild the railway bridge over the river and launch a cavalry probe toward Culpeper Court House. No one knew how the Rebels might respond to this

---

8   OR 29, pt. 2, 624.

9   Ibid, 1072-73; Seymour, *Reminiscences of a Louisiana Tiger*, 82; Trout, *Galloping Thunder*, 333.The guns were a section from Moorman's Battery and 3 pieces from Breathed's battery.

10   J. Gary Laine and Morris M. Penny, *Law's Alabama Brigade in the War between the Union and the Confederacy* (Shippensburg, PA, 1996), 130-31.

provocation, but if the Federals were lucky, Lee would abandon the Rapidan for a line farther south.

The Army of the Potomac spent the last three days of July preparing to strike across the Rappahannock. Intelligence had located Rebel cavalry positioned behind the Hazel River to the west and Confederates guarding all the Rappahannock fords. Scouts sent behind enemy lines reported Longstreet's corps and Stuart's cavalry concentrated around Culpeper Court House, Brandy Station, and Stevensburg. Neither these facts nor the necessity of shipping regiments to New York City nor the lack of reinforcements dissuaded Meade from pursuing his plans. If Halleck wanted the army to keep up a threatening attitude, creating bridgeheads was as good a way to do so as any.[11]

On July 30 Maj. Gen. Henry W. Slocum's XII Corps advanced to within a mile of Kelly's ford. At the same time Maj. Gen. John Newton's I Corps moved close to the river opposite Rappahannock Station. The Federals were careful to conceal their movements behind the high ground north of the waterway.[12]

At 11 p.m. that night Meade issued detailed instructions for the coming operation. Slocum was to seize Kelly's Ford after nightfall on July 31 and establish a beachhead on the opposite shore. Next, Federal engineers would lay down a pontoon bridge and Buford's cavalry division would cross the river and sweep northwest toward Rappahannock Station. Once Buford was on his way, Slocum would advance a division of infantry and fortify Kelly's Ford. The XII Corps was to also occupy Ellis's Ford (five miles southeast) and Wheatley's Ford (about a mile north) before establishing a picket line along the riverbank between those two points.[13]

Once Buford cleared the south bank of the river at Rappahannock Station, engineers would lay pontoons close to the destroyed railroad bridge. Newton would then send troops over the river with orders to fortify a defensive perimeter behind which Haupt's workers could safely reconstruct the railway span. After Newton's infantry was in place, Buford's division was ordered to advance toward Culpeper Court House. The enemy's response to that push would reveal much about Lee's position and intentions.[14]

The first phase of the operation worked perfectly. Shortly after nightfall on July 31 the 66th Ohio seized Kelly's Ford in a daring amphibious assault that drove off 100 or so Rebel cavalrymen guarding the crossing. They then pushed far enough inland to

---

11 OR 27, pt. 3, 781-82.

12 Powell MS, 66th Ohio Collection, Ohio Historical Society (OHS); ibid., 783.

13 OR 27, pt. 3, 784.

14 Ibid.

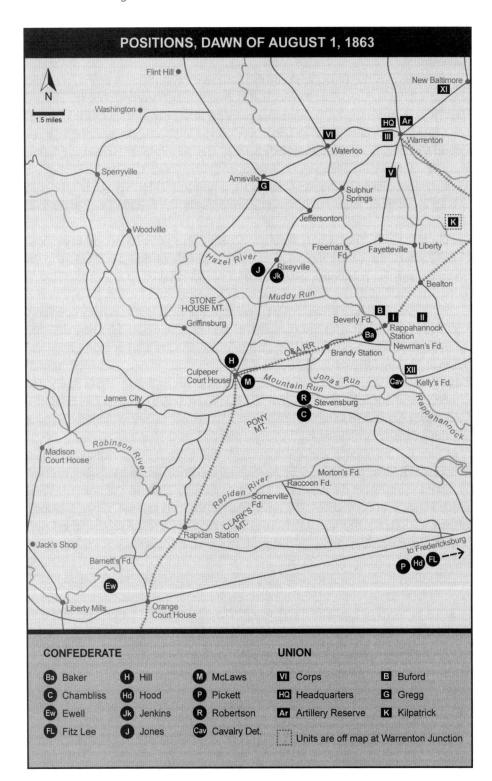

POSITIONS, DAWN OF AUGUST 1, 1863

N

1.5 miles

Flint Hill

New Baltimore
XI

Washington

HQ Ar

VI

Waterloo

III Warrenton

Sperryville

V

Amisville
G

Sulphur
Springs

Woodville

Jeffersonton

Freeman's
Fd.   Fayetteville Liberty

K

Hazel River

J Rixeyville
Jk

Bealton

Muddy Run

STONE
HOUSE MT.

Beverly Fd.   B I   II

Griffinsburg

Ba

Rappahannock
Station

Newman's Fd.

O&A RR   Brandy Station

H

Culpeper
Court House
M

Mountain Run

Jonas Run

XII

Cav   Kelly's Fd.

James City

R Stevensburg

C

Rappahannock

PONY
MT.

Robinson River

Madison
Court House

Morton's Fd.

Raccoon Fd.

Rapidan River   Somerville
Fd.

CLARK'S
MT.

Jack's Shop

Rapidan Station

to Fredericksburg

Barnett's Fd.

P Hd FL

Ew

Liberty Mills   Orange
Court House

CONFEDERATE

Ba	Baker	H	Hill
C	Chambliss	Hd	Hood
Ew	Ewell	Jk	Jenkins
FL	Fitz Lee	J	Jones

M	McLaws
P	Pickett
R	Robertson
Cav	Cavalry Det.

UNION

VI	Corps	B	Buford
HQ	Headquarters	G	Gregg
Ar	Artillery Reserve	K	Kilpatrick

Units are off map at Warrenton Junction

keep the ford out of rifle range and prepared to fight off a counterattack, which never materialized. With the enemy gone, Yankee engineers went to work assembling their bridge, and by 11 p.m. Slocum had one infantry brigade on the western bank and two more preparing to cross. Simultaneous with the attack at Kelly's Ford, Federal troops had seized Ellis' and Wheatley's fords without opposition and occupied each with a full brigade.[15]

This was when John Buford's cavalrymen were supposed to pass through Slocum's infantry and sweep up the river to uncover Rappahannock Station. But Buford had misconstrued his crossing point as Beverly's Ford, a few miles west of the destroyed railroad bridge. The resulting confusion took some hours to sort out, and it was 11:15 a.m. before the 1st Cavalry Division reached the south bank of the Rappahannock.[16]

As Buford's troopers began advancing down the O&A toward Brandy Station, Union engineers placed a pontoon bridge just upstream from Rappahannock Station. With the bridge finished, Maj. Gen. Newton ordered Brig. Gen. John C. Robinson's 2nd Division to move across the river. Brigadier General John R. Kenly received instructions to send one of his brigades to assist Robinson. The mission of these two commands, which totaled some 2,200 men, was to support the cavalry and establish a foothold at Rappahannock Station. Moving south to defensible ground, the Union troops immediately began constructing protective earthworks in anticipation of the arrival of railroad repairmen who—much to Newton's disgust—didn't get there until nightfall.[17]

As the Yankee infantry dug in, Buford's troopers moved south behind a screen of mounted skirmishers, and a few miles from the river they ran into Wade Hampton's cavalry brigade on Fleetwood Heights. With Hampton still recuperating from a serious Gettysburg wound, 33-year old Brig. Gen. Laurence S. Baker had charge of the brigade. A North Carolina native, Baker's promotion to brigadier had become official just eight days ago. He had a mere 935 men in six regiments at his disposal, many mounted on half-starving horses because of an extended dearth of grain. Rebel officers, in fact, had

15 Powell Ms, OHS.

16 OR 2, pt. 3, 787-88, 819, 820; Henry Norton, *Deeds of Daring or History of the Eighth New York Volunteer Cavalry* (Norwich, NY, 1889), 72. Hillman Hall, et al., *History of the Sixth New York Cavalry (Second Ira Harris Guard) Second Brigade–First Division–Cavalry Corps, Army of the Potomac: 1861-1865* (Worcester, MA, 1908), 15; *National Tribune*, Oct. 11, 1888.

17 OR 27, pt. 3, 822; Charles Camper & J. W. Kireley, *Historical Record of the First Regiment Maryland Infantry* (Washington, DC, 1871), 108; John Dominque Vautier Diary, August 1, 1863, www.wikitree.com/wiki/Vautier-28#Transcript_of_John.27s_ Civil_War_Diary, accessed Apr 30, 2018. Kenley sent the 3rd Brig of his 3rd Division.

to send some troopers to the rear because their mounts were too weak to go into battle.[18]

Not long after the opposing skirmishers opened fire Jeb Stuart arrived on the scene and took control of the struggle. He quickly realized that Baker could do little more than put up a stubborn delaying action against Buford's 2,800-man division. When the Federals took advantage of their numerical superiority to threaten the Confederate flanks, Stuart had no other choice but to order a fighting withdrawal. As the gray troopers pulled back, couriers dashed off to the south and west to summon reinforcements.[19]

Until help arrived the Confederates were begrudgingly compelled to abandon one position after another—yielding first Fleetwood Heights and then Brandy Station—before turning to make yet another stand on Kennedy House Hill. The fighting exacted a heavy price among Confederate officers. A Yankee bullet ripped into Brig. Gen. Baker's right arm and knocked him out of action. Colonel Pierce Manning Butler Young of Cobb's Legion assumed command after Baker went down, only to have a pistol ball hit him in the chest just a few minutes later. Control of Hampton's brigade devolved now onto Col. John L. Black of the 2nd South Carolina Cavalry. Black, however, could do little to stem the blue onslaught. Even the arrival of another battery of horse artillery could not prevent the Federals from pushing the Confederates off Kennedy House Hill.[20]

---

18 [Salem, NC] *Peoples Press*, August 13, 1863; Mays, "Journal of a Confederate Soldier" *Tyler's Quarterly*, July 1923, 5:97. Lieutenant Colonel James Gordon took command of the 1st NC Cavalry after Baker's promotion. [Washington, DC] *Daily Morning Chronicle*, August 14, 1863; Eleanor McSwain, ed., *Crumbling Defenses or Memoirs and Reminiscences of John Logan Black, Colonel C.S.A.* (Macon, GA, 1960), 56. *Editor Union*, August 5, 1863; Samuel Elias Mays " Sketches from the Journal of a Confederate Soldier" *Tyler's Quarterly Magazine*, 5:97, 99. Mays says Baker had about 1,000 men on Aug. 1.

19 *New York Daily Tribune*, August 13, 1863; Weld, *War Diary*, 253-54; [Washington, DC] *National Tribune*, October 11, 1888; Trout, *Moorman's and Hart's Batteries*, 220; Mays, *Tyler's Quarterly #5*, July 1923, 98; Black, *Crumbling Defenses*, 56. Buford's actual strength is unknown. My 2,800 figure is a rough estimate: on July 31 Pleasonton reported 8,646 officers and men "present for duty equipped" in his corps (exclusive of the horse artillery). Since the cavalry had 3 divisions I simply divided the total present equipped by three to get a most imperfect estimation of the 1st Cavalry Division's Aug. 1 strength.

20 Eleanor D. McSwain, ed., *Crumbling Defense or Memoirs and Reminiscences of John Logan Black, Colonel C.S.A.* (Macon, GA, 1960), 56, 59; Service Records, Confederate, M. B. Young Pierce www.fold3.com; Lynwood Holland, *Pierce M. B. Young: The Warwick of the South* (Athens, GA, 1964), 74; Harriet Bey Mesic, *Cobb's Legion: A History and Roster of the 9th Georgia Volunteers in the Civil War* (Jefferson, NC, 2011), 88; Jones, *Reminiscences of a Louisiana Tiger*, 82; Morrissett diary, ACWM; Trout, *Moorman's and Hart's Batteries*, 220; Mays, *Tyler's Quarterly #5*, 98.

The battered Southern horsemen fell back to Inlet Station, which stood next to the railroad tracks just north of the last ridge in front of Culpeper Court House. Although their extended fighting withdrawal had increasingly disorganized the Confederates, Black led his new command in a series of charges and countercharges against John Buford's aggressive Union troopers. The Rebel horsemen somehow managed to check the Federals for a time, but unless what remained of Hampton's brigade received substantial reinforcements, the Federals would surely storm into Culpeper before the sun set.[21]

*   *   *

Fortunately for the Confederates, help for Colonel Black was close at hand. Jeb Stuart's couriers and wigwag messages from the Rebel signal station on Mount Pony had kept General Lee appraised throughout the day of the battle's progress. As the combat drew near Culpeper Court House, Lee instructed Maj. Gen. Anderson to commit his veteran infantry to help drive back General Buford's troopers. The division commander immediately dispatched Brig. Gens. William Mahone's brigade of Virginians and Carnot Posey's Mississippi brigade toward Culpeper. Brigadier General William E. "Grumble" Jones' cavalry was also approaching the battlefield with the 6th, 7th and 11th Virginia regiments, together with Capt. Roger Preston Chew's battery of horse artillery.[22]

Jones and Chew had left their positions near Rixeyville earlier that day in response to Stuart's call for reinforcements. Although they had farther to travel than Anderson's infantry, the cavalrymen and gunners started earlier and reached the field first. After leaving the Rixeyville road at Chestnut Fork Church, Jones and Chew had moved across country in an effort to strike the exposed Federal right flank. The sudden appearance of these enemy formations to the west startled the Yankees. Buford swung part of his line back to confront this new threat to his flank while the rest of his command did its best to bludgeon Hampton's brigade into giving up Culpeper Court House.[23]

The struggle near Inlet Station showed no signs of slackening as Jones came onto line. Both sides traded mounted charges leading to bouts of vicious hand-to-hand combat. Colonel Black, fighting at the forefront until an extraordinarily painful gunshot wound to his right hand, had to leave the field, whereupon Col. Thomas J.

---

21 Black, *Crumbling Defenses*, 56.

22 *OR* 27, pt. 3, 820-1; Kirkpatrick diary, August 1, 1863, UT; *Richmond Whig*, August 12, 1863; A. L. Peel, War Diary, August 1, 1863, http://freepages.family.rootsweb.com/ ~peel.html.

23 Daniel Grimsley, *Battles in Culpeper Country Virginia, 1861-1865* (Culpeper, VA, 1900), 14.

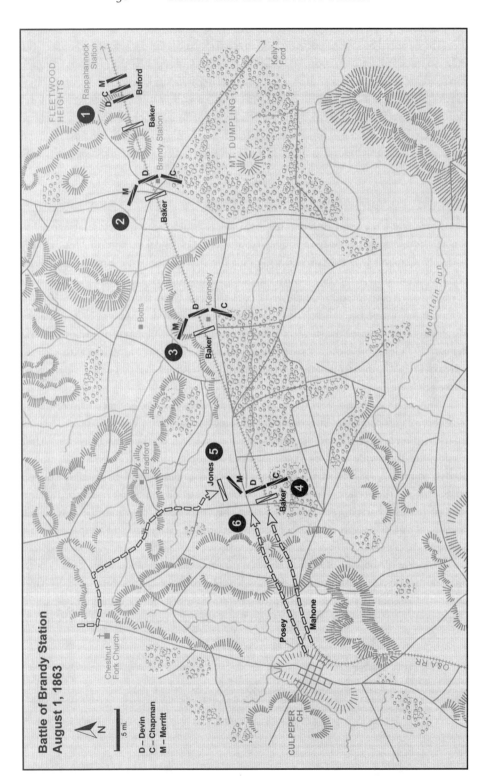

Battle of Brandy Station
August 1, 1863

D – Devin
C – Chapman
M – Merritt

5 mi

Lipscomb of the 2nd South Carolina Cavalry took charge of what was left of the brigade.[24]

Jones' attack relieved some of the pressure on the Rebel line fronting Culpeper, but the battle continued to hang in the balance until Mahone's and Posey's infantry arrived. The 12th Virginia and 12th Mississippi, each at the head of their respective brigade columns, moved parallel to one another and deployed as skirmishers just behind Hampton's cavalry. Relieved and excited at their approach, Jeb Stuart galloped over and ordered both regiments to charge. The infantrymen responded with a shout and surged forward, followed by a section of horse artillery.

The arrival of Jones, Chew, Mahone, and Posey swung the battle decisively in Stuart's favor. Outnumbered and out-gunned, Buford gave way. The blue troopers pulled back sullenly, contesting every hill and ridge much as the Rebels had done earlier. Stuart's cavalry joined the infantry in pressing the Federals back toward the river. As the fighting moved northward Col. Lipscomb took a bullet and command of Hampton's brigade passed to Lt. Col. William W. Rich of the Phillips Legion Cavalry.

The action finally petered out near Brandy Station, where a line of dismounted Yankee skirmishers made a stubborn stand in a large cornfield. A Confederate artillery barrage failed to dislodge them. As the sun began fading from view, the exhausted Rebels withheld further attacks. During the night Buford pulled his men back to Fleetwood Heights, and the Confederates chose not to follow.[25]

The day's obstinate combat had been costly for both sides. Northern newspapers listed 23 dead, 94 wounded, and 157 missing in Buford's three brigades.[26] Stuart suffered a great deal more. A private in the 2nd South Carolina Cavalry claimed that "in men and horses" Hampton's brigade "was reduced to about half its strength," although he admitted far more horses had been lost than men. Colonel William R. Carter, whose cavalry regiment did not take part in the battle, recorded in his diary that Hampton's

---

24 Stephen M. Weld, *War Diary and Letters of Stephen M. Weld 1861-1865* (Boston, MA, 1979), 253; Henry Brown to Parents, August 14, 1863, www.espd.com/letters/1863/Letter7_08_14_63.htm; Wittenberg, *Rush's Lancers*, 45; Black, *Crumbling Defenses*, 58-59.

25 Henry Brown to parents, August 14, 1863; Peel Diary, August 1, 1863, http://freepages.family.rootsweb.com/~peel/pellaugust.html; Grimsley, *Battles in Culpeper County*, 14.

26 *Daily Morning Chronicle*, August 4, 1864; George Chapman Diary, IHS; Wittenberg, *Rush's Lancers*, 103; Swank, *Sabres, Saddles and Spurs*, 86; Chapman says his brigade lost 5k, 13w, and 4 m, while noting "other Brigs lost more heavily." Norton in *Deeds of Daring*, 72, says that the 8th NY Cavalry lost 2k killed, 11w, and 1m. Frederick Phisterer in *New York in the War of the Rebellion*, 3rd ed., (Albany, NY, 1912), 873, lists casualties for the 8th New York as 18 total: 2k, 10w, and 6m. www.civilwardata.com shows Merritt's Reserve Brigade with 8w and 1m; Chapman's brigade with 3k, 11w, and 6m and Devin's brigade losses as 4k, 15w, and 4cap.

(Baker's) brigade lost 15 killed, 55 wounded and 130 missing. Casualties among the Southern infantry numbered 1 dead and 6 wounded.[27]

*   *   *

The Union cavalry had gained Meade some solid intelligence despite its failure to reach Culpeper Court House. The Federals now knew that A. P. Hill's corps was in Culpeper County, as were the Hampton and Jones cavalry brigades. Slocum's advance had confirmed the presence of Brig. Gen. Beverly Robertson's small cavalry brigade near Kelly's Ford. More importantly, Buford, Newton, and Slocum had secured the south bank of the Rappahannock, enabling Haupt's workers to rebuild the railroad bridge—a task they completed by August 5.[28]

Whatever the Yankees had gained, it had been bought with much misery. Searing temperatures characterized the day; one Confederate asserted the sun was hot enough to melt pewter buttons. The heat forced Federal cavalry to pull back within a mile of the Rappahannock so the troopers and their animals could be closer to water. Notwithstanding such harsh conditions there would be no relief from danger. Buford's advance had put both armies on alert and for several days the foes sparred fitfully, each trying to discern the other's intent.[29]

Meade's latest thrust confirmed Lee's intuition about Union intentions and the wisdom of getting his infantry out of the Culpeper V. On the morning of August 3, the general set Hill's corps in motion toward Orange Court House. Army headquarters directed McLaws' division of Longstreet's corps to the same point, while Pickett's and Hood's divisions marched for Fredericksburg. To protect the withdrawal, Stuart's cavalry advanced toward the Rappahannock and spent a couple of days skirmishing with Buford's troopers.[30]

27 [Washington, DC] *Daily Morning Chronicle*, August, 4, 1863; *Richmond Whig*, August, 12, 1863; John W. Moore, *Roster of North Carolina Troops in the War Between the States*, 18 Vols. (Raleigh, NC, 1882), 1:305- 42; Holland in *Pierce M.B. Young*, 74, says Phillip's Legion took 37 casualties and lost 50 horses; Compiled Service Records for Phillip's Legion in the National Archives show 1w and 7cap. The *Richmond Dispatch* estimated Confederate casualties as 15k and 60-70w. The 1st SC Cavalry recorded 4 k, 8 w, and 5m. Cobb's Legion lost 2k, 3w, and 1cap. Phillips Legion officially noted 1w and 7cap alongside 50 horses lost.

28 OR 27, pt. 1, 111; Haupt, *Reminiscences*, 254; *Editor Union*, August 5, 1863; Mays, *Tyler's Journal #5*, 101.

29 Munson, *Confederate Correspondent*, 93; OR 27, pt. 3, 827, 833; Robert K. Krick, *Civil War Weather in Virginia*, (Tuscaloosa, AL, 2007), 106. The temperature was 86 at 7 a.m., 92 by 2 p.m., and 84 at sunset.

30 OR 27, pt. 3, 832; Lee, *Wartime Papers*, 566.

At first Stuart's movements alarmed and mystified Union officers. That changed when Yankee signal corps observers began reporting telltale evidence of a Rebel withdrawal. This news created a frustrating situation for Meade. Washington's instructions to avoid bringing on a major battle, in league with the incredible heat, left him frozen in a defensive posture. The Federals could only watch as Lee pulled south of the Rapidan unhindered. Likely the Rebels were already building breastworks behind the river. At some future date, when he finally received permission to move, Meade would have to fight his way over a barrier he might have passed easily if only Washington had not interfered.[31]

The assumptions behind Meade's planning looked much less certain upon closer inspection, however. Buford was reporting Stuart's cavalry still in place north of Culpeper, in strength and apparently with every intention of holding its ground for some time to come. Stuart's presence rendered it almost impossible for Union cavalry to fix the precise location of the Rebel army. As long as Southern troopers occupied most of the county, Meade could not verify withdrawal of the entire Confederate army behind the Rapidan.

This was, of course, exactly what Lee desired. As his infantry shifted southward, he ordered Stuart to hold onto Culpeper County if he could do so without sacrificing his men. Lee wanted a buffer between the rival armies to complicate future enemy movements and shield his still-recovering command from harassment. Although unwilling to fight a major battle in the cramped space between the Rappahannock and the Rapidan, Lee saw no reason to yield that ground to the Yankees free of charge.

If George Meade wanted to control the territory separating the two rivers he would have to come and take it.

---

31 Krick, *Civil War Weather*, 106; George Aggassiz, *Meade's Headquarters 1863-1865: Letters of Colonel Theodore Lyman* (Boston, MA, 1922), 21.

Chapter 4

"Elastic Spirits"

Jefferson Davis—Robert E. Lee—A Shocking Request—Davis' Response—
Questions of Morale—Deserters and Firing Squads—Recovery

WITH Lee's infantry now behind the Rapidan, the South could take stock of all that had transpired during the last two months. For the Confederates, Gettysburg had ended another invasion of the North with mixed results. The South had achieved its intermediate campaign objectives by subsisting Lee's army on the rich farmlands of Pennsylvania, gathering enormous quantities of supplies to feed and equip it for future use, and drawing Union forces out of Virginia. But larger aims of forcing the Federals to weaken the siege of Vicksburg or winning a dramatic victory that might end the war had gone unfulfilled. Gettysburg, combined with Federal conquest of the final Rebel bastions on the Mississippi River, engendered despair and disappointment on the home front and in the army.

As weary Rebel soldiers camped on familiar ground around Orange Court House, the two men chiefly responsible for launching the Pennsylvania invasion and leading the Southern nation afterwards—President Davis and General Lee—could ill afford to dwell on broken dreams of victory. But neither could they disregard the reaction of the public or the army to the defeat of those imaginings.

Kentucky-born and Mississippi-raised, Jefferson Davis graduated from West Point in 1828. While serving as a young officer he met and fell in love with Sarah Taylor, the daughter of Col. Zachery Taylor. When Davis proposed marriage, the young lady was willing but her father, shunning an army life for his daughter, disapproved. Whereupon Davis resigned his commission in June 1835 and the young couple eloped. Tragically, malaria killed Sarah just three months later and almost claimed her new husband's life as well.[1]

---

1 Zachery Taylor would go on to become a major general and hero of the Mexican War. In 1848 he was elected to the presidency on the Whig ticket. The best biography of Jefferson Davis, by far, is William C. Davis' *Jefferson Davis: The Man and His Hour* (New York, 1991).

Davis recovered and became a successful Mississippi planter. In 1845 he married his second wife, Varina Howell, and was elected to Congress. He left politics to command a volunteer regiment known as the Mississippi Rifles in the Mexican War where he served with distinction and was wounded at the battle of Buena Vista. Following the war he won election to the US Senate, until resigning to run unsuccessfully for the governorship of Mississippi in 1850. President Franklin Pierce appointed him secretary of war the following year. In that role he received praise as an able and innovative administrator before returning to the Senate in 1857.

When Mississippi seceded in 1861, Davis resigned his Senate seat. Expecting war, he hoped to serve the South in a military capacity. But to his surprise, the Provisional Congress of the Confederate States of America unanimously elected him president of the new Southern nation in February 1861.

Jefferson Davis was 56 years old in June 1863 when he met Lt. Col. Arthur L. Fremantle, an officer in the British army touring the Confederacy. The president's "emaciated, and much wrinkled" face made him look older than expected, the Englishman thought, and he noted that the "nearly six-foot tall" Mississippian was "extremely thin" and slightly stooped. Though an earlier bout with fever had left an opaque film over Davis' left eye, the president's good eye was "very bright, and full of life and humor."[2]

Like Lincoln, Davis provoked strong emotions. An eloquent speaker with the refined manners of the South's planter class, he could be warm, gentle, witty, and outgoing with his friends, family, and those he respected. Opponents found him cold, aloof, stubborn, and unforgiving—inadequate to the task of leading the fledgling nation. His political enemies blamed him for every military reverse, disappointment, or difficulty even as they railed against the measures he urged to strengthen the central government's ability to wage war. His defenders praised his resolution, talent, and perseverance.

Fremantle credited President Davis for the rapid and successful formation of the Confederacy's armed forces. The Mississippian's long public service and tenure as a secretary of war, believed Fremantle, had fitted Davis especially well for the task of selecting military commanders based on merit rather than political connection. Once the president "formed his opinion with regard to appointing an officer," concluded the foreign observer, "always most determined to carry out his intention in spite of every obstacle."[3]

---

2   Arthur L. *Fremantle, Three Months in the Southern States: April-June 1863* (New York, 1864), 167-70.

3   Ibid.

General Robert E. Lee
Library of Congress

This same determination on almost any issue nurtured a stubborn rigidity as well. Extraordinarily loyal, especially in reciprocal loyalty, the president also had a knack for making bitter, often venomous, political enemies. Along with many Southern politicians, editors, and generals, Davis never turned his back on a friend, but when he made a foe it was for life. Fortunately for the Confederacy that was not a problem Davis had with the commander of the Army of Northern Virginia.

* * *

In August 1863 Robert E. Lee was the most famous soldier in the South and perhaps in all of America. Tall, gray-bearded, broad shouldered, and handsome, Lee exhibited the ideal traits of the perfect Southern gentlemen. A devout man, he did not drink, swear, gamble, or smoke. Despite his genteel manner and appearance, Lee was a man of strong passions with a sharp temper he did not always control. He dressed unpretentiously in dark blue trousers tucked into tall boots, a plain felt hat, and a gray frock coat modestly adorned with three stars on each collar. He never carried a sidearm and wore his sword and sash exclusively on ceremonial occasions.[4]

Duty and audacity were Lee's bywords. Indifferent to physical danger, hardship, and sometimes faltering health, he drove himself and his staff hard. His soldiers loved, admired, and trusted him, sometimes with near religious zeal. The feeling was mutual. Although Lee cared deeply for his troops and their welfare, he didn't hesitate to hurl them into battle against fearful odds. Lee was willing to incur heavy casualties to achieve great ends. But searching for good leaders constantly bedeviled him. The Army of Northern Virginia "would be invincible if it could be properly organized and officered," he wrote Maj. Gen. John Bell Hood in May, 1863. The general had supreme

---

4 Dowdey, *Wartime Papers of R.E. Lee*, 197; Fremantle, *Three Months*, 197-98.

confidence in his troops, however, and told Hood: "There were never such men in an army before. They will go anywhere and do anything if properly led."[5]

Lee put that faith to the test when he marched north in June 1863. The South's principal hope for victory, he believed, was defeating the enemy with such rapidity and regularity that the Northern people would conclude final victory impossible and abandon the war. None of the impressive victories he had won in Virginia had led to that result yet. Although logistical necessity played a large role in his decision to invade the North, Lee hoped the campaign would present an opportunity to crush the Army of the Potomac and deliver a fatal wound to the Union war effort. Gettysburg had derailed that desire.

Now came the reckoning. Davis sent Lee a clipping from the Charleston *Mercury* shortly after the Confederates returned to the Rappahannock line. The piece, fairly representative of the opposition press, harshly criticized the conduct of the Gettysburg campaign. Lee responded to Davis on July 31, saying he regretted the *Mercury's* condemnation "as it is calculated to do us no good either at home or abroad."[6]

Still, Lee recognized some truth in the criticism. None of his senior generals had performed to their customary standard at Gettysburg. His army—reorganized into three corps just a month before the invasion—had proven a bulky machine during the battle. Moreover, Lee feared that he had personally contributed to the defeat by asking too much of his men and expecting their accustomed abilities to overcome too many obstacles. Keenly disappointed, Lee didn't shy from taking the blame for failure nor did he deflect criticism onto his subordinates. Given his inability to achieve his aims, the general concluded that the critiques of his leadership had merit. His own self-appraisal was even more damning, and it led him to make an extraordinary request.[7]

On August 8, in one of the most remarkable letters he wrote during the war, Lee told Davis that, although to be expected, reverses and defeats were sent to teach "wisdom and prudence" as well as "call forth greater energies" to prevent future disasters. As long as the Southern people remained "true and united," and bore "manfully the misfortunes incident to war," Lee asserted, everything would "come right in the end." Obliquely referencing the recent criticism, he lamented that it was "unbecoming in a generous people" to blame others for the "non-fulfillment of our expectations." Fairly or not, the press had widely censured his conduct of the

---

5 John Bell Hood, *Advance and Retreat: Personal Experiences in the United States and Confederate Armies* (Philadelphia, PA 1879), 53; Gary Gallagher, *Lee the Soldier* (Lincoln, NB, 1996) is an excellent examination of Lee as a military commander and the historiography on his generalship.

6 *Charleston* [SC] *Mercury*, July 30, 1863; Dowdey, *Wartime Papers of R. E. Lee*, 564-65.

7 Dowdey, *Wartime Papers of R.E. Lee*, 564-65; Gallagher, *Lee the Soldier*, 515.

Pennsylvania invasion, and the general suspected similar opinions existed in the army, although his troops had been "too generous to exhibit it." The nation had a right to expect success, Lee admitted, and victory was the only real criterion for evaluating commanders. Regardless of an officer's abilities, lack of success would justify his removal—in fact it fairly demanded dismissal, for once a leader lost the confidence of his men "disaster must sooner or later ensue." Coming to his point, the general recommended "in all sincerity" that Davis assign someone else to command the Army of Northern Virginia. "I do this with the more earnestness, because no one is more aware than myself of my inability for the duties of my position." The triumph of the Southern cause, he said, was simply too important to allow any other course.[8]

Davis, who trusted Lee above all Confederate generals, was completely shocked by this self-effacing request. Moreover, in sharp contrast to the less than cordial relations Davis enjoyed with so many of his senior commanders, Davis and Lee genuinely got along. The Gettysburg campaign may not have been a brilliant success, but it certainly hadn't been a total failure. Besides, until Gettysburg, virtually every time the Army of Northern Virginia fought under Lee's command, it had been successful. Only when Lee's army crossed the Potomac had it met defeat.

Davis wasn't about to jeopardize this combination because of press grousing. He understood the frustrations of having to bear the "criticisms of the ignorant," he told Lee in a warm reply, "who pronounce everything a failure which does not equal their expectations or desires, and can see no good result which is not in line of their own imaginings." Lee had been correct about the axioms of command, wrote the president, but nothing the Virginian had written prepared him for his application to be replaced.

"[E]xpressions of discontent" in newspapers had no relation to the "sentiment of an army," he assured Lee. Vain men sought to deflect such criticism by surrounding themselves with sycophants. Stooping to such a level was simply beyond Lee's character, as Davis well knew. And it was unnecessary as well, because his "achievements would, alongside those of his army," make him "the subject of history and object of the world's admiration for generations to come."

[S]uppose, my dear friend," he wrote in a touching passage, "that I were to admit, with all their implications, the points which you present, where am I to find that new commander who possesses the greater ability which you believe is required?" He didn't doubt Lee's sincere readiness to "give way to one who could accomplish all that you have wished," and avowed that "if Providence should kindly offer such a person for our use, I would not hesitate to avail of his services."

---

8 Dowdey, *Wartime Papers of R.E. Lee*, 565.

But, Davis confessed, his sight was "not sufficiently penetrating to discover such hidden merit" even if it existed. To find a commander "more fit" or one who would better possess "the confidence of the army or of the reflecting men in the country" was, in his view, "an impossibility." Lee would remain at the head of the Army of Northern Virginia where he belonged. The president continued in "sober earnestness" to urge Lee to avoid "all unnecessary exposure to danger," because the country "could not bear" to lose him.[9]

*   *   *

Davis was no readier to part company with his Gettysburg general than Lincoln had proven to replace his Gettysburg commander. The circumstances that led each officer to request his replacement and the way in which his superior had responded were in striking contrast to one another, however. In the face of presidential criticism, the victorious Meade had tersely demanded his removal. The administration had refused that petition in equally terse fashion. Despite the efforts at rapprochement among Halleck, Lincoln, and Meade, it was clear that the wound inflicted by that incident had not healed and possibly never would. Lee, on the other hand, had humbly requested replacement in hope that a better leader might succeed where he had failed. Davis declared his complete trust in Lee despite Gettysburg and responded with warmth and affection. He could think of no one better suited to command.

The import of this contrast was as clear as it was significant. Lee would go into the next campaign knowing that he had the full confidence of his commander-in-chief. Meade enjoyed something a great deal less. In the coming months the Pennsylvanian would find himself constantly hampered by residual doubts sown by his failure to destroy Lee at Williamsport and Manassas Gap.

*   *   *

As Virginia sweltered under an August heat wave Lee and Meade grappled with the task of restoring their commands in the wake of Gettysburg. The two generals confronted a remarkably similar set of problems. The enormous casualties suffered in Pennsylvania had badly weakened their armies. Each desperately needed to rebuild its strength, yet each faced growing difficulties in obtaining men to fill the ranks. The loss of hundreds of officers and many senior leaders at Gettysburg had markedly decreased efficiency. Discipline had declined in many units. Troops on both sides realized that all their recent bloodshed and hardships had simply returned the Virginia Theater to its

9 Ibid, 589.

pre-Gettysburg status quo. Little wonder that in these circumstances the rival armies experienced a sudden surge in desertions, yet another factor that threatened to further undermine morale and short circuit efforts to rebuild combat power.

Although Meade's troops were justly proud of their Gettysburg victory, the last stages of the campaign had proven disappointing. The army's familiarity with its position north of the Rappahannock hardly boosted a sense of accomplishment. "Here we were back again within a short distance from where we started in June," grumbled a 106th Pennsylvania soldier. That the Federal host was no nearer Richmond than when the Gettysburg campaign began was bitterly ironic. Despite everything he and his comrades had endured, the Rebels still "resisted and prevented our advance as they did when here last."[10]

By all objective indicators, the war appeared to be running steadily in the Union's favor. However, the recent string of Yankee victories had spawned appalling casualties, draft riots, a burgeoning Northern peace movement, as well as a realization, at least within the ranks of the Army, that the end of the war was nowhere in sight. Private Oliver W. Norton feared that successes at Gettysburg and Vicksburg had stirred unwarranted optimism and over-confidence at home. "Every paper that I see lately is telling how nearly used up the rebels are and how soon the war will end. I think they are taking the wrong course, raising hopes and expectations that will be disappointed." Commanders worried too. Major Henry Abbott perceived an "awful feeling of indifference" among Northern civilians on the conduct of the war. He couldn't help "feeling devilish gloomy about the future," and how the conflict might be brought to a successful conclusion.[11]

Nonetheless, Meade's soldiers had the satisfaction of having won their most recent battle. The Confederates enjoyed no such balm. The campaign's rigors and their own heavy losses among officers and men at the Gettysburg had left Lee's army battered and bruised. The general knew he had to revive his command quickly or the prospects of future success would dim greatly.

The recuperation of his army would not be simple or easy. Morale and discipline had taken a beating. Private James Kirkpatrick of the 16th Mississippi confided to his diary that "camp life seems to have lost all its enjoyments. No amusement of any kind is indulged in and everyone seems clouded with grief." A gloomy pall hung over the Army of Northern Virginia. That already famous organization was unaccustomed to defeat and its men took the setback in Pennsylvania personally. The inactivity and

---

10 Ward, *History of the One Hundred Sixth Regiment Pennsylvania Volunteers*, 179.

11 Norton, *Army Letters*, 181; Scott, *Fallen Leaves*, 219.

tightening discipline which always followed a major action, accented the general feeling of disenchantment.[12]

That mood was only reinforced by letters from the home front recounting economic hardships, loneliness, heartache, and disappointment at the summer's defeats. Vicious editorial criticism of Jefferson Davis, the Confederate congress, and army leadership exacerbated matters. This was especially true in North Carolina where a number of dissatisfied citizens and public journals loudly denounced the edicts of the Richmond government and its conduct of military affairs.

All of this was reflected in a growing tide of soldiers forsaking their duty and heading for home without permission. Always a concern to some degree, desertions were now "becoming fearfully numerous" and threatening to "ruin" the army, according to one officer. News of hundreds of troops abandoning their units, said another, left men remaining at their posts "discouraged and disheartened."[13]

In the wake of Gettysburg and Vicksburg defeats, it was perhaps unsurprising to see an epidemic of desertion in Southern ranks. Desertion was not a uniquely Confederate problem, however; Meade too confronted an alarming upsurge in the number of men slipping away for home. But the source of his woes was not so much the aftereffects of Gettysburg as a systemic problem in the Northern government's effort to maintain Union military strength.

As 1863 had dawned the Lincoln administration faced a sharp decline in volunteer enlistments. The Congress responded that March by passing the nation's first conscription act. By that summer the draft had become the primary way to funnel large numbers of new men into the ranks. Although complicated, the conscription system ultimately proved a much more efficient way to strengthen the army than forming new regiments, as had been done earlier. The war department could send individual replacements to bolster the ranks of depleted commands. This in turn allowed veteran units to remain in the field and placed green recruits where they could learn the art of war from experienced soldiers.

The conscription law did create problems, however. Among these were provisions that allowed a man to buy his way out of service by paying a $300 fee or hiring a substitute to go in his place. Soldiers already in the field deeply resented both means of evading military duty. Substitutes were a mixed bag. Many entered the ranks and served well; others pocketed their fees and promptly disappeared. Draftees were, by definition, reluctant soldiers, and a goodly number of them deserted before they got to

12 James Kirkpatrick Diary, July 30, 1863, University of Texas at Austin (UT).

13 William A. Smith to fiancé August 6, 1863, UT; Mills Lane, ed., Dear Mother: Don't Grieve About Me: If I Get Killed, I'll Only Be Dead. *Letters from Georgia Soldiers in the Civil War* (Savannah, GA, 1977), 260-61.

the front or soon thereafter. Most veterans had little regard for either. Major Henry Winkler voiced the prevailing opinion, pronouncing substitutes "uncouth, untrained, insubordinate, mutinous, [and] everything bad."[14]

Despite the initial reservations of commanders and enlisted men alike, draftees and substitutes who stayed with the army generally went on to make good soldiers. Major Abbott found himself unexpectedly concluding that the conscripts brought into the 20th Massachusetts proved "better than the men that originally made up" the regiment. Drill instructors "put the screws to them like the devil," but only six or seven deserted. The major thought those who remained would become "excellent soldiers . . . in time."[15]

No one in uniform would say the same about a class of unscrupulous characters called "bounty jumpers." These scoundrels enlisted, often under an assumed name, for the sole purpose of pocketing the government-issued cash incentive to join the army and then deserting at the first possible moment. Commonly, they would repeat the process in a different location. The serious desertion problem they created was apt to spread demoralization that might induce homesick soldiers to desert as well.[16]

Faced with a similar crisis, albeit with different origins, Union and Confederate high commands moved swiftly to deal with their desertion problem. Each employed the same tactics to confront the issue. Newspapers vilified deserters as cowards and traitors in hopes of attaching a fearful public stigma to the crime. Both presidents issued proclamations of amnesty for deserters who would return to the ranks within a given period of time. Officers instituted strict roll call regimens and increased the number of pickets around their camps to discourage unauthorized departures. Lee instituted a system of furloughs to allow the most deserving men a brief trip to their homes. Some Federal commanders offered the same reward to any man who turned in a potential deserter. All of this helped a little. None of it helped enough.[17]

---

14 Frederick Winkler to wife, September 2, 1863, https://catalog.hathitrust.org/Record /009628680, accessed May 2, 2018. Some men entered the army with medical conditions rendering them useless as infantrymen. One officer feared turning even healthy conscripts into soldiers would be a "task which will bother us very much" and take a considerable amount of time. See Acken, *Inside the Army of the Potomac*, 327-38.

15 Scott, *Fallen Leaves*, 208.

16 Bruce Catton, *A Stillness at Appomattox* (Garden City, NJ, 1954), 23. A bounty could quickly add up to over $1000—a princely sum in 1863 equivalent to more than $20,230 in 2017. Local politicians used these monetary inducements to meet manpower quotas issued by state or national governments. Failure to meet that quota resulted in the conscription of enough men to fill the quota from within a county, city, or larger geographic district.

17 J. F. J. Caldwell, *A Brigade of South Carolinians* (Dayton, OH, 1984), 157.

This led both commanders, with the blessing of their respective administrations, to use the death penalty to punish desertion and underscore its consequences. Courts martial and firing squads were soon about their brutal business. Soldiers convicted of desertion met their fate in front of thousands of former comrades assembled to absorb the cautionary tale. Troops witnessing executions shuddered at what they saw but conceded the penalty's justice. The rival generals on either side of Culpeper County deemed the death penalty absolutely essential to the safety and effectiveness of their commands. More importantly, the tactic worked. By September 1863, the rate of desertions had fallen to more normal levels.[18]

*   *   *

The squelching of desertions allowed Lee and Meade to give paramount consideration to rebuilding the strength and morale of their armies. Both replaced officers lost at Gettysburg with promotions and new assignments. In almost every instance this quickly improved efficiency and discipline. The troops received pay for the months of May and June, and the two commanders ordered their subordinates to institute programs of serious and proper military routine, such as regimental and brigade drills. Commissary officers strove to increase and improve rations. This was an easy task in Meade's ranks, but even south of the Rapidan, Confederates enjoyed more bountiful and varied meals. Letters from Lee's army were soon referencing an abundance of food including beef, bread, beans, potatoes and "occasionally bacon." Despite sporadic disruptions in the supply chain, one soldier bragged that "the bugbear of starvation" was a thing of the past.[19]

On either side of the battle line quartermasters replaced clothing, footwear, equipment and other items lost or worn out during the recent campaign. The largess of Union supply depots made this task relatively simple in the Army of the Potomac. The provision of adequate supplies had never been quite so straightforward in the Confederacy. The Southern army had returned to Virginia with 10,000 soldiers barefooted and most wearing tattered uniforms. Once Lee's regiments reached Orange

18 Bell I. Wiley, *The Life of Johnny Reb: The Common Soldier of the Confederacy* (Baton Rouge, LA, 1986), 228; *Richmond Enquirer*, August 4, 1863; Waddell diary, August 15, 1863, VMI; J. B. Jones, *A Rebel War Clerk's Diary*, 2 Vols. (Philadelphia, PA, 1866), Vol. 2, 4; Dowdey, *Wartime Papers of R.E. Lee*, 591; Kirkpatrick diary, September 30, 1863, UT; James I. Robertson, *General A. P. Hill: The Story of a Confederate Warrior* (New York, 1987), 232; William A. Smith to fiancé August 2, 13, 1863, UT; OR 29, pt. 2, 102-103; *Harper's Weekly*, September 12, 1863.

19 Kirkpatrick diary, August 6, 1863, UT; Jeremiah Tate to sister, August 6, 1863, GLI; William Smith to fiancé, August 13, 1863, UT.

Court House, however, Richmond quartermasters went into overdrive to supply the troops' needs. Such large quantities of shell jackets, trousers, shirts, and shoes arrived in the camps that Maj. Jedediah Hotchkiss of Ewell's corps, boasted that Lee's soldiers were "being nicely clothed and shod" and would soon present the "appearance [of] a uniformed army."[20]

The onset of a religious revival that spread throughout Lee's command also boosted Rebel morale. The president called for a day of fasting and prayer on August 21. Although Lee urged his troops to observe the occasion, the results were mixed. Some men obeyed; others didn't. But if fasting didn't catch on among Lee's soldiers, prayers and sermons enjoyed an entirely different reception. Throughout the day chaplains preached to attentive crowds, and to the delight of many, the army's interest in religion intensified in the following weeks. Throughout the rest of the summer and into autumn religious gatherings proliferated. One soldier wrote that even "the most ordinary preachers drew large congregations" while "scarcely a day passed without a sermon." Few doubted that these meetings would help improve Southern spirits and discipline.[21]

Within just a few weeks, the atmosphere within the Army of Northern Virginia changed markedly from the one prevailing in early August. Talk of Lee's men being "clouded with grief" faded. Everywhere evidence of renewed strength and confidence met the eye. Second Lieutenant James F. Caldwell observed that the soldiers' "elastic spirits" had recovered from the "depression of July and satisfaction with the present and confidence of the future were almost unanimously expressed." Everyone appeared ready for the next battle. "The boys all seem cheerful and willing to meet the enemies of our country on any field" William Brand of the 5th Virginia assured his family.[22]

* * *

20 *Richmond Examiner*, August 13, 1863; For the shortage of shoes and blankets see OR 29, pt. 2, 759, 769, 784, 794, 800, 830, 835, also Dowdey, *Wartime Papers of R. E. Lee*, 595-96; Lee to Davis, 593-94. For the problems of keeping animals fed see OR 29, pt. 2, 665, 697-9, 816; see also Robertson, *A.P. Hill*, 230; Wise, *Long Arm of Lee*, 708; Jedediah Hotchkiss to brother, August 21, 1863, http://valley.lib.virginia.edu/papers/A2590, accessed May 2, 2018..

21 Kirkpatrick diary, August 21, 1863 UT; Wiley, *Life of Johnny Reb*, 181; *Richmond Enquirer*, August 15, 1863; Robertson, *A.P. Hill*, 231; Caldwell, *Brigade of South Carolinians*, 157; OR 29, pt. 2, 636; Jones, *Reminiscences of a Louisiana Tiger*, 82; Morrisett Diary, August 21, 1863, MOCW.

22 Caldwell, *Brigade of South Carolinians*, 157; See also: William A. Smith to fiancé August 13, 1863, UT; Kirkpatrick diary, August 11, 15, 1863, UT; William Francis Brand to "Kate," Sept. 16 1863, Albert H. Small Special Collections Library, University of Virginia (SCL/UV); Jesse Rolston, Jr. to Mary Rolston, Sept. 5, 1863, http://valley.lib. edu/papers/A6142, accessed May 3, 2018.

North of the Rappahannock, Rebel resiliency did not surprise Union soldiers. Although Yankee troops remained certain of their ultimate triumph, they in no way believed Gettysburg had put the enemy on the road to inevitable destruction. One infantryman predicted that the South "can & will stand more and still harder" blows than those she had suffered so far. As long as the Army of Northern Virginia remained in the field, there was "a chance for the Confederacy." The majority of Federal troops had concluded that nothing less than "hard war" could beat the secessionists into submission. Their defeat would require utter ruthlessness and total destruction of the South's economic and political infrastructure. Many were convinced victory would not come until the Union had driven Lee into the defenses of Richmond and starved his army to death.

Headquarters clerk Thomas Carpenter complained, though, that the Federals in Virginia maintained a "state of masterly inactivity" throughout August. The soldiers were ready to get on with it. Captain Francis A. Donaldson of the 118th Pennsylvania Infantry had no doubt Meade was anxious to "move upon Lee's army" and "fight it, no matter where" with the goal of its destruction. But he was being restrained. Donaldson and others blamed Washington for this. As they saw it, the administration, not the general, called the strategic tune, and Lincoln was using the army as "a political machine" to be "moved forward and backward to suit the political situation." So Meade's hands were tied. The army would continue "backing and filling, racing to the Rappahannock and back again to the Potomac" in an unrelenting stalemate that would "never end the war."[23]

Regardless of such sentiments, the August efforts of both armies' commanders allowed the resilient young men in the ranks to rebound swiftly from June and July's hardships and privations. In their swift recovery, the two armies performed like the veteran organizations they had become. They absorbed the carnage and punishment of Gettysburg just as they had those of Chancellorsville, Fredericksburg, Sharpsburg, or Second Manassas. The courage, flexibility, and grit of the common soldier endured. They would fight on until fate pronounced a victor to their bloody contest.

23 James Robertson, ed. "An Indiana Solider in Love and War: the Civil War Letters of John V. Hadley," *Indiana Magazine of History*, (Sept. 1963) 59:247-67; Oliver W. Norton, *Army Letters 1861-1865* (Chicago, IL, 1903), 181; Donelson, *Inside the Army of the Potomac*, 345.

Chapter 5

"If Meade Does Not Move
I Wish To Attack Him"

Regaining Strength—Meade's Detachments—Tennessee Crisis—
Confederate Strategy—Lee Plans an Offensive—Longstreet Goes West

As their respective armies recovered, Meade and Lee plotted strategy. The two men confronted one other across the familiar landscape embraced by the Rappahannock and Rapidan rivers. Although the advantages and disadvantages of a position in Culpeper County were obvious, its rolling countryside remained at the center of their chess board. For the next several weeks both antagonists contemplated possible opening gambits for the next campaign. To their irritation, however, a variety of strategic, political and logistical difficulties threatened their preferred move.

Since the Army of the Potomac stood on the defensive it became a ready source of reinforcements for areas the war department deemed more active. Halleck had assured Meade at the end of July that beyond the 1,600 men already taken to enforce the draft, there would be no further reduction of his force. This proved untrue. On August 5, Meade received orders to send the XI Corps' 3,708-man strong 1st Division to Alexandria. There it would be loaded on ships and sent to bolster the on-going assault against Charleston, South Carolina.[1]

A week later, on August 12, Secretary of War Edwin Stanton called Meade to the capital for consultation. The general left for Washington at noon the next day. After arriving in the city around 5 p.m., Meade attended a gathering of the cabinet. This was Lincoln's and his department heads' first chance to meet the victor of Gettysburg.

---

1 OR 29, pt. 2, 7. This move not only reinforced the effort at Charleston, it also separated from Meade's command a hard-luck division which had lost the confidence of most of the army. Elsewhere the division would get a fresh start and might do better.

Secretary of the Navy Gideon Welles confessed that he had formed "unfavorable impressions" of Meade since Lee's escape back into Virginia. Once he met the general, he softened somewhat. Meade "demonstrated intelligence and activity," Welles noted, and admitted he was "as well or better pleased" with him than anticipated. Nonetheless, doubts remained. Welles thought Meade "would do better as second-in-command than as General-in-Chief." Doubtless Meade was "a good officer," but he saw no evidence the general was "a great and capable commander."[2]

Meade failed to perceive these qualms. After returning to his headquarters, he wrote his wife that "the manner" in which he was "received and treated" in the capital had proven "most gratifying." The president and cabinet's politeness, professional courtesy, and respect impressed him: "I really believe I have the confidence of all parties and will continue to retain it, unless some great disaster should overtake me."[3]

Although Meade missed the reservations attached to administration expressions of support, the purpose for which Stanton had called him to the capital was perfectly clear. While no detailed record of the cabinet session survived, apparently ensuring an orderly recommencement of the draft was a principle topic. The administration, desperately needing conscription to resume, decided that New York and other places required soldiers to guarantee it resumed smoothly. The war department concluded that the only available source for the required troops was Virginia.

Meade's army soon felt the consequences of that decision. On August 12, he ordered the VI Corps' 2,000-man strong Vermont Brigade to Alexandria for transport to New York City. More units soon followed. On August 14, six regiments, some 1,300 men, sailed for New York. The next day another twelve regiments went north. By the middle of August, Meade had dispatched around 9,200 men to enforce the draft. "I have sent you my best troops and some of my best officers," he told Halleck, and stressed that he did not plan to send more unless specifically ordered.[4]

Presumably the administration would repay the Army of the Potomac for the temporary loss of these regiments with a steady flow of men to bolster its thinning ranks. Meade doubted this, however. The first handful of replacements the draft brought in were "miserable creatures" some of whom were veterans previously discharged for "physical disability." These men had returned to the ranks as substitutes hired by draftees, Meade complained. As far as he was concerned, this sort of additional manpower was "worthless."

---

2   OR 29, pt. 2, 35, 37; J. T. Morse, ed., *Diary of Gideon Welles*, 2 Vols., (Boston, MA, 1911), Vol. 1, 404. The Vermont Brigade consisted of the 2nd, 3rd, 4th, 5th and 6th Vermont regiments.

3   Meade to wife August 19, 1863, *Life and Letters*, Vol. 2, 143-44.

4   OR 29, pt. 2, 39, 42, 46, 50.

The concept of conscription troubled Meade. "If the draft is not heartily responded to, the Government had better make up its mind to letting the South go," he wrote Margaret. He wanted a "vigorous prosecution of the war" but admitted that it couldn't be "prosecuted with any hope of success" without a "great many willing men." Reluctant draftees wouldn't do. What the army needed were "men who have their hearts in the business and who are determined to fight and to conquer, or die." Whether the draft could ever provide that was an open question, but at least there was some solace in the belief that Lee found it "as hard to recruit his army" as did Meade.[5]

Whatever the future utility of conscription, the manpower levels of the army remained stable. Despite the detachment of the equivalent of a corps, Meade's numerical strength hardly changed at all. On the tenth of August, 90,522 officers and men were present for duty. At the end of the month, Meade had 89,950 troops on hand. Soldiers returning from wounds or sickness had maintained the balance, and as a result, Meade was now as strong as it had been on the opening day of Gettysburg.[6]

*   *   *

Lee could make the same boast for the same reasons. Rebel ranks swelled dramatically as convalescents returned to their regiments. The ANV had listed only 53,611 men present at the end of July. The returns for August 10 showed an increase to 68,104 troops, and by the end of the month 71,954, supported by 246 pieces of artillery. This was just a few thousand soldiers shy of Lee's Gettysburg strength.[7]

In little more than 30 days, the high command and Richmond authorities had managed to rejuvenate the Confederacy's main eastern army. Most observers saw its improved condition and revived spirit as a means to an end—the honing of a rapier that Robert E. Lee could wield to strike another blow at the enemy.

Striking a blow was certainly on his mind. The ANV's current position behind the Rapidan was an ideal line of defense which protected the critical Virginia Central railroad and provided secure communications with Richmond. The river, buttressed with fortifications erected at important fords, posed a significant military challenge to an attacker. Together they gave Lee a tactical edge that helped offset superior Federal numbers.

---

5   Meade to wife, August 19, 1863, *Life and Letters*, Vol. 2, 143-44.

6   *OR* 29, pt. 2, 28, 118.

7   *Richmond Enquirer*, August 14, 1863; *OR* 29, pt. 2, 659, 681; *Richmond Examiner*, August 13, 1863; Kirkpatrick diary, August 6, 1863, UT; Caldwell, *Brigade of South Carolinians*, 157.

The strength of the Rapidan line aside, the general didn't intend to sit passively behind the river awaiting the enemy's next move. On August 22, just three weeks after his return to the Rapidan and a mere seven since the start of his Gettysburg retreat, Lee wrote Davis that "if General Meade does not move, I wish to attack him."[8]

Should the Yankee general beat him to the punch, Lee would fight a defensive battle. But he remained convinced that only offensive campaigns could keep the Federals off balance, dilute their material superiority, and offer the chance to strike a death blow that might force the North to the peace table. The last couple of months had not shaken Lee's resolve. Unbowed by Gettysburg, he would continue to operate aggressively not just to win battles but to inflict potentially war-winning blows on his opponent. The Rapidan provided security until he found the opportunity to attack—then the river would help obfuscate and shield his movements.

*   *   *

What the Federals might do in Virginia wasn't the only factor influencing Lee's eagerness for the offensive. As the Vicksburg and Gettysburg campaigns had reached their zeniths, Maj. Gen. William S. Rosecrans' Army of the Cumberland had maneuvered Gen. Braxton Bragg's Army of Tennessee out of the center of its namesake state back to the stout defenses at Tullahoma, Tennessee. Then Rosecrans maneuvered Bragg out of those works by threatening the single railroad along which the Confederates transported their supplies. At the end of June the Southern army withdrew once again, this time all the way behind the last line of mountains shielding the strategic railroad junction of Chattanooga, Tennessee.

Rosecrans paused at Tullahoma for six weeks to stockpile supplies and plan his next move. The delay irritated Washington, and Halleck urged Rosecrans to continue pushing south. He ignored this prodding and insisted on waiting until everything was in order before resuming his campaign on August 15. At that same instant Maj. Gen. Ambrose E. Burnside's Army of the Ohio began advancing from its camps around Lexington, Kentucky, into eastern Tennessee's rugged mountains.

The dual Federal campaigns posed great danger for the Confederacy. While Rosecrans clearly aimed at Chattanooga, Burnside's offensive potentially threatened Knoxville and the railways running northeast and southwest out of that city. If the North captured either, it would cut the only direct railroad line linking Virginia to the western Confederacy. Possession of Knoxville would give the Yankees virtual control

8 *OR* 29. Pt. 2, 661.

of eastern Tennessee, whereas from Chattanooga they would be poised to invade the very heartland of the Southern nation.

Bragg had only 40,000 men with which to defend Chattanooga; his enemy boasted 68,000 troops. Thirty miles of incredibly difficult mountainous terrain known as the Cumberland Plateau separated the two forces, but the Federals unquestionably held the initiative. Bragg had neither manpower nor supplies to launch a counterattack through this formidable barrier. Rosecrans task was far from easy, but he had ample resources to attack, and could choose to strike anywhere along a 150-mile front. Bragg would need to move quickly and decisively to turn back any Federal thrust.

The commander of the Confederate Department of East Tennessee, Maj. Gen. Simon Bolivar Buckner, found himself in an even more awkward predicament. He had just 15,000 troops to confront Burnside, not to mention holding onto a vast swath of mountainous territory populated by a significant number of Union sympathizers. On July 25, 1863 the Confederate war department put Buckner under Bragg's command and designated his force the III Corps of the Army of Tennessee. The reorganization allowed Braxton Bragg to harmonize Buckner's operations with his own. This, of course, included drawing Buckner to Chattanooga if the need arose—an eventuality both generals fully anticipated.[9]

When or even if Buckner would move toward Chattanooga remained an open question. Murky intelligence and clever Federal maneuvering left the Confederates uncertain of Union plans. Was Burnside aiming for Knoxville or a link up with Rosecrans before an attack on Chattanooga? No one could say for certain, but Southern generals most feared a juncture of the two Union armies. Together Rosecrans and Burnside would have 90,000 men—nearly double Bragg's and Buckner's combined strength. Against those odds it would be all but impossible to hold Chattanooga.[10]

* * *

News of the growing crisis in Tennessee was slow to arrive in Richmond, and at first somewhat dimly perceived. But the South's worsening strategic circumstances were abundantly apparent. President Davis faced some difficult choices in the immediate future, and before making them, he wanted the advice of his best commander. On August 24, Davis wired Lee that he had been hoping to visit his headquarters for several days to "consult . . . on military questions of a general nature."

---

9 *OR* 30, pt. 4, 512.

10 Ibid., 526, 529.

But rapidly unfolding events beyond Virginia had prevented it, so Davis asked Lee to come to Richmond. Sensing serious matters stirring, the general left James Longstreet in charge along the Rapidan and hurried to the Confederate capital.[11]

Citizens quickly noticed Lee's presence in the city. Many supposed he was visiting to confer with Davis on the Virginia army's next move. Actually, Lee was there to talk grand strategy. Davis had precise, succinct questions: What could be done to help Bragg and save Chattanooga? What about other points that were under pressure? Federal forces besieged Charleston; the commander at Wilmington, North Carolina, one of the nation's few remaining open seaports, was warning of imminent attack. Knoxville was vulnerable. And of course Meade's army remained a menace.

Clearly Bragg and Buckner defended the most threatened points. They obviously needed reinforcements, but from where? Was it safe to draw troops away from Charleston, Wilmington, or Virginia to strengthen Tennessee? If such a maneuver was possible, was it the wisest move or was there a better alternative?[12]

General Pierre G. T. Beauregard, in command at Charleston, could continue to hold his own, Lee thought. Wilmington, though perhaps ripe for attack, was not in any immediate danger. But it would be inadvisable to remove men from either of those positions to reinforce Bragg. Unquestionably, whatever spare units existed in the western theater should march for Tennessee. It was unlikely, however, that these would provide enough manpower to allow Bragg to hold Chattanooga and Knoxville. The only other possible source of meaningful reinforcements was the ANV. If sufficient troops were detached from Lee and moved west, they should give Bragg the strength to launch a counteroffensive. The only other alternative was for Lee to attack Meade in hope of hurting him so badly Lincoln would shift Federal troops from Tennessee to protect Washington and aid the Army of the Potomac.

This dilemma was hardly new. The South had faced a similar situation just four months ago at Vicksburg. Rather than move troops westward to reinforce Gen. Joseph E. Johnston's force attempting to relieve the besieged fortress, Lee had invaded Pennsylvania at least partially in hope of drawing Union strength out of Mississippi and easing the Yankee menace to the city. The result had been the defeat at Gettysburg, the fall of Vicksburg, the loss of Port Hudson, and Federal control of the Mississippi River.

When faced with an almost identical problem now, Lee and Davis favored an identical solution. Both men felt it best for Lee to attack in Virginia. Because the poor condition of the army's livestock presented a serious obstacle to any offensive, Lee

---

11   *OR* 51, pt. 2, 759; Douglas Southall Freeman, *R.E. Lee: A Biography*, 4 vols. (New York, 1935), Vol. 3, 163.

12   Jones, *Rebel War Clerk's Diary*, Vol. 2, 25.

extracted a commitment from the quartermaster department to ship 3,000 bushels of corn to the Rapidan every 24 hours. The corollary to that promise was the unloading and return of the cars to Richmond each day. This was the only way logisticians could keep their word and the horses get proper forage for an arduous campaign.[13]

With the quartermaster's assurance in hand, Lee told Longstreet to prepare the army for a movement and use "every exertion" to get the troops and animals in condition for combat operations. Lee knew that Meade was dispatching regiments from his command, if not necessarily why, and he sensed opportunity in the slackening odds. He could "see nothing better to be done than to endeavor to bring General Meade out and use our efforts to crush his army while in its present condition."

Longstreet obeyed but counseled against an offensive. He warned that any attack would simply chase Meade into one of his fortified positions. Although the Georgian admitted knowing little about the situation in the west, he "inclined to the opinion that our best opportunity for great results is in Tennessee." Longstreet was certain Confederate fortifications would allow two corps to hold Meade at bay while Lee's remaining corps reinforced Bragg and destroyed Rosecrans' army.[14]

Longstreet's analysis wasn't without merit, nor was his suggestion a moot point. News filtering in from the west painted an increasingly dim picture of the situation in Tennessee. Despite Lee's preparations, the future course of Confederate strategy remained uncertain.

Then on August 29 Davis received an alarming dispatch from Confederate Senator Landon C. Haynes from his home in east Tennessee, claiming that the Federals had taken Knoxville. Davis hoped Haynes exaggerated his blunt message since the government had received no other information concerning Knoxville's capture. Nonetheless, the president asked Secretary of War Seddon to ascertain the facts, telling him the situation in eastern Tennessee "presents a serious matter for consideration." Davis pointedly expressed his anguish over the possible loss of Knoxville by scribbling a note on Haynes' dispatch: "What is to be or can be done?"[15]

*   *   *

Seddon telegraphed Davis' inquiry on August 31. Bragg responded on September 2, wiring that in his opinion Burnside was moving to join Rosecrans rather than threaten Knoxville. Reports of that city's capture were false, and any loss of

---

13 Dowdy, *Wartime Papers of Robert E. Lee*, 594.

14 Freeman, *R.E. Lee*, Vol. 3, 165.

15 *OR* 30, pt. 4, 565-66.

communication was the result of saboteurs damaging railroad and telegraph lines. General Buckner's troops had already joined the Army of Tennessee. This concentration of forces had required abandoning a portion of eastern Tennessee. But Bragg and Buckner were confident they could save Chattanooga and recapture any lost territory.[16]

Notwithstanding Bragg's assurances, a flood of disturbing reports flowed into Richmond during the first days of September. On the 5th, Brig. Gen. Alfred Jackson, commanding a small brigade Buckner had left to guard the railroad east of Knoxville, informed the war department that he had lost all telegraphic communication west of Jonesborough, Tennessee. Union forces in his front were increasingly aggressive, and the widening scope of their activity convinced him that the enemy was about to overrun the entire region. To prevent such a calamity Jackson informed Richmond that he was preparing to destroy a critical railroad bridge to "check the advance of the Federals until reinforcements arrive."[17]

Jackson's message crystallized the confusing situation in Tennessee for Davis. He was determined to prevent the Yankees from cutting the railroad line between Virginia and Chattanooga. Only troops from Lee's army could provide the necessary strength to accomplish that task. After directing Jackson to leave the railway alone, Davis told Lee it was imperative for him to send Longstreet's corps to eastern Tennessee to save Knoxville and secure the railroad. After accomplishing that mission, Longstreet would march to Chattanooga and join with Bragg to defeat Rosecrans. This bold decision would require speed and daring to produce results. Hard pressed on many fronts, the Confederacy could not afford to be sparing with the number of soldiers dispatched to Bragg. Only significant reinforcements could save Chattanooga, and Lee's army was the sole source from which they could come.[18]

Despite having his preferred plan sidetracked, Lee moved promptly to shift Longstreet's corps westward. Less than 24 hours after Davis made his decision, Lee forwarded detailed orders to put those troops on the road. The president, however, wanted to send more than these 19,157 men to Tennessee. The critical situation near Chattanooga also required the steady hand of the Confederacy's best military mind, and that meant sending Robert E. Lee as well. When Davis broached that subject with the general, however, Lee opposed the idea. He did not want to leave Virginia or his army and adamantly stated that his presence in Tennessee would make little difference.

16 *OR* 30, pt. 4, 575, 583-84.

17 *OR* 30, pt. 4, 598.

18 *OR* 30, pt. 4, 598; Longstreet, *From Manassas to Appomattox*, 436.

Apparently, he made his feelings abundantly clear to Davis. So clear, in fact, that he worried later that he had overstepped the boundaries of a soldier's duty.[19]

Concerned that he had left the impression he would refuse a transfer, Lee hastened to reassure the president he would follow orders. Before returning to the Rapidan, he wrote Davis reiterating his view that the officers already in Tennessee could best meet the challenge there. But the general also acknowledged that only the commander-in-chief had a grasp on the overall strategic situation. Which meant Davis could "come to a more correct conclusion" than he himself could, given his more limited perspective, on the question of who should command in the west.[20]

After promising Davis that he would serve wherever sent, Lee labored for several days under the impression that he would go to Tennessee. This was certainly rumored in Richmond, although not everyone believed it. Those who did felt certain such a transfer would lead to the loss of the capital and all of the Old Dominion.[21]

*   *   *

Word of a troop movement from Virginia to Tennessee, with or without Lee, could hardly remain secret. As early as September 5, rumors were afloat that Ewell's Corps was going west and that a division had already gone. One Rebel admitted that such stories caused "great excitement" throughout the army. But that was just one tale. Other hearsay claimed that the high command would order both Longstreet's corps and Hill's command to Bragg's assistance. The capital was rife with similar gossip.[22]

Few men in Lee's army evinced any desire for duty in Tennessee. This was especially true among Virginia troops, but even soldiers from the Deep South had little desire to shift their base of operations closer to home. Alabaman Jeremiah Tate hoped that Longstreet's command, rather than Hill's corps to which he belonged, would head to Bragg. "I never want to leave Virginia to reinforce any except Alabama," Tate wrote home, adding that he had but little desire for even that.[23]

As it turned out, the concerns in Ewell's and Hill's corps, as well as the streets of Richmond, were baseless. Only one of Lee's three corps was leaving Virginia, and General Lee would not be among those heading west. On September 8, Davis

---

19 *OR* 29, pt. 2, 681, 700.

20 Ibid., 700-701.

21 Jones, *Rebel War Clerk's Diary*, Vol. 2, 32-33.

22 Samuel Carson to Annie September 5, 1863, http://valley.lib.virginia.edu /papers/A3007, accessed May 3, 2018; Jeremiah Tate to "Sister Mary" September 12, 1863, GLI.

23 Ibid.

telegraphed Lee that he believed his presence with "the western army would be worth more than the addition of a corps." Although he did not doubt Lee's "willingness to do whatever was best for the county," Davis admitted he feared Lee's "absence from Virginia" and had decided to leave him in his current command. The ranking officer going to Tennessee would be James Longstreet.[24]

That selection was a wise choice in many ways: the Georgian was competent and unquestionably believed in the coming movement. He had advised such a maneuver last spring but was overruled. Now with the situation similar to that of May, Longstreet felt sure the transfer of troops from Virginia to Tennessee was the proper response to the threat aimed at Chattanooga. On the same day Davis decided to send most of his corps to Tennessee, Longstreet bluntly told Lee: "I think that it is time that we had begun to do something in the west, and I fear if it is put off any longer we shall be too late."[25]

Now Longstreet would get his chance. He would have to restructure his corps considerably before it moved west, however. Pickett's division had yet to recover from Gettysburg and was too weak to undertake such a campaign. Longstreet would exchange Pickett's command for the brigades of Henry A. Wise and Micah Jenkins, currently guarding the Confederate capital—a duty Pickett would now assume. Two of Longstreet's Georgia brigades were also detached to reinforce Charleston. Beyond the need to strengthen that imperiled bastion, fear of desertions by Georgia troops as they passed through their home state motivated this particular decision.[26]

Although this meant only two First Corps divisions would go to Chattanooga, their transfer represented a significant reinforcement for the beleaguered Army of Tennessee. Lee and Longstreet well understood the risks and opportunities this concentration of strength entailed. Before leaving for Richmond with his command, Longstreet stopped at Lee's headquarters for a final meeting. The parting of these two officers was not without emotion. They had served together for 15 months and fought through some of the most monumental campaigns of the war side-by-side. Longstreet's return to the Army of Northern Virginia wasn't certain. Both men appreciated the magnitude of the operation he was undertaking and the potential consequences of failure. Meaningful strategic results simply *had* to ensue. As Longstreet mounted his horse to leave, Lee told him he must "beat those people out

---

24 OR 29, pt. 1, 702.

25 Jeffry D. Wert, *General James Longstreet: The Confederacy's Most Controversial Soldier, A Biography* (New York, 1993), 304-305.

26 OR 29, pt. 2, 706.

west." Longstreet responded: "If I live, but I would not give a single man of my command for a fruitless victory."[27]

*   *   *

The First Corps cooked three days rations on the evening of September 7 and prepared to march at daylight for Hanover Court House to a rendezvous with trains bound for Richmond. The initial leg of that journey was a miserable ordeal. Troops practically suffocated in the scorching heat and clouds of dust kicked up by thousands of marching men. Both soldiers and their animals suffered intensely from a lack of water along their route. According to regimental surgeon Robert Myers a large number of Longstreet's heat- and thirst-stricken troops fell out of ranks and "laid on the roadside panting [and] exhausted" until they mustered the strength to keep moving.[28]

The First Corps divisions overcame these challenges and quickly gathered at Hanover Junction. Before long they crowded onto the railway cars and headed toward Richmond. From the capital city those regiments destined to reinforce Bragg expected to be transported southwest over four separate rail lines through Burkeville, Lynchburg, Bristol, and Knoxville to Chattanooga. The brigades reinforcing Charleston would travel south through Petersburg, then across North Carolina and on into the Palmetto State.

Unfortunately for the Confederacy events in Tennessee conspired against Longstreet's planned route. Union cavalry seized Knoxville on September 2, riding unopposed into the town. Official news of this calamity didn't reach Richmond until September 7. The city's fall severed the direct rail line to Chattanooga. With Burnside's 20,000 infantry and 5,000 cavalry in and around Knoxville, sending Longstreet directly through southwestern Virginia into Tennessee was out of the question.[29]

News of Knoxville's loss wasn't Bragg's only unhappy tiding. Once more Rosecrans had used his numerical superiority with great dexterity. The Yankees had breached the Cumberland Plateau in several places and proceeded to secure a bridgehead over the Tennessee River southwest of Chattanooga. If Rosecrans exploded out of that lodgment, he could quickly sever the single railway supplying Bragg's army. Lacking sufficient troops to both counter this threat and hold

---

27 Longstreet, *From Manassas to Appomattox*, 437. Longstreet advocated that he replace Bragg as commander of the Army of Tennessee; Davis did not approve that suggestion.

28 Myers Diary, September 7-8, 1863, Eleanor S. Brockenbrough Library, American Museum of the Civil War (ACWM), Richmond, VA

29 *OR* 30, pt. 2, 548; *OR* 30, pt. 4, 621.

Chattanooga at the same time, Bragg evacuated the city on September 8. Union forces occupied it the next day.

Even with the loss of Chattanooga, Davis determined to carry out the strategic plan already in motion. There was no other choice really. General Bragg would have to counterattack to regain the vital lost ground, and that was impossible without Longstreet. Now, however, his divisions would have to take a circuitous 700-mile-long route through the Carolinas and Georgia to reach the Army of Tennessee.[30]

Longstreet personally arrived in Richmond on the evening of September 10. He spent several days overseeing the replacement of Pickett's division and the brigades destined for South Carolina with those of Jenkins and Wise. Before leaving the city, the general penned a final letter to Lee. He would start west on September 14, he wrote, and promised "if I can do anything there, it shall be done promptly. If I cannot, I shall advise you to recall me." Then in an emotional passage he said,

> If I did not think our move a necessary one, my regrets at leaving you would be distressing to me, as it seems to be with the officers and men of my command. . . . All that we have to be proud of has been accomplished under your eyes and under your orders. Our affections for you are stronger, if it is possible for them to be stronger, than our admiration for you.

He signed the letter "most respectfully and affectionately, your obedient servant." And with that, Longstreet and his soldiers were officially gone from the Army of Northern Virginia.[31]

No one could say what impact they might make on western events. But the departure of an entire corps from Lee's army dramatically changed the strategic situation in Virginia. By September 10 Lee could muster only 54,000 soldiers on the Rapidan—a far cry from the 72,000 he had at the end of August. By contrast, the Army of the Potomac reported its strength as just over 89,000. The odds were now almost 1.5 to 1 against Lee. What George Meade would do once he realized this fact was likely to prove most dangerous to the Confederate cause.[32]

*   *   *

---

30 Robert C. Black III, *The Railroads of the Confederacy* (Chapel Hill, NC, 1998), 184-91; Longstreet, Manassas to Appomattox, 436. Just when Lee and Longstreet became aware of the change in plan is unclear. Longstreet maintained in his memoir that Richmond kept both him and Lee ignorant of the loss of Knoxville until the movement was too far advanced to allow recall.

31 *OR* 29, pt. 2, 713-14.

32 Ibid., 709,118.

Theoretically, the strategic shift of 20,000 troops out of theater should have been a strict military secret. But military secrets are the most fragile of creations, and this one never had a chance of surviving. Rumors of the movement were all over Richmond even before Davis actually decided to send Longstreet to Tennessee. The Yankees would certainly learn such news quickly. Not quite two weeks into September stories were already circulating in the Confederate capital that deserters had told the enemy about Lee detaching large numbers of troops for duty elsewhere. Almost everyone expected Meade to take advantage of their absence.[33]

The Federals found out about Longstreet's westward trek soon enough, with or without the help of deserters. Lee complained to Davis that the New York *World* of September 9 contained precise information on the marching sequence of Longstreet's divisions to Hanover Junction, as well as the news that Pickett's division had traded places with two brigades guarding Richmond. Lee had not even alerted the quartermaster department of Longstreet's movement until September 6. If New York newspapers could report on the operation so thoroughly just three days later, the general complained, there must have been "great imprudence in talking on the part of our people" or "improper persons" working for the railroad. [34]

With the Federals already spun up into a heightened state of watchfulness, evidence of the transfer of Longstreet's divisions couldn't help but garner swift Yankee notice. By uncanny coincidence, on the very day Lee ordered his First Corps to Tennessee, Halleck wired Meade that Rosecrans was reporting (erroneously) that some of Lee's troops had reinforced Bragg. Halleck wanted Meade to "employ every possible means to ascertain" if this were true.

None of his subordinates had observed any major activity by the Rebel army, Meade responded. The only change along Lee's front had been a retrograde movement by Brig. Gen. John R. Cooke's command, which had shifted to Fredericksburg from its usual post around Richmond during Lee's recent retreat. Meade supposed Cooke was returning to the city. He doubted any significant Confederate undertaking could happen without his hearing of it, although reliable information was admittedly "very difficult to obtain."[35]

However, the general agreed that it would be best to investigate the rumors, and he sent spies behind Rebel lines to determine the truth. As his agents went about their clandestine task, Meade held a grand review of each of his seven infantry corps. These pomp and circumstance occasions gave the commanding general a better look at the

---

33 Jones, *Rebel War Clerk's Diary*, Vol. 2, 37.

34 *OR* 29, pt. 2, 719-20. Improper persons meant spies.

35 *OR* 29, pt. 2, 158.

army he had led for barely two months and let his troops see him in return. The ceremonies also kept the army busy while it waited for Washington to remove the shackles of inactivity it had fastened around Meade's ankles at the beginning of August.

As the last of the reviews concluded, events rapidly began overtaking the army. On September 11, Meade learned that nine of the regiments sent to New York were on their way back to Virginia. Another 15 commands awaited the ships that would return them to the army. That the government no longer needed these units and that they were on their way to the Rappahannock was welcome news.[36]

But other reports that day weren't so cheering. Scouts returned from behind Rebel lines with the unsettling information that McLaws' division of Longstreet's corps had left its old camps. Eyewitnesses had seen Law's brigade of Hood's division marching southward. Meade dutifully telegraphed these troubling reports to Washington but confessed they only confirmed that some part of the enemy force had left the Rapidan-Rappahannock line. What was uncertain and hence more worrisome, Meade had "no positive evidence" as to *where* it had gone.

No fan of military uncertainties, Meade sought to quickly uncover firmer intelligence. On September 12, he ordered Maj. Gen. Alfred Pleasonton to deploy his entire cavalry corps into Culpeper County "to try and find something out." Gouverneur Warren—promoted to major general on August 8 and now temporarily commanding the II Corps—would cross his men over the Rappahannock in support. Newton's I Corps would stand ready to reinforce the move on short notice if needed.

Far to the south, Meade was preparing to investigate what Federal soldiers in North Carolina already knew. Major General John J. Peck, commander of the District of North Carolina, reported on September 12 that a Union sympathizer had just come into his lines with news that "a large body of troops passed from General Lee's army to the west for General Bragg, estimated at varying from 15,000 to 20,000." The informant, a Pennsylvania native visiting his son-in-law in Graham, North Carolina, had talked to some of the Rebel troops "and all said they were going to Bragg and that it would not be known at the North."[37]

*   *   *

Behind the Rapidan, the Rebels continued to wait. News of Knoxville's capture reached the ANV but seems to have aroused no special concern in the ranks. Lee's troops did wonder about their own lack of movement despite the excellent fall

36 *OR* 29, pt. 2, 167.

37 *OR* 29, pt. 2, 172-73.

weather. One soldier echoed his comrades' sentiments when he wrote "the time has come for action." The army, he predicted, would not remain idle much longer.[38]

The transfer of the First Corps had manifestly increased the danger that Meade might undertake an offensive. As a precaution, on September 6 Lee issued ammunition to his regiments and instructed them to cook three days rations. Such orders often portended battle, but despite the distribution of hardtack and bullets neither army stirred.[39]

Although the redeployment of Longstreet's corps had passed the initiative to the Federals, their army remained immobile and inactive. Lee, like Meade, decided to take advantage of the lull to hold a review of each of his corps. As a rule officers believed it beneficial for morale to have their men witness the army's strength arrayed. In the current circumstances this seemed especially apropos. Such a display might soothe nerves about Longstreet's departure and bolster everybody's confidence: soldiers, officials, and civilians alike.

For spectators these reviews were majestic, displaying exactly the kind of war one read about in books—all those brave men, their musket barrels shining in the sun, drawn up in their thousands under fluttering banners to attest to the power and spirit of the army and the Confederacy. The fact that many ladies attended, among them General Lee's daughters, enhanced the allure of the occasion. The soldiers had divided feelings about the exercise, however. Some were awestruck with the occasion and excited to take part; others considered the entire affair a lot of needless work.[40]

Whatever the rank and files' opinions, many observers were as taken with the élan of the Army of Northern Virginia as the pageantry of its display. One onlooker wrote that Lee's regiments showed "by their steady and firm step and soldierly bearing that they were not disheartened, but ready to go wherever their trusted and beloved commander might point the way."[41]

That spirit would be tested sooner than anyone anticipated. Following the September 11 review of Hill's Corps, one last quiet, lazy day passed along the Rapidan. The weather was hot, and on the night of September 12 a heavy drizzle began falling. While the Confederates slept and the rain came down, Meade's cavalry began to move south.[42]

---

38 Russell F. Stanley to wife September 5, 1863, WFCHS.

39 Ibid, September 6, 7.

40 John Worsham, *One of Jackson's Foot Cavalry* (New York, 1912), 179-181; William A. Smith to fiancé September 10, 1863, UT; Kirkpatrick diary, September 11, 1863, UT.

41 Freeman, *R.E. Lee*, Vol. 3, 167.

42 Kirkpatrick diary, September 12, 1863, UT.

Chapter 6

"Firing Pistols, Flashing Sabers
and Excited Men"

General Pleasonton—Federal Advance—Battle of Culpeper Court House—
Capture of the Guns—To the Rapidan

As a result of the Lincoln administration's need to resume the draft at bayonet point, the Army of the Potomac had marked time along the Rappahannock for six weeks. The long delay at least allowed Meade to rejuvenate his command after its Gettysburg ordeal. Apparently, the Confederates found the interval equally useful. Increasingly credible rumors of Lee's shipping troops to Tennessee had put the Federal high command on edge. Halleck was anxious for facts, so too was Meade who decided to dispel any doubt by sending Pleasonton's Cavalry Corps and Maj. Gen. Warren's II Corps into Culpeper County at first light on September 13.

Meade had suspected since late July that Lee would avoid a major battle around Culpeper Court House and might even abandon the Rapidan line if pressed. The coming movement would test that hypothesis. However the general stressed to Pleasonton that his task was only a reconnaissance "predicated" on reports that the enemy had made a "retrograde movement." He was to avoid bringing on a general engagement. Warren's infantry went along as insurance so that cavalry could withdraw safely if it ran into serious trouble.[1]

A 39-year old West Pointer (Class of 1844) with a long record on the frontier, Alfred Pleasonton had led a regiment during the Peninsula Campaign and earned promotion to brigadier in July 1862. Two months later he took command of a cavalry division. Pleasonton and other officers lobbied vigorously for the creation of a cavalry

---

1 *OR* 29, pt. 2, 175.

Major General Alfred Pleasonton
Library of Congress

corps until congress authorized one in April 1863. The disappointing performance of the corps under Maj. Gen. George Stoneman during the Chancellorsville campaign, led to his replacement by Pleasonton, who received a promotion to major general on June 22, 1863.[2]

The new cavalry corps commander was controversial and enigmatic. His waxed moustache, close-cut beard and habit of enjoying oysters and champagne gave him a reputation as a "nice little dandy," in the words of one II Corps officer. The jaunty angle of the general's hat, his white kid gloves, riding crop, and tendency to favor tall horses reinforced this impression. He was also something of a charmer who possessed fine social graces and a witty disposition. A headquarters aide described him as "a singular" sort of man: "cold-blooded yet kindly, ambitious but not soaring," with a "quick and ready brain," yet one strangely incapable of "judging things *en grand*."[3]

The cavalryman proved an able administrator with a knack for promoting talented subordinates. Shortly after taking command of the corps, he had made brigadiers of George A. Custer, Elon Farnsworth, and Wesley Merritt, men whose aggressiveness and swagger, prized by press and enlisted men alike, echoed his own. Although the cavalry corps had performed quite well under Pleasonton's command, some doubted that he deserved credit for its accomplishments. Indeed, more than a few subordinates

---

2 Tagg, *Generals of Gettysburg*, 165. Alfred Pleasonton's appointment to the West Point was due to the fame his father, Stephen Pleasonton, had earned during the War of 1812. As an employee of the State Department, the elder Pleasonton had saved the Declaration of Independence, Articles of Confederation, Constitution, and other priceless documents from capture or destruction by the invading British Army when it burned some of Washington, DC in August of 1814.

3 Ibid.; Lyman, *Meade's Army*, 116.

despised not only his consistently harsh discipline, but even more his unseemly scheming for rank or fame and propensity to take credit for the successful actions of others.[4]

Meade was aware of Pleasonton's negative aspects. But he also acknowledged that the cavalry had shown more promise under his leadership than at any point in the past. His confidence in the cavalryman was sufficient to deflect Secretary of War Stanton's offer to get rid of Pleasonton. Now the general would lead his corps into the field as a coordinated unit for only the second time in the war: its mission to find out what the Rebels had been up to behind the Rappahannock.[5]

Pleasonton's plan was straightforward. Buford's 1st Cavalry Division would attack southward down the O&A toward Brandy Station. At the same time Brig. Gen. Judson Kilpatrick's 3rd Cavalry Division would cross the Rappahannock River at Kelly's Ford and move northeast to link up with Buford. Together the two divisions would push on toward Culpeper Court House. Meanwhile Brig. Gen. David M. Gregg's 2nd Cavalry Division would cross the Hazel River near Rixeyville, seize a bridge over Muddy Run, and move on Culpeper from the northwest. All three divisions should converge on the court house around noon. If circumstances seemed favorable, Pleasonton intended to continue his advance toward the Rapidan. The Confederate response to all this would tell Meade much of what he needed to know.[6]

Unfortunately for the Federals, they would not catch the Confederates by surprise. At 3 a.m. on September 13 word reached Stuart that enemy cavalry was assembling north of the Rappahannock River. Within 30 minutes Rebel buglers were sounding boots and saddles. Not long after that, Southern horsemen began moving into position to resist the enemy's pending advance.[7]

Stuart had only two full brigades and part of another to defend a 20-mile front stretching from Rixeyville on the Hazel River to Kelly's Ford on the Rappahannock.

---

4   Pleasonton has received little attention from scholars despite the fact that he commanded the AOP's Cavalry Corps for almost a year and during one of the war's most famous campaigns. No biography of the man exists. Historians have concluded that Pleasonton grossly inflated or embellished the importance of his actions at Chancellorsville. Peter G. Eidler, *Army of the Potomac: The Civil War Letters of William Cross Hazelton of the Eighth Illinois Cavalry Regiment* (Seattle, WA, 2013), 116. Pleasonton's career has been discussed in Tagg, *Generals of Gettysburg*, 165; Warner, *Generals in Blue*, 373; Longacre, *Lincoln's Cavalrymen*, Vol 1, 96, 149, 249; Stephen Z. Starr, *The Union Cavalry in the Civil War*, 3 Vols. (Baton Rouge, LA, 1979), 1:313, 327.

5   Meade to wife, March 9, 1864, *Life and Letters*, Vol. 2, 176, 71.

6   *OR* 29, pt. 1, 118.

7   J. H. Stine, *History of the Army of the Potomac* (Washington, DC, 1893), 560; Henry B. McClellan, *I Rode With Jeb Stuart: The Life and Campaigns of Major General J.E.B. Stuart* (Bloomington, IN, 1958), 373; Beale, *A Lieutenant of Cavalry*, 124.

Hampton's and Robertson's brigades (the latter just two regiments strong) were near Stevensburg, both under the command of Col. James B. Gordon. The bulk of Jones' brigade, under Brig. Gen. Lunsford L. Lomax, was bivouacked south of Muddy Run on the Rixeyville Road, with the 11th Virginia Cavalry picketing the Hazel River. Half of W. H. F. "Rooney" Lee's brigade was camped southwest of Brandy Station. The other half deployed as skirmishers from Fleetwood Heights eastward. Colonel John R. Chambliss had led the command since Lee's wounding in June. However, on September 13 Chambliss was absent, and Col. Richard L. T. Beal commanded the brigade.[8]

Major Robert F. Beckham had distributed his battalion of horse artillery across the front to support the Confederate horsemen. Capt. Wiley H. Griffin's battery was stationed south of Muddy Run with General Lomax. The batteries under Capt. Roger Chew and Capt. William M. McGregor and a two-gun section from Capt. Marcellus N. Moorman's battery were not far from Culpeper Court House. Captain James F. Hart's battery was in camp with Col. Gordon near Stevensburg. Three fieldpieces operating under the personal direction of Capt. Chew stood ready on Fleetwood Heights.[9]

When General Lee pulled his infantry behind the Rapidan River, he directed Stuart to occupy Culpeper County as long as he could do so "without sacrificing" his men. Although the general didn't want his cavalry to engage in a major action north of the Rapidan, the fact that it had stockpiled a considerable quantity of supplies at Culpeper Court House complicated that desire. If Stuart did not intend to abandon those precious stores, he would have to keep the Yankees away from the town until his rear echelon could pack and whisk the depot's contents away to safety. That meant a fight was inevitable.

By 4:00 a.m. quartermasters in Culpeper were loading boxes and barrels of supplies into wagons that would carry them south of the Rapidan. Stuart also directed the removal of his command's broken down and spare horses. Once the loaded wagons were on their way, sweating men began transferring remaining materiel into boxcars parked at Culpeper's railroad station. The departure of the O&A's rolling stock

---

8 OR 27, pt. 3, 1075; George Beale, *A Lieutenant of Cavalry in Lee's Army* (Boston, MA, 1918), 124; Daniel E. Sutherland, *Seasons of War: The Ordeal of a Confederate Community 1861-1865* (New York, 1995), 234. Brig Gen Beverly Robertson had asked for and been granted reassignment. NY State Military Museum, Unit History Project, 2nd Regiment Cavalry, New York Military Museum, "The Late Cavalry Advance" http://dmna.ny.gov/hisotric/reghis/civil/cavalry/2ndCav/2ndCavCWN.htm, accessed May 6, 2018; hereinafter cited as "NYMM."

9 Trout, *Galloping Thunder*, 333. Two of the guns were from McGregor's battery. The other was a 3-inch gun from Chew's Battery.

would have to await the noon arrival of the regularly scheduled locomotive, which meant Stuart's troopers would have to hold the Yankees at bay for the six next hours[10]

*   *   *

Dawn on September 13 broke cheerlessly with torrential rain sweeping through the Culpeper area around 4 a.m. For the next two hours a violent thunderstorm drenched Federal and Confederate troopers massing for the fight everyone knew was coming. The saturated ground hindered and slowed the Yankees as they struggled through deepening muck toward their assembly areas. By 6 a.m., however, the rain had stopped and Pleasonton's offensive got off to a quick start.[11]

Gregg's 2nd Cavalry Division moved first, crossing the Hazel River unopposed and easily occupying Rixeyville. By 9 a.m. Gregg's regiments were riding south toward Muddy Run. There the 11th Virginia Cavalry put up a stout 30-minute defense of the only bridge over the stream. The Federals eventually outflanked the position and forced the Virginians to withdraw. Rebel troopers set the span on fire as they fell back, but their opponents quickly extinguished the flames and continued their advance. Upon learning of Gregg's thrust, a troubled Brig. Gen. Lomax sent the 7th and 12th Virginia cavalry regiments and Griffin's battery to reinforce the 11th Virginia.[12]

Despite his focus on Gregg, which he believed to be the main Federal effort, Lomax wisely did not neglect the probability of a Union attack from Rappahannock Station. He dispatched his remaining regiment, the 5th Virginia Cavalry, to Fleetwood Heights, where the 6th Virginia Cavalry and a squadron of sharpshooters from the 9th Virginia Cavalry—both from Rooney Lee's (Chambliss/Beale's) brigade—stood guard. Meanwhile the bulk of Beckham's battalion of horse artillery and the rest of the Beale's command (the 9th and 13th Virginia cavalry regiments) received orders to advance to Brandy Station. If the Yankees lunged south, the troopers near Fleetwood Heights had orders to fall back on these reinforcements and make a stand.

---

10 Elijah Johnson diary September 13, 1863, VHS; Beale, *A Lieutenant of Cavalry*, 124; Walbrook D. Swank, ed., *The Civil War Diary of John William Peyton* (Shippensburg, PA, 2003), 87.

11 Aggassiz, *Meade's Headquarters*, 14; Moore, *Rebellion Record*, Vol. 7, 503.

12 Moore, *Rebellion Record*, Vol. 7, 504; *Philadelphia Inquirer*, September 16, 1863; Walter S. Newhall, *A Memoir* (Philadelphia, PA, 1864), 116; William Lloyd, *History of the First Regiment Pennsylvania Reserve Cavalry* (Philadelphia, PA, 1864), 71; Wells A. Bushnell, "Sixth Regiment Ohio Volunteer Cavalry Memoir 1861-1865," unpublished manuscript, Western Reserve Historical Society (WRHS). The 11th Virginia Cavalry withdrew from the Hazel that morning and was already on the way to Muddy Run when the Yankee offensive began.

While Lomax did what he could to deal with Gregg and prepare for Buford, Pleasonton's 3rd Cavalry Division under Judson Kilpatrick crossed the pontoon bridge at Kelly's Ford. The Federals captured a few Rebel pickets and then moved toward Stevensburg. At the cut off to Brandy Station, Kilpatrick directed his column to the northeast, and to shield his flank sent Lt. Col. Peter Stagg's 1st Michigan Cavalry toward Stevensburg with orders to test Rebel strength in the area. Stagg subsequently skirmished with Hampton's brigade under Col. Gordon, but the antagonists broke contact when word of a serious engagement to the west reached them.[13]

This engagement was a growing action along the O&A line. Earlier that morning Buford had allowed both Gregg and Kilpatrick to get a good head start before leading his division south out of the Union bridgehead around Rappahannock Station. With the rain clouds having finally dissipated, sunshine blanketed the landscape as the Federal troopers moved forward behind the 9th New York Cavalry's mounted skirmishers.[14]

Only three enemy field pieces on Fleetwood Heights, a squadron of sharpshooters from the 9th Virginia Cavalry and the 5th and 6th Virginia cavalry regiments stood in Buford's path. Although the Rebel cannon engaged briefly with Yankee guns, the Confederates were hopelessly outmatched; the Virginians had no choice but to retire slowly toward Brandy Station and to waiting reinforcements. The 15th Virginia Cavalry, which had been picketing the Rappahannock east of the railroad, also fell back towards the station.[15]

Under steady pressure from Buford, the Confederates withdrew all the way back to Brandy Station where Lunsford Lomax and six fieldpieces from Beckham's horse artillery awaited them. With five regiments at his disposal the 27-year old Lomax deployed the 5th, 6th and 13th Virginia cavalry regiments to the west of the tracks and the 9th and 15th Cavalry to the east. General Lomax assumed personal command of

---

13 OR 29, pt. 1, 120, 124, 129, 130; Willard Glazier, *Three Years in the Federal Cavalry* (New York, NY, 1870), 313.

14 OR 29, pt. 1, 111; David W. Lowe, *Meade's Army: The Private Notebooks of Lt. Col. Theodore Lyman* (Kent, OH, 2007), 34-35. Merritt's Reserve Cavalry Brigade had returned to Washington, DC, its usual duty station. Therefore, Buford, like Gregg and Kilpatrick, only had two brigades. Exactly how many and which batteries from the horse artillery accompanied Pleasonton on Sept. 13 is unclear. Only three batteries (Martin's, Counselman's, Fuller's) are named in official reports or memoirs, and two (Butler and Williston) are identified in an Oct. 3, 1863 edition of *Harper's Weekly* by Alfred Waud. A division usually had two batteries attached, but as the entire cavalry corps was involved, all of the horse artillery batteries may have crossed the Rappahannock. Buford's advance began at 7:30 a.m.

15 Newel Cheney, *History of the Ninth Regiment New York Volunteer Cavalry, War of 1861-1865* (New York, 1901), 132; Lyman, *Meade's Army*, 13; Grimsley, *Battles in Culpeper County*, 15.

his left flank and assigned his right to the highly competent 44-year old Col. Beale, who had once represented Virginia in the US Congress.[16]

The 3rd Cavalry Division arrived to reinforce Buford at the same instant Southern forces consolidated around Brandy Station. As the advance guard of Kilpatrick's column (Lt. Col. Otto Harhaus's 2nd New York Cavalry) neared the railroad, it failed to spot Beale's units and Beckham's guns in the heavy woods east of the tracks. The sudden roar of Rebel artillery took the Federals by surprise and inflicted several casualties before the Virginians launched a furious attack upon them. Harhaus kept his wits about him and avoided being surrounded by ordering a quick retreat.[17]

Luckily for the New Yorkers, the rest of Kilpatrick's command arrived before Harhaus's regiment was destroyed. As Kilpatrick established communication with Buford, Battery K, 1st US Artillery engaged Beckham's guns and the 3rd Cavalry Division deployed for action. The Union generals agreed to use the railroad as the boundary between their units—the 1st Division to the west and the 3rd to the east.[18]

Under this pressure the badly outnumbered Confederates pulled back once more. Lomax and Beale made a brief stand around the Kennedy House, but gave way when Union formations began to curl around their flanks. They turned to fight again in the woods in front of the last ridge before Culpeper Court House, the same spot where they had stopped Buford on August 1. Beale held the enemy in check for a time from the cover of a heavy forest east of the railroad, but General Lomax's men on the other side of the tracks lacked cover, and enemy pressure forced them to retire. Colonel Beale thus had to order his regiments to give ground as well, and just as his withdrawal began an enemy bullet knocked Beale out of the fight.[19]

As his staff carried their wounded chief to the rear, the battle's pace accelerated dramatically. The outnumbered Confederates fell back over the last ridge shielding Culpeper Court House and slipped down its rear slope toward Mountain Run. The creek's rugged banks snaked through a small valley separating two parallel 400-foot high ridges. The outskirts of Culpeper sat on the southernmost ridge. As the Federals

---

16 Lyman, *Meade's Headquarters*, 15; Luther Hopkins, *From Bull Run to Appomattox* (Baltimore, MD, 1914), 115; Moore, *Rebellion Record*, Vol. 7, 504; Beale, *History of the Ninth Virginia Cavalry*, 99. The CS guns were a section each from Moorman's, McGregor's and Chew's batteries, a total of nine guns.

17 Willard Glazier, *Three Years in the Federal Cavalry* (New York 1870), 312-13; Elijah Johnson Diary, September 13, 1863, VHS. The 2nd New York Cavalry was also known as the Harris Light Cavalry.

18 OR 29, pt. 1, 118, 120.

19 Aggassiz, *Meade's Headquarters*, 16; Beale, *Ninth Virginia Cavalry*, 99, 125. Beale would need 3 months to recover before returning to duty.

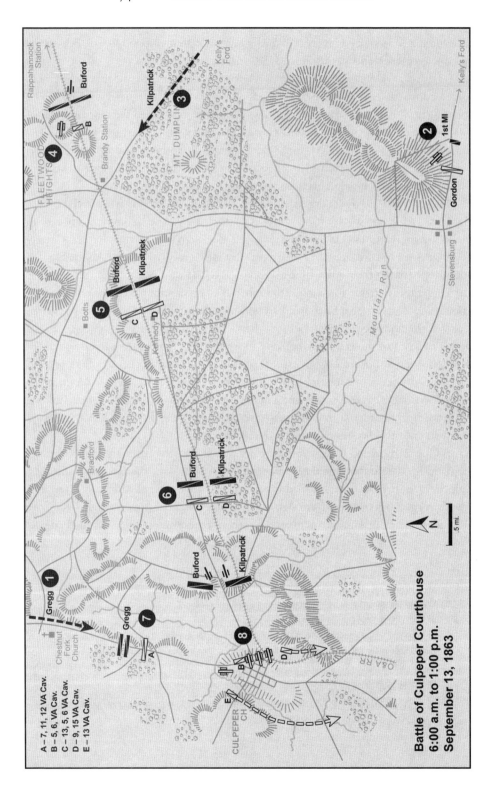

A – 7, 11, 12 VA Cav.
B – 5, 6, VA Cav.
C – 13, 5, 6 VA Cav.
D – 9, 15 VA Cav.
E – 13 VA Cav.

Battle of Culpeper Courthouse
6:00 a.m. to 1:00 p.m.
September 13, 1863

rushed toward the height north of the stream, the Confederates hurried to a railroad bridge spanning the waterway and in a somewhat disorganized fashion, crossed the creek via two fords located on either side of the trestle. Once over the creek the Rebels rushed to the top of the ridge and the town.

Whether on orders or by instinct, most of the Confederates did not draw up to defend the village. The 15th and the 9th Virginia Cavalry retreated down the eastern flank of Culpeper Court House and took position on a hill southeast of the town. The 13th Virginia Cavalry slipped below the town to the west. Only the 5th and 6th Virginia Cavalry along with Beckham's horse artillery made a stand on the northern border of Culpeper. Behind them they could see workmen coupling the just arrived O&A locomotive to boxcars.

Even as the Confederates deployed to defend the court house, the sound of firing off to the northwest heralded the approach of Gregg's Union division, which had been slowly fighting its way toward Culpeper in the face of a vigorous delaying action by the 11th, 7th, and 12th Virginia cavalry regiments. Griffin's battery had broken away from that running fight and retired to the northwest corner of Culpeper, where the artillery command had unlimbered and taken up a good position facing down the Rixeyville Road.

To Griffin's right, four guns from McGregor's battery and a pair of fieldpieces from Chew's outfit unlimbered west of the railroad tracks. The remaining three guns from Beckham's battalion—a section from Moorman's battery and a 3-inch rifle from Chew's battery—took up a position east of the rails. A pair of mounted squadrons from the 6th Virginia Cavalry stood nearby the cannon west of the O&A in support of the guns. Dismounted troopers from the 5th Virginia Cavalry spread out along the tree-lined banks of Mountain Run to defend the fords on either side of the railroad bridge.[20]

Minutes after the Rebels took up these positions the massed might of Buford and Kilpatrick's divisions swept onto the ridge north of the creek. As nearly 6,000 Yankee troopers went into line, Union artillery spun into position and began firing. Some of the Federal guns focused on the enemy cannon and horsemen in front of Culpeper Court House. Most, however, bombarded the town's railroad depot, where a locomotive was just beginning to pull a train of boxcars southward. Much to their disappointment, the artillerymen were able to fire only a few ineffective shots at the accelerating target

---

20 Above paragraphs based upon Grimsley, *Battles in Culpeper County*, 16; Moore, *Rebellion Record*, Vol. 7, 501, 503. A newspaper account of the positioning of the Rebel guns and the fight at this point is at 2nd NY Cavalry, "The Late Cavalry Advance" http://dmna. ny.gov/hisotric/reghis/civil/cavalry/2ndCav/2ndCavCWN.htm, NYMM accessed May 13, 2018.

A locomotive at Culpeper's Train Depot. *Library of Congress*

before it drew out of range. Elsewhere along the front, a handful of errant Yankee projectiles overshot their targets and exploded in Culpeper's streets. [21]

Confederate gunners were more accurate. Rebel shells slammed into the ranks of the 6th Michigan Cavalry, felling men and horses at every discharge. Apparently this galling fire came from three enemy fieldpieces located to the east of the tracks. Colonel Henry Davies, whose brigade was suffering the most from this barrage, ordered Col. Harhaus's 2nd New York horsemen to take the troublesome guns. Almost simultaneously, Gen. Kilpatrick gave George Custer's brigade the same mission.[22]

Custer instructed Col. Russell A. Alger's 5th Michigan Cavalry to launch a dismounted attack across Mountain Run toward the Rebel cannon. Then the young brigadier galloped over to Col. William D. Mann and issued orders for his 7th Michigan to cross the creek farther east and outflank the enemy. He himself would lead the column. As the movement began, Kilpatrick sent word for Maj. William Wells' 1st Vermont Cavalry to ride east, attempt to ford Mountain Run, and cut off the Rebel forces retreating to the south.[23]

21 Beale, *A Lieutenant of Cavalry*, 125; Moore, *Rebellion Record*, Vol. 7, 502; Nunnelee Diary, September 13, 1863, ACWM; *Richmond Enquirer*, September 18, 1863.

22 *OR* 29, pt. 1, 118, 120, 124; Grimsley, *Battles in Culpeper Country*, 16; Trout, *Galloping Thunder*, 350; *Orleans Independent Standard*, October 9, 1863. Griffin's Battery had 3 guns; Chew's 3 guns; Moorman's 2, and McGregor's 4.

23 2nd NY Cavalry, "The Late Cavalry Advance," http://dmna.ny.gov/hisotric/reghis/civil/cavalry/2ndCav/2ndCavCWN.htm, NYMM accessed May 6, 2018; *OR* 29, pt. 1, 118-19, 126, 128, 129; Moore, *Rebellion Record*, Vol. 7, 502-503; Elliott W. Hoffman, *History of the Frist Vermont Cavalry Volunteers in the War of the Great Rebellion* (Baltimore, MD, 2000), 133. It is possible the

As Custer's men rode off, a battalion from the 2nd New York led by Maj. Samuel McIrvin charged out of the center of the Federal line toward the enemy cannon. Confederate shells tore through the air around the blue column of fours as it dashed toward Mountain Run. When McIrvin's men neared the creek, withering fire from the 5th Virginia Cavalry forced the Union regiment to veer left for cover behind an embankment leading to the railroad bridge. As the New Yorkers redeployed, the 5th Michigan chased away the Southern troopers defending the ford east of the bridge. Seizing the opportunity, McIrvin ordered his column to charge over the crossing and uphill toward the Rebel guns.[24]

Custer was closing on those same cannons. Mountain Run's rain-swollen, steep and miry banks had thwarted the 7th Michigan's effort to cross. The brigadier told Col. Mann to dismount his regiment and get across the waterway as best he could. Meanwhile, the general and a handful of troopers managed to force their mounts over the creek. After slithering out of the muddy waters, Custer's small party surged uphill toward the Confederate fieldpieces.

At the height's crest, they charged the 3-inch gun from Chew's battery commanded by Lt. James W. Thomson. The Rebels pivoted their weapon in Custer's direction and fired a shell that detonated among the brigadier's cavalcade. The explosion wounded Custer slightly in the leg while killing his horse and a bugler riding alongside. As the general and his slain mount tumbled to the ground, the rest of the tiny band kept charging. Realizing that Thomson could not get off another shot before the Yankees reached him, Capt. Chew ordered the lieutenant to abandon his gun.[25]

Unfortunately for the Rebels at that exact instant the 2nd New York suddenly thundered over the crest of the hill to their rear. These troopers had managed to gallop up the hillside unseen thanks to its steep slope and the distraction provided by Custer's attack. The New Yorkers quickly assailed Thomson's gun. A few crewmen managed to jump on battery horses and flee, but the Yankees captured the remaining seven graycoats along with their cannon.

With these guns silenced, the Northerners turned toward a nearby two-gun section from Moorman's battery, which had limbered up and was trying to get away. The Federal cavalrymen descended on the closest of these guns with a demonic fury. Union sabers slashed through the air as gunners fought back desperately with whatever

---

Vermont regiment moved first. The commander of the 1st VT, Colonel Edward B. Sawyer, was on a three day leave. When he heard vague rumors of an advance he hurried back to the army but did not reach his regiment until Sept. 14.

24 Grimsley, *Battles in Culpeper County*, 16; OR 29, pt. 1,120, 124, 125; Moore, *Rebellion Record*, Vol. 7, 503.

25 OR 29, pt. 1, 120; Neese, *Three Years*, 211.

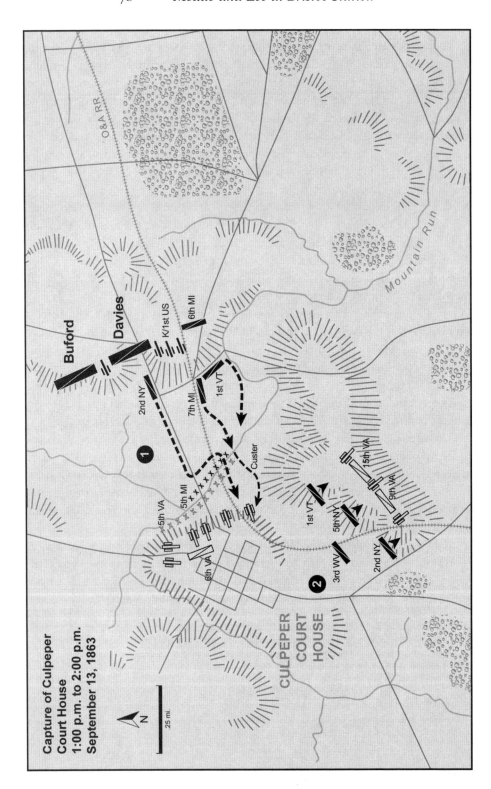

Capture of Culpeper
Court House
1:00 p.m. to 2:00 p.m.
September 13, 1863

25 mi

weapon or implement was at hand, according to an eyewitness there followed a "mixed-up affair of firing pistols, flashing sabers, and excited men." The unequal contest ended quickly, leaving 14 Confederates and another cannon in Union hands. Moorman's other gun managed to make its escape during the mêlée.[26]

The loss of these guns and the hilltop shattered the Rebel position in front of Culpeper, and the outmatched Southerners began a rapid retreat through the town. The 6th Virginia Cavalry held the Yankees back long enough to allow the rest of Maj. Beckham's guns to limber and flee. Not all his pieces escaped, however. The 1st Vermont Cavalry, unable to find a way across Mountain Run east of town, had reversed course and galloped back to the railroad. Spying dismounted troopers of the 5th Michigan Cavalry swarming uphill on the other side of the creek Maj. Wells followed in their wake. After crossing the ford, he received orders to strike the town from the east. The Vermont troopers surged into the village so quickly they overran and captured one of Capt. Griffin's guns and a caisson. But to the blue cavalrymen's disappointment, the rest of the Southern fieldpieces escaped after a hard chase.[27]

*   *   *

The Federals rode into Culpeper Court House at 2 p.m., but the battle was hardly over. A few hundred yards beyond the city limits Confederates were making dispositions to resist any further Union advance. Just below the southeast corner of the town, where the Fredericksburg Road emerged from the village toward the Rapidan, the 15th and 9th Virginia Cavalry regiments along with most of Beckham's surviving guns made a stand. A short distance to the west, the 5th, 6th and 13th Virginia along with a section of guns from Griffin's battery took up position on a ridge blocking the road from Culpeper to Rapidan Station. James Gordon's command—which had withdrawn southward after its earlier Stevensburg skirmish—took up position on Pony Mountain behind these battered units. The North Carolina colonel deployed Hampton's brigade, along with the 4th and 5th North Carolina regiments from Robertson's brigade and Hart's battery, on the elevation's northernmost lower slope. Meanwhile the 7th, 11th and 12th Virginia cavalry regiments, cut off from the rest of

26 OR 29, pt. 1, 120, 126-129; Gregory Urwin, *Custer Victorious: The Civil War Battles of General George Armstrong Custer* (Edison, NJ, 1983), 97; Agassiz, *Meade's Headquarters*, 17; Neese, *Three Years*, 210-211.

27 2nd NY Cavalry, "The Late Cavalry Advance," http://dmna.ny.gov/hisotric/reghis/civil/cavalry/2ndCav/2ndCavCWN.htm, NYMM, accessed May 5, 2018; Grimsley, *Battles in Culpeper County*, 16; *Burlington* [VT] *Daily Free Press*, Oct. 16, 1863; OR 29, pt. 1, 125, 129; Trout, *Galloping Thunder*, 351.

Lomax's command when the Yankees captured the court house, were retreating along a roundabout route west of town. Until they could link up with their comrades south of Culpeper, they were out of the battle.[28]

Although the Rebels had lost the village, Pleasonton knew they had not given up the fight. Enemy cannon on the Fredericksburg Road ridge could hit anything in the town, and until the Federals drove off those guns, Culpeper wasn't secured. He therefore ordered Col. Davies to push the Confederates away and capture the commanding terrain. The ensuing fight was vicious and the first Yankee attempts to take the hill were driven back in a series of wild charges and countercharges. Eventually, however, Union numbers prevailed, and the Southerners fell back over a mile to link up with Gordon on the lower slopes of Pony Mountain.[29]

As Davies' fight reached its climax, Pleasonton assembled his division commanders to assess the situation. He carried in his pocket a 2 p.m. message from Meade. The commanding general had not forgotten the intervention of Confederate infantry on this same battlefield during Buford's August 1 advance on the town. Meade wanted no repetition of that unhappy event. He reminded Pleasonton that his mission was a reconnaissance and that he should avoid stirring up a general engagement.[30]

The cavalrymen did not share Meade's concern. Neither Buford, Gregg, nor Kilpatrick had encountered enemy foot soldiers; each believed he could continue driving the enemy if given the chance. No one thought Confederate infantry would join the battle north of the Rapidan. Pleasonton, who wished to continue the attack and was urged to by a pair of headquarters signal corps officers, was inclined to agree. Having followed the cavalry's southward advance, Warren's II Corps was currently sheltering in the woods near Brandy Station; it was close at hand should the cavalry run into increased resistance south of Culpeper. Furthermore, capturing the signal station atop 791-foot tall Pony Mountain was a critical goal for the signalmen: until Union troops possessed it, the enemy could see every move Warren or Pleasonton made.

Persuaded, Pleasonton chose to continue the battle. He informed Meade at 3 p.m. that from all the information he could gather, Lee's army had retreated behind the

---

28 *Richmond Enquirer*, September 18, 1863; Agassiz, *Meade's Headquarters*, 17-18; Trout, *Galloping Thunder*, 353; Grimsley, *Battle in Culpeper County*, 17.

29 OR 29, pt. 1, 111-12, 120, 128; Vincent L. Burns, *The Fifth New York Cavalry in the Civil War* (Jefferson, NC, 2014), 146; *Galloping Thunder*, 352; Beale, *A Lieutenant of Cavalry*, 126; *Philadelphia Inquirer*, Sept. 18, 1863; Moore, *Rebellion Record*, 7:503; Hoffman, *First Vermont Cavalry*, 133; *Burlington* [VT] *Daily Free Press*, Oct. 16, 1863; Grimsley, *Battles in Culpeper County*, 17; Collea, *First Vermont Cavalry*, 197-98; Robert J. Trout, ed. *Memoirs of the Stuart Horse Artillery Battalion: Moorman's and Hart's Batteries* (Knoxville, 2008), 65; Mays, *Tyler's Quarterly* #5, July 1923, 102.

30 Lyman, *Meade's Army*, 35.

Rapidan. Having reassured his chief that the cavalry was following its orders, the general told Buford to seize Pony Mountain and an intersection near the height's western terminus. Custer would assist with that effort, while Gregg advanced simultaneously west of the railroad toward Rapidan Station.[31]

A little after 3 p.m. the Federals attacked and met stiff resistance from Stuart's troopers and guns. Buford had to pummel the Rebels with artillery to clear the slopes of Pony Mountain. Gregg had an even tougher struggle. A Confederate ambush savaged the leading elements of his division shortly after it trotted out of Culpeper Court House. However, a daring cavalry charge by Col. John Taylor's brigade ejected the determined Southerners from their position. By 4:30 p.m. Northern regiments controlled all their assigned objectives and Yankee signalmen were wigwagging messages from the top of the mountain.[32]

Combat ended at nightfall. As Pleasonton's worn out troopers made their bivouacs a terrific thunderstorm erupted over the battlefield. While the Yankees tried to get some sleep amid the downpour, miserable Confederate cavalrymen and gunners marched to the Rapidan. Late that night Hampton's and Robertson's brigades along with Hart's battery crossed the river at Raccoon Ford. Lomax led Jones' brigade and the bulk of Beckham's artillery to Rapidan Station. Tired Rebels prepared to resist the enemy's further advance, which was sure to come with the morning.[33]

31 *OR* 29, pt. 1, 111, 115.

32 *OR* 29, pt. 1, 115, 124; Abner Hard, *History of the Eighth Cavalry Regiment, Illinois Volunteers, During the Great Rebellion* (Aurora, Il, 1868), 271; *OR* 29, pt. 1, 124; Lyman, *Meade's Army*, 35; Grimsley, *Battles in Culpeper Country*, 17; 2nd NY Cavalry, "The Late Cavalry Advance" http://dmna.ny.gov/hisotric/reghis/civil/cavalry/2ndCav/2ndCavCWN .htm NYMM, accessed May 7, 2018; Mays, *Tyler's Quarterly* #5, 102; Lloyd, *History 1st Regt Penn Res Cav*, 72; Regimental History Committee, *History of the Third Pennsylvania Cavalry, Sixteenth Regiment Pennsylvania Volunteers in the American Civil War* (Philadelphia, PA, 1905), 340; Uzal W. Ent, *The Pennsylvania Reserves in the Civil War: A Comprehensive History* (Jefferson, NC, 2012), 324-25; Crowninshield, *First Massachusetts Cavalry*, 171; Wells A. Bushnell, "Sixth Regiment Ohio Volunteer Cavalry Memoir, 1861-1865," unpublished manuscript, The Western Reserve Historical Society (WRHS), Cleveland, OH; Regimental Committee, *Third Pennsylvania Cavalry*, 340; Maj. Delos Northway to Friends Sept. 27, 1863, Pearce Museum, Navarro College, Corsicana, TX.

33 *OR* 29, pt. 1, 132; Bushnell memoir, WRHS; Delos Northway letter of Sept. 27, 1863, Pearce Museum; Mays, *Tyler's Quarterly* #5, July 1923, 102; Nunnelee Diary, September 13, 1863, ACWM; Robert Kirk, *Ninth Virginia Cavalry* (Lynchburg, VA 1982), 28; Mays, *Tyler's Quarterly* #5, 102; Black, *Crumbling Defenses*, 67; Grimsley, *Battles in Culpeper County*, 17-18; Neese, *Three Years*, 211-12; Terry L. Jones, *Reminiscences of a Louisiana Tiger: The Civil War Memoirs of Captain William J. Seymour* (Baton Rouge, LA, 1991), 83; Beale, *History of the 9th Virginia Cavalry*, 100.

The weary Confederate troopers would not have to defend the Rapidan line alone. Robert E. Lee had tracked the battle's progress throughout the day. Late on September 13 he ordered A. P. Hill to send a division to reinforce Rapidan Station and told Ewell to dispatch a similar force to Somerville Ford, between Raccoon Ford and Rapidan Station. Hill detailed Maj. Gen. Richard Anderson's command to support the cavalry. His brigades moved from their camps near Orange Court House at nightfall and arrived at Rapidan Station before sunrise. Jubal Early's division from Ewell's corps marched to the Rapidan at dawn. Ewell also placed Col. Thomas H. Carter's artillery battalion at Early's disposal with orders to move toward the front at daybreak.[34]

As Lee's reinforcements headed to the river, Meade was evaluating the day's fighting. At 5 p.m. Pleasonton reported "slight casualties" and the advance of his cavalry to within a few miles of the Rapidan. He was certain the enemy's main body lay behind the river. Talkative prisoners claimed that "Longstreet's Corps had gone south, destination said to be Tennessee." The failure of Lee to send infantry to Stuart's aid, as he had done in August, lent credence to those assertions. Late that evening Meade telegraphed Halleck an account of the day's action and the intelligence gained thus far. Although Meade had authorized the army's mounted arm to press southward tomorrow, he reiterated his intention not to provoke a major battle. Whether Lee would allow that to happen was another question.[35]

*   *   *

The Federal cavalry rode for the Rapidan at dawn on September 14, and by 8 a.m. it had made contact with the enemy at Rapidan Station, Raccoon, and Somerville fords. At each place Rebel cavalry, infantry, and artillery occupied strong earthworks on high ground south of the river. Confederate gunners dominated the flat terrain north of the Rapidan and blasted away at Union regiments send to probe the secessionist's defenses. Venomous shellfire turned back the Yankees, who suffered numerous casualties for little gain. By 10 a.m. it was obvious that Lee fully intended to hold the Rapidan in the face of Northern cavalry attacks. Pleasonton quit trying to force the fords by mid-afternoon, but that didn't end the fighting. Rebel artillery and sharpshooters kept up a deadly fusillade against any Union unit close to a crossing point. The shooting didn't sputter to a conclusion until nightfall.[36]

34 Dobbins, *Grandfathers Journal*, 161; Seymour, *Civil War Memoirs*, 83; OR 29, pt. 1, 422.

35 OR 29, pt. 2, 175.

36 Lyman, *Meade's Army*, 36-37.

Some 20 miles north of the firing line, George Meade spent a day of uncertainty. At 10:30 a.m., satisfied with his current intelligence, he told Halleck that Longstreet's corps likely had left for Tennessee while two Rebel corps remained on the Rapidan. He promised to forward any additional "authentic intelligence" Pleasonton might uncover. The army commander spent the rest of the day marking time and worrying.[37]

There was certainly much to fret about. Under orders from Washington, the Army of the Potomac had remained stalled on the Rappahannock for six weeks, freezing the Virginia campaign in place since August 1. Now the strategic situation was thawing and no one could be absolutely certain of what lay below the ice. Whatever happened next, Meade faced a complex set of circumstances complicated by events in other theaters. A host of unknowns confronted him. What was the exact strength of the enemy on the Rapidan? Had Longstreet's corps really gone to Tennessee, or was it elsewhere in Virginia? Would Pleasonton's movement provoke an unwanted battle? Was Lee inclined to withdraw closer to Richmond? If so, would Federal cavalry pressure provoke the move or would it take an advance by Union infantry? If Lee did abandon the Rapidan, was he luring the Federals into a trap?

If, on the other hand, the Rebels made a stand along the river should the Army of the Potomac occupy Culpeper County? Was there a way to breech the Rapidan without suffering disastrous casualties? If the Union army could cross the river, should it, and if so to what end? Given Federal manpower problems and conditions in Tennessee, was a battle south of the river worth fighting or the risk of defeat? If the army won a battle below the Rapidan River, how should it follow up—especially if casualties proved heavy? Could the Army of the Potomac sustain itself farther south with the O&A as its line of supply? If it were unwise or impracticable to force the Rapidan, should the army shift its line of operations to a better, safer option offering more decisive results? Did that kind of an option even exist, and would the administration permit such a movement?

Meade had no obvious answers to any of these questions. For the moment, he deemed it improbable that his cavalry's success would "require" the entire army to advance to the Rapidan. But he could not rule out that possibility. So while he awaited more information from Pleasonton, Meade directed his infantry commanders to hold their troops "in readiness to march at short notice."[38]

By the evening of September 14, Meade knew little more than he had known that morning. Pleasonton had pushed the Rebels over the river only to encounter enemy infantry and artillery at every crossing point. The cavalry commander asserted,

37 *OR* 29, pt. 2, 177.

38 Ibid., 178.

however, that if Warren's corps moved to the Rapidan, the cavalry could force its way over and possibly compel the Confederates to abandon their defenses. Absent significant infantry support, however, Pleasonton said he could do no more between Raccoon Ford and the railroad. Prisoners taken today echoed the claims of yesterdays, insisting that Longstreet had gone south, but that Ewell and Hill remained on the Rapidan. It seemed clear that Lee intended to dispute Union passage of the river. In light of this, Pleasonton wished to know what headquarters desired him to do tomorrow.

At 8:30 p.m., Meade told his cavalry chief that he was "not prepared at present" to make a "general movement of the army," although that decision might change. As for tomorrow, Pleasonton should picket the river on a wide front and obtain all the information he could on enemy movements. Meade still hoped Lee might withdraw from the Rapidan as he had from the Rappahannock under similar circumstances. Therefore Pleasonton should probe the Rebel defenses on September 15. If he found a way to cross the river "without hazarding the safety" of his command he could do so, but by all means he should avoid a "severe engagement." Whatever happened, Meade wanted Pleasonton to "communicate frequently" by telegraph and fully advise headquarters "of all that transpires in your vicinity."

At 9 p.m., these instructions having been issued, General Meade sent his appraisal of the strategic situation to Washington. A variety of admittedly "meager and conflicting testimony," he told Halleck, had convinced him that Longstreet's entire corps, plus a few regiments from Ewell and Hill, had left Virginia. Though it was hard to say how strong Lee remained, the general-in-chief should not get the idea that the Rebels were now vulnerable. Whatever force his opponent had left, Lee undoubtedly "deemed sufficient . . . with the advantages of position, to check my crossing the Rapidan."

As Meade saw it, the Confederates held the advantage and would continue to until the troops detached to enforce the draft returned to Virginia. Only then would the AOP have the necessary strength to mount an offensive. Whether such an effort was worth undertaking was a different question. Meade thought it possible Lee would continue to fall back and decline battle until he gained an even more decided advantage in position or manpower. It was pointless, Meade contended, to chase the Confederates back to heavily fortified Richmond because the Union army wasn't large enough to besiege the city. Given these realities, Meade asked Halleck what he thought "had better be done, if anything."

The army commander had no idea how his superior would answer that important question. He was, however, positive that prudence required that he stand ready to meet any eventuality. Less than an hour after wiring Washington, Meade dispatched a confidential circular to his corps commanders reiterating his instructions that they keep their troops "prepared to move on short notice" and "everything in readiness for an advance."[39]

* * *

Robert E. Lee would have been greatly relieved to learn of Meade's concerns. The sudden Union thrust across the Rappahannock, so quickly after Longstreet's departure, prompted serious second thoughts about the wisdom of having sent one-third of his army elsewhere. On September 14, Lee warned Davis of the Federal concentration on the Rapidan and that Meade knew about "the large reduction of this army." Lee regretted that he had lost the use of Longstreet's troops in Virginia where they were "much needed" and feared they had "gone where they will do no good."

Referencing Northern newspapers, Lee complained that he had only just now learned that Chattanooga and Knoxville had been lost before Longstreet left Richmond. Had he known Burnside was headed to Knoxville, Lee wrote Davis, he would "have recommended that General Longstreet be sent to oppose him, instead of to Atlanta." Lee fretted that Bragg would not take advantage of his reinforcements to attack Rosecrans, or that Longstreet would arrive too late to be of help. In that event Lee thought it "would be better to return Longstreet" to Virginia so that the South might "oppose the advance of General Meade with a greater prospect of success."

Deferential as always, Lee was also frank: "Should General Longstreet reach General Bragg in time to aid him in winning a victory, and return to this army, it will be well. But should he be detained there without being able to do any good it will result in evil." In closing, Lee wrote he hoped the president would receive enough reliable information to allow him to decide "correctly" the future use of Longstreet's command.[40]

Fortunately for Lee, the one perplexed about what to do was Meade not Davis. No one could say what the future held in store. There was little doubt, however, that the relative quiet that had prevailed in Virginia over the last six weeks was at an end.

---

39 Previous paragraphs based on *OR* 29, pt. 2, 177-81. The Union signal corps had telegraph lines in operation as far south as Culpeper Court House on the evening of Sept. 14.

40 *OR* 29, pt. 2, 720-21.

CHAPTER 7

"What Can I Do With Such Generals?"

Pondering Commanders—Presidential Advice—Meade's Angst—
Washington Unhelpful—Chickamauga—Lincoln's Lament

T**HE** valley of the Rapidan was thick with tension on the morning of September 15. After two days of fighting no one knew what today would bring, including George Meade and Robert E. Lee, both of whom made provisions for further combat.

South of the river more Confederate infantry advanced to the front. Rodes' division and Carter's artillery battalion occupied Morton's Ford and took up positions to hold the crossing. Lee and his corps commanders detailed other troops to defend lesser fords. Everywhere Rebel infantrymen labored to strengthen fortifications or construct new defenses, cutting down groves of trees and clearing underbrush to create unobstructed fields of fire for newly laid out gun positions. Some men expected a big battle, others disagreed, but nobody argued against making preparations for a fight.[1]

Overnight, equally industrious Union soldiers dug rifle pits at the various fords. The Yankees also emplaced artillery to cover the river crossings. Tactically these were sensible defensive measures, but Meade was thinking offense not defense. At 9 a.m. on September 15 he instructed Pleasonton to scout the Rapidan for one or two undefended downstream locations where the riverbanks would allow laying pontoon bridges. The army commander cautioned his cavalry chief to be circumspect lest he tip off Lee to a possible movement against his right flank.[2]

---

1 Munson, *Confederate Correspondent*, 98-99; John R. Purifoy, "Jeff Davis Artillery," typescript, AL State Archives, 210.

2 2nd NY Cavalry "The Late Cavalry Advance" NYMM, http://dmna.ny.gov/historic/reghist/civil/cavalry/2ndCav/2ndCavCWN.htm; *OR* 29, pt. 2, 189.

Pleasonton's regiments thus renewed their efforts along the river. Skirmishing broke out everywhere shortly after sunup as troops on both sides of the Rapidan resumed yesterday's sharpshooting. The heaviest action occurred at Raccoon Ford where several Federal batteries deployed for action and began exchanging fire with Confederate guns. Buford's entire division and part of Kilpatrick's command demonstrated in front of the crossing to distract Rebel attention from reconnaissance efforts elsewhere. For a time many Southerners suspected the Yankees were organizing an attack.[3]

That fear never materialized. As was the case the day before, Rebel artillery posted on high ground had all the advantages while Yankee guns made no appreciable impact. At Raccoon Ford shells dismounted two Union fieldpieces from their carriages and wounded several men and horses. Across the front each side gained little tactical triumphs or suffered minor defeats. While intense enough for the men engaged, these local clashes did nothing to alter the state of affairs along the Rapidan.[4]

Whether he should try to change the status quo was very much on the mind of George Meade. His request for guidance had as yet received no response, and as the hours passed, the general became increasingly frustrated.

Distracted by the dangerous situation developing south of Chattanooga, Halleck didn't reply to Meade's September 14 messages until 11 a.m. the following day. Even then his telegraphed advice amounted to a suggestion that Meade make preparations to "threaten Lee and if possible cut off a slice of his army." That was a long way from detailed direction and no different than what Halleck had been saying since July 31. The general-in-chief did admit that the "exact condition of affairs" wasn't clear enough for him "to authorize any very considerable advance." No doubt sensing that Meade would find this of little help, Halleck promised to send a more thorough response later in the day.[5]

Despite a lack of useful counsel, at 1:30 p.m. Meade decided to take another step toward a potential southward thrust. He would leave Howard's XI Corps in place to guard the O&A and keep Newton's I Corps around Rappahannock Station. The rest of the army would concentrate at the various crossing points on the upper Rappahannock. Meade told Slocum to mass his XII Corps at Kelly's Ford and for French to assemble his III Corps at Freeman's Ford. Meade directed Sykes' V Corps to take position at Beverly Ford. Major General Sedgwick received orders to concentrate

---

3   Seymour, *Civil War Memoirs*, 83-84; *OR* 29, pt. 1, 119; Munson, *Confederate Correspondent*, 98-99.

4   Bushnell Memoir, WRHS.

5   *OR* 29, pt. 2, 186.

his VI Corps at Sulphur Springs, leaving enough troops in Warrenton to protect its supply depot until it was "broken up." For the moment Warren's II Corps would stay at Culpeper Court House.[6]

These orders set tens of thousands of Union troops and their accompanying batteries and wagon trains marching toward the Rappahannock throughout the afternoon of September 15. Many of Meade's soldiers had anticipated an eventual forward movement, but marching orders caught most by surprise. A good number of regiments had made substantial improvements to their camps during the lengthy repose north of the Rappahannock, and many men found leaving those recently constructed amenities quite disconcerting.

George Meade suffered from far greater anxieties. Despite Halleck's 11 a.m. pledge to provide more in-depth advice later in the day, by mid-afternoon Meade had still heard nothing from Washington. At 4 p.m. he informed Halleck that the army was massing at the Rappahannock fords. Perhaps hoping to spur a reply, Meade related that scouts just returned from behind enemy lines confirmed Longstreet's departure from Virginia, and were also reporting A. P. Hill and Ewell defending the Rapidan, ready to contest any Union movement. He also promised to await further orders before undertaking an additional advance.[7]

*   *   *

Well after nightfall, Meade finally received a response to the questions he had posed to Washington some twenty-four hours ago. For security reasons the general-in-chief had chosen to relay his views by letter rather than risk telegraphic interception by the enemy. An aide who took a train to army headquarters personally delivered the missive to Meade sometime between 10 and 11 p.m. on September 15.

Halleck went into some detail about the burgeoning crisis near Chattanooga. The Rebels were undoubtedly concentrating their forces against the Army of the Cumberland hoping to destroy it and recover Eastern Tennessee. The war department had instructed every Union commander in the region to cooperate with Rosecrans and had ordered all available troops in the Western Theater to his assistance. Consequently, the Army of the Potomac should not expect to receive meaningful reinforcement under "any contingency." Halleck stressed that "no rash movements" should be "ventured." Instigating a major battle was out of the question. If Lee's army had been

---

6   OR 29, pt. 2, 188-90.

7   OR 29, pt. 2, 186.

"very considerably reduced," Meade might attempt to further weaken it or force the Confederates "still farther back," but that was all.[8]

Halleck included with his letter a note from President Lincoln, who had also seen Meade's request for guidance. The commander-in-chief recommended that Meade "move upon Lee at once in manner of general attack" and let developments dictate whether to convert that movement into an actual offensive. Lincoln believed this was the surest, fastest way to discover if Lee had truly sent troops to Georgia. However, he wanted it understood that this was merely a suggestion and not an order.[9]

Such was the high command's advice. Halleck was telling Meade not to do anything rash. Lincoln was telling him to advance and see what happened. Once again the responsibility for determining what to do rested solely in Meade's hands and after careful consideration, he decided to occupy Culpeper County.

At 11:50 p.m. the general sent orders for the bulk of his army to cross the Rappahannock the next morning. Once over the river the infantry would occupy the areas around Stone House Mountain, Stevensburg, and Culpeper Court House. All supply depots north of the river would be concentrated at the latter place. General Haupt was told to put the O&A into operation as far south as Culpeper, near which Meade would establish his headquarters. Once the army attained these objectives, it could relieve Pleasonton's troopers along the Rapidan and free the cavalry for more reconnaissance work.[10]

At the moment that was as much as Meade intended to do and all he felt he could do. Since the end of July he had hoped, somewhat optimistically, that an advance by Union infantry would convince Lee to abandon the Rapidan and withdraw farther south. Now he increasingly doubted this would happen. Pleasonton's reports suggested that Lee had retained sufficient strength to hold the Rapidan's heavily fortified southern shore despite shipping an entire corps to the west. If the cavalryman was right, Lee would probably stand and fight.

Six weeks of Washington-imposed delay had worsened the strategic situation and robbed Meade of a success he might have had for the asking in early August. Nonetheless, he would march his army into Culpeper on the unlikely chance that the

8 OR 29, part 2, 186-7. Halleck postulated that the Rebel concentration resulted from their fear that while Rosecrans and Meade held their present positions in Virginia and Chattanooga, Grant and Banks would "clean out" the states west of the Mississippi and thus the "fate of the rebellion would be sealed." Such a statement implies that Halleck did not intend to move the armies under Grant and Banks against the heartland of the Confederacy until resistance west of the Mississippi ended.

9 OR 29, pt. 2, 187.

10 OR 29, pt. 2, 178, 191-92, 196-98.

enemy would yield the Rapidan without a fight. Meade couldn't say what he would do if the Confederates stood their ground, but he did know that any attempt to breech the enemy's defenses would provoke a major battle. Since Halleck had ordered him to avoid that outcome, Meade had few viable options. The only play he had left was to up the ante and bluff. If Lee called that bluff, all Meade could promise Halleck was that the Union army wouldn't attempt to assail the Rapidan line unless some unexpected opening appeared.

*   *   *

The Federals swarmed across the Rappahannock River at dawn on Wednesday, September 16. Some troops marched over pontoon bridges while others waded through waist-deep water. Generally speaking the roads were good and most units had only a dozen or so miles to march. It should have been a fairly easy hike, but many soldiers found the trek difficult. Six weeks of relative inactivity had softened their physical endurance. Army headquarters was urging corps commanders to hurry their men forward. Field officers, anticipating a possible battle, had issued extra ammunition, and large numbers of troops carried overcoats and spare blankets in anticipation of the cold weather just weeks away. Virginia's citizenry exacerbated the difficulties of the advance. Federals trudging into Culpeper noticed the women dressed in "deep mourning" and a "scowl or frown" on every face. Even the children, one soldier recalled, looked upon the Union invaders with contempt while the few white men still in the town "were saucy and ugly."[11]

George Meade's mood was not dissimilar. Several of his aides who had accompanied Pleasonton during his push to the Rapidan had received orders to rendezvous with army headquarters at noon near Culpeper Court House. Among them was Col. Theodore Lyman, a 30 year-old Massachusetts native from a wealthy and influential Boston family. A graduate of Harvard University and its prestigious Lawrence Scientific School, Lyman had first met Meade in Florida where the young second lieutenant was supervising light house construction and Lyman was doing field research on starfish. The two men instantly hit it off and continued to stay in touch after they parted company.

Tall and long-limbed, Lyman looked like the intellectual he was. A large expanse of bald forehead seemed to emphasize his thick hair while a pair of bushy sideburns came together in a well-groomed mustache above his upper lip. He had married just before

---

11 Ibid., 197; Henry N. Blake, *Three Years in the Army of the Potomac* (Boston, MA, 1866), 240; Alfred S. Roe, *The Thirty-Ninth Massachusetts Volunteers 1862-1865* (Worcester, MA, 1914), 104; Thomas Carpenter to father September 20, 1863, MHS.

the war began and spent the first half of the conflict honeymooning in Europe. Upon his return in 1863, Lyman asked to join Meade's military family as a volunteer aide. When the general agreed, Lyman secured a commission as a lieutenant colonel from the governor of Massachusetts and in early September took up his duties on Meade's staff. He became a close confidant of the general and a keen observer of events at army headquarters.

The colonel along with his fellow aides assembled at Culpeper Court house a little before noon. Meade didn't arrive until 2:30 p.m. Lyman thought he looked "haggard and worried," and indeed, his boss had gone sleepless the night before. The general's worry, Lyman discerned, came from an "abundance of good advice from Washington."[12]

Despite their punctual assembly, there was little for Meade's staff to do because the army's morning advance ground to a halt almost as quickly as it began. Sykes' V Corps along with the Artillery Reserve joined Warren's II Corps at Culpeper Court House around the same time Meade reached the village. Newton's I Corps camped east of the town halfway to Stevensburg, while Slocum's XII Corps pitched its tents around Stevensburg itself. Sedgwick's VI Corps and French's III Corps bivouacked west of Culpeper, the former at Stone House Mountain and the latter midway between there and the court house. The XI Corps remained spread out north of the Rappahannock guarding the railroad. That afternoon infantry from Warren's and Slocum's corps relieved the cavalry and took over the job of guarding the Rapidan.[13]

The arrival of foot soldiers on the river officially ended Pleasonton's reconnaissance. It had netted vital information, plus 120 Confederate prisoners and three captured cannon. The cavalry confirmed that Longstreet had left Virginia and that Lee still had the corps of Ewell and A. P. Hill on the Rapidan. The Federal troopers had driven Stuart's brigades south of the river and verified that the Confederates meant to defend the Rapidan line. Pleasonton had managed his corps well and his division commanders had performed aggressively and competently.[14]

The cost of those achievements had been 129 casualties including 27 listed as killed, 60 wounded, 38 captured, and 4 missing. The number of Southerners killed or wounded was impossible to say with certainty. Pleasonton's commanders conjectured

---

12 Lyman, *Meade's Army*, 1-15, 38. Elizabeth "Mimi" Russel, daughter of noted merchant and philanthropist George Robert Russell, and Theodore Lyman were married in 1858. Mimi was also the first cousin of the famed Col. Robert Gould Shaw who was killed commanding the 54th Massachusetts Colored Infantry in the assault against Fort Wagner outside Charleston, SC, on July 18, 1863.

13 *OR* 29, pt. 2, 191-192.

14 *OR* 29, pt. 1, 179; Neese, *Three Years*, 210.

Colonel Theodore Lyman
Massachusetts Historical Society, Boston, MA

that enemy losses were significant. Richmond newspapers reported Stuart's casualties as "not over" 50 men in killed and wounded, while admitting the Yankees had swept up "at least 75 prisoners." Incomplete Confederate service records list 7 dead, 54 wounded, and 111 captured for a total of 172 in the cavalry and horse artillery. Adding in the handful of killed and wounded from the Rebel infantry or artillery commands engaged at the Rapidan fords—at least 6 known dead and 17 injured—makes an overall Confederate casualty figure of 195 (13 killed, 71 wounded, 111 captured).[15]

Whatever the casualties, the recent fighting in Virginia generated much excitement in the press. The Union army had finally advanced. But what did it have in mind? Although the *Richmond Enquirer* reported that Yankee prisoners claimed the movement was a mere reconnaissance-in-force, Northern and Southern newspapers agreed that the battle for Culpeper Court House must be the opening maneuver of a Union offensive and that "a big battle will occur soon."[16]

The prevailing atmosphere along the Rapidan certainly portended trouble. For three days and nights, recalled Pvt. Jacob Raymer of the 4th North Carolina, Rebel troops "lay in line of battle" expecting a Federal attack or orders for an assault of their

---

15 OR 29, pt. 2, 179-80, 112, 119; *Richmond Dispatch* September 17, 1863; *Richmond Enquirer* September 18, 1863; *Philadelphia Inquirer*, September 18, 1863. Federal casualty total from www.civilwardata.com which list losses by regiment from a variety of sources and provides names and details for each casualty. Losses are from Sept. 13-19, 1863. In his official report Kilpatrick listed 7k, 34w, and 17m in his command from September 12-15. Neither Buford nor Gregg submitted a list of casualties or an official report of the operation. On September 13, Pleasonton reported his losses as 3k and 40w. Southern papers listed losses in the 13th Virgina Cavalry as 12w and 1k. Total Confederate losses from www.civilwardata.com are added to this newspaper report and losses in the horse artillery to obtain Southern casualty figures.

16 *Richmond Enquirer*, September 13, 1863; *Harper's Weekly*, September 26, 1863.

own. From his picket post at Raccoon Ford, Cpl. Charles Engel of the 137th New York watched Confederates busily strengthening their earthworks on the opposite shore. As far as he could tell, the summer string of Northern victories had done nothing to demoralize the enemy, nor diminish their numbers. "They are thick as spatter and saucy as they can be," he told his family back home. Indeed the trigger-happy Rebel pickets were in a murderous frame of mind. Engel thought his sentry post the most dangerous he had ever occupied; "the Rebs fire at us every chance they have," he complained. Sharpshooting and occasional cannon fire were commonplace for several days after Meade's infantry reached the Rapidan.[17]

Hostilities along the river subsided somewhat when the Rebels realized that Yankee foot soldiers had replaced Pleasonton's troopers on the picket line. The failure of the Union army to thrust beyond Culpeper dealt an even more decisive blow to everyone's apprehensions. By September 24 anticipation of a battle had all but evaporated. North Carolinian Pvt. Raymer told his hometown *Carolina Watchman* newspaper that "contrary to all expectations" no battle has occurred. "As I have remarked before," he lectured, "military prognostications are utterly useless—to guess or conjecture about army movements is breath wasted."[18]

After a full week slipped by with neither Meade nor Lee advancing, muscles and nerves tensed for combat relaxed. Southern officers left pickets in the trenches and withdrew the rest of their troops into the woods behind the earthworks. Along the Rapidan routine replaced trepidation. When they weren't staring at the Yankees, standing watch, or working on the entrenchments, Confederate infantryman amused themselves by verbally harassing their cavalry counterparts, engaging in horse play, or raiding neighboring cornfields for something to eat. But the Rebels could hardly ignore their nearby enemies totally. They wondered what the Yankees were up to and what would happen next.[19]

Union troops were just as puzzled. They realized the possibility of moving again in a few days, but no discernible sign pointed in that direction. Some men thought the army's gyrations constituted a mere reconnaissance. Others surmised that the recent advance had been a feint designed to keep Lee from sending more help to Bragg. The only certainty was that Rebel fortifications along the river grew steadily stronger.

Eventually even sharpshooting died away. Officers allowed their troops to slip back into familiar habits, while enemy pickets stood in full view of each other and were

---

17 Munson, *Confederate Correspondent*, 98; Charles Engle to "Charlotte" September 20, 21, 1863, http://www.sugarfoottales.org/. Accessed May 12, 2018.

18 Munson, *Confederate Correspondent*, 98.

19 Kirkpatrick diary, September 15, 1863, UT.

content to leave one another alone. The weather continued autumn-like and pleasant with occasional heavy rains to break the monotony. Both sides launched intermittent forays across the river to gather prisoners and gain scraps of information. Commanders hoped these little actions sharpened their troops' aggressiveness and kept the enemy on edge.[20]

Despite these sporadic raids, the rival soldiers quickly fell into decidedly non-combative behavior. Brigades rotated to and from the front with each regiment taking a turn on picket duty, then on picket reserve, and then back to camp. Now and again men exchanged shots, but for the most part everything remained peaceful. When the outposts weren't jockeying for position, the opposing armies acted as if the war didn't exist. Sentries yelled greetings or traded barbs across the river, and occasionally arranged swap-meets. Southern tobacco, Yankee coffee, and newspapers were common trade goods.[21]

The high command frowned upon such activities. Conversations between sentries posed an unnecessary security risk on the eve of possible action. Generals became concerned that useful information might cross the Rapidan during careless banter. Orders came down for such exchanges to stop. To conceal troop positions, Rebel officers forbade their guards from building fires at night. Union commanders prohibited needless shooting for the same reason. Meade found it necessary to remind Kilpatrick that "no communication whatever" should take place between his vedettes and the enemies'.[22]

The measures taken to end fraternization were less than successful. The generals never managed to snuff out forbidden contacts, and some leaders declined to deal harshly with soldiers who engaged in them. Opposing troops who spoke the same language, shared a common heritage, often a common religion, and always the universal miseries of homesickness and military life had too much in common. No one could convince them to remain constantly hostile while active operations were suspended.[23]

---

20 Ibid.; *OR* 29, pt. 2, 189; McClellan, *I Rode with JEB Stuart*, 374; Glazier, *Three Years in the Federal Cavalry*, 316; The *Richmond Enquirer*, September 22, 1863, mentions a raid by the 7th Louisiana which took 30 prisoners at Raccoon Ford.

21 Kirkpatrick diary, September 19-October 7, 1863, UT; Caldwell, *Brigade of South Carolinians*, 156. Troops sometimes constructed miniature sailboats to convey goods from one shore to the other.

22 Kirkpatrick diary, September 19 and 24, 1863, UT; *OR* 29, pt. 2, 106; Charles Engle to Charlotte September 21, 1863, http://www.sugarfoottales.org/.

23 Robert Henry, *Story of the Confederacy* (New York, 1931), 301-2.

*   *   *

While front line leaders worried about talkative pickets, higher authorities vigorously resumed their debate over strategy. Meade had hoped his advance into Culpeper County would result in a Confederate retreat from the Rapidan. That hadn't happened. Now the Federals faced the consequences of occupying the problematic Culpeper V. On September 16, Meade warned Halleck that Union sentries constantly heard locomotives arriving behind enemy lines, each accompanied by much cheering. Doubtless Lee was deploying his entire force to defend the Rapidan and occupy the formidable entrenchments south of the river. Meade admitted he might be able to get around those defenses by a wide flank march, but this would expose his communications to attack. The only way to blunt that threat was to assign a significant number of troops to protect the O&A between Culpeper and Centreville—which in turn would weaken the army's combat strength and risk its defeat in detail.

Meade was "very doubtful about the expediency" of a southward advance "without some very definite and positive information" on the "position and numbers" of the enemy. If the Confederates weren't as weak as the Federals supposed Lee might go over to the offensive. Meanwhile Rebel raiders would try to sever the Union army's railroad supply line, lengthened now by an additional 20 miles after the advance to the Rapidan.[24]

Much to Meade's chagrin and continued uneasiness, Halleck—who was progressively more fixated by events on Rosecrans' front—didn't respond to his latest essay on strategic dilemmas. On September 18 he wrote Halleck again. Mindful of instructions to avoid a battle, the general said that, as things stood, he did not "feel justified in making a farther advance without some more positive authority" from the general-in-chief or the president. The army commander specifically wanted to know if he should convert his recent feint toward the Rapidan into a real offensive, as Lincoln had suggested. Before Washington answered that question, however, Meade wanted to make certain the administration knew all the pertinent facts.

Meade wired Halleck that Lee had 40,000 infantry ensconced on the south bank of the Rapidan, with artillery crowning "every available point." The enemy seemed quite prepared to dispute any Federal effort to cross the river, and although Meade was confident he could fight his way over the waterway, he was equally certain this would provoke a major battle.

The problem, as the general saw it, was that merely shoving Lee southward was not an end in itself. "The whole question," he wrote Halleck, "hangs upon the

---

24 *OR* 29, pt. 2, 194-95.

advantage to be gained and the course to be pursued in the event" of a successful engagement. Meade believed his army was too weak to pursue Lee to Richmond. After incurring the losses incumbent in a severe struggle the Federal army would be weaker still. Dwindling or suspect manpower reserves in the North might not make good those losses. Meade told his superiors that he could "get a battle out of Lee under very disadvantageous circumstances," but warned that Union casualties in such a fight might actually result in making Lee's "inferior force my superior." Even if this were not the case, Meade felt the outcome of any action was unlikely "to result in any very decided advantage." In closing he bluntly admitted he was "reluctant to run the risks" of a major engagement "without the positive sanction of the government."[25]

This doubt in the utility of battle was something new for Meade. In early January 1863 the general—then just a division commander—had written his wife that he was "tired of this playing war without risks." Pondering the course of the conflict in 1862 he sharply criticized George McClellan for insisting on having everything "just as he wanted before he would attack" and a "want of nerve to run what he considered risks." As Meade saw it such timid leadership had cost the Union army several chances to take Richmond and would continue to rob the Northern army of opportunities unless its leaders eschewed excessive caution. "We must encounter risk if we fight," Meade declared, "and we cannot carry on war without fighting."

In the aftermath of the Fredericksburg debacle he had advocated instigating the next engagement under any circumstances and regardless of "what results followed" in order to give the country the "immense advantage" of a victory—even one that came at a high price and bore little strategic fruit. But now, in the fall of 1863, with the responsibility for the army and the cause weighing on his shoulders, he felt differently. Meade was smart enough to recognize that fact and it gnawed at him.[26]

*   *   *

Once again Halleck replied by mail rather than telegraph; as a result Meade had to wait more than a day for a response. In the ensuing vacuum he vented his frustrations in a letter to Margaret. After reiterating his view of the military situation, Meade told his spouse of 22 years that he was "greatly embarrassed" about "what to do." He had asked Halleck for "clear and positive instructions," but confessed he had little hope of obtaining clarity and feared his superiors would not provide the guidance he desired. "They undoubtedly would be glad if I should attack and prove successful," Meade

---

25 Ibid. 201-202.

26 Meade to wife January 2, 1863, *Life and Letters*, Vol. 1, 344-45.

confided, before putting his finger on the crux of the issue: "They wish me to assume the responsibility," he wrote, "so that in case of disaster, I may be made the scapegoat."

The general had no intention of becoming a stooge and under no circumstances would he hazard defeat without being able to lay some accountability on Washington's doorstep. If the administration would give him complete authority to act as he saw fit, he was "willing to assume" total responsibility for whatever outcome his strategy might produce. But neither Lincoln nor Halleck had offered such latitude. Instead, Meade complained, he had "from time to time [been] controlled and directed" by his superiors, who had disapproved his preferred line of operation and taken pains to remind him that his "army involves other interests besides its own safety." Given these limitations and the present "critical" circumstances of the country, Meade felt he had "a right to acquire" clear instructions.

Despite all this, he expected the authorities would leave him dangling in the wind. This made him angry. "I am willing to do my duty and meet any risks or responsibilities that may be legitimately involved, but to be compelled to act one time at the bidding of others and at another time told to act for myself is, I think, unfair." Meade confessed that the "very heavy and oppressive" burden of managing a vast army, coping with the enemy, and trying to satisfy non-committal and demanding bosses had left him in a "state of anxiety . . . [and] so fretted and worried" by the course of affairs he might physically "wear down." In a passage sure to have alarmed Margaret he wrote, "Sometimes I almost wish a stray cannon ball would put an end to my troubles."

Despite his travails, George Meade was a good soldier and loyal subordinate. A preemptory order from the president had put him in the command of the army just eleven weeks ago, and the general believed it his duty to serve in whatever capacity his superiors directed. The fact that he occupied his current post through no effort of his own did give him some solace: he would do his best and that would have to be good enough.

As he reached the end of his letter, the general realized that what he had written might appear a powerful indictment of his chiefs and an exposé of his own doubts. In a touching but also cautionary tone, he confided to Margaret that she was "the only living soul I can write or speak to upon the subject." Begging her to "pardon" him for unburdening himself, he closed requesting that she give his love to their children and pray for him.[27]

---

27 Previous paragraphs based on Meade to "Margaret," September 19, 1863, George Gordon Meade papers, Historical Society of Pennsylvania (HSP); Civil War Women, "Margaretta Sergeant Meade," http://www.civilwarwomenblog.com/margaretta-sergeant-meade/, accessed May 10, 2018. After less than a year of courtship George Meade and Margaretta Sergeant were married in Philadelphia's St. Peter's Church on December 31, 1840, which was also the

*   *   *

Halleck's response to Meade's September 16 telegram arrived at army headquarters sometime on September 19 or the next day. It did not ease Meade's mind. If a lack of instructions from Washington frustrated the general, Meade's hesitance to demonstrate independent initiative or act aggressively equally frustrated the high command. Halleck refused to shoulder responsibility for bringing on a battle and didn't think it was his job to do so. His task, he reminded Meade, was to indicate "the objects which the government wishes accomplished" and then help army commanders get the job done. "Unless directed to do so, I never attempt to direct a general when, where, or how to give battle," he asserted. "He must decide such matters for himself. No one else can do it for him."

The general-in-chief would, however, provide strategic guidance and spell out the purpose of any campaign the army might undertake. He did not consider Richmond of "great military importance, nor as the objective point of the Army of the Potomac. Your objective point, in my opinion, is Lee's army, and the object to be attained is to do it as much harm as possible with as little injury as possible to yourself." If the Rebel position on the Rapidan was too strong to either attack or outflank, Meade must not be idle. He should strike at Lee's outposts and detachments, raid his communications, and seize the "supplies of the adjacent country" to feed his own army and starve the enemy's.

Rosecrans would soon be "hard pushed," Halleck predicted, and he also anticipated that Longstreet would quickly return to Lee after helping deliver a blow in Georgia. Therefore Meade should do whatever he could while the enemy First Corps was absent. "If you really think nothing of importance can be accomplished," he concluded, "then it seems to me that it will be as well to withdraw your army to some point nearer Washington." Whether the general wrote that sentence as a strategic calculation or a veiled insult designed to spur Meade into action was unclear.[28]

Accompanying Halleck's letter was one he had received from Lincoln responding to Meade's request for "clear instructions." The document ably demonstrated the president's keen grasp of his commanders' strategic dilemma. It also expressed his frustration with their inertia without offering a solution to their problem.

Lincoln acknowledged Meade's question about taking the offense, but confessed that he was not "prepared to order or even advise an advance" while he knew so "little

---

general's 25th birthday. She was six months his senior. They had seven children together. Meade referred to Margaretta as Margaret in all his letters.

28 OR 29, pt. 2, 206-207. The exact date and time Halleck's letter arrived is unclear.

of the particulars" of Meade's situation. Although the general had made it clear that he felt the risks of a battle "great and the promise of advantage . . . small," Lincoln admitted that the current stalemate perplexed him. With the precision of an accomplished lawyer, the president laid out the contradictions in Meade and Halleck's predicament.

> These two armies confront each other across a small river, substantially midway between the two capitals, each defending its own capital, and menacing the other. General Meade estimates the enemy's infantry in front of him at not less than 40,000. Suppose we add 50 percent to this for cavalry, artillery, and extra-duty men, stretching as far as Richmond, making the whole force of the enemy 60,000. General Meade . . . has with him and between . . . Washington, of the same classes of well men, over 90,000.

Given these figures Lincoln went on to reason that neither Lee nor Meade could bring their entire strength "into a battle, but each can bring as large a percentage as the other." This would give Meade odds of three to two against Lee. "Yet, it having been determined that choosing ground and standing on the defensive gives so great [an] advantage that the three cannot safely attack the two, the 60,000 are sufficient to keep the 90,000 away from Richmond." If this logic was correct, and Lincoln did not question its validity, he wondered why 40,000 Union troops couldn't keep Lee's 60,000 men away from Washington. This would free 50,000 men now with Meade to be "put to some other use."

President Lincoln's analysis brought him to a core truth. "Having practically come to the mere defensive [in Virginia]," he wrote, it seemed "no economy at all to employ twice as many men" to protect Washington than were needed. Lincoln assured his generals that he could "perceive no fault" with his reasoning unless the Federal commanders were willing to admit their troops were not "the equal of the enemy, man for man."

If Meade and Halleck could bring themselves to make an offensive movement, Lincoln wanted no "misunderstanding" of his own strategic calculations. "To attempt to fight the enemy slowly back into his entrenchments at Richmond, and there to capture him, is an idea I have been trying to repudiate for quite a year," he said. Indeed, Lincoln's "judgment was so clear against" such a strategy he would "scarcely allow the attempt to be made," even if Meade wanted to make it. The commander-in-chief reminded his subordinates that his "last attempt upon Richmond was to get McClellan, when he was nearer there than the enemy was, to run in ahead of him." McClellan failed to do so, and since then Lincoln had "constantly desired the Army of the Potomac to make Lee's army, and not Richmond, its objective." If Meade could not wreck Lee's army along the Rapidan, Lincoln saw no reasonable way to do it while "attempting to follow him over a succession of entrenched lines into a fortified city."[29]

Here the president ended his strategic treatise. Everything he said was unquestionably true. Both generals already knew all of it, and none of it gave Meade what he sought. He was exactly where he had been three days ago: Washington wanted action but would not order it. The administration acknowledged the challenges facing the AOP in its current circumstances. But Meade's proposal for overcoming them—to shift the army's base to Aquia Creek and advance on Richmond from Fredericksburg with a shorter, more secure, and mostly seaborne line of communications—had been rejected. Washington expected him to surmount all of his disadvantages and do as much harm to the enemy as possible. That he had not yet done so clearly irritated the president and general-in-chief. This left Meade alone to figure out a solution to an intractable military conundrum and with total responsibility for any failure or misstep he might suffer. Little wonder he asked his wife for her prayers.[30]

*   *   *

The same day Lincoln and Halleck wrote Meade, the battle of Chickamauga began in earnest. The fighting in northern Georgia continued on September 20, when part of Longstreet's corps, just arrived from Virginia, made a decisive breakthrough that routed most of Rosecrans' army. Confederate command difficulties and stubborn fighting by troops under Maj. Gen. George H. Thomas had barely prevented rout from becoming the Army of the Cumberland's destruction.

News of this disaster quickly reached Washington. On September 21 a despondent Lincoln sought out Gideon Welles. He reported the president "feeling badly" because the Confederates had clearly engineered a major concentration of their troops against Rosecrans. The two men agreed that while the Rebels were active, "Halleck has fritted away time and dispersed our forces." Many units of Grant's army had been shifted west of the Mississippi, "where a large force is not needed," Welles complained, while another Union force under Maj. Gen. Ambrose Burnside was "two hundred miles away from Chattanooga" in Knoxville. The Union high command had

---

29 *OR* 29, pt. 2, 207-208. Lincoln would allow Grant to employ just such a strategy in 1864.

30 In January 1863 Meade said he was convinced of the "impracticability" of the Fredericksburg axis of operation and believed the James River the proper line for an advance on Richmond. "But as they were determined in Washington that we should not go there," he continued, "I thought, rather than stand still we ought to attempt a practicable, though less desirable, line." Meade to wife, January 2, 1863, *Life and Letters*, Vol. 1, 344-45.

apparently missed evidence of Southern concentration. Welles (somewhat unfairly and inaccurately) laid this failure at Halleck's feet.

These facts distressed Lincoln. Although dissatisfied with his generals, his reaction had been subdued, more so than Welles thought proper. "He does not censure or complain. Better perhaps, if he did." Welles wondered aloud "what Meade was doing with his immense army and Lee's skeleton and depleted show in front." The president said "he could not learn that Meade was doing anything, or wanted to do anything." "It is the same old story of this Army of the Potomac," Welles recorded Lincoln as saying. "Imbecility, inefficiency—don't want to do—is defending the capital." The chief executive lamented to his cabinet secretary, "it is terrible, terrible, this weakness, this indifference of our Potomac generals, with such armies of good and brave men."

Welles asked Lincoln why he did not fire Meade, "who may be a good man and a good officer but is not a great general." Meade had allowed Lee to escape into Virginia after Gettysburg, he grumbled, and bluntly told Lincoln he had no confidence in the Pennsylvanian. According to Welles, Lincoln agreed with everything he had said. But the president had no solution to the problem. "What can I do with such generals as we have? Who among them is any better than Meade?" Mindful of political difficulties stemming from his dismissal of George McClellan in late 1862, Lincoln warned Welles that "to sweep away the whole" of the Potomac army's generals would cause a shock and likely lead to "combinations and troubles greater than we now have." Lincoln clearly felt himself on the horns of a dilemma. "I see all the difficulties as you do," he confessed, forlornly adding, "They oppress me."[31]

Although fate spared him from hearing these words, Meade sensed the administration's disappointment with his performance. But the failure of Lincoln and Halleck to provide the answers, guidance, and authority he so earnestly desired was equally disappointing. Left alone to solve his strategic and operational problems, the Pennsylvanian grappled with discerning how to get at Lee without wrecking the Army of the Potomac. Despite his own doubts, Meade felt duty bound to give his superiors the battlefield victory they seemed to desire so heartily. How to accomplish that without possibly losing the war was the puzzle Meade had to solve.

---

31 Paragraphs above based on Morse, *Gideon Welles*, Vol. 1, 438-40. As much of what Welles said was true, much was also not. The Federals *did* pick up evidence of what the Confederates were doing. Halleck *had* put in motion aid to Rosecrans. Longstreet's head start proved impossible to overcome, and the Federal reaction too slow to void it. Burnside's advance on Knoxville resulted from Lincoln's obsession with liberating largely pro-Union East Tennessee. His capture of the city greatly alarmed and mortified the Confederates.

Chapter 8

"One of the Very Fiercest Fights of the War"

Meade Looks Left—Yankee Reconnaissance—Battle of Jack's Shop—Stuart
Surrounded—Counterattack—Fight at Barnett's Ford—Chasing the Federals

AT the beginning of July 1863 after Federal victories at Vicksburg, Port
Hudson, and Gettysburg, the final triumph of the Union cause had
appeared at hand. The only question was *when* not *if*, with the *when* coming soon. Eleven
weeks later ultimate victory had not only failed to materialize, the tide of war seemed to
have reversed.

The Rebels had pulled off a masterful strategic feat by transferring Longstreet's
corps to Georgia. Braxton Bragg had employed it to deal a shocking defeat to William
Rosecrans' army, which was now trapped in Chattanooga. Meade's own belated thrust
to the Rapidan—delayed six weeks by home front unrest and administration orders—
had done nothing to help Rosecrans and much to complicate the Army of the
Potomac's situation.

As news of the Confederate triumph at Chickamauga spread throughout the
continent, problems from front and rear beset George Meade. With his usual skill Lee
had placed his army in a nearly impregnable position. The president was displeased.
Halleck wanted an advance but wouldn't order one or pose an alternative. Both men
expected him to do something, but each left the vexing question of just what to do in
Meade's hands.

The general shared the extent of this dilemma with Colonel Lyman, who recorded
his chief's assessment on September 20. The disparity of infantry numbers in the
Union's favor, about 65,000 to 40-50,000 wasn't enough "for offensive moves against
strong positions" or a siege of Richmond, if it came to that. Even if the Federals
crossed the Rapidan and won a battle, they "would not probably destroy Lee's army,
which could retreat on the fortifications of Richmond whither it was of no use to
pursue." And, of course, the Union might suffer a reverse "with new loss of life and

less than no good done." Meade felt certain the only way out of the tactical and strategic quandary Lee had imposed was to abandon the O&A as a line of advance. Shifting the Union army to Fredericksburg would compel the Rebels to "fall back, without a fight," while "giving all the moral result to be hoped for." But the administration had rejected this idea. After seeing the advice Halleck and Lincoln had provided in lieu of true strategic guidance, Lyman judged that Halleck "did not answer Meade's question at all," although the president's observations contained a "gist of common sense."[1]

Lincoln, Halleck, Meade and the general's staff briefly toyed with leaving just enough Union troops in Virginia to protect Washington while sending the AOP's surplus strength to other fronts. However, no one was willing to take that step because it essentially admitted defeat, would be unacceptable to the Northern public and politically disastrous for the administration. Moreover, it would cede the initiative to Robert E. Lee, who had proven on numerous occasions what he could do with inferior numbers. If the Rebels could shift troops from Virginia to Georgia to win success at Chickamauga, why couldn't they shift troops to Virginia so that Lee could gain a similar triumph? The nightmare scenario, of course, was that such a victory would lead to capture of Washington.[2]

Meade was thus condemned to solve the military puzzle in front of him. Halleck had designated his sole task as bringing Lee to battle wherever possible and damaging or destroying his army without suffering debilitating Union losses. Achieving that goal was far easier imagined than achieved. At least Halleck's declaration that Richmond was of no special importance freed the army from making the city's capture its goal.

*   *   *

If Halleck and Lincoln wanted fighting for fighting's sake then Meade would try to give it to them. Since an attack across the Rapidan into the teeth of Lee's defenses would be suicidal, outflanking the Confederate position by crossing the river well to the east or west of Lee's line appeared Meade's only possible move. But which way should the Union army lunge, left or right?

The Federals had recently operated in the general area east of the current Rebel position. More or less conversant with its advantages and disadvantages, they knew this

---

1 Lyman, *Meade's Army*, 38-40; OR 29, pt. 1, 118. On August 31, 1863, the Army of the Potomac had 76,219 officers and men present for duty. Meade had told Lyman twice in the previous day or so that he wished someone else were in command of the army.

2 Lyman, *Meade's Army*, 40; James Biddle to wife September 24, 1863, HSP.

sector fairly well. The region to the west was a different matter. Any offensive in that direction would carry the Union army across Robertson's River into Madison County, whose southern border was the Rapidan. Federal commanders knew little about this part of the state, much less its relative merits for offensive action. Only a large-scale cavalry reconnaissance could obtain the information army headquarters needed. On September 20, Pleasonton received orders from Meade to reconnoiter Madison County with two cavalry divisions and thoroughly scout the region between Madison Court House and the Rapidan. Additionally, headquarters wanted information on the river fords and the topography south of the stream. Any intelligence the troopers might garner about Lee's strength, dispositions, and intentions was also welcome. Once they accomplished these tasks the cavalrymen were to proceed to Orange Court House if possible.[3]

Pleasonton chose Kilpatrick's and Buford's divisions to carry out the mission under Buford's overall command. On September 21 the two units crossed the narrow Robertson's River, and late in the day they easily chased a squad of Confederate horsemen out of Madison Court House. That night the Federals bivouacked just outside the town. Buford planned to put his men in the saddle early the next morning, September 22. Once his force cleared the village it would split into two columns. Kilpatrick would head toward Wolftown, some six and a half miles west, then turn south toward the Rapidan. After fording the river near Burtonsville, he would move east to Liberty Mills, where he would re-cross the stream and rejoin Buford sometime during the evening.[4]

As Kilpatrick rode his circuit, Buford's division would undertake a pair of simultaneous tasks. The general would accompany Col. George Chapman's 1st Brigade due south toward Liberty Mills. Colonel Thomas Devin's 2nd Brigade would head southeast to scout Barnett's Ford on the Rapidan and the roads to Locust Grove on Robertson's River. Buford intended to open communication with Kilpatrick before their link up somewhere north of Liberty Mills later that afternoon. The united force would then ride east to join Devin near Barnett's Ford. No one could say how the Rebels might respond to these movements. Enemy cavalry was reported in Madison County, however, and Buford suspected he would have a fight before the end of the day.[5]

3   OR 29, pt. 2, 215.

4   George Chapman Diary, September 22, 1863, IHS; OR 29, pt. 1, 140; W. N. Pickerill, *History of the Third Indiana Cavalry* (Indianapolis, IN, 1906), 95. Chapman had temporary command of William Gamble's brigade.

5   OR 29, pt. 1, 140.

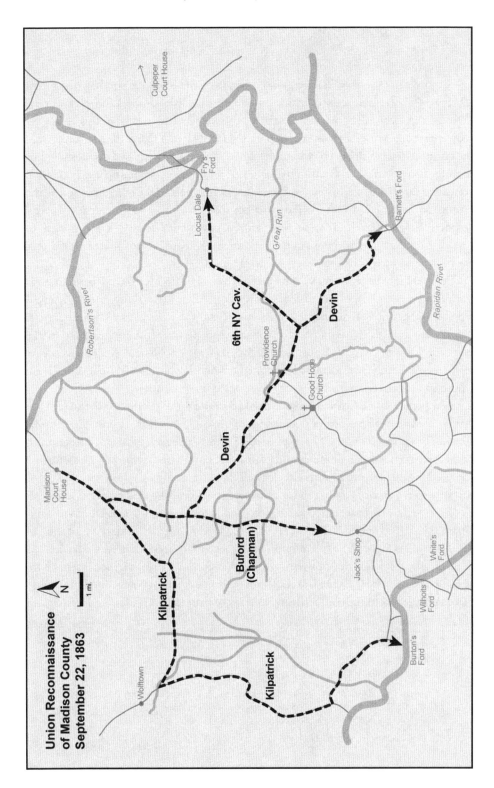

Union Reconnaissance
of Madison County
September 22, 1863

N

1 mi.

*   *   *

Buford's intuition was correct. Only a handful of miles to the south, a division of Jeb Stuart's horsemen was preparing to disrupt the Federal operation come dawn. During the last few weeks, Stuart's command had undergone significant reorganization. At Lee's recommendation, the Confederate Congress had authorized the creation of a cavalry corps within the ANV. This gave Stuart two divisions, led by recently promoted Maj. Gens. Fitzhugh Lee and Wade Hampton. Each division contained three brigades of four or five regiments. As part of the reorganization all the North Carolina cavalry units in the army consolidated into a single brigade. Several colonels assigned to lead these restructured commands gained a promotion to brigadier general. The coming confrontation with Kilpatrick and Buford would give the new cavalry corps its first test.[6]

It would also be another in a long line of challenges for Maj. Gen. Jeb Stuart, who remained one of Lee's most trusted subordinates. Since Gettysburg, the 30-year old Virginian had largely redeemed his missteps during the Pennsylvania campaign. His outgunned and vastly outnumbered troopers had performed commendably in the battle of Culpeper Court House just eight days ago. Solid and sometimes stellar regimental and brigade leadership had honed the fighting qualities of Rebel horsemen, whose spirit and dash mirrored Stuart's own style and philosophy.

The general's lighthearted persona masked a thoughtful realism. At the start of the war he told one of his brothers that the South could not win against the North's superior resources fighting "force to force." The Confederacy had to "make up in quality" what it lacked in numbers and "substitute esprit" for manpower. Therefore he had tried to "inculcate the spirit of the chase," in his men. Stuart's dress and demeanor served as much as a tool to that end as an expression of his own exuberant personality.[7]

War, with its challenges, hardships, and excitement, its martial pomp and circumstance, was Jeb Stuart's natural element. He was the perfect picture of the gay cavalier: well-built, with a full auburn beard accenting deep blue eyes. He dressed dramatically in knee-high boots, an ostrich-plumed slouch hat, a yellow sash, and a striking double-breasted shell jacket. Although his rank strongly suggested his proper place in battle was to the rear, Stuart reveled in combat, usually leading at the front and

---

6   *OR* 27, pt. 3, 1068-69. The new structure became official on September 9, 1863. It took several weeks for all the effected units to assume their positions in the new table of organization, however.

7   Susan Leigh Blackford & Charles Minor Blackford, *Letters from Lee's Army* (Lincoln, NB, 1998), 42; Thomason, Jr., "J. E. B. Stuart," *Scribner's Magazine*, Volume 87, No. 4, April 1930, 485-491. Stuart had 3 brothers and 6 sisters.

Major General James E. B. Stuart
Library of Congress

often on the actual firing line. He was one of the few major generals in either army to frequently discharge a weapon in close combat.[8]

Since its mid-September retreat behind the Rapidan, Stuart's cavalry had guarded the Rebel army's flanks. Fitz Lee's division occupied a position on the right between Fredericksburg and the lower Rapidan fords. Hampton's division (the one in Buford and Kilpatrick's path) held the left of the line. With Hampton still recovering from his Gettysburg wound, Stuart personally supervised the division.

A few days before Pleasonton ordered his troopers into Madison County, a Yankee deserter came into Early's lines claiming that within the week a large force of Union cavalry and an infantry corps planned to advance toward Madison Court House. This news put the Confederates on alert. During the afternoon of September 21, only hours after Kilpatrick and Buford had crossed Robertson's River, Stuart learned that infantry had replaced Yankee cavalry picketing the western Rapidan. Considering this news verification of the deserter's story, Stuart ordered Hampton's division over the river at Grinnan's Ford to deal with whatever mischief was afoot.[9]

An evening reconnaissance by the 11th and 7th Virginia Cavalry from Jones' brigade, currently under Col. Oliver R. Funsten, confirmed that Yankees were near Madison Court House. Armed with this knowledge, Stuart determined to move toward the enemy at first light on September 22. That morning, as Federal columns took their separate routes out of Madison Court House, he led 2,000 gray troopers northward on

8 John Esten Cook, *Wearing of the Gray* (New York, 1867), 166; Heros Von Brock, *Memoirs of the Confederate War for Independence*, 2 Vols. (Edinburgh, UK, 1866), vol. 1, 22. For an outstanding study of Stuart's operations in the Gettysburg campaign, see Eric J. Wittenberg and J. David Petruzzi, *Plenty of Blame to Go Around: Jeb Stuart's Controversial Ride to Gettysburg* (El Dorado, CA, 2003).

9 OR 29, pt. 1, 141; Harold R Woodward, *For Home and Honor: The Story of Madison County, Virginia During the War Between the States* (Madison: Skyline Services, 1990), 69-71.

Gordonsville Pike. Seven guns from Maj. Beckham's horse artillery rumbled along with the cavalry.[10]

At 8 a.m. Stuart's main body reached the spot where the 11th and 7th Virginia had spent the night. As the Rebels paused for a brief rest, those two units rejoined Funsten's brigade, and a pair of scouts went forward to fix the exact location of the enemy. It did not take either man long to report sighting a large Union force heading south from Madison Court House and another riding west toward Wolftown. The absence of Yankee infantry led Stuart to conclude that the Federals intended a raid against the Virginia Central Railroad.[11]

The general quickly formulated a plan to foil his opponent's scheme. He sent a dispatch to A. P. Hill requesting infantry support near Liberty Mills. Then he had signalmen wig-wag orders for Fitz Lee to rush westward and block any Yankee thrust toward the vital rail junction at Gordonsville. Stuart knew it would take Lee most of the day to travel the 20 some-odd miles from the army's right flank to its left. Hampton's division would have to keep the Yankees occupied until then. As usual, Stuart believed an attack was the best way to derail enemy plans. An aggressive movement should slow the Federals long enough for Lee and Hill to arrive.[12]

With his strategy devised, Stuart led Hampton's division straight toward Buford. Colonel Gordon's newly created North Carolina brigade rode at the front of the column. About 4 p.m. near the tiny village of Jack's Shop his advance guard ran into the 3rd Indiana Cavalry, which was the vanguard of Chapman's brigade. After an initial clash that surprised both parties, the combat escalated rapidly. Stuart threw the 1st and 5th North Carolina Cavalry into the action and in short order they pushed the Indiana regiment out of a skirt of trees bisecting the road.[13]

Once the Rebels gained the woods, however, they were shocked to discover Chapman's entire brigade going into line a short distance away and Lt. Edward B.

---

10 Edward B. Williams, *Rebel Brothers: The Civil War Letters of the Truehearts* (College Station, TX, 1995), 176-77. Baker's North Carolina brigade (commanded by Col. James B. Gordon) headed the column with Butler's brigade (under Col. Dennis D. Ferebee) following. The remaining units of Jones' brigade (under Col. Funsten) brought up the rear. Four artillery pieces from Hart's Battery, two from McGregor's and one from Mooreman's comprised the guns.

11 Ibid., 177.

12 James E. B. Stuart to wife Sept. 26, 1863, VHS.

13 OR *Supplement* 5, pt. 1, 585-86; Harrell, *Second North Carolina Cavalry*, 194-95; Clark, *North Carolina Regts.*, vol. 1, 452; Pickerill, *History 3rd Indiana Cav.*, 95. The official US Post Office name of Jack's Shop was Rochelle. Laurence Baker, recently promoted to brigadier, was the North Carolina cavalry brigade's official commander. His August 1 wound prevented him from ever taking up the post, however, and James Gordon eventually got the job and the promotion to general that came with it.

Brigadier General John Buford
Library of Congress

Williston's Battery D, 2nd US Artillery, unlimbering in support. After sending back word for help, the two North Carolina regiments gamely took the deploying Federals under fire. Stuart ordered the rest of Gordon's (Baker's) North Carolina brigade as well as the sharpshooters from Col. Dennis Ferebee's (Butler's) brigade into the fight as well.[14]

Try as they might, the Tar Heels couldn't hold the woods under the pounding of Northern artillery and the massing might of a full enemy brigade. Stuart realized he could only maintain his ground by committing the rest of Hampton's division, but he also sensed that idea most unwise. Kilpatrick lurked somewhere off his left flank or rear, and he had no way of knowing how rapidly Fitz Lee or A. P. Hill were moving to his assistance. Those circumstances dictated maintaining a sizable reserve as insurance against the unexpected.

Rather than reinforce the fight in the woods, it made more sense to pull the elements of Hampton's division closer together. The general ordered Gordon and Ferebee to withdraw several hundred yards to a new position on the far end of a large field in front of a small hill where the seven guns of Beckham's horse artillery had unlimbered and prepared for action. If Buford wanted Stuart out of his way, he would have to attack across a wide expanse of open ground. The Southern commander doubted his opponent would make the attempt, and he was right. The Federals occupied the recently-abandoned woods but pushed no farther. Buford seemed content to bring his artillery forward and duel with Beckham's fieldpieces while Chapman's troopers kept up a hot firefight against their Southern counterparts. The battle devolved into a stalemate.

A standoff fitted into John Buford's plans perfectly. The Kentucky-born 37-year old West Pointer (class of 1848) had an excellent decade-long record of service on the

---

14 Clark, *North Carolina Regts.*, vol. 3, 573 & vol. 1, 453; *OR Supplement* 5, pt. 1, 586.

western frontier. During the first year of the war his talents had been wasted in an administrative post and he didn't get a general's commission and a brigade until the summer of 1862. Buford took a bullet in his knee at the Second Battle of Bull Run and was knocked out of action for six months. He rejoined the army in time for Chancellorsville, and after that fight took command of the 1st Cavalry Division, which he led into action at the battle of Brandy Station in June 1863. He became famous at Gettysburg when his holding action on July 1 helped save the high ground near the town for the Union army.[15]

A no nonsense kind of officer, Buford's rugged appearance and simple work-a-day dress squared with his reputation for decisive action and hard fighting. Many officers throughout the army considered him the best cavalry leader in Virginia. His troopers appreciated his lack of pretension and willingness to make gutsy decisions wherever the bullets were flying.[16]

He evinced those traits today. As soon as his column encountered Stuart, he sent a courier with new orders for Kilpatrick: forego further exploration of the Rapidan, re-cross the river, and attack the Rebel rear on the Gordonsville Pike. If everything came together as Buford hoped, the Federals could destroy Hampton's division.[17]

The fight in front of Jack's Shop was now a contest of firepower. Federal guns concentrated on Beckham's pieces, which became the linchpin of Stuart's defense. Union shells shattered the axle on one cannon and knocked another out of action. Despite this pounding, the Southern artillerymen stood to their work and returned the Yankee barrage with feverish intensity.[18]

Meanwhile Chapman's regiments kept up the pressure on Stuart's dismounted troopers. Although the Federals declined to attack, the battle slowly tilted in Buford's favor. Gordon and Ferebee reported their men running low on ammunition. In response Stuart directed them to pull back several hundred yards to a stronger position. Sensing an advantage, the Yankees showed signs of trying to turn the Rebel flanks. Just as his situation grew more precarious, Stuart received urgent news from the scouts watching his rear. A force of Union cavalry had crossed the Rapidan and was approaching Jack's Shop from the southwest.

15 Tagg, *Generals of Gettysburg*, 168; Warner, *Generals in Blue*, 52.

16 Ibid; David W. Lyman, ed. *Meade's Army: The Private Notebooks of Lt. Col. Theodore Lyman* (Kent, OH, 2007), 34-35; Allan Nevins, ed. *A Diary of Battle: The Personal Journals of Colonel Charles S. Wainwright, 1861-1865* (New York, 1998), 309; Tagg, *Generals of Gettysburg*, 168.

17 Glazier, *Three Years in the Federal Cavalry*, 318.

18 Robert Trout, *Memoirs of the Stuart Horse Artillery Battalion: Breathed's and McGregor's Batteries* (Knoxville, TN, 2010), 109; *Galloping Thunder*, 359; McClellan, *I Rode with JEB Stuart*, 374-75.

This was Kilpatrick, of course, but only a small fraction of his division. Well before Buford's courier arrived with orders to join the battle north of the river, Kilpatrick had detached Custer's brigade (under Lt. Col. Peter Stagg while Custer recovered from his Culpeper wound) and the 1st West Virginia Cavalry to scout various roads or fords. Only the 2nd and 5th New York cavalry regiments from Brig. Gen. Henry Davies' brigade and Battery C, 3rd US Artillery were on hand to respond to Buford's request.[19]

Kilpatrick immediately turned these units north. Crossing the river at Wilhoits Ford, they traveled a series of side roads toward the Gordonsville Pike and Jack's Shop, the 2nd New York under Lt. Col. Otto Harhaus in the lead with Maj. John Hammond's 5th New York Cavalry and the artillery, both moving at a slower pace, some distance behind. Kilpatrick knew little about the situation and nothing about the size of the enemy force he approached. But he was certain that trouble lay up ahead.[20]

*   *   *

Although Jeb Stuart didn't know how many Yankees were threatening his rear, the approaching Federals didn't surprise him completely. Before the fight at Jack's Shop began, scouts had reported that a second enemy column was operating in Madison County. He had deployed vedettes to watch out for it and kept Funsten's brigade and part of Gordon's as a reserve just in case the bluecoats made an unwelcome appearance. This foresight now paid off.

While Ferebee's regiments along with the 1st and 5th North Carolina continued their fight with Chapman, Stuart hurried the 2nd and 4th North Cavalry regiments and Funsten's three Virginia units—the 7th, 11th and 12th Cavalry—rearward to confront Kilpatrick. The Confederate artillery also divided its attentions, with three guns maintaining their fire to the north, while the remaining two pieces swung around to face south. A nerve-wracking, almost desperate situation faced the Confederates. Officers didn't hide the dire nature of the situation and told the troops their survival depended upon driving off the Yankees threatening the division's rear. The men responded enthusiastically, promising victory or death in the effort.[21]

---

19 OR 29, pt. 1, 141-42. Davies received a promotion to brigadier on Sept. 16, 1863. Whites Ford was the likely destination of the 1st WV.

20 On period maps cartographers often misspelled Wilhoits as Wilhites or Whalhites. Wilhoits is the name of the modern road leading to the site of the mill on the Rapidan that gave the ford its name.

21 Daniel Coltrane, *The Memoirs of Daniel Branson Coltrane, Co. I, 63rd Regiment, N.C. Cavalry C.S.A.* (Raleigh, NC, 1956), 20; Clark, *North Carolina Regts.*, vol. 3, 573.

Stuart's prompt response to Davies' approach proved decisive, although that fact wasn't obvious for a while. The Federals hadn't expected to encounter a prepared foe. The sight of five Rebel regiments advancing to the attack shocked the 2nd New York's troopers as they neared the Gordonsville Pike. Instead of surprising the enemy, the enemy had surprised them. Within seconds dismounted Southern skirmishers hidden in some woods and a section of enemy artillery took the New Yorkers under fire. This fusillade caught the Northerners while they were traveling in a column of twos down a narrow road through dense forest. Both the terrain and this formation seriously inhibited the 2nd New York's ability to deploy for battle. In a frantic bid to buy time for his regiment to form up in the forest, Harhaus ordered his leading company to attack the oncoming enemy.[22]

Funsten threw his troopers forward so impetuously that the Union company proved little more than a speed bump. In the face of overwhelming numbers it fled the field, escaping destruction only by riding off to southeast and hiding in the woods for the rest of the battle. Nonetheless, its small assault had bought Harhaus the precious minutes he needed to shake his New Yorkers into a battle line and repulse Funsten's first wild charge.[23]

Slightly to the north, Buford heard the rising sound of battle below Jack's Shop. Realizing that Kilpatrick must be on the scene, he ordered Chapman to attack the Rebels facing his brigade. The combat along Stuart's front and rear rose to such a frenzied pitch one Rebel trooper later referred to the struggle as one of the "very fiercest fights of the war." With Beckham's artillery firing rapidly in both directions, Gordon and Ferebee launched a series of mounted charges to hold back Chapman, while Funsten repeatedly hurled his men against the 2nd New York. For a time the situation looked ugly. Rebel regiments charged, recoiled, reformed and charged again. The Confederate units virtually lost their organizational cohesion in the broiling action and Stuart later reported his men had fought almost en masse.[24]

Actually, things were not as bad as the Southerners believed. Kilpatrick realized his two regiments couldn't possibly stand up to more than a brigade of gray cavalry. He ordered Harhaus to hold off the enemy until the rest of Davies' column could turn around and get a head start for the Rapidan. The New Yorkers managed to resist long

---

22 Glazier, *Three Years in the Federal Cavalry*, 318.

23 *OR* 29, pt. 1, 142; William N. McDonald, *A History of the Laurel Brigade* (Baltimore, MD, 1907), 175-77; Glazier, *Three Years in the Federal Cavalry*, 319; Clark, *North Carolina Regts.*, vol. 3, 573.

24 Clark, *North Carolina Regts.*, vol. 3, 573-74; Harrell, *Second North Carolina Cavalry*, 195; *Fayetteville Observer* [NC], October 5, 1863; Mesic, *Cobb's Legion*, 91-2; McDonald, *Laurel Brigade*, 175-77.

enough, but just barely. A final charge by Funsten's ad hoc command finally drove the Yankees out of the woods and captured an entire battalion from the 2nd New York while the rest of the regiment scurried down the Gordonsville Pike in full retreat. Although it seemed longer to the men in it, the fight south of Jack's Shop and the threat to the Rebel rear had lasted a mere 20 minutes.[25]

*   *   *

Now Stuart became the aggressor. He told Ferebee to hold Chapman at bay while the rest of Hampton's division chased after Kilpatrick. The colonel accomplished this tricky task with a series of mounted attacks by the 2nd South Carolina and Phillip's Legion which temporarily disrupted Buford's efforts to press forward. By the time Ferebee got permission to pull back, Chapman's brigade had been played out. After following the Rebel rearguard a mile beyond Jack's Shop, Buford ordered his 1st Brigade to halt and retire to the village.[26]

The battle wasn't yet over, however. Kilpatrick withdrew down the Gordonsville Pike toward Liberty Mills with Stuart in hot pursuit. The Yankees barely managed to get over the Rapidan before leading elements of Maj. Gen. Cadmus Wilcox's infantry division arrived. Hampton's division, its men and horses worn out by a day-long battle, crossed the river not long after Kilpatrick. The Confederates had just missed the chance to trap and destroy a considerable portion of Union cavalry. Nonetheless, Stuart still worried about a Yankee effort to raid the Virginia Central. He felt compelled to maintain the pressure on Kilpatrick.[27]

The weary Rebels chased the retreating bluecoats for another two miles. At dusk the Northerners turned to make a stand behind Marsh Run. The Confederates made one final charge that captured some Yankee skirmishers before galling fire from Capt. Dunbar R. Ransom's Battery C, 3rd US Artillery, the stream's steep banks, and nightfall rendered further attacks impossible.[28]

The combatants now drew apart. Kilpatrick fell back to White's Ford, where he linked up with Stagg's (Custer's) brigade before retreating north of the Rapidan. Stuart

---

25 OR 29, pt. 1, 141; Clark, *North Carolina* Regts., vol. 3, 574; McDonald, *Laurel Brigade*, 175-77; Glazier, *Three Years in the Federal Cavalry*, 419; *Fayetteville Observer* [NC], October 5, 1863. Major McIrvin commanded the captured battalion. This was the same force that had taken two Rebel guns at Culpeper Court House on September 13.

26 Douglas, *Boot Full*, 281-82.

27 McClellan, *I Rode with JEB Stuart*, 374-5; Glenn McMullen, ed., *A Surgeon With Stonewall Jackson: The Civil War Letters of Dr. Harvey Black* (Baltimore, MD 1995), 61.

28 Harrell, *Second North Carolina Cavalry*, 196.

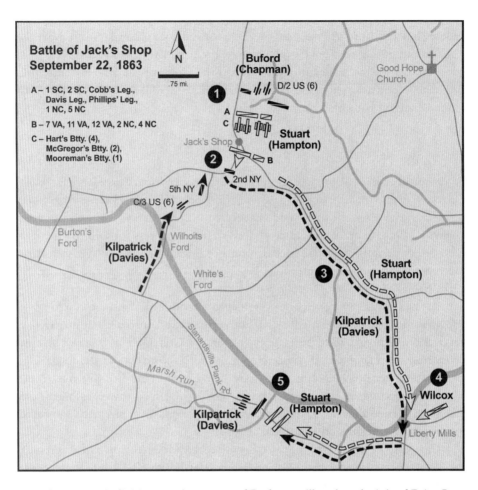

Battle of Jack's Shop
September 22, 1863

A – 1 SC, 2 SC, Cobb's Leg.,
   Davis Leg., Phillips' Leg.,
   1 NC, 5 NC

B – 7 VA, 11 VA, 12 VA, 2 NC, 4 NC

C – Hart's Btty. (4),
   McGregor's Btty. (2),
   Mooreman's Btty. (1)

N
.75 mi.

Buford
(Chapman)

Good Hope
Church

D/2 US (6)

Jack's Shop

Stuart
(Hampton)

2nd NY

5th NY

C/3 US (6)

Burton's
Ford

Wilhoits
Ford

Kilpatrick
(Davies)

White's
Ford

Stuart
(Hampton)

Kilpatrick
(Davies)

Stanardsville Plank Rd.

Marsh Run

Stuart
(Hampton)

Kilpatrick
(Davies)

Wilcox

Liberty Mills

turned Hampton's division southeast toward Barboursville, where he joined Brig. Gen. William C. Wickham's brigade awaiting him there. Fitz Lee had dispatched Wickham and Chew's battery of horse artillery to protect Gordonsville on Stuart's order earlier that morning. It had taken them all day to ride the 24 miles separating their camps east of Orange Court House and Barboursville, northwest of the vital railroad stop. Once at the village they blocked the road leading to Gordonsville, and for hours thereafter had listened to the distant boom of guns around Jack's Shop. Wounded men drifting south from the fight said the Yankees had surrounded Stuart, producing great apprehension for his fate. Unsurprisingly, Wickham's men gave Hampton's exhausted division a warm relief-filled reception when it arrived in Barboursville during the night of September 22.[29]

---

29 *OR* 29, pt. 1, 142; James E. B. Stuart to wife September 9, 1863, VHS; Neese, *Three Years,* 213-14; Lawson Morrissett Diary & Thomas Trussel diary fragment, both September 22, 1863,

*   *   *

Another fight also faded away as dusk descended. Before the struggle around Jack's Shop, Col. Thomas Devin had led his brigade and Battery D, 2nd US Artillery towards Barnett's Ford. Along the way he sent Major William P. Hall's 6th New York Cavalry and a section of artillery to Locust Dale near Robertson's River. They were to scout the roads to that place and hold nearby Fry's Ford as an escape hatch back into Culpeper County. After this detachment split off, Devin guided the rest of his regiments toward the Rapidan. Some miles from the river he ran into 50 troopers of the 7th Virginia Cavalry and three guns from Capt. Marcellus Moorman's horse artillery battery. The Rebels put up a running delaying action all the way to the ford, but couldn't prevent Devin from reaching his objective.[30]

Once at the river, the Federals got close enough to A. P. Hill's camps to hear beating drums and lob some shells at enemy wagons until they scampered out of range. That was the extent of Union success, however. Yankee skirmishers nearing the river came under fire from Confederate infantry (Scale's brigade, Wilcox's division) and could do little more than engage in a fitful firefight until dark. Devin then backed away from the ford and settled in to await the arrival of Buford and Kilpatrick, who were supposed to join him before morning.[31]

*   *   *

During the night, Buford decided that his reconnaissance had accomplished its primary mission and that a movement on Orange Court House was clearly

---

ACWM; Henry Watkins to Mary September 24, 1863, VHS; Elijah Johnson Diary, September 24, 1863, VHS; H.C. Lee papers, UVA; Pickerill, *History 3rd Indiana Cavalry*, 95; Lewis Nunnelee Diary, September 22, 1863, ACWM.

30 Hillaman A. Hall & William B. Besley, *History of the Sixth New York Cavalry (Second Ira Harris Guard)* (Worcester, MA, 1908), 158; Cheney, Newell. *History of the Ninth Regiment New York Volunteer Cavalry, War of 1861 to 1865* (Jamestown, NY, 1901), 133-34; Lewis Nunnelee diary, September 22, 1863, ACWM; Williams, *Rebel Brothers*, 177; David J. Petruzzi, "Hoofbeats and Cold Steel: Thoughts on Civil War Cavalry: the 3rd (West) Virginia Cavalry" www.http://petruzi.wordpress.com/2007/06/14, accessed May 13, 2018. Moorman had two 3-inch guns and one 12-pounder howitzer. Many accounts of the battle of Jacks Shop, including the historical markers on the battlefield in 2018 claim that the 6th NY turned around from Barnett's Ford and struck Stuart at the same time as Kilpatrick. This is incorrect as the regimental history and Parmelee letter makes clear. In an 8:30 a.m. message on Sept. 23, Buford tells Pleasonton that the 6th NY and a section of artillery are at Locust Dale (OR 29, pt. 1, 141).

31 Samuel Parmelee to Father, Sept. 24, 1863, DUKE; Cheney, *Ninth New York Cavalry*, 133-34. The skirmishers were from the 9th New York Cavalry.

impracticable. It was time to retire into Culpeper County. On the morning of September 23, the general dispatched riders with orders for Devin and Kilpatrick to rendezvous with Chapman several miles northeast of Jack's Shop between Good Hope Church and Providence Church. During the night Buford had received a report that Hill's corps had entered Madison County and was north of Great Run. Although that seemed highly unlikely, Buford felt the rumor's source was "so reliable," he felt compelled to dispatch scouts to "ascertain the truth." They were also to make sure the road to Locust Dale was open and that the 6th New York Cavalry still held Fry's Ford over Robertson's River. Once the 1st and 3rd Cavalry Divisions were concentrated and a clear path to the Locust Dale confirmed, the Federal column would head for home.[32]

Meanwhile, Jeb Stuart wasn't idle. He considered it highly probable that the enemy would renew his supposed raid on the Virginia Central. To increase the odds of defeating whatever the Yankees had planned, overnight the general had ordered Maj. Beckham to bring his remaining horse artillery batteries to Barboursville. With this additional firepower at hand, Stuart led Hampton's division and Wickham's brigade toward the river as the first streaks of daylight graced the eastern sky. Much to the corps commander's relief his patrols reported no enemy south of the Rapidan and indications that the Federals were withdrawing in the direction of Culpeper.[33]

The Confederate cavalryman did not intend to let his enemy get away peacefully and he pushed his units hard to catch up to the foe before he could escape. Luck was with Stuart. Although Buford managed to gather his force together at an early hour, it was 8:30 a.m. before scouts reported an unobstructed path road to Locust Dale and the 6th New York still holding Fry's Ford. The wait for that news allowed the Rebels to overtake Col. Stagg's 1st Michigan Cavalry, which Kilpatrick had detached for rearguard duty and positioned a mile or so west of Good Hope Church. Confederate skirmishers began pressing against Stagg's troopers just as Buford ordered his command eastward. Much to the distress of the Midwesterners, the Union column, burdened with 100 prisoners, 12 captured vehicles, a herd of confiscated cattle and several wagons of runaway slaves, moved at a snail's pace.[34]

That meant the Yankee rearguard had to fight vigorously to hold the Rebels back. The slow-paced battle continued all the way to Locust Dale. Here Kilpatrick told Stagg to maintain his ground for at least an hour in order to buy time for the main column to thread its way across Fry's Ford. Unfortunately for the 1st Michigan that necessity allowed Wickham time to bring up his entire brigade and attempt to turn the Federal

---

32 *OR* 29, pt. 1, 141-43; Hallaman, *Sixth New York Cavalry*, 158.

33 Ibid; Lewis Nunnelee diary, September 23, 1863, ACWM.

34 *OR* 29, pt. 1, 141-43; Lewis Nunnelee diary, September 23, 1863, ACWM.

left flank. Just as the enemy began to spring his trap, Buford's column finished crossing the river and Kilpatrick sent word for Stagg to pull back. That order almost came too late. As the Michigan troopers started to withdraw, a pair of Virginia regiments came storming down on their flank. Stagg had to wheel a squadron out of his column to blunt the enemy charge while the rest of his regiment hurried toward the river.

The Yankees squeezed their way out of encirclement, although just barely. As they chased after the fleeing bluecoats the Rebels cut off and captured Stagg's rearmost platoon. Once at the river, however, the Confederates encountered the 5th Michigan Cavalry and a battery of Union artillery drawn up on the opposite shore. These units covered Stagg's final withdrawal across the narrow waterway to safety. Stuart was unwilling to press the matter further. He called off the pursuit and led his men back to Orange County. The Federals continued on to Culpeper Court House.[35]

After two days of fighting, both sides declared victory. Buford bragged that he had successfully completed his reconnaissance. The cost of that accomplishment had not been light. Chapman reported 22 killed, wounded or missing in his brigade. Kilpatrick initially stated his losses as 1 dead, 12 wounded and 92 missing or taken prisoner. Most of those casualties came from Harhaus's 2nd New York Cavalry, which lost 87 men (4 dead, 6 wounded and 77 captured). Total Union losses equaled 127 men.[36]

Stuart made no official report on the two-day action and no firm record of Confederate casualties exists. Incomplete Southern regimental records show at least 20 dead, 39 wounded, and 62 captured in Hampton's division, for a total loss of 121 men. In all probability the number of wounded and missing was slightly higher.[37]

---

35 OR 29, pt. 1, 743; Henry Watkins to Mary September 24, 1863, VHS. Battery C was armed with six 3-inch Ordnance Rifles.

36 Lewis Nunnelee diary, September 23, 1863, ACWM; OR 29, pt. 1, 141; George Chapman diary, September 23, 1863, HIS; www.civilwardata.com lists 9th New York Cavalry losses at 2w, 1cap; 3rd Indiana losses at 1k, 1cap; Frederick Phisterer, *New York in the War of the Rebellion, 3rd edition* (Albany, NY, 1912), 753; OR 29, pt. 1, 141-43; Harrell, *Second North Carolina Cavalry*, 196. www.civilwardata.com records show 114cap and 2m in Kilpatrick's division: nine from the 1st Michigan, 73 from the 2nd New York, 12 from the 1st Vermont, one each from the 5th and 6th Michigan, and 18 from the 7th Michigan which also has 2 men missing.

37 Harrell, *Second North Carolina Cavalry*, 197; Mesic, *Cobb's Legion*, 93, 281-82. The 1st North Carolina, numbering only 130 men at Jack's Shop, counted 33 k, w, or missing–nearly a fourth of its strength. Cobb's Legion reported 4k, 6w, and 8cap. Capt. Williams of the 2nd South Carolina wrote home that the Richmond press reported CS casualties as "much greater" than they actually were and estimated Rebel losses at less than 100. He stated that the 2nd South Carolina had 4k and 8 or 10w, most of them minor.www.civilwardata.com , accessed 13 May 2018, shows CS losses as 1st North Carolina, 5k, 8w, 14cap; 2nd North Carolina: 2k, 4w, 8cap; 4th North Carolina: 1k, 3w, 2cap; 5th North Carolina: 3k, 1w, 25cap; 5th Virginia: 1w, 1cap; 6th Virginia: 1cap; 7th Virginia: 1k, 6w, 4cap; 10th Virginia: 1cap; 11th Virginia: 2k, 9w, 12cap; 12th Virginia: 1k; Jeff Davis Legion: 1cap.

Despite these casualty figures, the outcome pleased the Confederates considerably. They were certain that they had derailed a raid on the Virginia Central. Stuart had thwarted Buford's attempt to trap Hampton's division and badly hurt Kilpatrick before chasing the Yankees all the way back to Culpeper County. Lee heaped praise on his cavalry and its commander for their success, commending Stuart for his "usual energy, promptness and boldness." In a letter to his wife Stuart bubbled with glee over the compliments; he barely mentioned that the enemy had shot his horse out from under him at Jack's Shop.[38]

Of course, the Federals had not attempted a strike against the railroad, and Buford had accomplished his primary purpose. The intelligence Federal cavalrymen had gathered was the real result of the expedition. Buford reported both Madison County's roads and its fords in good condition. He also collected further proof that Ewell and A. P. Hill defended the Rapidan. If Meade wanted to swing around Lee's left, this was critical information.[39]

But the 48-hour struggle south of Madison Court House had also helped the Rebels. Buford's reconnaissance provided a useful insight into Meade's thinking. On September 23, Lee wrote President Davis that the Federal general had "apparently expected" the Army of Northern Virginia to "abandon the line of the Rapidan on his approach." That the Rebels had held their ground clearly perplexed Meade. Lee suggested that the Union "advance seems to be delayed by doubts as to our strength." Since the Federals had probed his left flank, he speculated they would next probe his right and cautioned: "We must be prepared for him there or prostrate him by a movement on his rear."[40]

As usual Lee wasn't content to await events. The best way to upset Meade's plans was to strike first and throw him onto the defensive. Whether Lee's weakened army could successfully undertake such an attack remained debatable. But if fate offered the chance to strike, Lee was determined to seize it.

---

38 Stuart to wife September 25, 1863, VHS; *OR* 29, pt. 1, 742-43.

39 Harrell, *Second North Carolina Cavalry*, 197; *OR* 29, pt. 1, 140-41.

40 *OR* 29, pt. 2, 742-43.

CHAPTER 9

"Matters Again Look a Little Complicated"

Two Corps Go West—Union Worry—Odds—
Lee Anxious to Strike—Southern Confidence—Confederate Plans

WHAT might happen in Virginia depended greatly on what was happening on the battlefields of Tennessee. The fate of Chattanooga remained the cornerstone of events. In August the Confederacy was trying vainly to avoid the city's capture. By the end of September the Federals were striving desperately to hold the place. Beaten at Chickamauga Maj. Gen. Rosecrans's Army of the Cumberland had fled into the city. Braxton Bragg's triumphant Army of Tennessee had followed. Against Longstreet's advice to outflank Chattanooga and compel Rosecrans to abandon the town, Bragg ordered his troops to besiege the vital railroad junction.

Confederate artillery perched on high ground around Chattanooga controlled the Tennessee River and virtually cut Union supply lines. The trickle of food managing to reach Rosecrans's trapped command barely kept it from starving. There was no chance the Federals could successfully escape their encirclement. The Lincoln administration had to do *something* to relieve pressure on the beleaguered army and hold the city. Whatever action it chose had to be prompt, otherwise the Union cause would suffer a defeat rivaling the Confederate loss of Vicksburg.

As a first step, Halleck ordered all available Federal troops in the Western Theater to Rosecrans' assistance. More importantly, the war department dispatched Maj. Gen. Ulysses S. Grant to Chattanooga to recover the situation with the authority to relieve Rosecrans and replace him if necessary. But this was only a start; to save the Army of the Cumberland more would have to be done.[1]

---

1 For a compelling examination of the Grant-Rosecrans relationship and their respective roles at Chattanooga, see Frank P. Varney, *General Grant and the Rewriting of History: How the*

The question of exactly what else the administration could do hung heavily over Washington. Since the Confederates had taken troops from Virginia to reinforce Bragg, Secretary Stanton and Secretary of the Treasury Salmon P. Chase favored replicating the Rebel effort by shifting significant force from the Army of the Potomac to Tennessee. Lincoln and Halleck, sensing opportunity amid misfortune, were reluctant to weaken the eastern army. They felt the transfer of Rebel troops from Lee to Bragg offered the Union a rare chance to achieve decisive results in Virginia. Obviously, Meade could not send massive reinforcements to Chattanooga *and* launch a major offensive against Lee at the same time. It was up to Lincoln to decide, and quickly, what Meade should do. Despite the obvious need for rapid action the president refused to let events stampede him into a rash decision. He was determined to thoroughly weigh the possibility that just now there was more to gain in Virginia than endanger in Tennessee.

On September 22, Meade received orders to report to Washington for a high-level consultation. The next day he met with Secretary of War Stanton (apparently alone) and with President Lincoln and General Halleck together. The seeming inactivity of the war department while the Confederates had beefed up their forces in Tennessee dismayed navy secretary Welles, who saw little or no reason for optimism. Upon learning that Meade was in the capital, Welles expressed hope that the army would strike "some efficient blows . . . now that Lee is weak." Although certain that "the opportunity should not be lost," he feared the current crisis was beyond Halleck's capabilities to handle.[2]

If Welles had sat in on Lincoln's meeting with Meade, he would have found little reason to abandon his gloom. Face to face with his general, the president repeated the position he had laid out in his letter to Halleck a few days before. If the war in Virginia had come down to a defensive stalemate, Lincoln saw no reason for Meade to have as large a force as he commanded and proposed detaching troops from it for use elsewhere. Meade responded by reiterating his willingness to step aside if Lincoln and Halleck thought he had been "too slow or prudent." Again, the general-in-chief rebuffed the offer.

Thus encouraged, Meade argued against any reduction of his army. Exactly how he made his case is unknown, although he likely hinted at an offensive movement in the near future. Whatever his argument, the general believed he had been persuasive. He

---

Destruction of William S. Rosecrans Influenced Our Understanding of the Civil War (El Dorado Hills, CA, 2014).

2 Morse, *Diary of Gideon Welles*, vol. 1, 442.

left Washington on the afternoon of September 23 convinced Lincoln would leave the Union's Virginia army alone.[3]

Nonetheless, his interlude with the commander-in-chief had been disturbing. Although he never recorded the content of his Washington discussions, he did relate them to Col. Lyman, who turned reflective in his journal entry for September 23. Pondering his chief's experience, the aide admitted:

> Geniuses do not grow on every bush, I know not when I have been so struck with it as here in the army. There are the finest tools for a genius to work with; men by the thousands who are brave, hard-working, honest, even able; but, of that rapidity and originality that mark the leading control of great minds, there is nothing, or almost nothing.

There was "little doubt Halleck is a mediocre man," he opined. The president inspired no greater confidence, and the colonel clucked that "Mr. Lincoln thinks he knows a great deal about war." This rather haughty assessment coming from a man who had first put on a uniform just six weeks ago, was likely influenced by Meade, who certainly had more standing to express such views.[4]

Meade also unburdened himself in a letter to his wife. Darkly warning of the "by no means favorable," news from Tennessee, the general told Margaret about the "feverish anxiety" in the administration for the eastern army to do something. As usual though, no one in the war department or the White House seemed to know "what exactly might or could be done."[5]

This was not a new lament: Meade might have written the very same words in late July or August, which hardly left him in a cheerful mood. Among the personnel at army headquarters word quickly spread that the general's infamous temper was in full bloom. Meade was "mad enough to bite iron bars in two" when he returned from the capital, Thomas Carpenter said. Although the staff had no way of knowing it, their commander's foul mood was justified for his optimism regarding Lincoln's intentions was ill-conceived.[6]

*   *   *

Sometime after midnight on September 23, just hours after Meade returned to Virginia, half a dozen powerful men met in the secretary of war's office: Lincoln,

3   George G. Meade to wife, *Life and Letters*, vol. 2,150.

4   Lyman, *Meade's Army*, 41.

5   Meade, *Life and Letters*, 150-51.

6   Carpenter to parents September 28, 1863, MHS.

Halleck, Stanton, Chase, Maj. Gen. Joseph Hooker (Meade's predecessor as AOP commander) and Col. Daniel McCallum, superintendent of military railroad transportation. Stanton opened the discussion with an explanation of the current situation in Chattanooga. He then proposed detaching and transferring 30,000 men from Meade to Tennessee. The secretary of war echoed Lincoln's own reasoning by claiming there was "no reason to expect that General Meade will attack Lee, although greatly superior in force and his great numbers where they are, are useless." In just five days, claimed Stanton, Northern railroads could deposit 30,000 troops at Chattanooga.[7]

Lincoln wasn't so hopeful. Long experience left him skeptical of any rapid movement by the Union army. "I will bet," he told Stanton, "that if the order is given tonight, the troops could not be got to Washington in five days." Halleck and the president still preferred some action in Virginia. Stanton's logic, combined with Chase's support and Meade's vague promises of impending action, proved impossible to overcome, however. After two hours of discussion, Lincoln assented to the transfer of the XI and XII Corps from the Army of the Potomac to Tennessee, so long as Meade wasn't on the verge of launching an immediate offensive.[8]

Halleck wasted no time in finding out Meade's plans. At 2:30 a.m. on September 24 the general-in-chief sent a curt telegram to Culpeper Court House asking if Meade had "positively determined to make any immediate movement." If the answer was no, the XI and XII corps were to prepare to move to Washington. Meade responded within the hour, confessing that he contemplated no "immediate movement" by the army. Perhaps suspecting what was behind Halleck's query, he tried to hedge his bet by explaining his "decision was not positive" and might change when intelligence arrived from Buford's reconnaissance of Madison County.[9]

Later that morning, Halleck showed Meade's response to the president. The Pennsylvanian's continued equivocation made Lincoln's decision easy. At 9:30 a.m. Halleck telegraphed orders directing that Meade ship O. O. Howard's XI and John Slocum's XII corps by rail to Washington "with the least possible delay."[10]

Those instructions hit Meade's headquarters like a lightning bolt. No one other than the army commander seemed to have expected such a directive. The general,

7   Hattaway, *How the North Won*, 456.

8   Ibid; Daniel Bauer, "The Rail Transfer of the 11th and 12th Corps to the Western Theatre of War," *Civil War: The Magazine of the Civil War Society* (Berryville, VA), vol. 12, 68.

9   *OR* 29, pt. 2, 147.

10 Ibid., 148.

however, had sensed it coming, even if at the last minute. He promptly responded that he would do whatever necessary to carry out Halleck's order.[11]

By 11 a.m. of September 24, both Slocum and Howard had instructions to have their men cook five days' rations and assemble for shipment by rail to Washington. The XII Corps would rendezvous with its trains at Brandy Station after the I Corps relieved it of picket duty along the Rapidan. Meade told Slocum to use the "utmost promptitude and dispatch" in executing his orders. The corps was to march all night if necessary to meet the railcars on time.

Howard's XI Corps, spread out along the railroad between the Rappahannock River and Bristoe Station, was not to delay even long enough to be relieved of duty guarding the tracks. Rather, Howard was to inform O&A management where he wanted his regiments loaded onto transports and be ready to embark the moment trains arrived.[12]

Once the two corps assembled in Washington, Joe Hooker would take overall command of both units and get them to Chattanooga as quickly as possible. The war department gave Col. McCallum extensive power to supervise the movement. By presidential order Hooker was granted authority to "take military possession" of all railroad track and property required to accomplish his urgent mission.[13]

Hooker's westward speed was all-important. Some feared it might already be too late. Welles was "more desponding" than he cared to admit: "The army management distresses all of us, but we must not say so." The secretary took some solace in the fact that reinforcements were in fact on the way to Tennessee.[14]

*   *   *

If the plan to transfer 13,641 soldiers from Virginia to Chattanooga reassured Secretary Welles, it had quite the opposite effect on Meade's army. The sudden reassignment of two corps unhinged whatever offensive plans Meade had in the works. Colonel Lyman declared that the general had been just 24 hours away from launching an offensive when Halleck's order arrived. The irritated aide felt that the administration was sending Slocum and Howard on a pointless errand instead of letting Meade take advantage of his best chance to fight Lee since the beginning of August. Lyman was

---

11 Lyman, *Meade's Army*, 41-42.

12 OR 29, pt. 2, 148.

13 Bauer, "The Rail Transfer," 68; *OR* 29, pt. 1, 151.

14 Morse, *Diary of Gideon Welles*, vol. 1, 442.

sure that the XI and XII corps would arrive in the west too late to do any good while their absence from Virginia spoiled a grand opportunity.[15]

The army's rank and file knew nothing of Meade's supposedly derailed plans, of course. Nonetheless they felt that they had been on the verge of doing something important. Abraham Bope of the 61st Ohio, like many other Union soldiers, was "anticipating a big fight." He and his compatriots had heard rumors about the departure of Longstreet's divisions and part of Ewell's corps. "If that is the case we can clean out Lee with his 80,000 men and go into Richmond," Bope reasoned. Thomas Carpenter, a clerk at army headquarters provided a better ability to see the strategic picture, had expected an impending campaign. "Everything was ready for a big move somewhere," he noted. "Every soldier had eight days rations and the trains were filled up with sixteen more and orders given to be ready at a moment's notice."[16]

Now, the administration's response to the bloody Chickamauga debacle made those preparations moot. In truth, however, the transfer of the XI and XII corps didn't spoil any concrete offensive plan. Meade himself acknowledged as much when he answered Halleck's telegram during the early hours of September 24. Even Lyman realized Meade had given his superiors no reason to forgo detaching troops for western service. Headquarters should have had "plans duly digested," he thought, to take advantage of any opening the reconnaissance into Madison County revealed. "But, as a fact," he glumly admitted, "the army was not so ready, and plans remained to be made."[17]

It did not take long for Meade's soldiers to feel the repercussions of the defeat in Georgia and the meetings in Washington. For days Union troops had felt anxious about developments in the west. Pleasonton's confirmation of Longstreet's departure from the Rapidan had foreshadowed trouble and its realization seemed almost the worst imaginable. Rosecrans' disaster almost certainly demanded that the Army of the Potomac to do something to help redeem the situation.[18]

Just what it could do was an open question. But many soldiers believed they knew what it *would* do, and that was fall back on Washington. This distressing prospect was far preferable to the rumor floating about that Halleck had ordered an attack on Lee's

15 OR 29, pt. 2, 118. Lyman, *Meade's Army*, 42; Field Returns for end of August showed 25,000 men present and absent, in the two corps; Hattaway, *How the North Won*, 456.

16 Abraham Bope to parents September 22, 1863, GLI; Thomas Carpenter to parents September 28, 1863, MHS.

17 Lyman, *Meade's Army*, 42.

18 Thomas Carpenter to parents September 20, 1863, MHS; John Hadley letters, *Indiana Magazine of History*, 254-56.

fortifications behind the Rapidan, which few men doubted would produce another calamitous defeat for the Army of the Potomac.[19]

Confusion proliferated as one rumor rapidly superseded another. But even amid swirling news of crisis, some Potomac soldiers couldn't help feeling vindication in the Army of the Cumberland's plight. Many of Meade's veterans believed that Grant, Sherman, and Rosecrans had won their laurels against the South's second team, while the eastern army had confronted the best the Rebels could offer. Now that western Federals had faced some of Lee's troops, they would better understand what the AOP had been up against. That might incline Rosecrans' men to brag less about their victories or criticize the Virginia army's lack of them.[20]

Whatever the necessity of reinforcing Tennessee, the movement didn't sit well with many of the commanders going west. The "whole body" of officers in the XII Corps was reportedly "quite furious" at having to leave Virginia and "indignant at being placed under Hooker, who they despise." Henry Slocum felt so aggrieved he tried to resign rather than submit to his new assignment. Lincoln mollified him by promising to solve the problem once the troop transfer was completed.[21]

The reaction of the XI Corps was markedly different. Major General Howard took a philosophical approach. A deeply religious man, he trusted the government was sending him west "for some wise and good purpose," and that the transfer would greatly benefit his soldiers. Their misfortunes at Chancellorsville and Gettysburg had besmirched their reputation. Reassignment promised the possibility of redemption and that his troops would be "better appreciated" in a new theater.[22]

Although the order to head north took virtually everyone by surprise, the XI Corps moved swiftly toward Washington. The march began at midnight on September 25 and continued without a let up, save a brief rest at dawn, until 5 p.m. the following afternoon when the corps began concentrating around Manassas Junction. By nine

19 Rufus Ricksecker to "My dear sister," September 25, 1863, The 126th Ohio Volunteers, Letters of First Lieutenant Rufus Ricksecker, http://www.frontierfamilies.net/family/ Rickpt1.htm, accessed May 16, 2018; Eseck Wilber to parents September 24, 1863, RICE.

20 John Hadley letters, *Indiana Magazine of History*, 254-56; Thomas Carpenter to parents October 2, 1863, MHS.

21 Lyman, *Meade's Army*, 42; OR 29, pt. 1, 156. Warner, *Generals in Blue*, 452. Slocum was given command of the Vicksburg garrison until after Hooker resigned just before the fall of Atlanta. At that point Slocum assumed command of the XX Corps and participated in the final struggle for Atlanta and Sherman's "march to the sea."

22 Lyman, *Meade's Army*, 42; OR 27, pt. 3, 778-80; Oliver O. Howard, *Autobiography of Oliver Otis Howard, Major General, United States Army* (New York, NY, 1907), 455. An outstanding history of the XI Corps is James Pula, *Under the Crescent Moon: The XI Corps in the American Civil War, 1862-1864*, 2 Vols. (El Dorado, CA, 2017).

o'clock that night all of Howard's troops were "packed into the dirty baggage cars" and speeding north.[23]

The XII Corps had to mark time until the I Corps assumed its position on the Rapidan, but the generals handled this shift expeditiously. Lincoln spent the 25th anxiously waiting and worrying at the war department and ended it pleasantly surprised with the promptness of the army's movements. Only 24 hours had elapsed between Halleck's order to send two corps to Washington and the departure of the first trainloads of troops for Chattanooga.[24]

The capital viewed the rapid dispatch of Howard's and Slocum's units as a triumph, but in Culpeper County many soldiers had premonitions of serious peril, if not disaster. Though some troops could hardly credit news that the XI and XII corps had gone west, even the most doubtful had to admit it was probably true. The overactive rumor mill left many men bewildered and uncertain. At army headquarters, a worried Thomas Carpenter admitted that "matters again look a little complicated." He didn't like "waiting for a turn in events elsewhere." What the future held, he couldn't say, but he doubted the Rebels would stand idly by as the Army of the Potomac was weakened.[25]

Whatever was going to happen in Virginia over the next weeks and months no longer concerned the XI and XII corps. They had already embarked on a roundabout 1,200 mile journey to save the Army of the Cumberland. Meeting an enthusiastic reception all along their route, they would cover 500 more miles than Longstreet had done. The first of Hooker's 13,600 men wouldn't arrive near Chattanooga for a week. The last of them took 11 and a half days. By contrast, the Confederates, speeding over a shorter route, consumed 10 days to get the first of Longstreet's troops to Bragg, while moving the entire 16,000-man force took 16. The Union shipped its men farther and faster than the Confederates. Given the conditions of their respective railroad networks, which of these movements rated the more remarkable is still debatable.[26]

There is no doubt, however, that the Rebel maneuver drew first blood. Longstreet's brigades helped win the battle of Chickamauga and drive the Union army back into Chattanooga. These troops also performed a great service to Lee *in absentia* by forcing Washington to shift troops from Meade to rescue Rosecrans. What had

23 Frederick Winkler to wife September 30, 1863, Hathi Trust Digital Library, Letters of Frederick C. Winkler, 1862-1865, https://catalog.hathitrust.org/Record/009628680, accessed May 16, 2018.

24 Morse, *Diary of Gideon Welles*, vol. 1, 443.

25 John Hadley letters, *Indiana Magazine of History*, 254-56; Thomas Carpenter to parents September 28, 1863, MHS.

26 Hattaway, *How the North Won*, 455.

happened, though, was the exact opposite of the strategy Davis and Lee preferred. Rather than an offensive in Virginia pulling Yankee divisions away from Chattanooga, a Rebel counterattack in Georgia had pulled a large Union force out of Virginia.

The detachment of two corps from Meade's army hardly altered its numerical strength at all, however. At the end of August the eight corps of the AOP counted 89,050 men present for duty. Thirty days later Meade's six corps had troop strength of 89,058. The return of units earlier detailed to New York City on draft riot duty offset the shift of the XI and XII corps to Chattanooga.[27]

Longstreet's absence, on the other hand, seriously weakened Lee. At the end of August he had 71,954 men present for duty, thirty days later, he was down to 55,221. The only reinforcement Lee received in the meanwhile was Brig. Gen. John Cooke's North Carolina brigade. The numerical odds for the Confederates in Virginia were better before the First Corps departed, and they certainly didn't improve with the shift of two Federal corps. Before both armies sent large contingents westward Meade outnumbered Lee by 17,000 men. After the rival transfers, the Yankees outnumbered Lee by 34,000 men—twice the previous margin.[28]

Although the departure of the XI and XII corps had not materially weakened the AOP, the reassignment of those units to Tennessee had an enormous impact on the war in Virginia. "The President is the best judge of where and how the armies can best be employed," Meade wrote, taking a philosophical tack in a letter to Margaret, "and if he chooses to put this army strictly on the defensive I have no right to object or murmur." Still, the general had no doubt he was now utterly incapable of undertaking aggressive action. The loss of two corps had reduced his army's manpower to a "figure a little greater only than Lee's," and the great natural strength of the Confederate position south of the Rapidan would "equalize the difference" between the rival armies. Under these circumstances, he complained, "I cannot do anything."

Meade was wrong. He now enjoyed a numerical advantage over Lee twice what it had been at the start of September. But the ghosts of past battles haunted him. The success of the tactical defensive at Fredericksburg and Gettysburg had imprinted itself on his mind. Even though Lee had stood solely on the defensive in just two battles—Fredericksburg and Antietam—Meade felt certain that if his army crossed the Rapidan, it would encounter well-entrenched Rebels ready to receive an attack. Without a solid, massive numerical advantage, the best Meade could do now was prepare to fight a defensive battle if the enemy dared issue forth.[29]

27 *OR* 29, pt. 2, 118, 239.

28 *OR* 29, pt. 2, 681, 764.

29 George G. Meade to wife September 24, 1863, *Life and Letters*, vol. 2, 150-51.

* * *

Lee quickly heard rumors of the dispatch of the XI and XII corps, of course—and by October 1 he was confident of it. He probably didn't realize his opponent's troop strength was unchanged, but he doubtless knew his army remained heavily outnumbered. But there was nothing unusual about that. Lee had faced long odds before and was used to running risks. He needn't proceed cautiously against an opponent who had failed to attack his wounded army during the Gettysburg retreat and who had behaved so warily over the last two months.[30]

Lee had been anxious to resume the offensive against the Army of the Potomac for some time and had said so in late August and again in early September. Even as Longstreet's corps was leaving Virginia, Lee had told President Davis that he wanted to drive Meade back on Washington.[31]

With his enemy weakened, Lee sensed an opportunity to "strike a blow" which might fatally injure the Yankee army. At a minimum he wanted to prevent Meade from sending more reinforcements to Tennessee. To do so he would emulate his successful campaign against Major General John Pope in August 1862 by making a flank march with his army through Madison County to attack Meade around Culpeper Court House. Should the Yankees refuse to stand and fight, the ANV would renew its march and seek to get between Meade and Washington or hit his retiring force while it was vulnerable to defeat in detail.

If the Southern army succeeded in pushing the Federals back toward their capital, it would automatically preempt whatever plans Meade may have for an offensive across the Rapidan. Moreover, news of the Union army retreating toward the Potomac would depress Northern morale and aid the growing peace movement in the United States on the eve of congressional elections. It might even convince Lincoln to recall the reinforcements Meade had sent to Tennessee. But more than anything, Lee wanted to seriously damage his adversary. A significant victory might cripple Meade and allow for another invasion of the North.[32]

The depression and despair pervading the South after Vicksburg and Gettysburg now gave way to optimistic enthusiasm. Along the banks of the Rapidan, hunger for news from Tennessee (nearly) replaced soldier concerns about food and weather. The reports reaching Lee's army were almost too good to be true. "The news is cheering from Bragg," a Rebel in the Stonewall Brigade wrote home, adding that he hoped the

30 Lee, *Wartime Papers*, 606; OR 29, pt. 2, 753-54, 756-59, 766.

31 OR 29, pt. 2, 661.

32 OR 29, pt. 1, 405; Freeman, *R.E. Lee*, vol. 3, 170 n71.

western general had the "skill to follow up his success and it will result in the entire annihilation of Rosecrans' army."[33]

*   *   *

Whether or not the victory in Georgia presaged the end of a Federal army, the Confederacy's improved strategic situation clearly pointed toward an offensive by Lee. October had begun in a hard rain that gave way to beautiful, cool weather, ripe for campaigning. Various headquarters in the Rebel camps instinctively issued orders to get everything ready for a movement.[34]

An indication of pending action came on October 3 when Lee rode to the 1,082-foot peak of Clark's Mountain. Here he held a "long consultation" with generals A. P. Hill, Richard Ewell, and Jubal Early, none of whom left a record of the meeting. But as they gazed down on the vast Union encampments, Lee briefed his subordinates on his plans and their roles in them, solicited advice, and addressed any questions. Maybe he also allowed his concerns about Ewell and Hill to cross his mind. With Longstreet absent and Stonewall Jackson in his grave, these men would be responsible for bringing Lee's strategic vision to fruition.[35]

Both his corps commanders were West Pointers who had enjoyed a solid if unspectacular military career before 1861. Ewell had spent most of his service with the 1st Dragoons and had been promoted to captain for bravery in the Mexican War. After that he spent years fighting Indians in the Southwest and had been slightly wounded in the hand during an 1859 skirmish with Apaches under Cochise. Hill saw brief cavalry service in Mexico before going on to fight Seminoles in Florida and spending five years with the U.S. Coastal Survey. When Virginia seceded, both men had resigned from the U.S. Army and offered their talents to the Confederacy.[36]

Their physical appearance contrasted sharply. A. P. Hill looked the part of a stylized romantic warrior. Just a month shy of his 38th birthday, the general stood about 5-foot 8-inches tall and weighed 150 pounds. His full auburn beard sat below a straight nose, deep set eyes and long, slightly curled hair that he wore parted to one side.

33 *Richmond Enquirer*, October 9, 1863; Charles W. Turner, ed., *Ted Barclay, Liberty Hall Volunteers: Letters from the Stonewall Brigade, 1861–1865* (Natural Bridge Station, VA 1992), 107.

34 Kirkpatrick diary, October 6, 1863, UT.

35 Peter Hariston diary, October 3, 1863, SHC/UNC.

36 The best biographies for Ewell and Hill are: Donald C. Pfanz, *Richard S. Ewell: A Soldier's Life* (Chapel Hill, NC, 1998) and James I. Robertson, Jr. *General A. P. Hill: The Story of a Confederate Warrior* (New York, 1987). Ewell graduated West Point in the Class of 1840, Hill in 1847.

Lieutenant General A. P. Hill
Library of Congress

Courtly and somewhat romantic, he typically dressed with dash, but especially when he donned a red flannel hunting shirt he liked to wear into battle. More careful observers, however, noted that Hill's narrow chest and thin face hinted at his increasingly fragile health.

It was hard to say exactly what malady or maladies afflicted Hill. He had contracted a serious case of gonorrhea during his time at West Point and later caught typhoid and yellow fever in Mexico. He had been with Jackson at Chancellorsville when the friendly fire that struck down Stonewall had wounded Hill in both legs. All of these misfortunes affected his health, but frequent urinary tract infections and an inflamed prostate induced by his untreatable gonorrhea caused the Virginian's greatest distress. After elevation to corps command Hill's health problems steadily worsened, occasionally rendering him so feeble he took to bed. This incapacity tended to manifest itself at moments of extreme stress, which meant that Hill often inclined toward illness on the eve of battle.[37]

The same height as Hill but nine years older, Richard Stoddert Ewell marked his 46th birthday in February 1863. A correspondent for the *Petersburg Express* described the Second Corps commander as "a tall, slim individual, with extremely sharp features" and a "Frenchified moustache and whiskers." The bald dome of the general's head was in many respects the most prominent part of his visage. But one reporter found Ewell's "most remarkable feature" to be his "restless" eyes, constantly darting about to take in every detail of his surroundings.[38]

Much to his troops' approval, Ewell liked to lead from the front and often put himself in the line of fire. But at the battle of Groveton, the general's élan resulted in a Union bullet smashing into his kneecap and inflicting a wound that required the amputation of his left leg above the joint. During his lengthy recovery, he missed the army's four major battles: Second Manassas, Sharpsburg, Fredericksburg, and

---

37 Tagg, *Generals of Gettysburg*, 301; James I. Robertson, Jr. *A. P. Hill*, 186-89; see also OU e-history, "Medical Information on General Officers," https://ehistory.osu.edu/exhibitions/cwsurgeon/cwsurgeon/generals, accessed May 17. 2018.

38 A Confederate, *The Grayjackets: And How They Lived, Fought and Died For Dixie* (Richmond, VA, 1867), 230.

Chancellorsville. Ewell could not mount a horse unaided and had to be strapped into the saddle. To avoid this difficult process, the general traveled in a carriage when his troops were on the move and rode a horse only in battle. He could walk with crutches but preferred to use an artificial leg. Unfortunately, this device caused Ewell frequent discomfort and tended to irritate the stump of his leg and produce complications.

Ewell was extraordinarily modest, whereas Hill was touchy about his reputation, which had led to difficulties with both Longstreet and Jackson. Somewhat high strung and remarkably brave, both generals were rugged fighters and good administrators who took care of their troops. Consequently they earned the admiration of their soldiers and were, for the most part, universally liked by their subordinates.

Before suffering his Groveton wound, Ewell was a bachelor of middling fortune, noted for his extensive use of profanity. That changed during his convalescence when he accepted religion and married a wealthy long-lost love who refused to let him curse in her presence. While most people applauded these transformations, some suspected that they had, along with the loss of his leg, shorn Ewell of some intangible quality of character and by so doing taken the keen edge off his military mind.

This possibility along with both men's suspect health worried Lee. So too did the occasional hints that corps command had stretched the limits of his two subordinates beyond their abilities. Both had been excellent as heads of a division. Ewell's leadership had been critical during Jackson's 1862 Valley Operations and in the opening stages of the Second Manassas Campaign. Hill's record was more spotty. His impatience had initiated the Seven Day's battles prematurely and a gap he had left in his front at Fredericksburg allowed George Meade's division to temporarily breach the Confederate line. At Cedar Mountain, however, he had rescued Jackson from a dire situation, and at Sharpsburg his rapid march from Harper's Ferry and timely attack on the Union IX Corps had saved the Army of Northern Virginia from destruction. Lee considered Hill his third best officer after Jackson and Longstreet.

The army and the press widely heralded the elevation of Ewell and Hill to corps command, and during the initial phase of the Pennsylvania campaign, both had seemed to vindicate their selection for larger responsibilities after Jackson's death. At the Second Battle of Winchester in June, Ewell displayed the same vigor and tactical acumen that had won him Stonewall's trust. Until Gettysburg Lee had no reason to doubt his decision to promote these men to lieutenant general.

But once the Pennsylvania fight started, both had fallen short of expectations. Hill had been sick and allowed his lead divisions to instigate an engagement Lee had told him to avoid. After that A. P. Hill virtually disappeared for the remainder of the action. Ewell was perfectly healthy at Gettysburg. His corps had helped rout the Yankees on July 1, but then, with some justification, he had failed to follow up that success and seize critical high ground on Cemetery and Culp's Hills. On the battle's second day his

Lieutenant General Richard S. Ewell
Library of Congress

performance had been subpar. Neither Ewell nor Hill had displayed firm control over his corps.[39]

Fortunately, the two generals behaved competently during the retreat from Pennsylvania. They had handled their men well during the risky redeployment through the Blue Ridge Mountains. Ewell had even shown a touch of his old aggressiveness in the lower Valley. Since the army's return to the Rappahannock and its subsequent withdrawal to the Rapidan, neither man had given Lee cause for complaint. But then again he had needed to ask little of Ewell and Hill during the two months since returning to central Virginia.

In Lee's mind Ewell's capabilities conjured more questions than Hill's health. Several men noted Ewell's tendency to lean heavily on the opinions of his division commanders, a trait that had manifested itself at Gettysburg and lingered ever since. It was natural and largely commendable that he conferred with his talented subordinates and sought their advice. What some officers noticed, though, Lee possibly among them, was Ewell's apparent over-reliance on their counsel. One of Ewell's perceptive and articulate artillery battalion commanders, Lt. Col. Thomas Henry Carter, observed in September 1863 that Ewell never did anything "except by the advice of Early or Rodes." Early's presence at the conference on Clark's Mountain might support that criticism, or, given Ewell's health, it might have been nothing more than the prudent attendance of his second in command.[40]

*   *   *

Whatever Lee's reservations, the two generals almost certainly faced a looming test. After returning to camp following the Clark's Mountain conference, Early remarked to his aide, Peter Hairston, that although the army had yet to fight a battle in

---

39 Pfanz, *Richard S. Ewell*, 322-24.

40 Graham T. Dozier, ed. *A Gunner in Lee's Army: The Civil War Letters of Thomas Henry Carter* (Chapel Hill, NC, 2014), 205.

the month of October, that might be about to change. Two days later, Hairston learned that scouting parties had gone across the Rapidan to gather information. To him this was final proof that Lee was about to "do something." His generals and the men in the ranks were obviously willing. "They look with longing eyes upon the well-filled knapsacks of the enemy" Hairston wrote. The troops needed blankets and didn't know where to get them "unless they take them from the Yankees." [41]

Few of Lee's soldiers could foresee what their commander had in mind, but they trusted his judgment implicitly. Obviously he would soon put them on the march, and consequently his need for secrecy was intensifying. Lee took every precaution to draw a cloak of obscurity around the army. Officers issued strict instructions to the pickets along the river prohibiting campfires and any communication with the enemy.[42]

North of the Rapidan a sense of apprehension suffused the air. Frustration consumed the staff at Union army headquarters. Expressing dismay that Lee was not being "either cut to pieces, or in precipitate flight on Richmond," Col. Lyman complained that "no particular prospect of a battle" appeared on the horizon. This fact he, and perhaps his boss, lay squarely at the feet of the government and Rosecrans. As far as he was concerned, Lincoln and Halleck's response to the mess made by the Army of the Cumberland at Chickamauga had cheated Meade of a chance to fight.[43]

However true, that wasn't the whole story. Meade's reluctance to seek a major battle contributed significantly to the army's inertia. Though hardly unwilling to fight—he still concocted schemes for crossing the Rapidan to tangle with Lee—Meade was convinced that any such battle would inflict heavy casualties and produce nothing better than driving the Rebels back to an even stronger position. Since the government was unlikely to replace the losses of such a battle, the probable risks outweighed the possible benefits.

George Meade certainly grasped the irony of his situation. On the morning of September 24 while reading a two-day-old copy of the Richmond *Sentinel* at breakfast with his staff, Meade suddenly burst out laughing. He then read aloud a paragraph from the paper: "From the Rapidan we learn that all is quiet. Meade is making '*I would*' wait on '*I dare not*.'" Meade chuckled again. "Sharp fellers, they have hit it precisely!"[44]

* * *

41 Peter Hariston diary, October 3, 1863, SHC/UNC.

42 Kirkpatrick diary, October 6, 1863, UT.

43 Lyman, *Meade's Headquarters*, 22, 25.

44 Lyman, *Meade's Army*, 41; *Richmond Sentinel*, September 22, 1863.

General Lee, unlike his counterpart, didn't fear to dare. The relative strength of forces or his opponent's greater advantage mattered not. Lee was determined to do now what he had ached to do since August. He would strike.

On October 8, after a night of heavy rain, the Army of Northern Virginia began shifting position. By relatively easy and short movements, Lee massed his troops in jump off positions for a campaign designed to turn Meade's line along the Rapidan. Many Confederate regiments headed southwest toward Orange Court House, whereupon they swung northwest towards Madison County. Although few outside army headquarters understood exactly what these maneuvers portended, the men knew—as they always seemed to—that a campaign had begun. Quietly, deliberately, and without instructions from their officers, restless troops began preparing bedrolls and arranging their equipment for a hard march.[45]

As Ewell's corps made camp on the evening of October 8, Reverend James Sheeran, a Catholic chaplain serving with the 14th Louisiana, found himself unexpectedly moved by the beauty of his surroundings. The glow of light cast by numerous campfires bounced off the stacks of "brilliantly polished" muskets and shot upward to be "reflected by the boughs of . . . majestic oaks." It reminded him of a cathedral's interior. After several moments of contemplation, Sheeran confessed that nothing else he saw did that. Instead of "devout worshippers" kneeling in a magnificent church "adoring the God of peace and praying for the salvation of their enemies," he saw "men drilled in the science of war" about to "meet their fellow man on the bloody field of battle." These thoughts, in stark contrast to the physical beauty of the regiment's camp, posed a "strange combination of ideas," to the chaplain.[46]

Whether anyone entertained similar reflections that night is uncertain. But what everyone understood was the grim reality that when Robert E. Lee put his army on the road, its usual destination was a battlefield.

---

45 Kirkpatrick diary, October 7-8, 1863; Lewis Nunnelee diary, early October, ACWM; William S Long ms, Breckinridge Papers, NA.

46 Joseph T Durkin, ed., *Confederate Chaplain: Rev. James B. Sheeran, C.SS.R. 14th Louisiana, C.S.A.* (Milwaukee, WI, 1960), 63.

CHAPTER 10

"The Long Glittering Hedge of Bayonets"

Lee Moves—Meade Uncertain—James City Duel—
Buford Crosses the Rapidan—Meade Changes His Mind

O N October 9, both armies awoke to a cool dawn after a night of steady rain. North of the Rapidan, Union troops worked on building winter quarters, contending with the usual camp routines and boredom. South of that storied stream the Confederate army began to move.[1]

Acutely aware of the long odds he was facing, Robert E. Lee had been proactive in making sure they didn't grow longer. Well versed in playing upon the enemy's strategic sensitivities—civil and military—he looked to operations in the Shenandoah Valley to confuse the Federals about his objectives and route of advance. In a letter to Brig. Gen. John D. Imboden, he stressed it a "matter of great importance" to keep Federals forces around Harper's Ferry from aiding "points more seriously threatened." Lee instructed him to use his cavalry brigade to harass Yankee garrisons in the lower Valley. This should at the least prevent Meade from drawing these troops eastward as reinforcements. In the best case, it might persuade him to believe Lee was launching a wide flanking movement into the Union rear or even an invasion of the North. If Meade could be misled in either direction, he might overreact and offer the Rebels the chance to inflict a meaningful wound.

Imboden was also to scout Manassas and Thornton gaps in the Blue Ridge Mountains and give early warning should a menace develop on Lee's western flank. If he could defeat any Federal force he met, Lee wanted him to do it, and then push

---

1 John Merrell Diary, October 9, 1863, www.barkend.com/documents/JMBK08.pdf Accessed 7/19/2007; Thomas Carpenter to Phil, October 3, 1863, MSH; George Patch to parents, October 4, 1863, VHS.

toward Washington. A threat to the Union capital would certainly cause Meade problems, and the more Lee could psychologically discomfit his enemy, the better.

Similar directives went to Maj. Gen. Samuel Jones, commanding Confederate troops in southwestern Virginia, a more distant region where operations would be less likely to immediately impact Meade. But the recent shift of Longstreet to Georgia and the ongoing siege of Chattanooga had undoubtedly increased Federal concerns that Lee would dispatch more troops to Tennessee. Aggressive action by Jones' brigades might prompt Lincoln to suspect a Rebel move against Knoxville, which in turn might lead Stanton to send reinforcements to Burnside and discount the seriousness of Lee's move. At the very least Jones' force could fix in place whatever Union troops he already opposed—preventing them from assisting either Rosecrans or Meade. Naturally, Jones should be alert for greater possibilities: "if opportunity offers to do more," Lee told him, "it should be made use of."[2]

Having done what he could to synchronize operations in the Valley with those between the Rapidan and Rappahannock, Lee focused on the advance of his own command. The Army of Northern Virginia had operated on these same lines just over a year ago. Lee envisioned doing in this campaign what he had done to Union Maj. Gen. John Pope in August 1862. That effort had led to the rout of a Yankee army at Second Manassas and the invasion of Maryland. A similar outcome would be most gratifying.

But critical differences distinguished the 1862 and 1863 offensives. The earlier campaign took place in late summer. October would afford Lee far fewer daylight hours in which to maneuver and Virginia's war-ravaged countryside would prevent him from living off the land. The general would have to keep his slow moving wagon trains close at hand and pause for resupply at some point. That time consuming effort might seriously disrupt the speed of the campaign and Confederate flexibility.

Beyond doubt the most significant difference between October 1863 and all previous campaigns was the absence of James Longstreet and Stonewall Jackson. Since Lee had first assumed command of the army at the end of May of 1862, one or both of those generals had always been by his side. The Army of Northern Virginia had never fought a battle without either Jackson or Longstreet. Although hardly flawless— Jackson had been slow during the Seven Days battles and Longstreet sullen at Gettysburg—Lee had always been able to rely on their talents and competence.

In this campaign Lee would need Ewell and Hill to emulate the wisdom, aggressiveness, and surefootedness Longstreet and Jackson had usually exhibited. Much to Lee's frustration, poor health hampered his ability to keep a close watch on his generals as the campaign began. "In addition to other infirmities," he complained of

---

2 OR 29, pt. 2, 780.

rheumatism in his lower back, so painful he "could scarcely get about." For the first two days of the offensive this condition forced him to ride in an ambulance.

Nothing, however, would stay Lee from moving against Meade, much less personal discomfort. On the night of October 8 he had met with Hill and Ewell. The objective of the campaign, Lee explained, was to execute a turning movement designed to force Meade back from the Rapidan toward Washington. The primary goal was to so threaten the Federal capital and the Army of the Potomac that Meade could dispatch no additional reinforcements to Tennessee. The movement might also offer a chance to fall upon the retreating Federals and inflict great harm. Lee directed A. P. Hill to lead the march with his corps; Ewell's would follow. Moving first to Madison Court House, the army would there turn northeast to threaten Culpeper and Meade.[3]

Stuart, leading Hampton's division, would precede Hill and cover the right flank of the infantry, screening it from interference and observation by Union troops. Fitz Lee's division, supported by two batteries of horse artillery and an infantry brigade from Rodes' division of Ewell's corps, would remain behind the Rapidan to guard Lee's rear as the army marched away. The cavalrymen were to convince Federal pickets that the Rebel army remained in place, or, failing that, cast doubt on its destination.[4]

Like many of Lee's stratagems, this one was risky. With Longstreet's troops gone, the manpower discrepancy between the two armies had become significant. Though Lee needed every man in the ranks, he recognized that this movement might be beyond the capabilities of some soldiers. Before setting out, officers informed their men that, although they expected everyone to do his duty, any soldier without shoes who so chose, would be allowed to stay behind. Like their commander, most of Lee's veterans disdained physical limitations. Only a relative handful remained in camp, while barefoot thousands took up the march.[5]

The Army of Northern Virginia filed onto the road before dawn on October 9. For the first time since Gettysburg Lee had assumed the offensive, and for many men keen to square accounts with the Yankees this thrilling moment had been too long in coming. Even Providence seemed to smile on their venture. The magnificent weather was all marching soldiers could ask, and panoplies of brilliantly colored fall leaves fashioned a stunning backdrop for the moving columns. One Rebel, inspired to poetic metaphor, marveled at "the crimson foliage of the woods," which "rivaled the tint of the red battle flags fluttering above the long glittering hedge of bayonets."[6]

---

3 Previous two paragraphs from Longstreet, *From Manassas to Appomattox*, 469.

4 *OR* 29, pt. 1, 439-40, 462-63.

5 Long "Reminiscences," in Breckinridge Papers, LC.

6 Ibid.; Robertson, *A .P. Hill*, 233.

But autumn's beauty also meant fewer hours of daylight, and the Confederates could not afford to waste a single minute of sunshine. By 4 a.m. Hill's corps was moving briskly—marching hard for 50 minutes and resting 10 out of every hour. Ewell's corps, starting later, strained to match Hill's pace. Despite moderate temperatures, the march was punishing. That first day the army traversed more than 20 miles of rough fields, piney woods, and rocky hills—a difficult route spawned by necessity. Preventing the enemy from discovering this first stage of his advance provided Lee's only real chance to steal a head start on Meade. If his opponent realized what was happening, he could withdraw along a straight line toward the defenses around Centreville or Alexandria, traversing much easier terrain on either side of the Orange & Alexandria RR in the process. With a superior path, Meade might be able to get his army out of harm's way and deny Lee an opportunity to strike.[7]

With stealth the key to success, the army studiously avoided giving away its position. Officers forbade bugle calls or cook fires and discouraged talking among the troops. In some areas, engineers built walls of pine brush to screen the moving formations. Whenever possible the columns avoided sandy and dry spots in the road, hoping to prevent tell-tale pillars of dust from alerting enemy scouts. Even civilians who watched the army pass seemed cognizant of the need for secrecy. Standing silently as the troops hustled by, they offered Lee's soldiers what food they could spare. Some even passed out cast-off shoes gathered from abandoned Federal camps.

Such efforts were of little avail. For some days, Yankee pickets along the Rapidan had noticed signs of a pending enemy move. On October 2 Warren reported "unusual activity" in Confederate camps, and the next day, Meade telegraphed Halleck of indications pointing toward some sort of maneuver by Lee. However, just when, where, or why the Southern general would move Meade could not say.

Although he had no idea what Lee might be up to, Meade sensed something was brewing and strove to prepare his army to react quickly if the need arose. On October 4, when John Sedgwick took his VI Corps on regular duty rotation to replace the II Corps along the Rapidan, Meade had cautioned him not to haul anything to the river "which cannot be got out of the way with facility and rapidity." When Sedgwick's regiments assumed their picket posts, Gouverneur Warren's corps positioned itself north of Culpeper on and around Fleetwood Heights. The rest of the army remained as before, with French's III Corps northwest of the Court House, George Sykes' V Corps near Stevensburg, and John Newton's I Corps guarding the Rapidan upstream and west of Morton's Ford.

7 Long "Reminiscences," LC; Kirkpatrick Diary, October 9, 1863, UT; Robert K. Krick, *Civil War Weather in Virginia* (Tuscaloosa, AL, 2002), 100. At 7 a.m. on Oct. 9 the temperature was 42 degrees, 67 at 2 p.m., and by 9 p.m., 52.

A Union signal station atop Pony Mountain, drawn by Alfred Waud in late September 1863. *Library of Congress*

By October 7, clearer evidence of a coming Confederate movement came to light. Having cracked their enemy's signal flag code, Union observers atop nearby mountains reported a sudden flurry of communication concerning the area around Madison Court House and James City. Even more worrisome, the signalmen noted "most of the Rebel generals" had met with Lee at his headquarters that evening. The next day, Union lookouts noticed Southern camps along the banks of the Rapidan beginning to disappear. Clearly Lee was up to something.[8]

In Washington, Secretary of War Stanton, basking in the successful transfer of the XI and XII corps to Tennessee, knew nothing of trouble developing on the Rapidan. In a letter to one of his generals on October 9, the secretary declared "all quiet along the

---

8 Previous paragraphs based on *OR* 29, pt. 2, 242, 251-52 (quote), 263, 266, 916.

Potomac," before predicting with unveiled sarcasm that nothing would disturb the "autumnal slumbers" of Meade's army. Stanton could not have been more wrong.[9]

*　　*　　*

The Confederates moved without hindrance throughout October 9. Hill's corps and Ewell's troops trailing behind cut across country, "following no particular road," in the words of one infantryman, until halting late in the day in a series of nameless fields. Bad roads and avoidance of every prominent hill and field made the going difficult. Whether the circuitous path succeeded in shielding the march from the enemy wasn't clear; that it made for a rough hike, none would argue.[10]

At least the trek north afforded relief from the familiar landscape south of the Rapidan. Any advance into new territory, friendly or hostile, meant a chance to forage, and the fields and farms along an army's route were fair game. Hungry soldiers took what they needed, if not always what they wanted. Officers were sometimes around to issue receipts for the provender carried away, sometimes not. Regardless, troops often felt entitled, as either defenders of the nation, or invaders punishing disloyalty, to do as they wished. The scavenging around Madison Court House proved disappointing, but as the march drifted farther north, chestnuts, apples and persimmons came to hand.

Foraging did not keep Lee's men from paying close attention to their itinerary. His army's enlisted ranks boasted many accomplished military observers and practiced strategists by this point in the war. It did not take them long to deduce Lee's plan to outflank Meade or get between the Federals and Washington. This didn't particularly trouble the general. He did, however, prefer to keep Meade guessing, and in this regard Southern newspapers were proving most unhelpful.[11]

In an October 7 article, the Richmond *Examiner* had refuted a report that Ewell's corps was crossing the Rapidan. Nonetheless, it stated "the impression prevails in the army that they are on the eve of important events." The next day the paper noted rumors circulating throughout the capital about Lee's next move; among these a story claiming Stuart's cavalry had forded the Rapidan near Liberty Mills. On the very day Lee began his turning movement, the *Examiner* told its readers that reports from Orange Court House stated the army on the march, although it admitted it had "no information from official quarters" about an offensive. By October 10, the

9 Bauer, "Rail Transfer," *Civil War Magazine* (Mar., 1988) 12:68.

10 Kirkpatrick diary, October 10, 1863, UT; Howard, *Recollections*, 233.

11 Previous paragraphs based on Kirkpatrick diary, October 10, 1863, UT; Howard, *Recollections*, 233; Long "Reminiscences," in Breckinridge Papers, LC.

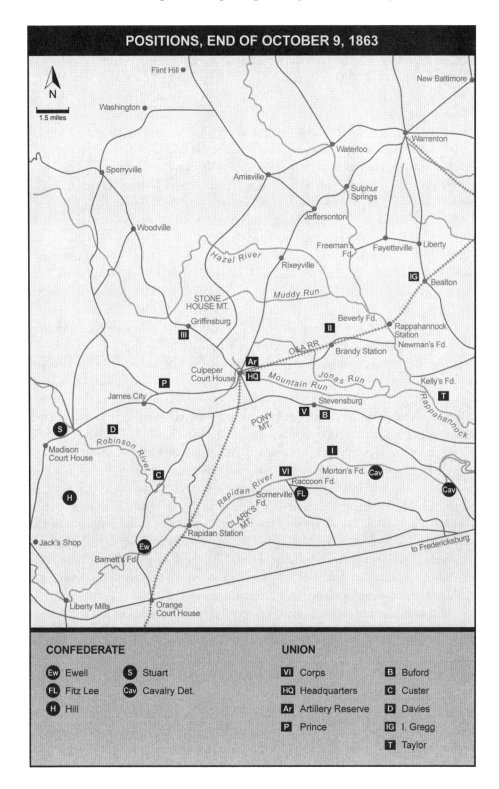

POSITIONS, END OF OCTOBER 9, 1863

N
1.5 miles

Flint Hill
New Baltimore
Washington
Waterloo
Warrenton
Sperryville
Amisville
Sulphur Springs
Jeffersonton
Woodville
Freeman's Fd
Fayetteville
Liberty
Hazel River
Rixeyville
IG
Bealton
Muddy Run
STONE HOUSE MT.
Griffinsburg
Beverly Fd.
Rappahannock Station
III
II
Newman's Fd.
O&A RR
Brandy Station
Ar
Culpeper Court House
HQ
Mountain Run
Jonas Run
Kelly's Fd.
P
James City
Stevensburg
T
V
B
Rappahannock
S
D
PONY MT.
Madison Court House
Robinson River
C
I
VI
Morton's Fd.
Cav
H
Raccoon Fd.
Rapidan River
Somerville Fd.
FL
Cav
CLARK'S MT.
Jack's Shop
Rapidan Station
to Fredericksburg
Ew
Barnett's Fd
Liberty Mills
Orange Court House

CONFEDERATE

Ew Ewell   S Stuart
FL Fitz Lee   Cav Cavalry Det.
H Hill

UNION

VI Corps   B Buford
HQ Headquarters   C Custer
Ar Artillery Reserve   D Davies
P Prince   IG I. Gregg
                  T Taylor

newspaper's evidence was firmer. "The long-talked of forward movement by General Lee has at last begun," it proclaimed, before prematurely announcing that "the Army of Northern Virginia is north of the Rapidan, in hot pursuit of the Grand Army of the Potomac, which has fallen back from Culpeper Court House, and is in rapid flight for Manassas or Arlington."[12]

After alerting its readers that Lee was attempting to outflank Meade via Orange Court House and Culpeper, the paper suddenly became skittish of military secrecy. "It would be most unwise, at present, to give even such meager particulars of our plans and movements as have come to our knowledge," it explained. "We may, however, say that Ewell's corps is in the advance, with General Edward Johnson's division as a vanguard." Although incorrect in part, some wondered what further "meager" details the paper could possibly possess it was not sharing.

Having all but telegraphed Lee's plan of campaign to Washington, a couple of days later the *Examiner* emphasized the potential importance of the army's movement. "The coming week will be one of great activity with General Lee, and doubtless also with his antagonist, whether he accepts or declines battle. If he has determined to run, no tortoise pace will avail him. He must fly, and we may expect to hear of great quantities of stores being burnt and much baggage thrown away."[13]

The Richmond paper endangered the very success it predicted by its boastful and informative story. General Lee, an assiduous student of both Union and Confederate newspapers, quickly learned of the *Examiner's* exposé. Although much of the paper's information was inaccurate, much was distressingly correct as well. Such reports might either forewarn Meade or corroborate other information he already had. None of this helped the Confederate cause. Secretary of War James Seddon soon heard from an angry Lee. These reports, he wrote, "are injurious to us [and] we have difficulties enough to overcome interposed by our enemies, without having them augmented by our friends." If nothing else, they served to put Meade "on his guard." Lee regretted the Richmond papers' failure to act with discretion. To prevent future problems of this nature he asked Seddon to "impress upon the editors the importance of rejecting . . . all mention of military movements until the result has been obtained." Lee's argument prompted Seddon to act swiftly on the general's request. The newspaper editors agreed to do as Lee asked, but some weren't happy about it.[14]

Meade didn't need the Southern press to tell him the Rebels were moving. He had abundant indications by late morning on October 8 that the enemy was marching into

12 *Richmond Examiner*, October 7-10, 1863.

13 Ibid, October 10, 12.

14 *OR* 29, pt. 1, 405-406; ibid., October 12.

Madison County. Meade ordered Kilpatrick's cavalry and a division of III Corps infantry to the vicinity of James City, a tiny village midway between Madison and Culpeper, with instructions to keep a sharp lookout for a possible attack.[15]

The dawning of October 9 only amplified Meade's concerns as a flood of messages poured into army headquarters. Signal stations on Thoroughfare, Stone House, Clark's, Pony, and Cedar Mountains were reporting the disappearance of tents and campfire smoke south of the Rapidan as well as movement of heavy bodies of Confederate troops and wagon trains around Orange Court House. Intercepted enemy signal flag communications confirmed that Lee was undertaking a major endeavor. Meade, accompanied by his chief of staff, Major General Andrew A. Humphreys, went out to see for himself, riding to the top of Cedar Mountain to examine the Rapidan line. From there they saw columns of Rebel infantry and cavalry moving in the direction of Madison Court House.[16]

Further reports coming in from I Corps pickets produced a stream of messages from Maj. Gen. Newton, including news that Rebel artillery had departed the defensive works along the river. Some of his subordinates also claimed that cavalry had replaced Confederate infantry guarding the fords at several locations. Union sentinels had heard the familiar sounds of Rebel drums beating reveille at an unusually early hour or, inexplicably, not at all that morning. In light of all this, Newton surmised the enemy was evacuating the Rapidan line in a rolling fashion from east to west.[17]

By that evening, Meade had no doubt his opponent was shifting position. But the intelligence gathered thus far shed no light on where the ANV was going or why. Pleasonton thought the Southerners were preparing to abandon the Rapidan and retreat to Richmond. Indeed, he told Meade he had information the enemy was preparing to evacuate his capital. Lee's westward march was merely a feint to buy time for the Confederate government to leave the city.[18]

Pleasonton's far-fetched theory aside, Meade could deduce only two logical conclusions from the available evidence. Either the Rebels had undertaken an offensive designed to turn the Federal right flank, or they were retreating from the Rapidan toward some defensive line further south. Neither Meade nor anyone else could determine which was taking place.[19]

---

15 *OR* 29, pt. 2, 266.

16 Humphreys, *From Gettysburg to the Rapidan*, 12-13; *OR* 29, pt. 2, 269-71.

17 *OR* 29, pt. 2, 269-73.

18 Humphreys, *From Gettysburg to the Rapidan*, 12-13.

19 James Biddle to wife, October 9, 1863, HSP.

For the commander of the Union army this frustrating situation distressingly resembled the one he had faced in the Loudoun Valley at the end of July. Uncertain whether Lee was plotting a post-Gettysburg offensive or attempting to slip through the Blue Ridge Mountains toward the Rappahannock, then, as now, contradictory intelligence reports had led him to vacillate between defensive and offensive action. Eventually proving more fearful of a counterstrike than willing to attempt a bold thrust of his own, Meade had halted his army for 35 critical hours to prepare for a Rebel attack that never materialized. When he finally had gone over to the offensive, it was too late and too feeble to foil Lee's plans. That lack of decisiveness had allowed the Confederates to escape the Shenandoah Valley and return to the Rappahannock virtually untouched—much to the frustration of the administration and the public.

Absent the intervening mountains, Meade's current circumstances were exactly the same. If Lee was on the offensive, the Federal army needed either to prepare for a battle around Culpeper or retreat to safer ground north of the Rappahannock. If, on the other hand, the Rebels were withdrawing, Meade could not allow them to escape without immediate, aggressive pursuit. Although he feared the Confederates were actually launching an attack, the ghosts of Falling Waters and Manassas Gap haunted Meade. That Lee might once again give his army the slip not only disturbed the general, it could well cost him his job.

Meade therefore determined to avoid the error he had made in July. He would refuse to let the dread of an enemy offensive prevent him from positioning troops for a vigorous pursuit of a retreating foe. Despite the evidence, and his own suspicions, the general decided to commit half his army to an offensive even as he prepared the other half to receive an attack issuing forth from Madison County.

*   *   *

At 6:30 p.m. on October 9, army headquarters directed Pleasonton to concentrate David M. Gregg's 2nd Cavalry Division at Culpeper Court House and expand Kilpatrick's zone of observation to include the Woodville Road, running northwest of town toward Sperryville. To the east, Buford's 1st Cavalry Division would force its way over the Rapidan at Germanna Ford "as soon as possible." After gaining the south bank, Buford would ride upstream and drive the enemy away from Morton's Ford so Newton's I Corps could cross the river. Meade's chief of staff, Maj. Gen. Humphreys, amended that plan an hour later. The new scheme called for Newton to move across the Rapidan as soon as Buford sent word that he was south of Germanna Ford.[20]

20 *OR* 29, pt. 2, 272.

The I Corps would wait for Buford at Morton's Ford. Once united, they were to "follow the enemy in the direction of Orange Court House" and report frequently on where the Rebels were going. Upon receiving word that both Buford and Newton were over the Rapidan, Sedgwick was to cross the river with the VI Corps at whatever point he thought practicable and join the I Corps in a drive on Rapidan Station. Once there, the infantry would take position on the heights overlooking the railroad crossing while Buford pursued the Confederates toward Orange Court House.[21]

If Lee's destination *was* Richmond, Meade saw an opportunity to shift his command eastward toward Fredericksburg. He had always preferred an axis of advance from Aquia Creek across the Rappahannock at Fredericksburg and then southward to the Rebel capital. If Lee was pulling back to the east, Meade would have to follow, necessitating a much desired change of base for the Army of the Potomac. So strongly did Meade hope this to be the case, he sent Brig. Gen. Henry W. Benham (commanding the army's engineer brigade) to Washington with orders to assemble equipment to bridge the Rappahannock at Fredericksburg. Benham was to be ready to ship his pontoons south the instant Meade called.[22]

Whatever was unfolding, the army would be moving soon and perhaps in hurried circumstances. Since September 21, Union troops had been under orders to carry five days' rations at all times. Though burdensome, this requirement would allow the army to travel suddenly and without supply trains, at least for a short time. With Lee on the march, Meade reiterated his order and told his generals to have their commands "in readiness to move at very short notice."[23]

At 7 p.m. Meade telegraphed Halleck a summary of the current intelligence and the steps he'd taken—both offensive and defensive—to meet any contingency. He could not yet say for certain whether Lee was trying to turn his flank or withdrawing to the south, but Meade did pass on news that Rebel pickets were overheard saying Lee had sent additional troops to Bragg. If this gossip was fact, it spelled more trouble at Chattanooga.[24]

---

21 Ibid., 268, 272-73, 276. This order is dated October 9, 6:30 a.m., but this must be incorrect. Humphreys in *From Gettysburg to the Rapidan*, 13, specifically says Buford's orders were issued on the evening of October 9. This is likely so: all other orders regarding this movement were issued between 7-8 p.m.

22 Ibid., 273; Humphreys, *From Gettysburg to the Rapidan*, 14. Actually Meade thought the James River approach to Richmond the one "true" approach, but he knew Lincoln disapproved of that line.

23 *OR* 29, pt. 2, 275.

24 Ibid., 276.

Halleck responded by telling Meade that Rosecrans was reporting that more troops from Lee's army were arriving in Tennessee. Of course, this wasn't true. But the shifting of Rebel units from east to west had burned Union commanders once, and they didn't want to get burned again. As for how Meade should discover Lee's real intentions, Halleck advised, "attack him and you will soon find out." Such counsel did nothing to help Meade make the decisions he now faced. Since he couldn't launch a full scale attack without knowing Lee's exact position, Meade hoped Buford's and Newton's pending thrust over the Rapidan might reveal something. At the moment, however, all the news was coming from the army's right flank.[25]

*   *   *

Chaos ruled the night of October 9 at Union army headquarters. At 10:15 p.m. Meade upped the ante on his push across the Rapidan River by instructing Sykes to move his V Corps closer to the river and to stand ready to support Newton and Sedgwick. But just 45 minutes later, Meade's uncertainty about what Lee *was* doing and what his own army *should be* doing began to get the best of him. In an 11 p.m. message to Newton, the commanding general reiterated that the thrust south had been based upon a possibly "erroneous" supposition that the Rebels were retreating. The I Corps' leader should "exercise prudence" and make no "unnecessary sacrifice in attempting to cross the river." Operating under the impression that he was to strike Morton's Ford regardless of how strongly it was held, this equivocation perplexed Newton. He diplomatically advised that the army should either launch a major attack or launch none at all. If the Confederates were retreating, the prudent course was to act audaciously. If the enemy intended to hold Morton's Ford, the position would be a tough nut to crack, and no half measures would do. In either case it would make sense to assault with maximum force. Newton urged Meade to firmly commit the V and VI corps to his support.[26]

General Newton's frustration with a lack of clarity from headquarters was shared in the bivouacs of the 1st Cavalry Division. Meade's imprecise orders for a mounted offensive across the Rapidan did little to facilitate coordination with the I Corps. Nothing in the written instructions to Pleasonton or Buford said whether Meade wanted his troopers to storm the river during the night or sometime early next morning. The high command anticipated that Buford would "probably be over the

25 Ibid., 278 (quote), 279.

26 *OR* 29, pt. 2, 274-76.

river by daylight," and the I Corps south of the Rapidan shortly afterwards. But no one seems to have communicated this expectation to the cavalry.[27]

That failure was soon irrelevant. The order issued from Pleasonton's headquarters at 7:20 p.m. on October 9 for the 1st Cavalry Division to seize Germanna Ford went astray during the night. Buford didn't receive the directive until sometime past sunrise on October 10, almost twelve hours after its dispatch.[28]

The timing could not have been worse. Buford's supply wagons were in Culpeper awaiting replenishment. The division didn't have a single bag of feed on hand. But with his orders already 12 hours old, the Kentuckian simply couldn't wait for either wagons or grain. Buford left word for his supply vehicles to be loaded as quickly as possible and then sent to Morton's Ford, where he assumed they would join him once Newton seized the crossing. Finally, at 8:30 a.m. his troopers rode out of Stevensburg for the Rapidan, accompanied by batteries D and B&L of the 2nd US Artillery.[29]

*   *   *

As Buford's horsemen belatedly moved south, Stuart's regiments delivered the first blows of Lee's offensive. The Confederate cavalry's job was to ensure its Yankee counterpart learned little of what the ANV was doing. Still seeking further redemption for his Gettysburg performance, Stuart was determined to succeed. On the evening of October 9, while Fitz Lee's command remained along the Rapidan guarding the army's rear and screening its absence, Hampton's division, still under Stuart's personal command, massed near Madison Court House and threw its picket line forward to Robertson's River.

When the army resumed moving next morning, Jones' brigade, under Col. Funsten's command, would be the vanguard of Hill's corps. Accompanied by Stuart and his corps headquarters, the other two brigades of Hampton's division, led by Cols. James B. Gordon and Pierce M. B. Young would cross the river at Russell's Ford. Their mission was to keep Meade's cavalry so occupied its prying eyes would remain far from the advancing gray infantry.[30]

27 Ibid., 274.

28 Ibid., pt. 1, 347; Krick, *Civil War Weather in Virginia*, 110, says sunrise on October 10 in Richmond occurred at 7:16 a.m.

29 *OR* 29, pt. 1, 347; Gilpin Diary, October 9, 1863, LC. Chapman continued in command of the absent William Gamble's brigade.

30 *OR* 29 pt. 1, 439. Jones was being court-martialed for insulting Stuart.

The Rebel troopers were in high spirits. Rumor had it the Federals had transferred four corps to Tennessee. If this talk were true, thought one trooper, "Lee will not be long in pitching into Meade." The concentration of Hampton's division left no illusions about what lay ahead, and the Southern horseman confidentially looked for "the ball to open in the morning."[31]

Events soon tested such prophecy. At 3:00 a.m. on October 10, Stuart led his brigades toward the river. The 4th North Carolina Cavalry riding at the head of the column quietly gobbled up a handful of Union pickets posted at Russell's Ford. The Federals charged with guarding the area had to decide quickly what to do. Companies C and D of the 5th New York Cavalry were familiar with these kinds of circumstances and wisely took a position on the road to James City in anticipation of fighting a delaying action. The far less mobile 120th New York Infantry formed a line of battle at Bethsaida Church about one mile from the river. Utterly outnumbered and terribly exposed, the regiment might have fled with no fear of reproach. It officers, however, refused: They would stand their ground as ordered. Despite this gritty decision, the New Yorkers were in a hopeless position and merely waiting for the predictable disaster to unfold.[32]

The wait was shorter than many expected. After ordering Gordon to dismount sharpshooters and move directly against the Federal line, General Stuart sent Young's brigade to turn the Union's exposed right. Seeing what was happening, one nervous bluecoat observed that, despite "imperative orders" to hold their ground, the ranks fidgeted in anticipation of the word to fall back. Unfortunately, their hesitant officers delayed delivering that inevitable command until it was too late. Just as the regiment got the order to withdraw, the Rebels struck, catching the enemy formation in mid-motion.

After circling through some woods, Young emerged to charge the Yankee flank and rear. At the same instant Gordon launched his men in an attack from the front. The 120th New York stood no chance at all to successfully repel the enemy and, as Stuart put it, managed only a slight resistance before it "broke and fled in all directions." Southern cavalry quickly chased down the fugitives. Though many were loath to surrender, with death the only alternative, one after another the Federals threw down their weapons and gave up. Young believed his troopers killed or captured nearly every man in the 120th. The total prisoner haul amounted to 115 men, plus "large numbers"

---

31 Corson, *My Dear Jennie*, 109.

32 OR 29, pt. 1, 460, 440; Van Santvoord, C., *The One Hundred and Twentieth Regiment New York State Volunteers. A Narrative of its Services in the War for the Union* (Rondout, NY, 1894), 87; *Daily Morning Chronicle*, Oct. 13, 1863.

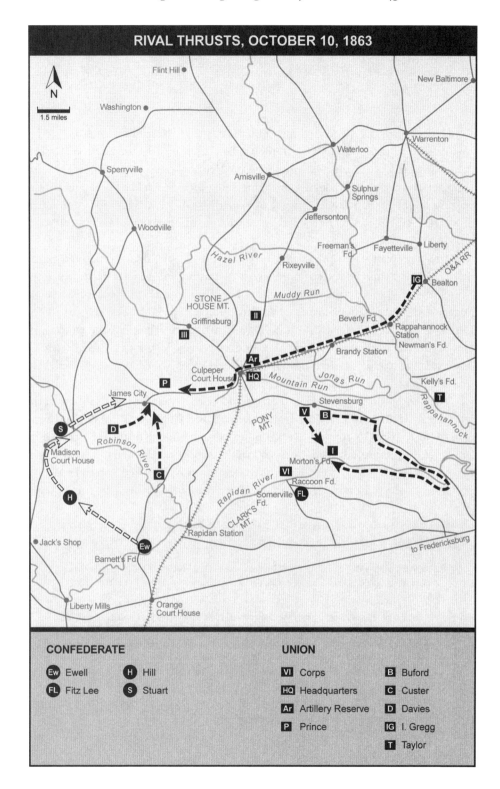

RIVAL THRUSTS, OCTOBER 10, 1863

N
1.5 miles

Flint Hill
New Baltimore
Washington
Waterloo
Warrenton
Sperryville
Amisville
Sulphur Springs
Woodville
Jeffersonton
Hazel River
Freeman's Fd
Fayetteville
Liberty
O&A RR
Rixeyville
Muddy Run
IG
Bealton
STONE HOUSE MT.
Beverly Fd.
II
Griffinsburg
Rappahannock Station
III
Newman's Fd.
Ar
Brandy Station
Culpeper Court House
HQ
Mountain Run
Jonas Run
Kelly's Fd.
P
Rappahannock
James City
Stevensburg
T
D
V
B
PONY MT.
C
I
Robinson River
Morton's Fd.
S
VI
Madison Court House
Raccoon Fd.
Rapidan River
Somerville Fd.
FL
H
CLARK'S MT.
Jack's Shop
Rapidan Station
to Fredericksburg
Ew
Barnett's Fd
Liberty Mills
Orange Court House

CONFEDERATE

Ew Ewell   H Hill
FL Fitz Lee   S Stuart

UNION

VI Corps   B Buford
HQ Headquarters   C Custer
Ar Artillery Reserve D Davies
P Prince   IG I. Gregg
                       T Taylor

of what one Rebel staff officer called "the newest, brightest and handsomest muskets ever handled."[33]

*   *   *

Having neatly dispatched this minor obstacle, Stuart detached a detail from the 5th Virginia to escort the captives to Gordonsville. The rest of his cavalry rode toward James City, which was the next stop between Madison County and Culpeper Court House, itself a mere eight miles distant. Skirmishing with the 5th New York most of the way, they soon ran into Davies' brigade of Kilpatrick's division, which Pleasonton had dispatched to James City several days ago to guard against the very threat now unfolding.[34]

The tiny town had a population of about 100 people, their homes and farms dotting the landscape around an impressive two-story inn and popular stagecoach stop. Kilpatrick hoped to deny the village to the Rebels. Unfortunately that exceeded a single brigade's capabilities. As Stuart's regiments approached, Kilpatrick sent word for Custer to hurry his regiments north to Davies' assistance. That message would take time to reach its destination, and it would take even longer for Custer's widely dispersed command to arrive near James City. Davies would probably need help sooner than his fellow brigadier could provide it.[35]

Theoretically, this unavoidable delay should be irrelevant for more substantial aid was close at hand. Army headquarters had detailed Brig. Gen. Henry Prince's III Corps division to Kilpatrick's support over 24 hours ago, and now Kilpatrick beseeched its assistance. But Prince, a half-mile east and worried about the strength of his own line, dragged his feet. Davies had no choice but to retreat across Crooked Run and take up a position on some hills northeast of town. These combined movements forced Capt.

33 OR 29, pt. 1, 457-458; 460; Escek Wilber to parents, October 24, 1863, RICE; John Esten Cooke, *Wearing of the Gray; Personal Portraits, Scenes and Adventures of the War* (New York, 1867), 265.

34 OR 29, pt. 1, 384 & pt. 2, 268; Van Santvoord, *120th New York*, 91; Louis N. Boudrye, *Historic Records of the Fifth New York Cavalry: First Ira Harris Guard* (Albany, NY, 1865), 78. Stuart reports that he skirmished with the 5th Michigan Cavalry, but this is incorrect. Davies makes clear it was the 5th New York from his brigade, and the regimental history confirms that point. The 5th Michigan, part of Custer's command, was well to the south at this time.

35 James City is modern day Leon, Virginia. Bill Backus and Robert Orrison, *A Want of Vigilance: The Bristoe Station Campaign, October 9-19, 1863.* (El Dorado, CA, 2015), 16. Custer regiments were spread out along Robertson's River south of James City.

Peter Taylor to abandon the Federal signal station on Thoroughfare Mountain—a major coup in Stuart's effort to blind Meade to Lee's movements.[36]

Although the Federals had lost the town and their observation post, they occupied a powerful line on high ground, with Crooked Run between them and the Rebels. Upon looking it over, Stuart decided against an attack. Seeking to hold the enemy's attention, rather than stirring up a fight, the general spent the rest of the day demonstrating in front of the Union position.[37]

Confederate regiments moved back and forth, sometimes exposing themselves to view then disappearing, in an elaborate version of hide and seek designed to confuse Kilpatrick about his enemies' numbers and intentions. Shortly after noon, two guns from Capt. William H. Griffin's Maryland Battery of horse artillery unlimbered and began periodically engaging the cannon of Capt. Samuel S. Elder's Battery E, 4th US Artillery, on a hill east of town. As the Yankee fieldpieces responded, the terrified remaining citizens of James City found themselves caught in the crossfire.

As the afternoon wore on, both sides brought up reinforcements. Captain James F. Hart's battery of Confederate horse artillery trundled forward to join the struggle. At 3 p.m. Custer's brigade arrived on the hills east of James City. Kilpatrick directed him to place his command on Davies' left, directly opposite the town. Upon doing so, Custer found his position dangerously exposed to Stuart's guns and quickly ordered Lt. Alexander Pennington's Battery M, 2nd US Artillery, into the fight.[38]

In the midst of the growing artillery duel, the ever-aggressive Custer decided to drive off or capture the Rebel cannon. At 4 p.m. a battalion of the 5th Michigan under Maj. John Clark dashed toward Griffin's Battery. Unfortunately for the Yankees, the Confederates anticipated such impulsiveness. As Clark's galloping troopers closed to within 200 yards of the guns, a body of 50 sharpshooters from the 1st South Carolina Cavalry rose up from behind a stone wall to fire into the attackers. Their deadly volley emptied several saddles and broke the charge, forcing the Yankees to beat a speedy retreat. After this, neither side tried to close with the enemy. Before long the firing sputtered to a halt although the rival battle lines sullenly held their ground.[39]

This stalemate was exactly what the Confederates wanted. Without much of a fight, they had frozen a good portion of Meade's cavalry in place, keeping it a long way from the gray infantry. Content that they were accomplishing their mission, Stuart and his staff dismounted to rest behind a fringe of trees gracing a hilltop west of town. They

---

36 OR 29, pt. 1, 380-81, 389-90, 230.

37 Ibid., 440.

38 Ibid., 380-81, 389-90.

39 Ibid., 458, 389-90.

could see Yankee cavalry on the other side of the valley but believed their own position immune to observation. They were wrong.

Although the Rebel horses and their riders were out of sight, Stuart's headquarters flag floated lazily in the breeze above the scattering of timber. Union artillerymen spotted this telltale evidence of enemy troops and fired a single projectile in its direction. The Southerners were causally lying on the ground napping when they heard the Yankee missile whistling toward them. Before the Confederates could react, a percussion shell struck the ground within four feet of Captain John Esten Cooke of Stuart's staff.

The round burst instantly, gouging a hole in the earth and showering Cooke with dirt. Fortunately the shell's fragments whirled through the air harmlessly, striking neither man nor beast, although startling both. The Federal battery sought to capitalize on its outstanding aim by throwing more ordnance in Stuart's direction. By the time additional shells rained down on the area, however, the general and his companions had scattered—each laughing at Cooke's distress and their own narrow escape from Kilpatrick's gunners. Although harmless in and of itself, this little bombardment renewed the shooting, which continued until nightfall without inflicting damage or altering the standoff between the two forces.[40]

*   *   *

Meanwhile, eight miles away in Culpeper Court House, Meade grew more apprehensive about Lee's menace to his right. When the Army of the Potomac had first occupied the vulnerable Culpeper V a few weeks ago, the general prudently laid out a defensive front for his divisions to assume should the enemy cross the Rapidan. Now, with the Rebels active along Robertson's River, Meade decided it was time to occupy at least the western flank of this line.

He ordered Warren's corps and most of French's command to take their pre-designated positions west and northwest of Culpeper. Prince's division would maintain its station supporting Kilpatrick, but should be prepared to fall back on the III Corps if necessary. Meade warned Sedgwick, Sykes, and Newton that, although the planned attack across the Rapidan was still on, enemy activities might necessitate dropping the offensive at any moment: they should be ready to pull back to positions near Culpeper Court House on short notice.[41]

40 Cooke, *Wearing of the Gray*, 265-66.

41 Van Santvoord, *120th New York*, 87; OR 29, pt. 2, 279, 280-81.

Yet Meade wasn't altogether positive he should be preparing to fight a defensive battle. Rebel actions to the west might be the start of an offensive or nothing more than an elaborate ruse. He desperately needed to know which, but until Buford told headquarters what was happening south of the Rapidan, Meade couldn't unravel the mystery. But here was the rub. Despite the fact that the movement of three corps was waiting on the progress of the 1st Cavalry Division neither Pleasonton nor Meade had received a single report from across the river.

Inexplicably, army headquarters had no idea that Buford hadn't marched until well after sunrise on October 10. Meade assumed the thrust south had been well underway for many hours. Thus the total want of communication from Buford was unnerving. At 9:15 a.m. Humphreys, queried Sykes—whose V Corps, had been positioned to support the attack southward since 8 a.m—asking the location of the I Corps and whether Sykes had heard from Buford. The corps commander's response was hardly enlightening. He could say only that the I Corps maintained its position north of the river and that he had no information about Buford, nor did Newton.[42]

*   *   *

While frustration and worry swirled about Meade's headquarters, at 11 a.m. the head of Buford's column finally came within sight of the Rapidan River. It took an hour for his command to fully deploy opposite Germanna Ford. But to their relief, few Confederates were around to challenge them. Just one squadron of the 1st Maryland Cavalry, a mere 110 men, defended the five miles between Mitchell's and Germanna fords on the Rapidan. With the Rebels so thinly spread, Buford saw no need for finesse and ordered a direct frontal assault.

At 1 p.m. the 8th Illinois Cavalry plunged into the river and charged across the ford. If even a few cannon still occupied the Rebel earthworks, such an attack would have been little better than suicide. But there were no enemy guns, and the horsemen easily seized the opposite shore, capturing fifteen dismounted Marylanders before they could get back to their horses. With Union troopers at last on the Rapidan's south bank, Buford ordered the rest of his division over the river. After crossing "in haste," as one Northerner put it, the Federal regiments turned west toward Morton's Ford.[43]

At almost the same instant, the context of the attack across the Rapidan began unraveling dramatically. The Union high command had become increasingly certain

42 *OR* 29, pt. 2, 281, 284.

43 *OR* 29, pt. 1, 465, 347-348, 463; Hard, *8th Illinois Cavalry*, 277; Gilpin Diary, October 10, 1863, LC, Chapman Diary, October 10, 1863, ISHS.

Lee wasn't retiring southward. Meade telegraphed Halleck at noon that although he had yet to hear anything from Buford, he knew Stuart had spilled over Robertson's River in force and was skirmishing heavily with Kilpatrick on the army's right flank. "[E]very indication" pointed toward a "large force of infantry" supporting the Rebel cavalry. Moreover, some signs suggested Lee might be slipping into the Shenandoah, which could mean another invasion of the North. The only good news Meade had was that no additional troops had left Lee's army for Tennessee.[44]

Neither in Culpeper or Washington could this have been reassuring. Meanwhile, engulfed in the fog of war around army headquarters, Meade sweated out the arrival of information from the cavalry on both his flanks. Nervous reports from the III Corps accentuated his worries about enemy activity near James City. But from the direction of Germanna and Morton's fords there came only a disconcerting silence.[45]

*   *   *

On the other side of the Rapidan, John Buford knew nothing of the angst at headquarters. His men moved over the rough country on the south bank of the river, skirmishing with a detachment of 5th Virginia Cavalry sharpshooters led by Lt. Col. Henry Pate. These annoying Rebels aside, he met no significant opposition and easily captured surprised enemy pickets at several other fords. Throughout the afternoon the Union cavalrymen hurried toward a link up with Newton's I Corps, which they trusted had fought its way over the Rapidan without too much difficulty. They need not have worried: Newton had not assaulted the enemy's river defenses nor did he await the cavalry's assistance. In fact, when Buford reached the vicinity of Morton Ford's, the I Corps was nowhere near there or even the Rapidan itself.[46]

Newton was absent because Meade finally decided Lee was maneuvering to turn his flank, not withdrawing southward. At 3:15 p.m. on October 10, army headquarters ordered Sykes' V Corps back to a defensive position in front of Culpeper. Shortly thereafter, Meade alerted Newton and Sedgwick to be ready to follow Sykes at "a moment's notice." At 4 p.m. the entire army was ordered to move its supply trains along with all railroad rolling stock north of the Rappahannock. The quartermaster depot at Culpeper Court House would be broken up and its stockpiles shifted to Bealton. Within the next thirty minutes, Sedgwick and Newton received orders to retreat as soon as it was dark, the I Corps to Stevensburg, the VI toward Culpeper.

---

44 *OR* 29, pt. 2, 278.

45 Ibid., 282-84.

46 Hard, *8th Illinois Cavalry*, 277; ibid., pt. 1, 347-48, 463; Gilpin Diary, October 10, 1863, LC.

Pleasonton dispatched couriers to find Buford and also order him back across the Rapidan.[47]

Almost as if he intuitively sensed something amiss in the Culpeper V, less than an hour later, at 4:55 p.m., a concerned President Lincoln wired Meade to learn what was happening. He tried not to sound too anxious: "Am interested with your dispatch of noon. How is it now?" A quick reply was not forthcoming. Meade's headquarters and telegraph stations were all on the move; he could neither receive nor reply to telegrams from the capital. The general wouldn't answer Lincoln's inquiry until 8:30 a.m. the next morning—and the news would not be good.[48]

*   *   *

With the Army of the Potomac coiling itself defensively around Culpeper—a fact of which John Buford was completely unacquainted—the 1st Cavalry Division was left without support and to its own devices. After reaching the environs of Morton's Ford after nightfall, Buford's cavalrymen drove Southern pickets into a ring of entrenchments overlooking the river. The Yankees suspected that a considerable Rebel force occupied this final bulwark commanding the crossing. Confident that an attack by the I Corps the next day would force the Rebs away, Buford declined to press his assault and ordered his men into bivouac.[49]

That night both Meade and Buford remained ignorant of the other's situation. The Confederates, however, knew exactly where the 1st Cavalry Division was and were moving to meet it. Brigadier General Fitzhugh Lee got word of Buford's whereabouts sometime during the night and ordered Brig. Gen. Lomax to send a regiment to Morton's Ford immediately.

 Lomax swiftly dispatched Col. Thomas L. Rosser and his 5th Virginia Cavalry to make contact with Pate's sharpshooters already opposing Buford. Together they would, if possible, deny the ford to the Yankees. As Rosser's men rode out, Fitz Lee instructed Lomax to move the remainder of his brigade toward the ford at first light. What else Fitz Lee might do depended almost entirely on the state of affairs along the Rapidan come daylight. If he was to have his way, however, dawn would herald the annihilation of Buford's division.[50]

---

47 *OR* 29, pt. 2, 234, 284-85.

48 Ibid., 279, 278, 290; Luther A. Rose diary, October 10, 1863, LC.

49 *OR* 29, pt. 1, 348.

50 Ibid., 465.

CHAPTER 11

"They Came Near Bagging the Division"

Yankee Infantry Disappears—Fitz Lee's Plan—Battle for Morton's Ford—
Action at Stringfellow Farm—Devin's Fight—Buford's Withdrawal

DAWN on October 11 crept in quietly. Not long after sunrise surprised Confederates discovered the northern shore of the Rapidan deserted. Apparently the enemy had slipped away during the night, departing, one Rebel said, "like a ghost when it scents the morning air." That could only mean that Meade's infantry was withdrawing toward Culpeper; leaving Fitzhugh Lee free to concentrate his division in hopes of destroying Buford's interlopers south of the river.[1]

The morning presented Federal horsemen with an entirely different prospect. Without so much as a hint of a Union infantry assault across Morton's Ford, they were both mystified and disturbed. Clearly, the strategic situation had changed or something had gone badly wrong. An apprehensive Buford scribbled Pleasonton a message at 6 a.m.: the 1st Cavalry Division had been at Morton's Ford since eight last night, but its supports were "not to be found." Troubling rumors were drifting about that the AOP had retreated to Culpeper. Buford didn't know what was happening, but he promised to stay put and await "further instructions."[2]

The mystery at Morton's Ford wasn't resolved until 7 a.m. when a stunned Buford learned from couriers dispatched hours ago that the I Corps had retired during the night. Buford dryly observed that Meade had clearly "changed the program." The infantry slated to cooperate with his troopers was gone. Army headquarters had sent the division's supply train and horse fodder across the Rappahannock. With no new orders Buford admitted himself "at a loss to know what course to pursue."

1 Neese Diary, October 11, 1863, ACWM.

2 *OR* 29, pt. 1, 346. The source of those rumors is unclear.

Fortunately he didn't have to ponder his dilemma long. A second courier arrived carrying a long-delayed message from Pleasonton countermanding the October 10 directive to cross the Rapidan. The 1st Cavalry Division's new orders dictated a retreat north of the Rappahannock, but they said nothing about how Buford should accomplish that mission. The cavalry commander quickly realized he had only two practical options. His division could retrace its steps all the way to Germanna Ford, or it could force its way over the Rapidan at Morton's Ford. The first option would take far too much time; the general thus determined to drive the Rebels away from Morton's and cross the Rapidan at the closest point available. He struck quickly, hitting the entrenchments around the ford shortly after 7 a.m. To Buford's great relief his troopers easily drove the enemy away from the river. However, as the Federals got their first real look at the crossing point they confronted a new concern.[3]

Morton's Ford lay on a sharp northward bulge of the Rapidan that resembled a broad brimmed hat when seen on a map. Lyman called the river "a narrow affair," no more than 25 yards wide and typically just 4 feet deep. Its severely steep six to eight-foot high banks created a trench-like channel for the waterway. The colonel noted that this rendered the river "hard to get in or out" of. The actual ford centered on a small wooded islet in the middle of the Rapidan.[4]

The land north of the river was cultivated and rose gradually over a distance of 700-800 yards to a ridge and the site of the elegant two-story Greek-revival style home of Powhatan Robinson. A single road ran down to the ford from the north, tracing a path through a cleft in the bluff. The ridge west of this road rose to a height of 250 feet and ran parallel to the Rapidan for nearly three miles.[5]

The really formidable terrain lay south of the Rapidan. Here the land rose abruptly in what Lyman described as a series of three "rolls" culminating in a high ridge about a mile from the river. This heavily wooded elevation stretched from side to side of the river bend to create a cul-de-sac that reminded the colonel of an amphitheater. The Rebels had dug a strong line of earthworks atop the ridge that commanded the ground between their position and the center "roll" of ground. Beyond that spot, however, the terrain sloped so sharply toward the river that it created a large defilade space safe from observation or direct fire from the entrenchments.[6]

---

3   Ibid., 348

4   Lyman, *Meade's Army*, 95-96; Terence G. Crooks, *Rochester's Forgotten Regiment: The 108th New York in the Civil War*, NYMM, https://dmna.ny.gov/historic/reghist/civil/infantry/108thInf/108thinfRFR_Crookes_Chap7.htm.

5   Ibid; *OR* 3, pt. 1, 115.

6   Lyman, *Meade's Army*, 95-96; *OR* 33, pt. 1, 115.

Morton's Ford in 1891. This view is from the north bank and looks toward the high ground on the south shore. The Buckner house is visible. *From Souvenir of the 14th C.V. Excursion to the Battlefields, 1891 by Chaplain H.S. Stevens.*

Inside these fortifications stood two farms, one belonging to Dr. Jeremiah Morton (a wealthy agriculturist and former congressman) and the other to Calhoun C. Buckner, with their houses and out-buildings on the same line roughly two miles apart. Both sat upon the second elevation rising up from the Rapidan about three-quarters of a mile from the river. Morton's house stood close by the waterway on the western side of the cul-de-sac, Buckner's occupied a steep knoll in the center of the space.[7]

Two roads entered the area at acute angles from the south, one coming in from the east and passing near Buckner's house, while the other came in from the west and traced a course close to Morton's home. North of Buckner's residence the roads joined and followed a common path toward the river. After crossing over a shallow creek and then a small hillock, the roadway turned sharply northwest towards the ford. Once the road stuck the island, it veered west for a few hundred yards before making a right angle bend to head inland past the Robinson house.[8]

---

7   OR 33, pt. 1, 115, 135; Lyman, *Meade's Army,* 95-96; H. S. Stevens, *Souvenir of Excursion to Battlefields by the Society of the Fourteenth Connecticut Regiment and Reunion at Antietam, September 1891, with History and Reminiscences of Battles and Campaigns of the Regiment on the Fields Revisited.* (Washington, DC, 1893), 108.

8   Ibid.

The Morton farm as seen from the Buckner house in 1891. This area was the focal point of combat on October 11, 1863. *From Souvenir of the 14th C.V. Excursion to the Battlefields, 1891 by Chaplain H.S. Stevens.*

The paths down to the Rapidan and the ford itself had been little used and undergone no maintenance for many months. The Yankees would have to make extensive repairs to both before their artillery could even attempt to cross the river. Colonel Devin ordered his commissary officer, 1st Lt. Edward McKinney, to take charge of the brigade's pioneers and get the work done as quickly as possible. A swift completion of their difficult task was unlikely, however. Labor parties would have to cut through the bank on both sides of the ford to allow horses and vehicles to get into and out of the river. They would also need to corduroy the muddy roads with looted fence rails to keep cannon from bogging down on their way to the river's edge. This kind of axe and shovel work would require a considerable amount of time, and that commodity unfortunately favored the Rebels.[9]

*   *   *

General Lomax, accompanied by a pair of squadrons from the 1st Maryland Cavalry (140 men) and the 15th and 6th regiments of Virginia cavalry, marched from Raccoon Ford toward Morton's Ford at daylight. Two infantry units under overall command of Col. Thomas Toon—the 20th North Carolina and five companies from the 12th North Carolina—trudged along behind the cavalry in support.[10]

As Lomax's troopers neared Morton's Ford they linked up with Rosser's 5th Virginia Cavalry and Lt. Col. Pate's sharpshooters, whom Buford had ejected from the

9   OR 29, pt. 1, 348; Edward P. McKinney, *Life in Tent, Camp and Field, 1861-1865* (Boston: Badger, 1922), 35.

10 OR 29, pt. 1, 465; Clark, *North Carolina Regts*, vol. 1, 639, and vol. 2, 119, 240; Neese, *Three Years in the Confederate Horse Artillery*, 217.

ford earlier that morning. By the time Lomax came within view of the crossing, McKinney's work details had improved the site enough to allow part of Chapman's brigade and both batteries of Federal artillery to gain the north shore. To cover the retreat of Devin's brigade, some of the Yankee guns went into position on the bluff running along the north bank of the river west of the ford. From here, Union troops spotted the approaching Rebels and quickly took them under fire.

While a squadron from the 15th Virginia acted as a screen, Lomax ordered the rest of his men to occupy the earthworks and some woods on the ford's Western side. Once the Rebels manned these fortifications the 15th's squadron dismounted and joined them there. With their skirmishers thrown forward, the Confederates hunkered down to await the arrival of the rest of Fitz Lee's division.

Fighting on foot from inside earthworks was an atypical experience for Southern horsemen, who quickly discovered it as dangerous as mounted combat. Enemy sharpshooters maintained a severe fire from the shelter of the Morton and Buckner farm buildings. A section of Yankee artillery shooting from across the river inflicted several casualties and kept Lomax's men pinned in their ditches. The Rebels returned fire in hopes of preventing Devin's brigade from retreating across the Rapidan.[11]

With only part of his division over the river, Buford's tactical circumstances grew steadily more difficult. After spending the early morning assembling his command at Raccoon Ford, Fitzhugh Lee was now on the offensive. Sending Chambliss' brigade and a gun from Chew's battery to reinforce Lomax, Lee took the remaining infantry of Johnson's brigade and Wickham's four regiments north of the Rapidan via Raccoon Ford. Because Wickham had been hurt badly in a horse fall ten days ago, Col. Thomas H. Owen had command of the brigade. The infantrymen, somewhere near 600 soldiers, were under the direction of Col. Thomas M. Garrett.[12]

Fitz Lee hoped to reach the northern end of Morton's Ford before Buford could affect his escape. This would allow the Confederates to attack the Yankees simultaneously from front and rear in a pincer that would destroy the 1st Cavalry division. Unfortunately for the Rebels, Buford had anticipated this plan and moved to thwart it by sending Chapman's brigade along the north bank of the river to blunt any enemy thrust from upstream.

The ensuing battle morphed into two equally vicious fights, with Chapman's brigade trying to fend off Fitz Lee north of the Rapidan, while Devin's regiments

11 *OR* 29, pt. 1, 465-67, 469.

12 *OR* 29, pt. 1, 462-63, 414-15 Morrissett Diary, October 11, 1863, ACWM; Clark, *North Carolina Regts*, vol. 1, 639, vol. 2, 119, 240; Johnson Diary, October 11, 1863, ACWM. The Johnson brigade remnant consisted of: the 5th and 23rd North Carolina along with the remaining five companies of the 12th.

fought Lomax and Chambliss south of the river. Devin had the more dangerous task, because he would have to disengage while crossing a difficult ford under fire. Buford didn't attempt to hide the grim situation from his troopers, who, he later recalled, "fought more savagely than ever" to prevent the Rebel trap from slamming shut.[13]

*　*　*

Devin's ultimate fate depended on Chapman's ability to negate whatever threat emerged north of the Rapidan. Fitz Lee had led his force of infantry and cavalry across Raccoon Ford that morning intending to fall upon the flank and rear of the Yankees fighting Lomax. Buford's decision to send Chapman to preempt this strategy succeeded. The Federals had moved earlier that morning and consequently when the two forces collided near the Stringfellow farm, Chapman wasn't far from Raccoon Ford.[14]

Both sides reacted quickly to the sudden appearance of the enemy. Union artillery swung around and went into battery on high ground overlooking the river road. Owen watched these guns unlimbering but spied no more than a handful of enemy cavalry hovering nearby in support. He decided on an immediate attack to hit the Yankee guns before they went into action. The ersatz brigadier ordered the 1st and 3rd Virginia Cavalry to charge while still mounted in fours. At the same time the 2nd and 4th Virginia regiments turned into an open field north of the road and went into line alongside Breathed's battery, which was also deploying for action.[15]

Unfortunately for the Confederates, Owen's hurried observation had failed to spot the arrival of most of Chapman's brigade. The Federals, on the other hand, had clearly seen their opponents and hurried to meet them. Consequently, the 8th Illinois Cavalry managed to establish a line of dismounted sharpshooters mere seconds before the Virginia troopers thundered down the road.[16]

Just as the charging Rebels got within range of the Illinois carbines, Fitz Lee grasped the actual strength of the Yankee position and quickly countermanded his attack order. Owen relayed the command, but with the two regiments already under fire and going at full speed, turning them around wasn't easy. Somehow, though, their officers managed it before the Virginians absorbed significant damage. The abrupt

13 Samuel Gilpin Diary, October 11, 1863, LC.

14   OR 29, pt. 1, 471, 348. The extended Stringfellow family owned many properties north of the Rapidan and there were several farms that bore that name.

15 OR 29, pt. 1, 471.

16 Hard, *8th Illinois Cavalry*, 278; OR 29, pt. 1, 349, 471.

about face naturally threw the attackers into some confusion, forcing them momentarily out of the fight until they could rally in the rear.

Uncertain of how many Federals he faced, Owen now proceeded more cautiously. He dismounted sharpshooters from the 2nd and 4th Virginia and threw them northward into some woods to protect his left flank. As these men deployed, the reformed 1st and 3rd regiments returned to the battle. Owen posted their dismounted sharpshooters behind a rail fence and ordered the remainder of both regiments to draw sabers and support Breathed's battery, which was banging away at the Federals and doing "good execution," in Owen's opinion.

Unintimidated by the Rebel guns and believing its fire had broken the enemy's first attack, the 8th Illinois pressed forward to enlarge its initial success. Owen spotted the oncoming threat and sent the mounted squadrons of the 4th Virginia at the Yankee skirmishers to break their line. The assault succeeded, but at a cost. Union bullets instantly killed the regiment's commander, Capt. William Newton, and Capt. Philip William of Company A.[17]

Despite the check delivered to the 8th Illinois, Chapman had successfully blocked Fitz Lee's attack from Raccoon Ford. But this triumph proved temporary when Rebel foot soldiers suddenly appeared and dramatically altered the status quo near the Stringfellow farm. Chapman could only guess at the ultimate size of the growing enemy force in front of him, but he did know his troopers couldn't hold out for long against even a modest contingent of infantry. Clearly, the time had come to withdraw before the Southerners overwhelmed his brigade.

Preparing to retreat, Chapman ordered his battery to begin disengaging. As the Yankee teamsters hitched up their guns, more and more Rebel infantrymen appeared on the field. It had been impossible for the riflemen to match the pace of the cavalry during Fitz Lee's advance from Raccoon Ford that morning. Their strung out column was now arriving piecemeal. The 23rd North Carolina reached the battleground first and had to wait some minutes before the 5th North Carolina and the five companies of the 12th arrived. Once Col. Garrett had all of his men at hand and in line of battle, he launched them against the single Yankee gun still firing from the high ground where the fight had started.

Within 300 yards of the enemy fieldpiece, Garrett ordered a charge. As the North Carolinians surged forward, the enemy gun hurriedly limbered and made for the rear, followed by its supporting horsemen. As the pursuing infantrymen swept up onto the crest, they discovered enemies who were not running. Dismounted Union cavalrymen sheltering in some trees opened an effective enfilade fire into Garrett's right flank when

---

17 OR 29, pt. 1, 47. Company A was also known as the Prince William Company.

it topped the ridge. A battalion of the 12th North Carolina under command of Lt. Col. William Davis was holding that side of the line. Fearing an enemy charge, Davis ordered a change of front to the right on the first company.

The well-drilled Carolinians executed the command instinctively and perfectly— no small feat under fire. The right flank company immediately wheeled 90 degrees to its right and halted facing the Federals to its south. Each succeeding company advanced until it reached the left flank of its sister company then wheeled right and advanced to form a front on the line marked by the first company. The effect was something like a line of falling dominos, and in the matter of a minute it threw Davis' battalion into position parallel to the attackers. As soon as his last company came onto line Davis ordered a charge. In the face of this aggressive maneuver, the enemy horsemen quickly withdrew.

When Fitz Lee's cavalry came up to support Garrett's flank, Chapman forfeited his dominant position. Outnumbered and unable with his carbines to answer the long range fire of infantry muskets, the colonel began withdrawing northeastward toward Stevensburg, hoping he had bought enough time for Devin to get over the river and retreat in the same direction.[18]

*   *   *

While Chapman dueled with Fitz Lee and Garrett, Gen. Lomax ratcheted up the pressure on Devin's brigade, which sooner or later would have to abandon its defenses around the Buckner and Morton farms and retreat downhill toward the ford. Hopefully, once that withdraw began, the rearguard could keep the enemy at bay long enough for the rest of the brigade to get over the Rapidan without being shot to pieces. Those final detachments south of the river, however, would have no option but to run the gauntlet protected only by Buford's artillery.

The 1st Maryland (CS) anchored the Rebel flank closest to the river. Just inland of the Marylanders was the 5th Virginia and on the extreme right of the line, the 15th Virginia. Along with Col. Toon's North Carolina infantrymen, the Rebel troopers maintained a fierce fusillade against Devin's stubbornly-resisting Federals. The arrival of Chambliss' brigade and Chew's cannon increased the fury of the struggle. The Yankees hit the Rebel reinforcements with carbine fire, but couldn't prevent a squadron of the 9th Virginia from dismounting and going into line alongside Lomax's men, while Chew's gun swung into action.[19]

18 Previous paragraphs based on *OR 29*, pt. 1, 416, 349.

19 Ibid., 466-69; Neese, *Three Years in the Confederate Horse Artillery*, 100.

Devin, realizing he could not hold his ground much longer, tried to move the bulk of his brigade to the ford. Chambliss responded by launching a mounted charge to cut the Yankees off. The 6th New York Cavalry at the head of Union column had little choice but to counter-charge in an effort to drive back the enemy. Although successful in arresting the Rebels, Lomax's attack had managed to stymie the Federal movement completely. Obviously, if these conditions persisted, none of Devin's regiments would escape.[20]

Like nearly everyone else in blue that day, Lt. McKinney of the brigade staff realized the critical nature of the situation at Morton's Ford. And to him a seemingly innocuous action by Col. Devin revealed the full extent of the Federal predicament. Thomas C. Devin, a 40-year old somewhat deaf New Yorker, could barely hear enemy bullets zipping overhead—not an altogether bad thing, and perhaps one reason why he always presented a picture of calm professionalism in combat. However, McKinney had noticed that in extremely stressful and dangerous situations, his boss habitually tried to light his already lit pipe. Devin "would strike a match on the seat of his pantaloons and hold it right to his pipe," although smoke was already "pouring out of his mouth." With the Rebels now pushing ever harder against the Yankee perimeter, McKinney noted Devin's pipe and habit in "full blast," a sure sign that "something was doing."[21]

The colonel's embattled troopers hardly needed Devin's nervous tic to confirm their trouble. Morton's homestead had become the focus of the fighting. As long as the Northerners held it they protected the ford and the bulk of Devin's brigade sheltering downslope from the buildings. If the Rebels gained possession of the structures, they could hit anything on either side of the river. Well aware of this fact, Lomax directed Toon's infantrymen to seize the farm.

When the foot soldiers tried to advance, however, intense fire from Yankee sharpshooters occupying one of Morton's barns pinned down the Tar Heels. Rather than accept this repulse, Lt. John T. Gregory, adjutant of the 12th North Carolina, courageously gathered a volunteer force of 20 men and led it in a daring attack against the enemy marksmen. The bold assault forced the Yankees out of the building, which the Rebels quickly occupied. With the barn gone, Devin's hold on the rest of Morton's property weakened. If the entire site fell into enemy hands, his brigade's position would

---

20 Hall, *Sixth New York Cavalry*, 159-60.

21 McKinney, *Life in Tent, Camp and Field*, 35. Born in New York City, Devin was a house painter and part owner of a paint and varnish company, as well as a Lt. Col. in the New York state militia before the war. His Irish forebears included veterans of the French and Indian War and the American Revolution.

Colonel Thomas Devin
Library of Congress

crumble. Devin ordered his troopers to counterattack, but Gregory and his men repulsed them and held onto their newly won gain.[22]

The capture of the barn brought the battle to its crisis. Now with a decisive advantage, Lomax ordered the entire Rebel line to advance. With the Rebels leaping out of their earthworks and pushing forward, Devin had no choice but to order his brigade over the river. In the face of the oncoming avalanche, the rearmost bluecoats relinquished their footholds on the Morton farm and dashed towards the riverbank.[23]

At this moment of maximum peril, the retreating Federals refused to panic. Instead, they put up a dogged struggle, maintaining a vigorous fire as they drew back to the ford. While urging his men to break Yankee resistance, Colonel Rosser heedlessly exposed himself to enemy fire. This display of gallantry nearly robbed him of his promotion to brigadier when a spent round thumped into his forehead. Stunned, he drifted rearward before realizing his wound was minor and returning to the fight.[24]

Despite Rosser's injury and the bluecoats' stubbornness, nothing could stop the gray tide rolling down toward the Rapidan. Company F of the 15th Virginia, on the far eastern flank of the Rebel line, attacked obliquely toward the left and drove the last few Yankees from the final hillock south of the crossing. With that position gone Lomax's line was poised to shove the enemy into the river.[25]

Fortunately for Devin's hard pressed troopers, a section of Union artillery firing from the opposite shore kept the Confederates at bay. To turn the Federal withdrawal

---

22 *OR* 29, pt. 1, 471; Beale, *A Lieutenant in Lee's Army*, 131. The 28-year old Gregory was a former merchant from Halifax, North Carolina.

23 *OR* 29, pt. 1, 465.

24 Beale, *A Lieutenant in Lee's Army*, 128; Beale, *9th Virginia Cavalry*, 100. Rosser's commission as a brigadier went into effect on October 11, 1863.

25 *OR* 29, pt. 1, 469.

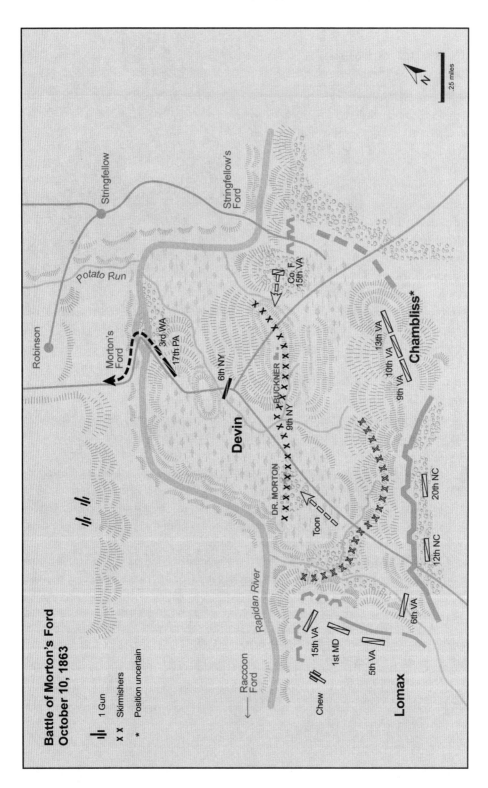

Battle of Morton's Ford
October 10, 1863

||| 1 Gun

x x Skirmishers

* Position uncertain

Stringfellow

Potato Run

Robinson

Morton's Ford

Stringfellow's Ford

Co. F
15th VA

3rd VA

17th PA

6th NY

9th NY

BUCKNER

Devin

DR. MORTON

Toon

Rapidan River

Raccoon Ford

Chew

15th VA

1st MD

5th VA

6th VA

Lomax

12th NC

20th NC

9th VA

10th VA

13th VA

Chambliss*

25 miles

into a bloody rout, Lomax had to silence these guns. The only means of dealing with the Yankee cannons was Chew's lone fieldpiece, which heretofore had focused on the enemy cavalrymen withdrawing to the river. Now Lomax rode over and asked its crew to silence the Northern battery on the opposite shore.[26]

The Rebel gunners responded by bringing their piece to within 1,000 yards of the opposing artillery and opening a rapid fire. With one cannon against two and the Federals in a better position on higher ground, the duel was inherently unequal. Nonetheless, the Southerners refused to relinquish the contest even though "shell and shrapnel shot raked the sod and tore the ground" around their gun. The obstinate Yankee artillery detained Lomax's troopers long enough for Devin to get the last of his men across the river. Once they cleared the Robinson house, the colonel reorganized his command and retreated toward Stevensburg to link up with Chapman.[27]

The Federals had, for the moment, given Lomax the slip, though clearly Devin's command had barely avoided annihilation. Neither side recorded a separate tally of casualties for the three-hour battle. Without stating numbers, Lomax claimed to have inflicted "considerable loss" on the Yankees before they crossed the Rapidan. Buford lent credence to this claim by admitting that Devin suffered "quite severely."[28]

Whatever the casualty figures, both Chapman and Devin were now withdrawing speedily along a converging course toward Stevensburg, with the Confederates following closely. Buford's troopers were in a sour mood. Riding south on October 10 they had anticipated the start of a march on Richmond. Twenty-four hours later they were instead retreating once again to the Rappahannock. Someone in the high command seemed to have thoroughly bungled, and the cavalry had paid the price. The Rebels had come "near bagging the whole division," as one Federal put it, and the Northern troopers realized they were lucky to have escaped Fitz Lee's trap.[29]

Their salvation might yet prove temporary, however. Buford had only a vague notion of the whereabouts of the rest of Pleasonton's cavalry corps. The only thing for certain was that Meade had ordered a withdrawal behind the Rappahannock. It was improbable that the 1st Cavalry Division could gain the river's north shore without encountering more Rebels. With the day only half spent, plenty of time remained for more fighting, and it was highly likely that some survivors of the recent battle would not live to see the sunset.

26 Neese, *Three Years in the Confederate Horse Artillery*, 217.

27 Ibid.

28 Beale, *9th Virginia Cavalry*, 100; OR 29, pt. 1, 348, 465, 467, 469, 470, 474. The 1st Maryland Cavalry (CS) did list 3 killed and 8 wounded in the fight.

29 OR 29, pt. 1, 465; Samuel Gilpin Diary, October 11, 1863, LC.

Chapter 12

"Meade Seems Unwilling to Attack"

Meade Orders a Retreat—Difficult March—Unfriendly Fire—Cavalry Convergence

As Fitzhugh Lee and John Buford began their fight at Morton's Ford on the morning of October 11, the Army of Northern Virginia resumed its advance. Marching at sunrise Hill's corps wound its way through the countryside until reaching the road connecting Front Royal and Culpeper Court House. Here it turned east toward the concentrated mass of the Army of the Potomac. So rapid was the movement, Rebel officers called a halt at 11 o'clock to give their weary troops an hour's rest and allow the column to close up.[1]

To the surprise of many Federal officers, the Union army was also marching hard that morning. All indications till now suggested Lee meant to outflank the AOP and force it into battle around Culpeper Court House. Many of Meade's commanders expected, even desired, a clash and the chance to perhaps finish what had been started at Gettysburg. If Lee was really looking for a fight in the Culpeper V, Meade had already selected the place to have it, and his army seemed eager for the contest.

The administration also appeared to welcome a renewal of combat between the Virginia armies. Although news of Longstreet's detachment had convinced Lincoln and Halleck that Meade ought to fight Lee, both shrank from actually ordering him to do it. Such a directive shouldn't have been necessary. Meade had long maintained his willingness to tackle Lee provided his army could meet the Rebels on a fair field, which in Meade's mind probably meant the chance to receive battle on the defensive. Now at last, with the Confederates on the attack, fate seemed ready to present Meade his opportunity.

---

1   Kirkpatrick Diary, October 11, 1863, UT.

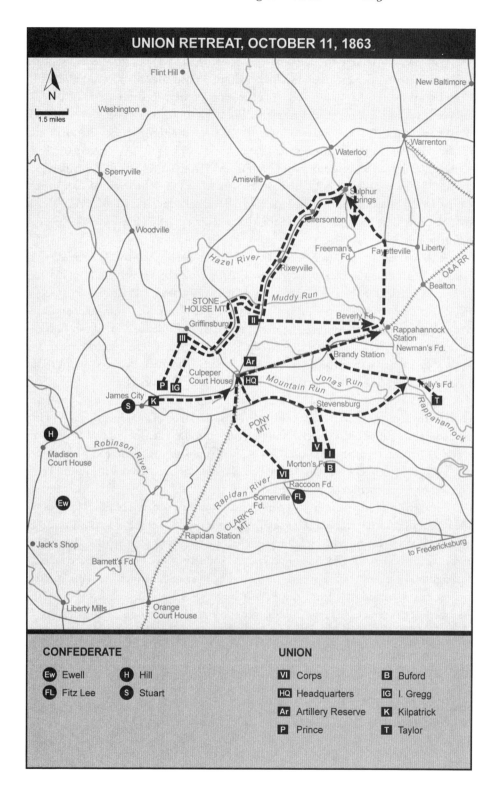

As the long-expected collision neared, however, the commander of the Army of the Potomac chose not to fight. At 3 a.m. on October 11, the Federals began abandoning their position around Culpeper Court House. Meade ordered French's III Corps north of the Rappahannock River instructing him to form a line of defense between Sulphur Springs and Freeman's Ford. Headquarters directed Warren's II Corps, Sedgwick's VI, and Sykes' V to cross the river at Rappahannock Station. Once on the north shore, the II Corps would extend on French's left, from Freeman's Ford to Beverly Ford. Sykes' position would run from Warren's left flank to Rappahannock Station. Sedgwick's line would stretch from there to the right flank of Newton's I Corps, which headquarters directed to cross the Rappahannock at Kelly's Ford. Meade told Newton to tie his right flank to Sedgwick and cover Kelly's Ford with the I Corps' leftmost units.[2]

Such movements always appeared logical and simple on the map. They hardly ever were in actual execution, especially when a night march was involved. Meade's men suffered considerably before getting across the river. Warren's II Corps had stood in line of battle around Culpeper throughout much of October 10, at one point enduring a violet rainstorm while waiting the next turn of events. Meade's pre-dawn order to retreat forced its weary soldiers to form up in utter darkness. The already sodden and miserable regiments then had to move cross country from their battle positions to the road that would carry them north. Inevitably things went wrong.

The experience of the 20th Massachusetts presented an extreme, but fairly characteristic, example of the difficulties that ensued. Many of its soldiers got lost while contending with swollen creeks and moving through dense underbrush-choked woods. Groping through dark forest, men stumbled over rocks and roots or fell into ditches full of water, emerging soaked to the skin and covered with mud. These conditions threatened to demoralize the entire regiment.[3]

In an effort to help various lost commands, someone ordered bonfires lit. Despite the recent downpour, these well-meaning beacons quickly set the woods on fire. The ensuing scene resembled something out of Dante's *Inferno*. "Sparks flew in all directions," recalled a regimental surgeon, "and soon tongues of fire were everywhere." "[F]rightful heat" and dense smoke produced a "mad rush of men" seeking to "free themselves at any cost," from the hellish blaze. Not until daybreak did the 20th Massachusetts extract itself from this danger and link up with the rest of the II Corps.[4]

---

2 OR 29, pt. 2, 286-87.

3 Martha Derby Perry, *Letters from a Surgeon of the Civil War* (Boston, MA, 1906), 104-105.

4 Ibid.

Such episodes undoubtedly unnerved but did not seriously delay the army's withdrawal. Throughout the wee hours of October 11 and beyond the Federals steadily moved north. At 8:30 a.m. Meade telegraphed Lincoln news of the retrograde march, explaining "the enemy are either moving to my right and rear or moving down on my flank, I cannot tell which, as their movements are not developed." He was "prepared for either emergency," Meade reassured the president. By nightfall the entire army would be behind the Rappahannock River.[5]

Meade's refusal to hold his ground perplexed many of his officers and men, including Col. Lyman. "[T]he idea of the enemy, 50,000 or 60,000 strong, marching about," he complained, "and we not know[ing] whether they were going one way or another, seems incredible." Although he conceded that hills and woods effectively hid the Confederate columns from view, it was fairly obvious that the Rebels were "paddling along, in the general direction of Warrenton," between Culpeper Court House and the Blue Ridge Mountains. Lee had made a serious mistake by taking the offensive, Lyman thought, telling his wife, "Our army, I say with emphasis, ought to be able to whip the gentleman."[6]

If Lyman's letter hinted that the AOP should stand fast and give battle, Maj. Gen. Halleck was positive that's what Meade should do. The general-in-chief told Maj. Gen. John G. Foster, who commanded the Department of North Carolina, that since Lee had sent a large force to Tennessee, Meade was "greatly superior" in numbers to his opponent. Yet "Meade seems unwilling to attack . . . without positive orders." Though he had the authority to issue such commands, Halleck saw little point in doing so. Directing "a general to give battle against his own wishes and judgment" would be assuming "the responsibility of a probable defeat," he wrote Foster, adding that "if a general is unwilling to fight, he is not likely to gain a victory."[7]

Halleck had outlined the crux of the Union's problem in Virginia. The Army of the Potomac had always been, by some degree or other, numerically and materially stronger than its enemy. Lincoln and many others believed, then and now, that such odds provided the foundation for aggressive action and victory; yet seldom had this been the case. Triumphs came infrequently while defeats had proliferated. Now no one in the Northern high command wanted to take responsibility for launching a bloody battle that might bring another disaster.

Past reverses had typically resulted from poor generalship, real or perceived, and Lincoln habitually removed, replaced, or reassigned beaten leaders. Five generals had

---

5 *OR* 29, pt. 2, 290.

6 Aggassiz, *Meade's Headquarters*, 28; Lyman, *Meade's Army*, 48.

7 *OR* 29, pt. 2, 277.

preceded Meade in command of the Union's eastern army. Each lost his job after failure on the battlefield and fell into disfavor. Who could blame George Meade for believing that all that kept him from a similar fate was one battle gone wrong?

This reason was but one of several why Meade hesitated to fight, and certainly the least of them. Acutely conscious of the North's manpower woes, the general was reluctant to absorb the massive casualties any battle would produce. He refused to do so unless he saw a good chance of significant gain or something approaching surety of victory—a rare commodity indeed.

Meade would not run any risks until he positioned his army in such a way as to give it the necessary advantages for success. That meant following the dictates of accepted military science: a secure line of communications, a viable line of retreat, concentration of force, and a decent knowledge of the enemy's whereabouts and movements. Meade didn't believe any of this possible in Culpeper County, so he ordered a withdrawal to better ground. In his professional view, he'd taken the safe, sane, and prudent course necessity imposed. Unfortunately, his superiors in Washington did not agree.

The perplexities of their high command didn't concern the common soldiers, but Meade's order to retreat baffled them as much as it did any general. One Federal officer found it ironic that the entire army which "had marched all the way from Gettysburg for the purpose of engaging Lee" now withdrew the moment the Confederates offered to fight. A soldier and his compatriots in the 20th Maine wondered similarly why the Union army "hurried away."[8]

This criticism of Meade for failing to hold his ground near Culpeper was, perhaps, ill-considered. After all, Lee had retreated in August rather than do battle in the dangerous V of the Rapidan and Rappahannock. Why should Meade not feel the same? Two months ago, however, Lee had been badly outnumbered and his army still suffering the effects of Gettysburg. But now, at the start of October, 1863, Meade's numerical superiority doubled that of August, and the Union army had fully recovered from its Pennsylvania exertions.

Still, geography produced one stark, immutable military fact. The narrow end of the Culpeper V negated both Meade's room to maneuver *and* his superior numbers should Lee succeed in driving him there. Even a relatively minor tactical setback could occasion a desperate situation if it compelled Meade to retreat across the Rappahannock fords. That a Culpeper battlefield yielded few opportunities and required unnecessary risk was hardly an unreasonable conclusion for Meade to reach.

---

8 Martin McMahon, "From Gettysburg to the Coming of Grant," in *Battles and Leaders of the Civil War*, 4 vols. (New York, 1956), vol. 4, 81; John Pullen, *The Twentieth Maine: A Volunteer Regiment in the Civil War* (Dayton, OH, 1984), 160.

Hence the retreat; whether it halted on the north bank of the Rappahannock or continued depended on Lee. If his effort was limited and aimed at Culpeper Court House, Meade's movement would deny him his target. If Lee was playing a deeper game and seeking to interpose his army between Meade and Washington, the AOP would have to retire closer to the capital. In either contingency, placing the army on the Rappahannock's northern shore was a judicious decision.

*   *   *

Federal cavalry had a vital dual mission: covering this withdrawal and trying to discover Lee's intentions at the same time. The three Union cavalry divisions were relatively scattered on the morning of October 11: Buford was disentangling himself from the fight at Morton's Ford and withdrawing towards Stevensburg; Kilpatrick was retiring to Culpeper Court House from James City and covering the V Corps retreat; Gregg's division was shifting position to assume watch over the upper fords of the Rappahannock.[9]

For its part, the Confederate cavalry was chasing hard after Meade's army. Stuart left Young's brigade at James City to cover the approach of Rebel infantry while he took Gordon's brigade to Griffenburg and a link up with Jones' brigade. That junction accomplished, Stuart sent the 11th Virginia to scout the Warrenton-Rixeyville Pike and led the rest of his force toward Stone House Mountain.[10]

The Confederate's made these movements without interference, which allowed Stuart to confirm for Lee that no Union infantry was shifting to the northwest. It also meant that Meade was either preparing to make a stand near Culpeper or begin a withdrawal up the line of the railroad. Lee needed to know which of those options his foe had selected, and it was Stuart's job to provide the answer. Even though the famous cavalier had only five regiments with him, he had no choice but to press on toward Culpeper.

There the Rebels would find Kilpatrick's division of Yankee horsemen waiting for them. To discover what Meade's infantry was doing, Stuart would have to shove these Yankees out of his way. Both sides were spoiling for a fight, and as they converged on Culpeper Court House they rode into one of the most dramatic cavalry battles of the war.

9   Humphreys, *From Gettysburg to the Rapidan*, 16.

10 *OR* 29, pt. 1, 441.

CHAPTER 13

"A Situation to Try the Stoutest Hearts"

Stuart's Ploy—Race for the Rappahannock—Clash at Brandy Station—Custer's
Charge—Pleasonton's Escape—Heroes' Welcome—Battle Becomes Pursuit

JUST before noon on October 11, the citizens of Culper Court House watched with obvious satisfaction the retreat of the weary troopers in Judson Kilpatrick's 3rd Cavalry Division through their town. The commanding officer of the 1st Vermont, Col. Edward Sawyer, couldn't help but notice the hard "good riddance" stares of Virginia's civilians. To counter the visible hostility, the regimental band struck up *Yankee Doodle* just to annoy the unfriendly bystanders.[1]

Upon departing town, the division crossed Mountain Run and moved onto the ridge just north of Culpeper, where Kilpatrick faced his men about and formed a line of battle. Shortly thereafter, Jeb Stuart appeared at the northwest outskirts of town on the Rixeyville Road. It was almost a month to the day since Pleasonton had driven the Confederates out of the court house. Now, in a stark role reversal, the bluecoats were doing the back peddling. But the Yankees appeared unwilling to leave without a fight. Rebel horsemen approaching the oft-contested municipality could clearly see the mass of Kilpatrick's division sullenly standing its ground just beyond the county seat.[2]

Stuart sent a squadron from the 1st North Carolina Cavalry to occupy the village, and then led the rest of his dust-covered troopers northeasterly around Culpeper. The Rebel cavalrymen took up a position along the ridge just south of Mountain Run, which marked the northern boundary of the city limits. Stuart had only 1,500 troopers on hand; Kilpatrick had more than twice as many. Such odds were certainly grim, but to

1   *OR* 29, pt. 1, 441, 336-37.

2   McClellan, *I Rode with JEB Stuart*, 378-379.

a man like Jeb Stuart daunting odds only increased the exhilaration of the occasion. With his enemy so close, he would not hold back.[3]

Beckham's horse artillery raced up to the edge of town, and the crews quickly unlimbered their pieces and began shelling the Yankee guns on the opposite crest. A furious artillery duel was soon raging across the valley of Mountain Run. Despite this display of resistance, it wasn't clear to Stuart whether Kilpatrick meant to fight or was merely making a show of force. Determined to find out, Stuart ordered Col. James Gordon to probe the Federal line. The 4th and 5th North Carolina aggressively drove Kilpatrick's skirmishers away from Mountain Run, but when they crossed the creek, the gray troopers encountered a storm of Union artillery and carbine fire. The hail of Yankee lead wounded Col. Dennis Ferebee and knocked him from his horse. Another bullet ripped through the mouth of the 5th North Carolina's adjutant. Several junior officers and men fell wounded. Stuart had his answer: the Yankees would fight. The two Rebel regiments recoiled from their losses and fell back to their starting point, as both sides regrouped warily.[4]

Affairs had reached a tactical impasse. Stuart realized he had no chance of successfully attacking the well-positioned Federal cavalry. Stalemates, however, were not to his liking. He quickly decided to accomplish by maneuver what appeared impossible to achieve by combat.

Leaving Griffin's battery to fix the Federals' attention, Stuart withdrew his entire mounted force from Culpeper Court House. The general led Gordon's brigade, along with Funston's 7th and 12th Virginia cavalry regiments, westward for a short distance before turning the long column onto a series of back roads and meandering farm tracks toward Brandy Station. Stuart hoped to reach the former battlefield ahead of Kilpatrick and then spur his command north to occupy Fleetwood Heights. Once ensconced on that ridge, the Southern troopers would be between the Yankees and the Rappahannock.

Unfortunately for Stuart the open, relatively flat terrain around Culpeper Court House allowed the Federals to see his westward shift. General Pleasonton, now on the scene, surmised Stuart's purpose instantly. With no intention of allowing himself to be outflanked, he ordered Kilpatrick to pull back toward Fleetwood Heights. So as the

---

3 OR 29, pt. 2, 239. Precise figures for any unit on a battlefield are all but impossible to calculate. Field Returns of the AOP at the end of September 1863 show 13,888 officers and men present for duty in the Cavalry Corps. Dividing that number among Pleasonton's three divisions yields 4,629 for each command. That math is too simple: the divisions were not equal in numbers, various detachments and other factors would have reduced their strength by October 11. Nonetheless, it is safe to assume Kilpatrick had at least 3,000 troopers and perhaps several hundred more.

4 Ibid., 441.

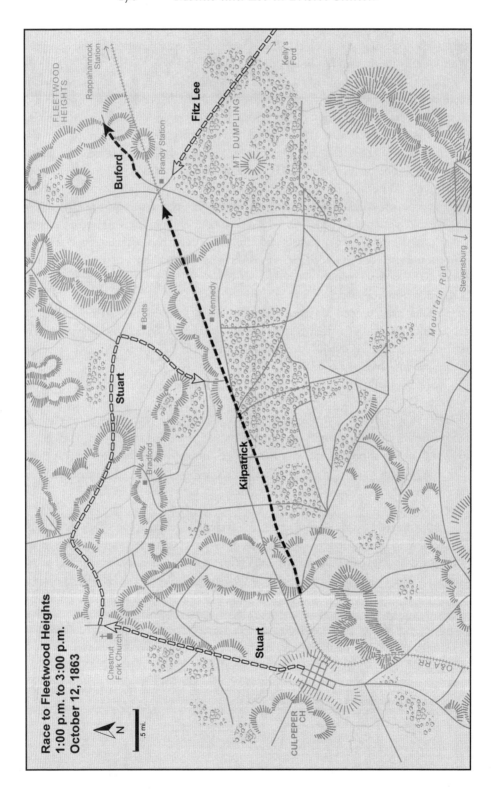

Race to Fleetwood Heights
1:00 p.m. to 3:00 p.m.
October 12, 1863

Confederates turned onto the Chestnut Fork Church road, which led to Brandy Station by way of Bradford's and Botts' farms, Federal horsemen began to move north. Although the Yankees withdrew along the straight line of the railroad and thus had a shorter distance to travel, it was not a certainty that they would reach the high ground ahead of the Rebels.[5]

If the Federal situation were not disconcerting enough already, the sound of artillery welling up from the southeast hinted at new dangers. Stuart heard it too and realized it heralded the approach of Fitz Lee's division from the Rapidan. Although the general had no idea of Lee's circumstances, his arrival might change the odds north of Culpeper considerably. If Stuart could seize Fleetwood and hold it, Fitz Lee could potentially assail Kilpatrick from the rear. Catching the Yankee division in such a vise would assure its annihilation. At the least, Fitz Lee might strike Kilpatrick's column from the east and slow it down long enough to allow Stuart's regiments to reach the heights. Everything depended on speed and whether the Yankees could retreat faster than the Confederates could advance. Whichever side won the race to Fleetwood Heights would carry the day.

Generals Pleasonton and Kilpatrick, hardly blind to these possibilities, pulled their commands back toward Brandy Station with all practicable haste. Davies' brigade moved on the eastern side of the railroad tracks, Custer's men on the west—while the sound of firing from the southeast came closer every minute. With a clear threat closing on the Federal left and disturbing evidence of enemy troops nearing on the right, the retreat of Kilpatrick's division became somewhat disheveled. Col. Sawyer of the 1st Vermont Cavalry sensed a definite air of apprehension as the Union horsemen raced north. Orders came to him "in such rapid succession" he later couldn't recall whether he had executed them all.[6]

The long column of Northern troopers presented an inviting target. The broad open fields and dearth of fences west of the railroad invited a Rebel flank attack. Such fine country for cavalry formations offered nothing to impede Stuart's regiments from crashing into Custer's column. Consequently Kilpatrick and Pleasonton focused most of their attention in that direction.

Davies' command was moving over quite different ground. Here the Federals encountered dense woods of heavy oak virtually impassible by anything other than a column of fours. Kilpatrick, though, seemed totally unaware of this. Fixated on the threat to his left flank, he issued instructions for his 1st Brigade to assume formations utterly impracticable in the terrain east of the railroad tracks. Riding northward as

---

5 Ibid., 441.

6 OR 29, pt. 1, 393.

swiftly as possible, Davies and his subordinates ignored the more senseless orders and negotiated the topography as best they could.[7]

As Kilpatrick's column raced toward Brandy Station, the open vista west of the railroad tracks filled with thousands of mounted men. Long columns of Union and Confederate cavalry were rushing northward, in full view of each other, and toward the same objective. As the parallel formations galloped forward, observers noted that the opposing soldiers "sent up shouts of mutual defiance, brandishing their sabers menacingly, [while] occasionally solitary horsemen rode out . . . and exchanged shots."[8]

Kilpatrick had the benefit of interior lines and a shorter route, while Stuart, per necessity taking a more circuitous path, operated at a serious disadvantage. After reaching Bradford's Farm, the Confederate commander could see dense columns of the Union cavalry dashing along the railroad towards Brandy Station. If the Federals passed through there first, and apparently they would, any hope of trapping them south of the Rappahannock River was ruined.[9]

The Yankees had their own problems, of course. Colonel Gordon had detailed the 1st North Carolina Cavalry to press Kilpatrick's rear, and the regiment relentlessly attacked the 7th Michigan at the tail of Custer's brigade. The Carolinians pressured the Midwesterners so stringently that their commander, Col. William Mann, constantly begged Custer for reinforcements. Intent instead on the ominous threat to his left, the young Union brigadier refused to strengthen his rearguard with anything other than a section of artillery from Lt. Alexander Pennington's Battery M, 2nd US Artillery.

A badly harassed rearguard proved a perilous place for Union cannon. After the two Federal guns unlimbered and opened fire, a small group of Rebel horsemen rushed out of a patch of nearby woods and momentarily captured both fieldpieces. The Yankee gunners refused to yield the cannon permanently and mounted their battery horses to launch an impromptu counter charge that reclaimed the guns. After this narrow escape the artillerists unilaterally decided their stint at rearguard duty was over. The cannons retreated to Custer's main body, once again leaving the 7th Michigan to fend for itself.[10]

While the 1st North Carolina harassed Custer's column from the south, the remainder of Stuart's command endeavored to interpose itself between Kilpatrick and the Rappahannock. Unfortunately for the Confederates, the hurried ride to outflank Kilpatrick had left Stuart's force badly strung out. The 7th Virginia Cavalry had taken a

---

7   Ibid, 393-94.

8   Starr, *Union Cavalry*, vol. 2, 25.

9   *OR* 29, pt. 1, 443.

10   Urwin, *Custer Victorious*, 101.

wrong road and was temporarily beyond the scene of action. This left the general with only the 12th Virginia Cavalry (at the head of his column) followed in turn by the 2nd, 4th, and 5th North Carolina cavalry regiments.

As the Rebel cavalrymen bore down on the head of Kilpatrick's column, Fitz Lee's division hove into view from the southeast, his troopers still engaging Buford's men. Although Stuart could distinguish distant friends from foes, Fitz Lee's artillery, looking westward, saw only a mass of moving horsemen, the closest of them wearing blue. The Rebel gunners in Chew's and Breathed's batteries began lobbing shot and shell toward a mark hard to miss, but one made up of friends as well as foes.[11]

*   *   *

Initiating friendly fire was merely the latest complication in Fitz Lee's advance to Brandy Station. After driving Buford away from Morton's Ford early that morning, the Rebels had followed the Federal cavalrymen toward Stevensburg. Close to the hamlet, Buford saw a long line of Union supply wagons retreating in the direction of Kelly's Ford. The Federal general felt compelled to halt his withdrawal and keep Fitz Lee at bay until the wagons were safe.

The Northern troopers, therefore, formed a mounted line of battle and stood their ground. Fitz Lee declined to charge such a dense formation of Union cavalry. Instead he brought up Lt. Col. Ridgely Brown's 1st Maryland Cavalry (CS), whose troops carried rifled muskets rather than cavalry carbines. With weapons that had greater range than those of his foe, Brown could take the Yankees under fire with minimum risk. Aided by shellfire from Chew's and Breathed's batteries, the Rebels stood out of range and peppered Buford's cavalry with accurate fire.

The Southern gunners did good work. One of Chew's shells exploded among a group of Union troopers, mauling four horses and three men. Fragments from the Confederate projectile ripped off the top of one Yankee's head, killing him instantly. A piece of shell ruptured an artery in the thigh of another Northerner who soon bled to death. The remaining Federal had been injured so badly his bowels and part of his spine protruded from his mangled body. Sadly it took this soldier some time to die. As he lay writhing in agony, Rebel troopers reached the scene, and he begged someone to shoot him and end his misery. None of the Southerners could bring themselves to do the

11 OR 29, pt. 1, 443. The movements of the battalion-sized 2nd NC Cav are unclear and thus I was unable to place them on any of the maps. They were often attached to the 1st NC Cav, but it is unknown if they were so assigned on Oct. 11.

deed. Instead they did what they could to ease his suffering through the dreadfully painful last few minutes of life that remained.[12]

Unable to respond adequately to Fitz Lee's harassment, Buford ordered his division to retire to Stevensburg, where he again turned to make a stand. Once more the Confederates deployed the 1st Maryland and artillery to drive off the stubborn Yankees. This time, however, the Federals stood stoutly, and for a time the two opponents exchanged a brisk fire. Wickham's brigade commander Col. Owen, eventually tiring of this game, impulsively ordered a series of mounted charges to dislodge the Federals. He personally led his own 3rd Virginia Cavalry in the first assault, which the bluecoats met with "a perfect shower of shot and shell." The colonel had his horse shot out from under him while his regiment pulled up 150 yards short of the Federal line and fell back. The 2nd Virginia Cavalry and then the 4th Virginia Cavalry followed with fruitless attacks of their own against the Union right flank. Owen's regiments struck with great élan, but their piecemeal assaults failed to make much of an impression on Buford's line.[13]

Although stung by the long-range fire of Maryland rifles and Rebel horse artillery, the Federal cavalry held its position until the supply wagons had safely departed. About the same time these vehicles drew out of range Col. Garrett's infantry arrived and once more tipped the balance of power in Fitz Lee's favor. Ordering his men to resume their retreat, Buford claimed he made a leisurely and unmolested retrograde movement toward Brandy Station, although admittedly with the Rebels close behind.

Colonel Owen perceived the Yankee withdrawal quite differently, reporting that "the enemy gave way under our furious attack and determined onslaught and fell back rapidly." Regardless of their manner, the Federals wasted little time in trying to get to the Rappahannock. One North Carolina officer complained that the dismounted Maryland sharpshooters and Garrett's infantry had to march "almost at the double quick" to maintain the pursuit.

Fitz Lee's division was not far behind Buford as he neared Fleetwood Heights. At first, the dense woods east of the railroad prevented Lee's troopers from spotting the mass of cavalry along the Orange & Alexandria Railroad. Unaware of Kilpatrick's position, Brig. Gen. Lomax directed his men to take possession of Brandy Station. As the Southerners hurried in that direction, the general noticed a small group of Federal ambulances and stragglers on the road leading to Culpeper Court House. Lomax told Maj. Charles Collins to take his 15th Virginia Cavalry and capture these isolated enemy troops.

---

12 Trout, *Galloping Thunder*, 368-69.

13 OR 29, pt. 1, 348, 471; Swank, *Sabres, Saddles and Spurs*, 92; Corson, *My Dear Jennie*, 111.

As Collins' Virginians reached the O&A tracks, however, they suddenly discovered a lot of Union horsemen heading northward out of the woods near the Botts house. This was Henry Davies' brigade, and it was obviously too much for the 15th to handle on its own. When Davies dispatched the 1st Vermont Cavalry to counter the Virginians, Collins decided to withdraw and seek a clearer understanding of the situation.

Jeb Stuart knew nothing of Fitz Lee's battle against Buford, but he had no difficulty discerning that Lee's artillerymen were mistakenly shelling their friends. With no time to send couriers and no signal flag communication at hand, the most expeditious method Stuart's men had to identify themselves was by attacking the Yankees. Thus the general ordered the 12th Virginia Cavalry, riding at the head of his column, to charge the nearest body of Federal troops.

The regiment's impetuous attack sliced across the path of Davies' brigade, cutting off more than 1,000 Union troopers from the rest of Kilpatrick's division. Determined to open the road, Davies directed the 18th Pennsylvania Cavalry to countercharge. A swirling mêlée ensued as the Confederates and Federals slammed into one another. Stuart desperately tried to bring more men into the fray, but Gordon's North Carolina regiments, hampered by the bad terrain, had fallen behind and no supporting units were close enough to lend weight to the assault.[14]

When the 4th and 5th North Carolina cavalry belatedly arrived nearby, Stuart sent word for them to reinforce the Virginians. But before this order arrived, disaster struck. The two Rebel regiments, formed in a column of fours, were sitting in a road cut through the railroad embankment intensely watching the mêlée between the 12th Virginia and 18th Pennsylvania. Blinded by the high embankment on either side of them and with their attention focused on the battle to their front, the North Carolinians were oblivious to the 2nd New York Cavalry charging down upon their right flank.

Sergeant Major Charles Haigh and bugler Frank Rose of the 5th North Carolina Cavalry were positioned on higher ground a little distance behind their regiment as the New Yorkers launched their attack. Horrified, they realized none of their comrades saw what was about to happen. They tried desperately to warn their fellows, but to no avail. One Confederate later recalled that the 2nd New York "fell like a tornado" on the unsuspecting Rebels, and several troopers were wounded or captured before both regiments broke and ran.[15]

---

14 Previous paragraphs based upon *OR* 29, pt. 1, 348, 443, 465, 467, 469, 471.

15 Ibid., 386, 443; Clark, *NC Regts*, vol. 3, 575-77.

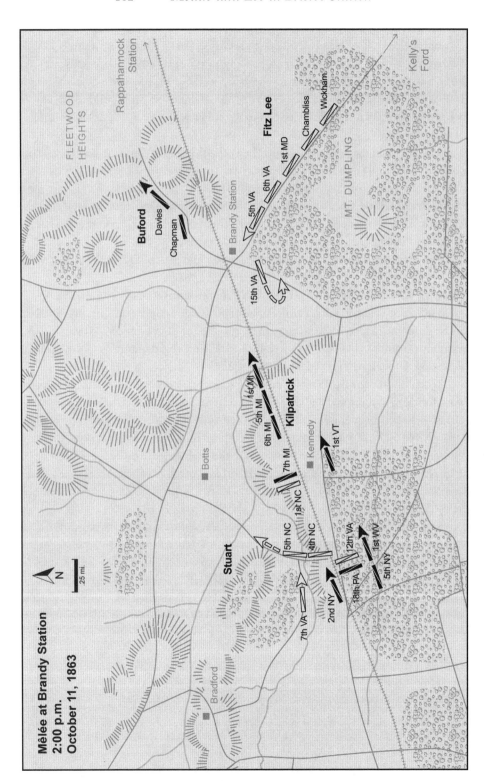

Mêlée at Brandy Station
2:00 p.m.
October 11, 1863

N

25 mi.

Bradford

Stuart

7th VA

2nd NY

18th PA

12th VA

1st WV

5th NY

5th NC

4th NC

1st NC

7th MI

6th MI

5th MI

1st MI

Kilpatrick

Kennedy

1st VT

Botts

FLEETWOOD HEIGHTS

Rappahannock Station

Buford

Davies

Chapman

Brandy Station

15th VA

5th VA

6th VA

1st MD

Chambliss

Wickham

Fitz Lee

MT. DUMPLING

Kelly's Ford

The terrified Tar Heels fled with gusto as Stuart and Gordon tried futilely to rally them. Not until officers with drawn pistols blocked their path along a narrow road did the panicked mass regain some semblance of discipline.[16]

Retribution for this insult to Southern arms came quickly. Even as the North Carolinians hurtled to the rear, the 7th Virginia Cavalry came up and struck the 2nd New York's flank. Disorganized by their own charge and completely unprepared to receive an attack, the New Yorkers bolted. Within a matter of minutes the Virginians killed or captured a large number of the audacious Yankees and drove the rest back in disarray.[17]

On the other side of the railroad tracks, as Fitz Lee's troopers neared Brandy Station, they finally caught sight of the struggle between Kilpatrick and Stuart. The sudden vista of four divisions of cavalry racing for Fleetwood Heights "all in the fastest motion, horsemen at the gallop, artillery at the gallop, battle flags borne swiftly above the dust" awed Lt. George Beale of the 9th Virginia Cavalry. It was, he thought, the most exciting scene he had yet witnessed during the war.[18]

Alas for the Confederates, by the time Fitz Lee realized the true situation Buford had the won the race for Fleetwood Heights. Although the enemy success was regrettable, Lee didn't dwell on it long. He quickly focused on a new goal—namely Kilpatrick's column still toiling toward the Rappahannock. Fitz Lee directed Col. Rosser to take a pair of regiments and get between Kilpatrick and Buford's commands. By preventing Pleasonton from uniting the two Federal cavalry divisions on the high ground, he hoped to aid Stuart in surrounding and destroying the 3rd Cavalry Division.[19]

As the 15th Virginia Cavalry backed away from its effort to capture Union ambulances and stragglers, the 5th and 6th Virginia cavalry regiments advanced on Brandy Station. Once there the Confederates turned south to face Kilpatrick's Yankees. Stuart's men had finally managed to cut off their foes from the Rappahannock. With ever more Rebels gathering around the 3rd Division's flanks, a New York chaplain admitted that the Federals were in "a situation to try the stoutest hearts."[20]

Fortunately for the trapped Northerners no stouter heart beat in the cavalry corps than George Armstrong Custer's. The boyish general, realizing that Rebels blocked the

---

16 *OR* 29, pt. 1, 443; Starr, *Union Cavalry*, vol. 2, 25-26.

17 *OR* 29, pt. 1, 443; Clark, *NC Regts*, vol. 3, 575-77.

18 Starr, *Union Cavalry*, vol. 2, 25.

19 *OR* 29, pt. 1, 394.

20 Ibid., 469, 465; Boudrye, *Fifth New York Cavalry*, 79.

way ahead, rode to Pleasonton and lobbied for permission to cut through the encircling Confederates and open a route to the Rappahannock. The corps commander quickly consented, telling the brigadier "to do his best." Ordering the 6th and 7th Michigan cavalry to hold back Stuart, Custer formed the 1st and 5th Michigan cavalry regiments into two columns of squadrons and commanded his troopers to draw sabers. In typically energetic fashion and with his usual flair for the dramatic, Custer rode to the front of his command and shouted to his men, "Boys of Michigan, there are some people between us and home. I'm going home! Who else goes?" The troopers responded with three hearty cheers. The regiments leveled their sabers; a nearby band broke into Yankee Doodle, and the Michigan troopers advanced to the attack.[21]

A hatless Custer and his small staff rode at the front of the columns, the general's headquarters flag and long blonde hair snapping in the wind. As the Federals moved forward, the brigadier turned in the saddle to survey his command. The sight thrilled Custer. A few days later he would refer to the moment as "Glorious War!" in all its majesty. Pleasonton and his staff, caught up in the excitement, drew their own sabers and accompanied the assault.

The Northerners first advanced at a trot and then sped up to a gallop as they neared the enemy. As soon as his men got within effective range of the Confederates, Custer gave the order to charge. The Union horseman, "whooping and yelling like demons," hurtled toward Rosser's troopers who met them with a fury of gunfire. Custer had two horses shot out from under him in just 15 minutes. But the momentum of the Yankee assault was too much, and the 5th and 6th Virginia fled sideways in retreat. The Michigan troopers kept Custer's promise to open the road and then kept it open. Thanks to the Michigan brigade's efforts, Kilpatrick extricated his division from encirclement and joined Buford on Fleetwood Heights.[22]

*   *   *

With the Federals massed on the high ground, both sides momentarily paused to catch their breath, gather in stragglers, and reform. After a short lull, the combat resumed with renewed fury. This second round of the struggle bore little resemblance to the first. The earlier contest, an intricate ballet of maneuver, now gave way to

---

21 OR 29, pt. 1, 390; Marguerite Merrington, ed. *The Custer Story, The Life and Intimate Letters of General George A. Custer and His Wife Elizabeth* (New York, 1950), 66; Eric Wittenberg, ed. *One of Custer's Wolverines: The Civil War Letters of Brevet Brigadier General James H. Kidd, 6th Michigan Cavalry* (Kent, OH, 2000), 61. Most likely each regiment was in a column of squadrons, but no historic records verifies that assumption.

22 Merrington, *Custer Story*, 66-67.

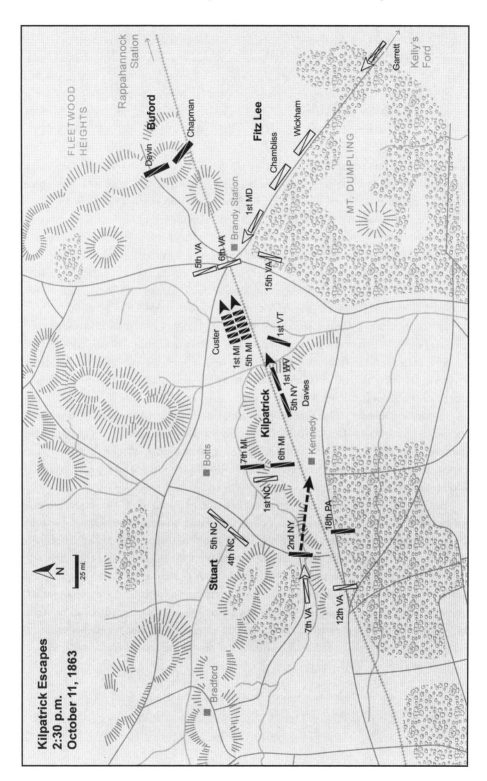

Kilpatrick Escapes
2:30 p.m.
October 11, 1863

nothing less than a bare-knuckled brawl with no orderly lines and seemingly no overall direction. One Union officer described it as a confusing "series of gallant charges made wherever the enemy appeared," a furious combat so fluid it was "hardly practicable" to describe the battle. The sweep of the struggle, however, was breathtaking. "As far as the eye could see over the vast rolling field," recalled a participant, "were encounters by regiment, by battalions, by squads, and by individuals, in hand-to-hand conflict."[23]

Lomax sought to dislodge the enemy from his perch on Fleetwood Heights by again dismounting the 1st Maryland Cavalry (CS) and deploying its men as long-range sharpshooters. Their job was to keep the Yankees pinned on the ridge while mounted Southern regiments moved to the attack. A seesaw contest with the Federals soon consumed the general's brigade. In wild and chaotic fighting Union regiments continuously attacked the pesky Maryland sharpshooters. More than once the dismounted Rebels found themselves surrounded and fighting at close quarters. Men on foot used their rifles against mounted troopers wielding sabers and firing pistols. Sometimes the Marylanders cut their way out of encirclement; at other times it took mounted charges by the rest of Lomax's brigade to save them.[24]

In front of the southern slope of Fleetwood Heights mounted charges swayed back and forth. When opposing regiments came within close range of one another, the rattle of pistol, and carbine fire rose briefly before flashing sabers dominated the struggle. Troopers used their edged weapons freely and many seemed to prefer the saber rather than a firearm in such close quarters.

Confusion reigned. The formations tore at each other so savagely it was often impossible for officers to maintain any semblance of control once a command was committed to action. At one point a mounted assault by one Virginia regiment was broken in two when another regiment charged obliquely through its ranks against a different target.

An assault by the 15th Virginia typified the fighting that afternoon. In the aftermath of an attack, the regiment rallied under the cover of some nearby woods while the enemy poured a heavy fire into the sheltering trees. Once the Virginians regained their organization, they charged out of the woods. As the Southerners rode over the tracks of the Orange & Alexandria toward a Federal battle line, the 1st Vermont and the 18th Pennsylvania hit the Virginians on both flanks simultaneously. Another Rebel outfit, seeing the onslaught of Union horsemen, raced ahead to strike the Vermont troopers. A vicious mêlée quickly entangled all four regiments until the Rebels disengaged only to fall back, reform, and repeat the charge moments later.

---

23 Hopkins, *From Bull Run to Appomattox*, 123; *OR* 29, pt. 1, 393, 384-85.

24 *OR* 29, pt. 1, 465, 467.

Yankee gunners rather than horsemen presented more danger to the 9th and 13th Virginia cavalry regiments of Colonel John Chambliss' (formerly Rooney Lee's) brigade. A Federal battery opened fire on these Virginians as they attacked Northern sharpshooters in the woods west of the railroad station. A terrible barrage of canister hurtled through the Confederate ranks bringing down horses and men. The Yankee cannons did effective execution, inflicting considerable loss and wounding the commanders of both regiments.[25]

As the rival bodies of horsemen continually charged, recoiled, reformed, and charged again, the enthusiasm of some participants naturally began to wane. As the mounted 6th Virginia stood its ground and prepared to receive a Federal cavalry assault, a young Rebel private named Luther Hopkins noticed that as the Yankee troopers neared, "quite a number" of the attackers were "reining in" their horses. Apparently the hesitant riders had lost their taste for hand-to-hand combat and were involuntarily signaling "I have gone as far as I mean to go." But others, recalled Hopkins, continued "dashing right into our ranks, firing as they came."

When the opposing battle lines collided, dust and gun smoke eddied thickly into the air, making it almost impossible to distinguish friend from foe. The tumult of gunfire, yells, shouts, rattling equipment, grunting men, and snorting horses combined with the metallic clanging of sabers to virtually drown out shouted commands. Sooner or later every cavalry charge devolved into single combat.

A Federal officer dashed directly for young Hopkins during the Union charge. With his saber drawn and ready to strike, the young trooper was nonetheless transfixed by his onrushing enemy and unable to act. "Somehow or other my arm would not obey me," he recollected. "It seemed too much like murder." Fortunately a nearby lieutenant had no such reservations. The officer rode forward until "his pistol almost touched" the Yankee and shot him in the side, no doubt saving Hopkins' life.

Terrible though it was, battle could also be exhilarating and dramatic. Amidst the noise, dust, confusion, and carnage, individual acts of courage occurred almost everywhere. Thomas Rosser's bravery attracted widespread notice. As he led the 5th Virginia into a charge that tore through the Federal ranks, the colonel's audacity caught the eye of men in another regiment. "The cry went up and down the ranks," said one Confederate, "Look at Rosser! Look at Rosser!" Such unvarnished bravery usually met a fatal end and "everybody expected" to see the colonel "tumble from his horse, shot to death." But luck rode with the ambitious Virginian this day and he did not fall.

A soldier fighting beside Luther Hopkins, perhaps as brave as Rosser, wasn't as fortunate. A bullet struck the trooper in the throat and ripped through his jugular vein.

25 *OR* 29, pt. 1, 469, 474.

"The blood spurted out like water from a spigot," remembered the horrified cavalryman. Hopkins himself had a closer call than he knew at the time: a bullet put a hole in his saber strap, which hung not an eighth of an inch from his leg.[26]

*   *   *

Despite repeated attempts, Stuart's horsemen could not drive Pleasonton's divisions from Fleetwood Heights. The Confederate general eventually abandoned that effort and instead tried to maneuver his command to get between the Federals and the Rappahannock. Realizing what the Rebels were up to, the Yankees frustrated their purpose by conducting a staged withdrawal to the river. One brigade at a time would retire a few hundred yards before turning to form line and cover the retreat of the next brigade, which in turn moved a little closer to the Rappahannock before itself forming to cover the movement of its predecessor. The Federal cavalry leapfrogged backward like this until it arrived safely north of the stream.

Thus the battle slowed and ultimately died out. Tactically the fight had been something of a draw. The Rebels had chased the Yankees all the way from the Rapidan to the Rappahannock. At the end of the day they held the field upon which the enemy had abandoned his dead, some of his wounded, and a large number of prisoners. On the other side of the ledger, Pleasonton's troopers had escaped destruction and managed to shield Meade's infantry from Stuart's observation or harassment.

Although the Confederates counted as a disappointment their failure to destroy Buford and Kilpatrick, Stuart's troopers never really had a chance to achieve that goal. The Federals had outnumbered the Rebels throughout the battle, and the terrain had favored the skilled and highly mobile Northern formations. Custer succinctly summed things up remarking to Pleasonton, "Alf, it's a pretty hard job to capture a division of cavalry."[27]

It had been a costly day for both sides, and the casualty lists reflected the severe nature of the fighting. Stuart did not report his losses for this specific engagement, instead tallying them for the entire campaign. However, an examination of a wide variety of sources reveals Confederate casualties of 27 killed, 169 wounded and 45 missing. To these figures must be added 33 casualties of an unspecified nature—total Rebel losses were 274 men from all causes. The number of horses killed is uncertain,

---

26 Previous paragraphs all based on Hopkins, *From Bull Run to Appomattox*, 118-119.

27 Wittenberg, *One of Custer's Wolverines*, 61.

but it was not uncommon to lose more animals than men in a large scale cavalry action.[28]

Federal losses were about the same. Neither Pleasonton nor either of his engaged division commanders reported specific casualties for October 11. A survey of Federal sources shows 30 dead, 47 wounded, and at least 153 missing: a total of 230 casualties from all causes. Stuart reported taking 233 Union captives around Brandy Station, 80 more than fragmentary Union records reveal. Possibly some of these extra prisoners were infantry stragglers, but cavalrymen most likely made up the majority of the captives. If that assessment is accurate, then Pleasonton's final losses were 310 men. As is the case with the Confederates, this total is incomplete, and the number of mounts which fell in the engagement is unknown.[29]

The struggles between Morton's Ford and Fleetwood Heights constituted a clear strategic victory for the Confederates. Stuart's primary job was to prevent Pleasonton's Union cavalry from observing or interfering with Lee's marching columns. The vigorous pressure Rebel troopers applied had kept the Federal horsemen focused on survival rather than the whereabouts of Confederate infantry. Moreover, Stuart had kept a constant stream of intelligence flowing to army headquarters. In fact, he sent so many couriers so frequently with information sometimes of little import that General Lee felt the need to caution Stuart against wearing out his horses unnecessarily.[30]

*   *   *

28 OR 29, pt. 1, 275; www.civilwardata.com; Walbrook D. Swank, ed., *Sabres, Saddles and Spurs*, 94. Carter broke down Wickham's losses as 1st VA: 1k, 18w; 2nd VA: 8k, 26w; 3rd VA: 5w, 4m; 4th VA: 9k, 40w. Although the 1st MD had been in the thick of the fight and had found itself encircled several times, it counted only 2w and 4cap. The 12th and 7th VA in Hampton's division lost 33 men between them. In the 6th VA, despite multiple charges and countercharges, losses were 2 men and several horses killed, alongside 15w. The 15th Virginia suffered 2k, 14w, and 4cap.

29 Ibid., pt. 2, 276; www.civilwardata.com collates casualties by regiment from a wide variety of sources and is thus an invaluable asset in determining often opaque casualty figures; Frederick Phisterer, *New York in the War of the Rebellion* (Albany, NY, 1912), entries for 2nd, 5th, 6th, 8th and 9th NY Cavalry regiments. The 1st VT counted 3 officers and 29 men k, w, or m. Davies' entire brigade reported only 4 k and 13 w. Its loss in missing and prisoners was 112 men.

30 Some felt Stuart was still trying to make up for his Gettysburg performance. For an excellent account of Stuart's operations during the Gettysburg Campaign, see Eric J. Wittenberg and J. David Petruzzi, *Plenty of Blame to go Around: Jeb Stuart's Controversial Ride to Gettysburg* (El Dorado Hills, CA, 2011).

The commander of the ANV was still not well, but finding it impossible to closely supervise his army's operations from an ambulance, Lee had bravely mounted his favorite horse, Traveler, that morning. As it turned out, he paid dearly for it. He later confessed that every motion of his horse and his own shaking body "gave much pain."[31]

Lee masked his suffering as best he could and accompanied Richard Ewell toward Culpeper Court House. Late in the day of October 11, the two men entered the town alongside Confederate infantry. At the start of the campaign Lee had issued orders for trainloads of rations to move to this point once his troops took the village. This foresight now allowed the army to replenish its supplies after three days on the road.[32]

The majority of Lee's troops were out of food, and as had often happened, hunger became a motivating obsession for Confederate soldiers. Most of Stuart's regiments had no feed for their horses, and their riders were little better off. Some troopers could do no better than collect hatful's of acorns to slake their stomach pains. According to one Rebel infantrymen, his comrades were speaking of little else than "the all absorbing question of Yankee haversacks full of rations and fat sutler stores."[33]

Although they could do little to help feed the Southern host, the good people of Culpeper Court House were delighted to welcome Lee's soldiers. As the general rode into town, old men, women, and children (all that remained of its white population) flocked around him. Many people simply wanted to see the great general or show their gratitude and admiration. Some residents, however, had issues to press upon the Confederate commander.

One matronly woman told Lee that some of the town's young ladies had attended a concert given by a band in Maj. Gen. John Sedgwick's VI Corps during the Yankee occupation. Union officers, she said, had escorted several girls to the affair. Worse yet, in the eyes of this female informant, most of the women appeared to have thoroughly enjoyed the event, despite the company.

The assembled crowd fell into a hushed silence. A number of young ladies cast their eyes downward, cheeks turning red with embarrassment and shame. Lee looked about with a stern expression on his face. Finally, he spoke. "I know General Sedgwick very well. It is just like him to be so kindly and considerate, and to have his band there to entertain them." Lee's expression softened as he enjoyed the reaction to his unexpected words. "So, young ladies, if the music is good, go and hear it as often as you

31 Freeman, *R.E. Lee*, vol. 3, 172-73; Longstreet, *From Manassas to Appomattox*, note, 469.

32 Ibid.

33 Howard, *Recollections*, 235; Swank, *Sabres, Saddles and Spurs*, 92.

can," he continued, "and enjoy yourselves. You will find that General Sedgwick will have none but agreeable gentlemen about him."[34]

No one recorded the disapproving matron's reaction, but the young belles were obviously relieved, and the great general was even greater now in their eyes. Lee had not forgotten the joys of youth, nor would he deny the ladies those few simple pleasures they might snatch in the midst of war.

As night fell on October 11, the Army of Northern Virginia concentrated around and to the west of Culpeper Court House. While some troops cooked newly issued rations, others went hungry. The Rebels were pleased despite empty stomachs and fatigue. Their army had done well thus far, and despite Gettysburg the Yankees still seemed to fear its might and audacity. [35]

The fighting at Brandy Station capped a satisfying day for Lee, although not nearly as satisfying as he wished. Meade's refusal to give battle had cheated the ANV of a chance to crush the Union army in the shallow V of the Rapidan and Rappahannock. No matter. If Meade wouldn't fight in Culpeper County, Lee would find a place where he would have no choice. Tomorrow his army would set out to cut off the Federal retreat. If all went well, it would catch a part of Meade's army out in the open and destroy it. Until sunset on October 11, Lee had maneuvered in hope of a battle. In the morning, his army would start in pursuit of a fleeing foe.

---

34 Freeman, *R.E. Lee*, vol. 3, 72-73.

35 *OR* 29, pt. 1, 471-72; Long "Reminiscences," Breckinridge papers, LC.

Chapter 14

"Almost Like Boys Chasing a Hare"

Meade Uncertain—Sedgwick Crosses the Rappahannock—Lee's
Offensive Resumes—Culpeper Crisis—Young's Bluff—Welles' Prediction

ONCE Kilpatrick's and Buford's cavalry divisions withdrew over the Rappahannock during the late afternoon of October 11, the Union army had safely exited the dangerous Culpeper V and with it the unpleasant possibilities of a battle within the constricting embrace of the Rappahannock and Rapidan rivers. But uncertainty still vexed Meade. Two days of fighting at James City, Brandy Station, and Morton's Ford had completely consumed the attention of two-thirds of his cavalry. Consequently, he had lost track of Lee's main body for forty-eight hours. He didn't know the exact location of the Rebel infantry or whether it was still on the move and, if so, where to.

The question of enemy intentions hung over Army of the Potomac headquarters like a sinister cloud. At Lee's first advance, Meade had been positive the Rebels would strike deeply intending to interpose themselves between Washington and the Federal army. Now he had doubts. Pleasonton and Sykes, whose units were among the last to cross the Rappahannock, reported seeing Confederates wearing knapsacks near Brandy Station. Since only infantry wore knapsacks, they naturally inferred that Lee's army was concentrating around Culpeper Court House.[1]

If they were correct, it might mean the Confederates didn't contemplate a deep offensive into the Union rear. If Meade discounted that strategic possibility, only two

---

1 OR 29, pt. 1, 415-16. They were right, but for the wrong reason. What they had seen was Garett's NC brigade which had followed Fitz Lee northward after the fight at Morton's Ford. A knapsack is a pack worn on a soldier's back. Men used it to carry blankets, spare clothing, personal items and extra rations. A haversack is a canvas or leather bag used for carrying rations. A soldier slung it over his right shoulder and wore it just above his left hip.

plausible explanations of Lee's strategy remained. Either the move was a feint designed to cover a withdrawal to a new defensive line farther south or it was a gambit seeking a battle near Culpeper. Given Lee's aggressive nature, the second possibility seemed more likely. Denied a battle in Culpeper County, the Rebel general might possibly, if somewhat improbably, strike across the Rappahannock on the morrow.

Throughout the evening of October 11, the AOP prepared for a fight along the river. Meade directed Sykes' V and Sedgwick's VI corps to occupy key hills on its south and north banks. He ordered all supply trains retired far enough inland to be out of artillery range. French received orders to mass his III Corps at Freeman's Ford. Gregg's cavalry division would assume French's former responsibility for Sulphur Springs, and keep an eye out for a Rebel flanking movement in that direction or an enemy shift toward the Shenandoah Valley. Kilpatrick's cavalry would relocate to Fayetteville with the dual task of supporting French and Gregg. Meade moved Warren's II Corps to Bealeton and told it to be ready on short notice either to reinforce the river line or counter a threat to the army's right flank. If Lee wanted to cross the Rappahannock anywhere between Freeman's and Kelly's fords, Meade would be ready for him.

At daybreak, however, no enemy advanced. Other than a small body of Rebel cavalry and a lone piece of artillery nonchalantly occupying Fleetwood Heights, no Confederates were in sight. After yesterday's tumult, the forenoon of the 12th was eerily quiet—a suspicious silence that made Meade worry his army was in the wrong place.[2]

Since the first indications of Rebel activity on October 8, some Federal officers had surmised Lee was making a feint to cover the withdrawal of his army closer to Richmond. Now the absence of enemy troops along the entire length of the Rappahannock lent credence to that possibility. First Lieutenant James Biddle, one of Meade's aides, echoed general opinion at headquarters when he concluded that "the mass of the rebels have fallen back." Biddle and others thought Lee's advance on Culpeper was merely meant "to conceal their real plans," i.e., to ship more troops from Virginia to Bragg so that he could finish off Rosecrans at Chattanooga.[3]

Meade acknowledged the possibility but wasn't quite ready to believe that Lee would voluntarily abandon so much territory without compulsion. The greater danger was that the Rebels might already be swinging west and north to cut the AOP's line of communication and retreat. If that were the case, Gregg's cavalry guarding the western

---

2 Ibid., pt. 2, 291-92, 295.

3 James C. Biddle to wife Oct. 12, 1863, James C. Biddle papers, HSP.

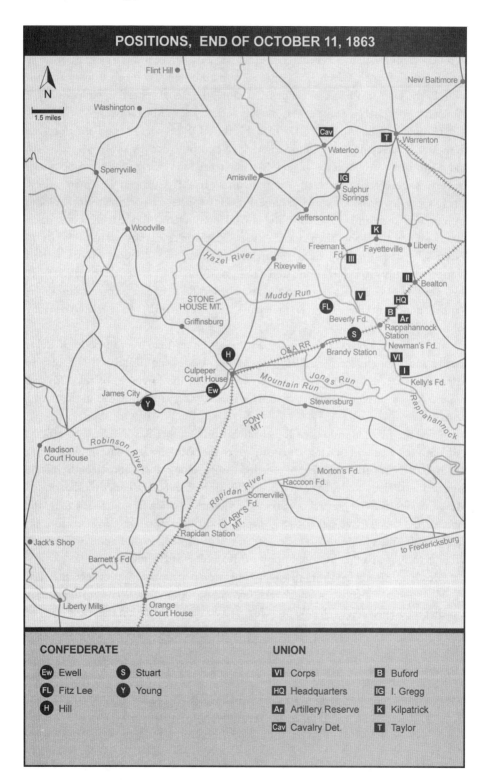

POSITIONS, END OF OCTOBER 11, 1863

CONFEDERATE

Ew Ewell
FL Fitz Lee
H Hill
S Stuart
Y Young

UNION

VI Corps
HQ Headquarters
Ar Artillery Reserve
Cav Cavalry Det.
B Buford
IG I. Gregg
K Kilpatrick
T Taylor

Major General John Sedgwick
Library of Congress

reaches of the Rappahannock should have spotted something by now. However, he had reported nothing.

Gregg's silence seemed to affirm Sykes' and Pleasonton's earlier assertion that Lee was concentrating at Culpeper Court House. Meade fretted over this possibility as the hours ticked by on the morning of the 12th. Finally, about mid-morning, his anxiety got the better of him. He decided to send an expedition across the Rappahannock to "ascertain" if Lee's army was in "position near Brandy Station or in the vicinity of Culpeper Court House" and "prepared to give battle."[4]

If so, this movement was apt to ignite a major engagement. No timid approach would do. The force crossing the river had to be strong enough to hold its own if it ran into trouble. Therefore Meade detailed two whole corps—Sykes' V and Sedgwick's VI (minus Brig. Gen. Henry D. Terry's 3rd Division which was guarding the railroad) to undertake the operation accompanied by all their ammunition trains and ambulances. Buford's cavalry division would precede the infantry. If he encountered no resistance at Brandy Station the column would push on into the vicinity of Culpeper Court House. Sedgwick would have overall command of the operation.

To support this effort, Meade told Gouverneur Warren to leave a brigade to guard the supply depot at Bealeton and cross the rest of his corps over the river to Rappahannock Station. There he would halt his command and keep it in readiness to move at a moment's notice. The II Corps' ordnance wagons and ambulances would remain on the north shore, deployed to follow Warren farther south if headquarters ordered him toward Brandy Station.

Meade made Sedgwick's mission clear, both personally and in writing: he was conducting a reconnaissance in force to determine if Lee's main body was near

---

4 *OR* 29, pt. 2, 296.

Culpeper and willing to fight. Should this be the case, Meade intended to rapidly advance the rest of the army and oblige the enemy. A telegraph operator would accompany Sedgwick to keep army headquarters speedily informed of unfolding events. Newton's I and French's III corps would stand ready to move quickly with little warning. If Sedgwick got into a battle he was to maintain his ground until Warren, French, and Newton could come up. Sedgwick could then direct their troops onto whatever battle line he had formed.

After issuing these orders Meade explained his actions to Halleck. Lee's intentions were "as yet undeveloped," he wired at 11:30 a.m. But since Gregg hadn't reported Confederates to the west, and given the size of the Rebel force attacking Pleasonton yesterday, Meade thought it "less probable" Lee was trying to get between him and Washington. After relaying his instructions to Sedgwick, he promised that "[i]f Lee will give me battle between the Rappahannock and the Rapidan I will fight him."

But this assertion of aggressiveness proved momentary. The next minute he was warning Halleck that the AOP would surely have to attack if it fought near Culpeper. Even the possibility of a tactical offensive conjured up phantoms for Meade. "From all the information I can get," he confided, "it is my opinion [Lee's] forces are nearly, if not quite equal to mine." This tone wasn't reassuring and implied a pre-mortem alibi for possible defeat or a sudden decision to forego offensive action. It sounded like last July to those who remembered. Meade had promised to assail the Rebel army then too, only to fail to attack when the moment came.

Moreover, Meade was flat-out wrong about the numbers. His 89,000-man command outnumbered Lee's 55,000 troops by a ratio of 1.6 to 1, and he could hardly plead ignorance of this. On September 15, he had told Halleck that Lee's army had "not less than 40,000 or 45,000 infantry and over 5,000 cavalry." Where and when the Rebels gained the additional 30,000 or 40,000 men required for parity with the AOP, Meade did not say. Indeed, how he came to this conclusion is hard to fathom. Perhaps because he himself was unwilling to assume the offensive with mere 1.6 to 1 odds, Meade couldn't conceive of Lee's doing it either.[5]

Meade's strategy was as dubious as his math. Twenty-four hours earlier, uncertain of Lee's intentions, the general had decided to withdraw north of the Rappahannock. Given the geographical perils of fighting a battle in the Culpeper V, this was a conservative but sound military judgment. Behind the Rappahannock, his army could avoid such a battle and prevent Lee from cutting its line of communication.

Meade now chose to undermine everything accomplished the day before while acknowledging Lee's intentions still remained unclear. What good purpose could

5   Previous paragraphs based on *OR* 29, pt. 2, 183, 293, 295-97.

Meade serve by ordering nearly half his army back to Brandy Station on October 12? Buford's cavalry was certainly capable of discovering if the Rebels hovered in strength near Culpeper and with far less risk. If Meade was crossing the Rappahannock to fight a major battle, why take just a portion of the army? If there remained a possibility the Rebels were striking more deeply, why run the chance of sending anyone across the river at all? If Meade thought it unwise to fight in the Culpeper V on October 9, 10, or 11 while occupying a pre-designated defensive line, how was it suddenly safer to assume the offensive there on October 12?

The general didn't ask these questions. Impatience was his only plausible reason for sending Sedgwick's force south of the Rappahannock, or perhaps a nagging feeling that his army should not have run in the first place. No doubt, how Washington perceived events played upon his mind. If Lee weren't pushing farther north, many influential people in and out of Lincoln's administration would interpret Meade's retreat as too cautious, his failure to fight as cowardice, and both as evidence he was no match for Lee. That just might cost the Pennsylvanian command of the army and ruin the reputation he won at Gettysburg.

*   *   *

On the morning of October 12, both commanding generals lacked information on the whereabouts of their enemy's infantry. Lee didn't know whether the Federals were still retreating or making a stand on the Rappahannock. Unlike Meade, however, this lack of information didn't impel hesitation or reconsideration for Lee. Whatever the Federals were doing, his stratagem would be the same—a wide flanking march that would turn any line on the river and, if successful, put the Army of Northern Virginia between Meade and Washington. Since the success of such a movement depended on speed, Lee decided to move his army on parallel routes toward Warrenton. Once there he would have the option of striking eastward toward the O&A or northward toward Manassas Junction.

A. P. Hill's corps would march through Newby's Crossroads toward Amissville en route to crossing the Rappahannock at Waterloo and then moving northeast to Warrenton and a link up with Ewell. Ewell's corps, marching northwest from Culpeper, would follow a path that ran through Rixeyville, Jeffersonton, and Sulphur Springs on the Rappahannock. Once over the river it would move on Warrenton. The ponderous Confederate supply train would trace a safer but slower path to the west of Hill's route. If everything went well, by nightfall Lee would be over the Rappahannock and in Warrenton before noon the next day.

When they took to the roads early on October 12, the Confederates were in a jubilant mood. As the sun arched higher in the sky, it became apparent to them that the Yankee army was retreating. "We all entered now fully into the spirit of the movement," remembered one Rebel, for "we were convinced that Meade was unwilling to face us, and we therefore anticipated a pleasant affair, if we should succeed in catching him." Hill's troops noted that their general was wearing the trademark red shirt which was his favorite battle attire. The men knew their commander sensed imminent combat, and they did as well. With the Yankees on the run and Lee's army in pursuit, one Rebel thought the march felt "almost like boys chasing a hare."[6]

*   *   *

Stuart's cavalry screened the movement toward the upper Rappahannock, with Funsten's brigade leading Ewell's column, Gordon's brigade covering its rear, and Fitz Lee's division guarding its right. After leaving his bivouac at Welford's Ford on the Hazel River, Lee led his command west to Stark's Ford (some two miles east of Rixeyville), where it crossed the Hazel before riding parallel to Ewell's column about three miles to its east. Lee's goal was Fox Mill Ford on the Rappahannock, about five miles southeast of Sulphur Springs, where his troopers would cross the river and camp for the night.[7]

While the ANV's infantry and most of Stuart's horsemen moved north, Col. Rosser with his 180-man strong 5th Virginia Cavalry and one fieldpiece from Chew's battery remained on Fleetwood Heights. Their job was to maintain the illusion that Lee's army had not marched away. Young's cavalry brigade, which had remained at James City during the fighting at Brandy Station on October 11, moved east toward Culpeper Court House to protect Lee's forward supply depot and screen the rear of his army. Since no one dreamed the fleeing Federals would suddenly undertake an offensive movement, especially south of the Rappahannock, Stuart anticipated Rosser and Young accomplishing their mission without undue difficulty or danger. But the Rebels hadn't foreseen Meade's sudden change of heart. When Yankee soldiers began flooding across the river around mid-morning, Rosser's cavalrymen suddenly found themselves in an unexpectedly difficult situation.

Buford's skirmishers struck the 5th Virginia's picket line at noon and quickly discovered no strength behind it. When Sedgwick heard this, he ordered his entire force to advance southward against Brandy Station. The Virginians, delaying the Union avalanche as best they could, fell back towards Culpeper all the while sending couriers racing rearward with desperate pleas for reinforcement.

---

6 James C. Birdsong, ed. *Brief Sketches of the North Carolina State Troops in the War Between the States* (Raleigh, NC, 1894), 80.

7 Cooke, *Wearing of the Gray*, 269; OR 29, pt. 1, 446, 460, 456, 472, 466, 474-75, 463.

The only hope of assistance within galloping distance was Colonel Pierce Young's command, making its unhurried way eastward from James City. In response to Rosser's appeal for help, Young rushed his brigade and the four guns of Moorman's and Hart's batteries the last few miles to Culpeper Court House. He found Rosser on a wooded ridge known ominously as Slaughter Hill, about a mile and a half north of town. Young immediately ordered his four field pieces into line next to Rosser's single gun and quickly took stock of the situation.

What he saw was fearsome. An entire division of Yankee cavalry, maybe 3,000 troopers, were facing his meager 680 sabers. Behind the Union horsemen was an enormous assembly of blue infantry. Young couldn't possibly say how many Federals had massed between the Rappahannock and Culpeper. But there were more than enough to swat his little command aside and go storming into the entrails of Lee's supply line if that's what they took a mind to do.[8]

The colonel dispatched an urgent message to Stuart detailing his situation and asking for reinforcements. But Young knew any assistance the general might send would be a long time coming. Until then he was on his own, with absolutely no hope that his diminutive force could stop even a minor Union attack.

Fortunately for the Confederates, the sight of overwhelming enemy numbers did not discomfit Pierce Manning Butler Young. The 26-year old colonel had graduated with honors from the Georgia Military Academy before attending West Point. His resignation from there when Georgia seceded prevented him from graduating. During the first two years of war, however, he had proven that he needed no more schooling to be an excellent soldier.[9]

After taking stock of his situation, Young concluded that his only option for holding Culpeper was to dupe the Federals into taking a more cautious approach. If the Rebels could create the impression of great strength, the enemy might delay long enough for Stuart to send reinforcements. Once he determined to rely on trickery, the wooded crest of Slaughter Hill spurred his inventiveness and served the Georgia colonel's purposes quite well.

Young ordered three-fourths of his brigade to dismount and form line alongside the 5th Virginia Cavalry. Gray sharpshooters took position at the edge of every available stand of trees. With luck the enemy would mistake this thin screen of dismounted cavalrymen for infantry skirmishers fronting a solid battle line. Young also dispatched details of mounted men to assume position in the various open spaces among the

---

8   Wiley C. Howard. *Sketch of Cobb Legion Cavalry and Some Incidents and Scenes Remembered*, SHC/UNC.

9   Warner, *Generals in Gray*, 348. Born in SC, Young moved to GA as a child and grew up there.

Colonel Pierce M. B. Young
Bartow Historical Museum, Cartersville, Georgia

woods. Twelve or 16 Rebel horsemen in a column of fours would trot up to each such spot and move just far enough forward so that the enemy could see the head of the tiny formation on the crest of the ridge. From the Yankee vantage point Young hoped this would appear to be the tip of an entire regiment mounted and waiting to attack.[10]

Moorman's and Hart's cannon also played a role in Young's grand charade. When the five available guns went into action, they speedily provoked Union artillery to return fire. The resulting noisy duel was just what the colonel wanted. Young took personal command of the battery and directed its fire, even sighting some of the pieces himself. As the cannons boomed and shells burst overhead, he ordered his men to yell "like hell and damnation" in order to enhance his illusion. Meanwhile, couriers raced back and forth in front of the woods as though carrying orders to elements of a formidable foe.

Throughout it all Col. Young sat calmly atop his iron-gray stallion near the guns, supervising their fire and shouting orders, unmoved by the exploding shells or his desperate circumstances. One Southern trooper, impressed by Young's display of "sublime courage," likened the colonel's personal and professional conduct to that of a "young Napoleon."

The sun had sunk well down the western sky when Rosser and Young united on Slaughter Hill. Only two hours separated the massively outgunned Confederates from nightfall. Would their elaborate bluff stave off disaster before darkness brought at least a temporary lessening of danger? Astonishingly, the answer appeared to be affirmative. The enemy had come to a complete stop "apparently dismayed," observed one Southerner, at the suddenly robust Rebel resistance. Young knew his amateur theatrical

10 Howard, *Sketch of Cobb Legion Cavalry*, UNC; Cooke, *Wearing of the Gray*, 269; OR 29, pt. 1, 446.

was enjoying only temporary success. Come morning virtually nothing could prevent the Federals from sweeping away the thin line of Rebel cavalry defending Culpeper.[11]

After nightfall, Southern troopers built a multitude of campfires across a front two miles wide. Federal pickets, it was hoped, would report the vast number of illuminations to Union leaders who would mistakenly deduce that Lee had massively reinforced Young and Rosser. To assist in the deception the regimental band of the 5th Virginia Cavalry moved from place to place, playing vigorously at each location to suggest that the Confederates on Slaughter Hill had a score of bands and hence a score of regiments. Hoarse Southern troopers lent weight to the façade by erupting with the Rebel yell at every tune. Not to be outdone, the Federals brought forward one of their own bands to counter the gray musicians.[12]

No one knew if this fakery would inspire caution in the minds of Sedgwick and his officers. If the Northerners undertook so much as a serious reconnaissance in the morning, they would certainly discover their enemy's weakness. Everything depended on what the Yankees would do at dawn. At least one Southerner, however, confidently predicted Young had little to worry about, and that was Jeb Stuart. After learning of the Federal advance on Culpeper late that evening, the general wrote back to Young that the danger would dissipate by morning. Once the enemy realized the ANV had crossed the upper Rappahannock, he predicted, the Yankees would retire from the vicinity of the court house as fast as they had come.[13]

*   *   *

Stuart might prove right. Neither Rosser's resistance nor Young's pretense had fooled John Buford. He passed his conclusions up the command chain to Sedgwick and Meade, who told Halleck at 8 p.m. on October 12 that Buford had encountered only trifling opposition. He also reported that civilians in the area swore Stuart's cavalry had ridden westward during the night of the 11th. The Confederates had claimed they were heading to Manassas Gap and the Shenandoah Valley to either cut Meade off from Washington or invade the North again.

What these civilians were saying hardly seemed improbable, and if they were telling the truth Gregg's cavalry would soon find out. Pleasonton had positioned his 2nd

11 Previous paragraphs based upon Howard, *Sketch of Cobb Legion Cavalry*, UNC; Cooke, *Wearing of the Gray*, 269.

12 McClellan, *I Rode with JEB Stuart*, 383-84; Howard, *Sketch of Cobb Legion Cavalry*, UNC; Cooke, *Wearing of the Gray*, 269.

13 *OR* 29, pt. 1, 446.

Division to the west, with orders to picket the upper Rappahannock fords and keep an eye on the roads leading to the Blue Ridge gaps. These outposts would be the first to encounter any Rebel force attempting to turn the Union right. Meade told Halleck he hoped to get some firm information from Gregg during the night. He promised to "fall back by forced marches" the moment he could "ascertain anything definite" proving that Lee was outflanking the Union army. In any event, Meade thought his chief "should be advised of this report, because if true, Lee may get between me and Washington and you may be annoyed then."[14]

Nothing in that dispatch was going to please either Lincoln or Halleck; not that anyone was happy at army headquarters either. Up to this point, October 12 had been an extremely frustrating day for the Federal high command. Meade desperately needed to know where Lee's army was and what it was doing. Sedgwick and Buford had confirmed that Lee wasn't at Culpeper. But Gregg's cavalry could produce no evidence that the Rebels were offensively maneuvering to the west. Clearly Lee was calling the tune now. Meade seemed frozen in place until someone could tell him the whereabouts of the enemy's army.

Much to the disappointment of the Union's political leaders, Meade's predispositions were apparent. Early on October 12, Lincoln had telegraphed Meade asking "What news this morning?" The president passed along a recent dispatch from Rosecrans claiming that more troops from Lee's army had reached Tennessee. "I send this for what it is worth," Lincoln said, unsure of its validity. Nonetheless the chief executive obviously thought it at least possible Lee had sent Bragg another corps, with the clear implication that a seriously weakened Lee was bluffing. If so, Meade knew his commander-in-chief expected him to act decisively and destroy the Rebel army.[15]

Secretary Welles had no illusions about what to expect from Meade. Noting the capital "full of rumors of fighting, and of Meade's falling back," Welles discounted much of what he heard as "trash for the Pennsylvania and Ohio elections" taking place next day. Nonetheless, the rumors smelled of truth—disquieting, disappointing truth. "I am prepared for almost any news from the front," Welles wrote in his diary that night, adding ominously that he would not be surprised if Lee outgeneraled Meade.[16]

---

14 Ibid. pt. 2, 293-94.

15 Ibid., 294.

16 Morse, *Diary of Gideon Welles*, vol. 1, 469.

Chapter 15

"A Bloody and Doubtful Contest"

Where are the Rebels—Collision at Jeffersonton—
Struggle for Sulphur Springs—Gregg's Crisis—Meade Reacts—Retreat

WHILE Sedgwick's October 12 reconnaissance in force plunged fruitlessly into Culpeper County, Brig. Gen. David Gregg's 2nd Cavalry Division kept watch over Meade's right flank and the upper Rappahannock River. The vast expanse of countryside between Culpeper Court House and the Blue Ridge Mountains had provoked Federal anxiety since the start of the campaign—and for good reason.

From the environs of Madison Court House Lee's army could march through Sperryville toward Thornton's Gap or through Gaines Crossroads toward Chester Gap. Using either pass the Rebels could enter the Shenandoah Valley where a network of excellent roads stretching all the way to the Potomac invited the enemy to launch another invasion of the North. Alternately, the Confederates might move into the Loudoun Valley, between the Blue Ridge and Bull Run Mountains. Once there they could cross the Potomac into Maryland or emerge from one of the passes in the Bull Run chain to come down on Meade's rear anywhere between Leesburg and Manassas.

Should Lee prove less ambitious, he could move through Amissville or Rixeyville to strike across the upper Rappahannock at Waterloo or Sulphur Springs. If the enemy got over the river at either point, he would outflank the AOP's line on the Rappahannock and position himself to make a quick march against Warrenton from whence he could move east to interdict Meade's O&A supply line. Unless the Federal army responded promptly to such a threat, Lee might interpose his command between it and Washington.

Every one of these alternatives was highly dangerous to Meade. As yet unable to determine just what Lee was up to, the Union commander knew that he would need the earliest possible warning of any such Rebel movements. Only his cavalry could sound the alarm if Lee moved west. To that end on the morning of October 11, army headquarters had directed Maj. Gen. Pleasonton to shift Gregg's 2nd Cavalry Division to the upper Rappahannock.

It had taken Gregg most of the day to reach this new position. His division's 1st Brigade, under Col. John P. Taylor, had left at daylight from Kelly's Ford for Brandy Station. When Taylor arrived there he received orders to take his regiments to Rappahannock Station, cross the river, then move west to Sulphur Springs and go into bivouac. The 2nd Brigade, led by Gregg's older cousin, Col. John Irvin Gregg, had ridden northwest from Culpeper Court House at 10 a.m. to the town of Jeffersonton, where it went into camp about 9 p.m.[1]

Gregg's activities on October 11 had kept him out of the cavalry fight at Brandy Station and positioned his division to guard the upper reaches of the Rappahannock River. At 9:45 p.m. that same evening Pleasonton had issued orders for the 2nd Cavalry Division to expand its scope of operations on October 12. Gregg was to post a brigade on the Sperryville road and watch for any sign of enemy troops. Pleasonton and Meade wanted this unit to report frequently, even if nothing was happening in its sector. Meade's chief-of-staff made certain Gregg understood that "information of Lee's movements" was the goal. He should avoid getting caught up in a battle. His mission was not to slow Lee down, but solely to discover his whereabouts and get that evidence to army headquarters "at the earliest possible moment."[2]

A 30-year old Pennsylvanian who hailed from a distinguished family, David M. Gregg's first cousin was Andrew Curtin, the state's governor. The general's grandfather, Andrew Gregg, had been both a US congressman and senator. After graduating from West Point in 1851, David had served on the western frontier and in California. He commanded the 8th Pennsylvania Cavalry at the war's outset and had quickly proved an excellent officer, gaining a brigadier's commission by November 1862. Since Chancellorsville he had led a division. Lyman remarked upon Gregg's "long, tawny beard" and "clear, dark blue eyes" before accurately summing up his essence: "less of dash in his expression," than Pleasonton's other commanders, but "more of judgment and sense." He was the sort of man Meade could count on to follow orders and carry out his mission.[3]

Complying with Pleasonton's instructions, Gregg awakened his division well before dawn on October 12. He directed Col. Taylor to move north and position his brigade to watch the roads leading into Warrenton from the west, and also to guard a

---

1   OR 29, pt. 1, 361, 365, 367, 369.

2   Ibid., pt. 2, 286; Humphreys, *From Gettysburg to the Rapidan*, 17.

3   Warner, *Generals in Blue*, 187; Lyman, *Meade's Army*, 35.

good ford at a place called Waterloo. The small town had grown into a thriving community after the 1849 completion of a canal linking it to Fredericksburg. Unfortunately, its prosperity ended quickly in 1852 when the O&A Railroad went into operation and killed the canal business. Military operations around the village during the past two years had destroyed or ruined most of Waterloo's buildings. The ford near the town, however, remained a useful crossing point on the Rappahannock River and a potential Confederate target.[4]

With orders issued to cover Warrenton and Waterloo, Gregg shifted his attention to the region south of the river. He gave the job of surveilling this area to his cousin, Col. Irvin Gregg. His instructions were specific. He should send one regiment to scout the zone between Amissville and Sperryville to detect any Rebel movement toward the Shenandoah Valley. Another regiment was to be deployed at Jeffersonton to provide early warning of an enemy thrust due north toward Warrenton. The rest of his command should take position behind the Rappahannock to protect the bridge at Sulphur Springs, 10 miles downstream from Waterloo.[5]

Established in 1798, the modest village of Jeffersonton was home to 160 people when the war began. It was a tiny place of just eight buildings, among them a school named the Jeffersonton Academy and a brick Baptist Church surrounded by a stone fence. A civilian traveling through the forgettable place in early 1863 referred to the town as a "poor deserted hamlet." Poor it might have been, but it was also an important transportation bottleneck. A pair of roads, including one leading to Rixeyville, intersected just south of town before sharing a route through the village. Once north of Jeffersonton the roads diverged again, one veering west toward Amissville and the other to Sulphur Springs.[6]

If Jeffersonton was unremarkable, Sulphur Springs was one of the most beautiful and renown spots in all Virginia. Sometimes called White Sulphur Springs, it boasted a pool of mineral water with reputed curative powers. The place had long been a popular tourist attraction. In the 1830s entrepreneurs built a spacious and magnificent four-story hotel near the spring. Combined with rows of individual guest cottages

---

4   OR 29, pt. 1, 361; Edward Tobie, *History of the First Maine Cavalry, 1861-1865* (Boston, MA, 1887), 193; Frederic Denison, *Sabres and Spurs: The First Regiment Rhode Island Cavalry in the Civil War, 1861-1865* (Central Falls, RI, 1876), 293-96.

5   OR 29, pt. 1, 361, 365, 367, 369; Tobie, *First Maine Cavalry*, 193. The 6-foot 4-inch tall chief of the 2nd Brigade went by "Irvin," but his men called him "Long John."

6   Daniel E. Sutherland, *Seasons of War: The Ordeal of a Confederate Community: 1861-1865* (New York, 1995), 7; Mrs. Burton (Constance Cary) Harrison, *Recollections Grave and Gay* (New York, 1911), 103.

Ruins of the White Sulpher Springs Hotel circa 1862. *Library of Congress*

flanking well-manicured and elaborately landscaped lawns, the resort could accommodate 800 guests.[7]

The town's splendor did not survive the war. In August 1862, Union and Confederate forces engaged in a nasty fight for control of the bridge at Sulphur Springs. Hit by shells from both sides, the hotel caught fire and burned to the ground. All that remained of its former glory were blackened walls, standing in stark contrast to majestic trees and untended gardens. But as was the case with Jeffersonton and Waterloo, the dilapidated condition of Sulphur Springs did nothing to lessen its importance as a military objective.

The significance of Jeffersonton, Sulphur Springs, and the road network south of the Rappahannock didn't escape Irvin Gregg. The colonel quickly put his brigade into motion upon receiving his orders. Gregg gave the critical job of reconnoitering

---

7   Pell Manning to parents Aug. 25, 1863, University of Washington; Fauquier White Sulphur
Springs history at https://www.hsl.virginia.edu/historical/exhibits/springs/fauquier.cfm

Sperryville to 35-year old Col. Charles H. Smith, a pre-war teacher who commanded the 1st Maine Cavalry.

These New Englanders and their leader were reliable veterans. Nonetheless, Smith recalled that Irvin Gregg carefully stressed the "important character" of this particular assignment. The Maine regiment was to travel through Amissville, Gaines Crossroads, and Washington on its way to Sperryville and it was to "promptly" report any sign of the enemy activity. Smith's simple task was also highly dangerous, because nobody knew how many, if any, Rebels lurked in that region. A careless misstep might lead to the regiment's destruction and the failure of its essential task.[8]

The 1st Maine Cavalry started its 22-mile journey to Sperryville before sunrise, traversing the 15 miles to Gaines Crossroads without stopping. There Smith detached Capt. Paul Chadbourne's Company I to keep watch on the surrounding area. Then, after a brief rest, he led the balance of his regiment three miles south to Washington, dropping off another observation detachment along the way. Once there, Smith told Lt. Col. Stephen Boothby and Maj. George M. Brown to select 100 men with strong horses and proceed to Sperryville. The balance of the regiment would remain in reserve at Washington. While Boothby and Brown headed south, Smith ordered Lt. William Harris and a 12-man escort to ride back to Sulphur Springs and inform Col. Gregg that the reconnaissance had encountered nothing but Rebel guerrillas thus far, and that the 1st Maine would rejoin the brigade later that night.[9]

*   *   *

As Smith and his regiment conducted their reconnaissance toward Sperryville, Federal cavalry spread out to monitor the upper Rappahannock. Colonel Taylor sent Capt. Joseph J. Gould with a 120-man strong battalion from the 1st Rhode Island Cavalry to guard Waterloo Ford.

Irvin Gregg deployed most of his brigade to defend the bridge across the Rappahannock at Sulphur Springs. The 4th Pennsylvania Cavalry and 10th New York Cavalry took post near the river. The 8th and 16th Pennsylvania cavalry regiments assumed a reserve position about a mile north of the bridge. Lieutenant Colonel Garrick Mallery's 13th Pennsylvania Cavalry remained in Jeffersonton with orders to picket the road between that village and Rixeyville. The regiment deployed vedettes along the Hazel River, some 5 miles south of Jeffersonton and waited for something to happen.

8 Tobie, *First Maine Cavalry*, 193.

9 Ibid., 193-194. Gaines Crossroads is modern day Ben Vue.

They didn't wait long: around daybreak, dismounted Rebels from Lt. Col. Mottrom D. Ball's 11th Virginia Cavalry encountered Mallery's outpost. The Virginians were the vanguard of Ewell's Corps and the advance element of Jones' cavalry brigade, commanded today by Col. Oliver R. Funsten. Their job was to displace any Yankees they found between Rixeyville and Sulphur Springs, and by 9 a.m. their skirmishers had driven the 13th Pennsylvania's pickets back into Jeffersonton.[10]

Ball had no idea how many Yankees held the town, but the surest way to find out was to poke the beehive and see what swarmed out. Even as his dismounted skirmishers continued advancing, Ball sent part of his regiment to launch a mounted charge toward the village. Colonel Mallery, anticipating such a threat, had kept a reserve force of about 100 men in the saddle, and as the Rebels came thundering forward, the Pennsylvanians counter charged. For a moment it appeared a classic cavalry mêlée was at hand, but then the 11th Virginia abruptly reversed course, leaving their erstwhile opponents with no one to fight.[11]

Not getting to cross sabers with the Rebels quickly proved the least of Mallery's problems. Lured out into the open, the Yankee cavalrymen now became easy targets for clandestinely deployed Southern marksmen. The Union troopers rapidly turned about and beat a hasty retreat. The men in blue could not outrun bullets, however, and a hailstorm of enemy fire emptied many saddles before Mallery's men made it into town. The survivors dismounted to fight on foot.[12]

As the struggle around the little village continued, Mallery sent word back to Irvin Gregg that Confederate cavalry was on the road between Rixeyville and Culpeper. Then, with no instructions to resist the Rebel advance, the Pennsylvania colonel ordered his regiment to abandon Jeffersonton and fall back toward the Rappahannock.

The 2nd Cavalry Division's commander didn't approve this decision. Mallery's men had seen no Rebel infantry. The presence of Rebel cavalry meant little and might amount to nothing more than a reconnaissance. Not willing to concede ground south of the river to Stuart's troopers, David Gregg ordered his 2nd Brigade to reinforce the Pennsylvanians. That task fell to Maj. George Covode's 4th Pennsylvania Cavalry, which was just going into camp between Sulphur Springs and Warrenton when the message to head south forced the men to reluctantly abandon their bivouac. Accompanied personally by Irvin Gregg, they were soon crossing the Rappahannock

---

10 Harold Hand, Jr. *One Good Regiment: The 13th Pennsylvania Cavalry in the Civil War, 1861-1865* (Victoria, BC, 2000), 82-83; Daniel Grimsley, *Battles in Culpeper County, Virginia* (Culpeper, VA, 1900), 22; *National Tribune*, December 15, 1898.

11 *National Tribune*, December 15, 1898.

12 Ibid.

and around 12:30 p.m., the 4th met up with the 13th Pennsylvania about a half mile north of Jeffersonton. Gregg promptly directed the two regiments to reoccupy the hamlet, which they soon did. At their approach, the handful of Rebel horsemen in the village meekly fell back into woods south of town.[13]

At 3 p.m. the Southerners renewed contact with the Pennsylvanians. The 11th Virginia Cavalry found the Federals posted behind hills, fences, and a stone wall surrounding the town's Baptist church. Ball dismounted his troopers and tried to dislodge the Yankees by a quick push. The attack went in with great vigor and fighting soon swirled around the church's stone wall, which became the epicenter of the struggle and the scene of several bouts of hand-to-hand combat.[14]

Despite this determined assault, a pair of Union regiments proved too much for Ball's Virginians to handle, and they fell back with some loss. Once more, however, it was only momentary success for the Yankees. Shortly after the regiment's repulse, Stuart, Ewell, and Robert E. Lee arrived on the scene, bringing with them the bulk of Funsten's cavalry brigade and Maj. Gen. Robert Rodes' infantry division, which was the leading element of Ewell's corps. Lee had no intention of acting as a mere bystander. After witnessing the retreat of the 11th Virginia, he told Stuart and Ewell to drive the Yankees away.[15]

They moved swiftly to execute Lee's orders. Rodes deployed Brig. Gen. Cullen Battle's six Alabama regiments and Maj. Eugene Blackford's sharpshooter battalion to surround the town. Battle dispatched the 3rd, 6th and 12th Alabama infantry regiments on a sweep to envelop Jeffersonton from the west, while the 5th and 26th Alabama moved to strike from the east. Blackford's command, careful to stay out of sight of its defenders, made a mile-wide circuit to get behind the town.[16]

As the infantry pressed forward, Stuart shook out Funsten's brigade, sending the 7th Virginia Cavalry to the left, while posting the 12th Virginia Cavalry to the right. The 11th Virginia remounted and took position in the center. The Federal troopers in Jeffersonton kept up a continuous and rapid skirmish fire, but once the Confederate regiments surged forward, the outcome of the fight was a foregone conclusion. Outnumbered and outflanked, those Pennsylvanians who could fell back. Most of the dismounted Federals discovered their horses gone, either captured or run off. With no

13 Stine, *Army of the Potomac*, 564; William Hyndman, *History of a Cavalry Company: A Complete Record of Company A, 4th Penn'a Cavalry* (Philadelphia, PA, 1870), 124-25.

14 McDonald, *Laurel Brigade*, 185; Hand, *One Good Regiment*, 82-83.

15 McClellan, *I Rode with JEB Stuart*, 385; Freeman, *R.E. Lee*, vol. 3, 175-178; Stine, *Army of the Potomac*, 565.

16 Robert Emory Park, "War Diary of Captain Robert Emory Park." *SHSP*, Vol. 26, 18-26; Eugene Blackford Diary, October 12, 1863, USMHI.

Jeffersonton Baptist Church, circa 1850. *Courtesy Jeffersonton Baptist Church*

officers in sight, some troopers decided to retreat to a nearby ridge. Having recently been clear cut, the height had cordwood thickly dotting its surface. Upon reaching this ground each man hurriedly stacked the timber into little individual fortresses.[17]

Rebel cavalry soon bore down on the ridge. After driving off five separate mounted charges, the isolated Pennsylvanians suddenly found themselves confronting Alabama infantrymen. Private John Hollis watched aghast as "large square bodies" of gray troops approached, battle flags fluttering in the breeze. With a sinking feeling he realized there was no escape. Nonetheless, just how quickly the Confederates overran the Federal position surprised him. Rebel infantry with fixed bayonets easily rousted the Yankees from their wooden forts and marched them away as prisoners.[18]

*   *   *

Gregg's horsemen seemed headed toward a similarly grim fate. About a half a mile north of Jeffersonton the road to Sulphur Springs passed through an expansive three-quarter mile long pine thicket. Amidst this dreadful tangle Funsten's regiments

17 [Washington, DC] *National Tribune*, December 15, 1898.

18 Ibid; Hand, *One Good Regiment*, 82-83.

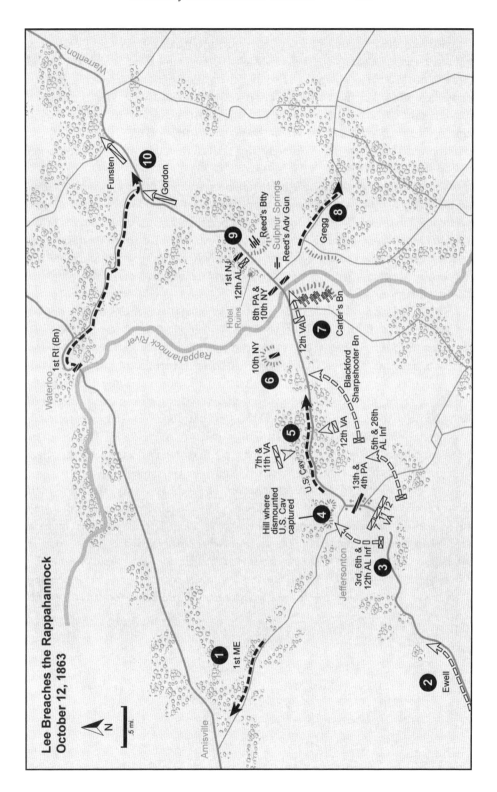

Lee Breaches the Rappahannock
October 12, 1863

N   .5 mi

Amisville

1 1st ME

2 Ewell

Jeffersonton

3rd, 6th & 12th AL Inf

3

13th & 4th PA

12th VA

VA 12

5th & 26th AL Inf

4 Hill where dismounted U.S. Cav captured

U.S. Cav

7th & 11th VA

5

Blackford Sharpshooter Bn

12th VA

6 10th NY

7 Carter's Bn

Hotel Ruins

8th PA & 10th NY

1st N.J.

12th AL

9

Reed's Btty
Sulphur Springs
Reed's Adv Gun

Gregg

8

Rappahannock River

Waterloo
1st RI (Bn)

Funsten

10

Gordon

Warrenton

slammed into the retreating Federals, who turned to make another stand. For thirty minutes a vicious close quarters struggle swayed back and forth. The Virginia and Pennsylvania regiments charged and countercharged one another across the difficult terrain in as mean a fight as could be imagined. One Rebel caught up in the struggle noted that the dense pines trapped the gun smoke and intensified the "rattle of small arms," shouts of command, and the "cries and oaths of the combatants." He characterized the struggle as a "bloody and doubtful contest" in which confusion reigned supreme.[19]

Gradually the relentless Confederate numbers pushed back the Federals. During the mêlée, Blackford's sharpshooters slipped between the bluecoats and the river, threatening their line of retreat. Once they grasped their situation, the Yankees broke and fled for the Rappahannock. Stuart's men pursued, and Blackford's sharpshooters, who had taken position parallel to the road, poured a hot fire into their fleeing foe. The Southern marksmen killed a dozen bluecoats and captured 20 more after shooting down their horses.[20]

With Rebel cavalry bearing down on the Federal rear and sharpshooters ripping into the Yankee flank, the Pennsylvanians' situation seemed critical. Without immediate help, the Confederates would certainly cut off and destroy both Union regiments. To stem the crisis, Col. Gregg ordered Maj. Henry Avery's 10th New York Cavalry across the river to do what it could to protect the battered commands desperately trying to reach the Rappahannock. Avery led his regiment to the south bank and deployed a squadron of skirmishers on the slope of a long ridge running perpendicular to the road and about a half mile from the river. Their sudden appearance diverted Confederate attention from Jeffersonton's fleeing defenders, thus saving what they could of the two shattered Pennsylvania regiments.[21]

This was a double-edged success, however. The Rebels now focused their wrath on the Federal newcomers, and the New Yorkers found themselves in exactly the same sort of jeopardy the battered Pennsylvanians were escaping. Luckily for Avery, his men were relatively fresh and his opponents somewhat disorganized by their clash at Jeffersonton. Still, the 10th New York barely held on long enough for the Pennsylvanians to get away. With his mission accomplished and enemy troops pressing closer, Avery eagerly sought to extract his regiment before it was too late. The 10th

19 McDonald, *Laurel Brigade*, 185-86.

20 Blackford Diary, October 12, 1863, USMHI; Fred Ray, *Shock Troops of the Confederacy: The Sharpshooter Battalions of the Army of Northern Virginia* (Asheville, NC, 2006), 82-83.

21 *OR* 29, pt. 1, 367-68.

scarcely managed to get back to the river, losing heavily in men and horses in the process.[22]

As Avery pulled back toward the Rappahannock, the first part of the afternoon's action ended. Gregg's cavalrymen had put up quite a fight and the cost of their stubbornness proved high. The Rebels cut all three of the engaged Federal regiments to pieces. The mangled commands collectively lost 17 men killed, 114 wounded, and 432 captured or missing.[23]

These were losses to little purpose. Irvin Gregg's mission had been reconnaissance, not combat. After the Yankees became embroiled in what seemed a routine fight against Rebel cavalry the sudden appearance of Rodes' infantry took them completely by surprise. With no hope of significantly slowing Lee's main body, the regiments defending Jeffersonton wound up fighting for mere survival. Their brave and utterly absorbing struggle unintentionally delayed transmission of the critical intelligence that Meade's entire army was waiting on.

The moment Union troops had spotted Rebels wearing knapsacks Federal officers in Jeffersonton had dispatched a courier to Sulphur Springs with reports of nearby Confederate infantry. Stuart's cavalry assault followed so closely on the arrival of Lee's infantry however, the courier had no chance to get away. The messenger blundered into the path of the 12th Virginia Cavalry which took him prisoner after killing his horse and severely wounding him.[24]

Only when the bloodied remnants of the 13th and 4th Pennsylvania safely crossed the river, could news of Lee's infantry finally start toward an anxious Meade. It was 4:50 p.m. before General Gregg got word that Rebel foot soldiers were at Jeffersonton and marching on Sulphur Springs. He immediately scrawled out a message to Meade that a large column of enemy infantry was "in plain sight" and moving to cross the Rappahannock.[25]

* * *

Buford's reconnaissance had informed Meade hours before that Lee wasn't at Culpeper Court House. Now Gregg had proof that the Southerners were moving to

22 Stine, *Army of the Potomac*, 565; McClellan, *I Rode with JEB Stuart*, 385; OR 29, pt. 1, 367-68.

23 OR 29, pt. 1, 359; Michael Dougherty, *Diary of a Civil War Hero*, (New York, 1960), 7-8; 169 of those casualties were from the 13th PA Cav according to *History of the Pennsylvania Volunteers 1861-65, Volume III*, page 1,269,

24 *Stine, Army of the Potomac*, 565.

25 Ibid, 566.

turn the Federal flank. The Army of the Potomac was in the wrong place and would have to react quickly to escape the trap Lee was carefully setting. Still, Irvin Gregg knew it would be hours before his couriers could reach Meade. It was imperative, therefore, that his brigade hold Sulphur Springs and delay the Confederate advance as long as possible.

Painfully aware that the uneven contest south of the river was ending, Col. Gregg ordered the 8th Pennsylvania Cavalry and Battery A, 4th US Artillery, into defensive positions covering the bridge over the Rappahannock. Lieutenant Horatio Reed deployed his four 3-inch ordnance rifles on high ground about a half mile north of the river. Major Joseph Wistar, commanding the 8th, stationed his troopers in previously dug rifle pits along the riverbank. He also ordered the bridge planking ripped up as soon as the survivors of the Jeffersonton fight passed over.

As Funsten's Southern cavalry drew near the Rappahannock River, Stuart sent the 7th and 11th Virginia regiments to cross at an upstream ford. Although this column would eventually outflank Gregg's defenses, Stuart had his enemy rattled and he intended to keep up the pressure. If possible, he also meant to have the bridge at Sulphur Springs.

The Federals, however, were no longer on the run. While most survivors of the 10th New York joined the 8th Pennsylvania in the rifle pits, Gregg ordered Reed to move one of his guns nearly to within canister range of the bridge. Wistar sent his 1st Squadron to support Reed's advanced piece. Ensconced in snug rife pits and backed by Reed's battery, the Northerners kept up a warm fire and refused to let the Rebels chase them away.[26]

The Confederates were going to have to fight their way over the Rappahannock against stout resistance. Since an opposed river crossing was among the most dangerous maneuvers a body of soldiers could undertake, Stuart sought to give his troopers every possible advantage. Because his horse artillery had been unable to keep up with the rapid advance, the general asked Ewell's chief of artillery, Brig. Gen. Armistead L. Long, for assistance. He was happy to comply and quickly deployed 20 cannon from Carter's Battalion to aid Stuart's effort.

Since Lee still desired to keep the Federals in the dark about the presence of his infantry, he ordered Carter's guns to take position on the reverse slope of a prominent ridge overlooking the river crossing. By posting the fieldpieces just below the summit, Lee intended the cannon to remain out of sight and beyond any possible counter battery fire as they lobbed shells mortar-like into the midst of Gregg's Yankees. It was an innovative approach, exactly the kind one might expect from Lee, who had first

---

26 *OR* 29, pt. 1, 369-70, 372-73, 368.

made his battlefield reputation building the gun emplacements that pummeled the Veracruz fortifications into surrender in 1847.[27]

Once in place, around 5 p.m., all 20 of Carter's guns opened simultaneously. The sudden shower of iron struck without warning, badly startling the enemy. Wistar's pioneers had to finish taking up the bridge planks under heavy bombardment. Meanwhile, the van of Rodes' division was coming forward and both Cullen A. Battle's and George P. Dole's brigades were deploying for an assault even as Blackford's sharpshooters stood ready to advance as soon as Rodes gave the order.[28]

For the moment, however, the Federals were holding their own. Impatient with this stalemate, Stuart hit upon a bold move to dislodge the stubborn Yankees. With Company B of the 12th Virginia Cavalry mounted and nearby, Stuart rode over to its commander, Lt. George Baylor, and directed him to charge across the bridge.

Baylor had been watching the firefight along the river for a while. Though highly doubtful a "cavalry dash" could win the day, he had no choice but to obey. He also knew that Lee, Stuart, and Ewell were observing the battle and had to admit, "It was the occasion of our lives." Certain that only conspicuous resolution would carry this assault, he placed four reliable men at the rear of his formation loudly ordering them to shoot the first man who wavered or turned to run. With any potential shirkers discouraged, he trotted back to the head of his column and prepared to attack.[29]

Although Baylor didn't know it, his pending assault couldn't have been better timed. Enemy troopers in the rifle pits had kept up such a rapid fire they had virtually exhausted their ammunition. The division's provost guard, busy deflecting a stream of stragglers all claiming to be trying to secure more cartridges, had twice turned back the orderly officially detailed to bring up ammo.[30]

Under supporting fire from Carter's guns, Company B galloped in a column of fours along the narrow causeway leading to the bridge. As the cavalrymen neared their objective, a final spasm of carbine fire erupted from the Federal rifle pits. The Virginians charged through the fusillade to the bridge abutment. But as the onrushing column reached the span, Baylor realized that the Yankees had removed its flooring. He immediately shouted: "By fours, right about wheel! Forward!" At this command his company, still at full gallop, executed a tight U-turn away from the bridge. As watching Southern infantry gave a wild rebel yell, Baylor led the column down from the

---

27 Blackford Diary, October 12, 1863, USMHI.

28 Ibid.

29 George Baylor, *From Bull Run to Bull Run; OR Four Years in the Army of Northern Virginia* (Richmond, VA, 1900), 169.

30 *OR* 29, pt. 1, 370-71.

causeway, u-turned it again toward the riverbank, then boldly splashed across the shallow Rappahannock and up the opposite bank. It was the sort of flawlessly and audaciously executed maneuver that had earned Stuart's troopers their reputation.[31]

Without pausing, the cavalrymen attacked the Union rifle pits, whose defenders, without carbine ammunition, could respond only with pistol fire. A handful of Yankees escaped. Most did not. The attackers virtually wiped out the two squadrons Wistar had deployed to the river. The 8th Pennsylvania lost 70 troopers killed, wounded, or captured trying to hold the bridge. As Yankee resistance sputtered out, the rest of the 12th Virginia Cavalry followed Baylor across the river. Other Rebel troopers rushed to re-lay the bridge planks, which the Federals had merely tossed onto the river bank.[32]

Even though the Federal position was rapidly collapsing, fighting continued. Some Northern troopers made a stand in the ruins of the old hotel, and Rodes sent Blackford's sharpshooters to root them out. Elsewhere along the front, Union stragglers with empty cartridge boxes scattered into the woods as Confederate artillery unrelentingly hammered the few enemy holdouts.[33]

The gunners of Lt. Reed's forward piece could no longer service their cannon and were lying prone under an intense storm of fire. General Gregg had already ordered Reed's battery to limber up and pull back, but word of the withdrawal hadn't reached them until Lt. Col. John Kester crawled forward to shout the order in the gun sergeant's ear.

Obviously, retreat was anything but easy. When the crew attempted to stand and move their gun, a hail of canister fire drove them back to the ground. The cannoneers resorted to crouching as low as humanly possible and painfully pulling their piece to the rear inch by inch. Once the artillerists got their gun into a little hollow, they could stand up and drag it back to the limber. After hitching up, the Yankees then ran a gauntlet of enemy fire to make good their escape.[34]

*   *   *

With his battered 2nd brigade pulling back east toward Fayetteville, Gregg warned Col. John Taylor, whose 1st Brigade was covering the roads to Warrenton, to prepare to resist a Rebel advance. Taylor had heard the clamor at Sulphur Springs around 4 p.m. and immediately ordered the 6th Ohio and 1st New Jersey Cavalry regiments and a

31 McClellan, *I Rode with JEB Stuart*, 385-86; Baylor, *Bull Run to Bull Run*, 169-70.

32 *OR* 29, pt. 1, 369-70.

33 Blackford's dairy, October 12, 1863, USHMI.

34 Henry Pyne, *History of the First New Jersey Cavalry* (Trenton, NJ, 1871), 175-76.

section of artillery toward the Rappahannock. Despite his prompt response, only Major Hugh Janeway's 360 man-strong 1st New Jersey would reach the field in time to engage the enemy.[35]

Although having to beg ammunition from other units to replace its own rain-ruined cartridges, the New Jersey troopers departed quickly, albeit with only ten rounds per man. They headed down the Warrenton Turnpike toward Sulphur Springs, completely unaware that the Confederates had already fought their way over the Rappahannock.

Fortunately, Janeway took care to send out an advance guard and dispatch some of his staff to ride ahead and determine the state of affairs at the river. Before getting there, these officers bumped into Rebel cavalry and quickly came pounding back to sound the alarm.

Unshaken by this unexpected news, Janeway deployed a squadron of skirmishers and pushed on through the woods toward Sulphur Springs. The Federals soon ran headlong into the 12th Virginia Cavalry. Now it was the turn of the Rebels to be surprised. The New Jersey squadron let loose a volley and instantaneously launched a charge that drove the Virginians back onto Rodes' infantry near the river.[36]

The Federal advantage did not last long. After encountering Battle's brigade around the ruins of the hotel, the Yankee skirmishers recoiled and formed line on a wooded hill nearby. Stuart tried to drive them off with the 12th Virginia, but Janeway threw another squadron into the fight and beat it back. Despite carefully parceling out his strength, the New Jersey major knew his command was in a dangerous spot. An increasing number of his troopers were running out of ammunition, while the opposing Rebel infantry force constantly grew. Only the swift-setting sun seemed to favor the Union regiment.

In the fading twilight Brig. Gen. Battle's Alabamians, with the 12th Alabama in the lead supported by the rest of the brigade, advanced against the obstinate enemy cavalrymen. They closed to within 50 yards of the Northern horsemen and fired repeated volleys into the Federal line. The return fire was weak and ineffective, not only because Janeway's men were low on ammunition, but also because they fired too high.[37]

Facing a solid line of infantry, and with Rebel skirmishers slipping around his flank and firing into his rear, Janeway knew he had done everything possible. As total darkness descended, the 1st New Jersey fell back, pursued for a short distance by

35 Ibid, Bushnell Diary, October 12, 1863, WRHS.

36 Previous paragraphs based on Pyne, *1st New Jersey Cavalry*, 175-76.

37 Park, *SHSP*, vol. 26, 19; ibid., 179-82.

Battle's cheering Alabamians. Despite his withdrawal from the field, Janeway had stalled the Rebel advance on Warrenton until nightfall, although at a cost of 3 men dead, 20 wounded, 7 missing, and a devastating loss of 170 horses killed or injured.[38]

Sunset did not end the litany of Union losses. The Rebel success at Sulphur Springs cut off the entire 120-man battalion of the 1st Rhode Island Cavalry that Gregg had sent upstream to guard Waterloo Bridge. After dark, the Rhode Islanders retreated toward Warrenton, mistakenly assuming Gregg's division would assemble there. Moving along a side road until they hit the turnpike between Sulphur Springs and Warrenton about halfway between the two towns, they unknowingly slipped into a gap between Funsten's and Gordon's brigades which Stuart had ordered to ride on to Warrenton.

Under no particular need to hurry or be on especial alert, the Yankee troopers were steadily moving toward Warrenton when the head of Gordon's column encountered the tail end of the Rhode Island battalion. The surprised Rebels demanded to know what regiment was in their way. The 1st Rhode Island, came the casual reply along with a demand for who wanted to know? The answer to that request was an unexpected volley of carbine fire. Abruptly aware of their danger, the Union horsemen galloped northward and quickly outran Gordon's troopers. But no sooner did they deem themselves safe than they blundered into the rear of Funsten's brigade.

It was about 10 p.m. and pitch black. Not imagining the enemy could be in front of them, the Northerners suddenly found themselves amid other horsemen. One Federal officer heard someone cock the hammer of a revolver, and instinctively warned the soldier to put away his pistol lest he accidentally shoot a comrade. To his dismay a disembodied reply came back, "You will be the man if you do not surrender." Belatedly realizing they were among Confederates, 47 of the Rhode Islanders surrendered. The rest of the Union battalion scattered and managed to escape.[39]

These additional losses brought the total casualties of the 2nd Cavalry Division up to something like 580 men—about 12 percent of its strength. This sacrifice had purchased little. Despite the heroics of Gregg's brigades, Ewell's troops were marching over the river with dry feet as dusk fell. Before midnight Funsten's and Gordon's brigades would bivouac on the outskirts of Warrenton. Once again the Army of Northern Virginia stood on the north bank of the Rappahannock with the road to the Federal rear open before it. Perhaps some among its ranks began dreaming about repeating their famous 1862 victory at Second Manassas. Meanwhile, less than a dozen

---

38 Park, *SHSP*, 26:19; *OR* 29, pt. 1, 361-62.

39 Frederic Denison, *Sabres and Spurs: The First Regiment Rhode Island Cavalry in the Civil War, 1861-1865* (Central Falls, RI, 1876), 293-96.

miles away, George Meade still had not the slightest inkling of the peril facing his command.[40]

*　　*　　*

At least word of Ewell's spearhead crossing the Rappahannock was making its belated way toward Union army headquarters. But the advance of A. P. Hill's corps, which was moving on parallel roads just a few miles west of Ewell's column, remained a total unknown.

The 1st Maine Cavalry under Col. Charles Smith had spent all day October 12 looking for indications that the Confederates were heading toward the Shenandoah Valley. Dropping off observation parties as it did so, the regiment had ridden through Amissville and Gaines Crossroads on its way to the town of Washington, the county seat of Rappahannock County, which one Yankee described as a "quite pretty" village "almost hidden" by trees. Although its 100 or so inhabitants proudly boasted that their town was the first named after America's greatest hero, most locals called the place "Little Washington" to differentiate it from the Union capital 70 miles to the northeast.[41]

It was an ideal central location for Smith to halt while Lt. Col. Boothby and a hundred troopers rode on to scout Sperryville six miles to the south. Shortly after this force headed out, Smith detailed a 12-man patrol under Lt. William Harris to return to Sulphur Springs, find Col. Irvin Gregg, and let him know that on the outward arc of its journey the 1st Maine had sighted no Rebels.

Although Smith's assignment had taken him far from the rest of the army and potentially exposed his regiment to great danger, he had encountered no cause for concern. Boothby's battalion returned from Sperryville late in the afternoon, reporting no sign of enemy activity. As far as Smith could tell, his reconnaissance had been a benign exercise of prudent caution. After giving Boothby's men an hour to rest, feed and groom their horses, Smith's troopers trotted out for their return to Sulphur Springs.

They journeyed back the way they had come, picking up their detachments as they rode toward Amissville, a planned stop for the night. As the regiment drew near the place, Smith ordered Capt. Paul Chadbourne to take a half dozen men and ride ahead

---

40 McClellan, *I Rode with JEB Stuart*, 385-386. Rodes and Johnson camped north of the river. Early's division camped south of it on the night of Oct. 12.

41 Charles F. Morse, *Civil War Letters of Charles F. Morse, 1861-1865*, (Big Byte Books electronic edition, 2016), no page number.

to Sulphur Springs. He was to find Col. Gregg and relay word that the 1st Maine had yet to see any Rebels.[42]

Everything seemed routine until 10 p.m. when Chadbourne's party ran into a Confederate picket line near Amissville. In the darkness the enemy opened fire on the small group of Federals. This unexpected challenge panicked several men, and they fled back to the regiment, breathlessly telling Smith what had happened.

At first the colonel supposed they had encountered Rebel guerrillas, wishful thinking that dissipated entirely when Chadbourne returned with news of a large force of foot soldiers around Amissville. Local civilians claimed the enemy was A. P. Hill's corps, which had been going into camp since three that afternoon.[43]

This was shocking information to say the least. Smith had no idea what might have happened to Lt. Harris and the 12 men he had earlier sent back to Sulphur Springs. Had they ridden across the oncoming Confederates' path without seeing a single enemy soldier, as the entire 1st Maine had apparently done that morning? Smith could only hope that Harris had spotted Hill and managed to warn Gregg, but it was highly probable that the Rebels had gobbled up the patrol. If that were the case, no Federal east of Amissville had any notion that Lee's army was nearing the upper Rappahannock.

Whatever had happened to Harris, Col. Smith realized that not only had he uncovered critically important intelligence he was likewise powerless to communicate it. Lee's whole army stood between the 1st Maine and the AOP. Completely cut off, Smith had only one escape route open to him: ride west and north in an attempt to get around Lee's flank and back to Union lines. Maybe this would allow the 1st Maine to save itself, but unless Lt. Harris had managed to elude Hill, it would do nothing to get the information Smith had to Gen. Meade.[44]

In fact, Harris's patrol had encountered dire trouble. He and his men had passed through Amissville just before Hill's column got there. As the Maine troopers closed on Jeffersonton's outskirts, however, they had run into the Rebel cavalry. Harris immediately turned around and tried to head back to the regiment. Nearing Amissville again, this time from the east, he found it occupied by Hill's corps. The tiny Union

42 Tobie, *First Maine Cavalry*, 193-201. According to a *New York Herald* writer, Sperryville was "a smart little town" with a population of 150 people, 6 wheat mills, 3 saw mills, a school, and a pair each of churches, stores, and taverns. As a result of the war, a reporter noted, the village was "dead now." *New York Herald*, July 21, 1862.

43 Ibid., 199-201.

44 Ibid, The story of this incredible adventure is told by Thaxter, Sidney, "No Trace of the Enemy," *Civil War Times Illustrated*, Vol. VII, 26-32. See also, Bill Backus and Robert Orrison, *A Want of Vigilance: The Bristoe Station Campaign, October 9-19, 1863*, (El Dorado, CA, 2015), 119-24.

detachment discovered itself trapped in a 6-mile-wide void between the two halves of the Army of Northern Virginia.

Harris led his men into a stand of thick pines where they hid out until nightfall. After weighing his options, he decided that riding out of this mess would be impossible. He had no feed for his animals, and the enemy would be sure to spot a small gaggle of Yankee cavalrymen roaming about. Evading the Rebels on foot appeared the only chance of escape; during the night, therefore, the Yankees turned their horses lose and destroyed their saddles and bridles. Then they began weaving their way westward through the woods, hoping to slip by the Confederates and find friendly forces somewhere in the Loudoun Valley. They failed. Although Harris and his men successfully fended off a small detachment of Col. John S. Mosby's partisans, a contingent of troopers from the 35th Virginia Cavalry Battalion overwhelmed and captured them near Thoroughfare Gap. The bulk of the 1st Maine Cavalry, on the other hand, safely returned to Union lines on October 14 after a roundabout 90-mile trek that took 30 hours.[45]

None of this did George Meade any good on October 12. Lee had outflanked his army, and its commander didn't know it yet. Sending Sedgwick with three corps and a division of cavalry across the Rappahannock and then leaving most of them near Brandy Station for the night had divided his force and allowed Lee to steal a march which now put Confederate infantry closer to Warrenton than the Federals, while two Rebel cavalry brigades actually occupied the town. Moreover, Lee and his army now had a clear and open path into the Union rear.

As darkness deepened over Virginia's countryside a courier on a lathered horse raced anxiously from the little burg of Fayetteville toward Meade's headquarters. He carried a message from Maj. Gen. Gregg warning that the Confederates were across the Rappahannock and bearing down on the Union flank. The rider galloped eastward in desperate haste, well aware that every passing minute brought the Federal army another step closer to disaster.

---

45 Ibid., 199-201. Lt. Harris managed to escape a few days later.

CHAPTER 16

"Move Immediately and With the Utmost Dispatch"

An Alarming Message—Great Danger—Meade Reacts—Retreat

THROUGHOUT October 12, the Army of the Potomac's high command had kept close tabs on Sedgwick's reconnaissance toward Brandy Station, but at the same time it had remained totally unaware of events on the upper Rappahannock. Although the fights at Jeffersonton and Sulphur Springs happened a mere eight miles as the crow flies from Meade's headquarters near Rappahannock Station, no sound of the furious struggles had drifted eastward. Lack of any report from Gregg, along with Buford's and Sedgwick's failure to find the Rebels, had engendered inertia and left Meade and his staff scratching their heads as to Lee's position.[1]

No clarification of the Union army's strategic quandary had occurred by twilight. Meade, not unreasonably, had left his troops where they had been at dusk, with one-half deployed defensively north of the Rappahannock River, the other half awkwardly concentrated for an offensive against an as-yet undiscovered enemy south of the river. The general and his staff were sitting around their campfires still pondering their dilemma. At 9:00 p.m., a courier from David Gregg galloped upon them with the alarming news that the 2nd Cavalry Division had been fighting since 11:00 a.m. that morning. Worse, his dispatch reported that Jeb Stuart had driven the Federal troopers

---

1 *Report of the Joint Committee on the Conduct of the War at the Second Session of the Thirty-eighth Congress*, 3 Vols., (Washington: Government Printing Office, 1865). Humphrey's testimony given March 2, 1864, Vol. 1, 400; *OR* 29, pt. 2, 286-287.

across the Rappahannock with heavy losses and that Rebel soldiers were swarming across the river.[2]

Gregg's message, written at Fayetteville some seven miles northeast of Sulphur Springs, answered the worrisome question of Lee's whereabouts while at the same time warning Meade in the bluntest terms possible of the grave danger he was in. The Confederates had breached the waterway nearly four hours ago and were poised to sweep around the Union right. The Federal army, divided by a river and with its front facing the wrong direction, had rarely been in a more vulnerable situation. And seldom had the Rebels placed themselves in a better one.[3]

From Sulphur Springs Lee could march on Warrenton or launch an attack down the north bank of the Rappahannock. The latter option might allow him to roll up Meade's army from west to east, smashing one corps after another before the Federals could concentrate to confront him. On the other hand, Confederate seizure of Warrenton would position Lee's troops for a southward drive toward Fayetteville, an eastward lunge at Warrenton Junction and Catlett's Station or a deeper strike northward into the Union rear. Should the Rebels get astride the O&A at any location, they would cut off the Northern army from its capital. Such a situation would likely force the Yankees into battle on unfavorable terms and on unfavorable ground.

Meade knew he had to guard against all of these possible moves. To his credit, the Pennsylvania general reacted quickly. But the extent of his surprise was palpable. The rapid stream of orders and counter orders flowing out of his headquarters during the night clearly indicated a general rapidly but astutely improvising a plan.

At 9:15 p. m., Meade telegraphed Sedgwick to pull the VI and V Corps as well as Buford's cavalry back across the Rappahannock immediately. The VI Corps would cross the river via the pontoon bridge at Rappahannock Station. Sykes' V Corps and Buford's horsemen were to use the pontoon bridge at Beverly Ford. Fifteen minutes after sending these directives, Meade ordered Warren's II Corps to retire from his post near Rappahannock Station to the north side of the river. As soon as his command was across, Warren was to "move immediately and with the utmost dispatch" to Warrenton Junction, and there deploy his troops to face a possible enemy advance from Warrenton.

Just 45 minutes later, Meade changed Warren's destination to Fayetteville to reinforce Gregg's and Kilpatrick's cavalry and fall in alongside French, who at 10 p.m. was ordered to swing his III Corps west to face Sulphur Springs and the nearest body

---

2 Ibid; Lyman, *Meade's Army*, 49. Gregg's message arrived one hour after Meade had telegrammed Halleck.

3 Ibid; *Report of the Joint Committee on the Conduct of the War*, Humphrey's testimony, 400.

Federal troops withdraw from Culpeper County over a pontoon bridge near Rappahannock Station in the pre-dawn hours of October 13, 1863. *Edwin Forbes*

of Rebel infantry. Warning French that the Confederates might attack his command in the morning, Meade then added in a less-than-reassuring display of flexibility, that if the enemy did strike, "I will immediately support you, but I may also send orders requiring you to fall back." French should "be ready for either contingency."

Meade feared that Lee's infantry would reach Warrenton by morning and then swiftly march east to cut the railroad. To blunt such a move, army headquarters turned to Brig. Gen. Henry D. Terry, whose VI Corps division guarded a substantial length of the O&A. Meade sent Terry orders to concentrate his troops at Warrenton Junction as a stop gap measure. Thirty minutes later John Newton received instructions to move his I Corps to the same point from Kelly's Ford. Since Meade had directed the army's wagon train to withdraw on roads paralleling the O&A, he cautioned Newton to choose a route that avoided that cumbersome traffic. Once the I Corps reached Warrenton Junction, Newton was to take control of Terry's division until further notice.[4]

---

4 OR 29, pt. 2, 298-300. Terry's division had been detached from the VI Corps during Sedgwick's thrust toward Culpeper Court House. Meade issued Warren's orders at 9:30 p.m., Terry's at 10:15 p.m., and Newton's at 10:45 p.m. Quote on 299.

Lieutenant Colonel Ira Spaulding's 50th New York Engineers received midnight orders to disassemble the pontoon bridges at Rappahannock Station and Beverly Ford as soon Sedgwick, Sykes, and Buford had crossed the river. Army headquarters also ordered Spaulding to destroy the railroad bridge at Rappahannock Station—a task he delegated to Capt. George Mendell's engineer battalion. Before these specialists could go to work Union generals commanding the three infantry corps and single cavalry division south of the Rappahannock would have to arouse 30,000 sleeping soldiers, form them up in pitch blackness, and get them moving quickly. These tasks took time, even under ordinary circumstances, and the Federals couldn't waste a minute.[5]

Commendably Meade's subordinates wasted none. The rattle of drums and blare of bugles sounded through the Yankee bivouacs shortly after Sedgwick got Meade's withdrawal order. Cursing and groaning as they rolled out of their blankets, weary soldiers threw on their accouterments and knapsacks while pointedly questioning the sanity of their high command.

Widespread grousing and disgust arose at the apparent mismanagement when officers told the troops to retrace their steps to a river they had crossed just 10 hours before. One 14th Connecticut critic snidely observed that this was the eighth time his regiment had marched over the Rappahannock during the war. "In fact, it would seem that crossing the Rappahannock had become a habit and that the troops were ordered back and forth over the river when the commanders could not think of anything else to do." Despite such fatigue-fueled complaints, the men quickly fell into ranks and began moving out.[6]

The hardships of the rank and file were not Meade's priority. It was imperative that he get his entire army north of the Rappahannock as soon as possible, and even more important that he got sufficient force into position facing Sulphur Springs and Warrenton to resist a possible dawn attack should Lee attempt one. If that meant marching most of the army through the night, then it would have to be done.

While the units south of the Rappahannock started to move, French's III Corps pivoted westward to block any Rebel advance along the river's north bank. This new position partially filled the gap between Freeman's Ford on the Rappahannock and Kilpatrick's and Gregg's cavalry divisions, some six miles inland at Fayetteville on French's right. The 3rd Division's troopers were unlikely to stop any Confederate attack, even with the aid of Gregg's men—who were just now in no condition for another fight. Hence Meade had ordered the II Corps to reinforce the cavalry as rapidly as possible.

5   Ibid. pt. 1, 999.

6   Page, *Fourteenth Connecticut*, 193.

Harper's Weekly correspondent Alfred Waud made this drawing of the O&A Railroad bridge going up in flames after the last of the Yankees pulled back over the Rappahannock River on October 13, 1863. *Library of Congress*

Warren put his troops on the road at 11 p. m., just 90 minutes after being told to evacuate Culpeper County. Since his corps was camped at Rappahannock Station, the young commander used a pontoon bridge near there to get his men rapidly over the river and reach Fayetteville at 1 a. m. after a speedy two-hour march. His dog tired troops had hiked 36 miles in the last 24 hours, but at least they were going into line where Meade needed them well before daybreak.

It took considerably longer to get the rest of Sedgwick's units north of the river. Buford's cavalry division had ridden almost all the way to Culpeper Court House on October 12. The V and VI corps had gone as far as Brandy Station. The southernmost elements of the Union army would have to traverse 11 miles to reach the Rappahannock. In broad daylight it would take exhausted men at least five hours to cover that distance. A night march was another matter entirely.

The Federal withdrawal across the river would eventually take almost ten hours. The tail of Sedgwick's VI Corps shuffled over the pontoon bridge at Rappahannock Station at 7:30 a.m. It was an hour later before the hindmost troops in the V Corps and Buford's cavalry tromped over the floating span at Beverly Ford. Once the last man in blue traipsed across the river, Federal engineers took up their pontoons and set fire to the nine-week old railroad bridge, thus putting a dramatic denouement to the army's misguided foray toward Culpeper.[7]

---

7   OR 29, pt. 1, 236, 286, 999. Fayetteville is modern Opal, VA. Three Mile Station is modern Casanova, VA. Company C of the US Engineer Battalion burned the railroad bridge, [Washington, DC] *National Tribune*, Feb. 4, 1909.

*   *   *

While his soldiers shifted position in the pre-dawn darkness of October 13, George Meade tried to divine Lee's strategy. He had taken precautions against an enemy attack eastward from Sulphur Springs or a southward strike from Warrenton, despite his serious doubts that the Rebels would attempt either. The area's terrain discouraged any meaningful offensive action. Meade understood his opponent well enough to know that Lee usually played for higher stakes. Rather than provoke a fruitless engagement, his masterful adversary would much more likely attempt a flanking movement to sever Meade's line of communication and compel him to fight on unfavorable terms. Lee had demonstrated his fondness for such maneuvers many times.

Meade was determined to foil such a scheme by eluding the Rebel trap. That required a retreat, although Meade refused to concede that's what it was. Instead he characterized his withdrawal as "maneuvering to get into proper position to offer battle" and preventing Lee from obliging the Federals to fight "at a disadvantage." Whatever the terminology, at 12:50 a.m. on the morning of October 14, Meade issued orders for his army to commence a retrograde movement toward Centreville, some 35 miles farther north and only 25 miles from Washington, DC.[8]

French was to march at daylight from Freeman's Ford on the Rappahannock, sidestepping Warren's battle line at Fayetteville by sliding behind the II Corps. He would then continue to Three Mile Station on the Warrenton branch of the O&A. As soon as French had passed, the II Corps was to fall in behind him and follow his march north. Meanwhile, the V and VI corps would move from Beverly Ford and Rappahannock Station to Warrenton Junction (where Terry's division would rejoin the VI) and go into line of battle facing west. Once either Sykes or Sedgwick reached the junction, Newton's I Corps would move five miles up the railroad towards Bristoe Station.

Pleasonton received instructions to protect the army's left flank and rear. He was also to detail a "sufficient force of cavalry" to guard the army's main wagon train, which was ordered to Weaverville. The Cavalry Corps commander gave Buford the job of escorting the trains. Gregg would serve as rear guard and move with Warren. That job required the 2nd Cavalry Division to send its wagon train to Catlett's Station under the escort of the 1st New Jersey Cavalry. Kilpatrick would cover Warren's left and shield the army's western flank.[9]

---

8   Meade to wife, October 30, 1863, *Life and Letters*, vol. 2, 154.

9   *OR* 29, pt. 2, 302-303; Pyne, 1st New Jersey Cavalry, 188.

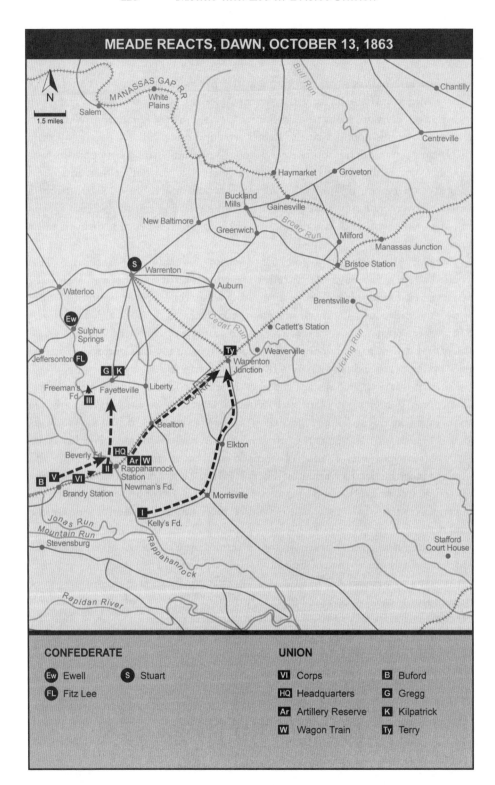

MEADE REACTS, DAWN, OCTOBER 13, 1863

CONFEDERATE

- Ew Ewell
- FL Fitz Lee
- S Stuart

UNION

- VI Corps
- HQ Headquarters
- Ar Artillery Reserve
- W Wagon Train
- B Buford
- G Gregg
- K Kilpatrick
- Ty Terry

These directives divided Meade's command and sent each half northward on parallel routes to Bristoe Station. This tiny hamlet was located on the O&A just south of a little creek called Broad Run, about 22 miles north of Rappahannock Station. Meade arranged his columns so as to keep his various corps within supporting distance of one another just in case Lee made a sudden lunge toward the railroad.

Meade didn't expect a major action south of Centreville, however. Early on October 13, he told French that "the object of both armies now is to gain certain points" and that a "serious attack" on the III Corps as it trekked north was unlikely. What mattered now was speed, and Meade warned French that the Rebels might seek to delay his march with "partial attacks." He was to ignore this harassment if possible. Should the Rebels strike with strength, the III Corps should fall back toward the railroad and the army's main body.[10]

Meade's decisiveness in the wee hours of October 13 contrasted starkly with his indecisiveness over the previous 76 hours. Finally obtaining clarity about his enemy's intentions, had transformed the general's demeanor. What he needed to do was now manifest, and he moved promptly to do it. His withdrawal orders had been clear, thoughtful, and well-designed—an impressive accomplishment given that his staff had drawn up and promulgated them in a span of just 4 hours.

Nonetheless, the Union general was in a reactive stance. Lee had held the initiative, and still did, since the start of the campaign. Gregg's misfortunes and Meade's fruitless reconnaissance toward Culpeper had allowed the Rebels to steal a march and get a head start in the race for Centreville. If the Federals couldn't outrun the Rebels, they would intercept the retreating Union columns with a good chance of mauling some part of the Army of the Potomac.

10 Ibid., 303.

Chapter 17

"A Spectacle Such As Few. . . Had Ever Beheld"

A Fleeing Foe—Move on Warrenton—A Difficult Retreat—
Meade Divides His Column—Stuart's Discovery and Distress

GEORGE Meade's pre-dawn decision to order a retreat toward Centreville deprived Union soldiers of any pause for rest on the morning of October 13. Having marched half the night, the exhausted men would simply have to press on lest the enemy cut their line of retreat. So columns of filthy, sweat-soaked infantrymen in dirt-stained clothes trudged norward alongside mud-spattered batteries and wagons. The foot soldiers moved through the fields, while the vehicles, heaped high with bags of forage, kept to the roads. Incongruous necessities such as coffee pots and frying pans jostled with cartridge boxes, knapsacks, and muskets on soldiers' bodies. Colonel Lyman thought that except for their weapons and uniforms, the men looked like refugees fleeing some natural disaster rather than an army on the march.[1]

Surgeon John Perry complained about the lack of decent food for both the troops and their animals. "What hardtack we had was so full of maggots," grumbled the doctor, "that it had to be baked, which hardened it still more." Quartermasters did not issue any meat during the movement, and the only water many troops had time to secure came from roadside puddles on "almost impassable" rain-soaked routes. The brutal pace of the Federal withdrawal caused utterly exhausted soldiers to fall asleep while still marching. Mounted officers dozed in their saddles. Although daytime

---

1 Lyman, *Meade's Headquarters*, 30.

temperatures in the 60s were well-suited to a forced march, the 40-degree nights were uncomfortably cold.[2]

As the troops strode north they frequently passed the skeletons of dead horses and the shallow graves of dead men—many with a skeletal arm or a leg protruding from mounds of hastily shoveled earth. Large flocks of turkey buzzards hovered around, understandably regarding the passing parade as a candidate for their next easy meal. Meade's soldiers didn't need these macabre spectacles to warn of impending danger. Indeed, the men were as quick to deduce the strategic situation as their Confederate counterparts. The Federal rank and file understood, as one of them put it, that Lee was trying "the same game" on Meade he had played on John Pope in August 1862.[3]

Whether the Rebel general would enjoy a similar success was as yet to be seen. But disarray in the Union rear seemed ominously suggestive of potential disaster. When the 122nd New York arrived at Warrenton Junction it found everything in a state of confusion. Temporarily assigned to guard a collection of loaded railway cars, the New Yorkers saw large numbers of contrabands intermingled among hospitals and supply dumps. "[S]tores of all kinds" lay in every direction seemingly without rhyme or reason. As the men stood watch over the railroad, rumors of fighting along the Rappahannock swirled through the ranks.[4]

The Rebels were making life difficult. Lee's thrust could not have come at a worse time for some Federal units. Many had recently absorbed large numbers of conscripts, all equally clueless about soldiering. Units like the 14th Connecticut were especially burdened, having 480 new recruits and a mere 100 veterans in its ranks. How well these novices would perform in a fight was anyone's guess.[5]

Yet the entire Yankee army seemed absorbed in the seriousness of the moment. The men knew what a retreat looked and felt like, and they all realized they were hurriedly retreating just now. But there was no panic. Well practiced in the art of withdrawal courtesy of many painful experiences, they went about their business with professional detachment. One infantryman remarked that he had never seen a "retreating army move so quietly," with everything going off "as regular as clockwork."[6]

---

2   Perry, *Letters from a Surgeon*, 107-108; Krick, *Civil War Weather*, 110.

3   John Merrill Diary, October 13, 1863; Robert Sneden Diary, October 13, 1863, VHS.

4   Alonzo Clapp diary, October 13, 1863, http://web.cortland.edu/woosterk/genweb/alonzoclapp/alonzoclapp1863.html. Contrabands was slang for runaway slaves employed by the Union army.

5   Page, *Fourteenth Connecticut*, 188-189.

6   John Merrill diary, October 13, 1863, VHS.

*   *   *

Whether operating like a well-oiled machine or not, the AOP appeared to be running for its life. The Confederates advanced in a totally different frame of mind. Meade was fleeing toward Washington, one Rebel remembered, and "we knew it, every man of us knew it!" The difficult march over rough roads at the start of the campaign faded into memory as the terrain they traversed gradually grew more gentle and familiar. Southern pioneers were bridging the streams lying in the army's path which allowed Lee's columns to march over creeks rather than waste time fording them.

As they often had, retreating Yankees proved to be the Southern soldier's best quartermaster. The Rebels picked up all manner of discarded equipment in the recently evacuated Union camps. Cast off shoes were a prize for many barefooted men. One South Carolinian reported some lucky soldiers managing to fill their haversacks with "Yankee crackers & pickled pork." More industrious troops collected the ubiquitous empty tin ration cans tossed aside by the Federals. Ingenious Rebel infantrymen turned these into cookware by attaching a wire handle that allowed them to suspend the can over a campfire for boiling food or coffee.[7]

Pauses to gather such booty proved all too brief as speed became more paramount. Ewell's command left Sulphur Springs at daylight on October 13. Pressing northward it passed a group of captured Union cavalrymen on a rest break. These Yankees had the "truly novel and interesting" experience of observing the entire Confederate Second Corps march by. Not that the ill-fated Northerners were impressed by their enemy's appearance. One Pennsylvanian likened the Confederates to "a dusty, tattered-looking gang of wretches, more like the accumulated outpourings of penitentiaries and poor-houses than . . . soldiers."[8]

The sheer size of the advancing Rebel columns and their attitude provoked a different reaction, however. A prisoner recalled watching an "innumerable array of dust-like hordes" sweeping forward behind dirty "battle-pierced" flags. The martial spectacle stretched out as far as the eye could see, and the Southerners were clearly men to reckon with. Each one wore a "look of terse determination" and "sinewy endurance," while the collective mass evinced "a general air of stern cheerfulness and deep-seated confidence in their own strength and valor," one captive noted. The advancing Confederates and Northerners naturally traded barbs and insults, but little

---

7 Kirkpatrick diary, October 13, 1863, UT; Long reminiscences (Breckinridge papers), LC; Caldwell, *Brigade of South Carolinians*, 114; Trout, *Galloping Thunder*, 372.

8 Seymour, *Civil War Memoirs*, 87; Hyndman, *History of a Cavalry Company*, 129-31.

of it proved mean-spirited. Indeed, some Rebel units cheered their enemies, leaving the surprised Federals certain they had the respect of their opponents if nothing else.

The compassion they were shown was even more amazing to the Yankee cavalrymen. One Rebel officer stopped to pray with the Union soldiers, asking God to show mercy and give aid to the captured bluecoats. A surgeon paused to dress the worst of the prisoners' wounds. The Federals, without rations now for more than a day, begged passing Confederates for hardtack. The hungry prisoners were immensely grateful but also astonished to get entire sacks of crackers from a battalion of South Carolinians. The Yankees had always supposed men from the Palmetto State "the bitterest rebels and most inveterate foes" of the Union. South Carolinians, they now had to admit, had proven themselves capable of "humanity and generosity" as well as "treason."[9]

* * *

The soldiers of both sides had not been so kind to the land for which they fought. Numerous campaigns had crisscrossed northern Virginia over the last two years. The region had sustained large armies for so long one observer described it as a "very desolate and forsaken country." A Richmond *Dispatch* correspondent traveling with Lee's army wrote that the northern reaches of the state were "a vast territory of ruin and desolation" with "not a house standing on the railroad from Manassas Junction to the Rappahannock River." Every fence on every farm had disappeared. "Extensive fields once yielding rich harvests" had been "cut to pieces by military roads." In lieu of crops, the correspondent continued, brambles and high weeds waved "triumphantly" over abandoned farmland.[10]

This devastation appalled observers of either side. Lyman noted that "houses that have not been actually burnt usually look almost worse than those that have." Nature had fared no better than manmade structures: Meade's aide lamented the sight of "hundreds of acres of stumps" occupying ground were "once good timber stood." Litter generated by the invading Union army lay scattered everywhere its camps had resided.[11]

Such devastation presented a military obstacle, especially to the advancing Confederates, who could not live off the land as they swept north. Hungry soldiers had stripped most trees of fruit and the untilled fields yielded nothing. Lee's slow-moving

9 Hyndman, *History of a Cavalry Company*, 129-31.

10 Kirkpatrick diary, October 13, 1863, UT; J. Cutler Andrews, *The South Reports the Civil War* (Princeton, NJ, 1970), 331.

11 Lyman, *Meade's Headquarters*, 48.

supply trains, which couldn't possibly keep pace with the troops, kept to the roads well west of the advancing infantry. Consequently some Rebels went hungry, especially the cavalry, which had to feed not only men but horses. Nonetheless, the Confederate army advanced from the Rappahannock at a brisk pace. One Mississippi infantryman in Hill's corps recalled that the columns "did not loll along the road; but went as though we were in a hurry to get somewhere."[12]

On October 13 the army was headed for Warrenton, the seat of Fauquier County established in 1810 and named after Revolutionary War hero Dr. Joseph Warren. Visitors described it as a pretty place graced with an impressive court house, many brick homes, stone sidewalks, and several hotels. The surrounding hilly but picturesque countryside was dotted with numerous farms, while the distant heights of the Blue Ridge Mountains lent a majestic backdrop to Warrenton's charms.[13]

Like every other area community, the war had not been kind to Warrenton. Its 1860 population of 2,000 had shrunk to around 600 souls. Most of its men were in the army, and many had become casualties, which hardly diminished the enthusiasm of Warrenton's remaining citizens for the Confederate cause. One Rebel soldier recalled that the townsfolk "were almost beside themselves with delight" at their arrival.[14]

*   *   *

Robert E. Lee reached Warrenton with Ewell's corps around 10 a.m. Since Hill's route from the Rappahannock was five miles longer, it would be noon before the first of his troops arrived nearby. The tail of his column probably wouldn't reach town until 2 p.m. What the ANV would do once its two halves reunited now largely depended on Yankee intentions and actions.[15]

---

12 Seymour, *Civil War Memoirs*, 87; Thomas D. Cockrell & Michael B. Ballard, *A Mississippi Rebel in the Army of Northern Virginia: The Civil War Memoirs of Private David Holt* (Baton Rouge, LA, 1995), 212.

13 Lyman, *Meade's Army*, 57. Holt notes that Hill's corps marched briskly, but then stopped near Warrenton "for more than a day." Dr. Joseph Warren of Boston, Massachusetts was a key leader of the Revolutionary cause in 1774-75. He was killed at the battle of Bunker (Breed's) Hill on June 17, 1775.

14 Durkin, *Confederate Chaplain*, 62; Stephen M. Weld, *War Diaries and Letters of Stephen M. Weld: 1861-1865* (Boston, MA, 1912), 248; George Beck Columns, Battery L, 1st New York Light Artillery, https://dmna.ny.gov/historic/reghist/civil/artillery/1stArtLt/1stArtLtBatLBreck Chap21Observation.htm, accessed June 3, 2018.

15 Just when Hill reached Warrenton is unclear. In his official report (OR 29, pt. 1, 410) Lee says the army reunited "in the afternoon." Holt (*A Mississippi Rebel*, 212) says that Hill's corps stopped at Warrenton for more than a day, clearly an exaggeration, since Hill left Warrenton

By this point Lee's knowledge of Meade's whereabouts was vague. The last meaningful intelligence that his headquarters had received came from Brig. Gen. Young. Late yesterday afternoon he had reported a large force of Union cavalry and infantry near Culpeper Court House. On the morning of October 13, Young had sent in word that the enemy had disappeared. But where had he gone? Was he still along the north bank of the Rappahannock? Was he retreating along the railroad toward Manassas Junction? Was he advancing on Warrenton looking for a fight?

Lee suspected a retreat, but he needed answers to these questions as soon as possible. Until he knew the location of Meade's main body and what it was doing, he couldn't formulate his own strategy intelligently. Lee thus ordered Jeb Stuart to reconnoiter toward Catlett's Station, which lay east of Warrenton on the Orange & Alexandria Railroad. Hill's corps should be up by the time Stuart's troopers completed their mission. Since Lee had directed the army's supply train to join the infantry at Warrenton, his troops could draw and prepare rations while they awaited results of the cavalry's reconnaissance.[16]

When Stuart received his new instructions he had only Gordon's, Funsten's, and Lomax's brigades available. Chambliss' and Owen's brigades under Fitz Lee were still making their way northward from Fox Mill Ford on the Rappahannock, while Young's brigade remained near Culpeper Court House. After two day's hard fighting, both Gordon's and Funsten's men were nearly out of ammunition, and would have to be resupplied before they undertook another operation. Lomax's men had full cartridge boxes, and Stuart ordered them to move off at once.[17]

Lomax's brigade promptly rode eastward toward Auburn, about 5 miles from Warrenton. Sometimes called Auburn Mills, the village sat on the north side of Cedar Run at a point where the creek's valley narrowed dramatically to a width of just a few hundred yards. Tall, partially wooded hills frowned over the spot from the north, west, and south, each of them forcing the roads in the area down steep grades toward the settlement.

Auburn had once been a significant manufacturing site for the McCormick Plow. The inventor of that revolutionary farm implement, 79-year old Stephen McCormick, still lived in a two-story house just north of Cedar Run. A bridge across the creek led

---

around 5 a.m. on October 14. Nonetheless it provides anecdotal evidence that Hill's troops spent considerable time around Warrenton on Oct. 13 and thus argues for at least an early afternoon arrival. The times given in the text are based on the distance Hill had to cover and the standard infantry marching speed of 2.5 miles per hour. It is possible that the approach of the army's supply train to Warrenton may have interfered with or slowed Hill's infantry.

16 OR 29, pt. 1, 410, 447; Seymour, *Civil War Memoirs*, 87.

17 McClellan, *I Rode with JEB Stuart*, 387.

almost directly to the elderly gentleman's front porch. Little was left of the town's former prominence other than McCormick's homestead, a post office, and a dilapidated stone mill. But this tiny unimpressive hamlet had significant strategic value as a road hub to all points of the compass: north to Greenwich, south to Three Mile Station and Fayetteville, west to Warrenton, and east to Catlett's Station.[18]

After reaching Auburn, Lomax learned from scouts that a large Federal force occupied Warrenton Junction, which was just six miles away down a branch of the O&A. Roads running along the track ultimately led there as well. Since the enemy might advance down either route to attack Lee's army, Lomax decided it was a good idea to occupy Auburn and wait for the rest of Stuart's column to appear. That pause took longer than expected because Gordon and Funsten had to await the arrival of their ordnance train before replenishing their ammunition and getting on the road. As a result, it was nearly 2 p.m. when Stuart finally reached Auburn.[19]

Upon his chief's arrival Lomax explained why he had halted there. In light of that report, Stuart and his officers rode up the hill behind the McCormick house to see what they could observe of the surrounding country. As he peered through his field glasses the corps commander noted a "large park of wagons and camp fires" three or four miles to the south near the home of a Mrs. Childs. This farm rested on the south side of the Warrenton Branch of the O&A about half way between Warrenton and Warrenton Junction. Apparently Union infantry was in the area, but headed east.

Stuart understood that this was vital information. At 3:30 p.m., he sat down to write a message notifying army headquarters of what he had thus far learned. The cavalryman also told his superior that the Yankees had a "considerable camp" at Warrenton Junction and were "burning stores along the railroad." Stuart thought it might be possible for the Confederates to "reach the rear" of the Union army if Lee could undertake a late afternoon or night march to get between Meade and the Federal capital.

Slowing the current enemy movement toward Bull Run would be key to buying Lee time to get into position. Therefore, Stuart hoped to disrupt the Yankees' northward progress. Correctly supposing the enemy had deployed units to defend the O&A, he suspected that the Yankees might let their guard down at nightfall. He would

18 Walker, *Second Army Corps*, 327-328; Sneden Diary, October 13, 1863, VHS; Auburn Civil War Battlefield National Historic District Preliminary Information Form, VA Dept. of Historic Resources; accessed June 3, 2018, www.citizensforfauquier.org/images/Auburn_Nomination_Preliminary_Information_Form.pdf

19 *OR* 29, pt., 1, 447. McClellan, *I Rode with JEB Stuart*, 387. McClellan says it might have been as late as 4 p.m. when Stuart reached Auburn, but his memory is mistaken, as Stuart was already in Auburn by 3:30 p.m. according to *OR* 51, pt. 2, 776-77.

be "pushing on toward Catlett's," he told his chief, and promised that he would "find out all I can and strike if an opportunity offers."

Before he left Auburn, Stuart also sent a dispatch to Maj. Gen. Fitzhugh Lee, whose division should be close to Warrenton by now. The corps commander told his subordinate that for the moment the Federals were "quietly encamped" at Warrenton Junction. His "impression" was that the enemy planned on shifting away from the railroad to retreat northeast toward the Occoquan River. This course would take him beyond easy reach of the Confederate army. He was "very anxious to get to Catlett's Station in time to do something before dark," Stuart said, and he wanted Lee's division to join him and hoped it would "come up in time." It was vital, however, that he "keep pickets on the road leading toward Warrenton, so that the infantry may not be surprised." After Fitz read this message he was to pass it on to army headquarters.[20]

Once Stuart entrusted these dispatches to couriers, he led Gordon's and Funsten's brigades toward Catlett's Station. Seven pieces of horse artillery, a handful of wagons and a few ambulances accompanied them. Lomax's command held its position at Auburn, simultaneously maintaining control of the road junction and covering Stuart's rear. In cooperation with Fitz Lee, the brigadier also had to mind his responsibility to screen the Rebel infantry at Warrenton adequately.[21]

*   *   *

As Stuart led his force down the Saint Stephens Church Road toward the O&A he was certain of the enemy's presence somewhere up ahead. With Union troops near Warrenton Junction, the general decided to exercise caution. He detailed his staff engineer, Capt. William Blackford, to take a few men and scout ahead of the main column. Soon enough the Confederates found plenty of Yankees. Upon arriving on high ground east of Saint Stephens Church, Blackford happened upon an awesome sight. There, spread out along the road below, he could see the balance of the Army of the Potomac retreating toward Centreville. Also visible was an immense park of vehicles occupying the fields between Warrenton Junction and Catlett's Station.

---

20 Previous paragraphs based upon *OR* 51, pt. 2, 776-77. The only means by which Stuart could have seen anything near the Warrenton Branch Railroad is to have ridden to the top of what everyone would later call Coffee Hill at Auburn. Stuart was probably looking at part of the III or II Corps wagon train, which was near Three Mile Switch and close to Mrs. Childs' house at 3 p.m.

21 *OR* 29, pt. 1, 447; McClellan, *I Rode with JEB Stuart*, 387; Clark, *NC Regts*, vol. 1, 454. The batteries were Chews (2 guns), McGregor's (3 guns) and Griffin's (2 guns). Trout, *Galloping Thunder*, 373-74; Robert J. Trout, *Memoirs of the Stuart Horse Artillery: Moorman's and Hart's Batteries* (Knoxville, TN, 2008), 223-234, 279.

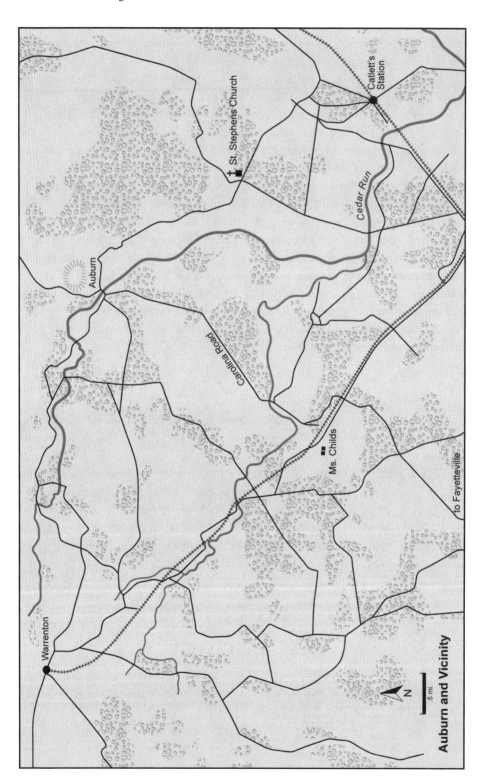

Auburn and Vicinity

Concentrated just out of sight, a few miles to the east around the village of Weaverville, were the pontoon wagons of the entire enemy army.[22]

The Rebels gazed at something Col. Lyman had chanced upon the day before and labeled "a spectacle such as few even of the old officers had ever beheld," i.e., the principal supply train of the Federal army assembled in one place. The massed wagons, perhaps 1,200 of them, covered 300 acres on a "great, open, prairie-like piece of ground" so completely hidden by white canvas-topped vehicles one Union sergeant thought the scene "resembled a plain covered with snow."[23]

Peering down on this magnificent panorama from the concealment of a clump of trees, Blackford scribbled a hurried note to Stuart telling him what he had found. That news soon brought the general himself to the scene. After sneaking up to Blackford's observation point, Stuart marveled at the vista spread out along the railroad.

The Yankee wagons presented a tempting target for the Rebel general. He was of course eager to launch an attack that would interrupt Meade's retreat, but also highly conscious that two cavalry brigades and a handful of guns could accomplish only so much. Even if Fitz Lee arrived to beef up his force, the Southern horsemen could likely do no more than create a temporary panic. That kind of minor success might convince the enemy to head east beyond Lee's reach, as Stuart already feared they planned to do.

Considering his options, Stuart concluded Catlett's Station presented an opening for "a more decided result" than frightening a lot of Yankee wagons. The most important thing now was informing Lee what the cavalry had discovered. If Confederate infantry could move up to Saint Stephens quickly, they might be able to launch a night attack on the Union column and possibly destroy some part of Meade's army.[24]

Everything now depended on surprise and speed. To avoid alerting the unsuspecting Federals, Stuart cautioned Gordon and Funsten to keep their horsemen quietly out of sight. Then the general ordered Maj. Andrew R. Venable to carry an urgent dispatch to army headquarters. Venable was to find Lee with all possible haste and give him word of the great opportunity just east of Stuart's position.[25]

---

22 Ibid., 447, 999; McClellan, *I Rode with JEB Stuart*, 387; W. W. Blackford, *War Years With Jeb Stuart* (Baton Rouge, LA, 1993), 238.

23 Lyman, *Meade's Headquarters*, 34; Devlin Bates to father, October 15, 1863, www.rootsweb. com/~necivwar/CW/bates/genbate2.html, accessed July 24, 2007; Edward K. Cassedy, *Dear Friends at Home: The Civil War Letters of Sergeant Charles T. Bowen, Twelfth United States Infantry, First Battalion, 1861-1865* (Baltimore, MD, 2001), 338.

24 OR 51, pt. 2, 776.

25 Blackford, *War Years*, 238; ibid. 29, pt. 1, 447; McClellan, *I Rode with Stuart*, 387. Venable was Stuart's inspector general.

This photo taken at Brandy Station in May 1863 shows 219 vehicles. This was approximately the number of wagons that made up a corps train. The main supply train of the Union army consisted of something like 1,245 vehicles—623 for carrying forage, rations or quartermaster stores, 177 for small arms ammunition, and 445 for hospital supplies. See Gen. Meade's August 21, 1863 announcement regulating the army's transportation. *Library of Congress*

Along with several aides, Maj. Venable hurried west. But he sensed something amiss as he galloped down the road toward Auburn. There was no sign of Lomax's vedettes. Instead came the sound of a growing murmur, as if some vast host were moving up ahead. With the sun sinking into the horizon ahead of him, Venable grew cautious, and well that he did. As the young officer neared the hamlet he saw not Lomax's troopers but, to his great shock, a dense horde of Union infantry moving northwest through the village. What had happened to Lomax's brigade was a complete mystery, but Venable understood that he must warn Robert E. Lee and Jeb Stuart that the Yankees were in Auburn.

Venable immediately dispatched a courier to Stuart with news of this startling development. Then he determined to carry on with his mission by detouring north in search of a way around the Yankee column and a clear road to Warrenton. Such a daring strategy risked the profound consequences of capture, but there was really no other choice. Fortunately for Venable and his companions, the enemy failed to discern a few horsemen in the fading light. The major's party was able to slide into the lengthening shadows unseen and take up its desperate race toward Warrenton.

The fate of a large portion of Stuart's cavalry, and perhaps the entire Army of Northern Virginia, now hung on Andrew Venable's ability to reach Lee before it was too late.[26]

---

26 *OR* 29, pt. 1, 447; Douglas Southall Freeman, *Lee's Lieutenants*, 3 vols. (New York, 1944), vol. 3:254-55.

CHAPTER 18

"A New and Decidedly Unpleasant Sensation"

Collision Course—Ambush—William French—
Seeing the Elephant—Counterattack—Possibilities for Disaster

GEORGE Meade's pre-dawn order for a general retreat to Centreville put Maj. Gen. William F. French's III Corps in motion at 5:00 a.m. on October 13. The corps had abandoned its battle line around Freeman's Ford on the Rappahannock and hiked northward to Fayetteville with Brig. Gen. Joseph Carr's 3rd Division marching in the lead. The meandering Union column bypassed the rear of Warren's westward-facing II Corps before continuing on to Three Mile Station, where Meade had ordered General French to halt and form a line of battle.

This movement presented several serious complications. Through some unexplained mistake, Brig. Gen. Henry Prince's 2nd Division never received orders to move that morning. French's headquarters had alerted Henry Prince the previous evening that the corps would march north on the 13th, and that Prince's command would march at the end of the long column. Prince claimed this communication included no information about a starting time. When the III Corps began moving just after sunrise, French somehow failed to notice that his column was short an entire infantry division.

Prince didn't learn that the rest of the III Corps had left Freeman's Ford until about 7:00 a.m., when a messenger sent to French's headquarters discovered the headquarters, along with the rest of the corps, had simply disappeared. At a loss for what to do, Prince requested instructions from General Meade. How the famously short-tempered army commander reacted to this foul up passed unrecorded, but he quickly relayed the III Corps' route to the perplexed division commander and told him to get moving, and quickly. These illuminating instructions arrived at the 2nd Division's command post at almost the same instant as did a courier from General

French, who had belatedly realized he was missing a few thousand men who all belonged to Prince's command.[1]

Prince had to hurry to catch up to the rest of the crops. His division reached Fayetteville just as Warren was putting the II Corps on the road to follow French. Much to everyone's irritation, Warren's men had to yield the road to Prince's command as it hustled northward. That general's woes did not end there. He had no guide, and what he called "the perplexity of the roads" confused him. Looking for the correct route caused further delay.[2]

It was almost 3 p.m. before Prince's troops rejoined their comrades at Three Mile Station. The 2nd Division hardly had time to form line alongside the rest of the corps before French ordered his men back onto the road. As the Union column lurched into motion, its leaders could not have guessed that, at that very moment, Jeb Stuart was catching a glimpse of their wagon train from his hilltop perch near Auburn.[3]

The III Corps was en route to the town of Greenwich. To get there it would march north along a colonial-era trade route known as the Carolina Road, but which also went by the name Rouges Road or sometimes the Three Mile Switch Road. Along the way the corps would have to negotiate the narrow crossing of Cedar Run at Auburn. Major General Birney's 1st Division would lead the column, followed by Carr's 3rd Division, the corps supply train, and finally, Prince's 2nd Division. Warren's II Corps and Kilpatrick's and Gregg's cavalry divisions were under orders to accompany the III Corps as it marched north. Kilpatrick would guard Warren's left flank, while Gregg acted as rearguard.[4]

Intelligence reports indicated most of Lee's army moving on Warrenton along roadways parallel to French's column. But the III Corps commander didn't seem overly concerned about the possibility of danger. Meade had told him to expect little more than Rebel harassing attacks on his march north. Undoubtedly the nearby presence of Warren, Gregg, and Kilpatrick reassured French of ready help if needed. Whatever the cause, French advanced toward Greenwich in a complacent frame of mind.

---

1   OR 29, pt. 1, 302, 312, 315. Meade sent his retreat order at 12:50 a.m. on October 13. The assigned position of Prince's division placed his command at the rear of the III Corps wagon train.

2   Ibid.

3   OR 51, pt. 2, 776-77.

4   Established in 1747 the Carolina Road ran from Frederick, MD to the Virginia-North Carolina border. http://www.loudounhistory.org/history/carolina-road.htm. Accessed June 3, 2018.

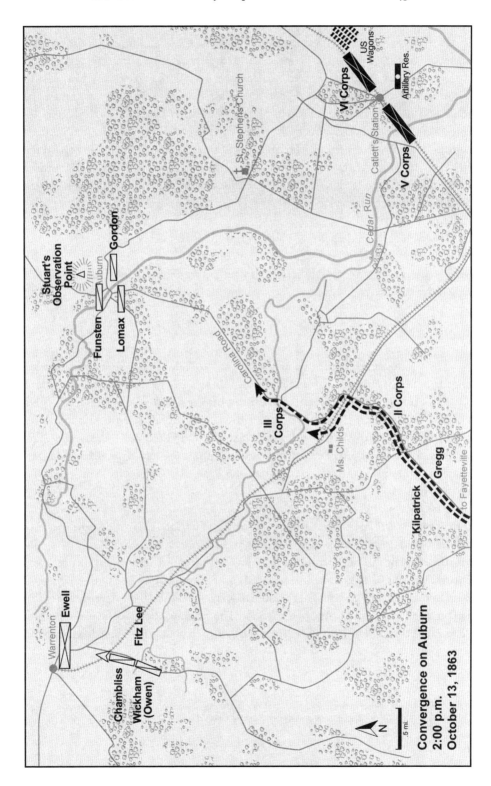

Convergence on Auburn
2:00 p.m.
October 13, 1863

N

5 mi.

A small body of cavalry formed the III Corps vanguard, followed a short distance behind by General French and his staff. The 57th Pennsylvania, with companies A and K thrown out as an advance guard, trailed along behind the general and was in turn followed by a two-gun section of the 10th Massachusetts Light Artillery under the command of 24-year old Captain Jacob Henry Sleeper. Colonel Charles Collis 1st Brigade of Birney's division was next in line, with the remaining four guns of Sleeper's battery plodding along behind. The balance of Birney's command and the bulk of the III Corps, its wagon trains, the entire II Corps, and Gregg's cavalry, stretched for miles back down the road leading toward Three Mile Station. Kilpatrick's division moved parallel to Warren, the cavalrymen weaving their way through the woods as best they could.[5]

It was highly unusual for a corps commander to personally lead his column through territory likely to contain the enemy, but that is exactly what French did. He would have reason to regret this bravado, for unknown to him, a significant number of Rebel cavalry lurked up ahead.

*	*	*

The Confederates French would soon run into belonged to Lunsford Lomax's brigade, which Stuart had left behind to hold Auburn while he led a larger force toward Catlett's Station. When his chief rode off toward the O&A railroad, Lomax led his troopers across Cedar Run and up onto a broad plain above the creek valley. After deploying his regiments into some woods bisecting the Carolina Road, he sent a few vedettes forward to provide sufficient early warning of any approaching danger. Sometime around 5:00 p.m. they spotted the head of a Yankee column marching toward Auburn.

The 28-year old Lomax knew nothing about the enemy force nearing his position. It might be a reconnaissance party or something much larger. He did know that Fitz Lee was riding toward Auburn, so help might therefore be close at hand. Holding the town was essential, Lomax realized, if he was to prevent the enemy from cutting off Stuart. Determined to hold his ground, and comforted that Fitz Lee must be drawing near, Lomax ordered his regimental commanders to dismount their sharpshooters and station them on the south edge of the woods. The mounted men took up a reserve line deeper in the forest and near the edge of the 80-foot high bluff looking down into the valley of Cedar Run. Now came the tense waiting for the Yankees to come within effective range before opening fire.[6]

*   *   *

The Federals approaching Lomax didn't expect an ambush. As soon as the leading cavalry element of French's column came close enough, the concealed Rebels let loose a volley from the thick woods. This initial fusillade sent the Union troopers scurrying backwards in shock which in turn triggered terror in a number of raw recruits in the leading infantry formations. These frightened soldiers went "running back in confusion, every man trying to get out of range." Luckily for Maj. Gen. French, the sight of fleeing men was nothing new to the veterans in his ranks and the rest of the column stayed steady.[7]

Fitz Lee reached Auburn just as the firing began. Upon hearing the popping of carbines south of town, he quickly directed Chambliss' and Wickham's brigades (the latter still under Col. Owens' command) across Cedar Run to join the fight. Chambliss went into position on the right of Lomax's line, while Owen's troopers took station on the left. Both men dismounted their sharpshooters and sent them forward. Breathed's horse artillery battery galloped to the top of the hill behind the McCormick house, quickly unlimbered and began firing on French's column. Their shells knocked tree limbs down onto the Union formations and forced the Yankees to keep their heads low.[8]

Meanwhile, the Federals were not idle. As the lead companies of the 57th Pennsylvania deployed to both sides of the road, French cantered back to the leading section of Sleeper's Massachusetts battery and ordered it into position. A 48-year-old pre-war veteran of the regular army, French had made a good record as an artilleryman

---

6 OR 29, pt. 1, 463, 466-68.

7 Ibid., 463, 466-70; Martin, et al, *History of the Fifty-Seventh Regiment*, 99. Among those heading to the rear were Marie Tebe and Anna Etheridge, two vivandiéres—female camp followers wearing stylized uniforms and unofficially attached to the 114th Zouaves and 2nd Michigan. They had been riding with French's staff. Veteran campaigners, these ladies were renowned for their courage and care of the wounded on many battlefields. They well understood their place of duty was not on the firing line and unlike their panicked male counterparts they were heading to, not away, from their battle station.

8 In his report on the action General Birney (*OR* 29, pt. 1, 312) refers to a Rebel battery positioned on the hill behind the McCormick house north of Cedar Run. Sneden writes in his diary that Confederate artillery opened fire on French's column, knocking tree limbs down onto Union troops sheltering in the road. (Sneden Diary, Oct. 13, 1863, VHS). Beside these two accounts, there is no reference to Southern artillery at Auburn. But since the two sources are mutually supportive, I have accepted each as valid.

and had fought in the Mexican and Seminole wars. During the current conflict's first year he had done well enough with a brigade to earn a promotion to major general. In that post he led a hard luck II Corps division which always drew bloody assignments such as attacking the sunken road at Antietam or Marye's Heights at Fredericksburg.

At the start of the Gettysburg campaign he was in command of the garrison at Harper's Ferry. After the battle, Meade assigned French's troops to the III Corps and he had taken on corps command as a result of seniority. The red faced, portly, sleepy-eyed general with a bushy mustache wasn't popular with most of his troops. They would have preferred a "homegrown" commander from one of their own division leaders. Some judged French's late July performance at Manassas Gap as unnecessarily cautious, and camp rumor held him overly fond of his liquor. But no one ever doubted William French's courage. When he and his small entourage came under fire on the outskirts of Auburn, the general didn't flinch. One Vermont soldier recalled seeing him calmly astride his horse, "brushing away the bullets with his hand as he would have brushed away flies." As his infantrymen rushed forward the corps commander shouted "shoot 'em, damn 'em, shoot 'em!"[9]

To suppress enemy fire French directed Sleeper's lead section to load canister and blast the Rebel position in the woods. He was probably unaware that this was the baptism of fire for the 10th Massachusetts cannoneers. The gunners certainly weren't. One of their number admitted that the "hostile hiss" of Rebel bullets was "a new and decidedly unpleasant sensation" for the greenhorn combatants.[10]

Union infantrymen shared the sensation. General Birney had a bugler riding next to him hit by enemy fire. Seconds later Rebel sharpshooters struck two of the general's orderlies. Lomax's troopers concentrated their fire on Sleeper's artillerymen and inflicted a number of casualties. A bullet slammed through the mouth of one sergeant, breaking two teeth and lodging in his neck before knocking him from his horse. Enemy marksmen hit another gunner in the arm and seconds later in the hip. A round that tore through the open lid of a limber chest injured a crewman getting ammunition. Other bullets smacked into the limber and its carriage. Several wounded horses went down screaming in pain or terror.[11]

Despite this punishment, the Bay State artillerymen performed as coolly as veterans and soon had their two pieces belching loads of canister towards the Confederates. Colonel Collis brigade went into line on the right side of the road in front

---

9   Edwin M. Haynes, *A History of the Tenth Regiment Vermont Volunteers* (Lewiston, ME, 1870), 45.

10 Billings, *10th Massachusetts Battery*, 95-96.

11 Sneden diary, October 13, 1863, VHS; ibid., 96-97.

of the guns, while part of Col. Regis De Trobriand's brigade took position on the other side of the thoroughfare. Prone on the reverse slope of a small knoll, the Union infantrymen began trading fire with Fitz Lee's sharpshooters. Meanwhile the remaining four guns of Sleeper's battery came forward at the gallop; the infantry in the road giving way to allow the cannons' passage down the narrow dirt lane. Deployed alongside their comrades they soon added their weight to the swelling contest.[12]

The excited Yankee gunners were firing as fast as they could load their guns, a wasteful practice typical of men in their first engagement that aroused the ire of Capt. George E. Randolph, chief of the III Corps artillery. One crewmen remembered Randolph riding up behind the battery and "as cool as if on review," ordering its crews to slow their fire and wait for the flash of enemy rifles before selecting a target. Ironically, just as Randolph delivered his sage advice the battle began to slacken, even though minutes before it had seemed sure to escalate.[13]

The increasingly obvious mismatch of forces contesting the road to Auburn hastened the abrupt finale. Even with the arrival of Fitz Lee and his two additional brigades, the Rebels remained hopelessly outnumbered. Surprise had allowed them to deliver a quick punch. But as ever more Federal troops joined the battle, the tide had dramatically swung against the Confederates.

Sleeper's guns, which one officer said were "pouring canister through the woods furiously," had a profound impact on the Southern cavalry, as did the realization that at least an entire Federal division, if not more, was strung out on the Carolina Road. Certain that his few brigades of horsemen could accomplish little in the face of such a "superior force of infantry," Fitz Lee ordered his men to disengage and withdraw.[14]

Just as the Confederates decided to abandon their uneven contest, Union infantrymen under Collis and De Trobriand rose from cover to charge. The gray cavalry hit Collis troops with a "murderous volley" which knocked several men to the ground, killing two and wounding nine in the 140th Pennsylvania alone. Heedless of the losses, the Federal regiments swept forward, and the Southern horsemen rapidly gave ground. The Yankees kept coming until they had cleared the woods from which Lomax had sprung his ambush. Their advance stopped only after reaching the edge of the bluff overlooking Cedar Run.[15]

---

12 Billings, *10th Massachusetts Battery*, 95-96; Sneden Diary, October 13, 1863, VHS; Regis De Trobriand, *Four Years with the Army of the Potomac* (Boston, MA, 1889), 541-49

13 David Craft, *History of the One Hundred Forty-First Regiment Pennsylvania Volunteers, 1862-1865* (Towanda, PA, 1885), 149; Billings, *10th Massachusetts Battery*, 97.

14 *OR* 29, pt. 1, 463, 466, 468, 472, 475, 570.

15 Craft, *141st Pennsylvania*, 149-50; ibid., 312; De Trobriand, *Four Years*, 541.

The Confederate cavalry got away with virtually no damage. Fitz Lee's retreat order gave most of the Rebel sharpshooters time to reach their led horses before the Yankees struck—a fact that spared De Trobriand's brigade from any casualties in its charge. Once mounted, the cavalrymen disappeared down the Dumfries Road toward Warrenton and soon outpaced any possibility of Federal pursuit. The Rebels did not go far, however. Fitz Lee backed up just enough to yield the Carolina Road to the Yankees and put his men into camp for the night within earshot of the enemy's drums.[16]

Although the Federals had won the contest at Auburn, the Confederates had inflicted considerably more damage than they had suffered. Neither Owen nor Chambliss, who saw only marginal combat, reported casualties. Lomax's command, which had carried the bulk the fight, recorded 2 killed—one in the 1st Maryland Cavalry (CS) and another in the 15th Virginia Cavalry, which also listed 1 man wounded. Birney's division lost 11 dead and 42 wounded—virtually all of them from Collis' brigade and Sleeper's battery.[17]

In the overall course of the campaign the number of casualties was insignificant, but the outcome of this little fight had important and potentially dangerous consequences for both sides. Fitz Lee's withdrawal opened the Carolina Road for the III Corps to continue its march toward Greenwich and for the II Corps to bivouac around Auburn later that night. A considerable number of Federals now stood between the Confederate army and Stuart's horsemen near the railroad. Depending on how fully the rival forces grasped and reacted to this situation, happenstance had spawned circumstances that might lead to the destruction of Warren's corps or, alternatively, two brigades of Rebel cavalry.

---

16 OR 29, pt. 1, 463, 466, 468, 570. It is unclear whether he had taken all of Wickham's and Chambliss' brigades south of Cedar Run or just their sharpshooters. Given the terrain, a rapid retreat by three brigades of cavalry over the creek near Auburn would have been difficult. The speed and ease of the Rebel retreat suggests that only Lomax's brigade and sharpshooters from Lee's other two brigades were south of the creek. Colonel Owen said that his men fired only a "few shots" before withdrawing.

17 Ibid., 467, 470; Sneden Diary, October 13, 1863, 882, VHS; Billings, *10th Massachusetts Battery*, 98.

CHAPTER 19

"Never Was the Voice of A Mule So Harsh!"

A Tense Night—Watching Yankees—Daring Couriers—Lee Worried—A Rescue Plan

JEB Stuart would be among the first to comprehend the importance of the late afternoon skirmish near Auburn. As that event played out, he and his accompanying troops had continued to hover near Catlett's Station. They were still carefully observing the movements of the Union army when a courier from Maj. Venable arrived in "hot haste" with the alarming news that Yankees had taken the crossroads in the Stuart's rear. Although Lomax had sent an earlier dispatch when French first threatened Auburn, the message never got through. Venable's belated warning was the first to alert Stuart that the enemy had him cut off from Warrenton.[1]

Grasping his now threatened circumstances, the Rebel general immediately turned his force westward and headed back toward Auburn. It was sometime between 8 and 9 p.m. The total darkness of October 13's new moon had already enveloped the landscape. As the Rebels slipped away to the west, a flutter of firing broke out at the rear of Stuart's column as Federal pickets near the railroad reacted to dimly perceived movement. Fortunately the scattering shots motivated only passing interest. The Southerners faded away, leaving enemy sentries convinced that they had been shooting nervously at shadows.[2]

Far greater danger loomed ahead. With Gordon's brigade in the lead, the Confederates carefully made their way to Auburn. Near the hamlet the Rebel advance guard bumped up against Federal pickets, precipitating a brief twilight exchange of fire.

---

1 Blackford, *War Years*, 238; McClellan, *I Rode With Stuart*, 388-89; OR 29, pt. 1, 447.

2 OR 29, pt. 1, 447; McClellan, *I Rode With Stuart*, 388-89; Moon phases for October 1863 can be found at https://www.timeanddate.com/calendar/?year=1863&country=1.

Still not entirely convinced a substantial enemy force barred his way, Stuart trotted up to Gordon and asked about the strength of the Yankees in his front. The brigadier calmly told Stuart to follow him and he would see for himself.[3]

A few seconds later, the sight of Union troops steadily marching in the flickering light of lanterns across his only path to Warrenton dispelled all doubts. These Federals must have turned off the routes alongside the O&A and swung west to avoid the clogged principal roadway, Stuart surmised. Likely these bluecoats would continue through Auburn and then head northward to Greenwich and perhaps Bristoe Station where they could rejoin the primary Federal column.

Whatever brought so many Yankees to this place was beside the point, however: they were here. Stuart understood that the large enemy formations to his front and rear had trapped his command. He lacked the strength to cut his way through the encircling Union infantry in either direction, even in a night attack. His only option, it appeared, was to abandon his cannons, wagons, and ambulances, and attempt to save his force by directing his men to sneak through Yankee lines in small groups and reassemble somewhere near Warrenton. Such a desperate move would knock a third of the Southern army's cavalry out of action for at least a day, perhaps longer, even if most of the troopers got through, which was hardly certain.

Jeb Stuart was in no mood to abandon anything, of course. Instead he sent staff officers back down the column with instructions for everyone to quietly move into an opportune little valley which offered a hiding place just north of the road. The general drew in both his advance and rear guards. Within minutes and in virtual silence, two brigades of Confederate cavalry, seven artillery pieces, and a handful of wagons vanished from view. With his command thus cloaked, Stuart dispatched a series of couriers to explain his predicament to army headquarters. Two of the riders wore uniforms taken from Union prisoners so as to increase the odds that at least one reached Robert E. Lee.[4]

Despite his delicate position, Stuart perceived opportunity in his circumstances. The general's dispatches suggested hitting the enemy on both flanks at the same time in the morning, with Southern infantry assailing the Federals at Auburn from the west, while the Rebel cavalry attacked from the east. Such an assault might yield rich results. But it could only happen if Stuart's force remained undiscovered and survived until Lee's infantry arrived.[5]

---

3   Clark, *NC Regts*, vol. 1, 453.

4   McClellan, *I Rode With Stuart*, 389; Thomas P. Nanzig, ed., *The Civil War Memoirs of a Virginia Cavalryman: Lt. Robert T. Hubard, Jr.* (Tuscaloosa, AL, 2007), 110.

5   OR 29/1:448; Freeman, *Lee's Lieutenants*, vol. 3, 256-57.

As the Rebel troopers stealthily dismounted in the darkness, officers detailed some men to form a skirmish line and told the rest to prepare for a long, worrisome evening. Stuart's troops were incredibly tense. Major Henry B. McClellan of the general's staff was one of those sweating through the long night. After placing the artillery into position and deploying the regiments, nothing "remained but to watch and wait and keep quiet," he recalled. Although the soldiers understood the need for silence, the "weary, hungry, headstrong mules of the ordnance train" didn't. The troopers stationed with every team to keep the animals quiet labored mostly in vain. Now and then the "discordant bray" of an animal would pierce the night. "Never," McClellan exclaimed, "was the voice of a mule so harsh!" Fortunately for the Rebels, vocal beasts of burden served both flags and the complaining livestock attracted no attention from Union lines.[6]

Nonetheless, the danger of discovery by the mass of enemy soldiers within hearing distance remained more than simply possible. Should even one Northern company commander send his men to gather firewood in the thin forest bordering Stuart's little valley, the entire game would be up. Fortunately, most of the Yankees stayed at arm's length.

Once during the night a pair of Union officers wandered into the Confederate position. As soon as the Yankees were inside the woods a Rebel trooper emerged from hiding and placed the "cold muzzle of a pistol" against the head of the nearest enemy. That chilling sensation along with a "whispered threat that the least move or outcry would bring instant death" ensured the new captives' cooperation. But this incident certainly accentuated the looming menace. No one wanted to contemplate what would happen if the captured Yankees' comrades came looking for them.[7]

As the long night wore on, Stuart's officers proffered various proposals for escape. In hushed conversation they weighed and then rejected each scheme in turn. There was no good alternative to waiting until dawn in hope of an attack by Lee's infantry or the sudden appearance of some fortuitous opportunity to escape. Throughout the night Stuart remained calm and appeared almost relaxed. As Capt. Blackford lay on his belly observing the lantern-lit passage of the Federal host through Auburn, the general laid down beside him, then placed his head on the small of Blackford's back and instantly fell asleep. The sympathetic staffer understood his chief's need for rest and selflessly refrained from moving for several hours. Eventually the strain became too much, and

6   McClellan, *I Rode with Stuart*, 390.

7   Edward S. Ellis, *The Campfires of General Lee: From the Peninsula to Appomattox Court-House* (Philadelphia, PA, 1885), 324; Robert J. Trout, *Memoirs of the Stuart Horse Artillery: Moorman's and Hart's Batteries* (Knoxville, TN, 2008), 223-34.

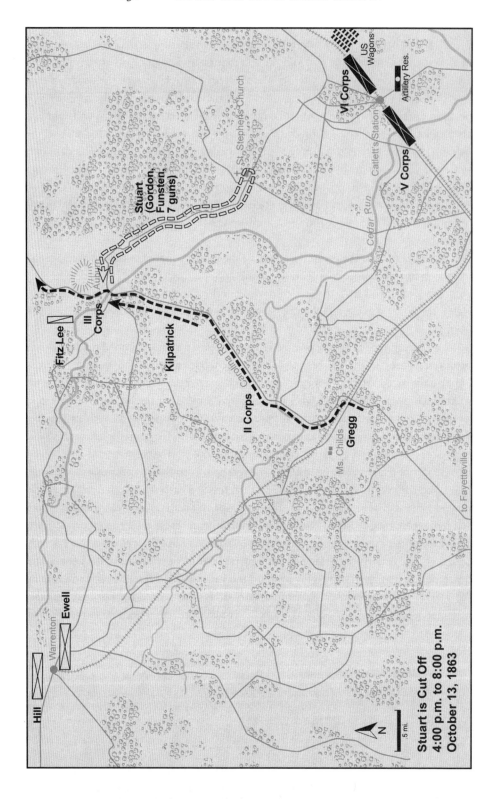

Stuart is Cut Off
4:00 p.m. to 8:00 p.m.
October 13, 1863

Blackford carefully tried to transfer Stuart's skull to a different spot: at which point the general awoke.[8]

Now it was the captain's turn to find temporary refuge in sleep while Stuart marked the slow passage of time, which seemed to drip like thick molasses through an hourglass. As he pondered his situation the general must have wondered whether the dawn would find his troopers rescued by friends, scattered in rout, or prisoners in Federal hands.

*   *   *

Five miles to the west another general shared Stuart's apprehension. As darkness had fallen on October 13, Robert E. Lee intuitively sensed something was wrong. The day had been somewhat frustrating for him. Despite putting his divisions on the road at dawn, it had taken until mid-afternoon to unite the army. Ewell's corps had massed south of Warrenton while Hill's later arriving troops had concentrated north of the town. Lee had wanted to launch them either north or east as soon as possible, but not without better knowledge of Meade's position. He had hoped Stuart could provide that information by the time Hill joined Ewell at Warrenton. Unfortunately, the ordered reconnaissance to Catlett's Station had gotten off to a late start, and Lee still knew nothing by late afternoon.[9]

As usual, the Confederate general didn't let time slip away uselessly. When the army began crossing the upper Rappahannock River in its effort to outflank Meade, Lee ordered his main supply train to rendezvous with the infantry at Warrenton. Once the wagons rumbled into the town, the general directed Generals Ewell and Hill to provision their troops. Although this would take some time, it would also enable the army to maneuver for the next several days without reliance on the slow-moving trains.[10]

Lee received his first reports from Stuart after 4 p.m. Written at 3:30 and 3:45 and passed along by Fitzhugh Lee, they had indicated a strong Yankee presence near Warrenton Junction. He was heading east, Stuart said, to gather information and launch a strike "if an opportunity" offered. The army could "reach the rear" of Meade's force, the cavalry chief thought, if Lee launched a late afternoon or night march to get between the Federals and Washington, DC—a suggestion the commanding general

8   Blackford, *War Years*, 239.

9   *OR* 29, pt. 1, 410.

10   Ibid.

apparently didn't consider practicable in the hour or so of daylight remaining after he read Stuart's message.[11]

Since those dispatches, army headquarters had heard nothing from the general. News that Yankee troops had shoved Fitz Lee out of Auburn and were marching north through the village exacerbated the commanding general's unease. Although still bothered by the pain in his back and undoubtedly needing sleep, Lee stayed awake late into the night concerned about his cavalry's whereabouts and well-being. Not until 1 a.m. did the reason for Stuart's uncharacteristic silence became clear.

That's when one of Stuart's favorite scouts, Pvt. Robert Goode of the 1st Virginia Cavalry, trotted into army headquarters. By boldly riding straight through the Union columns, rather than seeking a way around them as Venable had done, Goode became the first of Stuart's several couriers to deliver his urgent plea for help. He explained the situation of the cut off cavalry brigades and relayed his chief's suggestion for a two-sided attack on the Auburn Yankees in the morning. He also recounted what Stuart had seen along the O&A some eight hours ago.

Goode's report presented a lot for Lee to absorb. Combined with what the general knew about Union forces pushing through Auburn, he must have realized that Meade was swiftly retreating along the railroad toward Manassas or Centreville. The nearly day long pause around Warrenton had erased most of the head start the Confederates had gained on October 12, bringing the race between the two armies to almost a dead heat. Whichever one moved more swiftly on October 14 would win the day.

This argued for an early start and a rapid northward march by the entire ANV in the morning. However, Lee could hardly ignore Stuart's current predicament, unwelcome distraction that it was. As soon as the general had gleaned all he could from Goode, he ordered Ewell to march his corps to Stuart's assistance as quickly as possible. He hoped and expected that the Second Corps would quickly relieve Stuart while at the same time avoid getting entangled in a time consuming affair.

Lee also issued orders for A. P. Hill's corps and Fitz Lee's cavalry division to renew the army's flank movement at daylight. These units would march north on the Warrenton Turnpike to New Baltimore and then on to Greenwich. Once there Hill would swing east to strike the railroad, while Fitz Lee's cavalry protected his left flank. As soon as Ewell accomplished his mission to Auburn, he was to follow Hill toward Greenwich and the O&A.

After dispatching messengers to deliver those directives, the worried and weary army commander retired to his tent. Fatigue and anxiety had frayed Lee's nerves, though, as soon became apparent. While lying on his cot, he overheard Goode

---

11 OR 51, pt. 2, 776-77; Krick, *Civil War Weather*, 110. Sunset was at 5:36 p.m.

speaking about the situation at Auburn. The private was expanding upon the tactical deployments in the area and suggesting the best placement for artillery to assist the cavalry. Lee could hear only part of the conversation through the wall of his tent, but he heard enough to get angry about what he perceived to be the scout's loose talk in camp. The famed Virginian rose from his bed, stepped to the entry of his shelter, and scolded Goode for speaking of things he ought to share only with the army's commander. Returning to his bed, he left the poor private fairly trembling at having earned the general's displeasure.

The aide to whom Goode had been talking swiftly interceded on his behalf. He went to Lee and explained that the scout had not been speaking out of turn but providing important information for the dawn's coming operation. Mortified at his overreaction, Lee quickly made amends. He offered his own camp chair to the private and ordered the headquarters' staff to cook a hot meal and brew some coffee for the courier. According to one observer, the general then hovered nearby to perform "all the duties of a hospitable host" while the soldier ate.[12]

Goode's sojourn at army headquarters added another anecdote to Lee's growing legend. More importantly it put infantry in motion to Stuart's relief. Per instructions, Ewell's Corps was awake before dawn and on the road at 4 a.m. Major General Robert Rodes' division led, followed by Maj. Gens. Jubal Early's and then Edward "Alleghany" Johnson's commands. Moving southeast out of Warrenton, the gray column would approach Auburn from the south bank of Cedar Run. Its route carried it down the Double Poplars Road, which ran perpendicular to the Carolina Road the Federals were using. The two routes intersected at Auburn on the south end of the bridge over Cedar Run. Whether Ewell would arrive in time to save Stuart's cavalry was anyone's guess. It was certainly possible, however, that his corps was marching toward a fight that might spark the climactic battle of the campaign.[13]

12 A. L. Long, *Memoirs of Robert E. Lee* (Secaucus, NY, 1983), 308-309.

13 OR *Supplement*, 5, pt. 1, 505; Jubal Early, *Lieutenant General Jubal Anderson Early, C.S.A. Autobiographical Sketch and Narrative of the War Between the States* (New York, 1994), 304.

CHAPTER 20

"For God's Sake Hold . . . Them for Ten Minutes Longer!"

General Warren—Frantic Preparations—Rodes' Advance—Surprise Encounter—
Sudden Alarm—Desperate Orders—A Doomed Charge

IN between Jeb Stuart's hiding place east of Auburn and Ewell's bivouacs west of there, Union columns had continued moving up the Carolina Road for a good part of the night of October 13/14. The afternoon skirmish between Fitz Lee and French had not seriously delayed the Yankees. David Birney's 1st Division at the head of the III Corps column covered the five miles between Cedar Run and Greenwich in good time, reaching the town at 8 p.m. The movement of French's 200-vehicle wagon train, however, was so slow that Prince's 2nd Division, marching behind the wagons, didn't go into camp at Greenwich until 3 a.m.—some seven hours after Birney's command and Joseph's Carr's 3rd Division arrived in the town.[1]

The creeping pace of French's vehicles slowed the advance of Warren's troops to such an extent, the II Corps' commander brought his column to a halt at Three Mile Station rather than crawl along at a snail's pace behind French. While Warren waited for the III Corps to clear the road, some of his staff found a byway enabling him to put his regiments back into motion. Via this alternate route the II Corps could move alongside French's column to within a short distance of Cedar Run. By the time Warren reached the vicinity of Auburn at 9 p.m., it was dark and troops, batteries, and wagons packed both the bridge and the ford near the village.[2]

---

1 OR 29, pt. 1, 312, 315. The number of vehicles in French's corps train is inferred from Warren's count of the number of vehicles in his corps train, which numbered 225.

2 Ibid., 237.

The traffic snarl involved elements of both the III Corps and Kilpatrick's 3rd Cavalry Division. The horsemen had been moving on the left flank of the II Corps for most of the day, "making their own road" through the woods, in Warren's words. The logjam at Cedar Run had allowed Kilpatrick to outpace the II Corps' column and reach the village ahead of it. The cavalryman's orders directed him to make Buckland Mills, approximately eight miles north of Auburn, before going into camp. Since Judson Kilpatrick had no intention of needlessly wasting time before proceeding to his objective, he squeezed his troopers, artillery, and wagons over the creek and headed north. When the 3rd Cavalry Division rode into Buckland Mills at 11 p.m. the III Corps wagon train was still creaking across the bridge at Auburn.[3]

*   *   *

Gouverneur K. Warren was just as impatient as Kilpatrick on October 13. The New York-born II Corps commander was just 33-years old. An 1850 graduate of West Point ranked second in his class, he had taught mathematics at his alma mater before serving in the topographical engineers. When the war began he took the post of lieutenant colonel in the 5th New York Infantry and become its colonel in August, 1861. Warren earned high marks for handling a brigade at the battles of Gaines Mill and Second Bull Run. Although his command saw no action at Antietam, he received a promotion to brigadier general on September 26, 1862. His regiments were in reserve during the Union debacle at Fredericksburg twelve weeks later.[4]

In February 1863, Maj. Gen. Joseph Hooker named Warren chief topographical engineer of the AOP, and he proved so valuable to Hooker during the Chancellorsville campaign the general made him the army's chief engineer shortly after the battle. When Lincoln replaced Hooker with George Meade on June 28, 1863, the new army commander invited Gouverneur Warren to become his chief of staff.

Although well-suited to that position, the ambitious brigadier declined for a variety of reasons. Foremost among these was his preference for the relative independence of his engineer job, which he was unwilling to give up for anything other than the opportunity to lead troops in the field. That choice left him free to ride to Little Round Top on July 2, 1863 where his quick action summoning units to that critical height helped save the battle of Gettysburg for the Union. It also led to his earned promotion to major general on August 8 and temporary assignment to command the II Corps.

3   OR 29, pt. 1, 386.

4   Warner, *Generals in Blue*, 541. For an outstanding biography of Warren, see David M. Jordan, *Happiness is Not My Companion: The Life of General G. K. Warren* (Bloomington, IN, 2001).

Major General Gouverneur K. Warren
Library of Congress

Warren did not look like a warrior. Although of medium height, he was slightly built. Observers variously characterized him as boy-like, delicate, or wiry. His facial hair mimicked that of George B. McClellan—a carefully trimmed mustache which completely covered his upper lip paired with a diminutive tuft of hair right below the center of his lower lip. Lyman wrote about Warren's "small, dried up, pointed nose" and "a restless black eye" which reminded Meade's aide of a weasel. Colonel Charles S. Wainwright, commander of the I Corps artillery, thought that Warren's dark complexion and youthful head of "straight black hair" gave him "a little of the look of an Indian." Colonel Horace Porter noted Warren as one of the "few officers who wore their sashes in a campaign or paid much attention to their dress."[5]

Extremely intelligent, with a quick, active mind that Col. Lyman said was "never still," the general was an outstanding engineer, courageous battlefield leader, and a careful steward of his men. He impressed Meade and the army's chief of staff, Maj. Gen. Humphreys, a lifelong friend who had served with Warren before the war. Lyman thought Warren a "most original officer" whose mind was "extremely ready and sure on all points." Unfortunately, that confidence wasn't totally unsullied: there was more than a touch of arrogance in Warren's makeup. At times impatient with those he considered his intellectual inferiors, he could express harsh criticisms of fellow officers (including superiors) when their ideas or actions didn't live up to his standards.

He was also susceptible to bouts of depression. Possibly he harbored too sensitive a soul for the brutal profession he had chosen. Though he craved recognition and rank, he disdained courting either via newspapers or politics. Nonetheless, Warren needed frequent validation of his worth and talents. He was thus prickly about the prerogatives of rank and sometimes uppity or petty with subordinates and equals. In the

---

5   Allan Nevins, ed., *A Diary of Battle: The Personal Journals of Colonel Charles S. Wainwright, 1861-1865* (Boston, MA, 1998), 338-39; Lyman, *Meade's Army*, 29; Horace Porter, *Campaigning With Grant* (New York, 1897), 51.

not-too-distant future these traits would cause him much trouble. In the fall of 1863, however, his talents and potential were far more notable than latent personality flaws.

Warren had almost missed the current campaign. He had married Emily Chase Forbes on June 17, 1863, after a long distance 14-month courtship. The wedding took place just as the Gettysburg campaign began, and Warren had returned to the army only two days after the ceremony. He missed his bride terribly but put off requesting a furlough through August and September. Not until October 8 did he secure a leave to visit Emily in Baltimore. Lee's offensive cut the newlyweds' plans short, and the general felt compelled to hurry back to the army. He had reached Culpeper on October 10, barely in time to lead the II Corps in its gyrations across the Rappahannock.

The III Corps' inefficiencies and tepid pace from Fayetteville had thoroughly vexed Warren, who was acutely aware that his troops had not slept in 24 hours and desperately required rest and food. Although his column was still south of Auburn, the general decided a little after 9 p.m. that his command was close enough to satisfy Meade's order for the II Corps to camp there. His totally fagged out troops agreed. When Warren ordered a halt for the night they stepped to the side of the road, cooked and ate a hurried supper, then lay down for much needed sleep. Not even the rain that began falling an hour later disturbed their slumber.[6]

*　　*　　*

As October 13 faded into October 14, the thousands of Federal soldiers marching through Auburn or sleeping nearby remained oblivious to the fact that two brigades of Rebel cavalry lurked just a few hundred yards to the east. To the west, however, a small contingent of Union troopers was quite alive to imminent danger. The 10th New York Cavalry, already worn down thanks to yesterday's fight at Sulphur Springs, got the job of picketing the Double Poplars Road which ran westward to Warrenton. Just after nightfall, Maj. Avery sent companies H and L under 24-year old Capt. George Vanderbilt to establish the required outpost. Although led by a guide, the small force had to weave its way through the II Corps' tangled mass of wagons before taking an almost four-mile roundabout route to reach its destination, which, as it turned out, lay only half a mile beyond the eventual bivouac of Gregg's division.

Vanderbilt led his 40-man command into a dense wood stretching on either side of the Double Poplars road not far from where it veered sharply left to descend a ravine

6   Josiah Marshall Favill, *The Diary of a Young Officer* (Chicago, IL, 1909), 265; Thomas M. Aldrich, *The History of Battery A First Regiment Rhode Island Light Artillery in the War to Preserve the Union 1861-1865* (Providence, RI, 1904), 245-46; Thomas Myer, "Incidents and Anecdotes of the War Between the States," 78, Penn State.

into the valley of Cedar Run. He stationed most of his troopers near the eastern end of the timber, before taking 8 men to the western edge of the forest to establish his picket post. When this tiny detachment got to the desired location, the Federal horsemen were taken aback to see the horizon gleaming with Rebel campfires. Their number and scope clearly indicated a large enemy force just a few miles away. The captain immediately sent an officer to alert Avery and the rest of Gregg's division. Unfortunately, the courier got lost in the darkness, and Vanderbilt's critical warning wouldn't reach his superiors until the next morning, almost too late to be of any good.

Unaware that his message was going astray the young captain did what he could to prepare for certain trouble. He had both his picket and reserve force tear down the stout fences lining the road and construct substantial barricades across the path of any probable attack. As they worked the Union cavalrymen could hear loud voices from the Rebel bivouacs and see Southern sentries silhouetted against their campfires. Luckily, the thick woods shielded the Yankees from similar observation. Nonetheless, the men in blue took extreme care to make no unnecessary noise.[7]

* * *

At 2 a.m., a courier from Meade reached Warren with new instructions for tomorrow's march. The commanding general announced that the army would mass at Centreville on October 14. Newton's I Corps would lead the way, marching on the north side of the O&A and going through the little village of Milford—about a mile northwest of Bristoe Station—before moving on to Manassas Junction and crossing Bull Run at Mitchell's Ford. From there the I Corps would advance to Centreville and occupy the works around the town. Meade directed Sedgwick's VI Corps to follow a parallel route on the south side of the railroad which would lead it over Bull Run at Blackburn's Ford. Brigadier General Henry J. Hunt's reserve artillery would trail Sedgwick but cross the creek at McLean's Ford.[8]

French's orders instructed him to move the III Corps from its Greenwich bivouac to Milford and then follow the same route as Newton. Sykes had orders to take his V

7 Paragraphs above based upon N. D. Preston, *History of the Tenth Regiment of Cavalry New York State Volunteers* (New York, NY, 1892), 147-48; Ron Matteson, *Civil War Campaigns of the 10th New York Cavalry, With One Soldier's Personal Correspondence* (Lulu.com, 2007), 167; Clifton W. Wiles, "A skirmish at Little Auburn, Va." *First Maine Bugle Campaign II, Call X* (Rockland, ME, 1892), 71-74. The distance between the picket post and the camps of Ewell's corps near Warrenton was about 3 miles. Seymour, *Civil War Memoirs*, 87.

8 OR 29, pt. 2, 306-307, and pt. 1, 237. The O&A angles northeast from Culpeper Court House, so north of the tracks is also west of the railroad, etc.

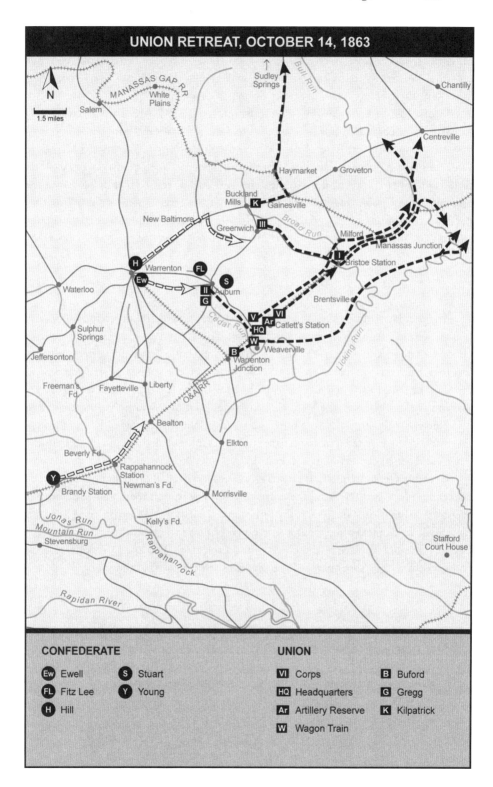

UNION RETREAT, OCTOBER 14, 1863

N
1.5 miles

MANASSAS GAP RR

Salem
White Plains
Chantilly
Sudley Springs
Bull Run
Centreville
Haymarket
Groveton
New Baltimore
Buckland Mills
K Gainesville
Broad Run
Milford
Greenwich
III
Manassas Junction
H Warrenton
FL
I
Bristoe Station
Ew
II
S Auburn
G
Brentsville
Waterloo
Cedar Run
V
VI
HQ
Ar Catlett's Station
Licking Run
Sulphur Springs
W
B
Warrenton Junction
Weaverville
Jeffersonton
Freeman's Fd.
Fayetteville
Liberty
O&ARR
Bealton
Elkton
Beverly Fd.
Rappahannock Station
Newman's Fd.
Y
Brandy Station
Morrisville
Jonas Run
Mountain Run
Stevensburg
Kelly's Fd.
Rappahannock
Stafford Court House
Rapidan River

CONFEDERATE

Ew Ewell
FL Fitz Lee
H Hill
S Stuart
Y Young

UNION

VI Corps
HQ Headquarters
Ar Artillery Reserve
W Wagon Train
B Buford
G Gregg
K Kilpatrick

Corps to Milford as well, with the discretion to wade Bull Run at Blackburn's Ford if Mitchell's Ford were too crowded for a quick crossing. Buford would continue escorting the army's trains and pontoons, while Kilpatrick's division was ordered to move "by way of Haymarket to Sudley Springs if practicable."[9]

Meade told Gregg's cavalry division to remain with Warren and directed the II Corps to turn east at Auburn and march to Catlett's Station. From there it was to proceed along the south side of the O&A through Bristoe Station toward Manassas. The commanding general cautioned his subordinates to "keep their flankers well out on the left" and to picket all the roads leading west. Meade sensed that Bull Run was the primary danger point. He ordered his generals to exercise "great caution" as they neared the infamous creek and to deploy their troops at the fords so as to "meet any attempt" by the Confederates to interrupt the army's passage of the watercourse.[10]

*   *   *

The pre-dawn of October 14 ushered in a dense fog which clung to the valleys and hollows around Auburn like a soupy blanket. The seemingly endless movement of Union regiments and wagons through the hamlet had ended sometime after midnight, and for a brief time all had been silent. Now, however, the sounds of an army echoed through the darkness as sergeants shook the men of the II Corps and Gregg's cavalry division awake. By 4 a.m. the Federals had started to move. Warren passed word that his vehicles should cross Cedar Run via the bridge. The infantry would wade through the two-foot deep stream at the adjacent ford. Bonfires lined the roads to help the troops and teamsters see the way forward.[11]

Brigadier General John C. Caldwell's 1st Division headed the column, followed by Alexander Hays' 3rd Division, the corps' 225-vehicle wagon train, and Alexander S. Webb's 2nd Division. Gregg's cavalry screened the tail of the II Corps as well as its left flank. Caldwell's picket line, deployed the night before to guard the approach to the bridge, remained in place as the corps took to the road. The line of infantry pickets connected to Gregg's troopers, whose bivouacs stretched off to the south.[12]

---

9   Ibid., pt. 2, 306-307.

10 OR 29, pt. 2, 306.

11 Theodore Reichardt, *Diary of Battery A, First Regiment Rhode Island Light Artillery, Oct. 14, 1863* (CreateSpace Publishing, 2016), 81-82. Reichardt recorded that one of Battery A's caissons and another from Battery B 1st Rhode Island Light were "upset in crossing the stream."

12 OR 29, pt. 1, 237.

Warren directed Caldwell once over Cedar Run to deploy his division on the hill just behind the McCormick house at Auburn. This position would shield the bridge and ford against any threat from the north bank of the creek. Captain Bruce Ricketts' Batteries F&G, 1st Pennsylvania Light Artillery, would unlimber alongside the infantry. Both commands were to face west toward the supposed danger of an enemy advance from Warrenton.

Southwest of Auburn, the Rebels were also astir in the fields west of Capt. Vanderbilt's picket post. These were Robert Rodes' men, aroused a little before 4 a.m. for the purpose of marching to Stuart's rescue. A detachment of cavalry from Lomax's brigade preceded them. In the foggy gray dawn, the Federal troopers could vaguely make out the enemy column slowly coming down the Double Poplars Road. Behind them the countryside began to fill indistinctly with Confederate infantry.

The trouble Vanderbilt had anticipated all night was now at hand. He quickly hid his eight pickets among the trees in front of his westernmost barricade. They deployed obliquely so that every man would have a clear field of fire onto the road. There the Federals waited until the ominous body of Southern horsemen drew within hailing distance. At seemingly the last minute the captain shouted "Halt! Who comes there?" The sudden challenge threw the Rebels into startled confusion, at which point Vanderbilt yelled the order to open fire.[13]

Stunned by the sudden volley, the Rebel cavalrymen recoiled and fell back, but only for a moment. Recovering from their surprise, they drew sabers and charged. The men of the 10th New York rushed to take cover behind their breastwork and braced for the coming onslaught. They could hear the thundering hooves of the attackers, but it was too dark for anyone to see the assailants until they closed to within 50 yards of the barricade. Once more the order to fire rang out as the Rebels slammed into Vanderbilt's makeshift fortification. Totally unprepared to encounter such an obstacle, the Southern column disintegrated into swirling confusion as men and horses tried to stop, turn, and find a clear path to the rear. In an instant the Rebels were gone, beaten back a second time by a handful of Union troopers.[14]

For the Yankee pickets this was an exhilarating but obviously temporary triumph. Dawn was breaking and the cloak of semi-darkness would no longer conceal their paltry numbers. The Confederates would not underestimate their enemy a third time, and were already deploying into a line of battle across the fields on either side of the road. The enemy would gobble up Vanderbilt's outpost with ease on their next assault.

13 Preston, *10th New York Cavalry*, 147-48; *Maine Bugle*, Campaign II, Call X, 72-75.

14 Ibid.

The time had come to retire, and the Federals speedily withdrew to their second barricade.[15]

*   *   *

The attack on Vanderbilt's outposts was the first hint to the Federal troops around Auburn that Confederates were nearby. Neither Warren nor Gregg had any idea that a corps of Rebel infantry was approaching from the west, let alone that two brigades of enemy cavalry lay concealed a few hundred yards to the east. The Southerners who initiated the morning combat belonged to Lunsford Lomax. At some point (exactly when is unclear) his troopers had crossed to the south side of Cedar Run and gone into line between the creek and the Double Poplars Road. Still smarting at losing Auburn the day before, they were especially anxious to break through to Stuart's relief.

After assigning a contingent to screen Rodes' column, Lomax had dismounted most of his command and posted his skirmishers within easy rifle shot of Gregg's and Warren's pickets. At about the same time Confederate horsemen collided with Vanderbilt's outpost, some of Lomax's soldiers close to the creek heard footsteps approaching their position in the murky pre-dawn light. They came from men of the 6th Ohio Cavalry groping their way toward Cedar Run to fill canteens. The instant these Yankees became visible, a Virginia cavalryman raised his carbine and fired.[16]

That single shot ignited a chain reaction as nervous men all along the line did likewise and a ragged rattle of musketry spread instantly across the front. The outbreak of gunfire and the sounds of the first clash along the Double Poplars Road occurred at almost the same instant Capt. Vanderbilt's long delayed warning about enemy troops reached Maj. Avery. Muzzle flashes twinkled along a front stretching from the banks of Cedar Run all the way to Vanderbilt's position.

The enemy assault hit the Federals with thunderclap surprise. Hearing the shooting, General Gregg hurriedly ordered his division to form up. Shouts of command mingled with the urgent notes of "Boots and Saddles" as buglers sounded the alarm. The 10th New York Cavalry scrambled desperately to mount up and rush help to Vanderbilt before the enemy overran his outpost. Major Avery forwarded a desperate entreaty to his subordinate: "For God's sake[,]Van, hold them for ten minutes longer, if possible!"[17]

---

15 Ibid.

16 Bushnell memoir, WRHS.

17 Preston, *10th New York Cavalry*, 147-48; *Maine Bugle*, Campaign II, Call X, 72-75.

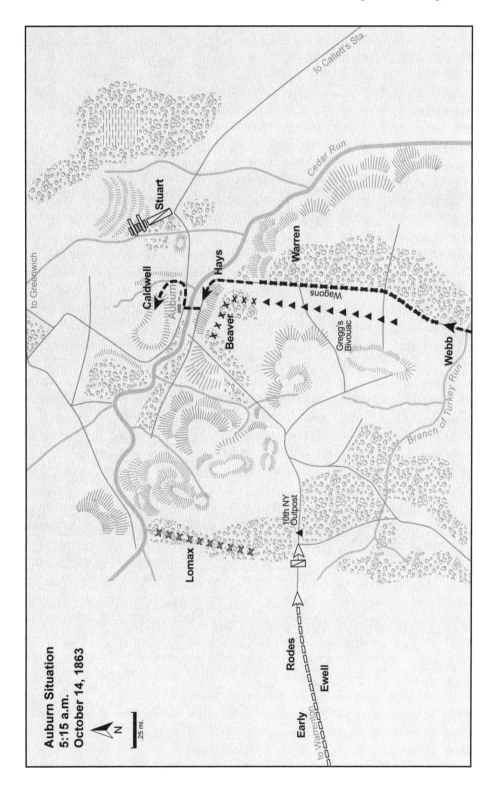

Auburn Situation
5:15 a.m.
October 14, 1863

N

25 mi.

Stuart

to Catlett's Sta.

Cedar Run

Warren

Hays

Caldwell

Auburn

to Greenwich

Beaver

Wagons

Gregg's
Bivouac

Webb

Branch of Turkey Run

Lomax

10th NY
Outpost

Rodes

Early

Ewell

to Warrenton

The sudden onset of combat rattled Union infantry as much as it did Gregg's horsemen. General Warren feared a Rebel attack might cut off his column from the Cedar Run bridge. As an initial step to prevent that calamity, he rode to Col. James Beaver of the 148th Pennsylvania—officer of the day for Caldwell's division and commander of the picket line stationed on the high ground overlooking the creek. Warren told the 25-year old pre-war lawyer it was imperative he hold the crest of the 80-foot tall bluff above the bridge until all the trains had passed. The importance of this mission was preeminent: Warren stressed that Beaver must accomplish it even if he lost every man in his command.[18]

The possibility that such a sacrifice might actually be required seemed more certain with each passing moment. Brigadier General David Gregg certainly felt that way. As he looked down the Carolina Road behind his assembling division, he could see a two-mile long train of wagons and ambulances, as well as most of the troops in the II Corps still clogging the route to Auburn. The cavalryman knew he had to maintain his position astride the road "at any cost." Gouverneur Warren underscored the urgency, issuing the same order to Gregg he'd given Beaver: the line had to hold until the II Corps was safely across the creek.[19]

Much closer to the danger than the generals, the situation appeared downright desperate to Vanderbilt and Avery. The Rebels had swarmed unopposed around the now deserted first barricade on the Double Poplars Road and were swiftly approaching the second. Convinced his position was about to be enveloped, Vanderbilt called for a dozen volunteers to undertake a spoiling attack in hopes of slowing the enemy's inevitable assault on this last barricade. Lieutenant Marsh Woodruff and a dozen men instantly mounted and sprang into line. Vanderbilt pointed down the road, not even wasting time to give verbal orders, and Woodruff and his men, "yelling like demons," dashed toward the attackers.

Once again the New Yorkers surprised the Rebels, who gave way and fled in the direction they had come with Woodruff's little band in hot pursuit. But when the Yankees approached the barricade formerly held by their own pickets, they discovered that breastworks were useful from either direction. Enemy troops waiting behind the obstruction poured a volley into the attackers which killed nine of their 12 horses, but

---

18 Joseph Muffly, *The Story of Our Regiment: A History of the 148th Pennsylvania Volunteer* (Des Moines, IA, 1904), 100. Wounded at Fredericksburg, Beaver returned to his regiment just before Gettysburg but was too weak to take command during the battle. In June 1864, he received a slight wound at Cold Harbor, a more serious injury at Petersburg, and in August 1864 finally lost a leg at the second battle of Ream's Station. After the war he served as a trustee for Pennsylvania State College and as governor of Pennsylvania from 1887-91.

19 Muffly, *The Story of Our Regiment*, 100.

oddly enough, missed every Union soldier. Nonetheless, Woodruff's charge had been crushed, and his men, most now afoot, ran for dear life back to their starting point.[20]

The Confederates quickly followed, and Vanderbilt abandoned his final barricade—as well as all his command's tents and camp equipment—and fell back toward the Carolina Road. The main body of the 10th New York Cavalry was finally coming on line behind him as were several mounted regiments from Col. Irvin Gregg's brigade. These Federal moves were timely, because the small body of Rebel cavalry that had tangled with Vanderbilt had been replaced by Ramseur's infantry brigade now filling the forest on both sides of the Double Poplars Road. Shortly after Avery's horsemen got into position, the command "forward" rang out from the woods in front of them. Seconds later, two lines of Confederate skirmishers emerged from the trees.[21]

They came on boldly, pushing Vanderbilt's men to within 300 yards of Gregg's main line before Maj. Avery sent a squadron to reinforce them. Elsewhere along the front, Northern cavalry officers told their troopers not to shoot until the Rebels got within easy range. Once the butternut uniforms drew near enough, the command to fire unleashed a volley which briefly checked enemy progress.[22]

A moment later the Confederates surged forward again. A Yankee soldier recalled that the Rebs came on "yelling and firing" as they advanced. The mounted Federals made good targets and enemy bullets were smacking into men and animals with distressing frequency. Outgunned and outnumbered, the Yankees could withstand such an unequal contest only so long before being overwhelmed. Under growing pressure Avery yielded another 100 yards to the attackers and then attempted another stand. The Northerners had barely gotten into line when the right of the 10th New York gave way, a collapse that forced the rest of the regiment to fall back all the way to Gregg's main body near the Carolina Road.[23]

To prevent a rout, the Yankees needed someone to stall the enemy advance long enough for the 10th New York to reach safety. Avery knew only an attack could do that, and he ordered Lt. Thomas Johnson, who commanded the regiment's fifth squadron, to charge the Confederates. This would be little better than a suicide mission. A few score cavalrymen weren't going to turn back an oncoming Rebel infantry brigade. But Johnson's squadron could make the foot soldiers pause long

20 Preston, *10th New York Cavalry*, 147-48.

21 Bushnell Memoirs, WRHS; William A. Smith, *The Anson Guards: History of Company C, 14th Regiment, N.C.V., Army of Northern Virginia* (Charlotte, NC, 1914), 216.

22 OR 29, pt. 1, 368; Preston, *10th New York Cavalry*, 147-48; *Maine Bugle*, Campaign II, Call X, 78; Bushnell Memoirs, WRHS; Raymer, *Confederate Correspondent*, 100-101.

23 Ibid.

enough to shoot a mounted charge to pieces. The few minutes thus purchased with lives might make all the difference.

Johnson, who couldn't have been ignorant of this, immediately led his men in a frantic saber charge against the enemy—with predictable results. Rebels came "pouring out of the woods" as the New Yorkers attacked across a field cluttered with "stumps and scrub oaks" which broke up their formation. Without attempting realignment, they galloped forward, driving enemy skirmishers backward until the riders topped a slight rise and came within full view of the Rodes' battle line.

The Confederates instantly blasted a murderous volley into the ranks of Union horsemen. Lieutenant Johnson fell along with several others. After responding with a weak volley of their own, the "shattered remnant" of the now leaderless squadron wheeled about and made for the rear, "with as much promptness," one soldier confessed, as they had gone forward. The survivors could not be reformed and returned to the fight for several hours.[24]

Johnson's effort had been expensive but it was also successful. By the time the Southerners resumed their advance, the 10th New York had reached Gregg's division, which was now deployed for battle. Colonel John Taylor's 1st Brigade formed a dismounted skirmish line atop a ridge parallel to the Carolina Road, while Col. Irvin Gregg's brigade deployed as a mounted reserve behind Taylor. More importantly, Capt. Joseph Martin's 6th New York Light Artillery had gone into battery alongside Taylor's troopers. The ability of his artillery to sweep the broad and open fields across which the Confederates must approach strengthened the Federal position immeasurably.[25]

Although the fight was by no means over, Brig. Gen. Gregg now had a reasonable expectation of holding his ground, at least for a while. North of Cedar Run, however, a new crisis confronted the Federal column—one even more surprising and far more serious than the danger Gregg had barely fended off moments ago. From out of nowhere a torrent of enemy shells had come screaming out of the woods east of Auburn. Somehow the Rebels had gotten between the II Corps and the rest of Meade's army along the railroad. Warren had no idea how many Confederates lay in his path, but if their numbers were considerable his command was in serious trouble. Unless he could effectively deal with them, everything the Union cavalrymen had achieved thus far would be for naught.

---

24 Previous paragraphs based on Preston, *10th New York Cavalry*, 149.

25 OR 29, pt., 1, 361, 366, 369; Bushnell memoir, WRHS; Richard Griffin, ed., *Three Years A Soldier: The Diary and Newspaper Correspondence of Private George Perkins, Sixth New York Independent Battery, 1861-1864* (Knoxville, TN, 2006), 142.

Chapter 21

"The Muskets Began to Crack"

General Caldwell—Danger and Opportunity—Bombardment—
Coffee Hill—Warren Surrounded—Hays' Advance—
Charge of the 1st North Carolina—Stuart Escapes

AROUND 5:00 a.m. on October 14, Batteries F&G, 1st Pennsylvania Light Artillery finished their climb to the top of the hill behind the McCormick house at Auburn. Captain Bruce Ricketts ordered his gunners to unlimber and go into position facing west toward Warrenton. As the Yankee fieldpieces spun into place, Brig. Gen. Caldwell began massing his 1st Division into a column of regiments on the eastern slope of the same hill.[1]

As each unit of infantrymen halted, the troops were directed to stack arms, break ranks, and prepare breakfast. Many soldiers stripped off their equipment before heading out to gather fence rail firewood or rummage through haversacks for rations. Since they had just forded the cold waters of Cedar Run, scores of men removed wet shoes and socks, hanging the soaked stockings on sticks and then suspending them over campfires in hope they would dry before the march resumed.[2]

Caldwell, who dismounted with his staff to eat his own breakfast, was inspired by the scene. Open and pastoral terrain spilled out from the crest of the hill eastward for almost 1,000 yards. The surrounding woods, bright yellow and crimson red with fall leaves, provided a colorful backdrop to the innumerable knots of men hovering over

1 A column of regiments consists of regimental lines of battle positioned one behind another. This was a good formation for Caldwell to assume. It placed his men on the east side of the hill, which at that time the Federals believed was the side opposite the most likely enemy approach. Should an attack from the west develop, a column of regiments would allow the general to quickly deploy fighting formations to the hilltop and/or his left and right.

2 Thomas Meyer, *Incidents and Anecdotes of the War Between the States*, Penn State.

Brigadier General John C. Caldwell
Library of Congress

their cook fires. Horses and mules grazed all about. The general took his repose beneath a moss draped apple tree and approved the "glorious picture" spread out before him. Everything seemed peaceful, any danger far away.[3]

An appreciation for autumn's beauty came naturally to John C. Caldwell, a 30-year-old Vermont-born graduate of Amherst College. He had been the principal of Washington Academy in Maine before the secession crisis. Like many prominent civilians, he suddenly became a solider after the outbreak of war. In November 1861 Caldwell received a colonel's commission in the 11th Maine Infantry. Presented a general's star and command of a brigade in April 1862, he earned high marks for his performance in the Peninsula campaign, especially at the battle of Glendale.[4]

Chaplain John H. W. Stuckenberg of the 145th Pennsylvania described Caldwell as "an agreeable man and well-liked" by his troops. They appreciated his lack of "assumed dignity of importance so common among officers." Some of his peers judged his performance mediocre at the battles of Antietam and Fredericksburg (where he received two minor wounds). But everyone admitted he had done well in dire circumstances at Chancellorsville, where his brigade had simultaneously faced in two different directions to cover the Union retreat at the height of the battle.[5]

When Winfield S. Hancock assumed command of the II Corps on May 22, 1863, Caldwell took charge of its 1st Division. Seven weeks later, on the second day at Gettysburg, the Vermonter might have had his best moment as a solider. After Longstreet's Rebels wrecked the III Corps, ripping a giant hole in the Union left flank, Caldwell got orders to plug the breech. The general had his four brigades in motion just

3   Josiah Marshall Favill, *The Diary of a Young Officer* (Chicago, IL, 1909), 265-66.

4   Warner, *Generals in Blue*, 63-64.

5   Sears, *Gettysburg*, 287-88; D. Scott Hartwig, "No Troops on the Field Had Done Better" John C. Caldwell's Division in the Wheatfield, July 2, 1863 in Gary Gallagher, ed. *The Second Day at Gettysburg: Essays on Confederate and Union Leadership* (Kent, OH, 1993), 136-71.

four minutes later. After a quick 20-minute march and with only the vaguest information about the terrain, the situation, and the enemy's strength or dispositions, he launched the only division-sized Union counterattack of the entire battle. His 3,200 troops hurled themselves across the famed "Wheatfield" into an overwhelming number of Confederates. The furious assault briefly stopped the onrushing Rebels in their tracks. Caldwell's action was one of the fastest command responses of the war.[6]

Unfortunately his success proved temporary. Without meaningful support in a chaotic environment, his outnumbered division was in a hopeless position. A vicious Southern counterattack hit Caldwell's troops from the flank and rear and drove them from the field. Though the same fate befell many Union units that bloody day, the reverse damaged Caldwell's reputation. Major General George Sykes witnessed the collapse of his command, but not its gallant attack, and he roundly criticized Caldwell's conduct.

An investigation into Sykes' allegations later cleared Caldwell and proclaimed that "no troops on the field had done better" than his division. Despite this verdict, his wounded reputation didn't heal easily. Hancock never forgave him for temporarily staining his old division's record. The fact that Caldwell was a division commander but a non-West Pointer exacerbated the situation. Nonetheless, he had proven on numerous occasions that neither he nor his men scared easily, which would shortly prove useful indeed.

*   *   *

Jeb Stuart's cavalrymen didn't give a damn about the Army of the Potomac's internal affairs. From their hiding place a few hundred yards away they watched Caldwell's infantry go about their domestic chores. The enemy were so close to the Confederate refuge that one Southerner claimed he could hear their "every word." Though substantial, the pending Yankee menace wasn't without vulnerabilities. Peering through the thin skirt of trees masking their position, Stuart's gun crews salivated at the dream target before them: a dense mass of blue gathered on the hillside. They longed to put their cannons to work. But with ever-more Union troops crossing the creek, they knew it would be suicidal.

Jeb Stuart also itched to strike his unsuspecting enemy—but only in conjunction with a Rebel infantry attack from the west. Absent such an assault, the general's primary goal was to ensure the survival of the two brigades then with him. Nothing

6 Sears, *Gettysburg*, 287-88; Hartwig, "No Troops on the Field Had Done Better," in Gary Gallagher, ed. *The Second Day at Gettysburg*, 136-71.

M^cCORMACKS HOUSE and OLD MILL. AUBURN. Virginia. Scene of Skirmish with the Rebels by 3rd Army Corps 16th Octr 1863.

Opposite page: The McCormick House and Coffee Hill at Auburn. This view looks north from the bridge over Cedar Run. Private Robert Knox Sneden, of the III Corps staff, made this painting from memory after the war. The mill should be to the right of the McCormick house, but otherwise this image gives a clear view of the rugged and mostly treeless nature of the hill Caldwell's division occupied on the morning of October 14, 1863. Today, the hill is densely wooded private property and inaccessible. The McCormick house no longer stands. *Virginia Museum & History Center, Richmond, VA. Author*

---

indicated that the Yankees had, as yet, any inkling of his position. With the sun rising higher by the minutes, Stuart knew his night-long sojourn must soon come to a close. If he didn't hear the sound of a Confederate infantry assault shortly, circumstances would compel him to undertake some type of desperate act of escape. For the moment, though, all he could do was watch and listen.[7]

*   *   *

As Caldwell's soldiers continued with their tasks, Alexander Hays' 3rd Division began fording the creek. Instead of veering left along the route French's men had traveled the night before, the blue column swung right toward Catlett's Station. Yankee infantrymen heard the outbreak of shooting when Lomax and Rodes struck the 10th New York Cavalry's outpost, but paid the outburst no more attention than a dispute between cavalry pickets deserved. Unperturbed, Caldwell's men continued cooking breakfast. Some of his soldiers watched idly as a battery of artillery rumbled into position on a hill just 300 yards east of their position. The arrival of the guns caused them no concern because they knew the Rebel threat was off to the south and west. These guns, therefore, had to be friendly.[8]

Or so they thought. Those fieldpieces actually belonged to Maj. Robert Beckham's Confederate horse artillery, and their crews were wheeling them into place in momentary expectation of killing a lot of Yankees. Unlike the Federals, Gen. Stuart was sure the gunfire below Cedar Run was significant. Obviously his couriers had reached army headquarters the night before, and Lee was launching the infantry assault

---

7   OR 29, pt., 1, 448; McClellan, *I Rode with JEB Stuart*, 392-393; Blackford, *War Years*, 239.

8   OR 29, pt. 1, 448; Thomas P. Meyer, *Incidents and anecdotes of the war between the states, 1861-1865: marches, skirmishes, and battles of the 148th Regt. Penna. Volunteers, also a complete historical itinerary of the regiment, experiences of the rank and file, life in confederate prisons, etc.* (n.p., 1904), 77-78, courtesy Penn State University Archives.

Stuart had proposed. The moment had come! He promptly ordered his eager artillerymen to open fire.[9]

Those Northerners still glancing off to the east saw a sudden flash and a blossom of white smoke smudging the horizon. A heartbeat later came the echo of a cannon shot, the frightening crack of a nearby explosion, and the sickening thud of shell fragments penetrating human flesh. The Rebel gunner who aimed that first shot knew his business, and his projectile burst right above a group of bluecoats huddled around a campfire, killing four instantly. Before anyone's mind could register what had just happened, a storm of grape and shell enveloped Caldwell's unsuspecting division.

The Confederate bombardment took the Yankees completely by surprise. The unexpected fire was simply "astonishing," said a Rhode Island gunner. It left everyone utterly "bewildered," a Pennsylvanian agreed. Startled mules and horses, some pulling their reins from the hands of equally startled officers, "dashed madly across the field." Infantrymen jumped to their feet, overturning "promising tins of coffee" as they hurriedly abandoned their half-cooked breakfasts. Some commanders ordered their men to lie down, while others shouted contradictory orders to flee. "Neither officers nor men seemed to know just what to do," admitted a future regimental historian. Rebel fire killed several Union soldiers literally before they had time to know what hit them.[10]

For a short time a great deal of running and skirting about ensued. But there was no panic. The majority of Caldwell's men were veterans, and they reacted with levelheaded professionalism, thereby setting an example for the recruits and draftees around them. Although still under fire, within a minute or two, the savvy old soldiers hurriedly put on their shoes, scooped half-cooked food into haversacks, buckled on their accouterments and slung knapsacks over their backs before forming ranks and unstacking their muskets. Then they did what came naturally to veterans and moved to the reverse (western) slope of the hill to escape the enemy's missiles. There they found a measure of safety and the chance to regain their composure before a totally calm Caldwell ordered the 57th and 66th New York regiments to outflank and capture the offending Rebel guns.[11]

---

9   OR 29, pt. 1, 448; Meyer, *Incidents and Anecdotes*, 77-78; Caldwell, *Brigade of South Carolinians*, 253-254; OR 29, pt. 1, 357; Trout, *Memoirs of the Stuart Horse Artillery: Moorman's and Hart's Batteries*, 223-234.

10   Stewart, *140th Pennsylvania*, 158; Meyer, *Incidents and Anecdotes*, 77-78; Favill, *Diary of a Young Officer*, 266; OR 29, pt. 1, 254; Reichardt, *Diary of Battery A*, 81-82; *Columbia Democrat and Bloomsburg* [PA] *General Advertiser*, October 31, 1863. "Letter From the Army of the Potomac" by Lt. Charles B. Brockway, Batty F&G 1st PA Artillery, signed as Artillerist.

11   Ibid.

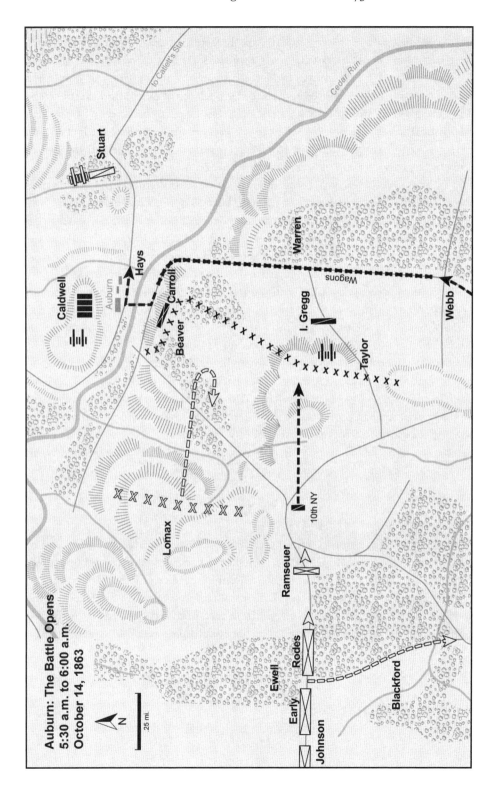

Auburn: The Battle Opens
5:30 a.m. to 6:00 a.m.
October 14, 1863

N

.25 mi.

As the Federal infantry regrouped, Capt. Rickett's battery, which had been facing west when the shooting started, coolly turned its cannon eastward to engage the Southern artillery. This maneuver produced a singular moment, when, as one Union gunner remembered, his officer gave the order, "seldom, if ever, heard except on the drill ground—Fire to the rear! Limbers and caissons pass your pieces!" Upon that command, the gunners wheeled their cannon in an about face, while the limbers and caissons rolled between the guns to take their proper position behind the line of artillery. Seconds later Rickett's crews opened fire on their enemy.[12]

Captain John G. Hazard, commander of the II Corps' artillery brigade, ordered Capt. William Arnold's Battery A 1st Rhode Island Light, to Rickett's support. The New England artillerymen hurried to ascend the rugged slopes of the hill under Rebel bombardment. Even as the artillerists exchanged shells, the tempo of battle to the southwest escalated. The reports of muskets and the crack of carbines soon became "rapid and incessant." While Warren listened to the noise of this latest attack, a cavalry officer he did not recognize raced up to warn him that "three overwhelming columns" of Confederate infantry were advancing down the road from Warrenton. With fire coming from the south, west, and east this worrisome information apparently confirmed that the Rebels were about to cut the II Corps in two.[13]

The general galloped into Auburn where he found Alexander Hays and ordered him to send Col. Samuel S. Carroll's brigade back across the creek to defend the bluff shielding the bridge over Cedar Run. Then Warren told Hays to turn the rest of his 3rd Division toward whatever blocked the road to Catlett's Station and push it out of the way. At almost that same instant Alexander Webb appeared. He had rushed several miles ahead of his 2nd Division to find Warren and get orders. Warren directed Webb to move his brigades on the double quick past the wagon train to Hays' support.[14]

*   *   *

Like Warren, Lunsford Lomax perceived ominous portends from the sound of Confederate guns bombarding Caldwell's hilltop. Quickly concluding that Stuart was hard pressed and in need of immediate help, the brigadier ordered his dismounted skirmishers forward. The advance of these butternut cavalrymen ratcheted up the sound of battle south of Cedar Run, which in turn further convinced Stuart that his plan to strike the Yankees simultaneously from both flanks was unfolding as designed.

---

12 Francis Walker, *History of the Second Army Corps* (New York, 1887), 336.

13 Aldrich, *Battery A, 1st Rhode Island Light*, 247; OR 29, pt., 1, 305, 308.

14 *OR* 29, pt. 1, 238-39.

That, however, was not the case. As Lomax's troopers pressed toward the bridge over Cedar Run they headed squarely into a killing zone. The ground over which the Rebels advanced rose gradually but significantly to the north and east until it formed a right-angled ridge that paralleled the Carolina Road before jutting westward to conform to the south bank of Cedar Run. The Confederates, absorbed in skirmishing with Col. Beaver's Yankee pickets in front of that stream, failed to spot enemy infantry behind a fence on the high ground adjacent to the road.[15]

It was a critical oversight. First Lieutenant Thomas Galwey of the 8th Ohio recalled that from this height the Federals could easily see the Southerners moving through a "very picturesque valley full of farmhouses and barns." Unwittingly the Rebels had exposed their flank to a lethal surprise. Galwey and other officers readily seized this unexpected opportunity and ordered their men to commence firing. About that same time Capt. Joseph Martin's 6th New York Light Artillery sent a blizzard of canister toward the oncoming Rebels.[16]

Lomax's advancing line pulled up as abruptly as if it had encountered an impassable chasm and then rapidly went back the way it had come. The Confederates retreated to the cover of a fence before turning to answer the Federal volleys. From here the gray troopers kept up a constant fire, but declined to essay another advance. Lomax's attempt to rescue his boss had come up short. Practically speaking it hardly mattered. Dismounted cavalry, no matter how determined, could do little to aid Stuart. He required infantry support, and that was not forthcoming.

From almost the beginning, Ewell's rescue mission had run into unexpected difficulties and delays. Intense darkness and fog had initially slowed its march, and only three miles from Warrenton, the corps had run into Gregg's cavalry outposts. As Ewell's infantry waited for Lomax to knock aside the stubborn Yankee troopers, stray artillery shells began bursting in uncomfortable proximity to Rodes' regiments at the front of the corps' column.

These were actually friendly shells originating from Stuart's artillery which was overshooting Caldwell's division. Of course that didn't matter to Ewell's Confederates, who couldn't understand how Yankee gunners had spotted their advance in the fog. Frustrated with the delay, Rodes detached Blackford's sharpshooter battalion and told it to scout the ground to the front of Ewell's stalled column.

The major immediately led his men off to the right and headed southeastward through the fog. The axis of Blackford's advance fortuitously carried his sharpshooters

15 Thomas Francis Galwey Diary, Oct. 14, 1863, LC; Thomas Francis Galwey, *The Valiant Hours: An Irishman in the Civil War* (Harrisburg, PA, 1961), 152-54.

16 Bushnell Memoir, WRHS; *OR* 29, pt. 1, 256-57, 372; Galwey Diary, October 14, 1863, LC.

past the left flank of Gregg's skirmishers and unwittingly toward Webb's infantry division hurriedly toiling toward Auburn. Blackford kept his battalion moving until he neared a spot where the Carolina Road passed over a stream. In the continuing fog he carefully arrayed his men in the roadside underbrush from whence they could see the last elements of Warren's corps rushing to the north. The enemy presented a ripe target for a flank attack, but Blackford, uncertain of the overall situation or the plans of his superiors, hesitated to strike. He feared that a premature thrust by his small force might ruin the opportunity for a more devastating blow.[17]

Rather than do nothing, however, the major pondered how best to position his marksmen to support the big assault he felt must be coming. After vainly waiting awhile for the fog to lift, he ordered his troops to move by their left flank toward Auburn. Blackford, accompanied by his bugler, personally led the way. The single file column crept through the haze until the 24-year old Virginian suddenly found himself standing just a few yards from the Carolina Road, which he recalled later, teemed with Yankees "hurrying along with all their might." He was so close to the enemy column a suspicious Yankee stepped out of the line to ask his identity.

A nearby Rebel sharpshooter silently leveled his musket at the enemy figure looming in the mist, an instinctive but dangerous movement. The last thing Blackford wanted was to ignite a firefight, and before his well-meaning subordinate could squeeze his trigger, the major identified himself as a Federal officer. The curious inquisitor accepted that at face value and turned away.

Shaken, Blackford backed away from his encounter as quickly as dignity permitted. Unwilling to further tempt fate, he placed his skirmish line a short distance from the Carolina Road and sent word of his discovery to Rodes. The major hoped reinforcements would arrive in time to attack the unsuspecting Federals. Until then he and his battalion had to content themselves capturing stragglers who stepped off the road to urinate or rest.[18]

*　　*　　*

Elsewhere on the field both Ewell and Rodes were having a hard time figuring out what they were up against. Jeb Stuart had the same problem. He had surmised the night before that the Federals marching through Auburn were en route to Greenwich,

---

17 Previous paragraphs based on Galwey Diary, LC, & Blackford Diary, USMHI, both entries October 14, 1863; Seymour, *Civil War Memoirs*, 87; Ray, *Shock Troops of the Confederacy*, 84-85.

18 Blackford Diary, October 14, 1863, USMHI; Ray, *Shock Troops of the Confederacy*, 84-85. Blackford had arrayed his men in a single line as skirmishers. A movement by their left flank means everyone faced left and moved in single file toward Cedar Run.

Buckland Mills, or Bristoe Station to speed Meade's northward retreat. French's path last evening had verified that analysis. This morning, however, a large Yankee force had turned east at Auburn apparently intending to march to Catlett's Station. By happenstance Stuart was blocking their path. Did the enemy know he was in their way or were they merely blundering blindly in his direction? Whatever the case, the general was about to have a fight he hadn't anticipated against odds he didn't like.

Warren could say the same thing. His command was taking simultaneous fire from two directions. The assault from the southwest was alarming, but at least from an expected direction; the Rebel attack from the east, on the other hand, presented a potentially disastrous surprise. The size or composition of that enemy force were unknown, and if it were a significant body of troops, the Confederates had already cut off the II Corps from the rest of the Union army. For all Warren knew, he was surrounded and about to be annihilated. The only way out of the trap lay to the east. The Federals had no alternative but to cut their way through whatever threat lay in that direction and to do so in short order.

Fortunately for Warren, Hays' 3rd Division had been crossing Cedar Run when the shooting began, and already heading toward the Rebel obstruction. Nonetheless, this crisis had caught Hays' men by surprise. Most of them had no hint of danger until their regimental officers unexpectedly ordered everyone to load their weapons. Seconds later, recalled one Connecticut soldier, "bang, bang, went the artillery and the muskets began to crack." Only then were Hays' Yankees jolted into realizing they were in a fight. The fog added a surreal aspect to the abrupt battle. An invisible enemy assailed them, but the muzzle flashes of his cannon were quite visible in the hazy atmosphere. Fire seemed to be coming from every direction, and many feared that the Rebels had the II Corps trapped. Officers knew these circumstances might easily inspire panic, but thankfully the 3rd Division contained some of the best soldiers in the Union army. Warren would need every ounce of their steadfastness soon.[19]

*   *   *

Jeb Stuart knew his artillery had surprised and momentarily embarrassed his enemies, but also that this advantage was fleeting. Yankee counterbattery fire had been prompt, and the Federal gunners were already gaining the advantage over Beckham's cannoneers. The infantry attack Stuart anticipated sweeping in from the west had not arrived. The musketry he assumed coming from Ewell's troops was in fact from Lomax's cavalrymen, and they had ceased shooting shortly after Beckham's horse

19 Page, *Fourteenth Connecticut*, 190.

artillery had opened fire. Worse, the presence of Union troops on Stuart's front exposed both the vulnerabilities of his position as well as his apparent lack of support.

Those troops—Hays' 3rd Brigade under Brig. Gen. Joshua Owen—were edging ever ominously farther down the road. Two companies of skirmishers from the 125th New York were already nearing the valley that concealed the Rebel cavalry. Five more companies from that regiment were deploying as skirmishers on either side of the road a few hundred yards farther back. The entire 126th New York was extending the Union skirmish line toward Cedar Run. Behind these units Col. Thomas Smyth's 2nd Brigade was forming into a battle line with some of its troops taking position on the slope of the hill where Caldwell's men had abandoned their breakfasts.[20]

The time had come for the Rebel cavalry to think about escape. With no other alternative, a reluctant Stuart was compelled to withdraw eastward until he could find a way to cross Cedar Run and break out to the south. Aides quickly relayed orders for Beckham to cease fire and limber up his guns. Teamsters got instructions to move their ambulances and wagons toward the Saint Stephens Road. Gordon and Funsten told their cavalrymen to mount and prepare to move. It would take at least 15 minutes to shift so many men and vehicles 300 yards from their wooded hiding place to the road. To buy that time Stuart had to halt the advance of enemy infantry. Only a vigorous counterattack could knock the Yankees back on their heels long enough to give the Confederate column an urgently needed head start.[21]

It was a desperate but necessary choice, and Maj. Gen. Stuart readily made it. He turned to James Gordon and told him "For God's Sake, take the 1st North Carolina and cut through." The brigadier relayed the directive to the regiment's 43-year old commander, Lt. Col. Thomas Ruffin. Without a second's delay he wheeled his 180 men into position then gave the command to draw sabers and charge.[22]

The 125th New York's skirmish line lay directly in Ruffin's path. For the last few minutes its men had been walking gingerly into a dense fog toward the flash of Rebel cannons. The skirmishers were several hundred yards in advance of their regiment and moving with a caution born of dread. They were already understandably edgy when the

20 OR 29, pt. 1, 299-300, 308, 304; Morris Brown Jr. to parents October 15, 1863, http://contentdm6.hamilton.edu/cdm/compoundobject/collection/civ-let/id/1265/rec/40 accessed

21 "The Cavalry Fight at Buckland Mills," Whitmel Hill papers, SHC/UNC; Trout, *Memoirs of the Stuart Horse Artillery: Moorman's and Hart's Batteries*, 223-234. The Whitmel Hill papers are a set of personal reminiscences that deals with the role of Stuart's cavalry throughout the entire Bristoe Station Campaign.

22 Morris Brown Jr. to parents, October 15, 1863, Hamilton College; OR 29, pt. 1, 299; Clark, *NC Regts*, vol. 1, 456. The exact formation of Ruffin's regiment is unclear. Mostly likely it was in a column of squadrons.

sound of thundering hooves and the unnerving screech of a Rebel yell pierced the mist to their front. Seconds later the 1st North Carolina cavalry emerged from the haze like some spectral banshee.

Ruffin's troopers had already jumped a ditch and fence and were moving at full speed when they exited the woods. This was too much for a pair of skirmish companies to handle, and they immediately turned and ran. A few men fired their muskets before fleeing; others threw down their weapons and shouted their surrender. Most scrambled rearward "like sheep" pursued by a pack of wolves, in the words of one observer.[23]

After scattering the skirmishers, Ruffin's North Carolinians surged across an open field toward the bulk of Joshua Owens' brigade, which had taken up a position on the other side of the clearing. The 126th New York's skirmish line lay between Owens and the charging Confederates. Unlike their unfortunate comrades in the 125th, these New Yorkers had forewarning of impending danger and were standing firm.

The onrushing Rebels were heading for Captain Morris Brown, Jr's Company A on the regiment's right flank. The 21-year old ordered his men to rally by company on their right. Other field officers did the same. (This was the standard defense of skirmishers against a cavalry assault. It required the men to rush quickly to their right flank, fixing bayonets as they ran, and form a perimeter around their company officers.) Within seconds each of the regiment's companies was standing in a circle, their bayoneted muskets pointing upward at a height designed to impale a horse's neck. The New Yorkers barely had time to form their defensive hedgehogs before the 1st North Carolina was on top of them. Instinctively the infantrymen let loose a volley at virtually point blank range. The barrage of bullets slammed into the Rebels with incredible force and knocked Col. Ruffin off his horse with apparently fatal wounds in his forehead, shoulder and knee.[24]

---

23 Edward Longacre, *To Gettysburg and Beyond: The Twelfth New Jersey Volunteer Infantry, II Corps, Army of the Potomac, 1862-1865* (Highstown, NJ, 1988), 154. Some students of the battle deduce from vague reports that a single Rebel gun supported Ruffin's charge by going into position on a little knoll north of the road. Archeological evidence conducted during the early 21st Century show some indication that a gun or two was engaged on this spot. However, no Confederate account supports the forward movement of a gun, which under the circumstances would have been a highly dangerous move likely to lose the gun. It is far more likely that the artifacts found in the area are connected to a section of guns from Battery A 1st Rhode Island Light, which retired by prolonge to cover the final retreat of Brooke's brigade later in the day. See http://Jenningsgap.com/images/Auburn_Report-FINAL_0_05_20_Section_11.pdf& Aldrich, The History of Battery A: First Regiment Rhode Island Light Artillery, 249-50.

24 Morris Brown, Jr. to parents Oct. 15, 1863, http://contentdm6.hamilton.edu/cdm/compoundobject/collection/civ-let/id/1265/rec/40 , accessed June 5, 2018; Clark, *NC Regts*, vol. 1, 456-57. Brown was killed at Petersburg on June 22, 1864, while leading an attack for which he was awarded the Medal of Honor.

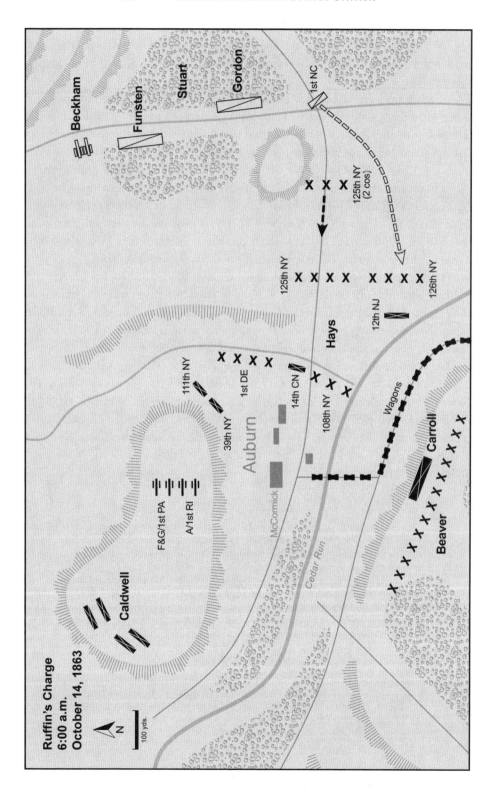

Ruffin's Charge
6:00 a.m.
October 14, 1863

Captain Morris Brown, Jr.
Hamilton College, Clinton, NY

The loss of their leader and the blaze of enemy rifles brought most of the attackers to an unexpected halt and sent them scurrying rearward in retreat. However, about 50 men and a handful of officers led by Maj. Rufus Barringer kept going, either undismayed by or ignorant of Ruffin's fall. Behind them Capt. William Cowles assumed command of the troopers who had fallen back and tried to rally them to resume the attack.[25]

Barringer had only returned to duty a few days ago after recovering from a wound received last June at Brandy Station. Although he was still using a cane to walk, his injury and long convalescence had not diminished his aggressiveness in the least. Waving the cane overhead rather than a sword, the major led his resolute little band through the line of the 126th New York.

The North Carolinians swerved between the rallied companies of enemy skirmishers before plowing into the 12th New Jersey Infantry, half of which had hurriedly taken cover behind a fence, while the other half sheltered a little to the rear in a line of scattered trees. The 12th was armed with .69 caliber smoothbore muskets—rather than the rifled pieces carried by most outfits—loaded with buck and ball cartridges (one .69 ball with three buckshot). Such ammunition was incredibly deadly at short range and lethal against a swarm of charging cavalry.[26]

As Barringer's troopers loomed in front of them the Jersey men aimed low and fired. In the blink of an eye a number of horses and men tumbled to the ground. The surviving attackers heaved forward, leaping the fence, and slashing at the infantrymen with their sabers. After the Confederates cleared the 12th's first line, the regiment's second line struck the Rebels with a volley bringing down even more men and animals.

The survivors of this second fusillade turned south toward Cedar Run. Still at the gallop they ran parallel to the Union front in a hazardous and audacious bid to escape

25 Longacre, *Twelfth New Jersey*, 156-57. Morris Brown, Jr. to parents Oct. 15, 1863, http://contentdm6.hamilton.edu/cdm/compoundobject/collection/civ-let/id/1265/rec/40 Hamilton College.

26 Longacre, *Twelfth New Jersey*, 152-53; Barringer papers, SHC/UNC; "Cavalry Fight at Buckland Mills," Whitmel Hill papers, SHC/UNC; Clark, NC Regts, vol. 1, 427.

the storm of lead which had decimated their ranks. Incredibly, some of them made it. With a wounded Barringer still leading, they slipped around the enemy flank and fled across the creek—their withdrawal aided by the lingering fog. Only about 15 of the Carolinians who had charged with Barringer managed to get away. Several of the escapees were injured, including Pvt. John Carver, still in his saddle despite seven wounds.[27]

As the Yankees blasted apart Barringer's assault, Capt. Cowles mounted a second charge with his own company and whoever else in the 1st North Carolina had the fortitude to sortie against a now utterly alert mass of Union soldiers. Not nearly as aggressive as the first attack, this second effort met solid volleys of enemy rifled-musket fire. It was quickly obvious that nothing more could be accomplished. Cowles ordered his men back into the shelter of the woods from which they had emerged mere minutes ago.[28]

Brigadier General Gordon had watched the entire fight unfold from a slight rise nearby. He was thinking about what to do next when Capt. Cowles rode up for further orders. Just as Cowles drew near, the general unexpectedly swayed backward in his saddle and threw his hands up over his face, blood gushing between his fingers and down onto his uniform. The general's staff and a horrified Cowles stared wide-eyed at their commander. Most expected the worst—a mortal wound—but to everyone's relief, Gordon removed his hands to reveal that a bullet had merely skimmed his nose and ruptured a small blood vessel. Although his injury produced a great deal of bleeding, it caused no serious damage. The general had been extraordinarily lucky: a millimeter's difference in the flight of the round or the tilt of his head might have left him dead or disfigured. Gordon reacted to this near miss with cool aplomb, exactly in the style expected of an officer and in a way that won men's hearts. The injury was a mere scratch, he remarked casually, before turning his attention back toward the enemy.[29]

Gordon's allotment of luck at this juncture proved generous indeed. As he gazed grimly out onto a field strewn with his dead and wounded, the crisis of the battle appeared to have already passed. The steep sacrifice of Ruffin and his men had not been in vain. Their sudden vigorous assault had kept the Federals at a distance for the moment. The brief fight had allowed Stuart's vehicles to pull back out of immediate danger. Seconds later Blackford arrived with orders for Gordon to retire his regiments

---

27 Clark, *NC Regts*, vol. 1, 456; Compiled service record for John Carver on www.fold3.com. Carver would die of his wounds some weeks later.

28 Clark, *NC Regts*, vol. 1, 456-57.

29 Blackford, *War Years*, 240; *OR*, 29, pt. 1, 457, 448.

and follow the artillery and wagons, which were already on the road. Funsten's troopers would constitute the rearguard.[30]

Much to Stuart's surprise he successfully withdrew his endangered command without further difficulty. Free from pursuit, the Rebel column traveled eastward a short distance on the Saint Stephens Road. Once out of sight of the Yankees, the Confederates turned south. After crossing the millrace alongside Cedar Run via a hastily constructed makeshift bridge, the troopers successfully forded the creek with their full complement of artillery, wagons and ambulances. Stuart now led his command toward the Carolina Road, where they captured a number of Yankee stragglers before stopping to cook a belated breakfast and feed their horses. Leaving his troopers, Stuart rode ahead to locate army headquarters and report to Lee.

*   *   *

Back at Auburn, the 126th New York advanced into the woods that a short time ago had held and hidden the Rebel brigades and paused to take stock of what had just happened. The sharp fight had lasted 20 minutes. General Owen counted 7 dead, 17 wounded, and 1 missing in his brigade. Caldwell had 11 men killed and 12 wounded in Stuart's surprise barrage. Together the two commands had taken a total of 48 casualties.

Confederate losses were about the same and almost exclusively in the 1st North Carolina Cavalry. Beside the several injured men who had escaped with Barringer, Federal troops counted something like 8-10 Rebel dead and 28 prisoners, some wounded, some not. Among the former was Col. Ruffin, whose capture naturally created a sensation in the Union ranks.

It was always a big thing to take a high ranking enemy officer, but Ruffin had been a former US congressman to boot (some incorrectly thought a senator), and hence everyone wanted credit for his capture. Captain Morris Brown attributed his actual apprehension to Company A of the 126th New York, whereas Company D claimed to have fired the shots that unhorsed him. First Lieutenant William Taylor took the ultimate prize by picking up Ruffin's sword as a souvenir.[31]

---

30 OR 29, pt. 1, 457, 448-49; Clark, *NC Regts*, vol. 2, 580-81.

31 Previous paragraphs based upon: OR 29, pt. 1, 238, 299; Morris Brown Jr. to parents, October 15, 1863, http://contentdm6.hamilton.edu/cdm/compoundobject/collection/civ-let/id/1265/rec/40, accessed June 5, 2018; Ezra Simons, *A Regimental History. The One Hundred and Twenty-Fifth New York State Volunteers* (New York, 1888), 156. Thomas Hart Ruffin served in the US Congress from 1853-61 as a North Carolina congressman. He also represented his state in the Provisional Confederate Congress in July 1861.

Before long a considerable number of soldiers were hovering around the semi-conscious Ruffin gawking at their prominent adversary. Among them was Sgt. Henry Avis of the 12th New Jersey, who along with several others spotted the colonel's "very fine gold watch and chain" lying partially exposed beneath his prostrate body. Here was a prize both beautiful and useful, and certainly more practical for an enlisted man than an officer's sword. Many of the onlookers wanted the watch, but no one could bring himself to take it from a man still alive. That would be stealing personal property in plain sight, and even these hardened soldiers could not bring themselves to this. But avarice is a strong emotion and sometimes finds a voice. Eventually one Yankee soldier spoke up, politely, indeed almost tenderly, requesting, "Colonel, do please hurry up and die; we want that watch."[32]

But Ruffin did not die, not yet anyway, and the 125th New York's surgeon, Dr. Washington Akin, soon arrived to dress his wounds, the most serious of which was the blow to his head. Placed in an ambulance, the retreating II Corps would carry the wounded North Carolinian northward where he would eventually be transferred to a military hospital in Alexandria. There doctors did what precious little they could, and on October 18, Ruffin succumbed to his injuries. Sympathetic Federal officers sent his coveted watch, jewelry, and personal effects back to his family.[33]

The loss of Ruffin was a hard blow to the Confederates, but only one of Stuart's laments that morning. He was irritated at the inability of the army to truly launch his proposed simultaneous assault, convinced that someone had wasted an opportunity to smash a large part of the Army of the Potomac. But supposed missed chances aside, the Rebel cavalry had made a clean, near-miraculous get away from an apparently hopeless situation. For that at least Stuart and his men were grateful.

The still somewhat shell-shocked Union regiments near Auburn were grateful too. The Rebel withdrawal appeared to have opened the road to Catlett's Station for them. But their relief was short lived, however. Even as the Southern cavalry withdrew, Ewell's corps began to pose an even greater threat to the Yankee rear.

*   *   *

For both Union and Confederate forces the early morning of October 14 had thus far been chaotic, frightening, and baffling. Everyone—Ewell, Stuart, Warren, Caldwell,

---

32 Longacre, *Twelfth New Jersey*, 154.

33 Simons, *One Hundred and Twenty-fifth New York*, 156; *Biographical Directory of the American Congress*, http://bioguide.congress.gov/scripts/biodisplay.pl?index=R000499 accessed June 6, 2018.

Gregg, Hays, Rodes, Lomax and Blackford—had been surprised in one way or another. Chaos and confusion appeared to have robbed the opponents of unseen opportunities while at the same time allowing them escape from easily imagined disasters. The II Corps had managed to fight off two surprise attacks, but in the process Warren's command now faced every point on the compass.

North of Cedar Run most Federal troops now looked east. Caldwell's division remained hunkered down on the western side of what the troops had spontaneously named Coffee Hill. His men along with Rickett's and Arnold's batteries still faced towards Stuart's now absent cavalry. To protect his new rear Caldwell deployed Col. John R. Brooke's 4th Brigade on the Carolina Road just west of Coffee Hill with its front toward Warrenton. Hays' division cautiously probed down the Saint Stephens Road toward Catlett's Station to verify that no Confederates were lurking behind Stuart's former position. After hurrying his division several miles past the corps' wagon train, Webb was massing his winded regiments east of Auburn behind Hays' command.[34]

South of the creek, Federal troops were still actively skirmishing with Lomax's brigade. The Yankee line resembled a stiff number 7. The pickets of Caldwell's division formed the bar of the 7 along the 80-foot bluff overlooking Cedar Run. These men were under command of Col. James Beaver, who as the division's officer of the day had placed them in position on the night of October 13. Samuel Carroll's 1st Brigade from Hays' division stood behind Beaver's men. Warren had ordered Carroll to protect the bridge at Auburn soon after the first outbreak of fighting that morning. After consulting with Beaver, Carroll had stationed his troops in a reserve position behind the 1st Division's pickets.

David Gregg's cavalry held the shank of the 7 which was on high ground parallel to the Carolina Road. Colonel John Taylor's brigade and Capt. Martin's 6th New York Artillery held the front line and were exchanging fire with Lomax's Rebels. Colonel Irvin Gregg's brigade was in reserve. The 1st Pennsylvania Cavalry on the far right of Gregg's front connected to the left flank of Beaver's picket line. These units had to hold their ground until the II Corps' two-mile long wagon train made its way over the Cedar Run bridge into Auburn.[35]

For Warren the situation remained unclear and dangerous. He had no idea how many Rebels he faced, where they were, or what they were doing. No doubt the general would have been alarmed to know there were twice as many Confederates as Yankees on the field. But it was clear to just about everyone that more enemy troops were

---

34 OR 29, pt. 1, 254, 238.

35 OR 29, pt. 1, 254, 238, 269, 261-64; Muffly, *148th Pennsylvania Volunteers*, 100.

arriving and massing for an attack. It was altogether possible they might yet surround and obliterate the II Corps.

In reality, the Federal position was rather solid, and the Northerners enjoyed significant advantages, although that hardly seemed evident at the time. The Rebels were in as much doubt about the actual location of Warren's troops as he was of theirs. Unlike the Confederates, the Union general knew the lay of the land and the route he had to travel. And since the Northerners were on the move, their positions were in flux, a constantly shifting target. Then, too, nature was proving a potent Yankee ally. Coffee Hill provided an excellent bulwark against any attack from the west or north, while Cedar Run substituted quite nicely for a moat to the south.

The Confederates would have to scout the fast shifting Union positions before deploying for an assault. It would take considerable time for the enemy to form his line of battle; those hours might allow the Federals to slip out of whatever snare the Rebels were trying to set. But first Hays had to clear the road to Catlett's Station. Then the II Corps' ponderous wagon train had to get through Auburn and go far enough beyond the town to allow the infantry brigades and horsemen south of Cedar Run to pull north of the creek. Once Warren accomplished all this, he still faced the challenge of sustaining a constant rearguard action all the way to the O&A Railroad.

Fortunately, Hays soon reported that the Rebels who had shelled Coffee Hill were gone. The enemy had not even left a token rearguard to harass the cautious Federal skirmishers. A relieved Warren ordered his corps eastward. Hays would take the lead, followed by Webb and the wagon train. Caldwell and Gregg would constitute the rearguard and would hold their current positions until Hays, Webb, and the wagons were well on their way. Then they would pull out as quickly as enemy would permit.

By the time Warren issued these orders, it was nearly 8 a.m. Several hours had been lost, but the II Corps was at last moving toward the railroad. After the morning's various scares the Federals seemed to have the situation well in hand. They had even found time to bury the men killed in the fighting around Coffee Hill. All Warren needed now was another hour or two, and he would be out of immediate danger.

Lieutenant General Richard Ewell had no intention of granting his adversary those hours. Despite numerous delays, most of his infantry was finally at hand and several battalions of Rebel artillery in position and ready to open fire. Warren had not escaped yet; the fighting at Auburn was a long way from being over.[36]

---

36 *OR* 29, pt. 1, 238-39.

CHAPTER 22

"Wherever We Turned the Confederates Were Ready For Us"

Ewell Attacks—Warren Withdraws—Confederate Pressure—Crisis on Coffee Hill—The Noose Tightens—Flight of the Rearguard—Ewell Turns North

THE morning of October 14 had been frustrating and befuddling for Lt. Gen. Richard Ewell. His troops had marched from Warrenton before sunrise toward an enemy of unknown strength and dispositions. Yankee cavalry had surprised the vanguard of Maj. Gen. Robert Rodes' division at the front of Ewell's column. The efforts of Ramseur's brigade had been required to drive the Federal horsemen back onto their reserves. An attempt by Lomax's dismounted cavalry to push the enemy away from the roads leading into Auburn had come up short. Meanwhile the brief flurry of firing from Stuart's reported position east of town had died away shortly after it had begun. The only thing Ewell and his subordinates had been able to ascertain for sure was that there were a lot of Federals around Auburn and a significant force of Yankees still south of Cedar Run.

The uncertainty plaguing the Confederates did not evaporate until the rising sun burned off the pre-dawn fog, allowing Rebel officers to perceive what they were up against. Now that he could see his enemies, Rodes ordered some batteries forward and began deploying his brigades south of Cedar Run for an attack. As these troops maneuvered Gen. Ewell rode up to get a good look at the field, and he didn't like what he saw.

The terrain south of Cedar Run and the hills on the other side of the stream posed a formidable defensive barrier. Ewell's troops would have to attack across open fields toward an enemy stationed on commanding ridges. Even if Rodes' men took those heights, they still had to get down a bluff and cross the creek under cannon fire from

Coffee Hill. Ewell's chief of artillery, Brig. Gen. Armistead Long, pointed out that the Union batteries commanded all the direct approaches to Auburn. Any assault from Rodes' current position was unlikely to succeed against those guns. Rebel artillery would have to silence the Yankee fieldpieces for an infantry assault to even be practicable.[1]

After examining the ground, Ewell concluded the best way to carry the Federal position was a double envelopment. He ordered Rodes' division to sidestep to the right (east) in search of a way around the enemy troops along the Carolina Road. Maj. Gen. Early's division, which stood in column behind Rodes, would move slightly northwest to ford Cedar Run a little upstream from Auburn. Lieutenant Colonel Hilary P. Jones' artillery battalion would accompany Early on a swing around the Federal right flank designed to descend on the enemy rear atop Coffee Hill. "Alleghany" Johnson's division at the tail of Ewell's column, would assume Rodes' current position and form the center of the Confederate line.[2]

In hopes of bringing a converging fire on the Federal guns defending Auburn, Gen. Long directed Col. Thomas Carter to shift his artillery battalion eastward to support Rodes. Long then sent word for Lt. Col. Richard S. Andrews to bring forward his battalion's long-range pieces and emplace them on the ridge earmarked for Johnson's position. As soon as Rodes' infantry seized suitable ground, Carter would put his guns into action supporting Andrews. Col. John T. Brown's and Lt. Col. William Nelson's artillery battalions would form a mobile reserve which Long planned to deploy "at the most favorable points" once the action started.[3]

*   *   *

Yankees observed these Rebel machinations with interest. On Coffee Hill, Pvt. Thomas Aldrich and several other gunners with Battery A 1st Rhode Island Light spotted the arrival of mysterious cannon on the ridge to their south. They alerted Capt. William Arnold to this surprising sight, warning it looked like trouble. Arnold agreed and ordered his battery to face about toward the possible threat. When Gen. Caldwell saw this, he quickly upbraided the captain for giving credence to his enlisted men's

1   OR 29, pt. 1, 418, 428.

2   Early, *Memoirs*, 304; Seymour, *Civil War Memoirs*, 87; Terry Jones, ed. *Campbell Brown's Civil War: With Ewell and the Army of Northern Virginia* (Baton Rouge, LA, 2001), 234-235.

3   OR 29, pt. 1, 418.

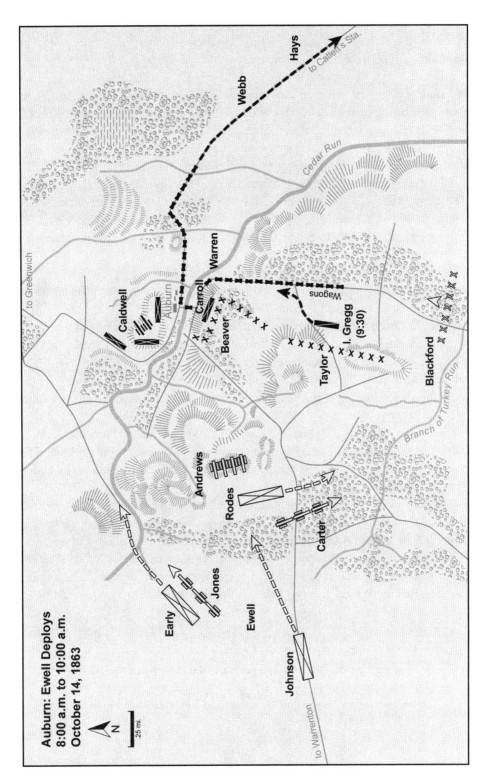

Auburn: Ewell Deploys
8:00 a.m. to 10:00 a.m.
October 14, 1863

N

.25 mi.

uninformed opinions. "Captain, make that man shut up; they are our own troops," he pronounced, just as the Rebel artillerists across the way commenced firing.[4]

Under Long's direction, Andrews had assembled a formidable force of three 10-pounder Parrot rifles, three 3-inch ordnance rifles, and two 20-pounder Parrots. As these guns began shooting, a torrent of Confederate shells surprised Federal soldiers on Coffee Hill for a second time that morning. The extraordinarily accurate enemy fire caught Arnold's battery completely unprepared. As the Southern gunners poured it on, Pvt. Aldrich thought he had never seen "shell come so thick and fast."[5]

However, Andrews' intensely accurate barrage was more frightening than deadly. The rugged and irregular shape of Coffee Hill gave Union troops plenty of defilade in which to take cover. Exploding shells damaged limbers, cannon wheels, harnesses, and even stripped the haversack off one Yankee's shoulder, but it wounded only three men and a few horses.

The Federals didn't suffer their punishment meekly. Battery F&G of the 1st Pennsylvania Light quickly went into action. Arnold's Rhode Islanders recovered from their surprise and were soon working their pieces alongside them. The ensuing artillery duel was brisk and the simultaneous roar of 20 guns echoed across the valley.

Yankee fire proved as accurate as the Rebels', and it almost scored a lucky hit when a burning ember from a bursting shell fell into an open Confederate limber chest. The red-hot fragment set alight the cotton bag holding a spare powder charge, threatening to explode the ammunition chest's entire contents. That detonation would have killed or injured dozens of men and horses besides destroying any number of guns. An alert Pvt. John Sawyer of the Alleghany Artillery saw the danger and courageously reached into the chest to grab the burning bag and throw it aside before it could explode. His courageous act narrowly averted serious disaster and kept Andrews' guns hammering away at Coffee Hill.[6]

Unfortunately for the Confederates, their savage bombardment didn't begin until 10 a.m.—far too late to truly imperil the II Corps, which had been moving toward Catlett's Station since 8 a.m. Although the fight with Stuart had delayed its advance, both Hays' and Webb's divisions along with the corps' trains were out of sight before the first Southern cannon fired. The Federal retreat proceeded with impressive dispatch, because Warren's troops believed they had been surrounded several times

---

4   Aldrich, *Battery A, 1st Rhode Island Light*, 248.

5   OR 29, pt. 1, 254, 418, 424-25; Aldrich, *Battery A, 1st Rhode Island Light*, 249.

6   OR 29, pt. 1, 424-25. Fixed cartridges had powder bags attached to projectiles. Each ammunition chest had separate projectiles and powder bags that could be married as circumstances dictated.

that morning. "[E]veryone was perfectly well disposed to march," reported one Union officer, "and there was no complaint as to the pace set by the head of the column."[7]

For the men under Caldwell, Gregg, Beaver, and Carroll, escape wouldn't be so easy. They had to fend off the encroaching Confederates long enough to allow the bulk of the II Corps to move a substantial distance toward Catlett's Station. Then they would have to make a fighting withdraw across Cedar Run and away from Coffee Hill, a task that would get harder as fewer and fewer Union men remained on the field.

After the last vehicle in the II Corps supply train trundled over the bridge at Auburn, Gen. Gregg ordered his cavalry brigades and Martin's 6th New York Battery to move by their right flank and cross Cedar Run. Blackford's Alabama sharpshooters viciously harassed the mounted column's flank as it headed north. Some Rebel marksmen pressed after the blue troopers almost all the way to the creek.[8]

Gregg's effort to disengage vastly increased the danger to Warren's rearguard. It was highly probable the Rebels would take advantage of the Union cavalry's withdrawal to launch an attack. If the enemy struck with enough force he might capture the bridge, and an orderly retreat would become a rout. To prevent this frightening scenario, Caldwell ordered Col. Patrick Kelly's famous Irish Brigade back over Cedar Run to guard the crossing point.

Kelly formed his men where the Double Poplars and Carolina roads joined at the southern end of the bridge, just below the bluff where Carroll and Beaver were fighting. Here they provided some insurance against disaster as Gregg's column pulled back into Auburn. As soon as the last cavalryman crossed the creek, Kelly withdrew over the bridge and formed a line of battle to cover the retreat of Carroll's brigade, which quickly faced left, slid down into the Carolina Road and hustled over the bridge.[9]

The Confederates quickly took advantage of shifting Federal dispositions. Gregg's withdrawal allowed Rodes to occupy favorable ground east of the Carolina Road and bring up Carter's artillery battalion. Captain Hazard had pulled Rickett's fieldpieces off Coffee Hill and sent them to join Hays' division. Only Arnold's battery remained to contest the fire of an increasing number of Rebel guns. Carroll's retreat left Col. Beaver's picket line unsupported against Alleghany Johnson's division then maneuvering into attack position. Already its skirmishers along with those of Lomax's brigade were pressing toward Cedar Run. Early's division had crossed the creek and was swiftly swinging into position to strike the Yankee rear. Generals Caldwell and

---

7   OR 29, pt. 1, 448; McClellan, *I Rode with JEB Stuart*, 392-93.

8   Blackford Diary, October 14, 1863, USMHI.

9   OR 29, pt. 1, 290-91, 254-55, 261-64.

Gregg could see the jaws of the Rebel trap beginning to close. Their margin for error was shrinking rapidly and any bungle or delay might prove disastrous.[10]

With Gregg and Carroll north Cedar Run, the only Union units still in contact with the enemy were Beaver's pickets south of the creek, Arnold's battery atop Coffee Hill, and Brooke's brigade along its western base. All these formations faced an increasingly desperate situation. The once cautious Confederate advance grew bolder, while increasing confusion amongst the Federals was spawning the very type of mistakes the Yankees had to avoid.

Gregg's division was supposed to relieve Arnold and Brooke, but fumbled its mission. The horse artillery battery that was to replace Arnold headed toward Catlett's Station instead. Gregg's horsemen formed up 100 yards behind, rather than in front of, Brooke's infantrymen. South of Cedar Run, Col. Beaver had troubles of his own. In preparing for a retreat over the stream, he had ordered his skirmishers to assemble by their right (western) flank. His men were dutifully moving in that direction when the colonel discovered to his dismay that the Rebels had slipped down the Double Poplars Road behind cover of a stone fence and a ravine. Now they were moving rapidly toward the bridge and already had Auburn and the crossing under fire.[11]

If his troops continued to obey his most recent order, they would blunder into a steadily gathering mass of Rebels. Desperate to avoid that catastrophe, the colonel dispatched Lt. Louis J. Sacriste of the 116th Pennsylvania to tell the men to reverse course and assemble on their left (east) by the Carolina Road. With the Confederates so near and advancing steadily, this was a hazardous but essential mission. If Sacriste failed, most of Beaver's pickets would meet disaster. Fortunately, the 20-year old lieutenant successfully brought the remaining skirmishers back to the left—a feat which merited him the Medal of Honor.[12]

This narrow escape was simply a first step. Now Beaver's pickets had to find a way across Cedar Run and back to the withdrawing II Corps. Since the Rebels had the bridge under fire, the fugitives had no alternative but to ford the creek wherever a chance of reaching the opposite shore seemed possible. The Confederates didn't neglect the opportunity thus offered. Rodes now held the high ground overlooking

---

10 Ibid., 305, 307.

11 Though unknown, these Confederates were probably some of Lomax's dismounted cavalry. Beaver ordered his men to assemble on their right because 1) units typically moved by their right and 2) to avoid congestion on the Carolina Road where Carroll had already led his troops.

12 St. Clair Mulholland, *The Story of the 116th Regiment Pennsylvania Infantry: War of Secession, 1862-1865* (Philadelphia, PA, 1899), 158-59; Muffly, *148th Pennsylvania Volunteers*, 247-48. Sacriste did not receive his medal until 1889.

Cedar Run that Gregg had just vacated, and Carter's guns were already firing from there toward Auburn and the creek.

Under this bombardment, the Federal pickets took to the stream, as one of them put it, "wherever they could get into it," waded across, and scrambled up the opposite bank. It was dangerous business: a Rebel bullet smashed Beaver's canteen while another lodged in his saddle before he and his men managed to make it to the north bank and reform. A quick cross-country march brought them gratefully back into the main body of Caldwell's division.[13]

*   *   *

Apparently Brooke's brigade wouldn't be so fortunate. To defend the road running along the western slope of Coffee Hill, the colonel had deployed the 53rd Pennsylvania, 2nd Delaware, and the attached 57th New York as skirmishers, while keeping the 45th Pennsylvania and 64th New York as a reserve. Brooke's men had dutifully held their ground as the II Corps' main body marched away. Although the brigade had only engaged in some light skirmishing, its soldiers could see ample evidence of a heavy body of enemy troops and artillery moving parallel to their line. Undoubtedly these Rebels were trying to outflank Coffee Hill and cut the road between Auburn and Catlett's Station.[14]

With the situation worsening by the moment, Caldwell still had orders to hold his ground until Gregg relieved him, and he never intended otherwise. Eventually, a section of guns from the 6th New York Light, supported by the 1st Massachusetts Cavalry and 6th Ohio Cavalry, arrived to replace Arnold's battery on Coffee Hill. As the Rhode Island gunners disengaged, the New York artillerymen took up an unequal duel with Long's cannon south of Cedar Run.

Much to the Rebel artillerymen's approval, the two newly-arrived mounted regiments on Coffee Hill presented much better targets than Caldwell's infantry, and their shells soon came crashing into the cavalrymen's ranks. One projectile burst dead center in the 6th Ohio's line, wounding one man and killing several horses. Understandably, the Yankee troopers didn't like their new position. Caldwell, on the

13 Mulholland, *116th Regiment Pennsylvania Infantry*, 158-59; Muffly, *148th Pennsylvania Volunteers*, 247-48.

14 *OR* 29, pt. 1, 254, 268. The heavy body of troops was Early's Division. Gen. Caldwell had attached the 57th New York from Col. Beaver's 3rd Brigade to Brooke shortly after Stuart's surprise bombardment that morning.

other hand, was glad to see them. The order to withdraw his brigades could not be long off now; he would not have to defend Coffee Hill forever.[15]

The general was quite relieved when Warren sent word to pull back. The swift withdrawal of the rest of the II Corps had left Caldwell's division virtually isolated. The enemy might easily cut the road before it could escape. To keep the route open, Caldwell ordered the Irish Brigade and Battery G, 1st New York Artillery, to occupy some high ground alongside the thoroughfare east of Coffee Hill and hold it until the rest of the command had passed. Once these units were in place, Caldwell ordered his 1st and 3rd brigades toward Catlett's Station. Waiting long enough to allow them a decent start, he then dispatched orders for Brooke's brigade to retreat.[16]

Those instructions arrived not a second too soon. Early's division was at that moment sweeping around the other side of Coffee Hill and angling through the forest toward the road to Catlett's Station. South of Cedar Run a line of Confederate skirmishers emerged from the woods and swarmed toward the creek. Recognizing a bad situation when it saw one, the 6th New York gun section ceased fire and hurried down the hill. As they made for Auburn, Rebel infantry came pouring across the stream. One Federal gunner remembered he and his fellows being so fearful of capture they whipped their horses to a "furious gallop" and tore through the village "amid a storm of lead." Remarkably, the artillery got through unscathed. With the battery gone, the 6th Ohio and 1st Massachusetts horsemen quickly headed east with equal urgency right behind the gunners.[17]

The sudden cavalry withdrawal dealt a blow to Col. Brooke. By the time he had assembled his skirmishers, the 4th Brigade's situation was near critical. The Rebels were pressing down on its line from the west and north while their artillery was deploying to its front. Rebel troops advancing from the south threatened to sever his route through Auburn. A considerable gap had developed between Brooke's command and the rest of the division. The cavalry which was supposed to cover the brigade's retreat had hightailed it even before his skirmishers could reassemble. Brooke's men were now the rearmost element of the entire II Corps.[18]

To bolster his rearguard's safety, Caldwell ordered Arnold to send a gun section back to support Brooke. The assistance was more encumbrance than aid at the

---

15 Ibid., 254-55, 308; Bushnell memoir, WRHS; Benjamin Crowninshield, *A History of the First Regiment of Massachusetts Cavalry Volunteers* (Cambridge, MA, 1899), 180-81; Griffin, *Three Years a Soldier*, 142.

16 OR 29, pt. 1, 254-55.

17 Bushnell memoir, WRHS; Crowninshield, *First Massachusetts Cavalry*, 180-1.

18 OR 29, pt. 1, 254-55.

moment, however, for escape, not resistance, had become the overriding goal. Alive to his danger, the colonel ordered his men to double-quick around the southern edge of Coffee Hill and hustle back through Auburn to reconnect with the rest of the division.

The Confederate gunners who had been pounding Coffee Hill were just congratulating themselves on driving the Yankee guns away when Brooke's infantry suddenly came jogging out of the woods. They immediately turned their fire onto this new target and forced the brigade to run what one fleeing Yankee termed a "destructive" gauntlet of solid shot and shell which did "considerable damage" to the moving column. The aim of the enemy cannoneers was excellent, and a cascade of missiles continually burst over and around the retreating Federals.

While Brooke's brigade sprinted through Auburn, Confederate infantry closed in on the Saint Stephens Road from the north and south, forcing the Federals to flee through the fast narrowing eye of a needle. It was a close race. Brooke's regiments, thoroughly winded after their lengthy double-quick, had been leaking stragglers—many of them raw conscripts wearing heavy knapsacks stuffed with spare clothes and shoes.[19]

Most of Brooke's regiments got through, but not all of them. A gap had opened in the brigade's column during its long run, and the Rebels exploited it. As some of Early's infantry surged in the direction of the Union left, other Confederates slipped behind the enemy column and poured a "terrific volley" into the Federal rear. Within seconds the Southerners had crossed the road, and the tail-end of the 148th Pennsylvania and the entire 57th New York suddenly found themselves cut off. "Wherever we turned," Sergeant Thomas Meyer lamented, "the Confederates were ready for us." Adding to the Yankees' woes, Jones now had two batteries in action to pester the isolated Northerners.[20]

Denied the road, Lt. Col. Alford Chapman led his 57th New York across a field to his left, making for the cover of some distant woods. From only 150 yards off Confederate skirmishers opened a "very severe" fire into his flank, while Jones' cannon pursued his men with exploding shells. Twenty-one New Yorkers fell before the regiment reached the trees. Lucking into a farmer's lane which seemed to point in the right direction, Chapman gambled and led his regiment down the unknown path.

19 Previous paragraphs based upon OR 29, pt. 1, 268, 270-73, 278-89, 274-75, 361; Griffin, *Three Years a Soldier*, 142; Meyer, *Incidents and Anecdotes*, PSU; George Nichols, *A Soldier's Story of His Regiment (61st Georgia) and Incidentally of the Lawton-Gordon-Evens Brigade, Army of Northern Virginia* (Tuscaloosa, AL, 2011), 129.

20 Meyer, *Incidents and Anecdotes*, PSU; Muffly, *148th Pennsylvania Volunteers*, 366-67; OR 29, pt. 1, 272, 421.

Fortuitously it intersected with the Saint Stephens Road which was full of Union soldiers: his New Yorkers were safe.[21]

The 148th Pennsylvania similarly dashed for protection. Badly shaken by a volley into its rear, some of the regiment's men rushed pell-mell out of the road and across an open field toward a strip of woods some distance away. The regimental pioneers at the end of the column, at a loss for what to do, pleaded with Sgt. Meyer for their orders. There were no orders, Meyer hollered, and "every man who can, will save himself from capture!" Rebel fire cut down many of the soldiers running for the woods. Meyer and his companions realized too late that the enemy already occupied the timber. The Confederates captured everyone who reached the trees. Most of the Pennsylvanians, however, kept to the field and managed to get away.[22]

The Confederate trap finally slammed shut, but too late to do much damage. Jones' battalion got off only a handful of shots before the Federals drew out of range. Although the Rebel infantry did rip into the rear elements of Caldwell's column, almost all of his division had already escaped. Brooke's brigade and the attached 57th New York lost 134 men—8 dead, 41 wounded, and 85 missing. Although some few had fallen victim to Stuart's shelling earlier in the morning, the final hectic retreat from Auburn produced most of the casualties and all of the prisoners.[23]

*   *   *

Despite Brooke's successful exodus from Ewell's envelopment, fighting hadn't ended. Rebel infantry followed Caldwell's rearguard long enough to keep it nervous. Gregg's horsemen (nearly out of ammunition by now) and Warren's flankers engaged in some hot skirmishing along the wooded roadside. The rearmost Union brigades alternately formed line and then displaced, leapfrogging backward to cover each other's withdrawal. At one point a section of guns from Battery A 1st Rhode Island Light retired by prolonge, each piece being loaded as horses pulled it rearward, then stopping to fire when ready before repeating the process.[24]

General Warren stayed in the rear to oversee the rearguard. His chief of staff, 28-year old Lt. Col. Charles H. Morgan, led Hays, Webb, and the corps' trains to the railroad. Although the enemy didn't push his advance with much vigor, Caldwell halted his division two miles east of Auburn and threw it into line of battle. He hoped this

---

21 OR 29, pt. 1, 268.

22 Meyer, *Incidents and Anecdotes*, Penn State.

23 OR 29, pt. 1, 248.

24 OR 29, pt. 1, 240, 261; Aldrich, *Battery A, 1st Rhode Island Light*, 249-50.

"brave show of force" would hold Ewell at bay until the rest of the corps could put some distance between itself and the Rebels. As it turned out, Caldwell's stand wasn't necessary. Ewell's goal had been to rescue Stuart, in consonance with the larger Confederate objective of disrupting Meade's retreat, not tangling with his rearguard. Just as the 1st Division turned to make its stand, Ewell abandoned his pursuit, such as it was, and allowed the Federals to depart without further molestation.[25]

The Auburn affair had consumed Ewell's corps for half the morning. Other than Stuart's successful escape, the effort had little to show for it beyond a modest haul of Yankee prisoners. Ewell ordered his troops to turn northeast and move back to the Carolina Road and then on toward Greenwich. With luck, he could pull ahead of Warren and hit him somewhere along the O&A on terrain more favorable to a decisive result.[26]

Through his field glasses Warren watched the Confederates occupy Auburn and then break off their pursuit. He was justly proud of his troops who had remained calm and acted with exemplary professionalism in a confusing and perilous situation. Their performance had denied the enemy a triumph. Now most of Ewell's units were moving away. Although a battalion of sharpshooters from Rodes' division hovered close to the tail of Warren's column, for the moment the danger to the II Corps had passed. It was free to march toward Catlett's Station and link up with the rest of Meade's army. At this point Confederate intentions were obvious.

Everything now depended on Federal soldiers outmarching their enemy. If they failed, the successful withdrawal from Auburn would become little more than an ironic prelude to disaster.[27]

---

25 OR 29, pt. 1, 240-41. A native New Yorker, Morgan graduated from West Point in 1857 and was commissioned in the artillery corps. Before the war he served on the frontier. A lieutenant in the 4th US Artillery during the Peninsula Campaign, he was promoted to Captain in Oct. 1862, and commanded the II Corps artillery at Fredericksburg. He became II Corps chief of staff on Jan. 1, 1863 and remained in that role until Winfield S. Hancock relinquished command of the II Corps in Nov. 1864. At that point he followed Hancock to the Headquarters of the Middle Department, where he served as chief of staff. Morgan remained in the army after the war, obtaining the rank of major before dying on duty at Alcatraz Island in San Francisco Bay on Dec. 20, 1875. See https://www.findagrave.com/memorial/5888409, accessed 13 Jun 18.

26 Walker, *Second Army Corps*, 336; OR *Supplement* 5, pt. 1, 594.

27 OR 29, pt. 1, 240-41, 449. The Confederate force that maintained contact with the II Corps is identified in the official record only as a battalion of sharpshooters from Rhodes' division and later Stuart's escaped force from Auburn.

CHAPTER 23

"Everything Went With a Rush"

Hill's March—Henry Heth—Sykes' Apprehension—
Hill and Warren Converge Opportunity—Battle Begins—II Corps' Plight—
Warren Abandoned—Heth's Advance—Critical Decision

THE

tempting aroma of hot food drifted through the bivouacs of A. P. Hill's corps as it shook itself awake on the chilly 45-degree morning of October 14. Warrenton's patriotic ladies had spent the night cooking or baking and as a result the lucky soldiers closest to town enjoyed an unusually bountiful breakfast. The majority of the corps made do with haversack rations. The Rebels, sensing that today would likely determine the outcome of the campaign, were in a high state of anticipation. Either they would catch up to the Federal columns or the enemy would make good his escape. Everyone anticipated the former rather than the latter outcome. Either way, by nightfall Robert E. Lee's entire army would be concentrated only 35 miles south of Washington, DC.[1]

The eager Southern troops took to the road from their bivouacs one mile above Warrenton at 5 a.m. or shortly afterwards. Major General Richard H. Anderson's division, accompanied by Maj. David G. McIntosh's artillery battalion, had the head of Hill's column. Behind them came Henry Heth's division and William T. Poague's battalion of artillery. Wilcox's division, three additional artillery battalions and the corps' wagon train brought up the rear.[2]

---

1 Krick, *Civil War Weather*, 110; Durkin, *Confederate Chaplain*, 62; Kirkpatrick Diary, UT; Howard, *Recollections*, 233; Long "Reminiscences" Breckinridge papers, LC.

2 OR 29, pt. 1, 426, 430. Since Hill's entire corps was using a single road, the last artillery battalions didn't depart Warrenton until 9 a.m. See Ken Wiley, *Norfolk Blues: The Civil War Diary of the Norfolk Light Artillery* (Shippensburg, PA, 1997), 96.

Hill set a brisk pace and pushed his men hard. He refused to allow even a single rest break during the first four hours of the march. After trekking northward five miles on the Warrenton Turnpike, the front of the Rebel column reached the little town of New Baltimore, which one soldier called "a mean, insignificant affair." There the road jogged to the east for a half mile before reaching Broad Run Church. Federal troops had burned this Baptist sanctuary, but its charred ruins still marked the point where the turnpike split in different directions. The main thoroughfare veered north toward Buckland Mills while a lesser byway angled due east to intersect with the Carolina Road between Auburn and the town of Greenwich.[3]

The approach to New Baltimore carried the Rebel infantrymen through familiar surroundings. Many had traversed this same route just 14 months ago before the battle of Second Manassas; now they suspected history was about to repeat itself. The enthusiasm of local Virginians enhanced that impression. "Hundreds of ladies often scattered along the road to see us on the march," remembered one Floridian, fondly recalling pretty girls waving their handkerchiefs and "giving Huzas for the Rebels." Other women urged the smiling troops "to go and kill all the Yankees and throw them into the river." The effect on morale was predictable.[4]

Upon reaching the ruins of the church around 7:30 a.m., Hill received reports from "various sources" of Federal activity to the northwest around Buckland Mills. Since the general could distinctly hear the rumble of wagons in that direction he believed those rumors. Hill had no way of knowing the strength or composition of the enemy his ears discerned. Nonetheless, he sensed opportunity rather than danger. If the Yankees were moving a large supply train in the area there might be a chance to strike a vulnerable Union column in the flank.[5]

Never one to pass up an opening to throw a punch, Hill directed Anderson's division to continue up the Warrenton Turnpike to Buckland. If there was a prospect for launching a meaningful attack, Anderson should seize it. If instead "nothing could be accomplished," he should move east to rejoin the rest of the corps at Greenwich.[6]

As Anderson headed out, A. P. Hill led the remainder of his Third Corps east from Broad Run Church toward the Carolina Road, where the column would turn north

3 Ibid., 426, 430. Durkin, *Confederate Chaplain*, 62; Kirkpatrick Diary, UT; Howard, *Recollections*, 233; Long "Reminiscences" Breckinridge papers, LC; Wiley, *Norfolk Blues*, 96. A History of Broad Run Church can be found at https://broadrunbaptist.wordpress.com/history/. Exactly when the Federals burned the church is unclear. Some sources say 1862, others 1863.

4 Mellon, Knox, Jr. ed. *"A Florida Solider in the Army of Northern Virginia: The Hosford Letters."* (Florida Historical Quarterly, Vol. 46, No. 3, Jan., 1968); Wiley, *Norfolk Blues*, 96.

5 OR 29, pt. 1, 426. The Union force was Kilpatrick's division moving toward Sudley Springs.

6 Ibid.

Major General Henry Heth
Library of Congress

toward Greenwich. The general expected a fight before the day was out, and he wanted his command to go into it with maximum mobility. Thus, Hill ordered his supply train to forego the turn at Broad Run Church and continue straight toward Buckland, where he ordered the wagons to go into park. Hill had Wilcox detail a single battery and a brigade of infantry from his division to protect the wagons—a thankless task Wilcox delegated to Brig. Gen. Alfred M. Scales and his five regiments of North Carolina infantry.[7]

*   *   *

Anderson's detachment placed Heth's division at the front of Hill's column. The 37-year old major general was a relative newcomer to the ANV. His father had been a US Navy captain during the War of 1812 and his grandfather a colonel in the Revolutionary War. As a young man Henry, who everyone called Harry, turned down an appointment to the US Naval Academy so he could attend West Point. He graduated in 1847, ranked last in his class. Assigned to the infantry, he nonetheless compiled a good record as a solider and saw significant action against hostile Indians and during the Mexican War.

Heth resigned from the US Army after Virginia seceded. During a brief tenure as the state's quartermaster general he caught the attention of Robert E. Lee, who thereafter took a keen interest in Heth's career. After his election as colonel of the 45th Virginia Infantry, Heth served in western Virginia. In January 1862 he received a promotion to brigadier general. His modest early résumé included the rout of his troops at the small battle of Lewisburg, Virginia on May 23, 1862. That embarrassing event didn't affect his reputation or prevent him from getting command of a division in

---

7   Ibid. The identity of the battery Wilcox sent is not known.

Maj. Gen. Edmund Kirby Smith's Army of East Tennessee, in which post he took part in the fall 1862 invasion of Kentucky but saw no combat.

In February 1863 the war department transferred the handsome and affable Heth to the Army of Northern Virginia. As a brigade commander in A. P. Hill's division, Heth fought in his first big battle at Chancellorsville where he performed adequately before taking charge of Hill's division after its commander fell in the same friendly-fire incident that badly wounded Stonewall Jackson.

When Lee reorganized the Army of Northern Virginia on May 30, 1863, Hill took command of the newly created Third Corps while Heth, promoted to major general, received a division in the same unit. Four weeks later, his advance on Gettysburg, Pennsylvania, ran into Union cavalry under Brig. Gen. John Buford setting off a skirmish that eventually swelled into the biggest battle ever fought on the North American continent. Some felt that Heth's clumsy handling of his division had allowed the action to grow until Lee was compelled to undertake a major engagement at a time and in a place not of his choosing. During the first day of fighting, an enemy bullet struck Heth in the head, fractured his skull, and knocked him out of action until July 7. Since then he had performed capably, but there was no denying an unlucky star seemed to follow him around.[8]

*   *   *

Once Hill's corps turned onto the Carolina Road it began wading through the backwash of William French's III Corps. Evidence of the enemy's hurried retreat was everywhere. Guns, knapsacks and blankets lay scattered along the road; abandoned camp fires still burned in the fields. The Confederates covered the 5-mile march to Greenwich so quickly that Hill's artillerymen rode their limbers rather than walk alongside the guns as usual. As the Rebels neared their destination, they captured 20 footsore Federal stragglers, and at 10 a.m. when Hill arrived on the southeastern edge of the village local citizens informed him that French's Yankees had left only a few hours ago.[9]

Hill had not been in Greenwich long before Anderson showed up. His diversion to Buckland Mills had uncovered nothing but elements of Kilpatrick's cavalry division in the vicinity. The Federals were already drawing off to the northwest when Fitz Lee had arrived with Chambliss', Owens', and Lomax's brigades. After the 5th Virginia

---

8   Warner, *Generals in Gray*, 133; Tagg, *Generals of Gettysburg*, 340.

9   Kirkpatrick Diary, UT; Long "Reminiscences" Breckinridge papers, LC; *OR* 29, pt. 1, 426; Wiley, *Norfolk Blues*, 96.

Cavalry drove the Yankees away from the hamlet, Anderson concluded that Fitz's horsemen had everything under control and marched his division to Greenwich.

* * *

About 10:30 a.m. Hill turned his reunited corps toward Bristoe Station, eight miles to the east along the O&A. Heth's division and Poague's artillery battalion remained in the lead. Anderson's division and McIntosh's artillery battalion fell in behind Heth. Wilcox's division (minus Scales' brigade) and the rest of the corps' batteries continued at the rear of the column. Heading southeast the Confederates scooped up another 150 Union stragglers.[10]

No Rebel cavalry moved in the front of Hill's troops. Fitz Lee might have sent over a regiment, but no one requested his support. Hampton's division, which Stuart still led personally, had the responsibility for screening the army's right flank. However the time-consuming affair at Auburn that morning, and a subsequent chain of unhelpful events, had prevented Stuart from assuming his assigned station.

When the fight at Auburn ended, Lomax's brigade—having lost touch with Stuart—rode north with Fitz Lee. After the cavalry corps commander had escaped from his predicament near Coffee Hill, he led his force to safety west of the Carolina Road. Soon thereafter Stuart made contact with Robert E. Lee and received orders to screen the army's right flank as it moved toward Greenwich and Bristoe Station. After returning to his troopers, Stuart led Funsten's and Gordon's brigades along with Beckham's seven guns back to Auburn.

Stuart's mission—creating a mounted buffer between the enemy and the main Rebel column—required that he advance on the eastern side of the infantry's flankers. Almost all of Ewell's corps had left by the time Stuart reached Auburn. But the general did spot a battalion of sharpshooters from Rodes' division moving through the woods. Assuming they were acting as flankers for Ewell's corps, he fell in on their right.

Stuart had assumed incorrectly. The infantry battalion had been detached to harass Warren's retreat to Catlett's Station and then along the O&A to Bristoe Station. Consequently, when Stuart's two brigades and their accompanying artillery moved to the right of the sharpshooters they veered far off Ewell and Hill's path. Stuart's troopers were thus chasing the tail of Meade's army rather than screening the eastern flank of Lee's infantry.

How Stuart could have so uncharacteristically allowed a battalion of skirmishers to divert his command is puzzling. Apparently he didn't communicate with the

10 *OR* 29, pt. 1, 376, 426.

Brigadier General John R. Cooke
Library of Virginia

sharpshooters well enough to discover their mission or the whereabouts of Ewell's corps. Or maybe by the time he learned the answers to those questions, his cavalry had veered so far off course it was impossible for the horsemen to reach their proper position. Either way, fatigue, if not sheer exhaustion, probably explains the error. Neither Stuart nor his troopers had gotten much sleep in the woods near Auburn the night before. Since the dawn of October 14 they had been almost constantly either fighting or on the move. It would not be surprising if the general and his men had gotten a little careless and sloppy by the time they reconnected with the infantry.[11]

Whatever the reason, no Rebel cavalry shadowed the eastern flank of either Hill's or Ewell's command throughout their entire march toward Bristoe Station. Thus the Third Corps' leading infantry division advanced blindly toward the enemy, just as it had on July 1, 1863 at Gettysburg. And like then, Harry Heth's command led the way.

Cooke's brigade, which had recently joined the army from the defenses of Richmond, was the vanguard of Hill's corps. Lee had assigned the 2,500-man unit to Heth's division only days before the campaign started. The brigade's four North Carolina regiments were all new to the ANV. By contrast their leader—30-year old, Missouri-born, Harvard-educated, Brig. Gen. John R. Cooke—was a hardened veteran who had already suffered seven wounds during the war and won a stellar reputation for bravery and competence. At the September 17, 1862 battle of Sharpsburg, then Colonel Cooke had led his 27th North Carolina in a counterattack that many believed saved Lee's army from destruction. The Confederate Senate approved Cooke's well-deserved promotion to general just six weeks later on November 1. He was as good a brigadier as Lee's army possessed.[12]

---

11 *OR* 29, pt. 1, 449. Stuart said little about the mistake in his official report.

12 James Robertson. *General A.P. Hill: The Story of a Confederate Warrior* (New York: Random House, 1987), 234; Warner, *Generals in Gray*, 61. Cooke was Jeb Stuart's brother-in-law and the son of Union general Philip St. George Cooke, who was Stuart's father-in-law and had been Maj. Gen. George B. McClellan's chief of staff.

After Cooke's formation came William W. Kirkland's brigade of North Carolinians. This 1,500-man outfit contained some of the best soldiers in the army. James Pettigrew had commanded the unit at Gettysburg where it participated in the brutal fighting on July 1 and the fateful attack of July 3. Kirkland took charge of the brigade after Pettigrew's mortal wounding at Falling Waters, Maryland, on July 14.

The command's new leader had entered West Point in 1852, but been expelled for poor conduct in 1855. Still desiring a military career, Kirkland managed to get an appointment as a 2nd lieutenant in the US Marine Corps. He served in that branch from 1855 until he resigned his commission in August 1860. As Colonel of the 21st North Carolina, Kirkland had fought at First Manassas and in Jackson's Valley Campaign. On May 25, 1862 at the First Battle of Winchester he ordered an ill-advised bayonet charge during which he took a Yankee bullet in the thigh. His wound necessitated a long recovery, but Kirkland wasn't willing to remain idle even while he healed and served as Maj. Gen. Patrick R. Cleburne's chief of staff at the battle of Murfreesboro in December 1862. Kirkland returned to Lee's army in time to fight at Gettysburg. Promoted to brigadier general on August 29, 1863, he was battle-tested and experienced.[13]

Next in line was the brigade led by Henry Harrison Walker. A graduate of West Point (Class of 1853) and a veteran of the pre-war Kansas troubles, the native Virginian had resigned from the US Army in May 1861 and become a lieutenant colonel in the 40th Virginia Infantry. Wounded twice at the battle of Gaines' Mill in June, 1862 he received praise from A. P. Hill for his conduct in that action. Walker became a brigadier on July 1, 1863, and his current assignment was his first field command since the Peninsula Campaign. He led the 13th Alabama, 1st Tennessee, 55th Virginia, and 14th Tennessee regiments along with the 22nd Virginia Battalion. His brigade somewhat awkwardly consolidated two units badly shot up at Gettysburg—Brig. Gen. James Archer's Tennessee brigade (whose commander had been captured on July 1) and John Brockenbrough's Virginia brigade, whose commander's performance during at Gettysburg had been found wanting.[14]

Joseph R. Davis' brigade brought up the rear of the division. The 39-year old lawyer and nephew of the Confederate president had won a seat in the Mississippi State Senate in 1860, but left politics to enter the army as lieutenant colonel of the 10th Mississippi once the war began. Promoted to colonel and transferred to President Davis' staff early in the conflict, he received his general's wreath on September 15,

---

13 Warner, *Generals in Gray*, 171-2; http://www.northstaterifles.com/kirkland.htm; Peter Cozzens, *Shenandoah 1862: Stonewall Jackson's Valley Campaign* (Chapel Hill, NC, 2013), 354-55.

14 Robertson, *A.P. Hill*, 234; OR 29, pt. 1, 433; Warner, *Generals in Gray*, 318; Lee, *Wartime Papers*, 563.

Brigadier General William W. Kirkland
State Archives of North Carolina

1862, but only after the Confederate Senate initially rejected his nomination under charges of nepotism.

His brigade was the smallest in Heth's division, numbering only four regiments, one of which was on detached service. A fairly new command, it had seen its first combat and been badly mauled at Gettysburg on July 1. The battered brigade received a similar pummeling while taking part in the famous Confederate charge on July 3, during which Davis had been wounded. He had just returned to the army after a long convalescence and a bout with typhoid fever.[15]

A lack of cavalry to reconnoiter ahead of their column didn't concern Henry Heth and his brigadiers. They were certain their men were snapping at the heels of the Yankee rearguard and convinced the enemy was on the run. Nobody had any inkling Hill was on a collision course with Warren's II Corps.[16]

* * *

The Union retreat alongside the O&A Railroad was not going flawlessly, and George Meade wasn't happy about it. His headquarters had been at Catlett's Station throughout the night of the 13th, and it was still there on the morning of October 14. Intelligence received the previous evening confirmed that Lee was swinging west. The obvious need to reach Centreville before the Confederates barred the way was paramount, and the Federal columns had resumed their march at dawn.[17]

Much to Meade's annoyance the army's ponderous wagon trains, which Col. Lyman called the general's "particular detestation," were proving a huge encumbrance.

15 Warner, *Generals in Gray*, 68-69.

16 *OR* 29, pt. 1, 426.

17 Lyman, *Meade's Army*, 50-51.

Moreover, some of his corps commanders seemed a little too anxious to retreat at an unseemly pace. With Rebels nearby and drawing closer, Sykes' infantry had left Catlett's Station at sunrise and covered the distance to Bristoe Station so quickly they had out-paced their wagons. This left the V Corps train completely vulnerable to attack, and Meade had to send Lyman to Sykes with orders to slow down and let his teamsters catch up.[18]

When the bulk of the II Corps reached Catlett's Station around 9:30 a.m., Meade immediately instructed its wagon train to head north in the wake of the V Corps. To make sure the same problem just occasioned by Sykes did not happen again, the army's commander detailed Col. De Witt Baxter's Philadelphia Brigade of Webb's division to accompany the wagons. Meade told Baxter not to stop until the corps' trains reached Centreville, 20 miles to the north. Hays' division, along with Webb's remaining two brigades, would wait for Warren, Caldwell, and Gregg before following in the wake of their vehicles.[19]

After issuing these orders, Meade rode north with his headquarters, leaving Catlett's Station about 10:30 and arriving at Bristoe Station around noon. There he found that the V Corps had already crossed Broad Run and was resting just north of the stream around Milford. French's III Corps had forded the creek some time ago. Stragglers from both commands could be seen in abundance, most still trudging north to catch up to their regiments. The II Corps wagons and their infantry escort had reached the station about the same time as Meade. While Baxter's brigade paused to cook a hurried lunch, the train rumbled gradually northeastward towards Wolf Run Shoals, a route that would take it away from the infantry's line of march and probably along a safer path as well.

Pleased enough to see the wagon trains moving steadily toward Bull Run, Meade wasn't quite ready for his foot soldiers to follow suit. He told Sykes to hold his corps at Milford until Warren arrived. The army commander also sent orders to French instructing him to halt the III Corps until Sykes resumed his march. In this way the V Corps would stay in supporting distance of Warren and the III Corps in supporting distance of Sykes.[20]

Meade sent word back to Warren telling him the road between Catlett's and Bristoe was clear and that he should "move forward as rapidly as possible." The general also cautioned the II Corps commander to be on his guard, as the Confederates might

---

18 Lyman, *Meade's Army*, 49-51.

19 Ibid., 50-51.

20 Joseph R. C. Ward, *History of the One Hundred Sixth Regiment Pennsylvania Volunteers 2nd Brigade, 2nd Division, 2nd Corps* (Philadelphia, PA, 1883), 184.

dispatch a column from Gainesville to intercept the Union line of retreat near Bristoe Station.[21]

*   *   *

Warren reached Catlett's Station with Caldwell's division and Gregg's cavalry about the same time Meade arrived at Bristoe. He didn't need his superior's urging to hurry north, and quickly put all three of his divisions on the road. The general again assigned Lt. Col. Morgan to guide the column. To speed his corps' pace, Warren directed that Webb's division and two batteries of artillery march on the northwest side of the railroad. Hays' division, followed by the corps' ammunition wagons and ambulances, as well as Gregg's ambulances and artillery, would move on the other side of the tracks. Caldwell along with the Gregg's cavalry continued as rearguard.[22]

As he had during the withdrawal from Auburn, Gouverneur Warren elected to remain toward the rear of his column, where everyone imagined danger the greatest. Although Meade had warned him to watch out for Rebel troops near Bristoe Station, Warren wasn't overly concerned. The V Corps had orders to wait at Milford for his arrival. Moreover the young New York general had complete confidence in Lt. Col. Morgan and the two men in charge of his leading divisions—brigadier generals Alexander S. Webb and Alexander Hays.

Webb, a 28-year old native of New York City and an 1855 graduate of West Point, hailed from a distinguished blood line. His grandfather had served on Washington's staff during the Revolution, while his father had been a US Army officer, a prominent newspaper publisher, and US minister to Brazil. A "handsome man, with regular features," the always well-groomed and "neatly dressed" Webb looked like a general. The division commander also had a pleasing personality, which Col. Lyman pronounced "effervescent" and "very jolly."[23]

Webb had spent the first part of the war on staff duty, for which he was well suited. Most of his service was with the artillery branch. During the Antietam campaign he temporarily served as the V Corps chief of staff. Although he did a stint as inspector general of artillery in Washington, DC afterwards, his Antietam comrades did not forget his talents. When George Meade assumed command of the V Corps after

---

21 Lyman, *Meade's Army*, 51; OR 29, pt. 1, 241.

22 OR 29, pt. 1, 241. These dispositions were against Meade's order to move entirely on the southeast side of the O&A.

23 Lyman, *Meade's Army*, 38; Tagg, *Generals of Gettysburg*, 49; Lyman, *Meade's Headquarters*, 307; Warner, *Generals in Blue*, 544.

Fredericksburg, he selected Webb as his chief of staff, a capacity in which the New York officer excelled. He got his first combat command experience when Meade sent him to direct forward operations during the battle of Chancellorsville. Webb's performance in that role impressed his boss and soon had dramatic ramifications.

On the same day he assumed control of the Army of the Potomac, George Meade put Webb in command of the II Corps' Philadelphia Brigade, whose leader was under arrest for failing to maintain discipline in the unit. Meade expected Webb to fix that problem promptly, but the troops resisted his initial efforts. He made little headway in the three days between taking charge of the brigade and the start of the battle of Gettysburg.

Webb's performance on July 3, 1863, changed everything. The 2nd Division of the II Corps held Cemetery Ridge, which was the target of first, an enormous artillery bombardment, and then a massive infantry assault by Rebel troops under George E. Picket, James J. Pettigrew and Isaac R. Trimble. Holding the center of the division's line, Webb's brigade was squarely in the bullseye of the enemy attack. Throughout the thunderous 150-gun barrage preceding the Confederate infantry charge, Webb had stood bolt upright, leaning on his sword, while his men lay down for cover. This display of courage won the respect and admiration of his troops and many others.

When Pickett's division tore into Webb's line, the brigadier's heroic, capable, and fearless leadership helped ensure the Rebels' repulse and enshrined Webb's reputation. It certainly vindicated Meade's appointing him to temporary command of the 2nd Division to replace Brig. Gen. John Gibbon, who had been wounded at the height of the fighting on Cemetery Ridge. In the span of six days Webb had gone from staff officer to division commander, and his behavior since Gettysburg had proven the wisdom of his rapid advancement.[24]

Alexander Hays, a 44-year old native-born Pennsylvanian and son of a congressman and militia general, had played an equally brave and stellar role in repulsing Pickett's and Pettigrew's charge. That didn't surprise those who knew him. Called Alex by his friends, Hays had sought out a military career. He left Allegheny College during his senior year to go to West Point. After graduating in 1844 he served on the frontier and distinguished himself in the Mexican War.[25]

Peacetime soldering held little appeal for Hays. He resigned from the army in 1848 and entered the iron business in Pittsburg. When that didn't work out as planned, he took part in the California Gold Rush. After success eluded him on the west coast, Hays returned to Pittsburgh and began a new career as a civil engineer specializing in

---

24 Previous paragraphs based upon Tagg, *Generals of Gettysburg*, 49

25 Tagg, *Generals of Gettysburg*, 53; Warner, *Generals in Blue*, 223.

Brigadier General Alexander Webb
Library of Congress

building bridges. When the Civil War erupted, he rejoined the army and became colonel of the 63rd Pennsylvania, which he handled well throughout the Peninsula campaign and during the battle of Second Bull Run where he took a bad wound in the leg.

It required more than six months for Hays to recover from his injury, but a promotion to brigadier general came through during his convalescence. When he returned to duty in early 1863, Hays received command of a brigade in the Washington defenses. When the war department transferred that unit to the AOP in June 1863 it became the 3rd Brigade of the 3rd Division in the II Corps. When that division's commander, Maj. Gen. William French, took charge of the garrison at Harper's Ferry, Hays' seniority placed him in command of the 3rd Division.

In contrast to Webb's experience, Hays troops took to him instantly. He was the kind of officer volunteer soldiers admired. The six-foot tall general looked like a fighter. His husky build and thick sandy red beard and hair, matched Hays' boisterous personality. One of his men summed up the general as "a very rough customer, but equally brave and full of fun." Another called him "a princely soldier" as "brave as a lion" and a "dashing, reckless, enthusiastic" general "idolized" by his troops.[26]

Hays thrived on the battlefield, where his exuberance sometimes boarded on excess and showboating. If the general occasionally exercised little restraint over his emotions, it never affected his decision making. He shone as combat leader, but had no aptitude for any post that took him off the firing line. Hays did not care for George Meade and believed he had made a huge mistake letting Lee get back into Virginia after Gettysburg. On July 18, 1863 Hays had written that the war "ought to have been settled

26 Wayne Mahood, *Alexander "Fighting Elleck" Hays: The Life of a Civil War General from West Point to the Wilderness* (Jefferson, NC, 2005), 121, 126; Tagg, *Generals of Gettysburg*, 53.

Brigadier General Alexander Hays
Library of Congress

in Pennsylvania. We are tired of scientific leaders and regard strategy as it is called—a humbug. Next thing to cowardice. What we want is a leader who will go ahead." [27]

With men like these at the head his column, Warren had no need to be concerned about his leading divisions blundering into a disaster. Nonetheless, in current circumstances it paid to be careful and avoid surprise. Warren therefore asked Gregg to deploy mounted vedettes on both flanks of the II Corps.

As the Federals hustled off to the northeast, Jeb Stuart appeared behind them with the same force he had led at Auburn—the brigades of Funsten and Gordon and Beckham's horse artillery. Along with a sharpshooter battalion from Rodes' division they clung to the Federal rear, but didn't venture too close and generally stayed out of the range of Gregg's troopers. But whenever the terrain permitted, Beckham unlimbered and threw a few shells at the withdrawing Yankees.[28]

The sound of this rolling fight could be heard from some distance away. Hill's troops, having listened to the rapid cannonading at Auburn earlier that morning, concluded this new round of firing indicated that Ewell was vigorously pressing the Union rearguard. If this were true, Lee's strategy was working as planned. The Confederates were on the verge of slamming into Meade's retreating horde and wrecking some part of the Union army.[29]

* * *

27 Mahood, *Alexander "Fighting Elleck" Hays*, 121, 126; Tagg, *Generals of Gettysburg*, 53.

28 OR 29, pt. 1, 241; Humphreys, *From Gettysburg to the Rapidan*, 23; Pyne, *First New Jersey*, 190. Warren's march dispositions were in contradiction to Meade's orders issued on the night of October 13/14, which instructed the II Corps to march on the southeast side of the O&A.

29 OR 29, pt. 1, 449; Kirkpatrick Diary, October 14, 1863, UT.

Major General George Sykes
Library of Congress

Major General George Sykes could hear the sporadic gunfire as well. At 41-years of age, Sykes was as regular army as a man could be. Born in Delaware in 1822, he had married into a prominent Maryland family and adopted that state as his home. After graduating from West Point in 1842 he fought against the Seminoles in Florida before serving in the Mexican War and later on the southwestern frontier. Lieutenant Frank Haskell described him as "a small rather thin man" whose thick brown hair and full beard surrounded a face of "red, pinched, rough looking skin, feeble blue eyes [and a] large nose." Although Sykes dressed well and had mastered the social graces, Haskell thought the general evinced the "air of one who is weary and a little ill natured."

When Meade became commander of the Army of the Potomac on the eve of Gettysburg, Sykes had assumed control of the V Corps. Before this assignment he enjoyed the distinction of leading primarily United States Army regular troops throughout the first half of the war as a regimental, brigade, and division commander. He had performed proficiently on the battlefield. One contemporary wrote that "it would have been hard to find a better officer" in the entire army. The second day at Gettysburg had been Sykes finest hour yet. His troops had played the pivotal role in saving Little Round Top and with it the battle and, some might argue, the war.

The army was Sykes' entire life. Although he could be personable with his peers and kindly to his underlings, the general was a stern disciplinarian utterly dedicated to his concept of duty. Perforce he came across as a man totally lacking in emotion. Some suspected Sykes cultivated this apparent coldness as a facade to ease the burden of ordering men to their deaths. His strict and meticulous adherence to regulations while at West Point had earned him the nickname "tardy George," a moniker that followed him throughout his life and reinforced the perception that he had what old soldiers called "the slows."[30]

30 Previous paragraphs based on Tagg, *Generals of Gettysburg*, 81-82; Warner, *Generals in Blue*, 492-93.

On the afternoon of October 14, however, Sykes didn't appear lethargic. The echo of skirmish fire welling up from the south made him anxious to get his corps moving again. In fact, the general appeared fixated on the idea of hurrying his men back to Centreville. At 2 p.m. he sent Warren a note saying that French was at Manassas, while his own troops at Milford awaited "the head of your column" and stood ready to resume their march the moment the vanguard of the II Corps approached Bristoe Station.

Perhaps feeling a bit sheepish at his seeming anxiety to continue the retreat, he further explained: "There is a long interval between French and I, which I ought to close up as soon as possible." Apparently only the presence of the III Corps could make Sykes feel secure, a junction with the II failing to suffice. Whatever the reason, his impatience was obvious. "Are you delayed by anything?" he asked Warren, before somewhat plaintively requesting, "let me hear from you." [31]

Shortly after Sykes sent this dispatch one of his officers reported seeing the front of Warren's column. The V Corps commander immediately ordered his men into motion. This, in turn, triggered the northward march of French's III Corps. But Sykes moved too soon. His aide had seen an advance patrol from the II Corps, not the main body which was still some miles away. The V Corps was pulling out of supporting distance well before Warren neared Bristoe Station, leading one of his officers to complain bitterly, "Sykes was told the II Corps was coming. So it was, and so was Christmas."[32]

*   *   *

As the V Corps began marching away from Milford, the Confederate Third Corps neared Bristoe Station. A. P. Hill's men recognized the road they were traveling and where it led. "We all knew the game now," noted Sgt. William Long of the 44th North Carolina, and every man expected a battle before the day ended. The pangs of empty stomachs disappeared as apprehension replaced hunger. A low murmur ran up and down Hill's column, and without instructions the troops closed ranks and quickened their pace. Intuitively sensing the nearness of combat, some men began checking their muskets to confirm they were in operating condition; others reached into cap pouches and cartridge boxes, fingering the contents to ensure their ammunition was in order.[33]

31 *Walker, Second Army Corps,* 343.

32 Humphreys, *From Gettysburg to the Rapidan,* 24; Walker, *Second Army Corps,* 343.

33 Long, "Reminiscences," Breckinridge papers, LC.

Hill rode forward to reconnoiter. When the general topped a rise a mile or so west of Bristoe Station, he could see Broad Run and the tiny hamlet of Milford which sat in an expanse of flat open ground nearly three-fourths of a mile wide. Masses of Union soldiers crowded around the little village, most of them already across the creek. For a brief moment Hill thought that he had missed his chance.[34]

But a closer look revealed the V Corps just starting to march away. Columns of Yankee troops and wagons were disappearing into the woods lining the north side of the plain—all of them moving rapidly toward Manassas and safety. Closer at hand, a great multitude of Federal stragglers could be seen resting on the south side of Broad Run, while others were in the process of crossing.

Hill thought he was looking at the rearguard of the Union army and realized this was the moment Lee's entire strategy aimed for. Perhaps it wasn't too late to land a blow! If he could attack swiftly, while the Yankees were still near Broad Run, he might wreck their rearguard, or at least fix it in place until Ewell came up. Then the united Rebel army could destroy a significant part of Meade's command. Hill would have to act quickly, however. The Federals were already moving, and would soon be beyond reach.

Feeling, as he put it, that "no time must be lost," Hill galloped back a mile and a half to the head of his corps. He found Henry Heth and ordered him to deploy three of his brigades in line of battle, leaving the fourth, Davis' brigade, in reserve. Hill also directed Walker to detach the 14th Tennessee from his brigade and deploy it as skirmishers to protect the right flank of the forming battle line. Then the Virginian sent a courier back down the road with orders for Poague's battalion of artillery to hurry forward.[35]

One of Heth's soldiers recalled that to avoid alerting the unsuspecting enemy, officers ordered their troops to maintain complete silence. The commands for shifting formations from column into line where given in hushed tones. Cooke's brigade formed to the right, the 48th North Carolina's left resting on the Greenwich Road, with the 27th, 15th, and 46th regiments stretching off into the woods. Kirkland's brigade deployed to the left of the thoroughfare, its rightmost regiment, the 44th North Carolina, just across the road from Cooke with the 26th, 47th, 52nd, and 11th North Carolina extending the line to its left. As the regiments uncoiled amid the tall pine trees, men piled knapsacks, bedrolls, and anything nonessential to the deadly business of fighting.

---

34 John W. Urban, *My Experiences Mid Shot and Shell and In the Rebel Den* (Lancaster, PA, 1882), 356.

35 *OR* 29, pt. 1, 434.

Despite Hill's desire for haste, it took time to form a battle line in the wooded terrain. Once Cooke and Kirkland were in position, officers quietly passed the order to move forward. As the Rebels advanced, the only sound was that of thousands of feet shuffling through the thick carpet of leaves lying on the forest floor. The unnatural silence surrounding the movement of two brigades merely intensified the already palpable tension. No man dared even break a twig for fear its snapping would echo like thunder.

The woods began to thin as the Confederate infantrymen moved east, the pines becoming shorter and scrawnier as the soldiers neared the edge of the forest. Just shy of the wood line, Heth's brigades halted. The men knelt and waited. Those not lost in thought spoke in half whispers despite the dryness in their throats. From somewhere beyond the trees the notes of a Yankee bugle drifted over the Rebel line, sending an electrifying sensation through the Southern ranks.[36]

The regiments of Cooke's and Kirkland's brigades were wearing wool blue-gray shell jackets and royal blue trousers which they had drawn from Richmond's quartermaster depot just before the campaign started. Certain that they were on the eve of battle, some men took old uniforms from their knapsacks and began changing clothes. Better to wear worn out and tattered garments into a fight, they reasoned, than risk ruining their new suits.[37]

After 30 minutes or so, the sound of Poague's batteries pounding along the road at full gallop broke the quiet. The cannons, limbers, and caissons raced through the waiting infantry then wheeled into line just beyond the trees. After finding suitable ground on the rise from which Hill had first seen the enemy, Poague's gunners unlimbered their pieces, stripped to the waist and prepared for action. No one had to designate their target. Poague noted that the "whole face of the earth in that vast plain seemed covered with Yankees."[38]

* * *

The sudden appearance of an entire battalion of Rebel artillery didn't go entirely unnoticed by the Federals. On the other side of Broad Run, Sykes' 3rd Division was

---

36 Previous paragraphs based on Long, "Reminiscences," Breckinridge papers, LC.

37 James Birdsong, ed., *Brief Sketches of the North Carolina State Troops in the War Between the States* (Raleigh, NC, 1894), 82. It is not certain that Kirkland's men had new uniforms. For details regarding Cooke's uniforms, see www.libertyrifles.org/research/regiments/27th-north-carolina-troops.

38 Humphreys, *From Gettysburg to the Rapidan*, 25; Robinson, *A.P. Hill*, 234; OR 29, pt. 1, 426-2, 430; Long "Reminiscences" Breckinridge papers, LC.

resting with stacked arms, some of its men preparing a hurried lunch while others dozed. A soldier in the 1st Pennsylvania looking back to the south alerted his commander to the arrival of artillery on a ridge about three-fourths of a mile beyond Broad Run. So totally unexpected was the sight, recalled one Federal, he and his momentarily "dumbfounded" comrades began to debate the meaning of this sudden apparition. Some men claimed the guns must belong to Warren's corps, others, warning they were Rebel cannon, hastily gathered up their equipment in preparation for a rapid retreat.[39]

The Pennsylvanians did not have to puzzle long. Only moments after dashing out of the woods the Confederate artillery was ready to open. Hill and his staff appeared on the road nearby. Their horses, caught up in the moment, reared and plunged as the general motioned to his bugler to sound commence firing. Before the musician could remove the instrument from his lips, Poague's 16 guns roared to life. The sudden burst of fire shattered the stillness with thunderclap surprise. As shells exploded in the air all around Broad Run, panic seemed to seize the Union troops. It now being "painfully evident," in the words of one Yankee, that the distant cannon belonged to the enemy, the Federals scrambled to get out of the line of fire. Commands to form orderly columns and double-quick to the rear instead produced "an inglorious flight to get out of range of the murderous guns."[40]

Sergeant Long, together with the rest of Harry Heth's troops, watched as the enemy "broke into a mad rush to get somewhere, anywhere, out of that hell." As Union officers vainly tried to rally their men, some Rebels convulsed with laughter at the "ludicrous" sight of Yankees fleeing toward Washington. Blue uniformed stragglers forgot their weariness and crowded across the creek as fast as possible. Major Poague, delighted at the effect of his shells, declared that he never saw "such scampering and skedaddling."[41]

Despite the seeming chaos, Hill's unexpected bombardment failed to halt Sykes' retreat. Even before Poague opened fire, most of the V Corps was already on the road and heading north—its first and second divisions, followed by the corps' artillery, having just disappeared into woods along the northern edge of the plain. The bursting shells merely convinced the Union column to quicken its pace toward Manassas.[42]

---

39 Urban, *My Experiences*, 356-57.

40 Long "Reminiscences" Breckinridge papers, LC; Poague had 7 smoothbore 12-pounder Napoleons, 6 x 12-pounder howitzers, 1 x 3-inch ordnance rifle and 1 x 10-pound Parrott gun.

41 *OR* 29, pt. 1, 426; Robertson, *A.P. Hill*, 234; Long "Reminiscences" Breckinridge papers, LC.

42 Robert Carter, *Four Brothers in Blue* (Austin, TX, 1979), 355.

The entire V Corps did not scurry away, however. Brig. Gen. Samuel Crawford's 3rd Division retired only as far as the shelter of the woods before halting. The two Pennsylvania brigades with the division—both temporarily under the command of 29-year old Col. William McCandless while Crawford was on leave—were under orders to follow the rest of the corps. Their substitute leader, however, recognized the threat posed by Heth's appearance and the fact that it might put Warren's troops in great danger.

Born in Ireland and orphaned while still a baby, McCandless had immigrated to the U.S. at the age of 6 with an uncle. Nicknamed "Buck," he first made his living as a locomotive engineer but in 1858 became a successful lawyer. Appointed a major in the 2nd Pennsylvania in 1861, the Irishman earned praise the next year for his performance during the Peninsula campaign. In August 1862, a Rebel bullet struck him in the groin at the battle of 2nd Bull Run. He missed Antietam because of his wound but was back in the field in time to fight at Fredericksburg, where his regiment—a part of Meade's division—briefly penetrated the Confederate line before being repulsed. McCandless assumed charge of his brigade when its commander went down with a wound. On July 2 at Gettysburg the colonel led his regiments in the final spasm of fighting around Devil's Den.[43]

McCandless was not the sort of man to panic, and after holding what he called a "hasty consultation" with his brigade commanders, he made the gutsy decision to stay put. This not only violated orders but ensured his division would lose contact with the rest of the V Corps almost immediately. But the colonel was certain circumstances required him to stand fast, regardless of consequences.

That decision resulted in the almost instantaneous isolation of his division. As soon as the first Rebel shells exploded north of Broad Run, Col. Martin Hardin, commanding McCandless' 3rd Brigade, sent a courier racing after the V Corps column to request artillery support. Despite the urgency of Hardin's appeal, several more couriers were required before someone sent a single battery to the division's assistance. The rest of the V Corps left its own 3rd Division and Warren's II Corps to their fate.[44]

*   *   *

---

43 Friends of Mount Moriah Cemetery, "Col. William 'Buck' McCandless—Soldier and Citizen from Philadelphia, http://bit.ly/2sWZiZQ, accessed 14 June 2018.

44 M. D. Harden, *History of the Twelfth Regiment Pennsylvania Reserve Volunteer Corps* (New York, NY, 1890), 165-7.

From A. P. Hill's vantage point, the Confederate barrage had not only startled the Yankees but sped them on their retreat as well. That foreseeable result threatened to deny Confederate infantry the opportunity Hill envisioned. If his troops did not move forward speedily the Yankees would escape.

At this point Heth had two brigades in line of battle, Cooke's on the right side of the Greenwich Road and Kirkland's on the left. Walker's brigade was still forming behind Kirkland, its right flank resting on the road. Due to the great disparity in numbers between the two brigades and the detachment of the 14th Tennessee as skirmishers, Walker's line stretched only half as far as Kirkland's. Since they had just shifted formation, Walker's regiments had not yet moved into position on Kirkland's left.

Hill, sensing his chance for a significant victory slipping away, could wait no longer. He ordered Heth to advance his division at once. Walker, still trying to form on Kirkland, would have to do his best to get into position while on the move. Heth directed Kirkland and Cooke to go forward immediately; then he rode to Walker and personally explained the situation. The enemy was running; there was no time to wait for his brigade to extend the line. He would have to gain Kirkland's left while on the march.

Buglers sounded the advance, and the Rebel line began to move. Hill told Heth to take his command to Broad Run then march by his left flank to cross the ford at Milford before pursuing the fleeing enemy. But just as Heth turned to give that order, Federal skirmishers unexpectedly appeared on his right flank and took position along the crest of a knoll to the south and about 400 yards from the O&A railroad tracks. Concerned, Heth rode to Hill. Pointing at the blue skirmish line, he asked if the advance should continue. General Hill, confronted with this unanticipated development, hesitated and "directed that it should be deferred for the present."

*   *   *

The Union skirmishers whose presence gave Hill pause were the leading element of Warren's II Corps, which was now closing on Bristoe Station from the south. In fact, it was almost as close to Broad Run as the Rebels. After leaving Catlett's Station, Warren had set a brisk pace. Although Gregg's cavalry and Caldwell's infantry maintained a running rearguard skirmish with Stuart's cavalry and Rodes' detached sharpshooters, the II Corps' route to Bristoe Station remained unobstructed. Confident that the V Corps was waiting up ahead, Warren's officers felt little anxiety for their front. The danger lay in the rear. Mindful of Warren's desire to establish strongpoints to fend off a more aggressive Rebel pursuit, Lt. Col. Morgan detached Carroll's brigade and Battery I, 1st US Artillery from Hays' division and ordered them to hold a hill at the intersection of a road leading south toward Bristersburg. Carroll was to remain in place until the tail of the corps had safely passed.

Warren and his subordinates thought the movement to Centreville was going off smoothly. General Meade finally thought so, too. Just a short while ago he had telegraphed Halleck that his withdrawal had been "successful" thus far. Despite ongoing skirmishing around the edges of the army and Lee's advance from Warrenton, Meade assured the general-in-chief that the Confederates would "hardly be able to arrest" the Union army's progress at this late stage of the campaign.

Meade was wrong, or at least potentially so, and Warren's soldiers would be the first men in blue to realize that fact. Their officers erroneously but understandably assumed the V Corps was at Milford and awaiting their approach. With that comforting thought in mind Warren's column had marched blissfully along until it was within two miles or so of Bristoe Station. Then, as suddenly as if a bolt of lightning had struck from a clear blue sky, the sound of Poague's cannon startled everyone in the II Corps.[45]

Unable to see what lay ahead because of a neck of dense woods and the gently rolling terrain, Webb, whose troops were marching on the northwest side of the railroad tracks, took the immediate precaution of throwing the 1st Minnesota to his front as skirmishers. He also deployed the 59th New York and 7th Michigan as flankers to protect the left of the 2nd Division's column. As those three regiments fanned out, Webb's main body approached the southern terminus of a railroad embankment which jutted like an earthen scar northeastward toward Broad Run. Recognizing the advantage of using this topographical quirk to protect his men, the general led his column over the tracks and onto a trail running along the eastern side of the embankment. Once behind this shelter, Webb ordered his troops to double-quick toward Broad Run, still more than a mile away.[46]

---

45 Previous paragraphs based upon OR 29, pt. 1, 242, 290, 430, 433; pt. 2, 313.

46 George A. Bruce, *The Twentieth Regiment of Massachusetts Volunteer Infantry, 1861-1865* (Boston, MA, 1906), 308; James A. Wright, *No More Gallant a Deed: A Civil War Memoir of the First Minnesota Volunteers* (St. Paul, MN, 2001), 362-363; Edward Walker to Knight, Nov. 5, 1863, Lewis Leigh Jr. Collection, USMHI; ibid., pt. 1, 281, 287, 288, 283. There is some ambiguity about the deployment of Webb's and Hays' columns as they approached Bristoe Station. In his official report, Warren stated that Webb marched on the northwest side of the tracks and that Hays moved on the southeast side. Bruce, in *Twentieth Regiment*, claimed that Webb and Hays marched in parallel columns on the "northwest and northeast" sides of the railroad. Meade's orders were to move on the south side of the railroad. Wright, in *No More Gallant a Deed*, says that Union soldiers marched on the railroad tracks while wagons, officers etc., kept to the roads alongside the rails. Colonel Wass, commanding Webb's third brigade, was specific about Webb throwing his division to the east side of the tracks and getting ahead of Hays. Marching on railroad tracks is a difficult exercise for troops, and Webb would have had no reason to do so, although it is probable large numbers of stragglers may have walked down the railroad bed in

As the 2nd Division shifted position, Warren and Hill's troops continued on their collision course. Men in both corps vaguely began catching sight of distant bodies of unknown soldiers between gaps in the trees. Almost imperceptibly an ominous, foreboding atmosphere descended on the valley of Broad Run.[47]

Into the increasingly dangerous void between the opposing columns went the 1st Minnesota. Major Mark Downie had formed his regimental skirmish line west of the railroad perpendicular to the division's direction of march. His line faced northeast with its right flank resting on the tracks. While Webb's column moved along the railroad embankment to Broad Run, Downie ordered his men to advance obliquely to the left at the double-quick. Although he tried to keep his right flank apace with the head of the main column, Downie reasoned that sidling his line diagonally to the northwest and farther from the railroad would create a wider buffer between his regiment and the rest of Webb's division. But the Minnesota skirmishers had barely moved a few rods from the O&A when they saw a column of troops emerge from a wooded area about 300 yards distant from their left flank. Although it was too far to see well and no breeze unfurled the indistinct formation's flag, the Yankees could tell that the distant figures wore blue trousers. For a moment some of Downie's perplexed skirmishers thought the mystery troops must be part of Caldwell's division.[48]

The unpleasant truth swiftly became evident. The opposing column seemed as surprised to see the Federals as the Federals were to see it. After partially halting and turning to look at the Minnesotans, the anonymous formation suddenly rushed a line of skirmishers toward a piece of woods between the rival lines. Only an enemy would respond like this![49]

Downie sent word back that he had encountered Rebels in some strength. In response, Webb ordered the major to seize a knoll some 400 yards northwest of the railroad tracks astride the Gainesville Road. As the Minnesotans advanced they bore down on Confederate troops screening the forward movement of Heth's division. The two skirmish lines moved diagonally on a converging path until the left flank of the 1st Minnesota struck the right flank of the Rebel line in a growth of thick bushes. The rival

---

order to avoid the main columns on either side of the tracks. During the Civil War, any manmade feature along a railroad line was referred to as a "cut." These could be embankments used to get tracks over low ground (technically a "fill"), or a trench-like excavation through high ground (technically a "cut").

47 OR 29, pt. 1, 277, 434, 426; Perry, *Letters from a Surgeon*, 110.

48 Wright, *No More Gallant Deed*, 363; Edward Walker to Knight, Nov. 5, 1863, USMHI. One rod equals 5.5 feet.

49 Edward Walker to Knight, Nov. 5, 1863, USMHI.

skirmishers reflexively blazed away at one another as each side momentarily came to a surprised halt.[50]

Downie had encountered a significant number of Rebels, and he decided against trying to extend his line to the left. Instead the major ordered his men to pivot parallel to the railroad—pulling the left flank of the 1st Minnesota back while wheeling its right flank forward and to the west like some giant seesaw. For the men on the right of Downie's line this meant a rapid advance up the steep slope of the knoll Webb wanted them to occupy. The Yankees rushed forward at trail arms. One or two men with breath to spare gave a short yell as they ran for the crest. Once they reached the summit, the Federals could suddenly see most of Heth's division advancing toward Broad Run preceded by a thick cloud of skirmishers.[51]

The Union troops found themselves no more than a hundred yards away from a Confederate skirmish line, which had made a movement similar to Downie's and was heading directly toward his position. After quickly taking cover behind a considerable amount of rubbish scattered across the hill—the discarded refuse of former encampments—the Minnesotans opened fire. Although Orderly Sergeant James Wright doubted anyone was able to aim well after the long uphill run, the Yankee bullets had an effect. The Rebel line came to a halt and stepped backwards a few paces.[52]

As the rival skirmishers exchanged a brisk fire, Downie and his men could see large numbers of Confederates barely a quarter of a mile away. There must be a "million of them," cried one stunned Yankee. In fact, there were only about 4,000 Rebels in view, but under the circumstances none of the Minnesotans took issue with their comrade's assessment of the situation.[53]

*   *   *

While Confederate and Federal skirmishers "pelted away" at each other, A. P. Hill and Henry Heth pondered what to do for ten long minutes. The unexpected appearance of Downie's Yankee skirmishers was an obvious cause for concern. Hill

50 Ibid.; Wright, *No More Gallant Deed*, 363. The Confederate troops were probably the 14th Tennessee Infantry from Walker's brigade, but no source discovered thus far identifies them definitively. It is possible Downie decided to seize the hill on his own initiative.

51 Ibid. "Trail arms" was a common arms position used when troops were moving quickly. The soldier, with his right arm fully extended at his side, carries the musket in his right hand at a sloping angle of about 45 degrees.

52 Edward Walker to Knight, Nov. 5, 1863, USMHI; Wright, *No More Gallant Deed*, 363.

53 Wright, *No More Gallant Deed*, 364.

sent word to Brig. Gen. Cooke to watch out for his flank, but this was a stop gap measure. Knowing that he needed more troops to protect Heth's right, Hill sent a courier with orders for Richard Anderson to send forward McIntosh's artillery battalion as well as Carnot Posey's and Edward A. Perry's infantry brigades. Hill believed the arrival of these reinforcements would suffice to adequately protect his corps from any real danger.[54]

The ordered movements occurred swiftly and once Hill saw the head of Anderson's column appear he felt confident in telling Heth to resume his advance. Not everyone shared Hill's sense of security. General Cooke strongly believed that the skirmish line he confronted had to be screening something dangerous. He didn't want to move at all, and riding to Heth, warned against going ahead.[55]

Hill's order to renew the advance reached Heth just before Cooke did. Despite his subordinate's concerns, all Heth could do was reiterate his instructions. Cooke in turn could do nothing but obey. Still certain he was walking into a terribly perilous situation, the native Missourian told Heth: "Well, I will advance, and if they flank me, I will face my men about and cut my way out!" With that declaration, the resolute brigadier rode back to his regiments and ordered them forward.[56]

The "wonderful display of force" Heth's troops presented as they lurched back into motion awed Downie's skirmishers. Only a quarter of a mile behind the Confederate skirmish line, Cooke's and Kirkland's brigades steadily trod onward, the center of each command crossing open ground while their flanks remained hidden by woods. An eighth of a mile behind Kirkland, the Northerners could see Walker's advancing ranks and behind Walker a column of foot soldiers—probably the head of Davis' brigade—"leaving the road and marching out into the field." The smoke and thunder of Poague's batteries, which were still shooing the rear of the V Corps away from Milford, framed the movements of the Rebel infantry,[57]

Several hundred yards behind the 1st Minnesota, the Federals were scrambling to deal with this dangerously fluid situation. After crossing onto the eastern side of the railroad embankment, Alexander Webb had double-quicked his division's two brigades to the foot of a modest ridge overlooking the railway and just south of the creek. As the Federal infantry jogged forward, either Morgan or Webb ordered Lt. Thomas "Fred" Brown's Battery B, 1st Rhode Island Light Artillery to take position on the same ridge and "fire a few rounds" toward a line of Rebels now visible some 600 yards away.

54 *OR* 29, pt. 1, 426; Edward Walker to Knight, Nov. 5, 1863, USMHI.

55 *OR* 29, pt. 1, 434, 426.

56 Robertson, *A.P. Hill*, 236.

57 Wright, *No More Gallant Deed*, 364.

With no instructions to the contrary, Webb intended to frustrate the encircling noose of advancing Confederates by denying them control of the railroad and ensuring the II Corps had a viable route over Broad Run. As Brown's six 12-pounder Napoleons roared into life, Webb ordered his brigades to move forward and take shelter behind the railroad embankment. For a brief moment, the Federal troops pressed against the protecting wall of earth, gratefully catching their breath after a mile-long sprint.

Across the valley, Cooke's and Kirkland's brigades moved from the pines onto open ground while Walker was still moving through them. The Rebel line debauched from the woods and down into the valley of Broad Run. As more of the Confederate infantrymen appeared, the 1st Minnesota's skirmish line intensified its fire.

Colonel Edward Hall's 46th North Carolina, on Cooke's right flank and closest to the enemy, was the first to feel the brunt of the Union fire. "Much annoyed" by the musketry peppering his regiment, Hall sent word to Cooke that he was detaching a company to deal with the Union skirmishers. But a single company proved unequal to the task, there being far more Yankees than it could handle, and it was driven in. Hall responded in the only way possible: he halted his regiment, dropped out of Cooke's line, wheeled right, and faced the enemy skirmishers.

*   *   *

As the 46th North Carolina turned to confront its tormentors, the Federals continued shifting position. Webb knew the V Corps was to have been waiting at Milford just beyond Broad Run. He ordered his 1st Brigade led by Col. Francis E. Heath to hurry over the railroad bridge and connect with Sykes. Battery B was told to cease fire and find high ground north of the creek from which it could support Heath's infantry. Brown's guns and caissons forded the run a short distance east of the railroad and climbed up a steep hill a few hundred yards north of their original position. The gunners unlimbered near a derelict windmill on a barren knoll overlooking the railroad bridge. Here Brown's battery obtained a magnificent field of fire covering almost the entire valley. It also found itself unexpectedly alone and unsupported.[58]

Battery B's sudden isolation came courtesy of Gouverneur Warren who had been keeping watch on Caldwell's rearguard when he heard the sound of Poague's cannon. Instantly comprehending a new threat emerging, the general raced northward to Bristoe Station—an area he knew well from his time as the army's chief engineer. The war had not been kind to Bristoe. Soldiers had burned its few buildings during the 2nd

---

58 OR 29, pt. 1, 277, 280, 305, 309, 435; Perry, *Letters from a Surgeon*, 110. An Amtrak railway station sits on the hill Brown occupied.

Manassas Campaign, leaving only a couple of forlorn chimneys and foundations to mark their passing. A handful of old shanties—the remnants of some past encampment—and the ruins of a single house stood near the railroad bridge just west of the track. The fact that the former railway station's fields and hills were about to become a battlefield accentuated Bristoe's already melancholy appearance.

Warren quickly surveyed the unfolding scene and with commendable swiftness perceived a grand opportunity. He countermanded the order for Heath's brigade to cross the creek and directed Webb's entire division to form line behind the railroad embankment south of the bridge. There was no time for Brown's guns to limber and re-cross the stream, as the Rebels were already shifting toward the railroad. Battery B, unsupported but for a handful of stragglers it had dragooned into providing a modicum of protection, would have to make its fight alone.[59]

South of Broad Run the 1st Minnesota still clung to its knoll 400 yards west of the railroad embankment. As the regiment kept up a steady rifle fire, Cooke's and Kirkland's brigades paused to realign their ranks. Colonel Hall took the opportunity to reform his 46th North Carolina on the right of Cooke's battle line. As the Rebels again began moving, Capt. John Ball, commanding Company F of the Minnesota regiment, shouted to his men that they had to hold onto their knoll until the "last minute"—a minute, the Federal skirmishers knew, couldn't be long-delayed.[60]

They were right. John Cooke remained convinced that a serious threat lurked beyond his eastern flank. Stung by the fire of Maj. Downie's Minnesotans, Cooke decided to disregard Hill's orders to pursue the enemy north of Broad Run. Instead the general ordered a right wheel by his entire brigade so as to swing his command to face the bothersome Yankee skirmishers head on. Kirkland, seeing Cooke wheel, followed suit a few minutes later. Walker's brigade, several hundred yards to the rear, failed to perceive Kirkland's change of direction, and as the North Carolinians wheeled, their left flank moved ever farther and more quickly away from Walker's right. With no orders to change the axis of his advance, Walker continued to and across Broad Run, thus taking his regiments completely out of the coming fight.[61]

Meanwhile Cooke and Kirkland brought their front parallel to the railroad, their left and right flanks respectively resting on the road running westward to Gainesville and eastward over the railroad tracks to Brentsville. Once the Rebel lines completed their wheel, reported one Yankee, their skirmishers rose up out of the bushes and "came on firing." That was the last straw for Maj. Downie: he ordered his Minnesotans

---

59 *OR* 29, pt. 1, 242.

60 Ibid., 435; Wright, *No More Gallant Deed*, 365.

61 *OR* 29, pt. 1, 435, 433, 431, 427.

Lt. Brown's Battery B, 1st Rhode Island Artillery firing from north of Broad Run by Alfred Waud. The upper left inset shows Arnold's Battery firing from its hilltop position behind the railroad embankment south of the creek. *Library of Congress*

to fall back at the run. The Confederates were coming fast, racing up the west side of the knoll with unstoppable force. With no time to reform the regiment, Downie passed the command to make for the railroad while still deployed in open order. Standing up with the enemy so close took considerable courage, for just then it was more dangerous to run than to lay still. But a Southern prison held even less appeal, and to a man the Yankees decided it was better to seize a chance to escape if possible. The thin line of blue skirmishers fired one last volley, jumped to its feet, and ran for all it was worth.[62]

Everything "went with a rush" wrote a Union man. The Federals had barely abandoned the crest when Rebels took it. Screaming their trademark yell, they hurled a storm of bullets at the fleeing Minnesotans. Sergeant James Wright thought it an "intensely exciting moment" as he strained to sprint at his best speed back toward the railroad. Firing downhill, the Confederates mostly overshot their targets. Wright marveled at the "little puffs of dust" popping up in front of him as bullets plunked the earth, sometimes ricocheting with a "peculiar whining sound" he had never heard on any battlefield. Not every round went astray. Rebel fire killed or wounded a number of Downie's men during their desperate dash. Most of those the Minie balls spared had close calls as projectiles passed through their hats, clothing, and knapsacks.[63]

*   *   *

Along the railroad, the 82nd New York and part of the 15th Massachusetts of Col. Heath's 1st Brigade had already crossed the bridge over Broad Run when Webb received Warren's message to hold south of the creek. By now Confederate skirmishers

---

62 Wright, *No More Gallant Deed*, 365; Edward Walker to Knight, Nov. 5, 1863, USMHI.

63 Wright, *No More Gallant Deed*, 365; Edward Walker to Knight, Nov. 5, 1863, USMHI; M. H. Bassett, *From Bull Run to Bristow Station*, 32.

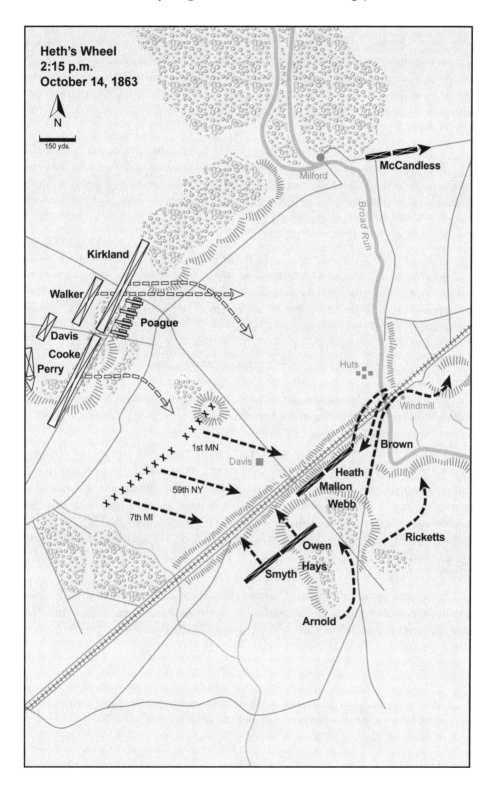

had taken possession of some huts near the creek about 100 yards from the railroad. These sharpshooters were firing on Heath's men as the colonel ordered his troops to halt, turn around, and hurry back across the bridge. In the resulting to and fro, the 1st Brigade connected with the right flank of Col. James E. Mallon's 3rd Brigade, still occupying the eastern side of the railroad embankment. By the time the two commands joined, however, a 150-yard gap yawned between Heath's right flank and the stream.

With Heath and Mallon connected, Webb had a solid battle line behind the railroad embankment. His left flank stretched several hundred feet south of the intersection of the O&A and the Brentsville Road. Although strong, it was hardly a perfect position. The substantial interval between Webb's right flank and Broad Run exposed his line to a flank attack. A potentially greater weakness was the lack of an embankment where the road crossed the tracks. The gap was no wider than a typical company front (20-25 men wide). But by a quirk of fate the 42nd New York—which contained a large number of conscripts going into their first battle—occupied this spot. That meant raw recruits would face the oncoming Rebels without the protection afforded the rest of the Union line by the railroad's impromptu breastwork. If they panicked and ran, the enemy might pour through the opening and rupture Webb's line.

Perhaps worse, only Brown's remote guns were providing artillery support, and Webb's left flank dangled in the air—guarded by nothing more than the thin skirmish line of the 7th Michigan and 59th New York. These skirmishers had given way more quickly than the 1st Minnesota and had already retreated behind the railroad. If the Rebels struck now, Webb's flanks might be enveloped, the railroad captured, and the II Corps cut off from Broad Run and the rest of Meade's army.

Luckily for the Union, Warren was already taking steps to prevent those calamities. While musket balls whistled around him, the general sent staff officers rushing to Capt. Robert Bruce Ricketts with orders for battery F&G, 1st Pennsylvania Light Artillery to take position on the high ground Brown's cannon had previously occupied. As Rickett's six 3-inch ordnance rifles raced towards Broad Run, similar orders reached Battery A, 1st Rhode Island Light Artillery. Its commander, Capt. William Arnold, told his gunners to mount the limbers and caissons before ordering his teamsters to whip their horses to full gallop to reach the field as fast as possible.[64]

Until these guns were in place, Warren realized the chance of total disaster quite likely. He could only trust his judgment and hope the Rebels would allow him the minutes he so desperately needed before battle was joined in earnest.

---

64 Previous paragraphs based upon *OR* 29, pt. 1, 242, 280, 282, 288, 287, 308.

Chapter 24

"I Expect We'd Better Charge"

The Railroad Cut—Minnesota Race—Kirkland and Cooke Turn—McIntosh Enters the Fray—Charge—Brief Breakthrough—Devastating Fire—Repulse—Guns Captured

As the boom of cannon and rattle of skirmish fire grew in intensity amid the warm afternoon temperatures on October 14, increasing numbers of troops moved toward Bristoe Station as if drawn to slaughter by some malevolent invisible force.

While Union artillery hastened to join the struggle, Hays' division reached the field after having double-quicked more than a mile to catch up with Webb's brigades. Hays' command came to a halt standing in column east of and parallel to the railroad embankment, some 150 yards to their left. Warren noted that the 3rd Division was in a perfect position to lengthen Webb's line and he quickly told Hays to left face his column and "run for the railroad cut." Hays instantly shouted to his brigade commanders "By the left flank, double quick; railroad cut!" It was hardly a textbook order, though effective it in no way produced a movement of parade ground precision.[1]

The troops executed a left face, undoubling their ranks to form a line of battle facing the railroad and then the entire line ran at full speed for the embankment. Unfortunately for Hays, the long jog into position had exhausted many of his men. Well before the division stopped, a significant number of winded soldiers had fallen behind. For the moment, every regiment was understrength and slightly disorganized.

---

1 OR 29, pt. 1, 242, 289; Morris Brown Jr. to parents, October 15, 1863, HC. "By the left flank" was an improper order, as it is given only while troops are in motion. From a standing position the proper command is "Front!" Both orders, however, have the same effect of causing the troops to left face, undoubling their files as they do so and forming a two-rank deep line of battle. Both commands can only be given if the column in moving "right in front."

Numerically at least, this deficit was overcome by the swarm of stragglers who happened to be between the railroad and Hays' command as it lunged for the embankment. Much to their dismay these men were caught up in the rush of the 3rd Division and involuntarily absorbed into its line as it swept forward. "Consequently," reported an observer, "the regiments went into action in any order but military." With gaps in their own ranks and random stragglers mixed into their formations, the officers would have a challenge forming a manageable line once they reached the tracks.[2]

Nonetheless it was a dramatic moment. Warren was one of the few in position to see the movements of both sides. From his vantage point he believed "a more inspiring scene could not be imagined" than the one playing out now, with "the enemy's line of battle boldly moving forward," against Webb's division "steadily awaiting it." At the same instant Hays' brigades were racing toward the Rebels at the double-quick, flags snapping in the wind, even as Federal artillery "was taking up position at a gallop and going into action."[3]

The scene didn't impress the Northern troops rushing toward the railroad. Minie balls "flew about our heads like hail," recalled one soldier, while another thought the "shower of bullets" he encountered on his sprint to the railroad the worst he had "ever passed through," surpassing even Gettysburg. As Hays' command advanced across a flat open plain without even so much as a single bush for cover, numerous bluecoats fell dead or wounded before reaching the embankment. The rest, "gasping for breath" as they ran, placed percussion caps on their unloaded muskets and unleashed a "crackling volley" as they "popped" caps to ensure the nipple and breech of their weapons were clear of moisture or obstruction.[4]

Heedless of its losses or lack of breath and thorough organization, Hays' division plunged forward. Warren and his staff dismounted and stood among the troops urging them on with shouts of "To the railroad ditch! Quick! Quick!" In just a few minutes, the 3rd Division stood behind the embankment, its men rapidly loading their muskets as officers worked to bring something like regular order to their formations. The II Corps now had four brigades facing Heth. Alexander Webb's 1st Brigade (Heath) stood nearest the railroad bridge with Webb's 3rd brigade (Mallon) to its left. Hays' 3rd Brigade (Colonel Joshua Owen) held the line between Mallon and Hays' 1st Brigade (Colonel Thomas Smyth), stationed on the far left flank.[5]

---

2   Cheryl Wells, ed., *A Surgeon in the Army of the Potomac* (Montreal, Canada, 2008), 73.

3   *OR* 29, pt. 1, 242.

4   Simmons, *One Hundred and Twenty-fifth New York*, 157-58; Morris Brown Jr. to parents, October 15, 1863, Hamilton College, Wells, *Surgeon in the Army of the Potomac*, 73.

5   Wells, *Surgeon in the Army of the Potomac*, 73.

Alfred Waud drew this sketch of Lt. Brown during the battle of Bristoe Station. *Library of Congress*

Hays' arrival and the deployment of additional batteries immeasurably strengthened the Federal position. Harry Heth saw Cooke and Kirkland swerve toward the railroad tracks but could not see Warren's infantry concealed in scattered woods and behind the railroad embankment. The several 30- or 40- foot high hills behind the railroad *were* easy to spot, though, and Heth realized they provided "an admirable position" for the enemy's batteries. The railroad embankment, however, was the critical topographic feature. About as high as a man's head, it gave "perfect protection" to Warren's infantry. Heth admitted the position "was as strong, or stronger, naturally and artificially, than military art could have made it with many hours of work."[6]

As yet unaware of the formidable Federal position, the bulk of Heth's division continued moving east. The skirmishers screening Cooke's brigade were atop the knoll

6   *OR* 29, pt. 1, 431-432, 427; George Patch to parents, October 15, 1863, VHS. The average height of a Civil War soldier was between 5 feet 6 inches and 5 feet 8 inches.

recently evacuated by the 1st Minnesota and firing into the backs of their fleeing opponents. But neither Cooke nor Kirkland could yet spy the Union troops formed east of the railroad. Unfortunately for the Rebels, Capt. Brown's battery on the other side of Broad Run had both Confederate brigades in full view, and his guns immediately took the North Carolinians under fire. This sudden barrage led Hill to order Poague's gunners to shift to a better position and turn their sights on the rival cannon.

Meanwhile, Maj. Downie's 1st Minnesota skirmishers were still running diagonally down the slope of the knoll from which they had first engaged the enemy. They could discern no sign of life along the railroad—not a flag, man, or hat—but assumed friendly troops must be there. Hidden behind the embankment, Maj. Edmund Rice ordered his 19th Massachusetts to hold its fire until Downie's regiment got inside Federal lines. As the Yankee infantry waited with readied muskets, Rickett's and Arnold's batteries rolled into position atop the hills behind the railroad. About 100 yards to Arnold's left front, a single gun from Captain Nelson Ames Battery G, 1st New York Light was also unlimbering and preparing to join the contest.

On the western side of the O&A the Confederates too were bringing more artillery into action. As Cooke and Kirkland wheeled, 11 guns from Maj. David McIntosh's battalion reached the battlefield. The 27-year old South Carolinian sent Capt. William Hurt with two Whitworth cannon to find a position best suited to their exceptionally long range. Then McIntosh followed Hill's staff engineer, Maj. Robert Duncan, to the edge of the plain with his remaining nine guns. Duncan pointed to the hill just abandoned by the Minnesotans as the spot for McIntosh to post his guns.

The artilleryman did not like what he saw. The position would expose his men to crossfire from the Federal battery shooting from across Broad Run and another unlimbering beyond the railroad. Once all the Federal guns were in action, they would be in perfect position to concentrate on his cannon. McIntosh was having none of this; he ordered his batteries to take cover and then sent his ordnance officer to advise Hill that the indicated location was exceedingly disadvantageous. He also persuaded Duncan to ride to the general and bolster the case against deploying onto the knoll.[7]

While McIntosh's battalion hesitated, Cooke's and Kirkland's commands continued toward the railroad and the Federal line. Nobody could describe this as a grand, irresistible charge. The nine North Carolina regiments moved forward somewhat hesitantly, unsure what lay ahead. Depending on where a regiment stood in its brigade's line of battle, the oncoming Confederates were encountering vastly different kinds of terrain.

---

7 Preceding paragraphs based upon *OR* 29, pt. 1, 285, 306, 427, 436-37.

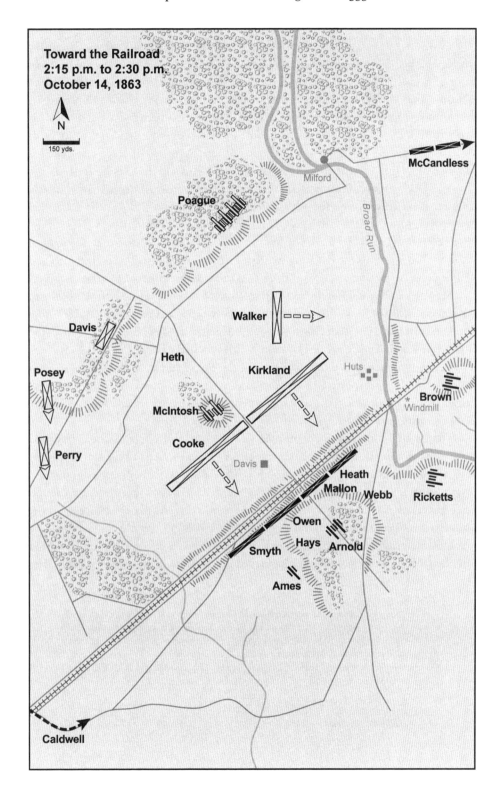

Toward the Railroad
2:15 p.m. to 2:30 p.m.
October 14, 1863

N

150 yds.

Two low ridges lay in front of Webb's command, for example, which initially shielded Kirkland's troops from enemy infantry fire. Cooke's men were not so lucky. In front of his battle line stretched the farm of T. K. Davis, the former sheriff of Prince William County. The war had ruined his once thriving establishment and turned his family into refugees. All that remained of Davis' former prosperity were the ruins of his two-story home, which sat immediately south of the Gainesville Road about 100 yards west of the railroad. His homestead, stripped of fences, devoid of crops and denuded of much of its timber, was now a large open plain—and a perfect killing zone.[8]

The Davis farm did not present a uniform field over which Cooke could attack. The left flank battalion of the 48th North Carolina advanced down the road over mostly flat ground, but its other battalion confronted the steep northern slope of the knoll recently defended by the 1st Minnesota. The 27th North Carolina, to the right of the 48th, had to climb the daunting western face of the hill itself, while the 15th and 46th regiments ascended a much more gradual and wooded ridge south of the height.

Moving at a slightly faster pace than the rest of Cooke's brigade, the 27th North Carolina crested the knoll first and its commander ordered a pause so the rest of the line could catch up. The 48th North Carolina, advancing more or less straight down the Brentsville Road, had a clear line of sight which revealed part of the 42nd New York standing in the open where the road crossed the tracks and no embankment offered concealment. Once it spotted these enemy troops the 48th opened fire. The rest of the brigade joined in, and the rattle of musketry spread rapidly from the left to the right of Cooke's entire line.[9]

The 1st Minnesota's sprint to the railroad ended just as the bulk of Cooke's brigade came into full view from the embankment. Major Downie's men tumbled into a slightly sunken road running along the eastern side of the O&A and then scrambled frantically up the embankment before sliding down the other side. To their great relief they found the Federal line standing just where they had supposed it had to be. The moment the Minnesotans cleared their front Hays' division and Mallon's brigade opened fire.[10]

Downie tried to reform his regiment, but that proved impossible. His men melded into the ranks of whatever unit they happened to encounter and joined the battle. The

---

8   Davis was a well-known Union sympathizer. In 1861-62 Confederate troops in the area had wrecked his nearby store. The family moved to Brentsville following the Aug. 1862 battle of Kettle Run, after which Rebel soldiers destroyed much of what remained of his farm. Eventually Davis relocated to Alexandria and then Washington, DC. US Southern Claims Commission, Disallowed and Barred Claims, 1871-1880. Thomas K. Davis, NARA RG 123, U.S. Court of Claims, Cong. Jur. #3575, Thomas K. Davis, Box 475.

9   OR 29, pt. 1, 435; Bassett, *Brief Sketch NCST*, 81-83.

10 Wright, *No More Gallant Deed*, 365.

7th Michigan and 59th New York had a similar experience. As Hays' troops took position along the embankment, the two regiments found themselves mixed in with the 3rd Division's line and essentially fought the battle as part of Hays' command.[11]

*   *   *

The contest was now fully joined along Cooke's front. The Rebels, having advanced over the summit of the knoll, could finally see most of the II Corps infantry behind the railroad. Undaunted, if somewhat surprised, the brigade came to an unordered halt about halfway down the slope. As they stood there firing toward the railroad, the North Carolinians presented Warren's line with an easy target. Intense fire quickly took a toll, especially among mounted officers. Not long after his brigade stepped onto the eastward slope of the knoll, a bullet shattered Cooke's left shinbone and knocked him out of the fight. Colonel John Gilmer, Jr., commanding the 27th North Carolina, also went down badly wounded. With Cooke disabled, the brigade staff sent word for Col. Edward Hall, the senior regimental officer, to take charge of the brigade. Lt. Col. George Whitfield assumed command of the 27th, while Lt. Col. William Saunders took charge of the 46th North Carolina from Hall.[12]

After learning that Cooke had been hit, Hall began to make his way toward the center of the brigade. Hoping to get control of the formation, he ordered the troops to cease fire as he passed down the line. The Federals, however, continued to pour a withering fusillade into the stalled North Carolinians and handfuls of men were falling killed or wounded every few moments. When Hall reached the rear of the 27th North Carolina he met Lt. Col. Whitfield, who had been moving down the line looking for him. The brigade would be slaughtered if it stayed put, Whitfield shouted; they either had to charge or retreat. With Union rifle and artillery fire tearing fearful gaps in his line, Hall could only agree and told Whitfield "I expect we'd better charge."[13]

McIntosh was still waiting for an answer from A. P. Hill about the placement of artillery when Hall's infantry began pressing toward the railroad embankment. The major felt he could delay no longer. He decided to advance at least some of his guns and directed five rifled cannon to deploy onto the knoll. Three of these pieces were from Lt. Samuel Wallace's 2nd Rockbridge Artillery. The remaining two-gun section belonged to Capt. William B. Hurt's Alabama Light Artillery. Just as McIntosh ordered

11 Wright, *No More Gallant Deed*, 365; Edward Walker to Knight, Nov. 5, 1863, USMHI; *OR* 29, pt. 1, 287, 288.

12 *OR* 29, pt. 1, 434-35; Bassett, *Brief Sketch NCST*, 81-83; *OR Supplement* 5, pt. 1, 599.

13 *OR* 29, pt. 1, 435; Bassett, *Brief Sketch NCST*, 82.

his men to open fire over the heads of Heth's infantry, word arrived from Hill that the battalion should deploy where previously ordered as quickly as possible.[14]

Now fully committed, McIntosh directed two smoothbore Napoleons from Capt. Robert S. Rice's Danville Artillery to join the rifled guns on the knoll. While Poague's crews concentrated on Battery B, 1st Rhode Island Light north of Broad Run, McIntosh's cannoneers dueled with Ricketts and Arnold east of the railroad. The latter's guns seemed particularly vulnerable to Rebel counterbattery fire. Confederate shells, complained one of Arnold's artillerists, came hurtling into the battery "lengthwise" from left to right. This same Federal characterized the shelling as the "most spiteful firing" he had ever seen. Fortunately for the Yankees, the Southern gunners were shooting just a "little too high," and most of their projectiles sailed harmlessly overhead. Nonetheless the Rebel fire forced the Rhode Islanders to pivot their cannon to confront McIntosh's fieldpieces directly.[15]

As the rival gunners blazed away, Kirkland's regiments could hear the rising tumult of infantry combat to their right. Still unaware of the Union infantry behind the railroad, his North Carolinians focused on the Yankee batteries unlimbering to the east. At about 400 yards from the Federal position, the Confederates opened fire. Up and down the line officers at the top of their voices ordered their troops to concentrate on the cannon, to shoot down the gunners and horses before they could go into action.[16]

While Kirkland's troops weren't yet under heavy fire, Hall's command was becoming disjointed. Lieutenant Colonel Whitfield had taken Hall's "we'd better charge" comment literally, and immediately lead the 27th North Carolina ahead at the double-quick. As the regiment swept forward, a motionless line of dead and wounded clearly marked where it had paused for a few terrible, costly moments.[17]

The 46th and 15th North Carolina moved forward on the 27th's right, but at the quick step, firing as they advanced rather than charging full tilt toward the dreadful torrent of lead issuing from the railroad embankment. The 48th North Carolina, awkwardly positioned on the northern slope of the knoll, was taking heavy fire from Federal infantry and Rickett's battery. Somewhat disorganized, the regiment had not moved, and Col. Hall ordered it to advance as quickly as possible.[18]

---

14 *OR* 29, part1, 436-37.

15 Aldrich, *Battery A, 1st Rhode Island Light*, 251.

16 Long "Reminiscences" Breckinridge papers, LC; *OR* 29, pt. 1, 435, 277.

17 Bassett, *Brief Sketch NCST*, 82.

18 *OR* 29, pt. 1, 435. The double quick is a slow jog. The quick step is basically a normal walking pace.

Some among the Union troops admired the enemy's courage. The attackers were "gallantly led," Warren remarked, and Capt. Robert C. Wright of the 42nd New York also noted their "unflinching bravery." Another Union officer marveled at the "steady force and . . . perfect coolness" of the advance, even as he and his comrades grimly went about the business of slaughtering as many of their brave enemies as possible.[19]

The Southerners kept coming. The 27th North Carolina's skirmishers covered the last few hundred yards toward the railroad under a "merciless shell fire." Nonetheless, they managed to reach the meager shelter of a slightly sunken lane running parallel to the embankment. Captain John Ball of the 1st Minnesota saw Rebels firing from this newly obtained position. Fearing that the enemy's battle line would merge with these skirmishers and swarm over the embankment, Ball cried out for his men to follow and jumped atop the railroad tracks. A handful of soldiers joined him as he emptied his revolver at the closest Confederates and then hurled the weapon at them in desperation. Silhouetted on the top of the embankment, neither Ball nor his comrades could long survive such a suicidal, albeit courageous, gesture. A Southern bullet ripped through the captain's groin. Several other Federals fell killed or wounded at almost the same instant, while the fortunate survivors quickly sought the cover of the embankment.[20]

Captain Ball's and his compatriots' sacrifice had been needless: once the advancing enemy came within 40 yards of the tracks hundreds of Federal soldiers rose up and poured a searing volley into them. Dozens fell, including Sgt. William Summer, the 27th's regimental color bearer. Cpl. Edwin Barrett, a member of the color guard, caught the flag before it could hit the ground and tried to take it the last few yards toward the enemy. Within ten paces the Yankees shot him in the right thigh, and he too went down. Corporal William C. Story grasped the banner, and somehow the 21-year old miraculously survived the storm engulfing what remained of his regiment. Others were not so lucky: Lt. Col. Whitfield went down, shot in the right leg, and Sgt. Maj. Robert Weatherly, fell mortally wounded. With Whitfield down, Maj. Joseph C. Webb assumed command and managed to stay with his troops despite three slight wounds.[21]

All across the field west of the railroad Yankee shells were "bursting fair" among the long lines of gray infantry. The effect, one Northerner observed, was akin to

19 Ibid., 242, 435, 287; Morris Brown Jr. to parents, October 15, 1863, HC.

20 Wright, *No More Gallant Deed*, 366. Although the bullet carried away one of his testes, Ball survived his wound and returned to duty in 1864. He died in 1875 of tuberculous. For more info see "First Lieutenant John Ball," http://www.1stminnesota.net/#/soldier/753, accessed 15 June 2018.

21 Bassett, *Brief Sketch NCST*, 82-83; John A. Sloan, *Reminiscences of the Guilford Grays, Co. B, 27th N.C. Regiment* (Washington, D.C., 1883), 71-73.

Captain John Ball
Minnesota Historical Society

throwing a rock into "a shoal of fish." Each detonation broke up the ranks of Rebel infantry, "spreading [men] in every direction." On the receiving end of this fire a North Carolinian admitted that the Union shelling was "terrific," but not as bad as the "murderous" Federal musketry. Rebel casualties rapidly mounted under such a "withering fire," and entire companies dissolved before the blistering Federal volleys. Men in the front rank of the 27th fell so quickly, a Southern soldier said they were "mowed down like grain before a reaper." In the face of this punishment, the gray line stalled and could go no further. But it refused to recede either. The stubborn Confederates stood their ground and returned fire as speedily as they could reload.[22]

On the extreme left of Cooke's brigade, the 48th North Carolina had finally managed to come forward and was approaching the ruins of the Davis house, near the road about 100 yards in front the Union line. One defender recalled that just as the regiment reached the building a "well-directed" Federal shell "swept away a large number" of attackers in a single explosion. This hit plunged the 48th into confusion and it began to unravel. A significant number of its men ran for the shelter of the house where they "huddled up around it like so many sheep." The tightly packed body of enemy troops presented a wonderful target for the Yankee guns which threw a torrent of canister and shell into the mass. This last was too much to endure and those who survived it turned for the rear in rapid flight.[23]

In the center of the Rebel line, Maj. Webb looked around and realized that the 27th had advanced much farther than the rest of the brigade. Most of the 48th North Carolina had already given way. The 15th and 46th trailed some distance to the rear, and Webb's own inherited command was breaking up. Some of his troops rushed for shelter in the ruins of a nearby cellar while others raced for the cover of a few

22 *OR* 29, pt. 1, 289; Robertson, *A.P. Hill*, 238.

23 Morris Brown Jr. to parents, October 15, 1863, HC.

abandoned huts. It was suicidal for the regiment to stay in such an exposed position without the prospect of support. Webb, therefore, ordered his men to retreat back up the shot-torn hillside they had so recently traversed.[24]

*   *   *

On the other side of the road, Kirkland's brigade was suffering a similar bloody fate. Behind the railroad, Hays' division and some of Mallon's 3rd Brigade troops from Webb's division were already hammering Cooke. Despite the blaze of battle to their left, most of Heath's 1st Brigade infantrymen remained unengaged. They simply could not yet see the Confederates coming toward the railroad. That soon changed. The 11th North Carolina on the extreme left of Kirkland's brigade, as well as the 52nd to its right, had the great good fortune of heading straight for the 150-yard gap yawning between Broad Run and the Federal right flank. Kirkland's other three regiments—the 47th, 26th and 44th—were not so fortunate.

Rebel skirmishers screening the brigade advanced until they reached a rise about 50 yards in front of the railroad embankment. At this point fire from some of Heath's Federals brought the Southerners to a halt. Major Henry Abbott, commanding the 20th Massachusetts, however, urged his men to hold their fire in order to lure the main Rebel line closer. Most of Heath's other regiments exercised no such restraint. Seeing the 11th and 52nd North Carolina advancing beyond the Federal right flank, the 82nd New York fired into them at the right oblique. Colonel George Joslin increased the 15th Massachusetts' rate of fire by having his rear rank load muskets and pass them forward to his front rank blazing away from the slope of the embankment.[25]

As the Confederates drew nearer, the Yankee volleys grew heavier and then erupted into a tempest of lead as the order to commence firing swept along Webb's entire line. The sudden fusillade came as a ghastly shock to Kirkland's men, who were still intent on shooting apart the Union batteries. In the ranks of the 44th North Carolina, Sgt. Long, likening the crash of Yankee rifles to a "roar as from the portals of hell," realized with horror that his troops couldn't "get at those guns." All around him men began to drop as enemy bullets tore through Kirkland's ranks. The colors of the 44th and those in the other regiments went down in quick succession.[26]

24 Sloan, *Guilford Grays*, 71.

25 OR 29, pt. 1, 277, 280, 282; Andrew E. Ford, *The Story of the Fifteenth Regiment Massachusetts Volunteer Infantry in the Civil War, 1861-1864* (Clinton, MA, 1898), 299.

26 Long "Reminiscences" Breckinridge papers, LC.

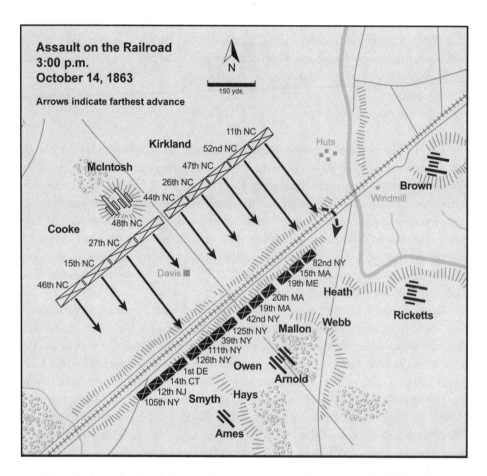

Nonetheless, the Confederates kept coming. As they neared the Union line, the left flank of Kirkland's brigade discovered that it overlapped the Federal right by more than 100 yards. Taking advantage of this happenstance, the 11th and 52nd North Carolina and about 50 of the brigade's skirmishers who had rallied to the left of the line surged up the embankment. Some men actually crossed to the other side and swung around to fire into the Union rear.

An even more immediate danger threatened the center of Webb's position. Despite the heavy fire from the embankment, small groups of Rebels got right up to the railroad. No sheltering wall of earth guarded the Brentsville Road where it crossed the tracks, which by pure chance was being held by a group of new conscripts in the 42nd New York. Fortunately, Col. James E. Mallon, in temporary command of the 3rd Brigade, recognized that this spot was especially vulnerable.

The colonel had just returned to the army after spending August and September in New York City forwarding conscripts to the 42nd, which was his own regiment. Mallon was a strict disciplinarian (perhaps even "to a fault" thought one of his men), and he anticipated the unsteadiness of the reluctant soldiers he had shepherded to Virginia. He was determined to hold them to their duty and purposefully positioned himself behind the draftees. Terrified by the demon-like onslaught of Rebel infantry, the green soldiers turned and ran for the rear. The fleeing novices didn't get far before encountering Mallon, sword in hand. His forethought succeeded in stopping "the stampede" before it unhinged the entire position.[27]

Despite Mallon, the conscripts' panic allowed the Confederates to penetrate the Union line. But their breakthrough was fleeting. There were way too many Yankees and far too few Confederates at the rupture for the North Carolinians to widen the breach. Most of the attackers never got nearer to the railroad embankment than 40 or 50 yards. One Southerner recalled that when they tried to push closer the Federals "poured a volley into our ranks which almost swept the remnant of us out of existence." Union fire was simply too intense for anyone to go farther. Those Rebels not gunned down or bayoneted, recoiled and fled.[28]

The Confederates had no better luck against the Union right. Major Thomas Baird's 82nd New York stood its ground despite the threat of being turned. A portion of his command refused the regiment's flank to confront the handful of North Carolinians who had actually crossed the tracks. Fire from the rest of the New Yorkers and Brown's battery kept the bulk of Rebels from assaulting over the embankment. But this success was tenuous, for once the two Southern regiments gathered themselves together, little would keep them from swarming over the rails to crumple Webb's line. What the 11th and 52nd needed was just a few more minutes.[29]

They didn't get them. The rain of Minie balls and shrapnel to their right soon became more than the rest of Kirkland's brigade could stand. A mere 75 yards or so from the railroad cut, the 44th North Carolina still struggled forward. Sergeant Long, seeing the regiment's colors struck down once again, leaned over to pick up the flag. As he stood up, 22-year old Lt. R. W. Dupree put his hand on Long's back and above the din shouted the order to fall back. As soon as those words left his lips, a Federal shell ripped away part of his skull, killing him instantly. Long, caught his slain friend and gently eased him to the ground. Kneeling beside the lifeless body, its chin still

27 Previous paragraphs based upon OR 29, pt. 1, 277, 282, 284; Perry, *Letters from a Surgeon*, 111; Irishacw, "Equaled by Few- Surpassed by None": Colonel James Mallon and the Battle of Bristoe Station," Oct 12, 2013, www.irishamericancivilwar.com/2013/10/12/equaled-by-few-surpassed-by-none-colonel-james-mallon-and-the-battle-of-bristoe-station/, accessed 16 Jun 18.

28 OR 29, pt. 1, 283; Robertson, *A.P. Hill*, 238;.

29 George A. Bruce, *The Twentieth Regiment of Massachusetts Volunteer Infantry, 1861-1865* (Boston, MA, 1906), 310; ibid., 282.

reflexively moving, the sergeant removed a small packet of letters and a pocket watch from Dupree's coat and grabbed his sword.[30]

This final kindness took only a moment, but by the time Long looked up, Kirkland's shattered brigade was in full retreat and already 50 yards closer to the sheltering trees. Still holding the 44th's colors, Long got the uncomfortable sensation of being an inviting target. The sergeant literally ran for his life, moving so fast he had "no feeling of touching the ground" until he reached the woods several hundred yards away.[31]

The withdrawal of the regiments directly opposite the Federals left the 11th and 52nd North Carolina completely unsupported. They had no option but to abandon their position along the embankment and make their way to the rear. Falling back, however, seemed far more dangerous than coming forward had been, because the Federal batteries now had full play of the field. Scores of men chose to stay where they were rather than risk the torrent of shells and bullets ripping up the ground behind them. The majority, however, braved the danger and fell back as fast as possible.

* * *

On both sides of the Brentsville Road the Rebel assault had been broken; however, the attackers hadn't been routed. Even Warren admitted the Confederates withdrew "sullenly." Cooke's right flank fell back in good order: indeed both the 46th and 15th North Carolina withdrew in textbook fashion. The 46th faced about, marched a short distance, halted, turned to fire a volley, and then turned about again, loading on the move before halting to repeat the process until it was out of range. At the same time, the 15th retired by alternate companies, firing as it pulled back. The 27th North Carolina, to the 15th's left, having lost between one-half and two-thirds of its men, retreated in what one survivor of the attack labeled "honorable confusion."[32]

By contrast, Kirkland's left flank, forced to run the gauntlet of enemy fire to retreat, fled in "utter confusion." His other three regiments retreated in tolerable order despite their losses. Two of these units rallied on Walker's brigade after it belatedly reached the scene of action after recrossing Broad Run. His regiments moved to

---

30 Long "Reminiscences" Breckinridge papers, LC. Dupree was adjutant of the 44th North Carolina Infantry. As the Sergeant Major of the 27th North Carolina he was wounded in the breast and captured at Sharpsburg. He was exchanged in October 1862. After his recovery he was promoted and transferred to the 44th NC Inf.

31 Ibid.

32 *OR* 29, pt. 1, 242, 435; *OR Supplement* 5, pt. 1, 601.

Colonel James Mallon *Library of Congress*

protect Poague's artillery, while about 20 men from Kirkland's brigade withdrew to the ruins of some nearby huts in front of Webb's division. They continued to shoot toward the Union lines from the dilapidated structures. These Confederates probably inflicted the highest ranking casualty on the Federal side of the battle.[33]

After his conscripts had beaten back the Confederate penetration at the gap in the railroad embankment, James Mallon ordered his men to lie down. Once his men were down the colonel did likewise just behind his nervous draftees. But he was not content to stay there.

A son of Irish immigrants, Mallon was a successful businessman and private in the 7th New York State Militia before the war. Since 1861 he had spent most of his service on detached duty making a solid record as a staff officer. Promoted to colonel on St. Patrick's Day 1863 and given command of the 42nd New York Infantry, he had led the regiment at Gettysburg and helped repel the Confederate infantry assault on the afternoon of July 3. Mallon's brother suffered a severe wound during the battle, a personal blow that hit the new colonel hard and left him ever more aware of the random, deadly dangers of combat.[34]

Since the battle of Gettysburg the Irishman had developed an extremely close friendship with Maj. Abbott of the 20th Massachusetts. As angry bullets continued to zip around Bristoe Station, Mallon became increasingly anxious about his friend's fate. Turning to surgeon John Perry next to him, the colonel said he intended to check on Abbott. Perry begged Mallon not to move and warned that standing up almost guaranteed getting shot. But Mallon, claiming the suspense too troubling and assuring Perry it would only take a moment, made the fatal choice to go anyway. As soon as he rose a Confederate bullet ripped through his abdomen. Perry dragged Mallon out of the line of fire and down to the relative cover of a little stream. The surgeon did what he could, but the wound proved too severe and Mallon died in Perry's arms within the

---

33 *OR* 29, pt. 1, 435, 433.

34 Irishacw, "Equaled by Few," www.irishamericancivilwar.com/2013/10/12/equaled-by-few-surpassed-by-none-colonel-james-mallon-and-the-battle-of-bristoe-station/

hour, probably from internal bleeding. As its senior field officer, Lieutenant Colonel Ansel Wass of the 19th Massachusetts took command of the brigade.[35]

The deadly fire that killed Mallon greatly annoyed the Yankees. Once Webb was certain the Confederates had been beaten back, he directed Colonel Wass to silence the enemy marksmen. In short order a detachment from the 42nd New York surrounded the buildings and compelled the Southern snipers to give up.

Other Federal advances were happening elsewhere on the battlefield. Just as the Rebel assault reached its high water mark, Gen. Hays had instructed Col. Thomas Smyth's brigade to cross the railroad and strike the flank of Cooke's battered command. Smyth had four regiments in line—from right to left, five companies of the 1st Delaware (the other five being deployed as skirmishers), the 14th Connecticut, the 12th New Jersey, and 108th Pennsylvania. They were busily firing at the right oblique into the faltering North Carolinians when the order to attack arrived. After fixing bayonets, the Federals climbed over the tracks and entered a dense pine woods which stretched along the railroad and extended out to the west for some distance.[36]

It was inhospitable terrain. Underbrush choked the woods and gun smoke hung densely among the trees. Smyth's Federals had considerable difficulty moving into position through this tangled mass. Still, the Yankees doggedly worked their way to the northern edge of the woods, where Smyth's regiments began to go "by the right flank into line." Poor visibility and the troublesome landscape made even this relatively simple movement exceeding challenging. Consequently, a gap opened between the 12th New Jersey and the 108th Pennsylvania on the brigade's far left.

Fortunately for the colonel, a portion of the 7th Michigan from Webb's division appeared to fill the void. The regiment had deployed as skirmishers at the start of the battle, but merged with Hays' units as they formed along the railroad embankment earlier in the fight. Once the Confederates began retreating, Maj. Sylvanus Curtis pulled the Michigan men off the firing line and ordered them to reassemble. Anxious to assist in the attack, Curtis offered his regiment to Smyth, who ordered it into the gap between the 108th's right and the 12th New Jersey's left.[37]

After struggling into position, Smyth's troops opened fire on the right flank of Cooke's brigade as it backed away from the railroad embankment. Lieutenant Colonel William Saunders of the 46th North Carolina promptly noted this new threat and

---

35 Perry, *Letters from a Surgeon*, 112; Scott, *Fallen Leaves*, 223-234; OR 29, pt. 1, 283-85; ibid. It had been just six weeks since Mallon's fourth wedding anniversary and a month after his own 27th birthday. He left behind a three-year old son and 18-month old daughter. Mallon's wife, Anna, never remarried.

36 OR 29, pt. 1, 277, 283-84, 294, 298-99.

37 OR 29, pt. 1, 294, 287.

moved to meet it. In a position on the far end of the Rebel line, his command had suffered much less than its sister regiments during the recent attack. It was in good condition and anything but demoralized. But it was still under heavy fire from Union artillery as well as enemy troops sheltering behind the railroad.

The appearance of Smyth's brigade required the 46th North Carolina to rapidly change front to face the new threat—a complex operation on a drill ground that was even more difficult in combat. Only a well-trained and disciplined regiment could maneuver to meet a flank attack under heavy fire from the front. Saunders' men pulled it off flawlessly. To the left of the 46th, the 15th North Carolina showed equal capacity by maintaining a hot fire toward the O&A to help shield the 27th as it fell back.[38]

*　　*　　*

The volleys of Smyth's troops helped encourage the Rebels to continue their retreat. Cooke's brigade did not halt until it was over the crest from which it had launched its impromptu attack a mere 20 minutes before. The extent of this withdrawal spelled doom for the seven guns McIntosh had deployed on the same knoll. As the major had warned, his position was horribly exposed.

With the repulse of the infantry, Federal batteries concentrated their efforts on McIntosh's battalion. Union fire quickly disabled two Napoleons from Rice's battery and killed more than 20 horses and wounded as many more. General Hill ordered up another battery to help, but it did not arrive in time to be of assistance. Bereft of support, McIntosh tried unsuccessfully to rally Confederate infantrymen streaming rearward past his guns.

The collapse of Heth's attack left McIntosh's fieldpieces vulnerable to capture. With most of his horses dead or disabled, he had no quick way to withdraw his guns, which he sorely wanted to do. To buy time, he ordered his remaining crewmen to fire canister toward the enemy, hoping to stave off the Yankees long enough to bring up help. The major sent a messenger to Hill for support. Then he himself rode to the rear looking for assistance. The courier never found Hill, but McIntosh did find Gen. Walker, who agreed to send a regiment to defend the battery.[39]

But it was already too late. Yankee cannon fire was "fast knocking to pieces" McIntosh's batteries, now the sole target of Union artillery. Since staying put meant obliteration, the Rebel gunners made "desperate attempts" to limber up their pieces

---

38 Clark, *NC Regts*, vol. 1, 743; vol. 3, 72.

39 *OR* 29, pt. 1, 433, 436-437.

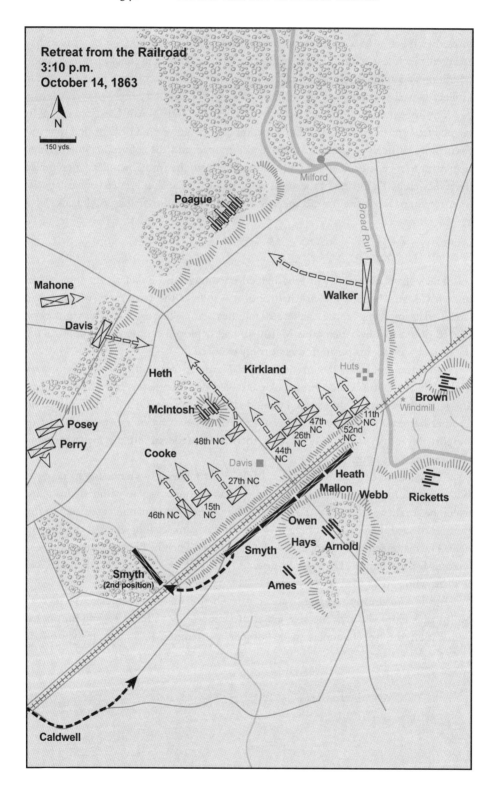

Retreat from the Railroad
3:10 p.m.
October 14, 1863

N

150 yds.

Milford

Broad Run

Poague

Mahone

Davis

Walker

Heth

Kirkland

Huts

McIntosh

Brown

Windmill

Posey

47th
NC

11th
NC

Perry

48th NC

26th
NC

52nd
NC

Cooke

44th
NC

Davis

Heath

27th NC

Mallon   Webb

Ricketts

46th NC   15th
NC

Owen

Hays   Arnold

Smyth

Smyth
(2nd position)

Ames

Caldwell

and retreat. So many battery horses had been killed, though, such efforts were fruitless, and the Confederates were forced to abandon their weapons.[40]

Witnessing this, a lot Union troops realized that they had an opportunity to capture the Southern cannons; which in turn led to a haphazard and spontaneous rush by several units to take the fieldpieces.[41]

McIntosh returned to his knoll about this time and instantly realized what the Federals were doing. The major ordered his limbers and caissons to the rear and told his men to drag their pieces down from the rise by hand. But the Yankees were already too close. The artillerymen barely managed to haul off one cannon when approaching Union infantry forced them to abandon the rest of their guns, this time for good.[42]

The Southerners departed just before Northern troops reached the hill. Yankee soldiers from a variety of units thronged over the battery. They found one gun still hitched to its team and drove it back into Union lines. "[Y]elling like Indians" the Federals dragged four additional pieces by hand to the other side of the railroad. All they left for the Rebels was a single damaged 12-pounder Napoleon. [43]

While the Northerners secured their booty, the Confederate infantry fell back into the woods that marked their starting point. Union fire followed them every step of the way. Heth ordered Davis' brigade to forego supporting Poague's artillery and instead hurry forward to shore up Cooke's command. Even as the Rebels rallied among the trees enemy fire continued inflicting casualties. A bursting shell obliterated one soldier who was laying prone for protection. Another Southerner bled to death from a bullet in the stomach. When comrades attempted to move his body to the rear, a round through the head killed a stretcher bearer. The continuing punishment forced the survivors of the railroad assault to seek better cover or retreat farther out of range.[44]

The withdrawal of the bloodied North Carolina regiments and the capture of McIntosh's guns brought a momentary end to the fighting. But with more troops reaching the field, the struggle was not likely over. Warren's initial success in smashing Heth's attack might have just been the first round of a battle only beginning.

40 Wells, *Surgeon in the Army of the Potomac*, 74.

41 *OR* 29, pt. 1, 285, 284; George Patch to parents, October 15, 1863, VHS.

42 *OR* 29, pt. 1, 437, 290. No less than 5 separate Union units claimed credit for capturing the guns. The great controversy this initiated was never resolved to everyone's satisfaction.

43 Wells, *Surgeon in the Army of the Potomac*, 74.

44 Long "Reminiscences" Breckinridge papers, LC.

CHAPTER 25

"No Little Confusion"

Reinforcements—Artillery Duel—Early Deploys—Gordon's Attack—
Gregg's Ordeal—Darkness Ends the Contest

A**FTER** the decisive bloody repulse of Cooke's and Kirkland's infantry attack and the loss of McIntosh's veteran guns, an uneasy lull settled over the Bristoe Station battlefield. Most of the shooting died away in a fitful cacophony that gradually gave way to silence. For a brief interval each side caught its breath and prepared to renew the struggle. Although they had handily driven back Hill's first assault, Union commanders knew they weren't out of danger yet. Warren and his subordinates worked frantically to consolidate their position before another onslaught.

Captain John Hazard, who commanded the II Corps' artillery, took an important step toward strengthening the Federal line by massing his batteries east of the railroad. The guns and crews that had helped beat back Heth's experienced infantry were ordered rearward to replenish their ammunition and get some much-needed rest. Arnold's battery retired below the crest of the hill it had recently occupied. Captain Brown brought his artillery pieces back from their isolated position north of Broad Run and parked them near Arnold's fieldpieces. Under Hazard's orders, Bruce Rickett's cannon prepared to follow suit and move to the reverse slope of their fighting position.

To replace these units, Capt. Hazard brought up Battery I, 1st US, commanded by Lt. Frank French, and deployed it on the hills behind Warren's infantry. Captain Ames' remaining guns also rolled into position and dropped trail on the high ground. One of his pieces unlimbered next to the battery's single cannon, which had helped repel the Confederate attack. Ames' remaining four guns deployed a short distance away. Hazard carefully aimed these fieldpieces southwest in the general direction of Kettle

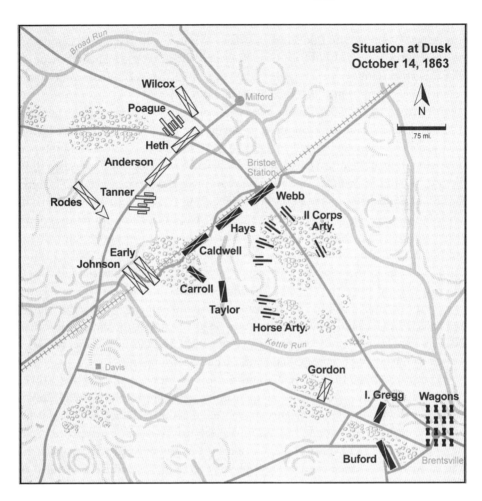

Run, which astutely allowed both batteries to cover the left and rear of the Federal position.[1]

These were timely moves given that the Confederates were working industrially to mass against Warren's southern flank. The van of Maj. Gen. Richard Anderson's division had reached the field just as Cooke and Kirkland began their advance. Initially Hill had instructed Anderson to strike Hays' II Corps division as it hurried to connect with Webb. Anderson had dispatched Brig. Gen. Carnot Posey's four Mississippi and Brig. Gen. Edward A. Perry's three Florida regiments to do that. But by the time these brigades were prepared to advance, Hays had not only reached the embankment, he

1   OR 29, pt. 1, 306, 308, 310; John H. Rhodes, *The History of Battery B, First Regiment Rhode Island Light Artillery in the War to Preserve the Union, 1861-1865* (Providence, RI, 1894), 249; Reichardt, *Battery A*, 81-82.

had helped Webb repulse Cooke and Kirkland. When he saw the North Carolinians retreating, Anderson ordered Brig. Gen. William Mahone's five Virginia regiments to plug the gap in Heth's front. Davis' brigade arrived to fill the breech and cover Cooke's regiments as they reformed before Mahone could get there.[2]

Meanwhile, other Confederates units were coming up on Anderson's right. After disengaging from the fight at Auburn earlier in the day, Ewell's corps had moved north to Greenwich, accompanied by Gen. Lee and army headquarters. Ewell knew this part of Virginia intimately: he had grown up on a 600-acre farm named Belleville just a short distance east of the town. To save time and avoid roads already clogged by Hill's corps, Ewell had led his men southeast of Greenwich along a route parallel to Hill's line of advance that passed by his childhood home. This path took Ewell's command down side roads until it emerged onto clear ground near the O&A just above Kettle Run a little south of Bristoe Station.[3]

It was 4 p.m. when the ANV's Second Corps reached the battlefield. Lee, Ewell, and Brig. Gen. William N. Pendleton, the army's chief of artillery, were riding near the head of the column as it approached Bristoe. The sound of the fight along the railroad had been clearly audible for some time. As soon as practicable the three officers had ridden forward to get some idea of what was happening, and shortly a courier from Hill arrived with news of his initial repulse and a request for support.[4]

This dispatch was disconcerting to say the least. Other than the fact that Yankee infantry and artillery were behind the railroad embankment south of Broad Run, it contained few details. The only encouraging thing about Hill's report was that his assault had halted the Union retreat. As usual Lee's first thoughts were opportunistic. Regardless of Hill's early misfortune, the opening Lee had pursued since crossing the Rappahannock seemed at hand. He had a chance to throw his entire command at an isolated portion of Meade's army. Determined to seize the moment, he assumed personal charge of the battle.[5]

Lee had to make some rapid decisions in the absence of critical information. He knew nothing about the casualties Hill had taken or the damage he had inflicted. The

---

2   OR 29, pt. 1, 429.

3   Ronald Ray Turner, "Prince William County Virginia," http://www.pwcvirginia.com/documents/BellView.pdf, accessed 21 June 2018. The spelling of 19th Century place names varied wildly. Such is the case with Ewell's childhood home, which variously went by Belleville, Belle View, or Belleview. After the war the farm's name changed to Stoney Lonesome. Craig Swain, "Stoney Lonesome Farm (Belleville)" https://www.hmdb.org/marker.asp?marker=21084, accessed 19 June 2018.

4   OR 29, pt. 1, 429, 418; Early, *Memoirs*, 305.

5   Early to Mahone, May 30, 1871, in Gibson Family Papers, Library of VA, Richmond.

Confederates didn't know the dispositions, identity, or size of the enemy force they had cornered. Throughout the day Ewell had captured prisoners from the Union II corps and Gregg's cavalry. Hill had taken captives from the III Corps. All or some of these Yankee commands might still be near Bristoe Station. At the very least, a considerable enemy force was east of the railroad.

As far as Lee was concerned, the identity or strength of the Federals did not matter. He would attack as soon as he could deploy his men and get some idea of the Union position.

The head of Ewell's corps was emerging from the woods south of Bristoe Station on a line of march toward the O&A Railroad bridge over Kettle Run. Various Rebel observers had glimpsed Yankee infantry moving along the tracks to join the enemy around Bristoe Station. How many Union regiments might be on the road between Kettle Run and Catlett's Station wasn't known: it could be a significant force. Lee instructed Ewell to do what he could to help shore of Hill's right flank. Next he ordered Jubal Early, whose command headed Ewell's column, to advance toward the railroad bridge over Kettle Run and form a line near the creek facing south. The rest of Ewell's corps and the remainder of Hill's were to come up and go into line as quickly as possible.[6]

General Early immediately rode to Brig. Gen. John B. Gordon. His six Georgia regiments led the division's column and were already within striking distance of Kettle Run. Early ordered the Georgia brigadier to get his men into line as quickly as possible and then move them into the woods not far from the creek's northern bank. Once there, cautioned the division commander, Gordon was to maintain his position until the rest of the division reached the field.

After relaying these orders Early rode back to expedite the deployment of his remaining three brigades under brigadier generals Harry Hays, Robert Hoke, and Col. John S. Hoffman of the 31st Virginia. The 42-year old Hoffman had worked his way up through the ranks from private to colonel. At least one member of 31st Virginia described him as a "hard, brave fighter, but a dull and slow man . . . unsuited" for his current position. If the next few hours went as Robert E. Lee wished, the accuracy of that assessment would soon be determined.[7]

---

6 Early, *Memoirs*, 305.

7 Ibid.; Krick, *Lee's Colonels*, 194. Hoffman had gained temporary command of William "Extra Billy" Smith's brigade as a result of Smith's resignation from the army following his recent election to the governorship of Virginia. Smith's nickname stemmed from the early 1830s when he ran a line of coaches and obtained a US government contract to deliver mail between Washington and Georgia's capital, Milledgeville. Smith expanded the line with many spur routes, each of which produced additional, "extra," fee revenue—hence the term.

*   *   *

While Early hurried to deploy his division, the fighting along the railroad flared back to life. Maj. Gen. Anderson was still trying to get his division into position on the right flank of Heth's command. Ewell's chief of artillery, Brig. Gen. Armistead Long, witnessing this effort, rode forward to offer Anderson artillery support. The general gladly accepted the help, and Long detailed his only immediately available battery— Capt. William Tanner's Courtney Artillery, which had come forward with Early's division—to go to Anderson's aid.

Before Tanner could act, however, Col. Smyth's brigade from Hays' division had lunged over the railroad to harass Cooke's withdrawing regiments. The sudden appearance of these Yankees west of the tracks worried General Anderson, who feared their advance might presage a serious counterattack. It also disrupted Tanner's effort to get into position and forestalled his first attempt to enter the battle. To blunt this threat, Anderson directed Carnot Posey's and Alfred Perry's brigades to confront the looming danger and seize the ground Tanner needed for his field artillery. As these commands moved into position to attack Smyth, they naturally attracted the attention of alert Union artillerists.[8]

Soon after going forward, Anderson's skirmishers spotted the 108th New York on the left flank of Smyth's line. At that moment the Yankees, still facing north, were entangled among the pines in front of the railroad. Although an indistinct target, it was a target nonetheless, and the Rebels opened fire at a range of about 500 yards. Even at that distance Southern bullets managed to inflict a few casualties and forced Col. Charles J. Powers, commanding the 108th, to look to his left rear. The sight of a "formidable body" of Confederate infantry bearing down on his position shocked the 30-year Canadian-born New Yorker. He immediately sent word to Smyth that the brigade's flank was in danger.[9]

Smyth promptly reported this development to Hays who ordered him to resist the enemy advance. The colonel then directed the 108th New York, 7th Michigan, and two companies of the 12th New Jersey to cease fire, form column, and move to the left so as to refuse his brigade's flank. Once in place the units went by the right flank into line of battle, thus forming a new front facing Posey and Perry. Now oriented to the west, the Yankees opened fire. Because they were shooting at more distant targets than usual,

8   *OR* 29, pt. 1, 418, 429, 421; *OR Supplement*, 5, pt. 1, 594.

9   *OR* 29, pt. 1, 294, 299; Clipping, n.d., "Killed and Wounded of the 108th New York Volunteers," NYMM, https://dmna.ny.gov/historic/reghist/civil/infantry/108thInf/108th InfCWN5.pdf, The 108th New York suffered 1k and 14w, including one officer, in the fight.

the regimental officers carefully instructed their men to adjust the sights on their rifled muskets to the proper range.[10]

Despite this Federal reaction, the advance of Anderson's brigades allowed Tanner's Courtney Artillery to finally get into position. Its two 12-pounder Napoleons and two 3-inch Ordnance Rifles deployed beside a pair of Napoleons commanded by Lt. Berryman Z. Price, whom McIntosh had sent over to assist Gen. Long. These six guns spotted Rickett's battery on the hill behind the railroad and opened fire on it just as his men began to hitch up their teams. The onset of exploding shells wounded several Union gunners and horses, while sowing "no little confusion" among the Pennsylvanians, who quickly got themselves and their guns out of the line of fire.[11]

The unexpected Rebel barrage provoked an instant return fire from French's and Ames' batteries. Brown and Arnold forgot about rest or resupply and raced their pieces back onto the high ground to join the fight. Soon 22 Federal cannon were blasting away against a meager half-dozen Confederate guns. A total of 18 Union tubes (4 from Arnold, 2 from Ames, and 6 each from Brown and French) focused on Tanner and Price's little force while 4 additional guns from Ames' battery shelled Perry's and Posey's infantrymen. Although Arnold lost a fieldpiece early in the fight when the axle tree of one gun snapped, the Yankees maintained a 3 to 1 advantage over their Rebel counterparts throughout the duel.[12]

The Southern artillerymen were indifferent to the hardly atypical long odds against them. After seeing the retreat of Rickett's battery, the Rebels mistakenly gave themselves credit for driving it from the field and drawing first blood. But in fact the Northern artillerists inflicted more significant and tangible damage than they took. Their fire wounded Capt. Tanner in the knee and forced him to retire from the field. Not long afterwards a shell fragment ripped into Brig. Gen. Posey's thigh. Although stretcher bearers successfully evacuated him from the field, the Mississippian's wound proved mortal. Within a month the 45-year Posey would die from an infection.[13]

---

10 *OR* 29, 294, 299. "By the right flank" means that the men in a marching column of fours (or twos) immediately face to the right, undoubling their files of four to form a two-rank deep battle line facing to the right.

11 Rhodes, *Battery B, First Rhode Island*, 249; ibid., 438.

12 *OR* 29, pt. 1, 306, 308.

13 *OR* 29, pt. 1, 421, 239; Richard Nicholas & Joseph Servis, *Powhatan, Salem and Courtney Henrico Artillery* (Lynchburg, VA, 1997), 236. An ambulance evacuated Tanner to Warrenton that night. His wound proved so bad, surgeons left him behind when the ANV retreated at the end of the campaign. The Federals captured Tanner on his sick bed a few days later. General Posey's fate was grimmer. Taken to a doctor for treatment in Charlottesville, his wound became infected, and he died on November 13, 1863.

Unfortunately for the Federals, their projectiles were not just hitting Confederates. Whether from defective fuses or poor gunnery, a significant number of Union shells burst above Yankee infantry. The 20th Massachusetts had one man killed and four badly wounded, while a soldier in the 148th Pennsylvania lost an arm to so-called 'friendly fire.' This assault from the rear incensed the commanders of both units who accurately declared it more demoralizing than the fire of the enemy.

Major Henry Abbott, whose Bay State regiment had similarly lost men on other fields, wrote a scathing indictment of the batteries in his official report. He charged that Union gunners seemed to "regard it as a matter of slight importance" if the infantry lost a few men "more or less, from fire of our own side." The adjutant of the 148th didn't wait to file an official complaint. Instead he jumped up from his position behind the regiment and charged after the officer commanding the offending battery. His fellow Pennsylvanians found the resulting confrontation "interesting both to see and hear."[14]

Sadly, such tragedies are the small change of battle. The cannons continued to buck and roar for a bit longer—their shells, if not their gunners, indifferent to whom they struck. With the time now somewhere between 4:30 and 5 p.m., twilight was rapidly approaching. Amid the growing shadows and the dense clouds of gun smoke, both sides aimed at barely seen enemies some 800 yards away. Under those conditions the chance of either combatant doing significant damage to its opponent was slight. With the fire of three Federal batteries concentrating on their position and the accumulating darkness rendering effective shooting impossible, the Rebel commanders ordered their pieces to cease fire. The Union gunners, certain that they had silenced an enemy battery, did the same. The end of the artillery duel led Hays to conclude that the immediate threat to his division had passed. Rather than leave Smyth's brigade exposed on the western side of the O&A, however, he ordered the colonel to fall back and resume his former position on the other side of the railroad embankment.[15]

Both sides believed this second round of combat near Bristoe Station accrued to their advantage. Federal artillery was credited with beating back Anderson's advance, while the brigades of Posey and Perry were lauded for stemming an assault by Smyth's brigade. Rebel gunners claimed to have driven off a Yankee battery, and Union cannoneers boasted that they had battered Tanner's guns to submission. None of this had happened. Neither body of infantry was about to launch an assault, and none of the rival batteries were compelled to retire. Rickett's fieldpieces were already under orders to head to the rear when the Rebels opened fire. The Confederate barrage merely

---

14 *OR* 29, pt. 1, 286; Muffly, *148th Pennsylvania*, 101.

15 *OR* 29, pt. 1, 306, 294; *OR Supplement* 5, pt. 1, 594.

hastened their appointed departure. Of course, neither side knew these facts and each merely drew what seemed to be obvious conclusions given their enemy's actions.[16]

*   *   *

The artillery contest had actually worked to the Federals' ultimate advantage. The duel delayed and complicated the Confederate effort to muster overwhelming force against Warren's still vulnerable position. It also helped mask the arrival of Caldwell's division on the field, which added badly needed strength to Warren's dangling left flank. So too did the appearance of two batteries of horse artillery (Battery A, 4th US and the 6th New York Light), that had accidentally lost contact with Gregg's division and followed Warren's ambulances and ammunition wagons to Brentsville.[17]

Since leaving Catlett's Station around noon, Caldwell's division and Gregg's horsemen had trudged drearily northward behind the II Corps vehicles and the 2nd Cavalry Division's wagon train. This tiresome but not overly difficult rearguard duty was interrupted by the unexpected sound of heavy firing from Bristoe Station as these troops had neared Kettle Run. Shortly afterwards one of Warren's aides, Lt. Frank Haskell, arrived with orders for the 1st Division to come up with the "utmost haste."

Caldwell ordered his men to the double quick. It was a tough jog for soldiers already fatigued by a dawn battle at Auburn and tedious rearguard duty ever since. Nonetheless, the troops responded well and in short order the division made contact with Hays' left flank. They also encountered a confusing situation much in flux, and at first Caldwell was unsure what his superiors expected him to do.

Warren cleared that up by ordering him to assign troops to support the Union artillery dueling with Tanner's guns. After detailing Col. Nelson A. Miles' 1st Brigade to that task, Caldwell shifted the rest of his command toward the railroad embankment. With nothing but a vague idea where the enemy was, he prudently threw out flankers and skirmishers. Rebel sharpshooters soon took these men under fire and thus revealed the presence of a large number of Confederates in front of the division.[18]

Smyth's brigade was still west of the railroad when the 1st Division reached the embankment. Since no one had issued orders to halt at the tracks, many of Caldwell's men thought they were about to launch an attack on the Rebels engaging Smyth's troops. Caldwell's 3rd Brigade crossed the O&A before instructions to stop reached

---

16 *OR* 29, pt. 1, 306, 421, 429.

17 Ibid., 372-3, 306; Griffin, *Three Years a Soldier*, 142.

18 Previous paragraphs based upon *OR* 29, pt. 1, 255, 256-57, 260, 266. Miles would go on to win great fame as an Indian fighter after the war.

Col. Paul Frank, the brigade's temporary commander. Smyth received orders to retire east of the railroad about the same time as Frank and the two brigades pulled back together. Their withdrawal placed Warren's entire corps behind the railroad embankment, which was some 15 feet high along Caldwell's front.[19]

Frank's (Beaver's) brigade occupied the right of the Caldwell's line and connected to Smyth's brigade on Hays' left flank. Colonel Patrick Kelly's Irish Brigade held Caldwell's center and Col. Brooke's 4th Brigade his left. Once Caldwell had his units in position, he ordered the entire division to lie down, both protecting his men and concealing their position from the enemy.[20]

Caldwell's deployment lengthened the Federal line, but did nothing to guard its flank. Col. Samuel Carroll's brigade, the last of Warren's infantry formations to rejoin the corps, assumed that task. Earlier in the day Carroll's command had been detached from Hays' division to guard a road intersection connecting Bristoe Station and Bristersburg to the south. Because Carroll's orders required him to hold his position until the rest of the II Corps had passed, his troops arrived near Bristoe Station after Caldwell's regiments. Although Carroll's brigade belonged to Hays' 3rd Division, Caldwell told Carroll to form his men perpendicular to Brooke's brigade and then go prone. This had the effect of slightly refusing Warren's southern flank and also massing a large body of troops at the point of greatest danger. In some places along Caldwell's line Union infantrymen were now stacked four or six ranks deep.[21]

Despite this concentration of troops, whether Warren could prevent the Confederates from crushing his left wasn't clear. The odds against his corps grew longer by the minute. Major General Cadmus Wilcox's division was already on the field and going into line behind Anderson's troops. More ominously, Ewell's entire corps, coming up fast, began deploying on A. P. Hill's right flank. Once assembled something like 40,000 Rebels would face roughly 9,000 Union infantry. Warren could count on just a few thousand troopers in Gregg's two cavalry brigades for reinforcements. Only the clock favored the Federals. It was already past 4 p.m. and the sun would set in 90 minutes. If light ran out before Ewell could attack, Warren's corps might survive the day.[22]

Robert E. Lee also knew what time it was, and he was anxious to mount an all-out attack before it was too late. Much to his frustration, however, numerous difficulties plagued the deployment of his army. Anderson's entanglement with Smyth's brigade

---

19 Ibid. The brigade's commander Col. James Beaver was serving as division officer of the day.

20 Ibid.

21 OR 29, pt. 1, 290-91, 255; Galwey Memoir, LC: Galwey, *Valiant Hours*, 157.

22 Krick, *Civil War Weather*, 110.

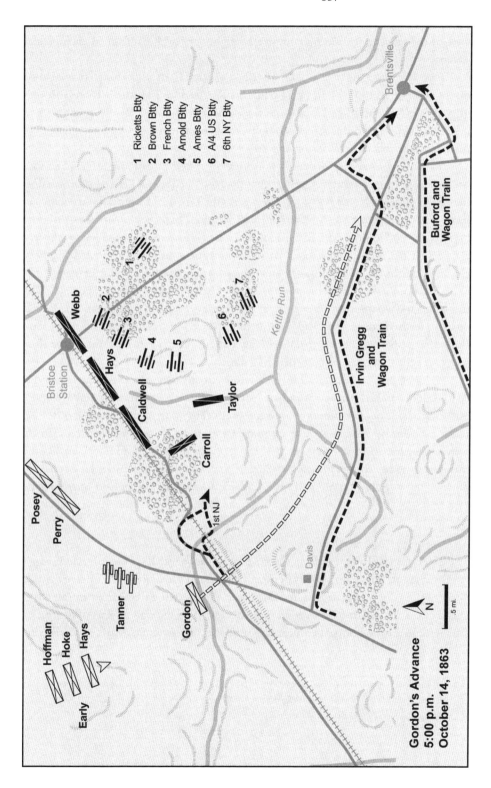

1   Ricketts Btty
2   Brown Btty
3   French Btty
4   Arnold Btty
5   Ames Btty
6   A/4 US Btty
7   6th NY Btty

Brentsville

Buford and
Wagon Train

Irvin Gregg
and
Wagon Train

Kettle Run

Webb

Bristoe
Station

Hays

Caldwell

Taylor

Carroll

1st NJ

Davis

Posey

Perry

Tanner

Gordon

Hoffman

Hoke

Hays

Early

N

5 mi

Gordon's Advance
5:00 p.m.
October 14, 1863

west of the railroad had been disruptive enough, but Ewell confronted even greater challenges.

Soon after reaching the battlefield Lee had ordered Early's division to block Union troops coming up the O&A toward Bristoe Station. Early quickly threw John Gordon's brigade into line and placed it in some woods near Kettle Run. Before going back to hasten the approach of his remaining units, the general had told Gordon to remain in place until the rest of the division arrived.

After Early rode off, Gordon's skirmishers spotted a scattering of Yankee foot soldiers along the railroad. Engaging what they assumed was a Federal skirmish line, they were surprised when it easily gave way. As the Georgians watched the enemy fall back, they noticed that the Northerners were wearing "big, heavy knapsacks." For the hungry, ragged Confederates the vision of luxuries contained in those knapsacks was akin to a child in a candy store. Anxious to capture desperately needed blankets, clothing and shoes, the Georgians quickly "took after" the fleeing Northerners.[23]

They eventually bagged most of their prey. Those Yankees who escaped did so by throwing away knapsacks, haversacks, and even guns to speed their flight. The Rebels quickly realized that they had captured a collection of Union stragglers, not skirmishers. Most of the prisoners were raw recruits, which explained the overstuffed knapsacks the Georgians eagerly began looting.

What might have been amusing in different circumstances had repercussions now. As Gordon watched his troops pursue Yankee knapsacks, he spotted Union cavalry escorting a large wagon train not far to the south. That was a provocative and fleeting target. The enemy vehicles would not remain within reach for long. Gordon's orders were to stay put and await the arrival of the rest of Early's division. But much like his men, the brigadier couldn't resist the allure of such a supply-laden prize. He decided to go after the wagons and ordered his battle line toward the bridge and across Kettle Run.[24]

*   *   *

The object of John Gordon's disobedient advance was Brig. Gen. David Gregg's cavalry division, which was slowly herding a column of wagons toward Bristoe Station. Col. John Taylor's brigade was moving west of the railroad embankment and well ahead of Col. Irvin Gregg's brigade which was escorting the wagons east of the tracks. By the time Taylor's horsemen neared Kettle Run it was almost dark, with visibility

---

23 George W. Nicholas, *A Soldier's Story of His Regiment (61st Georgia) and incidentally of the Lawton-Gordon-Evans Brigade, Army of Northern Virginia* (Jesup, GA, 1898), 129.

24 Early, *Memoirs*, 305.

rapidly decreasing in the fast fading light. As the Federals rode toward the creek they noticed a "long column" of infantry to their northwest. The Yankee cavalrymen assumed it must be a part of Warren's corps.[25]

That dark mass of troops was, of course, Gordon's infantry which entered a thick pine forest near Kettle Run before the Federals had a chance to grasp the true situation. From there the Southerners opened fire on the Taylor's brigade just as it was trotting over the railroad bridge spanning the creek. The 1st Pennsylvania Cavalry at the head of the mounted column turned to face the Rebels as soon as it reached the north shore. Even with virtually empty cartridge boxes, the Pennsylvania regiment covered the rest of Taylor's command as it dashed across the bridge and on to the relative safety of Caldwell's division.[26]

The 1st New Jersey Cavalry received no such assistance. During the approach to Kettle Run, the regiment had been supporting the 2nd Cavalry Division's rearguard skirmishers. With the regiment's commander, Maj. Hugh Janeway, in charge of the rearguard, Capt. William W. Gray commanded the New Jersey cavalrymen. When Janeway released Gray from his support duties, the 35-year old officer hurried his men to Kettle Run.

By the time the 1st New Jersey neared the stream Gordon's infantry had nearly reached the bridge. A hail of Rebel bullets swept over the structure and the ford just west of the span. Gray was in an awful spot, having to cross Kettle Run with no safe way of doing it. Riding over the railway bridge would make his men easy targets, and the ford was even closer to the enemy. Gray decided the ford the lesser evil—and even though its use would "be attended by fearful loss," he led his column in that direction.

An unidentified mounted Union staffer discovered an alternative escape route. The orderly had bravely slipped down into the creek and splashed his way to the bridge. Upon reaching its stone pillars, he began signaling frantically for the rest of the endangered Union column to follow. It took a minute or two, but an officer finally caught sight of the man's "earnest gestures" and grasped their meaning.[27]

The bulk of the 1st New Jersey dashed down into the creek's natural defilade and headed for the bridge while Gray and a smaller contingent raced across the ford. Rebel bullets continually smacked into the stone abutment as most of the regiment's men rode under the span. Remarkably, both parties managed to reach the northern shore without casualties and gallop out of danger to join the rest of their brigade.

25 Preston, *10th New York Cavalry*, 150; Matteson, *Campaigns of 10th New York Cavalry*, 189-90.

26 *OR* 29, pt. 1, 361; *OR Supplement* 5, pt. 1, 595; Bushnell Memoir, WRHS; Early, *Memoirs*, 305.

27 Payne, *First New Jersey Cavalry*, 190.

This drawing by Alfred Waud shows Federal troops retreating over Kettle Run prior to the fight at Bristoe Station. The railroad bridge is clearly visible in the background. The troops in the foreground are using the ford west of the bridge. The 1st New Jersey Cavalry crossed the creek via both routes under fire late on October 14. *Library of Congress*

If Taylor's regiments had made their getaway under hair raising circumstances, Brig. Gen. Gregg faced an even more difficult situation east of the railroad embankment. He was riding with Irvin Gregg's brigade, alongside the division's wagon train. Under cover of the embankment his force had initially avoided both enemy fire and direct Rebel observation. Now, however, it faced a more perilous situation. Gordon's advance had cut off the only direct route to Caldwell's division. Gregg may have briefly considered attempting to cut his way through to Warren, but with so many vehicles, he knew this would be foolhardy. Instead he turned his command away from the battle in a bid to outrace Gordon's Confederates and reach Brentsville.[28]

North of Kettle Run, Colonel Taylor watched as the Rebels captured the bridge and advanced south of the creek. Fearful that Gregg might not realize the enemy had gotten between his command and Warren's corps, Taylor ordered Capt. James Leeman to take a squadron from the 6th Ohio and carry an urgent warning to the general before he stumbled into unforeseen disaster.

28 OR 29, pt. 1, 366, 369, 372-73; Preston, *10th New York Cavalry*, 150; Bushnell Memoir, WRHS.

Leeman knew that the only way to speedily accomplish his mission was to cross the Kettle Run bridge and race to Gregg by charging through Gordon's brigade. In the face of this daunting prospect, the captain didn't hesitate. He figured that the audacity of such a move in the fading daylight might surprise the Confederates and allow at least some of the squadron to reach Gregg.

Fortune favors the bold, it's said, and it certainly seems to have blessed the 6th Ohio Cavalry on October 14, 1863. Leeman's men hit a soft spot in the Rebel line and managed to dash south of Kettle Run and reach Gen. Gregg without losing a man; they also rescued 15 II Corps prisoners from enemy hands in the process.

Ironically, the Ohioans' gallantry wasn't necessary. Keenly aware of his circumstances, Gregg had already diverted his column toward Brentsville. The Yankees managed to get a head start on Gordon's brigade, which staged a lengthy pursuit of Gregg's cavalrymen and their wagons. Despite the Rebels' persistence, the Federals moved two miles northeastward to Brentsville without real difficulty. The wagons went into park near the village, while Irvin Gregg's brigade and Maj. Janeway's rearguard skirmishers took up a defensive position close to the II Corps field hospital.[29]

*   *   *

Gordon's advance may have discomfited the Yankee cavalry, but it proved far more disruptive to his own side. Jubal Early returned to the spot where he had left the Georgians to find no one. After ordering Hoke, Hays, and Hoffman into line facing the creek, Early sent riders to locate his missing brigade, and that took a while.[30]

Wherever Gordon had gone, Early could no longer see any enemy force south of Kettle Run. He thus pivoted his division to face northeast toward Bristoe Station. While his brigades were shifting position a staff officer arrived to explain Gordon's absence and provide news of the Georgian's attack on Gregg.

Jubal Early was not pleased. Not only had the brigadier disobeyed orders, he now reported himself facing a significant force of Yankee horsemen defending a "very large train of wagons" around Brentsville, from which he could neither easily nor quickly withdraw. This unexpected news totally disrupted Early's nascent offensive plans.

By the time the general finished positioning his three remaining brigades onto a new axis of attack, at least part of his division stood east of the railroad tracks. The bulk of it, however, was on the other side oriented to the northeast with a thick stand of pines, barely navigable in line of battle, between it and the enemy. Any advance through

---

29 *OR* 29, pt. 1, 358, 361, 366.

30 Early, *Memoirs*, 305; *OR Supplement* 5, pt. 1, 595.

the pines would be slow and difficult. Federal infantry and especially artillery would undoubtedly pound the Confederates mercilessly as they traversed the woods.

A strong assault east of the tracks, where the ground was more conducive to offensive movements offered the only chance at evening the odds. An advance from that direction would strike the Yankee flank and rear, and it should deflect enough Union fire to give troops coming through the woods a better chance of reaching the railroad without being blasted apart. But Early lacked the strength for such an attack without Gordon's Georgians, who were fully a third of his divisional manpower.[31]

If Early could not strike alone in the absence of Gordon, it might be possible to attack in conjunction with Confederate forces west of the railroad embankment. Unfortunately most of those units were either too distant or otherwise preoccupied to help. Along A. P. Hill's front Wilcox's division was still going into position on Heth's left flank. At the moment Heth's division was incapable of resuming the offensive, and Anderson's division on Heth's right, already partially engaged, had not yet fully deployed. As for Ewell's corps, Rodes' division was too far back to reach the field before nightfall. Only "Alleghany" Johnson's division was near enough to join the fight.

If his command could lend its weight to an assault, the Confederates might yet overwhelm Warren's left flank. Darkness would magnify the resulting chaos in the Federal ranks and might lead to the rout, if not the destruction, of the Yankee II Corps.

It was not to be. Darkness had fallen by the time Wilcox had lined up on Hill's left and Johnson had deployed behind Early's division. Their troops engaged in a little light skirmishing and had a few shells sail over their heads, but that was all. One of Wilcox's soldiers recalled that his brigade's role at Bristoe Station consisted of lying prone on a brushy hill and watching the "lazy artillery firing on both sides."[32]

The seeming nearness of battle, followed by the anticlimax of inaction, was an experience shared by almost every unit that reached the field after the initial Confederate assault. As the sun slipped below the horizon the newcomers listened to the skirmishers pop away at one another. They marveled at what one man called the "grand sight" of cannon fire in the twilight, while Federal leaders puzzled over the failure of the Rebels to attack.[33]

*   *   *

31 Early, *Memoirs*, 305-306.

32 Caldwell, *Brigade of South Carolinians*, 160; Early, *Memoirs*, 305-306.

33 OR 29, pt. 1, 271-72; Worsham, *One of Jackson's Foot Cavalry*, 183; [Bloomsburg, PA] *Columbia Democrat*, Oct. 31, 1863.

During the evening the officers and men of Heth's division continued to sort themselves out and reform their regiments. Surgeon's assistants tended to minor wounds and stretcher bearers carried the more seriously injured to field hospitals. Commanders issued orders prohibiting campfires, lest they offer targets to enemy cannon. But with no rations to cook, fires were a moot point anyway. Unable to ignore the cries of wounded comrades left on the field, some men bravely crawled forward to aid those they could reach. The mournful hooting of a nearby owl deepened the already grim atmosphere west of the railroad.[34]

Sergeant William Long, like many others, marveled that he was still alive. He counted no less than 17 bullets holes in his uniform and was surprised to discover that he had a bruise from a shell fragment and a pistol ball lodged just beneath his skin. When Long learned that his cousin, Maj. Webb of the 27th North Carolina, was wounded, the sergeant secured permission to check on his relative's fate.[35]

He found the major being treated for a broken arm in addition to a flesh wound in one thigh and another in his unbroken arm. Despite these hurts, Webb had taken command of the 27th after the wounding of his superiors and then led it in the final attack and subsequent harrowing retreat. As the sergeant watched, the attending surgeon urged Webb to go to the rear. The major adamantly refused to do so and declared that he would not leave his troops while he still had one good leg and a horse to ride. As far as Webb was concerned, the fight at Bristoe Station was far from over and there would be "work to do when the sun comes up."[36]

That there was hard work ahead, no one in Cooke's or Kirkland's brigades doubted. Ordnance officers were busily resupplying the troops and ensuring that each man had 60 rounds of ammunition. As the battered North Carolinians laid down in line of battle to get what sleep they could, Webb told his cousin, "We've got to have those batteries over there . . . before breakfast."[37]

---

34 Long "Reminiscences," Breckinridge papers, LC.

35 Ibid.

36 Ibid.

37 Ibid.

CHAPTER 26

"No Fires, No Supper and No Sleep"

Looming Danger—Sykes Unaware—Warren's Plea—V Corps Reverses Course
Evacuating the Wounded—Union Escape—Buford's Travails

ALTHOUGH the fighting at Bristoe Station had ended for the moment, Gouverneur Warren knew that the Rebels might yet destroy his corps. The smallest in the Meade's command, it faced the concentrating might of the Army of Northern Virginia alone. Painfully aware that trying to withdraw over Broad Run before nightfall would likely be suicidal, Warren felt constrained to hold his ground. As long as his troops stayed behind the railroad embankment, the Rebels would remain cautious and probably uncertain of Federal strength and dispositions. Nonetheless, the odds against the Yankees grew longer. A concerted enemy attack might yet overrun the II Corps.

What Warren needed was help from George Sykes' V Corps, which Meade had instructed to stay within supporting distance. But other than its 3rd Division, which had remained out of sight and the fight, the V Corps had continued its retreat toward Manassas. Remarkably the sound of swelling battle had done nothing to make Sykes reconsider his course. He seemed utterly indifferent about any danger to the army's rearguard. Indeed, when the general discovered that McCandless' 3rd Division had stayed near Broad Run, he ordered it to get back on the road to Centreville at once. Colonel McCandless had no alternative but to obey. Around 4 p.m. the only element of the V Corps even remotely in position to aid Warren marched away just as the bulk of Ewell's corps arrived on the battlefield.[1]

About that same time, a courier from Sykes arrived at Bristoe Station with a dispatch for Warren, who read it with amazement. The V Corps was already at

1 Harden, *12th Pennsylvania Volunteers*, 167.

Manassas, Sykes wrote, but disposed to slow the pace of its withdrawal toward Centreville, unless Warren needed assistance. Apparently clueless that a major engagement had been raging all afternoon, Sykes warned Warren not to linger near Broad Run, for although he understood as yet "but few" Confederates were opposing the II Corps, that might change if Warren took too leisurely a pace. For now Sykes was confident Warren could "of course . . . manage" unaided the paltry number of Rebel infantrymen he might encounter.[2]

Lack of sleep and two battles in one day had frayed Warren's nerves. He had never been disposed to forgive what he perceived as blunders or incompetence. Sykes' message struck him as a gross example of both. The failure of the V Corps commander to sustain the II Corps, or even comprehend its situation enraged Warren to such a degree his temper boiled over, scalding the unfortunate V Corps courier. Although no one recorded what Warren said, it was evidently pointed and direct—so much so that the general later regretted berating the poor staff officer. At any rate, the man went back to report the true condition of things to Sykes. Warren also dispatched Maj. Benjamin C. Ludlow with instructions to impress upon Sykes and Army Headquarters the realities of the current situation and ask for assistance. The 32-year old Ludlow had been a physician before the war and a member of Hooker's staff at Chancellorsville. Meade had kept him on as an aide-de-camp and assigned him to accompany the II Corps during the retreat from Catlett's Station. Warren hoped Ludlow's gravitas would lend weight to his urgent appeal for help.[3]

* * *

Just how George Sykes remained unaware of what was happening at Bristoe Station on the afternoon of October 14 remains a mystery. Soldiers in the Newton's I Corps—the first to reach Centreville—had noticed the sound of "heavy cannonading" and columns of gun smoke wafting into the air from Bristoe at 2 p.m. Although they at first dismissed these telltale signs as evidence of a cavalry scuffle, by 3 p.m. it was clear something more than an "ordinary skirmish" was going on. At 4 p.m., as the clatter of

---

2 Warren to Sykes, October 29, 1863, Gouverneur Kemble Warren papers, NYSL; David M. Jordon, *Happiness Is Not My Companion: The Life of General G.K. Warren* (Bloomington, IN, 2001), 108-10.

3 OR 29, pt. 1, 243. Paul Eby Steiner, *Physician-generals in the Civil War: A Study in Mid-Century American Medicine* (Springfield, IL, 1966), 76; John Y. Simon, ed., 31 vols. *The Papers of Ulysses S. Grant: November 16, 1864-February 20, 1865* (Carbondale, IL, 1985),Vol. 13. n. 1, 81. Ludlow would become a brigadier general of cavalry in 1864 and had a horse shot out from under him sometime on Oct. 14.

combat continued to drift northward, many soldiers began to suspect something big brewing which might yet suck them into it. By 5 o'clock, however, the sound of battle had ceased, and whatever fight had taken place was obviously ended.[4]

The V Corps, which was nearer all this evidence than any other part of the army, seems to have either discounted the meaning of the gunfire or been indifferent to its portent. Certainly, nothing dissuaded its commander from his fervent desire to reach Centreville. Sykes was more fearful of the Rebels cutting off his command from the III Corps than he was of the Confederates separating the II Corps from his own. With single minded determination, he disregarded or rationalized away every scrap of evidence that suggested any course other than continuing north as quickly as possible.

Even when Ludlow and his own courier provided incontrovertible proof of Warren's predicament, Sykes did not change his mind immediately. In a return message to Warren, Sykes reported that he had just seen Ludlow, thus implying he knew the II Corps' circumstances. Nonetheless, Sykes still insisted it was "everything that the army should be concentrated at Centreville." He urged Warren to move toward Manassas "as soon as dark, if not before" and warned him that "two corps are little better than one" if Lee was nearby. Then he promised to "stay at Manassas until dark."[5]

Not long after he dispatched this message, Sykes changed his mind. For some reason he suddenly understood the II Corps to be in real trouble. At 5 p.m. he wrote Meade that Warren was in a fight at Bristoe Station, from where he could hear "sharp musketry." He passed along Warren's claim that the entire Rebel army was in front of the II Corps and then announced he was moving the V Corps back to Bristoe Station "at once."[6]

Despite this decisive tone, the general clearly felt conflicted and uneasy with his decision. Sykes admitted to army headquarters that he had no idea where the Rebel "main force" was located and repeated his opinion that if Lee's entire command were at Bristoe, the presence of the V Corps would make little difference. Nonetheless, he worried that if he didn't go to Warren's aid, the enemy might interpose between the II and the V Corps during the night. Moreover, by marching toward Bristoe Station, he would afford the Rebels a chance to slip between his own and French's III Corps, with

---

4   Lance Herdegen & Murphy Sherry, eds., *Four Years With The Iron Brigade: The Civil War Journal of William Ray, Company F, 7th Wisconsin Infantry* (Cambridge, MA, 2002), 226.

5   Ibid. OR 29, pt. 1, 243. Samuel Harris, commanding the cavalry escort for V Corps HQ, says that Sykes and his adjutant drank an entire bottle of whiskey between them on the afternoon of Oct. 14. It is possible to infer that this hindered the general's judgment; however, no account of that day makes any mention of him being in a drunken state, including that of Harris. *Personal Reminiscences of Samuel Harris*, 51-52.

6   OR 29, pt. 2, 313.

which he had no communication. Sykes obviously felt trapped by the situation, and he did not like it.

As he put his men on the road, the general didn't know whether his corps was going to join a battle or merely hastening to take the II Corps by the hand and lead it to safety. Sykes asked Meade if the V Corps should stay at Bristoe Station overnight or "unite with the army at Centreville" before daylight. Sykes obviously preferred the latter. His anxiety to head north, which had dominated his thinking throughout most of the day, remained paramount.[7]

*   *   *

The V Corps could have no immediate impact at Bristoe Station. Sykes had marched too far away and waited too long before choosing to return to Broad Run. Night would certainly have fallen before the V Corps neared the battlefield. The isolated II Corps would have to sweat out the remaining hours of daylight alone and fend off the gathering Rebel multitudes as best it could.

That might be a tall order. Warren's bone-tired soldiers were almost to the point of exhaustion. One officer complained that Meade's order to carry extra ammunition as well as five days rations instead of the customary three, had "weighed down [the men] with unusual burdens" throughout the retreat. Constant marching, with few breaks, had robbed everyone of sleep. These factors along with an "almost utter absence of cooked food for two days," a morning fight at Auburn and an afternoon struggle at Bristoe Station, sufficiently explained the physical state of the corps. With the Rebels so near, few men could find rest.[8]

The need to attend the wounded also cried out for attention. Many injured Confederates lay outside Union lines, beyond the reach of friend or foe. Their heart-rending pleas for help wore on the minds of everyone within earshot. The Federal wounded were more fortunate. Most of them had crawled off the firing line and found some safety in a ditch halfway between the railroad and the hills occupied by Union artillery. Here hospital stewards and friends did what they could to render aid before stretcher bearers and ambulances carted the worst of the injured to the rear.

The officer responsible for seeing to the proper care of these men was Maj. Alexander Dougherty, medical director of the II Corps. He was having as difficult a time as any line officer that afternoon. The McCormick house at Auburn had served as his first hospital of the day and his surgical teams had performed several amputations

---

7   Ibid., pt. 1, 243.

8   Walker, *Second Army Corps*, 345.

there and left behind a few mortally wounded soldiers when the retreat to Catlett's Station began. When Warren's corps reached the railroad later that morning, Meade's staff officers had sent most of Dougherty's ambulances northward with the II Corps wagon train. That army headquarters assumed there would be no more fighting and that none of these specialized vehicles needed to stay with the troops appalled Warren's medical staff. Captain Thomas Livermore, the II Corps chief of ambulance, protested this decision vigorously. Headquarters eventually allowed him to keep a meager 16 vehicles with the infantry.[9]

The outbreak of fighting at Bristoe vindicated the medical men's concerns. Dougherty and Livermore quickly established a field hospital in a barn near Kettle Run and began treating wounded men already "fast coming to the rear." Before long, however, the "rattle of carbines" from Gregg's cavalry announced Confederates bearing down on the Federal left. Dougherty ordered his hospital displaced to safer ground. After loading the wounded into the available ambulances, medical orderlies tossed most of the injured soldiers' muskets into the creek. But not all of them. In a testament to the confusion reigning near Kettle Run, the hospital staff felt the need to retain a number of weapons in case they had to defend their wards from a Southern attack.

The hospital moved northeast and attempted twice more to set up operations. The growing action around Bristoe Station compelled it to again retreat. Dougherty finally placed his hospital in a barn on the Porter farm, alongside the Brentsville Road about two miles east of the battlefield. The surgeons worked well into the evening tending the more than 180 stricken soldiers eventually collected at this location.[10]

The next day, if they were lucky, the wounded would be securely inside the lines of the Army of the Potomac and on their way to one of the hospitals around Washington, DC. But the injured would have to endure a long period of pain and discomfort first. Throughout the night the agonized moans and plaintive prayers of hundreds of mangled men hung over the valley of Broad Run, a stark testimony to the horrors of war.[11]

*   *   *

For General Warren, the one hopeful moment in that gloomy evening came when the V Corps arrived within a mile of Broad Run not long after night cloaked the field.

---

9   OR 29, pt. 1, 251-52.

10   Ibid., 251; Wells, *Surgeon in the Army of the Potomac*, 75.

11   Walker, *Second Army Corps*, 357.

Sykes' exhausted men had double-quicked nearly the entire five miles between Manassas Junction and Bristoe Station. On its southward journey the corps had linked up with McCandless' division, whose northward march Sykes had ordered suspended not long after it had resumed. The V Corps fanned out some skirmishers toward the creek as a precaution against any surprise from that direction. This probe provoked a brief exchange of picket fire, but the Rebels remained unaware that Union reinforcements were nearby.[12]

Although the V Corps presence was reassuring, technically Warren no longer needed its help. The battle was over; withdrawal was now the mission. If the V Corps came too near Bristoe Station it might clog the roads and fatally slow the II Corps' retreat. Sykes and Warren therefore agreed that the V Corps would hold its position until the II Corps could slip away from the battlefield and move north to join hands with Sykes' column.

While the V Corps waited, Federal soldiers south of Broad Run prepared their escape. Staff officers forbid anyone to give a command louder than a whisper. Bugle and drum calls were prohibited, and the troops were warned to muffle their canteens and tin cups before the corps marched. Warren had no choice but to withdraw his artillery over the railroad bridge and his infantry across the ford nearby. If the Rebels realized what was happening, they could easily sweep the bridge with artillery fire and turn orderly retreat into a rout or worse.[13]

Removing the wounded presented an especially difficult, disconcerting task. For a time, given the scarcity of ambulances, it looked as though the corps might have to leave a large number of casualties behind. The walking wounded would have to make their own way north, keeping up as best they could with the column. The more badly injured required vehicular evacuation. One doctor remembered that as few places in the available ambulances quickly filled, tortured glances from the eyes of those "poor fellows" threatened with abandonment became "clamorous" pleas for a spot on a wagon.

Fortunately, the trains of the 2nd Cavalry Division remained close by, and Gen. Gregg offered to loan Livermore 13 of his ambulances. This met most of the need. Although Maj. Dougherty felt certain "almost all" of the wounded were carried off, the assistant surgeon of 108th New York believed all but a few regiments left "more or less of their wounded on the field for want to transportation." Regardless of which claim

---

12 E. M. Woodward, *Our Campaigns; or the Marches, Bivouacs, Battles, Incidents of Camp Life and History of Our Regiment During Its Three Years Term of Service* (Philadelphia, PA, 1865), 299; Carter, *Four Brothers in Blue*, 355; Sidney Burbank Diary, October 14, 1863, LC; Bowen, *Dear Friends at Home*, 338.

13 Walker, *Second Army Corps*, 361.

was correct, Maj. Frederick Wolf, the 39th New York's surgeon, and assistant surgeon Gustavus Bingel of the 52nd New York, together with four hospital attendants, stayed behind to care for those men too grievously hurt to be moved.[14]

Once transportable casualties were loaded, the artillery teams hitched, and the infantry ready to march, Warren ordered his breakout into motion. Beginning at 9 p.m., Union regiments quietly started to make their way across the ford. The rearguard detachment of pickets maintained a protective screen west of the railroad embankment. They had orders to hold their ground until the column had passed and then fall in on its rear. One disconsolate Yankee recalled the appalling cries of "mutilated Confederates, lying where they had fallen" pursuing the Northerners as they silently withdrew.[15]

What one man described as "[D]ismal and wet" weather helped obscure Warren's otherwise noisy withdrawal. Somehow Southern pickets failed to detect the move, and the entire corps successfully snuck across Broad Run and made its dash for the north. Sykes ordered his troops to start marching as soon as the head of the II Corps column drew near the tail of the V Corps. For the men in both units this was no easy trek. Although Sykes' divisions were traversing the same ground for the third time in less than 12 hours, they set a brisk pace. One solider at the rear of the II Corps column complained that his regiment often had to "double-quick" to keep up. Before the night was over, recalled another Yankee, the two corps would ford four "cold and chilling" creeks.[16]

*   *   *

Several miles to the east of Bristoe Station, the vast wagon and pontoon trains of the AOP, escorted by John Buford's horsemen, were also on the move. After crossing the Rappahannock at Beverly Ford on October 13, the 1st Cavalry Division had ridden to Warrenton Junction and bivouacked for the night. Before dawn the next day, Gen. Pleasonton assigned Buford the job of escorting the army's main wagon and pontoon trains toward Centreville. To get the ponderous mass of vehicles out of the way of his infantry, Meade had directed that the trains veer east towards Brentsville. From there they would cross Broad Run on their way to Wolf Run Shoals, a few miles east of Yates Ford where Bull Run joins Occoquan Creek. Once they forded Bull Run at that point

14 Well's *Surgeon in the Army of the Potomac*, 76; OR 29, pt. 1, 251-52.

15 Cowtan, 10th New York, 224; Humphreys, *From Gettysburg to the Rapidan*, 30.

16 Cowtan, *10th New York*, 224; Page, *Fourteenth Connecticut*, 196.

the trains would travel through Fairview and Fairfax Station on their way to Fairfax Court House, northeast of Centreville.[17]

The wagons moved out at 2 a.m. on October 14. Buford's men were awake by three, but not on the march until 9:30 a.m. because it took so long for the massive assembly of vehicles and horses to uncoil itself and get out onto the road. Once underway the slow pace of its march led one Illinois cavalryman to proclaim that "Job's stock would have been exhausted at the outset."[18]

Lieutenant Colonel Spaulding's engineers agreed. They decided it would be faster to build their own road through the woods rather than wait for all the wagons to pass so that they could fall in at the rear of the column. Spaulding's men took up their axes and blazed a nine-mile-long road from Weaverville to Brentsville and still arrived there before the tail of the wagon train.[19]

The cavalry, on the other hand, was compelled to traipse slowly along beside the seemingly endless line of vehicles. Not until late in the afternoon of October 14 did the wagons reach Brentsville, where Buford was shocked to find the entire armada in the process of parking. Besides the main train and the pontoons, he discovered the wagons of the III, VI and Cavalry Corps all bunched up around the little village. The few quartermasters he could find evinced "little disposition" to resume their march, which frustrated Buford to no end. The entire situation was so dangerous the general felt compelled to send a 5:30 p.m. message to Pleasonton explaining the mess he had found. Buford apprehended great trouble in getting such a large and badly managed conglomeration to Centreville without mishap.[20]

The sound of battle at Bristoe and a twilight probe by Rebel cavalry convinced the teamsters that it might be a good idea to keep going. As the train lurched back into motion, the 1st Cavalry Division stood by its horses ready to mount as a precaution against a Confederate attack. At least one trooper would never forget the miserable night with "no fires, no supper and no sleep" that followed. David Gregg brought his brigades over to assist in protecting the wagon train. They remained on station until Buford deemed their support unnecessary, at which point Gregg's regiments rode off after the lumbering wagon train.[21]

17 Abner Frank diary October 14, 1863, USMHI; Cheney, *9th New York Cavalry*, 138-39; Hall, *6th New York Cavalry*, 162; Hard, *8th Illinois Cavalry*, 279.

18 Hall, *6th New York Cavalry*, 162; Hard, *8th Illinois Cavalry*, 279.

19 *OR* 29, pt., 1, 999-1000.

20 Ibid., 350, 346.

21 Pyne, *1st New Jersey Cavalry*, 193; ibid., pt. 1, 330; Hall, *6th New York Cavalry*, 163.

Besides being an unusually wretched experience for the Federal horsemen, the evening of October 14 was also a highly dangerous one. During the day's final contorted maneuvers around Kettle Run, the lines of the two armies had become badly intermingled. A portion of the 6th Ohio Cavalry discovered this when it tried to make its way from the railroad (where it had supported Caldwell during the Bristoe fight) to rejoin Gregg's division near Brentsville. As the men more or less felt their way along through the black night, they suddenly realized they were in trouble. An entire regiment of Confederate infantry had established a tentless bivouac on either side of the road down which they rode. The Northerners had unknowingly ridden right into the middle of an enemy camp!

Under the circumstances the commander of the lead squadron decided that boldness offered the best chance of escaping disaster. He ordered his men to charge through the mass of sleeping Southerners. The Confederates, taken by surprise—they had apparently failed to post sentries—offered no more than a sleepy resistance before the enemy disappeared into the night, untouched by scattered Rebel gunfire.[22]

This escape of the Ohioans was hardly the only heart-stopping moment that evening. From Brentsville northward difficult topography forced the Union army's wagon and pontoon trains onto a single, narrow lane. So many vehicles and animals passing over this route turned what had been a tolerably good dirt road into a rutted, muddy morass. The resulting difficulties and delays beggared description. One Federal remarked that in his whole military experience he "never saw a night" such as this.[23]

One Yankee cavalryman listed "precipitous" hills, slippery banks, swampy hollows, and "unfathomless mud holes" that ensnared vehicles and brought horses to a complete stop among the obstacles the column encountered. The unwieldy pontoon wagons were especially difficult to keep moving. A single stuck wagon halted the entire procession until men and animals could dislodge the vehicle. This happened at least 10 times over the course of the evening, and each time teamsters prepared to burn their wagons to prevent them from falling into enemy hands. Somehow, however, the obstacle was always freed, and the trains continued to crawl northward throughout the night.[24]

* * *

22 Bushnell Memoir, WRHS.

23 Aldrich, *Battery A, 1st Rhode Island Artillery*, 252; OR 29, pt. 1, 999.

24 Pyne, *1st New Jersey Cavalry*, 193; Bushnell Memoir, WRHS; Aldrich, *Battery A, 1st Rhode Island Artillery*, 252.

Along the line of the O&A Federal infantrymen, batteries, and ambulances encountered fewer impediments. The V and II corps, straining every muscle to reach Manassas, marched rapidly and without pause. This was as difficult a movement as the army had ever required, and it took extraordinary efforts to maintain the pace of the retreat. Leaders admitted that their troops "suffered severely . . . from fatigue and exhaustion." Some officers even carried the muskets of soldiers so worn out they could barely keep going. The provost guard at the rear of the column constantly had to awaken sleeping men alongside the road and prod them back into motion. Warren reported that even the horses were "nearly all worn out by their exertions."[25]

The dint of discipline and determination allowed the Federals to finally reach Manassas. Lead elements of the V Corps crossed Bull Run around midnight, and the hindmost units of the II Corps waded Blackburn's Ford about 4 a.m. Once attaining this measure of safety, the regiments filed out onto the side of the road, stacked arms, and broke ranks. Then the troops simply slumped exhausted to the ground. Despite the odds, Warren's II Corps had gotten away. It had been luckier than it realized.[26]

Before daybreak on October 15, Early's division as well as Cooke's and Kirkland's brigades formed line of battle without bugle calls or spoken commands. Officers in the Cooke's regiments instructed their men to move forward at a silent run—no shooting or yelling under any circumstance until they reached the railroad. With the signal to advance, the Rebels took off at the double quick. A man in Kirkland's brigade remembered "stumbling in the half-light" over the dead and wounded of yesterday's fight. As the North Carolinians neared the awful railroad they burst into a thunderous Rebel yell and swept up and onto the makeshift breastwork Warren had occupied only hours before—only to find the enemy gone. The Yankees had "crawled away" during the night, wrote one disgusted Southerner. They had taken with them Lee's best chance to destroy a substantial part of the Union army.[27]

---

25 OR 29, pt. 1, 244, 263.

26 Humphreys, *From Gettysburg to the Rapidan*, 30; Page, *Fourteenth Connecticut*, 196; Griffin, *Three Years a Soldier*, 143.

27 Long "Reminiscences," Breckenridge Papers, LC.

CHAPTER 27

"They Ought To Have Known Better"

Casualties—Lee's Reaction—A. P. Hill Condemned—
Confederate Reports—Presidential Verdict

Now in command of the field, the Rebels could calculate the price of the fight at Bristoe Station. The primary part of the battle had lasted a little more than one hour, with the critical infantry combat taking up a mere 40 minutes. Nevertheless, it had been a bloody affair. Casualties in Hill's corps totaled 1,378 men: 10 officers and 126 enlisted men killed, 65 officers and 732 enlisted men wounded, and 445 missing, virtually all of them taken prisoner. Most of the casualties were in the units assaulting the railroad embankment. Kirkland's brigade lost 547 men: 3 officers and 47 men killed, 19 officers and 201 men wounded, 277 captured. Cooke's losses were even heavier: 5 officers and 54 men killed, 30 officers and 409 wounded, 166 men captured, a total of 664 casualties.[1]

The battle had virtually wiped out some commands. Company F of the 26th North Carolina took 34 men of all ranks into the fight and lost 32 of them including six or seven killed. The 27th North Carolina listed 291 casualties from a roster of 426 men, including 33 of its 36 officers. The Yankees had also captured five cannons from McIntosh's battalion in addition to the battle flags of two North Carolina regiments. Union fire had disabled two other guns. Three generals—Cooke, Kirkland, and Posey—had been wounded, the latter mortally.[2]

The Federals suffered a great deal less. The combined casualties in the II Corps for the fighting at Auburn and Bristoe Station totaled 546: two officers and 48 men killed;

---

1 OR 29, pt., 1, 428.

2 Robertson, *A. P. Hill*, 239; *Confederate Veteran Magazine*, vol. 3, 109, vol. 6, 269; hereinafter cited as CVM; ibid., 279, 282, 243, 438. The identity of the two flags is uncertain.

29 officers and 306 enlisted men wounded, and two officers and 159 men missing and presumed captured. The North lost no guns or colors.[3]

On October 15, Lee examined the field at Bristoe Station with his staff. Out on the battleground stretcher bearers were still collecting the wounded. The bodies of Cooke's and Kirkland's slain North Carolinians lay were they had fallen. Nearby, Capt. William J. Seymour of Early's staff sensed that Lee was "in no good humor." The general sent for Hill and when he arrived sharply ordered him to bury his dead. Seymour noted that Hill "recognized a rebuke" in Lee's "tone and manner" and sought to take total responsibility for the debacle. "This is all my fault," Hill confessed, but his manful admission did nothing to deflect Lee's barely contained anger.[4]

Despite his courtly manner and idealized reputation, the famous Virginian was a man of strong passions and exacting standards of duty and performance. He managed to control his temper most of the time, but his staff knew well that it could boil over on occasion. Some of Lee's generals had felt its sting before. Now so did A. P. Hill. In response to his admission of responsibility Lee snapped, "Yes it is your fault; you committed a great blunder yesterday; your line of battle was too short, too thin and your reserves were too far behind."[5]

When Hill again tried to offer explanations, Lee coldly interrupted him and icily ended the interview: "Well general bury these poor men and let us say nothing more about it." Such a withering critique coming from Lee was devastating. Seymour, who overheard all of this, felt sorry for the corps commander who wilted under Lee's scolding. Later that day, he recorded in his diary that Hill "appeared deeply humiliated by this speech and no doubt wished that he could sink out of sight in the lowest depths of his capacious cavalry boots and there hide his diminished head."[6]

---

3 *OR* 29, pt. 1, 248-250, 282, 280.

4 Seymour, *Civil War Memoirs*, 89. Four Union soldiers earned the Medal of Honor at Bristoe Station. Pvt. Moses C. Hanscom of the 19th Maine, and Cpl. Thomas Cullen, an Irish immigrant in the 82nd New York, captured Rebel flags. Joseph Kirby Corson, assistant surgeon of the 35th Pennsylvania Infantry in McCandless' division, went back under artillery fire to rescue a badly wounded soldier. Michael Emmet Urell, another Irish immigrant and color bearer of the 82nd New York, was wounded during the battle and earned the Medal of Honor for "gallantry in action."

5 Ibid. Hopkins, *Bull Run to Appomattox*, 126. Hopkins states that his comrade, Frank Peak, also heard Lee's response to Hill.

6 Ibid. Several postwar accounts of this conversation report Lee as mildly rebuking Hill by cutting off his explanation of what happened and replying, "Well, well, general, bury these poor men and let us say no more about it." Seymour's account is contemporary and was written that same night. It fits with other examples of Lee sharply addressing his subordinates for failures and mistakes. Lee probably softened when he saw Hill's reaction and ended the conversation with the famous "let us say no more about it" phrase. This would not be out of character for

Edward Perry's Florida brigade of Anderson's division got the job of burying the dead at Bristoe Station. Among those carrying out this unpleasant duty was John Hosford of the 5th Florida Infantry. The carnage caused by Union artillery fire appalled him. A few days later he told a sweetheart it would "only make your heart ache for me to describe the battlefield." Hosford said that he and his comrades discovered few intact corpses to bury. Rather they could "only find some pieces of the body, such as a hand or two or three fingers. Sometimes a foot, or part of a foot, sometimes a whole arm, or half of the head." What complete cadavers the Floridians did discover were "mangled in every conceivable condition."[7]

This was hardly the glorious close to the campaign the Confederates had sought. The casualties at Bristoe Station had been so severe and the contest so unequal the entire Army of Northern Virginia reacted with outrage. James Kirkpatrick's regiment, the 16th Mississippi, arrived at Bristoe Station too late to take part in the fighting. That night he recorded in his diary that the "engagement had not been very favorable to us." Although "only a few troops had been engaged," he wrote, "Cooke's brigade was badly demoralized and used up." His fellow Mississippians got the impression that the Federals had lured Cooke and Kirkland "into an ambuscade, in cover of the RR embankment."[8]

The rest of the army agreed. Many blamed A. P. Hill for the bloody debacle. Responding to the controversy about the engagement, Hill ordered his commanders to provide written reports on the fight within the week. This was most unusual. Normally, officers wrote their after-action reports months after a battle ended (or longer), when a lull in campaigning afforded time to gather information and draft documents. Hill's subordinates obeyed, and all of their reports were in by October 24. After digesting the testimony of his officers, Hill forwarded his own account to Lee on October 26.

All these documents mention Hill's haste to attack the Federals retreating toward Manassas. They also admitted the failure of most Confederate leaders to see the Yankee troops forming near the railroad cut. Hall, who was the closest to the enemy on the extreme right of the line, wrote a fairly damning report. Although he didn't directly blame Hill—or anyone else for that matter—he made it clear that, as a mere colonel, he had sensed more danger in the order to advance than did the corps commander. No

---

Lee and much in the same vein as he had dealt with Stuart on the evening of July 2 at Gettysburg. For a discussion of the historiography of this incident, see Bill Backus and Robert Orrison, *A Want of Vigilance: The Bristoe Station Campaign, October 9-19, 1863* (El Dorado Hills, CA, 2015), 115-17.

7 Knox Mellon Jr. ed., *"A Florida Solider in the Army of Northern Virginia: The Hosford Letters."* (Florida Historical Quarterly, Vol. 46, No. 3, Jan., 1968), 254-55.

8 Kirkpatrick Diary, October 14, 1863, UT.

one, he argued, should blame the defeat on his troops. "I have been with the brigade during some of the heaviest engagements of the war," reported the colonel, "and have never seen the men more cool and determined." The repulse at Bristoe Station, he continued, "resulted from no fault of theirs, but from the great superiority in number and position of the enemy, and the entire want of support" for the attacking infantry brigades.[9]

Heth vividly described the ground the Federals defended and leveled a silent finger at Hill for so rashly attacking such a strong position. "No military man who has examined the ground, would attach blame to those two brigades for meeting with a repulse." Indeed, the division commander took pains to make certain no one felt his men inadequate. "My confidence in these troops is not shaken by the result," Heth stated, "and I feel satisfied on fields to come they will vindicate the high reputation they have gained on many a hard-fought battlefield."[10]

No one questioned the valor or skill of the regiments that attacked the railroad cut. No one suggested that division, brigade, or regimental commanders failed to faithfully and competently discharge their orders. By implication, then, blame for defeat rested with the man who gave those orders.

Lieutenant General Hill agreed. He acknowledged that his brigades had "advanced in beautiful order and quite steadily" during the attack, and he found no fault with his men or his commanders. Instead, he assumed entire responsibility for the defeat. "I am convinced that I made the attack too hastily," Hill admitted. But he did argue that his decision had been a reasonable one. "At the same time, a delay of half an hour, and there would have been no enemy to attack. In that event I should equally have blamed myself for not attacking at once."[11]

In his endorsement of Hill's report, Lee wrote, "General Hill explains how in his haste to attack the . . . enemy, he overlooked the presence of the Second [Corps], which was the cause of the disaster that ensued." Unfortunately neither time nor the result of the battle could be reversed. Lee accepted that Hill had made a mistake. He also knew that no man was perfect. Hopefully his corps commander would learn an important lesson and be a better general for it in the future. Secretary of War Seddon concurred with Lee's analysis of the battle. "The disaster at Bristoe Station seems due to a gallant but over-hasty pressing on of the enemy," he wrote in his endorsement. While the

---

9 OR 29, pt. 1, 436. Walker and Anderson submitted their reports on October 21; Col. Hall, in temporary command of Cooke's brigade, the following day, and Heth on October 24.

10 Ibid., 432. Of course, A. P. Hill had not ordered an attack on the railroad position; Cooke and Kirkland made that decision.

11 Ibid., 427.

ANV commander and the secretary were content to say no more about Bristoe Station, many others certainly were not.[12]

The Confederate rank and file labeled the battle a "slaughter pen" or a "gross blunder" and accused Hill of "unpardonable mismanagement." One staff officer called Hill "a fool & woeful blunderer." "Thus, by the most stupid bungling," Lt. Robert Hubbard, Jr., wrote, even more scathingly, "a well-conceived plan" for trapping Warren's corps and "crushing it was entirely thwarted." A 3rd Virginia Cavalry field officer complained that the fight at Bristoe Station had been a "badly managed affair." "Oh for Jackson to lead this corps [again]!" he exclaimed, neatly summing up the attitude of many veterans.[13]

In the end, Jefferson Davis probably penned the most concise, and perhaps the most accurate, observation on Hill's actions and the reason for defeat at Bristoe Station. "There was a want of vigilance," he scrawled on Lee's report of the battle.[14]

As is usually the case, mistakes were readily apparent after the fact. Potential dangers and pitfalls had been much more difficult to see in the heat of the moment. At any rate, the best man to judge what might or might not have been was on the scene. Lee believed Hill had fallen "too precipitately" on Warren—that haste had cost the Confederacy over 1,300 casualties. But Lee also knew that Hill's combative nature had saved the army from defeat on more than one occasion, and he didn't forget it amidst the outcry against his corps commander.[15]

Recriminations, reports, and explanations were for the future, of course. On the morning of October 15 the AOP was still retreating toward Washington. The Army of Northern Virginia had a campaign to complete, and A. P. Hill was too valuable an asset for Lee to be without. The battle at Bristoe Station likely produced many epitaphs. But one of the best came from 1st Sgt. Elnathan Tyler, whose 14th Connecticut helped repulse Hill's assault: "The Rebel attack . . . was spirited enough, but they ought to have known better."[16]

---

12 Ibid., 428.

13 Robinson, *A.P. Hill*, 239; Nanzig, *Memoirs of a Virginia Cavalryman*, 111; Swank, *Sabres, Saddles and Spurs*, 95; C. C. Chambers, "The Coahoma Invincibles," CVM, 1923, vol. 31, 461.

14 *OR* 29, pt. 1, 428.

15 Longstreet, *Manassas to Appomattox*, note, 469.

16 Page, *Fourteenth Connecticut*, 194.

Chapter 28

"Lee Is Unquestionably Bullying You"

Meade Concentrates—Concerns and Frustrations—Manassas Disappointment
Fighting At Bull Run—Escape of the Wagon Trains—Lee's Decision

T**HE** Army of the Potomac had managed to avoid being broken up during its retreat from Culpeper Court House. That had been a rather lackluster achievement. Now the question was when and where would it stop retreating and turn to fight? Since the evening of October 13, generals Meade and Humphreys had given this question a great deal of thought. Some Northern editors and politicians seemed to believe the answer a lot easier to find than did the two generals.

Humphreys noted that area between Auburn and Bristoe Station, bounded on the west by the Warrenton Pike and, seven miles to the east, by the O&A Railroad was "almost unknown" to Union officers. Based on his limited knowledge of the region, Meade had concluded it offered no tactical or strategic advantages and thus had foregone making a stand there. But if the Union army couldn't fight between Auburn and Bristoe, the next logical position was Manassas Junction, the site of two humiliating Federal defeats. That alone made everyone leery of Manassas. As Gen. Humphreys put it, any position near the old battlefield was "objectionable because of former operations."[1]

If Manassas was out of the question, the only other option was Centreville, less than 20 miles from Washington, DC. In July 1861 this little town had been the jumping off point for the first great Union campaign of the war, which had, of course, ended in rout at the First Battle of Bull Run. Since then Centreville had been heavily fortified and

---

1 Humphreys, *From Gettysburg to the Rapidan*, 30; *Report of the Joint Committee on the Conduct of the War*, Vol. 1, 400.

turned into a major Federal supply base. Those entrenchments beckoned to Meade, and he decided his army would halt its retreat within their comforting embrace.

The tired troops in Sykes' V Corps and Warren's II Corps had dragged themselves over Bull Run and reunited with the rest of the army before the morning of October 15. This left only part of the cavalry and the wagon trains beyond Federal lines. Meade expected both to be north of Bull Run by the end of the day. With most of his army concentrated, he began deploying for a defensive struggle around Centreville.

Sedgwick's VI Corps took position on the right (western) flank astride the Little River Turnpike near Chantilly. Newton's I Corps went into line on the VI Corps' left, with a division in the earthworks around Centreville and a contingent deployed to guard the bridge over Cub Run. Meade held the rest of Newton's command in reserve with orders to aid Sedgwick if necessary. Warren placed the II Corps in the center of the line to occupy the high ground behind Mitchell's and Blackburn's fords on Bull Run. Meade posted French's III Corps to Warren's left at Union Mills, where the O&A crossed Bull Run. French's mission was to cover McLean's Ford and send a division to hold Fairfax Station. Sykes' V Corps assembled at Fairfax Court House as a general reserve. Kilpatrick's cavalry division would cover the right flank, while Gregg's and Buford's divisions, once they were north of Bull Run, would cover the left.

Meade asked Halleck to send forward any troops he could spare from Washington's defenses. Merritt's Reserve Cavalry Brigade had left the city and joined Meade's army on the October 13. Other than this brigade, the general-in-chief had nothing to offer except 2,000 infantrymen under Brig. Gen. Rufus King, currently guarding the railroad between Fairfax Station and Alexandria. Beyond these, the only units in Washington were the heavy artillery regiments manning the capital's forts. Meade declined these, telling Halleck the army already had more artillery than it needed. Meade did accept King's infantry, but decided to leave his units where they were for the moment; although he attached them to Sykes' V Corps.

With his army arranging itself into a solid front, Meade felt prepared to receive an attack. He doubted, however, that the Rebels would be foolish enough to assault his troops in their chosen stronghold. Twice already in this campaign the Confederates had outflanked Meade. Would Lee try the same game or do something unexpected?

The 'what did Lee intend to do next' riddle had bedeviled Union commanders since October 8. In all probability the Rebel general proposed to make more mischief. Stuart's cavalry was already harassing the new Union line with artillery fire and small forays. It was difficult to know what to make of these probes. Whatever they foreshadowed, Meade was not about to abandon his defensive stance. At noon on October 15 the general wired Halleck that he awaited the enemy's movements.

Meade hoped his own cavalry might ascertain what the Rebels were planning; in the meanwhile he passed whatever information he did have back to the capital. "Hill's and Ewell's corps, re-enforced to a reported strength of 80,000 are advancing on me, their plan being to secure the Bull Run field in advance of me." By reaching Centreville, the AOP had foiled that enemy scheme, though Meade couldn't surmise whether Lee would continue his offensive. If he did, he would doubtless opt for another turning maneuver rather than assault Centreville.

Meade tried to put up an aggressive front but succeeded only in indicating he would probably continue retreating when pressed. If the Rebels did slip around the Union army at Centreville he would go over to the attack, Meade told Halleck, *unless* Lee's "movements indicate the probability of his being able to concentrate more rapidly than I can." At that point, Meade hedged, he would order the Federal army to "retire nearer Washington."[2]

Neither the White House nor the war department welcomed such language. Lee had already shoved Meade back 50 miles and transferred the seat of the Virginia war from the banks of the Rapidan to the outskirts of the Union capital. Another withdrawal would put Meade inside the city's defenses and Lee north of the Potomac. With Rosecrans trapped in Chattanooga, news of the Confederates invading Maryland or Pennsylvania could produce a serious setback for the Union cause.

Halleck was growing increasingly nervous about events. He had seen no need for the Federal army's retreat, and he told its commander so. Now his frustrations over Meade's performance burst forth in a scathing telegram. The general-in-chief scoffed at claims pegging Rebel strength at 80,000 men. Intelligence reports from Richmond put "Lee's present force" at a mere 55,000 troops. In light of this, "Is [Lee] not trying to bully you, while the mass of the rebel armies are concentrating against Rosecrans?" he asked. "Instead of retreating, I think you ought to give him battle. From all the information I can get, his force is very much inferior to yours."[3]

Other officials in Washington shared Halleck's aggravation. Secretary Welles described news from the front as "vague and unsatisfactory." While the newspapers constantly extolled Meade's "masterly movements," he told his diary, "street rumor glorifies him." Welles saw "nothing to authenticate or justify this claim of wonderful strategy." Suspecting the truth, he summed up the recent course of events: "Lee has made a demonstration, and our army has fallen back—'changed its base' they call it at the War Department, in the vernacular, *retreated*."

Although unhappy with Meade's conduct, Welles knew better than to voice his opinion publicly. "It is claimed Meade has shown great tact in not permitting the enemy to outflank him," the secretary reported, "Perhaps so. I shall not controvert, if I doubt it. I would not decry our generals, nor speak my mind freely if unfavorably impressed

---

2   Previous paragraphs all based upon OR 29, pt. 2, 324-25, 326, 347.

3   *OR* 29, pt. 2, 328.

concerning them." Nonetheless it was all quite distressing. Welles generously acknowledged that "Meade does the best he knows how." Halleck on the other hand, he complained, "Does nothing."[4]

The soldiers manning Meade's battle line cared not for Welles' or Halleck's concerns. But some few within the ranks echoed the angst of the administration and high command. "The papers say that Meade is only falling back to seek a field, but I don't believe it," one Pennsylvanian wrote. "If he had the force, the fields at Culpeper are just as good as those at Bull Run."[5]

By and large, however, the army seemed satisfied with its commander's latest course. One Irish soldier remarked that Meade had managed the retreat "neatly" if perhaps "rather cautiously." More importantly, the general had committed "no great blunder," which, while jousting with Robert E. Lee was "saying a good deal."[6]

Warren arrived at army headquarters just before dawn on October 15 not at all displeased with current events. Lyman described him coming into camp boasting: "We whipped the Rebs right out. I ran my men, on the double-quick, into the railroad cut and then just swept them down with musketry." That was as concise a report on Bristoe Station as one could wish. Lyman gave the weary officer a drink of brandy from his flask, after which Warren laid down and fell asleep in "about a minute."

Later that day the colonel got a chance to see the fruits of the II Corps' tidy victory. Lyman watched around 400 "gaunt and weary" Rebel prisoners march past. The campaign's rigors on the captives were obvious. "Many were mere boys," he wrote, "their clothes were poor, some of a dust-color, and others dirty brown, while here and there was a US jacket or a pair of trousers, the trophies of some successful fight." But if the enemy looked destitute, his spirit remained rich. "Some were wittily disposed," the colonel admitted. "One soldier of ours cried out: 'Broad Run is a bad place for you, boys.' 'Ya-as,' said a cheery man in gray, 'but it's purty rare you get such a chance.'"

Confederate livestock was far less impressive. When the five cannon seized at Bristoe Station trundled by, someone explained that a team of captured Rebel horses hauled one of the guns. Lyman could feel only pity for the half-starved beasts, "four miserable thin animals that had once been large and good."[7]

* * *

4   Morse, *Diary of Gideon Welles*, vol. 1, 470-71.

5   Norton, *Army Letters*, 184.

6   Galwey Memoir, LC; Galwey, *Valiant Hours*, 160.

7   Previous paragraphs based upon Aggassiz, *Meade's Headquarters*, 32.

The Rebel army hovering south of Centreville had its own dissatisfactions. The Yankee escape from Bristoe Station meant foiled strategy for the generals, but it had dealt ordinary soldiers a more tangible blow. One Mississippi private recalled that many of his fellows felt "badly disappointed at not getting an opportunity to capture blankets" and other comforts.[8]

This was, perhaps, a temporary setback. The Confederate rank and file didn't think the campaign was over. A Southern infantryman noted "marvelous stories" adrift about successes won by Stuart's cavalry, of guns thrown away by hordes of Yankee stragglers, and enemy rear guards captured. This Rebel was certain that the bluecoats were still on the run, and he "fully expected to be moved after them, and to attack them wherever they should make a stand."[9]

If Southern infantrymen anticipated battle, their mounted brethren entertained far more pleasant visions. Around noon, Stuart's cavalry advanced directly on Manassas Junction. "We were looking forward to Manassas with wild recollections of the rich haul that we had made there" in August 1862, wrote Luther Hopkins. "Everybody was saying we'll get plenty when we get to Manassas." But when they arrived at the fabled place Confederate troopers discovered that "everything had changed."[10]

Instead of a vast Federal supply dump, such as the one Stonewall Jackson's men had plundered on the eve of the 2nd Battle of Bull Run, the Rebels found nothing but desolation. "There was not a building anywhere," lamented Hopkins. "The soil, enriched by the debris from former camps, had grown a rich crop of weeds that came half way up to the sides of our horses, and the only way we recognized the place was by our horses stumbling over the railroad tracks." There were no stockpiles of rations, clothes, shoes, or fat sutlers stores. It was a grievous disappointment.[11]

The weather didn't lighten the mood. The forenoon of October 15 was heavy with clouds and occasional showers which increased in frequency as the day unfolded. The overcast skies promised more rain and the unwelcome mud that would accompany it.[12]

Despite the weather, Stuart was determined to test the Union line along Bull Run. After reuniting his entire corps on the evening of October 14—save for Young's brigade, still making its way north from Bealton—the Rebel general had sent the 11th Virginia Cavalry toward Brentsville to check out reports of a large Yankee wagon train in that direction. The rest of the cavalry rode north along the railroad. As the Rebels

8   Kirkpatrick Diary, October 15, 1863, UT.

9   Caldwell, *Brigade of South Carolinians*, 161.

10 Hopkins, *From Bull Run to Appomattox*, 127.

11 Ibid.

12 Elijah Johnson Diary, October 15, 1863, VHS.

reached Manassas around 2 p.m., Stuart held Gordon's and Funsten's brigades in reserve and directed Fitz Lee's division to probe the nearby fords across Bull Run.[13]

Lee led Lomax and Owen to McLean's Ford and sent Chambliss a few miles upstream to take possession of Mitchell's and Blackburn's fords. These maneuvers occasioned some heavy skirmishing between Rebel troopers and Union infantry. On higher ground and with heavier artillery, the Yankees had the advantage. Despite several attacks the Southern cavalrymen failed to drive the enemy from the fords.[14]

Near the end of Fitz Lee's efforts, Jeb Stuart received word that a more attractive target loitered nearby—namely the principal wagon train of the Army of the Potomac. Since the evening of October 14, Buford's and Gregg's cavalry divisions had shepherded a gargantuan train of Union supply vehicles north from Brentsville. The 11th Virginia Cavalry had shadowed the procession for miles as it crept north at a snail's pace, constantly hampered by bad roads, mud holes, steep hills, darkness, missed turns, and its own corpulence. The Union wagon masters managed their affairs so badly, Buford seriously doubted they would escape destruction or capture.[15]

Luckily for the Federals, the 11th Virginia wasn't able to relay the location of the Union trains to Jeb Stuart until late afternoon October 15. The Confederate cavalry commander responded by ordering Gordon's brigade eastward to intercept this lucrative prize. He would follow with Funsten's brigade as soon as possible.

Around 4 p.m. Gordon made contact with Capt. James Walsh's 3rd Pennsylvania Cavalry, the sole regiment constituting the wagon train's rearguard. The column's tailmost wagons were bottlenecking at Yates Ford and another portion of the train was diverting toward Wolf Run Shoals, when the Confederates appeared. Although badly outnumbered Walsh's men turned to make a stand. Fortunately, their commander, a capable soldier with 10 years of experience fighting Indians in the West, rose to the occasion. Astutely positioning his troops in a heavy forest to conceal their small numbers, Walsh used tactics learned on the frontier by constantly shifting a single squadron from point to point to create an illusion of greater strength.[16]

The subterfuge worked. With the sun sinking rapidly, Stuart feared an extended fight to break through the 3rd Pennsylvania's front would prevent Rebel troopers from striking the Yankee supply train. Hoping to get at his target before it escaped, Stuart

---

13 OR 29, pt. 1, 449.

14 Ibid., 330-31; 449, 463, 466, 472, 475; F. Halsey Wigfall to Lou, Oct. 16, 1863, LC; McDonald, *Laurel Brigade*, 201; McVicar Diary, October 15, 1863, Handley Library; Neese, *Three Years in the Confederate Horse Artillery*, 226.

15 OR 29, pt.1, 346, 350, 449-50, 999-1000.

16 OR 29, pt. 1, 350, 449, 1000; Pync, *1st New Jersey Cavalry*, 193; William Brooke Rawle, et al., *History of the Third Pennsylvania Cavalry 1861-1865* (Philadelphia, PA, 1905), 346.

instructed Gordon to keep Walsh busy while Funsten's brigade tried to outflank the enemy and assail his wagons.

Aided by a guide who claimed to know a way around the Union position, Stuart led Funsten's troopers on a roundabout route to reach the Federal rear. Meanwhile, Gordon dismounted his men and began applying pressure on the 3rd Pennsylvania. Buford called up reinforcements to Walsh's support, but these units found it extremely difficult to reach the battlefield because wagons choked the fords over Bull Run. Help for the Pennsylvanians would not arrive quickly.

Luckily for Walsh, Gordon's regiments pushed forward gingerly. Their primary mission was to keep the Yankees locked in place while Funsten got into their rear. They had no need to launch an assault. Steady pressure would do nicely, and if the Rebels were fortunate that alone might crack the Union position.

Gordon gradually extended his line until it overlapped the 3rd Pennsylvania's right flank. Just as it appeared the Rebels would crumple Walsh's front, Lt. Col. Coe Durland's 17th Pennsylvania Cavalry and a section of Federal artillery arrived on the field to help fend off the Southern attack. The Confederate thrust stalled in the face of increased resistance and shortly afterwards night put an end to the fighting.

Darkness also thwarted Stuart's effort to outflank the Union line and rampage into its rear. After following its guide along a circuitous, time-consuming route around Walsh's line, Funsten's brigade finally spotted the enemy. Despite the semi-darkness, the 12th Virginia Cavalry, at the head of the column, charged and overran a barricade the Yankees had constructed in the road. But the regiment could do nothing more. Union artillery threw a few rounds in Stuart's direction as the last beams of sunlight disappeared from the cloudy sky. Nightfall brought the action to a close.[17]

Waning daylight also marked the final escape of the Federal wagons over Yates Ford to safety. The wagon and pontoon train using Wolf Run Shoals didn't reach the north side of Bull Run until 3 a.m., October 16. Even then, whether the trains were permanently out of danger remained a question. Meade had again lost contact with Lee's infantry, and he had no idea what his opponent might do next. It was highly probable the Rebels would outflank the Centreville defenses. In which case, events might well carry both armies north of the Potomac and to the very outskirts of Washington, DC. This much was certain: the campaign was far from its conclusion, and the likelihood of another big battle on Northern soil loomed ever more possible.[18]

---

17 All previous paragraphs based upon *OR* 29, pt. 1, 350, 449, 450; Rawle, *Third Pennsylvania Cavalry*, 347, 350, 351-53.

18 *OR* 29, pt. 1, 350, 449, 450; Rawle, *Third Pennsylvania Cavalry*, 347, 350, 351-53.

CHAPTER 29

"I Desire To Be Relieved From Command"

Lee's Decision—Union Uncertainty—Lincoln's Urgings—
Telegraphic Tempers—Death of a Railroad—Flooded Creeks—Meade's Pursuit

THE Federals had avoided a third battle at Bull Run thanks to the Army of the Potomac's successful retreat. Meade had proven a better general than John Pope, who 14 months ago had suffered humiliating defeat at Manassas after falling victim to a maneuver similar to the one Lee had just used. In the aftermath of Pope's defeat, the Rebels had crossed the Potomac and entered Maryland. The question uppermost in Meade's mind was whether Lee would replicate his 1862 strategy and invade the North for a third time.

The commander of the Union army didn't know what to make of Jeb Stuart's aggressiveness along Bull Run. Reports of a large dust cloud near Manassas Junction, taken together with Rebel attacks on the various fords, might mean Lee's whole army was advancing—or not. Warren told Meade that Stuart's activity was "a blind to some other movement," and he was confident that no serious danger loomed near Bull Run.

Later in the day the II Corps commander assured army headquarters that he was "more and more convinced" that everything happening along his front "is mere humbug." The Rebel cavalry was trying either to cover a retreat or another flank march by Lee's infantry. Still, no one could say for sure what Lee was doing, and until that could be determined Meade felt it impossible for his army to react. Certainly his proximity to the Federal capital advised against his taking chances, not that he had shown a disposition to do so anywhere else.[1]

The Union commander would have been greatly relieved to learn that Lee had concluded his campaign had run its course. On October 15, he wrote Secretary of War

---

1 Previous paragraphs based upon OR 29, pt. 2, 327, 328.

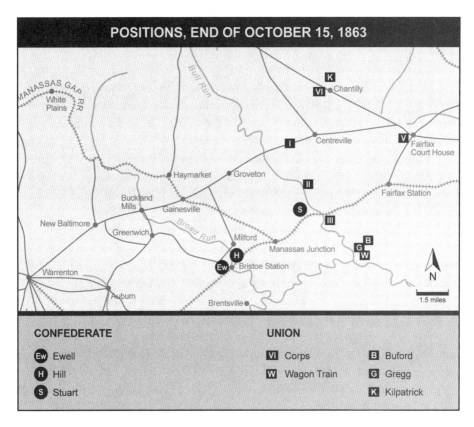

Seddon that Meade's retreat had been so rapid that his army had been "unable to do him any considerable damage." A further march to again turn the Yankee flank would bring little advantage, Lee explained. Meade could "retire under the fortifications of Washington and Alexandria" which the Confederates could not "attack advantageously." Since additional offensive action would be fruitless, a withdrawal to the upper Rappahannock seemed the only proper alternative.

Logistical difficulties as much as strategic considerations compelled Lee's decision. "It is impossible for us to remain where we are, as the country is destitute of provisions for men or animals," he told Seddon. The Yankees had destroyed the railroad bridge at Rappahannock Station as they retreated, while flooding had washed away the bridge over the Rapidan. This deprived the Confederate army of the O&A as a line of communication and the distance from the Rapidan to Bull Run precluded any reliance on wagons.

The condition of his troops also argued against further offensive movements. His "men were dreadfully off for shoes, blankets and clothes," Lee lamented in a letter to Longstreet, noting that "one division alone had over a thousand barefooted men." With the onset of severe weather near, the army was without shelter or food for "man or beast." Therefore, despite the Federals having "suffered less" than he wished, Lee would withdraw.[2]

But there was no need to hurry. As always, the commander of the Army of Northern Virginia would move at his own pace and on his own schedule. Throughout this campaign Lee had enjoyed the initiative, and he wasn't going to relinquish it simply because he was marching south. Stuart would continue to harass the enemy along Bull Run while Hill's corps continued hovering near Bristoe Station. Ewell's divisions meanwhile would spread out along the railroad between Broad Run and Warrenton Junction and then thoroughly wreck it by tearing up track, burning ties, and destroying the telegraph. This would seriously delay any Yankee pursuit and force Meade to rebuild the O&A before advancing any considerable distance southward.

So far no one outside the high command had any inkling of these plans. The first glowing reports of the campaign were just appearing in Richmond newspapers. Near Manassas, the soldiers in both armies simply waited. At dusk on October 15, infantrymen had heard heavy cannonading along Bull Run and watched the fireworks display an artillery duel between Fitz Lee and the Yankees had produced. The pyrotechnics seemed to suggest a continuation of the offensive.[3]

On the morning of October 16 nature decided to intrude on the plans of both armies. The previous day's showers turned into a storm. Heavy rain poured down almost hourly, and night brought more accompanied by heavy winds. Under the continuing deluge Bull Run's fords began disappearing. Despite the weather, some of Lee's troops withdrew southward and began dismantling the O&A: tearing up the rails, burning every bridge, hauling off the telegraph cable, and chopping down all the telegraph poles.[4]

The order to retreat and shatter the railroad surprised many Southerners. Most men had expected to continue moving north. Instead, one Rebel recalled, they endured a "most distressing march" to get into position to wreck the O&A. The day-long rain had turned the soil into a treacherous quagmire, and the troops trudged "far into the night, through the deep, slippery mud, along new, stumpy roads, and in the darkness of Egypt." When the columns finally halted they found little relief. Soldiers struggled in

---

2 Previous paragraphs based upon ibid., pt. 1, 406; Longstreet, *Manassas to Appomattox*, note, 470.

3 *Richmond Examiner*, October 15, 1863; Kirkpatrick Diary, October 15, 1863, UT.

4 OR *Supplement* 5, pt. 1, 595; Kirkpatrick Diary, October 16, 1863, UT; Glazier, *Three Years in the Federal Cavalry*, 334. Early's division would wreck the railroad between Broad Run and Kettle Run; Rodes' brigades from Kettle Run to Catlett's Station, and Alleghany Johnson's men from Catlett's to Warrenton Junction.

abject misery to build fires for a little warmth before lying down to sleep in the mud and rain.[5]

The elements made the hard work of demolishing the O&A harder. But its effects were instantly visible. Several thousand men could erase a railroad fairly quickly. The regiments lined up along the track and "prized up a length of cross-ties and rails equal" to their front. They then piled the ties, laid the rails atop the stacks, and set the ties on fire. The iron rails eventually softened, sagged, and warped in the flames, rendering them useless. Sometimes the troops would wrap the softened metal around a nearby tree trunk, considerably complicating its repair.[6]

The Rebels proved adept at their labor. The desolation they wrought amazed and impressed Federal troops later surveying the damage. Commissary Sergeant Rufus Ricksecker of the 126th Ohio marveled at the thoroughness of the devastation. The Confederates had not only removed every tie and ruined all the rails; they had even burnt the bridges and destroyed each culvert. A Massachusetts soldier admitted he "never saw anything so complete as the destruction of that RR."[7]

While Ewell's corps busily ripped apart the Orange & Alexandria, Southern cavalrymen kept careful watch on the enemy. Stuart left Fitz Lee around Manassas and took Hampton's entire division (Young's brigade having come up during the night) and four guns westward to cross Bull Run at Sudley Ford. Forging ahead over the muddy roads, he skirted past the right flank of the Union army, swung around behind Centreville, and skirmished with the VI Corps before putting his men into a wet bivouac near Stone Castle.[8]

Hill's corps experienced neither the challenge of a march, the labor of railroad destruction, nor combat with an enemy. Its men simply got drenched and did what they could to pass the sodden, dreary hours. Some few actually went sightseeing and strolled over the Bristoe battlefield.[9]

*　*　*

George Meade enjoyed no such leisure. Washington was again pressuring him to engage Lee. Halleck forwarded Meade a letter he had received from Lincoln which any

---

5　Herdegen, *Four Years in Iron Brigade*, 226; Kirkpatrick Diary, October 16, 1863, UT.

6　Caldwell, *Brigade of South Carolinians*, 161; George Patch to parents, October 15, 1863, VHS.

7　Rufus Ricksecker to family, November 1, 1863, www.frontierfamilies.net/Family/Rufus.htm Accessed 7/24/2007; George Patch to parents, October 15, 1863, VHS.

8　*OR* 2, pt. 1, 450.

9　Caldwell, *Brigade of South Carolinians*, 161-62; Kirkpatrick Diary, October 16, 1863, UT.

The results of Confederate efforts to wreck the O&A Railroad. *Library of Congress*

reasonable reader could only interpret as a plea for the Army of the Potomac to take the offensive. He didn't "believe Lee can have over 60,000 effective men," the president began. No doubt the Rebels had "gathered in all the available scraps, and added them to Hill's and Ewell's corps, but that is all." Federal intelligence indicated (incorrectly) that the Confederates believed four corps had been detached from Meade instead of the two actually sent to Tennessee. Meade's apparently shying away from contact, the president continued, would have confirmed this suspicion for the enemy. If indeed Lee had badly underestimated Union strength, a great opportunity beckoned. "If General Meade can now attack [Lee] on a field no more than equal to us, and will do so with all the skill and courage which he, his officers, and men possess, the honor will be his if he succeeds, and the blame may be mine if he fails."

There it was. The commander-in-chief finally acknowledged that the issue of "blame" in case of defeat was one factor inhibiting the Army of the Potomac's aggressive instinct. Further, he was now willing to face the problem squarely and tell Meade, through Halleck, the blame "may be mine" should the army fight and lose a battle.

But Lincoln's missive didn't convince George Meade. Surely he noticed the waffling "may be" on the question of ultimate blame in the president's letter. But Meade rejected the notion that the question of responsibility was an issue at all. He telegraphed a reply to Washington, asserting that he intended "to attack the enemy, if I can find him on a field no more than equal to us." The only reason he had not was "the difficulty of ascertaining [Lee's] exact position, and the fear that in endeavoring to do so my communications might be jeopardized." In other words, Meade wasn't disposed to abandon the cautious strategy he had pursued thus far.[10]

That didn't surprise Gideon Welles. After reading a copy of Lincoln's letter the secretary thought its meaning quite clear: the president was "urging [Meade] not to lose the opportunity to bring on a battle, assuring him that all the honors of a victory should be exclusively his, while in case of a defeat, he (the president) would take the entire responsibility." To a Republican partisan like himself, it was an incredibly significant gesture, but Welles was confident Lincoln was "tasking Meade beyond his ability." If the president were able to tell his general "how and when to fight," the secretary believed Meade would do well. But Lincoln couldn't do this. Expecting Meade to figure it out on his own was asking too much of the general's "capability and powers." It was Halleck's job to tell Meade what to do, Welles thought. "Where is . . . [the] general-in-chief, who should, if he has the capacity, attend to these things." If Halleck wasn't up to the job, he should be "got out of the way."[11]

Meanwhile, south of Washington evidence mounted that Lee's infantry wasn't advancing to Bull Run. As of October 16, Federal troops could confirm only that Stuart's cavalry and horse artillery occupied positions along the creek. Other Union reports placed Rebel horsemen in the vicinity of Centreville. The location of the Rebel infantry remained a troubling question.

In the Shenandoah Valley, Brig. Gen. John Imboden was diligently carrying out Lee's instructions to pressure the enemy and annoy the Yankee high command. Imboden's cavalry brigade was threatening Union forces near Charles Town, not far from Harper's Ferry. Some Northern officers interpreted these maneuvers as a precursor to Lee's entering the Valley on another march to invade the North. Others disagreed, arguing that the Confederates didn't need to swing so far west to get into Maryland.

Meade, too, was beginning to contemplate the possibility of an advance. But the severe rainstorm that plagued both armies considerably lessened the chance. Unceasing rain had turned fields into mud pits and flooded Bull Run. Most of the fords over that famous watercourse were impassable; there was no way for the opposing forces to even come to grips.[12]

The same weather hindered Rebel destruction of the railroad. One South Carolinian remembered "violent, almost blinding [rain] thoroughly drenching us and

---

10 Previous paragraphs based upon *OR* 29, pt. 2, 332, 333.

11 Morse, *Diary of Gideon Welles*, vol. 1, 471-72.

12 Humphreys, *From Gettysburg to the Rapidan*, 32.

raising the smallest branches to almost rivers." On the other side, a Yankee in the 18th Massachusetts complained of knee deep mud and water on every road.[13]

Rain continued falling throughout the night. The sun came out at dawn on the 17th, but yesterday evening's nearly half-inch of precipitation had already wreaked its mischief. Bull Run was overflowing, and the water stood six feet deep at McLean's Ford. Although Meade ordered his pontoon trains forward, they were far to the rear at Fairfax Station, and it would require some time for their worn out teams and engineers to bring them up over the torturous roads. Meade was now certain the Union army couldn't advance for at least another day.[14]

*   *   *

While the Army of the Potomac stood immobilized on the north side of a swollen Bull Run, the Confederates doggedly continued to withdraw. Ewell's corps was still working its way south, destroying the railroad as it went. Traveling backwards along the path of Meade's recent retreat, Rebel soldiers saw ample evidence of how hard the Yankee general had pushed his army to escape Lee's strategy. A South Carolina officer observed that, although his men found no human bodies, the "carcasses of horses" were "scarcely ever out of sight." North of Ewell, Hill's corps continued lingering near Bristoe Station, where many regiments busied themselves hunting rabbits to supplement meager rations.[15]

The only part of the Rebel army still in contact with the enemy was Jeb Stuart's cavalry. On October 17 he moved Hampton's division to the Little River Turnpike and the Union right flank. Near Frying Pan Church, Young's brigade ran into Yankee pickets and a "brisk" two-hour fight ensued. Neither side was able to do much harm in the miserable weather, but Stuart felt the skirmish allowed him to obtain the last necessary bit of intelligence to understand the extent of Meade's defensive line around Centreville. Following this, the Confederate horsemen withdrew after dark and headed south of Bull Run.

That night Robert E. Lee sent for Stuart and explained that the army was going to retire to the Rappahannock. He wanted the cavalry to cover the retreat and keep the enemy at bay so that the movement could take place unmolested. A. P. Hill received

---

13 Caldwell, *Brigade of South Carolinians*, 162; Hennessy, *18th Massachusetts*, 208.

14 Krick, *Civil War Weather*, 110; Caldwell, *Brigade of South Carolinians*, 162; OR 29, pt. 2, 339; pt. 1, 1000.

15 Caldwell, *Brigade of South Carolinians*, 162.

orders to begin his withdrawal toward the Rappahannock the next morning, October 18.[16]

Hill's corps started its march before dawn. Some brigades took to the road as early as 3 a.m. A Mississippian observed that the heavy rains rendered the route "very muddy & slippery" and that the overcast sky made daylight seem more like nightfall. Nonetheless, the Confederate regiments followed the destroyed railroad southward moving briskly, at "a steady gait all day" and "making but few rests." At the end of a 22-mile march they reached the river after dark, only to find Rebel engineers struggling to emplace a pontoon bridge. The resulting traffic jam prevented some of Hill's units from crossing that night.[17]

*   *   *

Well north of the Rappahannock, Meade remained uncertain of his future course and Lee's intentions. Imboden was doing Lee's army good service in the Valley by making his force appear much larger than it was. Since October 13 Federal commanders in that region had been reporting the presence of Lee's army near Martinsburg, Charles Town, Berryville, Strasburg, Harpers Ferry and even on the banks of the Potomac River.[18]

Those accounts fed Meade's suspicions. For several days he had thought the Confederates were possibly moving into the Shenandoah Valley. On the night of October 17, he wrote Halleck there were indications of an enemy movement into the Loudon and "probably, the Shenandoah Valley." But probably wasn't definitely, and Meade still felt he lacked the necessary intelligence to put his army into motion. As soon as he could get "any correct idea" of Lee's movements, he would act to "meet him."[19]

Halleck lost no time recommending the proper strategy if the Rebels were heading for the Shenandoah. "If Lee has turned his back on you to cross the mountains, he has seriously exposed himself to your blows, unless his army can move 2 miles to your 1. Fight him," the general-in-chief stoutly advised, "before he again draws you at such a distance from your base as to expose your communications to his raids." Halleck also

16 OR 29, pt. 1, 450.

17 Kirkpatrick Diary, October 17, 1863, UT.

18 OR 29, pt. 2, 309, 319, 332, 336, 338, 345.

19 Ibid., 338-39.

instructed Meade to pay particular attention to the Federal garrison at Harper's Ferry and not let it fall into Rebel hands.[20]

Meade quickly answered Halleck's telegram. Pleasonton's cavalry reported that Confederate infantry had abandoned Bristoe Station. A reconnaissance to Thoroughfare Gap found a strong enemy cavalry presence, but no evidence of Lee's main force having passed that way. Stuart's October 17 foray against Sedgwick worried him, though; as did reports that the Rebels had 4,000 cavalry and six guns near Aldie. Mosby's raiders were also active, moving into Fairfax County on October 15. In just four days they captured almost 100 prisoners, plus 100 horses or mules and several supply wagons. The sum of this information "doubtless" indicated a Rebel foray against the army's supply line, which Meade had dispatched all of Pleasonton's cavalry to counter.

Beyond that defensive measure, all he could do was complain once again of the impossibility of moving the AOP "until I know something more definite" of Lee's position. Some signs indicated Rebels advancing into the Shenandoah; others suggested them retreating to the Rappahannock. This conflicting evidence left Meade in doubt about what to do. If the Union army marched south and Lee moved into the Valley, he could neither save Harper's Ferry nor prevent Lee from invading the North. But if the Army of the Potomac shifted toward the Shenandoah while the Rebels were withdrawing to the Rappahannock, Meade would forfeit his chance to pursue them. Grasping for information, he asked Halleck if any new reports confirmed ANV troops in the Valley, before resignedly confessing that "whatever route [Lee] has taken, it is too late for me to overtake him in any short time."

Six hours later, Halleck wired Meade that an enemy force had attacked Charles Town and been repulsed. This was only partially correct. The Rebels under Brig. Gen. Imboden had captured the town and its garrison before withdrawing. But that had no effect on the strategic situation at all. At this point Halleck's patience with Meade gave out. The commander of the Army of the Potomac, reluctant to trust his own intelligence reports and paralyzed by uncertainty was letting Lee do whatever he desired. It was more than the general-in-chief could stand and he huffily snapped: "Lee is unquestionably bullying you. If you cannot ascertain his movements, I certainly cannot. If you pursue and fight him, I think you will find out where he is. I know of no other way."

That was about as much of Gen. Halleck's advice and prodding as George Meade's infamously short temper could take. He quickly shot off an angry response: "If you have any orders to give me, I am prepared to receive and obey them, but I must insist

---

20 Ibid., 345; pt. 1, 492.

on being sparred the infliction of truisms in the guise of opinions as you have recently honored me with, particularly as they were not asked for." Meade concluded by taking "this occasion to repeat what I have before stated, that if my course, based on my judgment, does not meet with approval, I ought to be, and I desire to be, relieved from command."[21]

Meade was truly angry. The campaign had imposed enough strain on its own without Halleck's lectures. The general was still agitated later that night. "I used to think how nice it would be to be General-in-Chief," he told Lyman, "[but] now, at this moment, I would [rather] go, with a division, under the heaviest musketry fire, than hold my place!"[22]

For almost 24 hours it was an open question whether Meade would keep his job. Halleck waited until noon the following day before responding to Meade's outburst. As was his custom after offending a subordinate, Halleck tried to mollify the general without apologizing. Rosecrans was "continually" reporting the arrival at Chattanooga of more troops from Lee, he reminded Meade, and was utterly positive the Confederates were concentrating to crush his army. "Under these circumstances," Halleck explained, the administration was constantly insisting that Meade "ought to ascertain Lee's forces and position, in order that the Government might at least know the actual facts." Since Meade hadn't been able to do this, Halleck "repeated the suggestion made to me of the necessity of giving battle."

In so many words, Halleck blamed Lincoln and Stanton for applying the pressure; he was merely the conduit for their advice. "If I have repeated truisms, it has not been to give offense, but to give to you the wishes of the Government." The general-in-chief concluded by telling Meade, "If, in conveying these wishes, I have used words which are unpleasing, I sincerely regret it." Despite the hint of sarcasm in Halleck's regret, it was regret nonetheless. Meade wired his superior accepting his explanation, "and I thank you for it." This ended the argument—for the time being.[23]

Despite his pseudo-apology, Halleck was right. Meade could have uncovered all the information he and the government needed by moving offensively against Lee, weather permitting. But Meade refused to play the game unless the Rebel general put all his cards on the table—and that was something Robert E. Lee never did. For fear of making a costly mistake, Meade was unwilling to run any uninformed risks.

Halleck saw this, and he could have ordered Meade to follow what he considered to be the proper course. But once again, the general-in-chief refused to issue direct

21 Previous paragraphs all based upon OR 29, pt. 2, 345, 346.

22 Lyman, Meade's Headquarters, 36.

23 OR 29, pt. 2, 354.

orders to his field commanders. This approach increased the self-imposed pressure on both generals, so it was little wonder frayed tempers snapped on both ends of the telegraph lines on October 18.

While Meade and Halleck sparred with one another, the Army of the Potomac's engineers emplaced a pontoon bridge at Blackburn's Ford. On the night of the 18th, Meade issued orders for his entire command to march south the next day.

The Confederates completed their retreat the same day that Meade began his pursuit. The final 24 hours of the Rebel withdrawal to the Rappahannock were no easier than the first 24 had been. Before dawn, a violent hail and rain storm slammed into the Rebel camps, rudely awakening the men to a thoroughly disagreeable morning. The traffic jam at the pontoon bridge had not broken up, and one irritated Southerner admitted that the troops waiting to cross the river were "much vexed & wearied by standing & 'closing up' in the mud & water." Eventually all the units Lee intended to cross to the south bank made it over the bridge. But the misery lingered, and that night, when the rain stopped, the weather turned uncomfortably cold.[24]

With Meade still at Centreville, and Stuart's cavalry providing a comfortable buffer, Lee positioned his army to defend the upper Rappahannock. Apparently he felt this line a great deal safer now than he had in August. Perhaps the lateness of the season and the prospect of winter quarters encouraged this outlook. Or possibly it was what he had learned about Meade during the recent campaign that convinced him to make a stand on the Rappahannock. Whatever the reason, the Army of Northern Virginia deployed along the river and waited once again for the arrival of its erstwhile foe.

---

24 Ibid., 348-59; Caldwell, *Brigade of South Carolinians*, 162.

CHAPTER 30

"Arms Glittering in the Bright Autumn Sunshine"

Cavalry Advance—Judson Kilpatrick—Stuart's Scare—Meade Moves—
Purloined Breakfast—Duel at Buckland Mills

NINE days after it had begun retreating toward Washington, the Union army finally reversed course and began moving south. Meade's plan of pursuit, if indeed worthy of the label, mirrored his plan of withdrawal a week earlier. He would split his command into two columns; one would advance on Warrenton while the other moved along the O&A to Rappahannock Station. Despite putting his army in motion, Meade still wasn't certain his opponent was retreating.

There had been no contact with Rebel infantry since the fight at Bristoe Station four days ago. Stuart's cavalry had been aggressive in the battle's aftermath. The hyper activity of enemy horsemen and the entire want of information were uncomfortably reminiscent of events around Culpeper Court House ten days ago. Meade couldn't shake visions of Lee marching west to outflank the Union army again. In such an environment it paid to be careful: that meant stationing cavalry to guard the Federal supply trains, flanks and rear. Which is what Meade did, deploying Gregg's and Buford's divisions to form a protective ring around the army.

This left only Wesley Merritt's Reserve Cavalry Brigade and Judson Kilpatrick's 3rd Cavalry Division to spearhead the southward advance and discover Lee's whereabouts. That was a fairly thin slice of cavalry for a tricky job. Meade discerned no cause for concern so long as his troopers didn't get too far in front of the infantry, and at 3 p.m. on October 18 he ordered Kilpatrick and Merritt to go ahead. Both commanders began to move forward shortly thereafter.

Merritt's brigade advanced down the O&A and before long encountered Chambliss' regiments north of Bristoe Station. Kilpatrick took longer to find the

Confederates. When his division left its Sudley Springs camp near Bull Run it headed for the picturesque hamlet of Groveton on the Warrenton Turnpike. To reconnoiter as much ground as possible, Kilpatrick split his force into two columns and sent each along a different route toward the village. Davies' command, with the 2nd New York Cavalry in front, marched due south from Sudley Springs. Custer's brigade, with the 1st Vermont Cavalry leading, rode southeast to New Market before turning west to move on Groveton via a road paralleling the pike. Both brigades encountered skirmishers from the 4th Virginia Cavalry as they neared the settlement. The Rebels put up only a token resistance before withdrawing below the town.[1]

Once Kilpatrick's two brigades united in Groveton, Davies' brigade took the lead and began pushing down the Warrenton Turnpike toward Gainesville, a small whistle stop on the Manassas Gap Railroad. As the sun sank into the horizon, the Yankees shoved the Virginians to within a short distance of the town before their resistance stiffened. After a brisk twilight skirmish the Federals broke contact and retired out of range before going into a cold, wet bivouac about 7 p.m.[2]

As his men groomed their horses and prepared supper, Judson Kilpatrick pondered the implications of the 4th Virginia's obstinate resistance. At 5-feet 5-inches tall, the 27-year old brigadier was a peculiar fellow. Colonel Lyman described him as a "spare, nervous, jerky man," with "colorless eyes, a big nose . . . narrow forehead" and "no upper lip, to speak of." The general had typically Irish red hair and a lantern jaw sporting a scraggly pair of sandy colored side whiskers. Kilpatrick set off his something less than handsome features with a sharp wardrobe. Between his snugly fitting uniform, knee-high boots and jaunty hat, the cavalryman displayed a unique, instantly recognizable style.[3]

A native of New Jersey, Kilpatrick compiled a solid record at West Point despite a tendency for getting into fistfights with fellow cadets. Smart, likeable, militarily aggressive, and occasionally brave, he was devoted to the Union cause. He was also highly ambitious, vainglorious, and seemingly indifferent to the death or suffering of his men. With little self-restraint, he indulged his vices at will. He drank, gambled, and

---

1   Previous paragraphs based upon *OR* 29, pt. 1, 382, 387, 391, 396, 472, 998. On August 28, 1862, the battle of Groveton set the stage for the battle of Second Manassas. The place was an important crossroads but little more than a collection of farms and orchards.

2   *OR* 29, pt. 1, 391, 396, 472, 998; *OR* 24, pt. 1, 333. See Gainesville, "History," http://gaines villeva.net/gainesville-history, accessed 24 Jun 18. Gainesville's railroad depot was burned in 1862.

3   Lyman, *Meade's Army*, 35, 103; Samuel J. Martin, *Kill-Cavalry: The Life of Union General Hugh Judson Kilpatrick* (Mechanicsburg, PA, 2000), 159-63. Kilpatrick's formal name was Hugh Judson Kilpatrick. He dropped the "Hugh" upon entering West Point.

Brigadier General Judson Kilpatrick
Library of Congress

consorted with ladies of ill-repute notwithstanding having married his sweetheart on the day of his West Point graduation.[4]

Kilpatrick was also corrupt. He accepted bribes and kickbacks from crooked contractors. As a lieutenant colonel in the 5th New York Cavalry, he sold confiscated horses and tobacco for personal gain and got thrown in jail for his troubles. Even Stanton recognized that the evidence against Kilpatrick unquestionably established his guilt. Nonetheless, his carefully constructed reputation as a gallant, hard fighting cavalryman saved him. The army whitewashed and explained away his behavior, and after three months the civil authorities dropped their charges and Kilpatrick returned to duty. In December 1862 he became colonel of his regiment. On June 14, 1863 he received a brigadier general's commission. Two weeks later Pleasonton appointed him commander of the 3rd Cavalry Division.[5]

The general's personal failings concerned his men far less than his military sins. His self-aggrandizing official reports often bore little relation to the truth. He was also a careless administrator and poor disciplinarian who failed to take proper care of his soldiers or horses. But these deficiencies paled by comparison to his pursuit of fame and advancement over the bodies of his men. A mediocre tactician, Kilpatrick had a notorious record for taking heavy losses for little gain other than newspaper headlines. Rash and impulsive on the battlefield, he had a proclivity for ordering near-suicidal charges. His troopers nicknamed their general "Kill-Cavalry" for good reason.[6]

Kilpatrick made great newspaper copy. Occasionally he achieved battlefield success, and he proved an audacious raider. More importantly, Kilpatrick's mantra of

---

4   Martin, *Kill-Cavalry*, 59-63, 128-130. In one infamous incident Kilpatrick shared his bed with a noted teenaged prostitute for some weeks in August 1863. He returned from an expedition to find his mistress had visited Rebel lines before moving in with his subordinate, George Custer. Incensed, Kilpatrick had the girl arrested as a spy.

5   Ibid., 57-58.

6   Warner, *Generals in Blue*, 266; Tagg, *Generals of Gettysburg*, 179-81, see Martin, *Kill-Cavalry*, 55-56, 92-96, 124-25, 140-43.

attack at all costs met the approval of Northerners who often felt frustrated by the AOP's perceived lack of aggressive spirit. His eagerness to fight and willingness to take casualties was what led Pleasonton to promote him to division command.[7]

Now Kilpatrick was where he most liked to be—out in front and on his own, with glory and headlines enticingly ahead. Which may or may not have been a good thing. The general's aggressiveness had always been double edged, with fame or disaster equally possible from his operations. The general was "a brave, vigorous man who is apparently deficient in judgement," Lyman wrote, before observing that his two brigadiers, Davies and Custer [did] "not much help him" with this "fault."[8]

For all of his unsavory qualities, Kilpatrick was no fool. After tangling with the 4th Virginia, he sensed that October 19 would prove more difficult than yesterday had been. That night he sent a dispatch to Pleasonton, informing him that scouts reported Stuart encamped with upwards of 1,000 men near Haymarket—a mere 3 miles northwest of Gainesville. Anticipating battle with the Rebels on the morrow, Kilpatrick requested reinforcements—which weren't forthcoming—from Merritt's brigade.

*   *   *

His foreboding was justified. Kilpatrick had barely missed a fight with Jeb Stuart on October 18. The Rebel general and Hampton's division had hovered around Gainesville most of that day anticipating a brawl. But when the Yankees failed to appear by mid-afternoon, Stuart decided to leave the 4th Virginia Cavalry to keep an eye on the Warrenton Turnpike while he led Hampton's brigades to Haymarket.

Severe logistical problems necessitated this move. Lee's recent order to cover the Confederate infantry withdrawal would put additional strain on the entire cavalry corps. Stuart's regiments had been on the move since October 8 and virtually without rations since then. Their horses hadn't eaten grain for nearly 10 days. Stuart needed to connect with Hampton's supply train to provision his soldiers and animals so they could withstand the rigors of their next mission. Stuart had left Gainesville for that rendezvous at almost the same time Kilpatrick had begun his advance on Groveton.

On the night of October 18, Hampton's brigades encamped a little northwest of Haymarket and only an hour's ride from Kilpatrick's bivouacs. Most of Fitz Lee's

---

7   Ibid.

8   Lyman, *Meade's Army*, 55, 103. By February 1864 Lyman's opinion of Kilpatrick had soured considerably and he referred to him as a "crack-brain" who was not "worth a fig as a general" and had the "indescribable air" of "a vulgarian."

division spent the night at Bristoe Station, with Merritt's cavalry not too far away. Wickham's brigade, still led by Col. Owen, remained at Langyher's Mill where it had spent most of the day. This spot was just seven miles from Kilpatrick's headquarters, roughly four miles northwest of Bristoe Station on the Gainesville Road.[9]

Despite the supply wagons and rations, Stuart's campsite was hardly pleasant. Federal troops had burned Haymarket in November 1862, reducing the town to a desolate gaggle of chimney stacks. Only 3 small houses and a church had survived the flames. After this calamity the village's entire population had fled.[10]

As if sleeping near such a gloomy place were not bad enough, it was a rainy, notably chilly night. While water-logged Rebel troopers tried to get some rest, Stuart received intelligence reporting Kilpatrick's cavalry and a significant force of Federal infantry had orders to move on Warrenton in the morning. As Stuart contemplated his strategy for the next day, an alarming dispatch reached him claiming that Yankee horsemen had driven the 4th Virginia Cavalry out of Gainesville.

If true, a crisis of serious proportions was at hand. Enemy possession of Gainesville would put the Yankees in a position to cut off Stuart's access to the Warrenton Turnpike—a road essential to his ability to cover Lee's withdrawal. Yankee control of it would place a huge Federal force between Hampton's division and the rest of the ANV. If that happened, Stuart would have to make a time consuming detour to rejoin the army during which he would be unable to screen the Southern infantry.[11]

Stuart couldn't afford to let the enemy occupy Gainesville before Hampton's division had taken a post on the Warrenton Turnpike. Preempting Kilpatrick required speedy action. Amidst a torrent of rain, Stuart ordered Brig. Gen. Pierce Young to saddle up his regiments and move to Haymarket immediately. From there he was to prepare to ride rapidly on Gainesville or Buckland Mills. Drenched and miserable, Young's troopers plodded east throughout the pre-dawn of October 19, which the rest of Hampton's division following shortly afterwards.

At Haymarket, Young discovered reports of Gainesville's capture false. The 4th Virginia still held the village, albeit with a lot of Yankee cavalrymen nearby. Relieved, Stuart decided it was time to unite his corps and dispatched a courier to Fitz Lee with instructions to that effect. The message informed Lee that Stuart would lead Hampton's division onto the Warrenton Turnpike before dawn on October 19 and

---

9   Previous paragraphs based upon *OR* 29, pt. 2, 349, pt. 1, 451, 463, 473, 998.

10   Williams, *From the Cannon's Mouth*, 244.

11   *OR* 29, pt. 1, 451. Haymarket and Gainesville were equidistant to Buckland Mills and New Baltimore, but using the Warrenton Turnpike the Yankees could move faster and along a straight line to both places.

would go as far south as Buckland Mills before halting. Fitz Lee was ordered to march toward the turnpike as soon after daylight as possible, on a route of his own choosing. The two Rebel cavalry divisions would unite somewhere along the pike that day, exactly where would depend on circumstances.

The messenger found Lee's division near Bristoe Station in a position it had held most of October 18. Chambliss' brigade had been stationed well north of Broad Run as an advance guard. But the approach of Merritt's Reserve Cavalry Brigade late in the day had compelled Chambliss to withdraw to within a mile and a half of the creek. The Federals were not in an aggressive mood, however, and they backed away and went into camp after Chew's battery fired a few warning shots in their direction.

After receiving Stuart's rendezvous order on the morning of October 19, Fitz Lee quickly sent word for Owen to shift Wickham's brigade from Langyher's Mill to Bristoe Station. Once he joined Lomax and Chambliss at the railroad, the division would move south to Catlett's Station, and from there ride west to Auburn, where Fitz Lee would then determine his final path to make a connection with Hampton's division.[12]

*   *   *

The sun rose on Monday, October 19, 1863 at 6:31 a.m. Heavy rain accompanied the dawn, but the sky soon cleared. The weather didn't prevent Stuart from pushing the brigades of Gordon and Funsten beyond Haymarket toward Gainesville. By the time the Rebels reached there, the 4th Virginia Cavalry—relieved of duty by Young's troopers—had already retired to Langyher's Mill to rejoin Owen's brigade. With no sign of Union forces in the immediate area, Stuart turned his column south toward Buckland Mills. Young's brigade lingered behind as rearguard.[13]

The Federals were also moving that morning. In obedience to an army headquarters circular issued the night of October 18, Newton's I Corps left Centreville via the Warrenton Turnpike at 6 a.m. headed toward Haymarket. French's III Corps and Warren's II Corps marched at the same time. The former crossed Bull Run at Union Mills on its way to Bristoe Station, while the latter traversed Mitchell's and Blackburn's fords en route to Milford. Sykes' V Corps marched from Centreville at 6 a.m. with instructions to cross Bull Run at Island Ford and proceed through New Market to Groveton.

---

12 Previous paragraphs all based upon OR 29, pt. 1, 353, 451, 463-64, 472-73, 475.

13 Ibid., 451; Carter, *Sabres, Saddles and Spurs*, 96; Krick, *Civil War Weather*, 110, Lyman, *Meade's Army*, 54.

In an attempt to lessen congestion on the Warrenton Turnpike, Sedgwick's VI Corps, destined for Groveton, didn't move until 7 a.m. Army headquarters and Brig. Gen. Hunt's reserve artillery advanced toward the same spot. The main supply trains moved to the north bank of Bull Run, where Meade had directed them to park, watched over by Gregg's and Buford's cavalry divisions.[14]

At daylight Kilpatrick received instructions to go "as far as possible [towards] Warrenton," while deploying units both west and east to "ascertain the movements of the enemy." The general dutifully put his men on the road, and at 8 a.m. they encountered Young's skirmishers north of Gainesville. The Rebels readily gave way and abandoned the town without a struggle. Once in possession of the village, Kilpatrick sent a scouting party to make sure the Southerners had evacuated Haymarket. The general also dispatched elements of the 7th Michigan Cavalry to ensure no graycoats lurked around Greenwich.[15]

Both these units soon reported the villages free of Confederates. Now certain of the security of his flanks, Kilpatrick was, as usual, more than eager to mercilessly press the enemy. He ordered Custer to move his brigade and Capt. Alexander C. M. Pennington's Battery M, 2nd US Artillery, to the head of the division column and then drive Young's troopers south. Davies' brigade, along with Capt. Samuel S. Elder's Battery E, 4th US Artillery, would follow. Major James Kidd's 6th Michigan assumed a position as the vanguard of Custer's brigade and trotted forward to engage the Rebels.[16]

Brigadier General Young deployed a single regiment as a rearguard and gradually fell back before Kilpatrick's much larger aggressive force. The Confederates continued withdrawing until Young's regiments reached the vicinity of Buckland Mills around 10:00 a.m. There, they found the rest of Wade Hampton's division preparing to cross a stone bridge over Broad Run in order to deploy along the creek's southern defensible shore.[17]

Stuart, on the scene and in a jovial mood, figured that Kilpatrick was operating independently and beyond any support. An opportunity to destroy his isolated force seemed possible, once Fitz Lee joined Hampton's division. To foster that result, Stuart arrayed Capt. William M. McGregor's battery along with Gordon's and Jones' brigades south of the stream. This would be Thomas Rosser's first fight as a general; he had led

14 *OR* 29, pt. 2, 349; Lyman, *Meade's Army*, 54.

15 *OR* 29, pt. 1, 362, 459.

16 James Kidd, *Personal Recollections of a Cavalryman* (Ionia, MI, 1908), 213-14.

17 *OR* 29, pt. 1, 459; U. R., Brooks, ed. *Stories of the Confederacy* (Columbia, SC, 1912), 205.

Jones' men almost since his promotion to brigadier on October 11. With Gordon and Young he would help hold the enemy in check until Fitz arrived.[18]

Stuart feared little from Kilpatrick and went about his business with a casual air. Hoping to get breakfast, he stopped at Charles Hunton's house, standing atop a 450-foot tall bluff called Cerro Gordo. Occupying a cleared imminence overlooking the north bank of Broad Run, it offered a splendid view of the surrounding countryside. The Huntons, happy to host the famous general, welcomed him into their home. He was still there when Young's rearguard brigade drew near Buckland Mills.[19]

Stuart sent a courier to fetch Young, who had been a brigadier for all of 20 days. Reporting as ordered, he found the general gaily playing the gallant cavalier while the Hunton daughters—25-year old Isabella and 15-year old Fannie—gleefully fussed over his breakfast. After introducing Young to the ladies, Stuart told his subordinate he had sent a unit to relieve his men from their rearguard work. Once that relief arrived Young's regiments were to fall back south of the creek and stand as a reserve for Gordon and Rosser.[20]

When Stuart finished with his instructions, he asked Young to join him for breakfast. The 26-year old Georgian happily accepted, but before the Hunton girls could prepare another meal, Stuart finished his and got up to leave. He cautioned Young not to savor his surroundings too long, because a fight was imminent, and the Yankees would be along to gobble him up shortly if he wasn't careful.

The youthful general almost failed to heed the advice. Enchanted by his female companions, of course, and eager for some hot food, he lost track of time. Just as the ladies were filling his plate, a Federal artillery shell burst over the house. Seconds later an aide dashed into the building shouting that enemy troops were nearby. With profuse and rapid apologies Young jumped up and rushed out the door. After mounting, he spun his horse around and gallantly promised his hostesses to return soon. Then he galloped down the hill and across the bridge just ahead of the advancing Federals.[21]

* * *

---

18 *OR* 29, pt. 1, 451.

19 Lynwood Holland, *Pierce M. B. Young: The Warwick of the South* (Athens, GA, 1964), 76.

20 Ibid; biographical details on the Hutton daughters are at: https://www.geni.com/people/Fannie-Hunton/6000000001180221033 and https://www.geni.com/people/Isabella-Hunton/6000000001180219989, accessed 25 Jun 18.

21 Holland, *Young*, 76.

The Yankees who chased Young away belonged to Maj. Kidd's 6th Michigan Cavalry which was nearing Broad Run along the Warrenton Pike. When he hit Stuart's picket line, Kidd dismounted part of his command to probe toward the creek. Pennington's battery unlimbered nearby and fired a shot at a cluster of Rebel horses near the Hunton household. Shortly thereafter the bluecoats went forward to test enemy intentions. The two sides were soon exchanging fire across Broad Run, and it rapidly became clear the Rebels were no longer retreating.

During the skirmish George Custer rode up the heights of Cerro Gordo to scan the surrounding countryside. Pennington's horse artillery rumbled onto the bluff behind him. As the gunners unlimbered their pieces, Custer walked his horse over to the Hunton house and politely asked if the family would cook him breakfast. A Confederate officer had just left, the ladies replied, and his breakfast was still on the table. Custer was welcome to it if he would like.

The general inquired as to the identity of the Rebel and upon learning that both Jeb Stuart and Pierce Young had been there, Custer smiled. He and Young had been cadets together at West Point; he knew the Georgian intimately. "Very well, ladies," Custer said. "Young and I are friends. I will take his breakfast." As the general enjoyed his fortuitous meal, he shared stories of his time with Young before the war. Then, as he got up to lead a battle against his former comrade, he asked the women to prepare dinner for him. He expected his command would still be around for an evening meal.[22]

This was hardly an overly pessimistic prediction. Stuart's men had taken a strong position south of Broad Run, which provided ideal defensive terrain. Its steep, heavily wooded, rugged banks rendered the rain-swollen stream impassable except at the turnpike's stone bridge and a ford one mile downstream. More importantly, the ridges south of the creek provided choice artillery platforms, and the stone buildings among Buckland's dozen or so structures made perfect emplacements for sharpshooters.[23]

Finishing breakfast, Custer, accompanied by his staff and escort, trotted down from Cerro Gordo onto the pike and stopped in the road to survey the situation through his field glasses. Rebel spotters on the other side of Broad Run noted the gathering of horsemen, and Capt. McGregor's gunners eagerly fired off a shot at such an irresistible target. Their shell dropped right into the midst of Custer's entourage, producing a "lively scattering" by the general's cavalcade. Luckily for the Yankees, the bursting ordnance inflicted no casualties.[24]

22 Ibid, 76-77.

23 Donaldson, *Inside the Army of the Potomac,* 372

24 Kidd, *Recollections of a Cavalryman,* 214.

Custer had seen enough to realize Stuart's troopers were making a stand. How long they were determined to hold their position was an open question. Whatever the answer, the young general determined to push forward. He promptly dismounted three regiments and ordered them to deploy for an attack against Broad Run.

Major Kidd's 6th Michigan Cavalry spread out across the turnpike. Colonel Russell A. Alger's 5th Michigan Cavalry took post south of the road, while Col. William D. Mann's 7th Michigan Cavalry formed north of the pike below the Cerro Gordo height. Colonel Charles H. Town's 1st Michigan Cavalry and Col. Edward B. Sawyer's 1st Vermont Cavalry remained in the rear as a mounted reserve. Once everything was ready Pennington's guns commenced firing from near the Hunton house.

McGregor's Rebel cannon responded, and as rival shells arched overhead, the Yankee troopers tried unsuccessfully several times to push the Rebels aside and force a passage of the creek. The stubborn defenders threw back every Union effort. Unable to shake Stuart's hold on Broad Run, Custer sent the 7th Michigan farther north to find a viable crossing and turn the Rebel left flank.[25]

* * *

While Kilpatrick confronted Stuart at Buckland Mills, Fitz Lee steadily approached the Warrenton Turnpike. After waiting for Owen's brigade to reach Bristoe Station early that morning, Lee had led his command south down the O&A to Catlett's Station. This route had two advantages: first, it was fast and from the station the cavalry would have an easy road to Auburn. From there it could head west to Warrenton, New Baltimore, or Buckland Mills. Second, moving south would pull Merritt's brigade out of supporting distance of Kilpatrick, while at the same time positioning Lee to go to Stuart's aid. Lomax's brigade, assisted by Chew's battery formed Lee's rearguard, which would keep Merritt occupied and prevent him from realizing what the Rebels were really doing.[26]

Owen's brigade and James Breathed's battery, followed by Chambliss' brigade, detoured toward Auburn as soon as they reached Catlett's Station. At some point during his ride, Lee received signal flag communication from Stuart and learned that Hampton's brigades were fighting Kilpatrick along Broad Run. Fitz Lee wigwagged a response that he wasn't far from Buckland Mills and suggested a stratagem to destroy Kilpatrick's division. If Stuart led a feigned retreat down the pike toward New Baltimore, he suggested, the Yankees would certainly pursue. Once the enemy was

25 Ibid.; *OR* 29, pt. 1, 387; 391.

26 *OR* 29, pt. 1, 463-64; 466, 473.

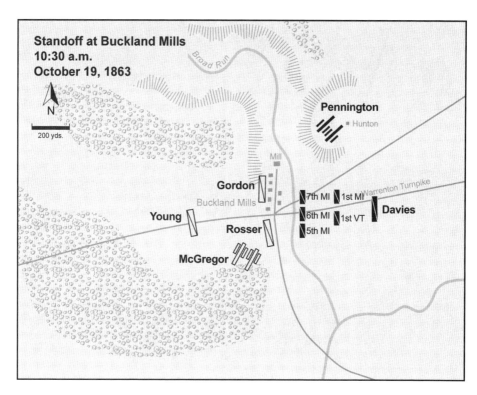

sufficiently distant from Broad Run, Lee's division could sweep in from the east, reoccupy Buckland, and fall against Kilpatrick's rear. Then, Stuart could turn and attack Kilpatrick in front. Caught between two Confederate cavalry divisions and cut off from any hope of support, the Federals would be ripe for annihilation.[27]

Stuart liked the idea. A little after noon Gordon, Rosser, Young, and McGregor left Buckland Mills and began retreating down the Warrenton Turnpike. Custer's men took advantage of this happy event to seize the stone bridge over Broad Run and swarm onto the creek's southern shore. About the same time, the 7th Michigan found a ford north of the town. The regiment swiftly waded over the stream and moved to rejoin Custer's brigade. The delighted general understandably concluded that the Rebel withdrawal had resulted from the 7th Michigan's turning Stuart's flank.

Anxious to capitalize on the enemy's sudden flight, Kilpatrick ordered Custer to reform his brigade and told Davies to pursue the retiring Rebels. As the Michigan and Vermont regiments assembled, the 1st Brigade and Elder's battery rode across the

---

27 Ibid., 463-64; Kidd, *Recollections of a Cavalryman*, 216; Charles Taylor, "The Signal and Secret Service of the Confederate States," *CVM*, 1932, Vol. 40, 303. When/where Lee used signal flags with Stuart is unclear. It may have been at Auburn, Greenwich, some point in between.

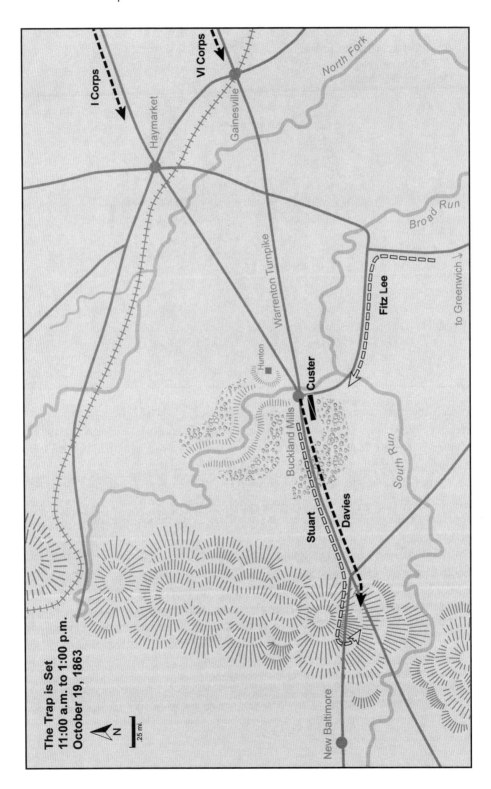

The Trap is Set
11:00 a.m. to 1:00 p.m.
October 19, 1863

N

25 mi.

I Corps

VI Corps

Haymarket

Gainesville

North Fork

Broad Run

Warrenton Turnpike

Fitz Lee

to Greenwich ↓

Hunton

Custer

Buckland Mills

South Run

Stuart

Davies

New Baltimore

Pennington's battery opens fire on Buckland Mills from the heights of Cerro Gordo. Buckland Mill, which gave its name to the town, is visible on the right. Smoke from McGregor's battery can be seen on the horizon. *Alfred Waud*

bridge and disappeared down the pike toward New Baltimore and Warrenton. Kilpatrick ordered Custer to fall in behind Davies and join the chase. Custer "respectfully but firmly" refused to comply. Neither his men nor his animals had eaten anything since last evening, he explained. His brigade should be allowed time to prepare and consume a late breakfast before joining the rest of the division.

Major Kidd, who witnessed the ensuing discussion between the generals, thought Custer's attitude "seemed obstinacy, if not insubordination." Although the young general had a reputation for caring "studiously for the comfort of his men," for Custer to refuse to press a retreating foe was highly unusual. But he would not budge. Finally, Kilpatrick relented and granted Custer time to feed his troops. The division commander insisted, however, that the 2nd Brigade's wagons and ambulances follow Davies' column at once so as not to slow Custer's march. Having issued his orders, Kilpatrick and his staff hurried after Davies' brigade.[28]

While Custer's troopers cooked bacon, boiled coffee, and fed their horses, Hampton's division continued its retreat. Davies' brigade followed as the Rebels surrendered five miles with only slight resistance. The advancing Federal horsemen presented a magnificent spectacle. At one point during the retreat, Lt. William Blackford of Stuart's staff paused to admire the enemy host. "As far as the eye could reach," he recalled, "their columns of splendidly equipped cavalry came marching on with flags fluttering and arms glittering in the bright autumn sunshine." Little did the men in blue suspect that the jaws of a trap were about to close upon them.[29]

28 Previous paragraphs based upon *OR* 29, pt. 1, 382, 391, 451; Kidd, *Recollections of a Cavalryman*, 215, 216.

29 Emory Thomas, *Bold Dragoon–The Life of J.E.B. Stuart* (New York, 1986), 268.

CHAPTER 31

"A Most Beautiful Trap"

.

Feigned Retreat—Surprise Fight—Custer's Stand—Kilpatrick Reacts—
Stuart Attacks—Desperate Situation—Buckland Races—
Evening Skirmish—Blame and Laurels

As Davies' brigade chased Jeb Stuart's retreating Confederates toward New Baltimore, Custer's troopers cooked and ate a badly needed meal. Some men found time to scrounge through the buildings of Buckland Mills for food and lucked in to discovering a honey-laden beehive. Uncharacteristically, their general seemed in no hurry to rejoin the division. Although content to take his time, Custer knew he could delay only so long. After two hours he ordered his men to saddle up and get ready to move.

Out in front of the Michigan brigade the Warrenton Turnpike ran arrow straight for a third-of-a-mile through rich farmland before disappearing into a forest. The cultivated fields east of the thoroughfare ended in a dense growth of trees. The Greenwich Road emerged from that wood line onto the open ground beside the turnpike. Although nothing indicated enemy troops nearby, those woods worried Custer.[1]

After his regiments fell in, the general rode over to Maj. Kidd and directed him to deploy the 6th Michigan Cavalry as a flank guard facing the forest east of the turnpike. Custer specified a point in the open field about 500 yards from the road as Kidd's position. The 6th Michigan Cavalry was to hold that spot until the rest of the brigade had passed by and then fall in at its rear. The brigadier warned his subordinate to be careful: elements of the 7th Michigan scouting near Greenwich might reenter Union

---

1   The Greenwich Road is modern Vint Hill Road, also known as Virginia Route 215.

lines via the road emerging from the woods. He wanted no casualties from friendly fire.[2]

As Custer's brigade started down the pike, Kidd led his regiment in a column of fours toward his designated station. Everything seemed oddly quiet; the only noise came from the Federal troopers. As the 6th Michigan approached a rail fence about 250 yards from the road, Capt. Don Lovell, riding next to Kidd, saw a mounted soldier sitting calmly astride his horse 200 yards closer to the trees. Alarmed by this unexpected sight, Lovell warned Kidd that something was amiss.

Unconcerned, the major replied that a scouting party was expected to return from that direction. The captain wasn't convinced, insisting that the suspicious character was a Confederate. As Kidd was reiterating his previous position, the unknown observer began riding his horse in a circle. This was all the proof Lovell needed: "Look at that! That is a rebel signal; our men don't do that," he exclaimed.

Whatever doubt Kidd still entertained disappeared seconds later when the suspect raised his weapon and fired a shot into the breast of one of the 6th Michigan's lead horses. As a spatter of gunfire erupted from the woods, the major immediately ordered his regiment to dismount and take cover behind the rail fence. While his troopers deployed, Kidd dispatched his adjutant to tell Custer that a large body of Confederates was swarming in the woods not far from Broad Run and the stone bridge.[3]

That was an understatement. Kidd and Lovell were looking at the spearhead of an entire division of Rebel cavalry. Colonel Thomas Owen had led Fitz Lee's column to Buckland Mills, and as he had neared Greenwich, sent the 2nd Virginia Cavalry ahead to scout the village. They had in turn captured a handful of Yankees from the 7th Michigan, probably preventing them from warning Custer of Fitz Lee's approach. From Greenwich the Rebel cavalry column had headed toward Buckland, just three-and-a-half miles west. As the Confederates drew near the town, Lee had ordered Owen to dismount his sharpshooters and deploy them in the woods parallel to the Warrenton Pike. The general also hauled up two guns from Breathed's battery and positioned them 1,200 yards from the road.[4]

The sudden exchange of gunfire caught everyone by surprise. Fitz Lee's division remained strung out on the road, with Chambliss still coming up, and Lomax too far in the rear to take part in the growing action. Fortunately for the Federals, Custer had not gone far from Broad Run, and he turned his brigade around as soon as he heard gunfire

---

2 Kidd, *Recollections of a Cavalryman*, 218.

3 Ibid. Kidd, *Recollections of a Cavalryman*, 218-220

4 OR 29, pt. 1, 473; Trout, *Galloping Thunder*, 378. Owen temporarily commanded Wickham's brigade, Chambliss led W.H.F. "Rooney" Lee's brigade.

in his rear. As his troopers rushed back to the creek, Custer sent the 1st Vermont and one artillery piece from Pennington's battery to hold the bridge. The 5th and 7th Michigan quickly dismounted and took up a position in some woods on Kidd's right. Pennington unlimbered a section of guns directly behind the 6th Michigan. As soon as his pieces were ready, the captain ordered them to open fire against Breathed's Southern artillery. The 1st Michigan Cavalry remained mounted as a reserve near Battery M.[5]

Confederate reinforcements reached the scene about the same time as Custer's regiments. As Chambliss' three Virginia regiments galloped onto the field, the colonel dismounted his sharpshooters and sent them into the woods alongside Owen's men. Fitz Lee now had seven regiments and a section of artillery fully engaged with Custer's five regiments and Pennington's six guns. Despite nearly equal odds, the Federals felt hard pressed. That Union gunners were firing over the heads of their own troopers emphasized the desperation of the moment.

*   *   *

As Custer and Fitz Lee clashed, the other half of the Confederate battle plan unfolded four miles to the south. Stuart had fallen back steadily since leaving Broad Run, all the while drawing Davies' brigade deeper into the Rebel trap. Two and a half miles short of New Baltimore, Stuart decided he'd gone far enough. Crossing over the wide crest of Chestnut Hill, he halted Hampton's division and turned it toward the enemy. His troopers, completely unaware of their general's plans, dismounted to rest their horses and await the resumption of the retreat. Few realized Stuart was laying an ambush.[6]

As the Southerners lounged, the Federals gained ground. The Rebels could distinctly hear the clink and rattle of Union weapons and equipment as Davies' men reached the opposite side of the ridge and began to climb. The rival forces were only two hundred yards apart when cannon fire erupted to the north. The inexplicable outbreak of shooting to his rear startled Kilpatrick. He sent an aide to Davies with orders to halt his advance and dispatch a regiment back along the pike to see what was happening near Broad Run. The rest of Davies' brigade would hold where it was and await additional instructions. But the general's impatience to personally find out what

---

5   Kidd, *Recollections of a Cavalryman*, 221; OR 29, pt. 1, 391.

6   Whit Hill Anthony, *Personal Sketch and reminiscences on the Cavalry Fight at Buckland, VA*, NC State Archives.

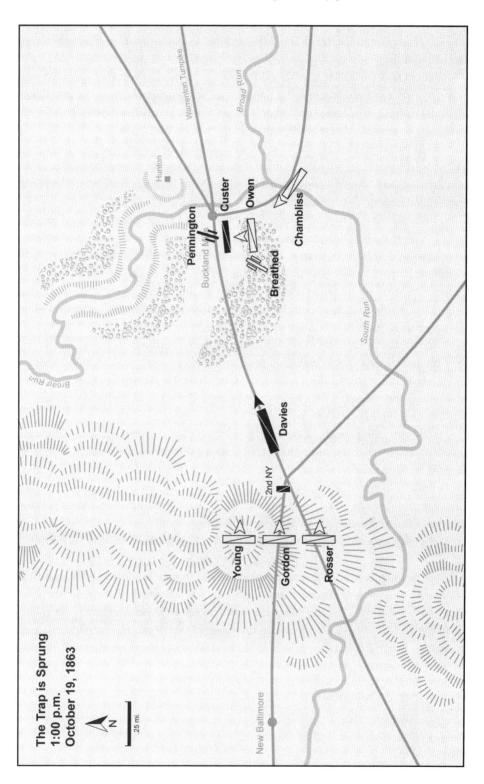

The Trap is Sprung
1:00 p.m.
October 19, 1863

N

25 mi.

was happening got the better of him. Minutes later he and his staff headed back toward Buckland Mills.[7]

Henry Davies shared his boss's sudden apprehension. The sound of fighting to the rear grew in depth and intensity by the minute. Uncomfortable with the way things were developing, he decided to forego further word from Kilpatrick. Deploying Lt. Col. Otto Harhaus's 2nd New York in a line across the Warrenton Turnpike, he instructed the rest of his brigade to turn about and head back from whence it had come. Harhaus had orders to hold his position long enough to give the column a head start and then pull back slowly toward Broad Run. The New York regiment, which had been the Federal column's vanguard, was now its rearguard.[8]

On the other side of Chestnut Hill, the boom of Lee's cannon had a galvanizing effect. Almost immediately, a dozen bugles sounded the call to mount. The Southern troopers—as surprised by events as Kilpatrick's—were in the saddle within seconds. Gordon's North Carolina brigade formed the center of the Rebel line, with Young and Rosser deployed on its flanks. As soon as his regiments were in the saddle, Stuart ordered an attack straight over the crest of the ridge into whatever Yankees stood on the other side.

General Gordon calmly trotted over to Maj. Rufus Barringer, commanding the 1st North Carolina, and simply said: "Charge those Yankees and break them." The major, at the head of his command, a bugler at his side, arrayed his regiment into a column of squadrons, and the rest of Gordon's regiments followed suit, forming a column of squadrons behind Barringer's men.

With everything ready, Barringer gave the order to draw sabers. With their characteristic metallic swoosh, hundreds of blades slid out of scabbards and into an upright position on the right of the gray cavalrymen. Seconds later the major signaled the advance, and his column trotted steadily forward for fifty yards before breaking into a gallop for the next one hundred. Then, with his formation gaining speed, Barringer ordered the bugler to sound the charge.

One Rebel recalled that as the familiar notes that "stirred men and horses to the deadly shock" rang through the air, buglers throughout the rest of Hampton's division echoed the charge. The 1st North Carolina leveled its sabers and surged forward. As Barringer's galloping men crested the ridge, they saw Davies' brigade in a column of fours on the turnpike. To their surprise, the Yankees were heading north, retreating. Only the 2nd New York Cavalry stood firmly astride the road. The men in this single regiment's line of battle were shocked to see the mass of enemy horsemen spilling over

---

7   Trout, *Galloping Thunder*, 377.

8   OR 29, pt. 1, 387.

the ridge in front of them. The startled troopers quickly fired a hurried carbine volley which flew over the heads of the oncoming North Carolinians.

Disregarding this ineffective fire, the Rebels thundered forward. Well aware that the rest of Davies' men wouldn't come to their aid, Colonel Harhaus's New Yorkers did the only thing they could do and hurriedly began pulling back, firing as they withdrew. The mounting sound of battle to the front, right, and rear strongly suggested the brigade had ridden into a snare from which it might not escape. As one Yankee in the 2nd New York observed "unexpected troubles were multiplying around the regiment with dizzying speed." Still Harhaus's men offered what resistance they could. At a slight rise of ground they turned to make a stand and were briefly able to check the enemy with rapid pistol and carbine fire.[9]

It was ephemeral success. The Rebels drew back, reformed, and charged again. This time no amount of gunfire could stay their assault. Gordon's troopers slammed into the New Yorkers, and after a short-lived and "fierce hand-to-hand conflict," the grossly outnumbered defenders were "hurled back by the overpowering shock" of the collision and driven rearward. The Confederates had not routed Harhaus's men, however, and they turned to resist their pursuers wherever the terrain provided an opportunity. The 1st North Carolina made at least four distinct charges during the running battle. Amid one mêlée in a small hamlet, the press of frenzied men and animals temporarily disabled Barringer by slamming him and his horse into a building. Captain Cowles took charge of the regiment and continued to press the attack as the Federals fled steadily northwards.[10]

* * *

Near Broad Run no one was retreating. Fitz Lee had hoped he could swing unopposed between Kilpatrick's division and Buckland Mills to cut off the Federal escape route. Instead the Confederates had stumbled unexpectedly into Custer, whose troopers were fighting desperately to hold open a line of retreat for Davies' dangerously exposed command. Before the Rebel trap could spring shut, the Confederates had to drive Custer from the bridge.

Fitz Lee was attacking with all his might. The gray line heaved forward, but Custer would not budge. Yankee gunners were winning their duel with Breathed's battery and virtually knocked one of his pieces out of action by wounding four of its crewmen. The

---

9 Previous paragraphs all based on Anthony, *Personal Sketch*, NC State Archives. A column of squadrons was a standard attack formation. Confederate accounts do not specify if it was used.

10 Ibid.; Glazier, *Three Years in the Federal Cavalry*, 336.

Southern artillery, by contrast, made little impression on Pennington's cannon. For the moment, the battle was stalemated; but it couldn't remain so long. "We were anxious," one Federal confessed, "for we knew we had got into a nest of hornets and were in a tight place."[11]

The arrival of Davies' retreating column did little to alleviate the situation. Once he had got about a mile and a half from Buckland Mills, the general turned his men about to face Stuart's attack. Amidst this crisis, Davies expected to receive orders from Kilpatrick detailing how the division would escape its dire predicament. But no instructions arrived; two separate couriers Kilpatrick dispatched to Davies never got through.

So Davies' men stood and fought. With Young and Rosser moving to outflank the Union line, only Gordon's troopers were trading blows with the enemy. It was a fairly even contest, at least for the moment. The 5th North Carolina, still furious over its October 11 rout at Brandy Station, was gratified the enemy dared to receive an attack. The Tar Heels had been looking for a chance to exact revenge on the 18th Pennsylvania—who they mistakenly believed had driven them from the field eight days ago. Now the hated Pennsylvanians sat right in front of them and, as one gray trooper later bragged, the Rebels "cut and slashed into their ranks furiously."[12]

No matter how staunchly Custer or Davies held on, the substantial gap separating their commands made Custer's line vulnerable to a flank attack. Should the Rebels plunge into the yawning void between the two commands they would cut Davies off from both Custer and the bridge over Broad Run. Kilpatrick realized this danger and ordered Col. Russell Alger of the 5th Michigan to plug the gap. The colonel did what he could, sending a 50-man battalion under Maj. John Clark from his hard-pressed regiment to do a job that required an entire brigade. Custer knew nothing of this detachment and in the crisis Kilpatrick had not been able to tell him.[13]

As Clark's men dismounted and took position in some woods, the Rebels under Owens and Chambliss attacked again, coming forward in dismounted as well as mounted formations. All along Custer's front, one Federal remembered, Confederates were "quite thick" and their bullets were coming "through the brush lively" as they relentlessly pressed forward. Heavy fire from dismounted Michigan soldiers couldn't stop them. When Fitz Lee's troopers got to within 20 yards of the rail fence held by the

11 Meyer, *Civil War Experiences*, 66; Eric J. Wittenberg, *Under Custer's Command: The Civil War Journal of James Henry Avery* (Washington, D.C., 2000), 53-54.

12 Clark, *NC Regts*, vol. 3, 582-83.

13 Marguerite Merrington, ed., *The Custer Story, The Life and Intimate Letters of General George A. Custer and His Wife Elizabeth* (New York, 1950), 68.

6th Michigan, Capt. Pennington feared his battery was about to be overrun. He gave the order to cease fire, limber, and retreat across the bridge. Custer couldn't continue to hold without artillery support. With Fitz Lee threatening to overwhelm his front and no help in sight, the general ordered a retreat.[14]

Astonished Confederates watched the Federal line quickly gave way. As soon as Pennington's guns raced over the bridge, Custer sent word for his regiments to follow. Colonel Sawyer's 1st Vermont Cavalry had spent the battle sitting its horses supporting the Union artillery. As he watched the guns clatter over Broad Run, Sawyer detailed Lt. Col. Addison Preston to stay behind with two companies and support Pennington's lone fieldpiece still defending the bridge. As Preston's men deployed, the rest of the 1st Vermont retreated across the stone span. The 7th Michigan galloped over the bridge seconds later. The 6th Michigan left its fence grudgingly and made a slow fighting retreat back to its horses. Major Kidd boasted that his men had withdrawn over Broad Run "leisurely, without hurry or flurry." The 1st Michigan followed them.[15]

Unlike most of Custer's regiments, the 5th Michigan barely eluded annihilation near Buckland Mills. Alger had shared the anxiety of his men throughout the fight, looking frequently to the rear for reinforcements. But now came a courier, his horse at a "dead run and covered with foam," racing forward with Custer's order to retreat "as quick as you can." The colonel, however, acted with deliberate calmness—directing his regiment to remount and wheel about, before trotting to the front of his column and leading it toward the creek and safety.[16]

Alger's retreat left Maj. Clark's battalion to its fate. After being detached from the rest of the 5th Michigan on Kilpatrick's orders, these men had been fighting dismounted in the woods on Custer's extreme right. As the Federal position rapidly collapsed, Clark failed to receive the order to retreat in time. Before his men could get to their horses Rebels swarmed all around them, capturing the entire battalion (some 50 men) along with the regiment's adjutant.

The rest of the 5th Michigan barely avoided a similar fate. Although its retreat began in an orderly fashion, the regiment soon discovered itself cut off from the bridge. Alger chose to lead his men to the creek and order them to get across it as best they could. One trooper recalled he and his comrades having no choice but to negotiate

---

14 Kidd, *Recollections of a Cavalryman*, 222-23; OR 29, pt. 1, 392; William Lee, *Personal and Historical Sketches and Facial History of and by Members of the Seventh Regiment Michigan Volunteer Cavalry* (Detroit: MI, 1902), 103.

15 S. S. Clark, "Buckland Mills." *The Maine Bugle*, Volume 4, January 1897 (Rockland, Maine, 1897), 108-10; Kidd, *Recollections of a Cavalryman*, 222-23; OR 29, pt. 1, 392.

16 James Henry Avery, *Under Custer's Command: The Civil War Journal of James Henry Avery* (Washington, D.C., 2000), 54.

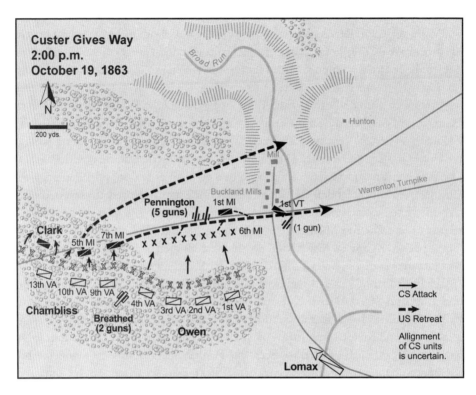

Broad Run's steep banks, swim their mounts across the rain swollen creek, and then slowly climb up the opposite shore as "shot and shell whistled and screeched and burst all around them." For the men running it, this gauntlet seemed to take forever. Remarkably, most of the regiment made good its escape and was able to rally on the north bank once beyond enemy gunfire.[17]

Successful withdrawal looked increasingly unlikely for Custer's last formations south of Broad Run. Rebels seriously threatened to overrun Pennington's remaining fieldpiece guarding the bridge. In a desperate effort to give this gun crew a chance to hitch up and escape, Lt. Col. Peterson took his two-company rearguard into a patch of woods south of the cannon. Here he had his men fire their revolvers as rapidly as possible, while shouting as madly as they could in hopes of fooling the Rebels into believing a counterattack was coming their way. The ploy worked long enough for the artillerists to limber up and scurry across Broad Run. Peterson's men had saved the

17 Kidd, *Recollections of a Cavalryman*, 222-23; OR 29, pt. 1, 392; James Henry Avery, *Under Custer's Command: The Civil War Journal of James Henry Avery* (Washington, D.C., 2000), 54; Merrington, *The Custer Story*, 68; Wittenberg, *Under Custer's Command*, 54.

gun, but in doing so they had positioned themselves so far from the bridge they were now isolated.[18]

Custer, unaware of Peterson's plight, stayed on the south side of Broad Run until the last of his squadrons scurried over the bridge. After dashing across the span himself, he spurred his horse up the Cerro Gordo heights, hoping to get some idea of the vigor of Fitz Lee's inevitable advance. Encountering the Hunton girls once more, he recalled his earlier request that they make him dinner. Since he wouldn't be around to eat the pre-ordered meal, Custer wittily explained to the ladies that since he had taken Pierce Young's breakfast, it was only fair that his old classmate help himself to Custer's dinner. The general handed a photograph of himself to one of the girls, asking her to give the image to Young with his compliments and request he send a photo in return. Then the general galloped away.[19]

Meanwhile Fitz Lee was busily organizing a pursuit. Within a few minutes of Custer's escape an entire brigade of Rebel cavalry pounded over the stone bridge. In their haste to catch the Michiganders, the Southerners utterly disregarded Peterson's two tiny Vermont companies. The Confederates assumed the isolated Yankees would have no choice but to surrender. Peterson had other ideas. Boldly forming his troops into line, he sent Sgt. Stephen Clark to find a way across the creek. He immediately rode off to explore a hunch that a nearby mill race dam might provide a viable route across Broad Run.

Clark's intuition proved correct—if the troopers waded the creek via the submerged dam, they could cross stream—and he rushed back to report that he had found a way out. The two stranded companies, taking advantage of the general confusion, followed Clark back to the mill race. There they managed against all odds to reach the north shore of Broad Run and then weave their way single file through thick woods back to Union lines.[20]

* * *

Custer's retreat spelled almost certain disaster for Davies. With the loss of the bridge the 1st Brigade's obvious line of retreat was gone. Withdrawal northeastward on the turnpike would take it into the clutches of Fitz Lee's entire division and certain destruction. Kilpatrick knew he had to warn Davies of this danger before it was too late.

18 Clark, *Maine Bugle*, "Buckland Mills", Vol. 4, Jan 1897, 108-10.

19 Holland, *Warwick of the South*, 77.

20 Clark, *Maine Bugle*, "Buckland Mills", Vol. 4, Jan 1897, 108-10.

That would not be simple. Finding themselves with Custer when his regiments began to pull back across Broad Run, Kilpatrick and staff had no choice but to retreat with them. But once over the bridge, he felt compelled to try one last time to alert Davies to his increasingly desperate position. Turning to his aide, Capt. Henry Meyer, the general said somebody had to get through to the 1st Brigade. Recognizing a preemptory order couched as a request when he heard one, the plucky officer instantly said he would go. As Meyer turned his horse to the southwest and began to hurry away, Kilpatrick shouted after him to tell Davies to get over the creek anywhere he could and then make his way to Newton's I Corps around Haymarket.[21]

Unable to use the bridge, Meyer made his way upstream hoping to find a path around the Rebels. By a stroke of luck he saw Peterson's Vermont troopers thread a path across the mill race and come ashore on the northern bank. Thus alerted to a way over the creek, the captain splashed into the water and galloped southward. Directed by the sound of Davies' fight, he reached the brigadier and found his line "hard pressed." Stuart's regiments were curling around the Federal flanks and relentlessly pushing the Yankees back toward Buckland. Davies now learned to his horror that the enemy had severed the turnpike and threatened to surround him.[22]

Reacting swiftly, the brigadier threw the 5th New York Cavalry out to guard his flank in the direction of Fitz Lee. With a few minutes to take stock of the situation, he realized that there was nothing left to do but retreat northeast as fast as possible across country in a diagonal flight for Broad Run. In a desperate bid to buy time for his wagons, ambulances, and artillery to escape, the brigadier ordered the 2nd New York Cavalry and 1st West Virginia Cavalry to charge the Rebels and delay the enemy long enough to allow the rest of his command to get a head start. The New Yorkers and West Virginians moved to the attack, while the remainder of the brigade, its vehicles, and Elder's battery made a dash for Broad Run.[23]

In Confederate eyes, the Yankee retreat looked like it was devolving into a rout. In the ranks of Kilpatrick's division it was not quite as bad as all that—but it *was* bad. Every Yankee knew his side had been defeated, and they were retiring under great pressure in the midst of a frighteningly fluid, dangerous set of circumstances. Major Kidd confessed that the Rebels had set "a most beautiful trap" for Kilpatrick and had come "within one of succeeding."[24]

---

21 Meyer, *Civil War Experiences*, 66.

22 Ibid.

23 OR 29, pt. 1, 387.

24 Eric J. Wittenberg, ed., *One of Custer's Wolverines: The Civil War Letters of Brevet Brigadier General James H. Kidd, 6th Michigan Cavalry* (Kent, IL, 2000), 63.

At the moment no one was pausing to reflect on the nature of victory or defeat. Escape and pursuit were all that mattered, and the Union troopers realized that they were on the wrong end of that equation. Luckily, Dr. Charles Capehart, a surgeon on Davies' staff, knew this area well. He led the column through the trackless terrain to a "most unpromising" ford which presented a dismal prospect for successful escape. There was no time to look for another passage, however. Davies' brigade and Elder's battery would have to cross here or face annihilation.[25]

For cavalry, the creek was a moat breaking up formations and disorienting men and mounts as they pitched into the water before emerging drenched and uncertain on the other side. The dense underbrush and steep creek banks meant every trooper had to find his own way to higher ground and ultimately his own line of escape. If Davies' brigade was *retreating* up to Broad Run, it is fair to say that after effecting a haphazard crossing, his command was so broken up it unquestionably met the military criteria for being *routed* once over the stream.

Elder's guns, limbers, and caissons somehow managed to use the ford and get away. So too did most of Davies' wagons. But the barely navigable crossing proved a natural bottleneck for the slow moving vehicles at the tail of the brigade's column. The Rebels caught up to them and captured a mixture of wagons or ambulances. Two vehicles from Davies' brigade and six from Custer's fell into Confederate hands, including the Michigan brigadier's headquarters wagon with all of the general's personal baggage.[26]

Custer's regiments had managed to get over Broad Run in much better condition than Davies' did. Nonetheless, they were still under enormous pressure. Breathed's horse artillery took position on Cerro Gordo and began shelling Federal units on the turnpike. Colonel Owen sent the 1st, 2nd and 3rd Virginia Cavalry across the bridge to harass the Union retreat. While these units advanced to within 100 yards of the Yankee line the 4th Virginia forded the creek upstream.

Maintaining the pressure, Owen threw his regiments against the enemy in a sequence of charges, first by the 3rd Virginia, then the 2nd, and finally by the 1st Virginia Cavalry. After fording Broad Run the 4th hurled itself against Custer's flank. Although the Federals fended off each of these blows, their only course was to continue retreating northward toward the lead elements of Meade's infantry.[27]

*   *   *

25 *Harper's Weekly*, November 14, 1863.

26 Ibid; Starr, *Union Cavalry*, vol. 2, 30.

27 *OR* 29, pt. 1, 472; Carter, *Sabres, Saddles and Spurs*, 96.

Stuart's pursuit of Kilpatrick didn't stop until the battered Union cavalrymen neared Gainesville and Haymarket, now occupied by Sedgwick's VI Corps and Newton's I Corps, respectively. These two commands had reached their separate destinations in late afternoon and promptly deployed pickets for the evening. Newton assigned the task of guarding the roads leading into Haymarket from Leesburg and Thoroughfare Gap to his 3rd Division, under Brig. Gen. John R. Kenly. The latter route ran due west out of Haymarket, while the former stretched off to the northwest.

Kenly detailed Col. Edwin H. Webster's 7th Maryland (US) Infantry to watch these critical avenues. Besides commanding a regiment of Maryland loyalists, its 34-year old colonel was also a current member of the US Congress. He placed outpost on each road about a mile-and-a-half from Haymarket and a strong picket line in the woods between the thoroughfares.

By the time the colonel finished posting his men, it was nearly sundown. Hopes for a quiet night abruptly vanished when the leading edge of a wave of fugitives from the Buckland Mills fight raced into Webster's line. From these frightened men, he learned that Confederate cavalry was driving in Davies' brigade. Once informed of the situation, Kenly immediately ordered his division to fall in and form a battle line.[28]

Within minutes the bulk of Davies' regiments were streaming through the 7th Maryland's picket line from the direction of Thoroughfare Gap. Southern horsemen appeared not long afterwards, and the foot soldiers quickly took the Rebels under fire. The sound of infantry muskets encouraged Elder's horse artillery to halt its retreat long enough to throw a few retaliatory rounds at the Confederates.[29]

The Union cannon and rifle fire brought the Confederates to a halt. Not that the fighting was over. Stuart's cavalry regiments had become fairly scattered during the long chase from Broad Run. Their commanders prudently declined to rush into a slapdash tangle with enemy infantry. They would pause long enough to consolidate their units and scout the Yankee position before renewing the contest. This delay was a godsend to Davies, who hurriedly sent a message to Brig. Gen. Kenly asking for support. He responded by dispatching the 143rd Pennsylvania to bolster the 7th Maryland's picket line.

Skirmishing between the rival forces which would continue till dark soon resumed. Shortly after it ceased, Davies withdrew his men and Elder's battery to the rear. The departure of the cavalry made Col. Webster nervous. The Confederates had been steadily probing the Union front, and they seemed to be slipping toward his left flank

---

28 Ibid., OR 29. pt., 1, 232, 234. Webster served in the US House of Representatives from 1859-65, as a member of the Maryland Legislature from 1855-59 and president of the Maryland Senate in 1858.

29 *OR* 29, pt. 1, 232, 234.

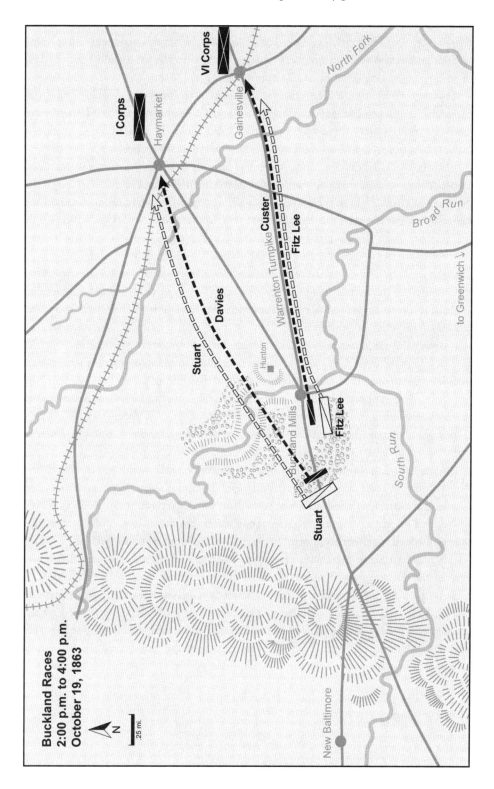

Buckland Races
2:00 p.m. to 4:00 p.m.
October 19, 1863

outpost on the Thoroughfare Gap road. Webster pled for assistance; Gen. Kenly responded by personally leading Lt. Col. John W. Wilson's 1st Maryland Infantry (US) to within supporting distance of its sister regiment.

Webster, Wilson, and Kenly had good reason to feel ill at ease. Unbeknown to all of them, no picket line east of the Thoroughfare Gap road adjoined their own. Through some mistake there was not a single Union soldier on guard for a distance of 500 yards between the Thoroughfare Gap road and a nearby creek.

Stuart's cavalry quickly discovered this critical flaw in the Federal line. The Confederates stealthily slipped past the 7th Maryland's left flank and then through the yawning gap in the Union picket line. This allowed them to swing around behind the Federals and get between the 7th Maryland (US) and 1st Maryland (US), which Kenly had put into line a few hundred yards behind Webster's regiment.[30]

At 8 p.m. the rising moon allowed the Rebels sufficient light to launch an attack. They hit the 7th's front, left and rear simultaneously, the flash of musket fire producing a dramatic pyrotechnic display in the darkness. To avoid being totally surrounded Webster ordered his left flank companies to refuse his line by falling back into some woods on the west side of the road.

Under the circumstances the Union infantry retreated in good order, but the Confederates believed they had the Yankees on the run. Hoping to turn the Federal withdrawal into rout, the gray cavalrymen charged the shifting enemy line. A column of Southern troopers hurled itself down the road, while a line of battle swept across the fields on either side of the roadway. In the face of this onslaught most of Webster's foot soldiers managed to escape by getting into the trees, but the Rebels ran down or captured more than 40 less fortunate Federals.

After pushing Webster back, the Southerners tried again to surround the Marylanders by assaulting their left and rear. To the Yankees' good fortune, the Confederate attackers slid into range of Wilson's 1st Maryland (US) which suddenly discovered its front now deployed perpendicular to the Rebel line. Volleys from this unseen Federal regiment convinced Stuart to break off his nighttime offensive.[31]

A little farther to the east, Fitz Lee's pursuit of Custer had also ended. He had chased the Yankees for 3 miles, all the way from Broad Run to the outskirts of Gainesville. Although his Virginians had severely harassed the enemy rearguard, the Rebels had been unable to do more than hurry the Federals along. Custer's men withdrew in good order until they were securely behind Sedgwick's VI Corps picket line. The Southern cavalrymen briefly skirmished with the Union infantry. But unlike

---

30 Ibid., 232, 234, 452.

31 *OR* 29, pt. 1, 233-34, 452.

Stuart, Fitz Lee had no opportunity to cause more mischief. After only a few minutes of fighting, he pulled his troopers out of range. Once his brigades encountered substantial numbers of Northern infantrymen, Jeb Stuart understood that he had accomplished all that was possible on October 19. His men had been in the saddle since before dawn. Both troopers and horses were exhausted and well-nigh spent. They had won enough laurels for one day. At 10 p.m. the general ordered both his divisions to retire to Buckland Mills where they could encamp behind Broad Run and get some badly needed rest.[32]

*   *   *

Bivouacked on the battlefield, the Rebels felt a surge of exhilaration and pride. Stuart had successfully concentrated his corps and landed an unexpected blow that had routed the enemy. Triumphant at the outcome of Fitz Lee's stratagem, the Southern troopers immediately labeled the affair "the Buckland Races." The disparity of casualties between victor and vanquished only reinforced the Confederate sense of triumph.

Kilpatrick's division had 199 men captured, 51 wounded (two mortally) and 12 killed, making a total loss of 262 men. (The enemy also captured close to 200 horses.) Davies' brigade suffered 98 casualties: 3 killed, 16 wounded, and 79 captured. Custer's brigade lost 9 dead, 28 wounded, and 104 captured for a total of 161. The Rebels captured fully half of Custer's prisoners when they overran Maj. Clark's detached battalion. The Federal batteries listed 2 men wounded and 1 captured.[33]

Major General Newton reported that his I Corps lost 50 men to all causes on October 19. Most of those casualties were in Kenly's division. According to Union regimental records the evening fight cost the 7th Maryland (US) 1 man killed and 8

32 Ibid., 473.

33 As always, precise casualty figures are virtually impossible to obtain. The 2nd NY Cav had 3k, 8w, and 48c; the 5th NY Cav had 4w and 17c. The 7th MI Cav lost 3w, 19 c. The 5th MI Cav lost 1k, 45c. These losses and those in the text are calculated from several sources: Stephen Fonzo, *A Documentary and Landscape Analysis of the Buckland Mills Battlefield (VA042).* (Buckland Preservation Society, 2008), 88-105; Some of the names of men lost by each regiment can be found at www.civilwardata.com; Phisterer, *New York in the War of the Rebellion,* 3rd edition, charts for 2nd and 5th New York Cavalry, available online at NYSMM, "5th Cavalry, Battles and Casualties, Civil War, New York," http://dmna.ny.gov/historic/reghist/civil/ cavalry/ 5thCav/5thCavTable.htm & NYSMM, "2nd Cavalry, Battles and Casualties, Civil War, New York," http://dmna.ny.gov/historic/reghist/civil/cavalry/2ndCav/2ndCav Table. htm, both accessed June 26, 2018.

wounded. Some 42 Federal foot soldiers fell into Stuart's hands. The combined cavalry and infantry loss included 312 men, 249 of whom became prisoners.[34]

Confederate losses were vastly fewer. Stuart suffered 43 total causalities—9 soldiers killed, 30 wounded, and 3 captured. One additional Southerner deserted during the fight. Hampton's division lost 10 men (2 dead, 6 wounded and 2 missing), while Fitz Lee lost 24 (4 killed, 18 wounded, and 2 missing). Yankee fire killed 9 horses.[35]

Comparing casualty lists makes it clear that Custer and Lee engaged in a more protracted gun battle, whereas Davies' and Stuart's contest was one of maneuver. The extent of the resistance Davies was able to offer is evident from the fact that Gordon's entire brigade reported only 3 casualties. The 1st North Carolina at the epicenter of the Rebel assault lost only 1 man killed and 1 wounded. The disparity in casualties between Hampton and Davies' commands—10 to 97 respectively—lend some credence to Confederate claims of a Federal rout.

*   *   *

The battle of Buckland Mills provided a welcome boost for Confederate morale after the debacle at Bristoe Station. In reporting the action Southern cavalry leaders penned a panoply of vivid phrases to describe the scope of their success. Major Henry McClellan boasted that the attack of Hampton's division had reduced Davies' brigade to a "crowd of fugitives among whom all order was cast aside," while it fled for a distance of five miles "in a manner worthy of the occasion." General Gordon wrote that the enemy had retreated "in great confusion" chased by his North Carolinians with "unrelenting fury." Stuart conceded that the Federals had made a "stubborn resistance" early in the fight. After that, however, the enemy had bolted from Chestnut Hill and run all the way to Buckland "at full speed" with his column "completely disorganized and retreating in confusion."[36]

Colonel Owen declared the fight "the most signal cavalry victory of the war." Lieutenant Colonel William Carter pronounced the success "particularly gratifying," because the "braggart Kilpatrick was completely outgeneraled and badly defeated." The men of the 5th North Carolina "joyously found that there is retribution in history,"

---

34 OR 29/1:232; some of the names of men lost by each regiment can be found at www.civilwardata.com, which gathers together information from a wide variety of period resources.

35 Historical records for Confederate cavalry losses are poor for most of the war. Fonzo, *A Buckland Mills Battlefield*, 105-10.

36 McClellan, *I Rode with JEB Stuart*, 394-95; OR 29, pt. 1, 461, 451-52.

and delighted in having evened a (mistaken) score with the 18th Pennsylvania. Stuart basked in the triumph and proclaimed "the rout of the enemy at Buckland the most . . . complete that any cavalry has suffered during the war."[37]

All of the Confederate boasting didn't really disguise the fact that the Rebels had failed to destroy Kilpatrick's command, even if by the most narrow of margins. Custer's fortuitous presence at Buckland Mills and his quick response to Owen's attack had prevented Fitz Lee from cutting off the 3rd Cavalry Division, thereby saving it from destruction. Davies had handled his brigade well until impossible circumstances forced his retreat. Although Stuart's troopers quite enjoyed seeing their foe flee in disarray, their enemy, under horrendous pressure, had managed to elude them.

Stuart had not, as he claimed, knocked the 3rd Division out of the war for a month. He had, however, deeply bruised the sensitive Yankee egos of Kilpatrick, Davies, and Custer. Those egos weren't assuaged when word of the affair quickly appeared in Northern newspapers. One correspondent described the dénouement of Kilpatrick's retreat as the "deplorable spectacle of 7,000 cavalry dashing riderless, hatless, and panic-stricken" through their infantry supports. Stuart got ahold of the quote and gleefully included it in his own account of the battle.[38]

Even before the press reports, Kilpatrick tried to downplay the defeat. On the evening of October 19, he invited all the division's officers to his headquarters, where he essayed what Custer called "a sorry attempt at merry-making over the events of the day." The general had always been a good host. The guests enjoyed their milk punch while a band provided excellent entertainment. Nonetheless, the effort fizzled. No matter how tasty the drinks or pleasant the music, nothing could "take away the bad taste left by the affair." The defeat weighed heavily on everyone, especially Davies' officers.[39]

Of course Kilpatrick blamed others for his fiasco. Union infantry was supposed to have been guarding his division's left flank, he claimed, but the foot soldiers hadn't been where they were supposed to have been, otherwise no disaster would have occurred.

Custer was having none of that. In a letter the next day he blamed Kilpatrick for the overall misadventure and the calamities that had befallen the 2nd Brigade in particular, including the loss of Maj. Clark's 5th Michigan battalion and the capture of

---

37 Starr, *Union Cavalry*, vol. 2, 30, note 82; *OR* 29, pt. 1, 452; Swank, *Sabres, Saddles and Spurs*, 97; Clark, *NC Regts*, vol. 3, 582-83.

38 *OR* 29, pt. 1, 452. Kilpatrick didn't have 7,000 men under his command. According to Humphreys, the 3rd Cavalry Division numbered roughly 3,500 troopers on October 19.

39 Kidd, *Recollections of a Cavalryman*, 226.

his own headquarters wagon. That important vehicle had contained his desk, various official reports and letters from his wife, some of which Richmond newspapers published. Moreover, Custer claimed to have warned Kilpatrick of Rebel troops threatening the division's flank, only to be disregarded.

No evidence indicates that Custer advised anyone of Fitz Lee's cavalry approaching Buckland Mills on October 19. Major Kidd's detailed account of the action relates nothing of his chief saying anything about Confederates lurking south of the Warrenton Turnpike. While Custer's accusation that Kilpatrick ignored his advice does not stand up, his other complaints weren't totally baseless. Certainly he was justified in pronouncing October 19 the "most disastrous day" the 3rd Cavalry Division had ever passed through.[40]

If Buckland Mills smudged Kilpatrick's reputation, Stuart's gained new luster. The Southern press gloried in reporting another triumph by Rebel horsemen, and noted that the cavalry had done all the "successful fighting" during the offensive. This latest success, along with Stuart's undeniable accomplishments earlier in the campaign, finally silenced the critics of his Gettysburg performance. Robert E. Lee warmly congratulated his cavalry chief for his most recent achievement.[41]

Actually, Jeb Stuart had done far more than anyone supposed on October 19. His victory—and the excuses Kilpatrick and his generals offered for their defeat—had a profound impact on George Meade. Consequently the Army of the Potomac would spend the next 24 hours concentrating in the wrong place to fight a battle against a non-existent foe.

---

40 Previous paragraphs based upon Merrington, *The Custer Story*, 68-69.

41 Starr, *Union Cavalry*, vol. 2, 30, note 82; OR 29, pt., 1, 452; Swank, *Sabres, Saddles and Spurs*, 97.

CHAPTER 32

"He Got the Advantage of Me"

Meade Visits Washington—Fighting for Iron—Proposal and Admission—
Casualties—The Generals Lament—Washington Dissatisfied—Meade's Future

THE defeat at Buckland Mills was the most humiliating setback suffered by Army of the Potomac's cavalry corps to date. The Confederates had lured the 3rd Cavalry Division into a clever trap and had come close to gobbling it up. This was the second time in eight days Kilpatrick's troops had been surrounded or cut off. The other occasion had been at Brandy Station on October 11. Then both Pleasonton and Buford had been on the field to share responsibility, and Custer's brigade had opened a way out of an encirclement not of the 3rd Division's own making. The fight at Buckland, however, belonged exclusively to Judson Kilpatrick, and he alone bore the burden of having placed his command in such dire straits.

Kilpatrick's nature did not allow accepting blame for any mishap. Neither he nor his brigadiers were disposed to concede the Rebels had outgeneraled or outfought them. Instead, they happily offered excuses for their debacle. Their principal defense argued that they had been attacked by what Custer called "a very superior force of infantry" deployed in a battle line "more than a mile in extent."[1]

Which wasn't true. No Rebel foot soldiers were at Buckland Mills. The Confederate infantry formation closest to the battlefield on October 19 was at Rappahannock Station, 22 miles away. Five brigades of Stuart's cavalry supported by a few guns, nothing more, had assailed the Federal horsemen. The most charitable explanation for Custer's claim is that he mistook the assault of Fitz Lee's dismounted troopers for a heavy attack by Southern infantrymen. That assertion spoke poorly of

---

1 OR 29, pt. 1, 387, 382, 391.

Custer. An officer with his experience should have been able to differentiate dismounted sharpshooters from a major infantry force.

Kilpatrick and his subordinates either truly misjudged the nature of the Rebel attack or they concocted a self-serving rationalization for their reverse. Since everyone understood that mounted troops could not stand up to infantry on a Civil War battlefield, the presence of enemy infantry was the best excuse for a cavalry defeat. Kilpatrick not only offered that explanation but beefed it up by claiming that the entire ANV was at Warrenton and had come to the aid of Stuart's hard pressed horsemen at Buckland Mills.[2]

Although pure fiction, Kilpatrick's report touched a sensitive nerve at army headquarters. Meade had been uncertain of enemy intentions for much of the campaign. From October 13-18, Union officers west of the Blue Ridge Mountains had buffeted the general with reports that all or part of Lee's army was in the Shenandoah Valley. As late as the night of October 17, Meade had considered it highly probable the Confederates were on their way into the Loudoun or Shenandoah Valley.

The next day, however, the general developed doubts about his opponent's destination. A recent deserter from Rodes' division swore the Rebel army was heading back to the Rappahannock. After thinking things over, Meade changed his mind. At 1 p.m. the general wrote Halleck that the Rebels were probably retreating toward the Rappahannock rather than marching for the Shenandoah. Almost 24 hours later, Maj. Gen. Warren reported further justification: a deserter from Stuart's horse artillery claimed the Confederates were withdrawing to the Rapidan.[3]

Less than eight hours after receiving Warren's message, Meade changed his mind again in the face of Kilpatrick's claim that Lee's army was at Warrenton. At 9:30 p.m. in an urgent telegram to Halleck, Meade explained that Kilpatrick had pushed as far south as New Baltimore before an enemy infantry attack had compelled him to retreat to Haymarket. Rebel foot soldiers had pursued the Union cavalrymen and were still in contact with I Corps pickets. Meade said that from "all the information" he could obtain, Lee had concentrated his entire command at Warrenton over "the last two days."

As usual the Pennsylvanian could not divine Lee's purposes. The Rebel army may have already slipped away leaving nothing but a rearguard behind, or it might be waiting at Warrenton prepared to give battle. Although Meade admitted that he couldn't discover the true state of affairs until the next day, he clearly expected a fight. Even

---

2   OR 29, pt. 2, 355. Humphreys wrote Warren that "information sent by General Kilpatrick indicates that Hill's and Ewell's corps were both at Warrenton." The text of Kilpatrick's message has never been found.

3   Ibid., 354; Lyman, *Meade's Army*, 54.

before sending his telegram to Washington, the general had his staff issue orders for the army to concentrate at Gainesville before dawn. Humphreys informed the corps commanders that "information sent by General Kilpatrick indicates that Hill's and Ewell's crops were both at Warrenton during the day" of October 19. This in turn indicated the "probability" of the Union army "meeting the enemy tomorrow morning" and the likelihood of a major engagement.[4]

Sedgwick's VI Corps was already at Gainesville with Newton's I Corps nearby at Haymarket. In anticipation of a battle, Sykes received orders to move from Groveton to Gainesville at 3 a.m. and mass his V Corps behind Sedgwick. Meade ordered Warren and French to bring their troops from Bristoe Station to Gainesville first thing in the morning. Newton's I Corps got instructions to march from Haymarket through Thoroughfare Gap and take up a defensive position at Georgetown in the Loudoun Valley.[5]

The Army of the Potomac was up well before dawn on October 20. At 6 a.m. the VI corps, followed by Sykes' V Corps, began advancing toward Buckland Mills and the enemy. Anticipation ran high at Meade headquarters, and Col. Lyman confessed that everyone expected "a great battle near Warrenton" today. Sedgwick's troops reached Broad Run without encountering Rebels and easily crossed the creek. Traversing the ground over which Kilpatrick and Stuart had fought the day before, the infantrymen discovered numerous bodies of Union cavalrymen who had been killed on October 19. One Federal solider remembered that "nearly all of the corpses" had been "stripped of their clothing" by the needy Confederates.[6]

Although these grim sights suggested more death and destruction ahead, the Yankees found no Southerners to fight. When an advance squadron of blue cavalry rode unopposed into Warrenton at noon, there was not an enemy in sight. For the third time since assuming command of the Army of the Potomac, George Meade had launched a morning advance expecting a major engagement, only to find that Lee's army had eluded him.

For Meade and his staff the resulting unpleasantly familiar sense of disappointment dredged up unhappy memories of similar misadventures at Falling Waters and Manassas Gap last July. At least this time Meade hadn't promised Halleck a decisive battle would take place, as he had on both those previous occasions. That fact did little to brighten anyone's spirits.

---

4 OR 29, pt. 2, 354, 355.

5 Ibid., 355-57; Lyman, *Meade's Army*, 56.

6 George Stevens, *Three Years in the Sixth Corps* (New York, 1870), 282.

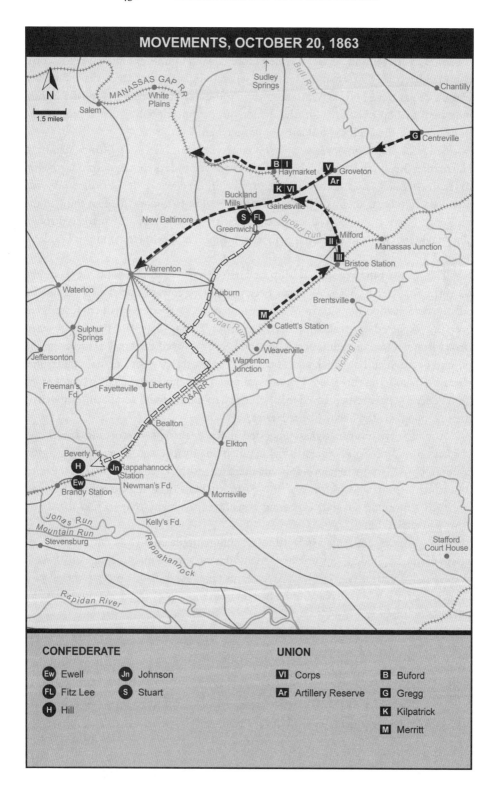

MOVEMENTS, OCTOBER 20, 1863

CONFEDERATE

Ew Ewell
FL Fitz Lee
H Hill
Jn Johnson
S Stuart

UNION

VI Corps
Ar Artillery Reserve
B Buford
G Gregg
K Kilpatrick
M Merritt

*   *   *

Despite its anti-climactic nature, occupying Warrenton finally gave Meade the clarity he had sought for five days. On the night of October 20, he wired Halleck that the Rebels had "all retired beyond the Rappahannock" and "completely destroyed" the O&A south of Bristoe Station and supposedly all the way to Culpeper County. The strategy behind Lee's offensive had become clear, Meade thought. He told Halleck that the destruction of the railroad "is significant of a purpose to detach troops to the southwest, based on the presumed delay in my advance."

If that was indeed what Lee had been after, he had certainly achieved his goal. When Federal engineers surveyed what was left of the O&A, they realized it would take at least a month to reconstruct the line from Bristoe Station to the Rappahannock. Meade knew exactly what that meant, frankly telling Halleck that "the time it will take to repair the road and the difficulty of advance without the railroad, will preclude my preventing the sending of troops to the southwest by the enemy."[7]

Believing "the campaign . . . virtually over for the present season," he advised withdrawing his forces to "some position in front of Washington" for the winter. This would allow Halleck to detach "such portions" of the Federal army "as may be required to operate elsewhere," which of course meant Tennessee. Although an idea both Lincoln and Halleck had contemplated in September, the suggestion came as something of a shock to the administration. Halleck promptly ordered Meade to Washington for consultation.[8]

On the morning of October 22, Meade accompanied by his son and aide, Capt. George Meade, Jr., Maj. Gen. Humphreys and Col. Lyman, left their Gainesville headquarters for the capital. Arriving there at 2 p.m. the party changed into their best uniforms and then traveled in what Lyman called "great state" to Halleck's office where the two senior generals met privately. Neither man left a record of what passed between them. Meade later wrote his wife that Halleck was "very urgent that something should be done" but had no useful ideas as to what that something should be.[9]

Following the meeting, everyone walked to the White House, where Meade and Halleck consulted for two hours with Lincoln. No minutes were made of this conversation either. Meade found the president "as he always is, very considerate and kind." According to Theodore Lyman, the commander-in-chief made quite clear his

---

7   OR 29, pt. 2, 358-59.

8   OR 29, pt. 2, 361-65.

9   Lyman, *Meade's Headquarters*, 37; George G. Meade to wife, October 30, 1863, *Life and Letters*, vol. 2, 154.

disappointment that no major battle had taken place during the last campaign. But he also concurred with Meade that the time required to repair the O&A meant "nothing more can be done this season."[10]

Neither president nor general-in-chief had any course of action to urge upon Meade. No one discussed any plans to detach more troops from the AOP. Apparently Lincoln didn't press Meade to explain his recent retreat or failure to fight. Perhaps, in light of his suggestion that the army retire to the Washington environs for the winter, Halleck and Lincoln just felt the need to look George Meade in the eye and make sure the man hadn't lost his nerve.

Whatever the motive behind it, the general left the meeting feeling slightly ill at ease. Later, Meade and his companions went to Willard's Hotel, one of the most famous—some might say infamous—Washington, DC establishments to eat dinner at the hotel's excellent restaurant. This plan worked well for Humphreys, Lyman, and Meade's son, who thoroughly enjoyed all manner of delicacies undisturbed. General Meade wasn't so fortunate. He was barely able to "snatch a mouthful of chicken," Lyman recorded, due to the constant questioning of politicians eager to hear the commander's views on the war's progress.

The evening worsened considerably when Meade and his aides discovered shocking reports in the Washington papers that the general had received "imperative orders" to give Lee battle during the campaign. By clear implication, Meade had failed to carry out direct commands from the president or the war department. This wasn't true, of course, but many believed what they read. These false accusations incensed Lyman; Meade said nothing.[11]

Although he feigned indifference to news reports and Washington's political opinions, Meade was infuriated. When Margaret wrote a letter containing verbiage from recent news stories, the general bristled. "You seem to be very much puzzled about my retreat, as you misname it," he groused. "It was not a retreat, but a withdrawal

---

10 Ibid; Lyman, *Meade's Army*, 57-58.

11 Lyman, *Meade's Headquarters*, 38; Lyman, *Meade's Army*, 58; Brig. Gen. John Gibbon, convalescing in Washington from a Gettysburg wound, was surprised to hear criticism of Meade and rose to the general's defense. Meade was being attacked, he thought, because he "was not quite so outspoken in what certain parties chose to denominate as loyalty, or did not indorse as fully as they did, what they considered the 'true policy' of the war." In other words, the assaults on Meade were political, not based upon his military record. Gibbon's defense didn't succeed. Meade's generalship reminded many of McClellan, which opened him to charges of incompetence or "disloyalty." Gibbon argued fruitlessly with people he considered friendly toward Meade, that all competent commanders followed the same military principles "irrespective of their . . . political opinions." His audience could not be convinced. The press had already classed Meade as a "McClellan-style" general. John Gibbon, *Recollections of the Civil War* (New York, 1928), 206-20.

of the army—maneuvering to get into a proper position to offer battle, and made to prevent Lee from compelling me to fight at a disadvantage."[12]

The administration's criticism stung even more keenly. On October 26 Meade told Lyman he wished Lincoln and Halleck would go ahead and replace him. He was more than willing to be fired, and reiterated, "I am sure I keep telling them if they don't feel satisfied . . . to relieve me."[13]

George Meade could correct his wife and complain to his aide. But trying to make Halleck, Lincoln and Stanton understand his point of view was almost as impossible as trying to set the capital press straight. Regardless of Meade's own certainty that he had acted wisely during the recent campaign, the general could not fend off the cumulative effect of negative press and the administration's displeasure.

*   *   *

The Army of the Potomac crept southward throughout the rest of October, its pace of advance dictated by the railroad repair crews. One last spasm of combat occurred on October 24 when Maj. Gen. "Alleghany" Johnson's division advanced northward from the Rappahannock. The purpose of the Rebel move was to allow Southern logisticians to lift and carry off five miles of railroad track that had not been ruined during Lee's retreat. A brisk day-long skirmish ignited when the Confederates ran into Devin's brigade and a battery of artillery from Buford's cavalry division. The Yankees temporarily feared Johnson's thrust was the opening gambit of an offensive. Meade sent Union infantry forward to support Devin, but nightfall closed the fighting. Confederate engineers succeeded in removing the rails and hauling them back over the river during the action. Johnson's troops withdrew after dark, and the Federals choose not to pursue the next day.[14]

With the conclusion of that engagement, the fighting and maneuvering that had characterized so much of October ended. From October 9-24 Meade reported a loss of 2,292 officers and men, including 1,385 troops listed as captured or missing, 136 killed, and 733 wounded. Among the infantry, Warren's II Corps had suffered the most with 548 killed, wounded or missing. Pleasonton's cavalry divisions sustained 1,251 casualties: 71 men killed, 312 wounded, and 886 captured or missing. A large number

---

12 George G. Meade to wife, October 30, 1863, *Life and Letters*, vol. 2, 154-55.

13 Lyman, *Meade's Headquarters*, 38.

14 *OR* 29, pt. 2, 378-80; Turner, *Letters from the Stonewall Brigade*, 110-111; Howard, *Recollections*, 234.

of horses were lost as well and many more broken down by the rigors of the campaign. In Buford's division alone, 107 animals had perished during the operation.

Confederate losses totaled 1,826, including 205 killed, 1,176 wounded and 445 missing. A. P. Hill's corps—907 dead or wounded with 445 missing—incurred most of these casualties during the battle of Bristoe Station, with the heaviest loss in Cooke's and Kirkland's brigades. Stuart's cavalry corps suffered far less than its Yankee opponent and listed only 54 men killed, 335 wounded, and a handful of troopers unaccounted for. Only Hill reported his number of missing, but as the Rebels were on the offensive, their loss in this category outside of Heth's division wasn't significant.[15]

In 1861 or early 1862, such casualty lists would have horrified the public and enthralled the press, but no longer. "The battles are nothing now unless the killed are counted by thousands," Union headquarters clerk Thomas Carpenter noted matter-of-factly. By the fall of 1863 both the army and the home front viewed the capture, death, or maiming of more than 4,100 men as almost inconsequential. What counted was ground taken or abandoned, cities saved or captured, battles won or lost, reputations made or wrecked. Casualties mattered only if the numbers were so huge as to appreciably weaken the foe.[16]

*   *   *

The outcome of the campaign pleased neither army commander. For his part, Meade confessed privately that Lee had outgeneraled him. His opponent had played a "deep game" and "I am free to admit that in the playing of it he got the advantage of me," he confided to Margaret.[17]

In a letter to Maj. Gen. Winfield Scott Hancock, Meade revealed the depth of his dissatisfaction with the recent course of events. Having been fellow division and corps commanders, the two men were close friends. The highly respected Hancock had led the II Corps at Gettysburg and was still recovering from a serious July 3 wound. Meade began by acknowledging Hancock's eagerness to return to his command. Although a pleasant prospect, he urged his comrade to be patient and allow his injuries to thoroughly heal before resuming the rigors of army life.

Meade then turned to the real purpose of his missive, which was to vent his feelings and explain the Bristoe campaign to an understanding ear. "God knows!" Meade wrote. "No one was more disappointed" than himself that no battle had been

15 *OR* 29, pt. 1, 226, 412-14.

16 Thomas Carpenter to Phil, October 26, 1863, MHS.

17 George G. Meade to wife, October 30, 1863, *Life and Letters*, vol. 2, 154.

Union work crews repairing the O&A, October, 1863. *Library of Congress*

fought. Compelled to guard his trains, he had refused to fight "without some opening to the rear in case of disaster." Which wasn't available until the army was behind Bull Run, but Lee had refused to engage him there.

At the time, the general felt that he had pursued the correct strategy. In hindsight, however, Meade admitted his mistake. "*After it was all over*, information was obtained, which, if I had possessed at the time, would have induced me to operate differently. Lee was *slow* and *ought* to have been farther ahead as I supposed he was, at the time." In light of such after-the-fact intelligence, it was little wonder the administration appeared to feel Meade had been too cautious.

"They are very polite and civil to me in Washington," Meade conceded, nevertheless he was prepared to be relieved and accordingly kept his "saber packed." Repeating his mantra that he had never wanted command of the army, Meade told Hancock it was merely a matter of time before Lincoln replaced him. Until then he would do his best, even if he knew that would never be good enough for the administration.[18]

Meade's performance unquestionably disappointed the authorities in Washington. But some Northern newspapers and more importantly, many Union soldiers, didn't

18 George G. Meade to Winfield Scott Hancock, November 6, 1863, Winfield Scott Hancock papers, Duke University, Durham, NC. Meade did not specify the nature of the information "obtained." Italics in the original.

feel the same. They believed Meade had prevented Lee from luring the Army of the Potomac into yet another battlefield disaster. None of the army's previous commanders had accomplished this feat. Meade might not have produced a victory, but he had avoided a defeat, and his troops appreciated that fact. As a result, one soldier said, "Meade's stock was rising in the estimation" of the army.[19]

Massachusetts infantryman George Patch bragged about the skill the army's commander had exhibited, claiming, "One thing certain is that a better retreat never was made, it fairly equaled the 7 days retreat." Artilleryman Thomas Cheney echoed the sentiment, claiming the entire army was in good spirits with "full confidence" in its commanding general. It was no secret why. Sergeant Charles Bowen of the 12th US Infantry explained it well: "Meade has taken us through with very little loss & also has given the rascals some hard knocks on the retreat."[20]

The respect and trust of his officers and men was important to George Meade, and he would have been gratified to learn of these sentiments. However, the feelings of common soldiers couldn't counterbalance the opinions of Lincoln, Stanton, Halleck, and Welles. How they reacted in the campaign's aftermath would determine the future course of the army and answer the question of whether Meade retained his command.

*   *   *

South of the Rappahannock, Robert E. Lee wasn't happy either. Meade's rapid retreat had foiled the Confederate plan to strike a hard blow. Lee was equally disgruntled about having to surrender the initiative to the Federals. He had wanted to hover near the Potomac for the winter and keep Meade pinned close to Washington. But a shortage of shoes, clothing, blankets, and an absolute dearth of supplies in Northern Virginia had rendered the army unfit for a winter campaign and forced it to retire to the Rappahannock.[21]

Like Meade, Lee expressed his discontent to an absent but trusted confidante. In an October 28 letter to James Longstreet he reviewed the campaign briefly and acknowledged his disappointment with its results. His offensive had "inflicted some punishment upon the enemy," he acknowledged, but the army had missed tantalizing opportunities to do more. Lee hinted that Ewell and Hill had been unequal to their

---

19 Hennessy, *18th Massachusetts*, 209.

20 George Patch to parents, October 15, 1863, George Patch papers, VHS; Thomas Cheney to Father, October 25, 1863, Thomas Carleton Cheney papers, University of New Hampshire, Durham, NH; Cassedy, *Dear Friends at Home*, 341.

21 OR 29, pt. 2, 794.

assigned tasks, and he feared the army "failed to manage as well as we might." In a poignant passage, the general sighed for what might have been and confided to Longstreet, "I missed you dreadfully, and your brave corps. Your cheerful face and strong arms would have been invaluable." Lee closed his correspondence by telling Longstreet, "I hope you will soon return to me."[22]

Like their commander, the rank and file had mixed feelings about the campaign. Some men grumbled that the army had accomplished so little. Others thought that the offensive "had a great moral effect" due to Meade's refusal to stand and fight. The performance of the cavalry occasioned universal praise. It had proven itself superior to the enemy's mounted arm once again.[23]

The overall impression, however, was a feeling of frustration. The army had failed to even the score for Gettysburg or capture large quantities of badly needed blankets, shoes, and other supplies. Sergeant John Garibaldi might have reflected the prevailing opinion best: "We were all disappointed because we expected the yanks would make a stand somewhere. If the thing had went on right, we could have got a big fight out of them, whipped them bad and got nearly all their wagons and commissaries and a large quantity of prisoners."[24]

* * *

On October 28 George Gordon Meade marked his four-month anniversary as commander of the Army of the Potomac. It is unlikely he noted the occasion. On that day he received a dispatch from Halleck, passing along an urgent message from Lincoln. Union spies had reported that Ewell's corps was moving toward Lynchburg with the evident intention of driving Burnside's troops out of Knoxville. Given Meade's own analysis that Lee had launched his offensive and destroyed the O&A to enable just this sort of maneuver, Lincoln believed what the spies said. The president wanted the Union army to force Lee to recall Ewell. If Meade didn't have any pending plan to launch an offensive, Lincoln suggested "that with all possible expedition, the Army of the Potomac get ready to attack Lee, and that in the meantime a raid shall, at all hazards, break the railroad at or near Lynchburg."[25]

22 Longstreet, *From Manassas to Appomattox*, note, 469-470.

23 Stanley Russell to sister, October 22, 1863, Stanley Russell letters, WFCHS; Lewis Nunnelee diary October 22, 1863, ACWM; Corson, *My Dear Jennie*, 113; Swank, *Sabres, Saddles and Spurs*, 95; Corson, *My Dear Jennie*, 112.

24 John Garibaldi to wife, October 21, 1863, John Garibaldi Letters, VMI.

25 *OR* 29, pt. 2, 375-76; Lyman, *Meade's Army*, 60.

Meade responded quickly, telling Halleck that no evidence verified anything Lincoln said. The army's own sources showed Hill and Ewell near Culpeper Court House. Rebel strength remained as before, and the enemy had fortified a north bank bridgehead near Rappahannock Station. Lee clearly intended to defend his current line and might even be contemplating another offensive. Nonetheless, Meade promised to do as the president wished and would proceed along that course until told otherwise.[26]

Halleck promised to relay Meade's views to Lincoln the next day, and apparently the information Meade provided satisfied the president. The raid never happened. Meanwhile the army continued a methodical, snail's pace advance toward the Rappahannock. The repair crews, however, were making more rapid progress than predicted. By October 30 the O&A was operational all the way to Warrenton Junction.[27]

From the viewpoint of the Lincoln administration the recent campaign had placed few laurels on George Meade's brow. His retreat without turning to fight had been distressing and the apparent lethargy of his pursuit equally unpalatable. Gideon Welles saw no merit in Meade's conduct and his tepid impression of the general had not been strengthened by his recent visit. "Meade's falling back was a weakness," the secretary declared. Future events would soon reveal whether the conduct of the war in Virginia resulted from Lee's strategy or Meade's.[28]

Many soldiers believed—and hoped—that the campaign season had ended. On both sides of the Rappahannock troops began building cabins in anticipation of imminent winter quarters. Assuming a defensive stance, the Confederates were obviously ready to respond to any provocation. But the issue of future combat depended wholly on Meade. If he decided that the post-Gettysburg campaign had run its course, then the next five months would be an interlude of relative ease and safety. If he determined to continue his strategic chess match with Lee, thousands of men now alive might not live to see Christmas.

Few observers would have guessed, Meade wasn't content to let 1863 wind down without another effort to best the Rebels. He had a movement in mind and was resolved to force Lee to retreat or do battle before winter shut down further operations.

26 OR 29, pt. 2, 376-77.

27 Lyman, *Meade's Army*, 60.

28 Morse, *Diary of Gideon Welles*, vol. 1, 472-73.

An Assessment of Command

Strategic Environment—Generals and Presidents—Dysfunctional Relationship
Lee's Daring—Meade's Prudence—Repercussions

AFTER Lee's army escaped across the Potomac into Virginia on July 13, 1863, Abraham Lincoln predicted that the war would go on indefinitely. The course of events between then and the end of October indicated he had been right. Gettysburg seemed to have changed nothing. Despite the 51,000-plus names on its awful casualty list, the battle did no more than previous blood-soaked contests to alter the military course of the war in the east. Other than forestalling some hypothetical chain of events, every preceding fight had merely reinstated strategic stalemate in the Virginia Theater. The Gettysburg campaign was no different. Indeed, its concluding weeks had reconstituted the stalemate in the exact physical location where it existed before the Pennsylvania invasion.

Neither Robert E. Lee nor George Meade nor, especially, the Lincoln administration liked this fact. Consequently, the commander of the Army of the Potomac remained under constant pressure to expand on his Gettysburg success. Often unspoken and accompanied by vague or unhelpful advice, the pressure never relented. Meade felt it acutely and it left him in a state of frustrated anxiety. He wanted to prove his critics wrong but wouldn't risk his army or his country's cause by rashly courting defeat or taking unnecessary chances.

Lee suffered under a slightly different burden. Sharp criticism of his handling of the Pennsylvania invasion faded quickly. The Virginian's stature as the South's best general easily restored confidence in his leadership. Nonetheless, Lee felt keen disappointment over the Gettysburg affair. Which in turn intensified his combative nature and made him especially eager to launch an offensive that would redeem the late defeat and inflict a crippling blow on his enemy.

The months of August and September offered neither Meade nor Lee opportunity to easily satisfy their impulses. The same problems afflicted both men upon their return to the Rappahannock. Each commanded an army mangled by the Pennsylvania campaign. Heavy casualties and the loss of key leaders negatively impacted morale, discipline, and efficiency. Horses were in short supply, and those with the armies were in bad shape. Desertion became an acute concern, even as serious manpower shortages appeared on the horizon. In the wake of Gettysburg both commanders had felt compelled to offer up their resignations as atonement for failures real or perceived.

If the symmetry of difficulties between the North and South was striking, so too was the similarity of responses by the generals and their governments. President Lincoln rejected Meade's demand for reassignment. President Davis refused to consider replacing Lee. Both sides effectively employed the firing squad to beat down a rising tide of desertions. A mixture of returning convalescents, draftees, and new recruits replenished the ranks so quickly that by the end of August each army was at pre-Gettysburg strength, or nearly so. A raft of appointments and promotions filled vacant leadership positions. Commanders tightened discipline while quartermasters resupplied worn out troops. The resilient young men in the ranks rebounded swiftly from the hardships and privations of early summer, and the two armies performed like the veteran organizations they were. Each absorbed the losses and effects of Gettysburg and fought on, just as they had fought on after Chancellorsville, Fredericksburg, and Sharpsburg.

Beyond successful restoration of their respective armies to fighting trim, Meade and Lee faced the larger challenges of strategy and command. From August through the beginning of October, the two men confronted one other across the familiar landscape embraced by the Rappahannock and Rapidan rivers. Like skilled chess masters they engaged in a cagey game of maneuver, but a variety of strategic, political, and logistical difficulties always prevented either from making his best move. Supply difficulties and the transfer of Longstreet's corps delayed Lee's desire to launch an offensive. Orders to stand on the defensive and dispatch troops to enforce the draft temporarily robbed Meade of mobility. Once Lee fell back behind the Rapidan, Lincoln refused Meade permission to shift his line of operations to Fredericksburg. Then the detachment of the XI and XII corps undercut his planning for a potential campaign.

Hamstrung by these circumstances, the generals dueled at arm's length throughout August and September. The rival cavalry forces fought three major engagements in seven weeks' time—Brandy Station on August 1, Culpeper Court House on September 13-14, and Jack's Shop on September 22-23—an unprecedented string of mounted combat in the absence of a major campaign.

These engagements damaged both cavalry forces, but each performed well under difficult conditions and battled with skill and tenacity. The commanders on both sides exhibited solid leadership and turned in competent performances on almost every occasion. Major Generals Alfred Pleasonton and Jeb Stuart accomplished the missions they were assigned with victory typically going to whoever brought the most force to bear at any given moment.

*   *   *

The ferocity of the cavalry fighting in August and September illuminated the foreground of momentous strategic and operational decision making by the rival high commands. The Jefferson Davis administration responded to the triple shock of Gettysburg, Vicksburg, and Port Hudson in much the same way as the Army of Northern Virginia responded to the shock of its Pennsylvania defeat. Despite dismay and criticism, the Rebel government did not panic or subscribe to impulsive measures.

In the aftermath of the Confederacy's July disasters, Davis maintained his trust in Lee and sustained the general in the face of censure. The Confederate war department did everything possible to strengthen Lee's command. The swift return of the ANV to offensive capability was as much a credit to the efforts of the Confederate government as it was to the officers and men of the army itself.

Lee and Davis worked together in a spirit of cooperation, trust, and mutual respect while facing the South's post-summer circumstances. The failure of the Gettysburg campaign to save Vicksburg stirred no doubts or second thoughts about the efficacy of their decision to invade Pennsylvania. In pondering how to deal with the threat to Chattanooga, Davis agreed with Lee's proposal to undertake an offensive against Meade. Both men continued to believe in the utility of seeking an eastern victory that might cripple the enemy's ability or willingness to carry on the war.

The loss of Knoxville caught Davis off guard. In the face of that crisis the Confederate president acted decisively by ordering Lee to send Longstreet's corps to Tennessee. Although this disrupted Lee's plan for an offensive, the general responded promptly and within days the movement commenced. It is hard to envision a swifter response by the Southern high command.

Despite its horrific blood-letting on his army, Lee was unbowed by Gettysburg. Once more in central Virginia, he astutely positioned his troops behind the Rapidan and the Rappahannock rivers. This gave him a tactical edge that helped offset the enemy's superior numbers. But the famous Virginian did not intend to sit passively behind his aquatic barrier awaiting Meade's attack.

The results of the Pennsylvania invasion had provoked no strategic or tactical epiphany in Lee. Nor did the departure of Longstreet change the Southern commander's intentions. As soon as Lee discovered that Meade had transferred two corps westward, he jumped at the chance to take the offensive. The geographic challenges he faced in the Culpeper arena left Lee undaunted. Nor did a dread of the heavy casualties sure to result from assuming the tactical offensive deter him. Lee's determination and the readiness to go over to the attack while indifferently supplied and badly outnumbered stood in stark contrast to Meade's strategic calculus.

Lee's October campaign was utterly characteristic of his previous offensive efforts. It sought to counterbalance numbers with audacity and aggressive execution. Lee's stratagem and the outstanding performance of Stuart's cavalry befuddled Meade about the real Confederate purposes for two days at the start of the campaign. The Rebel general's willingness to attack into the Culpeper V forced Meade to retire north of the Rappahannock.

On October 11 Stuart's aggressive cavalry again blinded Meade as to Lee's whereabouts. That led the Federal general to commit a potentially fatal mistake by sending half his army back into Culpeper County on October 12. His error was compounded when the Confederates made a rapid move to cross the upper Rappahannock that same day. Some bad luck and a swift, hard hitting attack by Stuart's troopers and Rodes' infantry, allowed the Rebels to bloody a Union cavalry brigade and leap the river without Meade discovering that fact for almost 12 hours.

For the first four days of the campaign, Lee's plan worked brilliantly. The speed, boldness, and competence of the Southern army mirrored its most impressive former successes. The first glitches in the Confederate program appeared on October 13, when Lee's army halted at Warrenton for almost an entire day. That pause allowed Meade to recover from his misguided offensive thrust toward Culpeper Court House by getting his entire army north of the Rappahannock.

The obvious question is whether Lee's Warrenton delay was necessary. Ewell's corps reached the village around 10 a.m. Hill's corps didn't arrive until midafternoon. Theoretically Ewell could have kept going. If he had marched north to Greenwich, he would have gained a substantial head start on the road to Bristoe

Station the next day. Or if Ewell had gone east toward Catlett's Station, he might have disrupted the Federal retreat at either Auburn or along the O&A.

Since Lee didn't know the location of Meade's army, either move would have placed Ewell's corps in potential danger of attack by a larger Union force before Hill could arrive on the scene. By the time Stuart revealed the Federal army's positions, not enough daylight remained to accomplish anything. The Union III Corps was already in Auburn, and Stuart had found himself trapped between two wings of Meade's army. Therefore, Lee's decision to concentrate his army and make no move until his cavalry could provide essential intelligence was reasonable, and as it turned out, prescient.

The events of October 14 indicate that Lee's Warrenton pause was not fatal to the object of his campaign. The morning fight at Auburn delayed the Union II Corps' northward march as much as it did Ewell's corps. Both halves of the Rebel army wasted no time and moved rapidly toward Bristoe Station. The Confederates reached Broad Run in time to cut off and potentially destroy Warren's command. If A. P. Hill's corps had arrived 30 minutes sooner, or 30 minutes later, the outcome of the fight might have been different. As it was, Hill's Corps appeared at Bristoe Station at almost the worst possible moment. Hill could see the V Corps retreating but not the II Corps approaching; it had not quite reached the field. Hill focused on the obvious prey to the virtual exclusion of anything else. His tunnel vision enabled the II Corps to occupy the railroad embankment a mere 10 minutes ahead of the Confederates. Fixated on his target, Hill discounted the growing signs of danger to his flank. He was bloodily repulsed as a result.

After the fight at Bristoe Station, the campaign reverted to its previous tenor, with Meade uncertain about Lee's location and strategy. Stuart's cavalry deftly blinded the Union general to Confederate purposes and administered a painful humiliation to Judson Kilpatrick's division in the process. The Rebel destruction of the O&A surprised the Yankees and led them to conclude that Lee had designed his offensive to enable the transfer of more troops from Virginia to Tennessee. This was incorrect, of course, but Meade's erroneous interpretation demonstrates that even in retreat Lee managed to get the better of his Yankee counterpart, at least for a time.

*   *   *

Robert E. Lee and Jefferson Davis shared a strategic vision and absolute trust in one another. No one could say the same about the relationship among George Meade, Henry Halleck, and Abraham Lincoln. Their dysfunctional dynamic put a great drag on Meade's performance, while exacerbating some of his own shortcomings.

Lincoln and Halleck forgave Meade's perceived failure to destroy the Rebel army north of the Potomac, but they could never forget it. In their eyes, that disappointment overshadowed everything the general proposed and did in the future. The trials and tribulations between the administration and Meade's forerunners in army command simply added a jaundiced tint to the interactions between the general and Washington. Meade found himself in the role of a young bride who must cope with all the emotional baggage carried by her thrice-divorced groom. No word or act could fail to touch on some sensitive or painful memory and possibly provoke an unexpected or perplexing response.

The core issue was that the president and the general-in-chief wanted Meade to fight Lee, but they shrank from ordering him to do so or giving him a free hand to operate strategically as he wished. This put Meade in an unpleasant predicament. He knew what Lincoln and Halleck desired and expected. He also knew that if he waged a campaign and failed, he would be the scapegoat. Despite all its civility, assurances of support and promises of good will, the administration was ruthless with generals who lost battles. The fact that George Meade was the fourth man to command the Army of the Potomac in 12 months spoke for itself.

This reality placed enormous pressure on Meade. And his stress was all the more burdensome because the Pennsylvanian had a firm grasp of strategic and tactical realities. He knew the AOP had a numerical superiority over Lee, but he was also highly conscious that (until Longstreet's detachment) this advantage was smaller than it had ever been. Convinced he would be the aggressor in the next battle against entrenched Confederates, Meade knew that defeating an enemy so disposed would produce heavy casualties which the North might not be able to replace.

Those truths transformed the Union army's O&A supply line into a significant encumbrance. Meade had to deploy 5,000 men to prevent enemy raiders from disrupting the flow of supplies to his army. That significantly weakened his already marginal manpower advantage over Lee. The detachment of troops to enforce the draft in New York City further decreased Federal numerical superiority in August. It also led Halleck to order Meade to stand on the defensive for six long weeks. Although that period allowed the Army of the Potomac to recover from Gettysburg, it granted the Rebels the same opportunity and enabled them to transfer Longstreet's corps to Tennessee.

When Washington permitted Meade to move forward in mid-September, he discovered the reduced Rebel army behind the Rapidan River. Lee's position presented Meade an extraordinarily difficult tactical nut to crack. The general quickly concluded he had little to gain and much to lose by attempting to breech the Confederate defenses. The best way to deal with the problem, he reasoned, was to avoid those defenses altogether.

Meade recommended a change of base to Aquia Landing on the banks of Chesapeake Bay and an overland advance from Fredericksburg toward Richmond, a strategic maneuver that would provide him secure waterborne communications, which would in turn vastly reduce the number of troops needed to guard the army's supply line and correspondingly increase available Federal combat strength. Such a shift would also force Lee to abandon the Rapidan and relocate his army to counter the Union move. From Meade's vantage point, the logic of his solution to the Rapidan challenge was compelling. It is therefore easy to understand why he was appalled when Lincoln and Halleck disapproved the proposal.[1]

Meade's superiors could not accept a change of base to Fredericksburg. It would carry the army back to the scene of its most humiliating defeat just six months after that debacle. The administration's political opponents would interpret this as an admission of strategic bankruptcy and wield that argument like a scythe in the upcoming elections. More importantly, transferring the seat of operations toward the lower Rappahannock appeared to make Richmond and not Lee the AOP's objective. Lincoln and Halleck believed that Meade's sole task was to destroy Lee's army. In the president's eyes, it didn't matter where the Union fought the battles to produce that result.

The commander-in-chief had summed up the gist of this strategic point of view after the battle of Fredericksburg in December 1862. William O. Stoddard, the president's assistant private secretary, remembered Lincoln propounding "a sense of awful arithmetic" in the wake of that bloody defeat. He acknowledged that the North had lost 50 percent more men than the Confederates in that dreadful engagement and then reflected that "if the same battle were to be fought over again, every day, through a week of days, with the same relative results, the army under Lee would be wiped out to its last man, while the Army of the Potomac would still be a mighty host. The war would be over. The Confederacy gone." Victory, then, was a matter of numbers and attrition the key to success.[2]

As Lincoln and Halleck understood it, where that attrition happened didn't matter, so long as the process of bleeding Lee to death was relentless. In the

---

1   George G. Meade to wife, January 2, 1863, *Life and Letters*, vol. 1, 344-45.

2   Carl Sandburg, *Lincoln: The War Years*, 4 vols. (New York, 1939), vol. 1, 632.

abstract this may have been true. Meade, however, could not plan and fight in the abstract. He had to select a battlefield and actually engage the enemy. But the administration refused the general the freedom to choose his ground and employ the assets of strategic mobility. In short, Lincoln and Halleck trapped Meade in an extremely difficult tactical conundrum and then exhibited great impatience when he did not quickly produce the requisite offensive campaign.

Condemned by his superiors to overcome the stout Confederate defenses behind the Rapidan, Meade wrestled with his dilemma through the last half of September. Since direct frontal assault had zero chance of success, Meade's only alternative was to outflank Lee by marching far enough west or east to cross the river beyond Rebel defenses. The Union general was confident he could do this and "get a battle out of Lee," but only under grossly disadvantageous circumstances.

Such a battle would gain little for the Northern cause, Meade feared, while realistically admitting that a Union victory wouldn't destroy the Rebel army. A serious battle would hurt each side equally in proportion to its strength. Lee would survive and withdrawal to an even stronger position closer to Richmond. When that happened, the Confederate supply line would shorten while Meade's lengthened, requiring him to detach even more troops to secure his communications and further reduce his combat power. This would render the outcome of the next fight even more doubtful and might enable the enemy to turn the tables on his army and even take the offensive.

All of Meade's concerns were valid, and the administration recognized and accepted them as such. Nonetheless, Halleck and Lincoln chafed whenever Meade reiterated his difficulties. They interpreted this as equivocation or procrastination and worried that it hinted at a lack of aggressive instinct in their field commander.

Since Gettysburg, the president and general-in-chief had wanted Meade to fight Lee and begin the process of grinding his army into oblivion. Meade wasn't afraid to fight, but he understood the on-the-ground challenge of provoking and winning a battle and coping with the manpower aftermath of either victory or defeat. If he were going to run those risks while advancing on a line of operations he opposed, the general demanded explicit orders to fight or explicit sanction of his operational plans. He refused to become a scapegoat like McClellan, Burnside, Pope, and Hooker. But Lincoln and Halleck wouldn't give Meade what he wanted.

Meade wouldn't give the administration what it wanted either. Although Lincoln and Halleck never put it so baldly, what they wanted was for Meade to act like Lee and do as Lee did. Like Meade, the Rebel general had to keep the enemy away from his capital and operate over the same ground. He faced the same tactical realities but did so while outnumbered and connected to a tenuous supply system with an even greater manpower crisis on his horizon. Despite all that, Lee was willing to take calculated risks. Always looking to fight regardless of the odds, he trusted that the initiative and battlefield success would cancel or obviate the many challenges under which his army operated. Fairly or not, the administration wondered why Lee, whose resources were dwarfed by those of the Union army, could do these things but Meade could not.

* * *

Meade's conduct of the Bristoe Station Campaign reinforced Lincoln's and Halleck's concerns about the AOP commander. Both were distressed when Meade refused to pitch into Lee after he emerged from behind the Rapidan in October. Understandably, they believed that the Rebel leader had released Meade from his September quandary. The Confederates had come out of their entrenchments and exposed themselves to superior Federal strength. For the president and Halleck, this was the moment to strike a blow.

But Meade did not strike. As had been the case in late July during his duel with Lee along the Blue Ridge Mountains, contradictory intelligence reports and an inability to trust his instincts rendered him irresolute, a tendency only worsened by his relationship with the administration. When Lee first began to move, Meade correctly suspected that the Rebels were outflanking the Union army rather than making a feint before a retreat. But he would not act on that instinct unless his cavalry and other intelligence sources absolutely verified his suspicion. The administration's prodding and evident dissatisfaction reinforced Meade's reluctance to go with his gut. The last thing the general wanted to report was that the Confederates had retreated toward Richmond without interference by the AOP. That had happened at Falling Waters and Manassas Gap in July. Because of his determination that it not happen on the Rapidan, Meade positioned half of his army for a pursuit south of the river, while the other half prepared to defend Culpeper from an attack issuing forth from Madison County.

After Meade extricated his army from that awkward stance by retreating north of the Rappahannock, he placed his troops in a solid position to respond to whatever Lee did next. But, just a half day later, on October 12, the Union general cancelled that accomplishment by sending half his army back into Culpeper County. His avowed purpose was to fight a battle on the offensive in the same place he had been unwilling to fight a defensive battle the day before. Maj. Gen.

Humphreys, the army's chief of staff, believed this was the only mistake his boss made in the entire campaign.[3]

Because of it, Meade was poorly situated to react when he belatedly learned that Lee had jumped the upper Rappahannock at Sulphur Springs. That ensured a much more perilous retreat than should have been necessary. Only quick thinking by Gouverneur Warren combined with a little luck and A. P. Hill's carelessness prevented the Rebels from wrecking the II Corps. To Meade's credit, once certain of his circumstances he acted intelligently, calmly, and decisively.

As the Union army assumed a defensive position behind Bull Run, however, the fog of war again led Meade into vacillation and unwillingness to act without certain knowledge of the enemy's position. Being so close to Washington he felt the full weight of responsibility for the country's cause and capital. His dread of making the wrong move kept him from making any move until opportunity had already departed. The general's dithering typically didn't last long, often only a day or so. But against an opponent like Robert E. Lee that could spell disaster.

His troops approved Meade's retreat from the Rapidan to Bull Run. They appreciated that he had avoided a similar disaster some of his predecessors had fallen into. The general had certainly frustrated Lee's purpose, although admittedly by a much narrower margin than should have been necessary. Meade's pursuit of the Confederates back to the Rappahannock failed even before it began. The Buckland Races merely aggravated that wound. Meade's own self-appraisal that Lee had gotten the better of him rings totally true.

All of this distressed Lincoln and Halleck no end. They didn't seem to realize that their subtle but constant nagging of Meade had helped to produce the uncertainty marking several of the general's choices during the campaign. It's hard to imagine Meade's decision to divide his army between potential offensive and defensive action on October 9/10 and 12 without suspecting that he was trying to avoid being blamed for failing to fight or letting the Rebels get away.

George Meade was certainly no coward. He could envision daring movements and bold strategies. As a division commander he had railed against "playing war without risks," advocating going out to whip the enemy "if there was any reasonable probability of our doing so, even though we should not be either able or desirous of following up our victory." It didn't matter if the fight took place on a "practicable, though less desirable, line" of operations. Battlefield success was all

---

3 Humphreys, *Gettysburg to the Rapidan*, 36.

that mattered and "would be of immense advantage" to the Union cause no matter when, where, or how it was won—or at what price.[4]

Meade had written those words to Margaret, his closest confidante, in January of 1863, six months before assuming the weight of army command. The responsibility for leading an army tempered the general's aggressive zeal. Now the obstacles in his way, the inevitable casualties, and the potential results of failure outweighed the possible benefits of less-than-predictable success. Although Meade had then proclaimed McClellan's "vice" as "always waiting to have everything just as he wanted before he would attack," it now appeared that vice was Meade's own. He would fight, but he would fight only when reasonably certain where his enemy was and when he could bring maximum force to bear on a target that offered a real chance of success.

The general knew that it took time to orchestrate such conditions. He knew his impatient masters in Washington and equally impatient editors in the press would grumble at the necessary delay. But he also felt wholly justified taking the necessary steps to make victory likely and ensuring that the thousands of inevitable casualties were not lost in vain.

If Lee was audacity, Meade was prudence. Whether the Meade of January 1863 or the Meade of September-October 1863 would show up wasn't clear. But the answer was not far off. As the last week of October 1863 slipped into history, the Union army closed on the Rappahannock River looking for a fight. The contest between Meade and Lee was entering a new phase.

* * *

The three months following Gettysburg unquestionably accrued to the benefit of the Confederacy in the Virginia Theater. Lee was able to restore his army and maintain the stalemate that had stymied and frustrated the North for two years. Furthermore, the South accomplished this without the casualties that would have resulted from a major battle. Lee had certainly wanted to do more and still sought the clinching battlefield victory. Nonetheless, continued stalemate could potentially help secure Lincoln's electoral defeat next fall and perhaps with it realization of Confederate independence.

Ironically, the Davis administration's transfer of Longstreet's corps to Tennessee proved detrimental to the long-term continuance of that stalemate. A

---

4 George G. Meade to wife, January 2, 1863, *Life and Letters*, vol. 1, 345.

daring and reasonable response to the loss of Chattanooga and Knoxville, that move highlighted the Western Theater in a way which many Southerners at the time, and many historians since, felt long overdue by Confederate leaders. Lee, however, intuitively feared that shifting Longstreet's corps to Tennessee would not only do no good, but rob him of an opportunity in Virginia. Ultimately Lee was correct. The primary result of the Confederacy's great strategic gamble, the costly victory at Chickamauga, produced no meaningful long-term benefit. Indeed, Longstreet had denigrated just that sort of fruitless victory before he set off for the West.

Had Longstreet remained in Virginia, Lee would have launched an early September offensive against Meade. The numerical odds between the armies at that point were almost equal. With the Federals positioned behind the upper Rappahannock, Lee would most likely have undertaken a flanking strategy similar to the one he used in October. The critical difference, however, would have been his ability to use one corps to misdirect Meade about his army's true intentions. Stuart's cavalry managed to do this twice during the October campaign with dangerous potential consequences for the AOP. Undoubtedly, had Stuart's efforts been assisted by a corps of infantry, they would have proven much more effective.

A large force of Rebel foot soldiers dangling in front of Meade might have left the Union commander uncertain of enemy intentions long enough to allow Lee's two remaining corps to gain the Federal rear with results impossible to determine. It may have led to pitched battle or perhaps a different version of Meade's rapid October retreat. Historians can only conjecture about the possible consequences. Nonetheless, it is reasonable to suspect that Lee, from great positional advantage, might have beaten Meade as he had beaten Hooker, Burnside, Pope, and McClellan. In exchange for forfeiting this opportunity, the South won a battle at Chickamauga which instead set in motion a chain of events that posed frightful dangers to the Confederacy.

The defeat of Maj. Gen. William Rosecrans' Army of the Cumberland at Chickamauga created a crisis for the Union in Tennessee. But it ultimately forced a critical and overwhelmingly successful response by the Lincoln administration: the firing of Rosecrans, the promotion of Ulysses Grant to general-in-chief, and the assignment of Maj. Gen. William T. Sherman to command of the armies around Chattanooga. The elevation of Grant and Sherman spawned the decisive 1864-65 campaigns that brought about the downfall of the Confederacy. If Lee had kept Longstreet in Virginia in 1863, those campaigns would not have unfolded as they did.

Between the fall of Vicksburg and the Tennessee crisis, Maj. Gen. Grant had no active assignment. On September 15, 1863, Halleck revealed his intentions for

Grant in a letter to Meade. The reason for the Rebel concentration of force near Chattanooga, he postulated, was because "the enemy probably saw that if you and Rosecrans could hold your present position till Grant and Banks cleaned out the States west of the Mississippi, the fate of the rebellion would be sealed." That statement and Halleck's insistence on campaigns in Arkansas and western Louisiana in 1864 indicate he intended to send Grant to the Trans-Mississippi Theater.[5]

Before the battle of Chattanooga no one considered making Grant general-in-chief. The campaign to elevate him to supreme command began *after* his success in lifting the siege of that city and routing Bragg's army at Missionary Ridge. Grant's role in the salvation of Chattanooga brought him to supreme command of all Union armies.[6]

Without the transfer of Longstreet's corps to Tennessee, Confederate victory at Chickamauga would have been less likely. Absent the Chickamauga defeat Rosecrans remains in command of the Army of the Cumberland, and no siege of Chattanooga takes place. Without a crisis at Chattanooga for Grant to salvage, how likely is it that Lincoln would have made him general-in-chief in early 1864? Without Grant assuming that position, Rosecrans, not Sherman, undertakes the Atlanta Campaign. Under these circumstances, it is easy to imagine that campaign playing out differently regardless of whether Braxton Bragg or Gen. Joseph E. Johnston led the Army of Tennessee. It is impossible to predict the outcome or political consequences of an 1864 Georgia offensive led by Rosecrans or an 1864 Virginia offensive led by Meade. But obviously those campaigns would have been completely different from those history now records.

At the time he took the decision, Davis made a logical move sending Longstreet to the West. In retrospect, however, the Confederacy would have probably benefited far more from putting maximum resources in the hands of Robert E. Lee.

---

5 *OR* 29, pt. 2, 186-87.

6 Ibid.; Ron Chernow, *Grant* (New York, 2017), 295-6, 300, 326-30. Chernow provides a good discussion of Grant's rise to general-in-chief. The victory at Missionary Ridge, of course, resulted from the spontaneous, unauthorized action of troops in Maj. Gen. George H. Thomas' Army of the Cumberland, not Grant's strategy. As overall commander of the Chattanooga operations, however, Grant got the credit. Grant, who detested Rosecrans, replaced him with Thomas soon after taking control of Union efforts at Chattanooga.

Primary Sources

Unpublished Manuscripts

Alabama State Archives, Montgomery, AL
    Purifoy, John R. "Jeff Davis Artillery" typescript
Albert H. Small Special Collections Library, University of Virginia, Charlottesville, VA
    Brand, William Francis: Letters
    Woods, Micajah Papers
Dolph Briscoe Center for American History, University of Texas, Austin TX
    Kirkpatrick, James Diary. Letters
    Smith, William Adolphus. Letters
Duke University Special Collections Library, Durham, NC
    Hancock, Winfield Scott. Papers
    Parmelle, Samuel Spencer Papers
Eleanor S. Brockenbrough Library, Museum of the Civil War, Richmond, VA
    Morrisett, Algernon S. Diary
    Morissett, Lawson. Diary
    Myers, Robert Pooler, Diary
——. Letter Copy Book
Nunnelee, Lewis T. Memoir
Fondren Library, Rice University, Houston, TX
    Wilber, Escek G. Letters
Gettysburg National Military Park, Gettysburg, PA
    Bailey, Thomas. "The Life and Times of Thomas Bailey: A Civil War Diary."
Gilder Lehrman Institute of American History, New York, NY
    Bope, Abraham. Letters
    Tate, Jeremiah. Letters
Hamilton College Library, Clinton, NY
    Brown, Morris. Letters
Historical Society of Pennsylvania, Philadelphia, PA
    Biddle, James Cornell. Letters, 1861-1865
    Meade, George G. Papers
Indiana Historical Society, William Henry Smith Memorial Library, Indianapolis, IN
    Chapman, George. Diary
    Van Dyke, Augustus M. Papers
Indiana State Library, Indianapolis, IN
    Bellamy, F. J. Diary
Library of Congress, Washington, DC
    Burbank, Sidney. Diary
    Galwey, Thomas Francis. Diary
    Gilpin, E. N. Diary
    Hatton, John William Ford. Memoir
    Long-Breckinridge Papers, Long, William S. "Reminiscences"
    Rose, Luther A. Diary
    Wigfall, Louis Trezevant. Family Papers
Library of Virginia, Richmond, VA
    Gibson Family Papers

Milne Special Collections and Archives, University of New Hampshire Library, Durham, NH
     Cheney, Thomas Carleton. Papers
Missouri Historical Society, Columbia, MO
     Carpenter, Thomas. Letters
National Archives, Washington, DC
     Bureau of Military Information File
New York State Library, Albany, NY
     Warren, Gouverneur. Letters
North Carolina State Archives, Raleigh NC
     Anthony, Whit Hill. "Personal Sketch and Reminiscences."
     Cowles, William H., Sketch.
     Foard, Noah. Memoirs.
Pearce Museum, Navarro College, Corsicana, TX
     Buford, John. Letter
     Northway, Delos, Letters
Pennsylvania State University, State College, PA
     Meyer, Thomas. Manuscript. "Incidents and Anecdotes of the War Between the States"
Ohio Historical Society, Columbus, OH
     Powell Manuscript, "Campaign on the Rappahannock"
Southern Historical Collection, University of North Carolina. Chapel Hill, NC
     Hairston, Peter Wilson. Diary & Papers
     McIntosh, David Gregg. Papers
The Handley Regional Library, Winchester, VA
     McVicar, Charles W. Diary
United States Civil War Collection, Western Michigan University, Kalamazoo, MI
     Harrington, George. Diary
University of Virginia, Richmond, VA
     Lee, H. C. Papers
US Army Center for Military History, Fort McNair, Washington, DC
     Blackford, Eugene. Diary
     Frank, Abner. Diary
     Walker, Edward A. Letter & Diary
US Military History Institute, Carlisle, PA
     Click, Jacob. Letters
Virginia Historical Society, Richmond, VA
     Johnson, Elijah S. Diary
     Patch, George H. Papers
     Sneden, Robert Knox. Diary
     Stuart, James E. B. Papers
Virginia Military Institute, Lexington, VA
     Garibaldi, John. Letters
Western Reserve Historical Society, Cleveland, OH
     Bushnell, Wells A. "Sixth Regiment Ohio Volunteer Cavalry Memoir, 1861-1865" typescript
Winchester-Frederick County Historical Society, Handley Regional Library, Winchester, VA
     Russell, Stanley F. Letters
Yale University Archives, New Haven, CT
     Furlow, Charles. Diary

Published Primary Sources

"A Confederate." *The Grayjackets and How They Lived, Fought and Died for Dixie. With Incidents & Sketches of Life in the Confederacy.* Richmond, VA: Jones Brothers & Co., 1867.

Acken, J. Gregory, ed. *Inside the Army of the Potomac: The Civil War Experience of Captain Francis Adams Donaldson.* Mechanicsburg, PA: Stackpole Books, 1998.

Aggassiz, George R., ed. *Meade's Headquarters 1863-1865: Letters of Colonel Theodore Lyman.* Boston, MA: The Atlantic Monthly Press, 1922.

Aldrich, Thomas M. *The History of Battery A First Regiment Rhode Island Light Artillery in the War to Preserve the Union 1861-1865.* Providence, RI: Snow & Farnham, 1904.

Avery, James Henry. *Under Custer's Command: The Civil War Journal of James Henry Avery.* Washington, DC: Brassey's, 2000.

Barber, Raymond G. & Gary E. Swinson, ed. *The Civil War Letters of Charles Barber, Private, 104th New York Volunteer Infantry.* Torrance, CA: Gary E. Swinson, 1991.

Bartlett, A.W. *History of the Twelfth Regiment New Hampshire Volunteers in the War of the Rebellion.* Concord, NH: Ira C. Evans, Printer, 1897.

Bassett, M.H. *From Bull Run to Bristow Station.* St. Paul, MN: North Central Publishing Co, 1962.

Baylor, George. *From Bull Run to Bull Run; or, Four Years in the Army of Northern Virginia.* Richmond, VA: B.F. Johnson Publishing Company, 1900.

Beale, George W. *A Lieutenant of Cavalry in Lee's Army.* Boston, MA: The Gorham Press, 1918.

Beale, R. *History of the Ninth Virginia Cavalry in the War Between the States.* Richmond, VA: B.F. Johnson Publishing Co., 1899.

Best, Isaac O. *History of the 121st New York State Infantry.* Chicago: Published by Author.

Billings, John D. *The History of the Tenth Massachusetts Battery of Light Artillery in the War of the Rebellion, 1862-1865.* Boston, MA: Hall & Whiting, Publishers, 1881.

Birdsong, James, ed. *Brief Sketches of the North Carolina State Troops in the War Between the States.* Raleigh, NC: Josephus Daniels, State Printer and Binder, 1894.

Blackford, Charles Minor III, ed. *Letters from Lee's Army.* Lincoln: University of Nebraska Press, 1998.

Blackford, W.W. *War Years With Jeb Stuart.* Baton Rouge: Louisiana State University Press, 1993.

Blake, Henry N. *Three Years in the Army of the Potomac.* Boston: Lee and Shephard, 1866.

Bowen, James L. *History of the Thirty-Seventh Regiment Massachusetts Volunteers.* New York: Clark W. Bryan & Co., 1884.

Boudrye, Louis. *Historic Records of the Fifth New York Cavalry: First Ira Harris Guard.* Albany, NY: S.R. Gray, 1865.

Brock, Heros Von. *Memoirs of the Confederate War for Independence.* 2 vols. Edinburgh, England: William Blackford & Sons, 1866.

Brooks, U.R., ed. *Stories of the Confederacy.* Columbia, SC: The State Company, 1912.

Bruce, George A. *The Twentieth Regiment of Massachusetts Volunteer Infantry, 1861-1865.* Boston: Houghton, Mifflin and Company, 1906.

Bryan, Charles Jr. and Lankford Nelson, eds. *Eye of the Storm.* New York: Simon & Schuster, 2000.

———. *Images from the Storm.* New York: The Free Press, 2001.

Byrne, Frank. *Haskell of Gettysburg: His Life and Civil War Papers.* Kent, OH: Kent State University Press, 1989.

Caldwell, J.F.J. *The History of a Brigade of South Carolinians.* Dayton, OH: Morningside Press, 1984.

Camper, Charles & Kirkley, J. W. *Historical Record of the First Regiment Maryland Infantry.* Washington, DC: Gibson Brothers, 1871.

Carter, Robert G. *Four Brothers in Blue.* Austin: University of Texas Press, 1978.

Cassedy, Edward K. *Dear Friends at Home: The Civil War Letters of Sergeant Charles T. Bowen, Twelfth United States Infantry, First Battalion, 1861-1865.* Baltimore, MD: Butternut & Blue, 2001.

Cheney, Newell. *History of the Ninth Regiment New York Volunteer Cavalry, War of 1861 to 1865.* Jamestown, NY: Martin Mere & son, 1901.

Coltrane, Daniel. *The Memoirs of Daniel Branson Coltrane, Co. I, 63rd Regiment, N.C. Cavalry C.S.A.* Raleigh, NC: Edwards & Broughton Company, 1956.

Cooke, John Esten. *Wearing of the Gray; Personal Portraits, Scenes and Adventures of the War.* New York: E. B. Treat & Co., 1867.

Corson, Blake W. Jr., ed. *My Dear Jennie.* Richmond, VA: Dietz Press Inc., 1982.

Cockrell, Monroe, ed. *Gunner with Stonewall: Reminiscences of William Thomas Poague.* Wilmington, NC: Broadfoot Publishing, 1987.

Cockrell, Thomas D. *A Mississippi Rebel in the Army of Northern Virginia: The Civil War Memoirs of Private David Holt.* Baton Rouge: Louisiana State University Press, 2005.

Craft, David. *History of the One Hundred Forty-First Regiment Pennsylvania Volunteers, 1862-1865.* Towanda, PA: Reporter-Journal Printing Company, 1885.

Crowninshield, Benjamin. *A History of the First Regiment of Massachusetts Cavalry Volunteers.* Cambridge, MA: The Riverside Press, 1899.

Denison, Frederic. *Sabres and Spurs: The First Regiment Rhode Island Cavalry in the Civil War, 1861-1865.* Central Falls, RI: The First Rhode Island Cavalry Veteran Association, 1876.

De Trobriand, Regis. *Four Years with the Army of the Potomac.* Gaithersburg, MD: Ron R. Van Sickle Military Books, 1988.

Dobbins, Austin, ed. *Grandfather's Journal.* Dayton, OH: Morningside Press, 1988.

Doster William E., *Lincoln and Episodes of the Civil War.* New York: G. P. Putnam's Sons, 1915.

Dougherty, Michael. *Diary of a Civil War Hero.* New York: Pyramid Books, 1960.

Dowdy, Clifford and Louis Manarin, eds. *The Wartime Papers of Robert E. Lee.* New York: Bramhall House, 1961.

Dozier, Graham, *A Gunner in Lee's Army: The Civil War Letters of Thomas Henry Carter.* Chapel Hill, NC: University of North Carolina Press, 2014.

Durkin, Joseph T., ed. *Confederate Chaplain: Rev. James B. Sheeran, C.S.S.R. 14th Louisiana, C.S.A.* Milwaukee: The Bruce Publishing Company, 1960.

Early, Jubal. *Lieutenant General Jubal Anderson Early, C.S.A. Autobiographical Sketch and Narrative of the War Between the States.* New York: Konecy & Konecy, 1994.

Eidler, Peter G. *Army of the Potomac: The Civil War Letters of William Cross Hazelton of the Eighth Illinois Cavalry Regiment.* Seattle: Coffeetown Press, 2013.

Favill, Josiah Marshall. *The Diary of a Young Officer.* Chicago: R.R. Donnelley & Sons Company, 1909.

Fleming, George. *Life and Letters of Alexander Hays, Brevet Colonel United States Army, Brigadier General and Brevet Major General United States Volunteers.* Pittsburgh: Gilbert Adam Hays, 1919.

Floyd, Dale E. *"Dear Folks at Home . . ." The Letters and Diary of Thomas James Owen, Fiftieth New York Volunteer Engineer Regiment, During the Civil War.* Washington, DC: US Government Printing Office, 1985.

Ford, Andrew E. *The Story of the Fifteenth Regiment Massachusetts Volunteer Infantry in the Civil War, 1861-1864.* Clinton, MA: Press of W. J. Coulter, 1898.

Fremantle, Arthur L. *Three Months in the Southern States: April-June 1863.* New York: John Bradburn, 1864.

Galwey, Thomas Francis. *The Valiant Hours: An Irishman in the Civil War.* Harrisburg, PA: The Stackpole Company, 1961.

Gibbon, John. *Recollections of the Civil War.* New York: G. P. Putnam's Sons, 1890.

Gienapp, William E. and Erica L. Gienapp, eds., *The Civil War Diary of Gideon Welles: Lincoln's Secretary of the Navy.* Urbana, IL: University of Illinois Press, 2014.

Glazier, Willard. *Three Years in the Federal Cavalry.* New York: R. H. Ferguson & Co., 1870.

Gracey, Samuel L. *Annals of the Sixth Pennsylvania Cavalry.* E. H. Butler & Co., 1868.

Griffin, Richard, ed. *Three Years A Soldier: The Diary and Newspaper Correspondence of Private George Perkins, Sixth New York Independent Battery, 1861-1864.* Knoxville,: University of Tennessee Press, 2006.

Grimsley, Daniel. *Battles in Culpeper County, Virginia, 1861-1865 and other articles by Major Daniel A. Grimsley, of the Sixth Virginia Cavalry.* Culpeper, VA: Exponent Printing Office, 1900.

Hall, Hillman, et al. *History of the Sixth New York Cavalry (Second Ira Harris Guard) Second Brigade—First Division—Cavalry Corps, Army of the Potomac: 1861-1865.* Worcester, MA: The Blanchard Press, 1908.

Handerson, Henry. *Yankee in Gray: The Civil War Memoirs of Henry E. Handerson.* Cleveland: Western Reserve University Press, 1962.

Hard, Abner. *History of the Eighth Cavalry Regiment Illinois Volunteers, During the Great Rebellion.* Aurora, IL: Published by Author, 1868.

Harden, M. D. *History of the Twelfth Regiment Pennsylvania Reserve Volunteer Corps.* New York: Published by the Author. 1890

Harris, Samuel. *Personal Reminiscences of Samuel Harris.* Chicago: The Rogerson Press, 1897.

Haupt, Herman. *Reminiscences of General Herman Haupt.* Milwaukee: Wright & Joys Co., 1901.

Haynes, Edwin M. *A History of the Tenth Regiment Vermont Volunteers.* Lewiston, ME: Journal Steam Press, 1870.

Hennessy, John, ed. *Fighting With the 18th Massachusetts: The Civil War Memoir of Thomas H. Mann*. Baton Rouge: Louisiana State University Press, 2000.

Herdegen, Lance and Murphy Sherry, eds. *Four Years With The Iron Brigade: The Civil War Journal of William Ray, Company F, 7th Wisconsin Infantry*. Cambridge, MA: De Capo Press, 2002.

Hewett, Janet; Suderow, Bryce; and Trudeau, Noah Andre, eds. *Supplement to the Official Records of the Union and Confederate Armies*. 100 Volumes. Wilmington, NC: Broadfoot Publishing Co., 1995.

Hoffman, Elliott W. *History of the First Vermont Cavalry Volunteers In the War of the Great Rebellion*. Baltimore: Butternut & Blue, 2000.

Hood, John Bell. *Advance and Retreat: Personal Experiences in the United States and Confederate States Armies*. New Orleans: Hood Orphan Memorial Fund, 1880.

Hopkins, Luther. *From Bull Run to Appomattox*. Baltimore: Fleet-McGinley Co., 1914.

Howard, McHenry. *Recollections of a Maryland Confederate Soldier and Staff Officer*. Baltimore: Williams & Wilkins, 1914.

Howard, Oliver Otis. *Autobiography of Oliver Otis Howard, Major General, United States Army*. New York: The Baker & Taylor Company, 1907.

Humphreys, Andrew. *From Gettysburg to the Rapidan—The Army of the Potomac, July, 1863 to April, 1864*. New York: Charles Scribner's Sons, 1883.

Hyndman, William. *History of a Cavalry Company: A Complete Record of Company A, 4th Penn'a Cavalry*. Philadelphia: Jas. B. Rodgers Co, Printers, 1870.

Jones, J. William. *Christ in the Camp: Religion in Lee's Army*. Richmond: B. F. Johnson Company, 1887.

Jones, John B. *A Rebel War Clerk's Diary*. 2 Vols. Philadelphia: J.B. Lippincott & Co., 1866.

Jones, Terry, ed. *Campbell Brown's Civil War: With Ewell and The Army of Northern Virginia*. Baton Rouge: Louisiana State University Press, 2001.

——. *The Civil War Memoirs of Captain William J. Seymour: Reminiscences of a Louisiana Tiger*. Baton Rouge: Louisiana State University Press, 1991.

Kidd, James. *Personal Recollections of a Cavalryman*. Ionia, MI: Sentinel Printing Company, 1908.

Lewis, George. *Battery E First Rhode Island Light Artillery 1861-1865*. Providence, RI: Snow & Farnham, 1892.

Livermore, Thomas. *Days & Events 1860-1866*. Boston: Houghton Mifflin Co., 1920.

Lloyd, William. *History of the First Regiment Pennsylvania Reserve Cavalry*. Philadelphia: King & Baird, 1864.

Long, A. L. *Memoirs of Robert E. Lee*. Secaucus, NJ: The Blue and Gray Press, 1983.

Longstreet, James. *From Manassas to Appomattox*. Secaucus, NJ: Blue & Gray Press, 1984.

Lowe, David, ed. *Meade's Army: The Private Notebooks of Lt. Col. Theodore Lyman*. Kent, OH: Kent State University Press, 2007.

Martin, James, et al. *History of the Fifty-Seventh Regiment Pennsylvania Volunteer Infantry*. Meadville, PA: McCoy & Calvin, n.d.

McClellan, Henry B. *I Rode With Jeb Stuart: The Life and Campaigns of Major General J. E. B. Stuart*. Bloomington: Indiana University Press, 1958.

McDonald, Archie P., ed. *Jedediah Hotchkiss: Make Me a Map of the Valley: The Civil War Journal of Stonewall Jackson's Topographer*. Dallas: Southern Methodist University Press, 1973.

McDonald, William N. *A History of the Laurel Brigade*. Baltimore: Sun Job Printing Office, 1907.

McKinney, Edward P. *Life in Tent, Camp and Field, 1861-1865*. Boston: Badger, 1922.

McMullen, Glenn, ed. *A Surgeon with Stonewall Jackson: The Civil War Letters of Dr. Harvey Black*. Baltimore: Butternut and Blue, 1995.

McSwain, Eleanor ed., *Crumbling Defenses or Memoirs and Reminiscences of John Logan Black, Colonel C.S.A.* Macon, GA: The J. W. Burke Company, 1960.

Meade, George. *Life and Letters of George Gordon Meade*. 2 Volumes. New York: Charles Scribner's Sons, 1913.

Merrel, John H., *Diary*. [Typescript copy in author's possession.]

Merrington, Marguerite, ed. *The Custer Story, The Life and Intimate Letters of General George A. Custer and His Wife Elizabeth*. New York: Devin-Adair, 1950.

Meyer, Henry C. *Civil War Experiences under Bayard, Gregg, Kilpatrick, Custer, Raulston, and Newberry: 1862, 1863, 1864*. New York: The Knickersocker Press, 1911.

Moore, Edward. *The Story of a Cannoneer Under Stonewall Jackson*. New York: Neale Publishing, 1907.

Moore, Frank, ed. *The Rebellion Record: A Diary of American Events with Documents, Narratives, Illustrative Incidents, Poetry, Etc.*, 12 Volumes. New York: D. Van Nostrand, Publisher, 1864.

Moore, John W. *Roster of North Carolina Troops in the War Between the States,* 18 Volumes. Ashe & Gatling State Printers: Raleigh, NC, 1882.

Morrison, James, ed. *The Memoirs of Henry Heth.* Westport, CT: Greenwood Press, 1974.

Morse, Charles F. *Civil War Letters of Charles F. Morse: 1861-1865.* www.bigbytebooks.com, 2014.

Morse, J. T., ed. *Diary of Gideon Welles.* 3 Volumes. Boston: Houghton Mifflin Co., 1952.

Moyer, H. P. *History of the Seventeenth Regiment Pennsylvania Volunteer Cavalry.* Lebanon, PA: Sowers Printing Co., 1911.

Muffly, Joseph. *The Story of Our Regiment: A History of the 148th Pennsylvania Volunteers.* Des Moines, IA: Kenyon Printing & Mfg. Co., 1904.

Mulholland, St. Clair. *The Story of the 116th Regiment Pennsylvania Infantry: War of Secession, 1862-1865.* Philadelphia: F. McManus Jr. & Co., 1899.

Munson, E.B., ed *Confederate Correspondent: The Civil War Reports of Jacob Nathaniel Raymer, Fourth North Carolina.* Jefferson, NC: McFarland & Company, Inc. Publishers, 2009.

Nanzig, Thomas P., ed. *The Civil War Memoirs of a Virginia Cavalryman: Lt. Robert T. Hubard, Jr.* Tuscaloosa: The University of Alabama Press, 2007.

Neese, George M. *Three Years in the Confederate Horse Artillery.* New York: The Neale Publishing Company, 1911.

Nevins, Allan., ed. *A Diary of Battle: The Personal Journals of Colonel Charles S. Wainwright, 1861-1865.* New York: Da Capo Press, 1998.

Newhall, Walter S. *A Memoir.* Philadelphia: C. Sherman Son & Company, 1864.

Nichols, George. A *Soldier's Story of His Regiment (61st Georgia) and Incidentally of the Lawton-Gordon-Evens Brigade, Army of Northern Virginia.* Tuscaloosa: The University of Alabama Press, 2011.

Norton, Henry. *Deeds of Daring or a History of the Eighth N.Y. Volunteer Cavalry.* Norwich, NY: Chenango Telegraph Printing House, 1889.

Norton, Oliver. *Army Letters 1861-1865.* Chicago: O. L. Deming, 1903.

Page, Charles. *History of the Fourteenth Regiment Connecticut Vol. Infantry.* Meridan, CT: Horton Printing Co., 1906.

Perry, Martha Derby. *Letters from a Surgeon of the Civil War.* Boston: Little, Brown and Company, 1906.

Phisterer, Frederick. *New York in the War of the Rebellion,* 3rd edition. Albany, NY: J.B. Lyon Company, 1912.

Pickerill, W. N. *History of the Third Indiana Cavalry.* Indianapolis, 1906.

Porter, Horace, *Campaigning with Grant.* New York: Century, 1897.

Preston, N.D. *History of the Tenth Regiment of Cavalry New York State Volunteers.* New York: D. Appleton & Co., 1892.

Pyne, Henry. *History of the First New Jersey Cavalry.* Trenton, NJ: J.A. Beecher, 1871.

Rawle, William Brooke, et al. *History of the Third Pennsylvania Cavalry 1861-1865.* Philadelphia: Franklin Printing Co., 1905.

Regimental Association Publication Committee. *History of the Eighteenth Regiment of Cavalry Pennsylvania Volunteers, 1862-1865.* New York: Winkoop, Hallenbeck, Crawford Co., 1909.

Regimental History Committee. *History of the Third Pennsylvania Cavalry, Sixtieth Regiment Pennsylvania Volunteers in the American Civil War, 1861-1865.* Philadelphia: Franklin Printing Company, 1905.

Reichardt, Theodore. *Diary of Battery A, First Regiment Rhode Island Light Artillery.* Providence, RI: N. Bangs Williams, Publisher, 1865.

Rhodes, John H. *The History of Battery B, First Regiment Rhode Island Light Artillery in the War to Preserve the Union, 1861-1865.* Providence, RI: Snow Farnham Printers, 1894.

Roe, Alfred S. *The Thirty-Ninth Massachusetts Volunteers 1862-1865.* Worcester, MA: Regimental Veteran Association, 1914.

Scott, Robert Garth, ed. *Fallen Leaves: The Civil War Letters of Major Henry Livermore Abbott.* Kent, OH: The Kent State University Press, 1991.

Simons, Ezra. *A Regimental History. The One Hundred and Twenty-Fifth New York State Volunteers.* New York: Ezra D. Simons, 1888.

Sloan, John A. *Reminiscences of the Guilford Grays, Co. B, 27th N.C. Regiment.* Washington, DC: R. O. Polkinhorn, Printer, 1883.

Smith, William A. *The Anson Guards: History of Company C, 14th Regiment, N.C.V., Army of Northern Virginia.* Charlotte, VA: Stone Publishing Co., 1914.

Sparks, David. *Inside Lincoln's Army: The Diary of Marsena Rudolph Patrick, Provost Marshal General, Army of the Potomac.* New York: Thomas Yoseloff, 1964.

Stevens, George. *Three Years in the Sixth Corps*. New York: D. Van Nostrand, Publisher, 1870.

Stevens, H. S. *Souvenir of Excursion to Battlefields of the Society of the Fourteenth Connecticut Regiment and Reunion at Antietam September 1891 with History and Reminiscences of Battles and Campaigns of the Regiment on the Fields Revisited*. Washington, DC: Gibson Brothers, Printers and Bookbinders, 1893.

Stewart, Robert L. *History of the One Hundred Fortieth Regiment Pennsylvania Volunteers*. Philadelphia: Published by the Regimental Association, 1912.

Survivors' Association. *History of the 121st Regiment Pennsylvania Volunteers: An Account from the Ranks*. Philadelphia: Catholic Standard and Times, 1906.

Swank, Walbrook D., ed. *Sabres, Saddles and Spurs: Lieutenant Colonel William R. Carter, CSA*. Shippensburg, PA: Burd Street Press, 1998.

——. *The Civil War Diary of John William Peyton*. Shippensburg, PA: Burd Street Press, 2003.

The Annals of the War Written By Leading Participants North and South. Philadelphia: The Times Publishing Company, 1879.

Tobie, Edward. *History of the First Maine Cavalry, 1861-1865*. Boston: Press of Emery & Hughes, 1887.

Turner, Charles W., ed. *Ted Barclay, Liberty Hall Volunteers: Letters from the Stonewall Brigade (1861-1865)*. Natural Bridge Station, VA: Rockbridge Publishing Company, 1992.

Urban, John W. *My Experiences Mid Shot and Shell and In the Rebel Den*. Lancaster, PA: Hubbard Brothers, 1882.

Van Santvoord, C., *The One Hundred and Twentieth Regiment New York State Volunteers. A Narrative of its Services in the War for the Union*. Rondout, NY: Press of the Kingston Freeman, 1894.

Von Brock, Heros *Memoirs of the Confederate War for Independence*, 2 Vols. Edinburg, England: William Blackwood & Sons, 1866.

Walker, Francis. *History of the Second Army Corps*. New York: Charles Scribner's Sons, 1887.

Wallace, Lew. *Lew Wallace, An Autobiography*. New York: Harper and Brothers, 1906.

Ward, Joseph R.C. *History of the One Hundred Sixth Regiment Pennsylvania Volunteers 2nd Brigade, 2nd Division, 2nd Corps*. Philadelphia: Grant, Faires and Rodgers, 1883.

Wells, Cheryl, ed. *A Surgeon in the Army of the Potomac*. Montreal: McGill Queens University Press, 2008.

Williams, Edward B., ed. *Rebel Brothers: The Civil War Letters of the Truehearts*. College Station: Texas A&M University Press, 1995.

Wittenberg, Eric, ed. *One of Custer's Wolverines: The Civil War Letters of Brevet Brigadier General James H. Kidd, 6th Michigan Cavalry*. Kent, OH: Kent State University Press, 2000.

——. *Under Custer's Command: The Civil War Journal of James Henry Avery*. Compiled by Karla Jean Husby. Washington, DC: Brassey's, 2000.

——. *"We Have It Damn Hard Out Here: The Civil War Letters of Sergeant Thomas W. Smith, 6th Pennsylvania Cavalry."* Kent, OH: Kent State University Press, 1999.

Worsham, John. *One of Jackson's Foot Cavalry*. New York: Neale Publishing Co., 1912.

Woodward, E. M., *Our Campaigns; or the Marches, Bivouacs, Battles, Incidents of Camp Life and History of Our Regiment During Its Three Years Term of Service*. Philadelphia: John E. Potter, 1865.

Wright, James A. *No More Gallant a Deed: A Civil War Memoir of the First Minnesota Volunteers*. St. Paul: Minnesota Historical Society Press, 2001.

The War of the Rebellion: A Compilation of the Official Records of the Union and Confederate Armies. 128 Volumes. Washington, DC: Government Printing Office, 1880-1901.

Online Primary Sources

Civil War Voices—Soldier Studies, "Soldier Profile, Bates, Delvan." http://www.soldierstudies.org/index.php?action=soldier_profile&Soldier=12.

Civil War Letters of George Bolton of New York. http://www.canton.org/canton/Civil%20War%20Letters%20of%20George%20Bolton%20of%20New%20York.htm.

New York State Military Museum and Veterans Center. "Unit History Project: 1st Artillery Regiment, Light, Battery L, George Breck Columns, http://dmna.ny.gov/historic/reghist/civil/artillery/1stArtLt/1stArtLtBatLBreckChap21Observation.htm.

——. "5th Regiment Cavalry, New York Volunteers." https://dmna.ny.gov/historic/reghist/civil/cavalry/5thCav/5thCavCWN.htm.

"The Civil War Letters of Thompson, Connecticut's Henry Washington Brown, 21st Massachusetts Volunteer Regiment, 1861-1865." https://www.thompsonhistorical.org/pdf/Private%20Henry%20W%20Brown%20Letters.pdf.

"The year 1863 from the diary of Alonzo Clapp." http://web.cortland.edu/woosterk/genweb/alonzoclapp/alonzoclapp1863.html.

The Civil War Letters of Charles Engle. 137th New York Volunteer Infantry. http://www. sugarfoottales.org/.

"Fauquier White Sulphur Springs. William Burke. The Mineral Springs of Western Virginia. https://www.hsl.virginia.edu/historical/exhibits/springs/fauquier.cfm

United States Civil War Collection. Western Michigan University. George L. Harrington Diary, 1863. http://bit.ly/2lK5Y9E.

The Valley of the Shadow. "Hotchkiss Family Letters—the War Years." http://valley.lib.virginia.edu/VoS/personalpapers/documents/augusta/p2hotchkissletters.html

Howard, Wiley C. "Sketch of Cobb Legion Cavalry and Some Incidents and Scenes Remembered." http://docsouth.unc.edu/fpn/howard/howard.html

The Central Rappahannock Regional Library. "Civil War Diary of A. L. Peel, Adjutant, 19th. Mississippi Regiment: April 29-30—May 1863, The Battle of Chancellorsville"http://www.librarypoint.org/civil_war_diary_alpeel

The 126th Ohio Volunteer Infantry. "Letters of First Lieutenant Rufus Ricksecker." http://www.frontierfamilies.net/family/Rickpt1.htm

Wikitree. "John Dominque Vautier (1843-1912)" www.wikitree.com/wiki/Vautier-28#Transcript_of_John.27s_Civil_War_Diary

Shotgun's Home of the American Civil War. "The Diary of Edwin B. Weist." www.civilwarhome.com/weistdiary.htm

Hathi Trust Digital Library. "Letters of Fredrick C. Winkler, 1862-1865." https://catalog.hathitrust.org/Record/009628680

Newspapers

Alexandria [VA] *Gazette*

Burlington [VT] *Daily Free Press*

Brookville [PA] *Republican*

Charleston [SC] *Mercury*

Columbia Democrat [Bloomsburg, PA]

Daily Morning Chronicle [Washington, DC]

Daily National Republican [Washington, DC]

Harper's Weekly [New York, NY]

Illustrated London News [London, England]

Memphis Daily Appeal

National Intelligencer [Washington, D.C]

Orleans Independent Standard [Irasburgh, VT]

Philadelphia Evening Bulletin [Philadelphia, PA]

Republican & Sentinel [Youngstown, OH]

Richmond Dispatch

Richmond Whig

Southern Watchman [Athens, GA]

The Abingdon [VA] *Virginian*

The Evening Star [Washington, DC]

The Gettysburg [PA] *Compiler*

The Daily Intelligencer [Wheeling, WV]

The National Tribune [Washington, DC]

The New York Daily Tribune

The New York Herald

The New York Times

The Peoples Press [Selma, NC]

The Philadelphia Inquirer

The Press [Philadelphia, PA]

The Richmond Enquirer

The Richmond Examiner

The Sun [New York]

The World [New York]

Wyoming Mirror [Warsaw, NY]

Secondary Sources

Books

Ambrose, Stephen E. *Halleck: Lincoln's Chief of Staff.* Baton Rouge: Louisiana State University Press, 1996.

Andrews, Cutler. *The South Reports the Civil War.* Princeton, NJ: Princeton University Press, 1970.

Bache, Richard Meade. *Life of General George Gordon Meade Commander of the Army of the Potomac.* Philadelphia: Henry T. Coates and Company, 1897.

Backus, Bill and Orrison, Robert. *A Want of Vigilance: The Bristoe Station Campaign, October 9-19, 1863.* El Dorado, CA: Savas Beatie, 2015.

Black, Robert C. III. *The Railroads of the Confederacy.* Chapel Hill, NC: University of North Carolina Press, 1998.

Burns, Vincent L. *The Fifth New York Cavalry in the Civil War.* Jefferson, NC: McFarland & Co., Inc., 2014.

Bushong, Millard and Dean. *Fightin' Tom Rosser, C.S.A.* Shippensburg, PA: Beidel Printing House, Inc., 1983.

Clark, Walter, ed. *Histories of the Several Regiments and Battalions from North Carolina in the Great War 1861-1865.* 5 Volumes. Goldsboro, NC: Nash Brothers, 1901.

Cleaves, Freeman. *Meade of Gettysburg.* Norman: University of Oklahoma Press, 1960.

Collea, Joseph D., Jr. *The First Vermont Cavalry in the Civil War.* Jefferson, NC: McFarland & Company Inc., 2010.

Douglas, David. *A Boot Full of Memories: Captain Leonard Williams, 2nd S.C. Cavalry.* Lexington, SC: Palmetto Books, 2003.

Ellis, Edward S. *The Campfires of General Lee from the Peninsula to Appomattox Court-house.* Philadelphia: Henry Harrison & Co., 1885.

Ent, Uzal W. *The Pennsylvania Reserves in the Civil War: A Comprehensive History.* Jefferson, NC: McFarland & Company, Inc., 2012.

Faust, Patricia, ed. *Historical Times Illustrated Encyclopedia of the Civil War.* New York: Harper & Row, 1986.

Freeman, Douglas Southall. *Lee's Lieutenants.* 3 Volumes. New York: Charles Scribner's Sons, 1944.

——. *R. E. Lee.* 4 Volumes. New York: Charles Scribner's Sons, 1935.

Fyre, Dennis. *The Second Virginia Cavalry.* Lynchburg, VA: H.E. Howard, 1984.

——. *The Twelfth Virginia Cavalry.* Lynchburg VA,: H.E. Howard, 1988.

Fonzo, Stephen. *A Documentary and Landscape Analysis of the Buckland Mills Battlefield (VA042).* Buckland Preservation Society, 2008.

Gallagher, Gary. *Lee & His Army in Confederate History.* Chapel Hill, NC: University of North Carolina Press, 2001.

——. *Lee the Soldier.* Lincoln: University of Nebraska Press, 1996.

Hand, Harold, Jr. *One Good Regiment: The 13th Pennsylvania Cavalry in the Civil War, 1861-1865.* Victoria, British Columbia, Canada: Trafford Publishing, 2000.

Harrell, Roger. *The Second North Carolina Cavalry.* Jefferson, NC: McFarland & Company Inc., Publisher, 2004.

Hartley, Chris. *Stuart's Tarheels: James B. Gordon and His North Carolina Cavalry in the Civil War.* Jefferson, NC: McFarland & Company, Inc., 2011.

Hattaway, Herman and Jones, Archer. *How the North Won.* Chicago: University of Illinois Press, 1983.

Henderson, William. *The Road to Bristoe Station, August 1—October 20, 1863.* Lynchburg, VA: H.E. Howard, 1987.

Henry, Robert S. *The Story of the Confederacy.* New York: Grosset & Dunlap, 1936.

Holland, Lynwood. *Pierce M. B. Young: The Warwick of the South.* Athens: University of Georgia Press, 1964.

Humphreys, Henry. *Andrew Atkinson Humphreys—A Biography.* Gaithersburg, MD: Ron R. Van Sickle Military Books, 1988.

Jones, Terry. *Lee's Tigers: The Louisiana Infantry in the Army of Northern Virginia.* Baton Rouge, LA: Louisiana State University Press, 1987.

Jordon, David M. *Happiness Is Not My Companion: The Life of General G.K. Warren.* Bloomington: Indiana University Press. 2001.

Kreiser, Lawrence, Jr. *Defeating Lee: A History of the Second Corps, Army of the Potomac.* Bloomington: Indiana University Press, 2011.

Krick, Robert. *Civil War Weather in Virginia.* Tuscaloosa: The University of Alabama Press, 2007.

——. *Ninth Virginia Cavalry.* Lynchburg, VA: H. E. Howard, 1982.

——. *Staff Officers in Gray: A Biographical Register of the Staff Officers in the Army of Northern Virginia.* Chapel Hill, NC: University of North Carolina Press, 2003.

Laine, J. Gary and Penny, Morris M. *Law's Alabama Brigade in the War Between the Union and the Confederacy.* Shippensburg, PA: White Mane Publishing Co., Inc, 1996.

Longacre, Edward G. *Lee's Cavalrymen: A History of the Mounted Forces of the Army of Northern Virginia.* Mechanicsburg, PA: Stackpole Books, 2002.

——. *Lincoln's Cavalrymen: A History of the Mounted Forces of the Army of the Potomac.* Mechanicsburg, PA: Stackpole Books, 2000.

——. *To Gettysburg and Beyond: The Twelfth New Jersey Volunteer Infantry, II Corps, Army of the Potomac, 1862-1865.* Highstown, NJ: Longstreet House, 1988.

Lonn, Ellas. *Desertion During the Civil War.* New York: Peter Smith, 1928.

Mahood, Wayne. *Alexander "Fighting Elleck" Hays: The Life of a Civil War General From West Point to the Wilderness.* Jefferson, NC: McFarland & Company, Inc., Publishers, 2005.

Martin, Samuel. *Kill Cavalry: The Life of Union General Hugh Judson Kilpatrick.* Mechanicsburg, PA: Stackpole Books, 2000.

Matteson, Ron. *Civil War Campaigns of the 10th New York Cavalry, With One Soldier's Personal Correspondence.* Self-published, Lulu.com, 2007.

Mesic, Harriet Bey. *Cobb's Legion: A History and Roster of the 9th Georgia Volunteers in the Civil War.* Jefferson, NC: McFarland & Co, Inc., 2011.

Munson, E. B., *Confederate Correspondent: The Civil War Reports of Jacob Nathaniel Raymer, Fourth North Carolina.* Jefferson, NC: MacFarland & Company, Inc., 2009.

Nicholas, Richard & Servis, Joseph. *Powhaten, Salem and Courtney Henrico Artillery.* Lynchburg, VA: H.E. Howard, 1997.

Pfanz, Donald. *Richard S. Ewell: A Soldier's Life.* Chapel Hill, NC: University of North Carolina Press, 1998.

Rafuse, Ethan S. *George Gordon Meade and the War in the East.* Abilene, TX: McWhiney Foundation Press, 2003.

Ray, Fred. *Shock Troops of the Confederacy: The Sharpshooter Battalions of the Army of Northern Virginia.* Asheville, NC: CFS Press, 2006.

Robertson, James. *General A.P. Hill: The Story of a Confederate Warrior.* New York: Random House, 1987.

Sandburg, Carl. *Abraham Lincoln: The War Years.* 4 Volumes. New York: Harcourt, Brace & World, 1939.

Scheel, Eugene. *The Civil War in Fauquier County Virginia.* Warrenton, VA: The Fauquier National Bank, 1995.

Sears, Stephen W. *Lincoln's Lieutenants: The High Command of the Army of the Potomac.* New York: Houghton Mifflin Harcourt, 2017.

Starr, Stephen Z. *The Union Cavalry in the Civil War: The war in the East, From Gettysburg to Appomattox, 1863-1865.* Baton Rouge: Louisiana State University Press, 1981.

Sutherland, Daniel E. *Seasons of War: The Ordeal of a Confederate Community, 1861-1865.* New York: The Free Press, 1995.

Tagg, Larry. *The Generals of Gettysburg: The Leaders of America's Greatest Battle.* Campbell, CA: Savas Publishing Company, 1998.

Thomas, Emory. *Bold Dragoon: The Life of J. E. B. Stuart.* New York: Harper Row, 1986.

Tighe, Adrian. *The Bristoe Campaign.* Self-published, 2011.

Townsend, Jan. *The Civil War in Prince William County.* Prince William County Historical Commission, 2011.

Trout, Robert. *After Gettysburg: Cavalry Operations in the Eastern Theater, July 14, 1863 to December 31, 1863.* Hamilton, MT: Eagle Editions Ltd, 2012.

——. *Galloping Thunder: The Stuart Horse Artillery Battalion.* Mechanicsburg, PA: Stackpole Books, 2002.

——. *Memoirs of the Stuart Horse Artillery Battalion: Moorman's and Hart's Batteries.* Knoxville: University of Tennessee Press, 1998.

——. *Memoirs of the Stuart Horse Artillery Battalion, Volume 2: Breathed's and McGregor's Batteries.* Knoxville, TN: University of Tennessee Press, 2010.

Urwin, Gregory. *Custer Victorious: The Civil War Battles of General George Armstrong Custer.* Edison, NJ: The Blue & Gray Press, 1983.

Warner, Ezra. *Generals in Blue.* Baton Rouge, LA: Louisiana State University Press, 1964.

——. *Generals in Gray.* Baton Rouge, LA: Louisiana State University Press, 1959.

Wittenberg, Eric. *Rush's Lancers: The Sixth Pennsylvania Cavalry in the Civil War.* Yardley, PA: Westholme Publishing, 2007.

Wise, Jennings. *The Long Arm of Lee: The History of the Artillery of the Army of Northern Virginia.* New York: Oxford University Press, 1959.

Woodward, Harold R, Jr. *Defender of the Valley: Brigadier General John Daniel Imboden, C.S.A.* Shenandoah Valley. Berryville, VA: Rockbridge Publishing Co, 1996.

——. *For Home and Honor: The Story of Madison County, Virginia During the War Between the States.* Madison, VA: Skyline Services, 1990.

Articles

Bauer, Daniel. "The Rail Transfer of the 11th and 12th Corps to the Western Theatre of War." *Civil War: The Magazine of the Civil War Society.* Vol. 12. March 1988. 66-78.

Chambers, C. C. "The Coahoma Invincibles." *Confederate Veteran Magazine.* Vol. 31, November 1923. 420-22.

Clark, S. S. "Buckland Mills." *The Maine Bugle.* Vol. 4, January 1897. 108-10.

Lane, James H. "History of Lane's North Carolina Brigade" in *Southern Historical Society Papers.* Vol. 9. January-December 1881.

Longacre, Edward. "Alfred Pleasonton: The Knight of Romance." *Civil War Times Illustrated.* Vol. 13. December 1974. 12-23.

Longstreet, James. "Lee in Pennsylvania," in *The Annals of the War Written By Leading Participants North and South.* New York: De Capo Press, 1994. 414-46.

McMahon, Martin. "From Gettysburg to the Coming of Grant." In *Battles and Leaders of the Civil War.* Vol. 4. 81-94.

Mays, Samuel Elias. "Sketches from the Journal of a Confederate Soldier" *Tyler's Quarterly Magazine,* Vol. 5. July 1923. 97-102.

Mellon, Knox, Jr. ed. "A Florida Solider in the Army of Northern Virginia: The Hosford Letters." *Florida Historical Quarterly,* Vol. 46, No. 3, January 1968. 243-71.

Miller, J. Michael. "The Battles of Bristoe Station." *Blue & Gray.* Vol. 26, August 2001. 1-26

Park, Robert Emory. "War Diary of Captain Robert Emory Park." *Southern Historical Society Papers.* Vol. 24. 18-26.

Robertson, James, ed., "An Indiana Solider in Love and War: The Civil War Letters of John V. Hadley," *Indiana Magazine of History* 59, No. 3, Sept. 1963. 247-67.

Thaxter, Sidney. "No Trace of the Enemy." *Civil War Times Illustrated.* Vol. 7. Harrisburg: Telegraph Press, August 1969. 26-32.

Thomason, John W. Jr., "J. E. B. Stuart: Portrait of a Cavalryman" *Scribner's Magazine,* Vol. 87, No. 4. April 1930. 485-91.

Wiles, Clifton W. "A skirmish at Little Auburn, Va." *First Maine Bugle Campaign II, Call X.* 1892. 71-74.

Government Documents

Auburn Civil War Battlefield National Historic District Preliminary Information Form, VA Dept of Historic Resources. 2007. Typescript copy in author's possession.

Biographical directory of the American Congress, 1774-1961 : the Continental Congress, September 5, 1774, to October 21, 1788 and the Congress of the United States, from the First to the Eighty-sixth Congress, March 4, 1789, to January 3, 1961, inclusive. https://catalog.hathitrust.org/Record/001142296

Bristoe Station and Kettle Run Battlefields Preservation Study. http://eservice.pwcgov.org/ planning/ documents/archaeology/BSKR_Study_ARPA.pdf

"Report of the Joint Committee on the Conduct of the War at the Second Session of the Thirty-eighth Congress," Vol. 1. Washington: Government Printing Office, 1865.

US Southern Claims Commission, Disallowed and Barred Claims, 1871-1880. National Archives RG 123, Thomas K. Davis, Box 475.

Note: Two very helpful websites used in researching this book were www.fold3.com and www.civilwardata.com. Both require annual memberships but are reasonably priced with memberships that can be cancelled at any time. Fold3 has digitized the Civil War service records collected at the National Archives. They are searchable by unit and name. Civil War Data is an aggregation of information on individual regiments and soldiers drawn from a wide variety of sources. Searchable by unit or name, it provides lists of engagements and casualties sustained in each action with the names and some biographic information on the men killed, wounded or missing. Both sites were invaluable tools.

Index

Jeffrey William Hunt is Director of the Texas Military Forces Museum, the official museum of the Texas National Guard, located at Camp Mabry in Austin, Texas, and an Adjunct Professor of History at Austin Community College, where he has taught since 1988. Prior to taking the post at the Texas Military Forces Museum, he was the Curator of Collections and Director of the Living History Program at the Admiral Nimitz National Museum of the Pacific War in Fredericksburg, Texas for 11 years.

Jeff holds a Bachelors Degree in Government and a Masters Degree in History, both from the University of Texas at Austin. In 2013, he was appointed an honorary Admiral in the Texas Navy by Governor Rick Perry, in recognition of his efforts to tell the story of the Texas naval forces at the Texas Military Forces Museum. He is a frequent speaker for a wide variety of organizations as well as documentaries and news programs. He is also the author of *The Last Battle of the Civil War: Palmetto Ranch*, and has contributed to *Essential Civil War Curriculum*, the *Revised Handbook of Texas*, and the *Gale Library of Daily Life: American Civil War*.

Jeff's last book, *Meade and Lee After Gettysburg: The Forgotten Final Stage of the Gettysburg Campaign, from Falling Waters to Culpeper Court House, July 14-31, 1863* (Savas Beatie, 2017), was awarded the Gettysburg Civil War Round Table's 2017 Distinguished Book Award.